FRANCE

DURING THE

GERMAN OCCUPATION

1940-1944

*A Collection of 292 Statements on the Government
of Maréchal Pétain and Pierre Laval*

Translated from the French by
PHILIP W. WHITCOMB

VOLUME II

DISTRIBUTED BY STANFORD UNIVERSITY PRESS FOR
THE HOOVER INSTITUTION
ON WAR, REVOLUTION, AND PEACE
Stanford University, Stanford, California

CHAPTER XI

JUSTICE

CHAPTER XI

JUSTICE

PROBLEMS OF THE JUDICIAL SYSTEM

MAURICE GABOLDE

Minister of Justice

To understand the attitude of the government presided over by Pierre Laval toward repressive judicial activity during the occupation, and the decisions taken by it, it is necessary to recall briefly the circumstances which created in France an atmosphere of public insecurity, characterized by repeated attacks not merely against members of the German army but against many French people suspected either of collaborationism or merely of a passive or indifferent attitude toward the resistance movements.

It was this evolution toward a sort of civil war that I had pointed out to Pierre Laval in 1942 before entering the government, when, deeply moved by an attack made in the rue de Bucy in Paris, only a few hundred yards from the Hotel Matignon [Paris residence of the president of the Council of Ministers], he had summoned me to see him about ways of aiding him to find legal means to prevent such attacks against the public peace. Members of the Paris police had been killed in trying to arrest those who were inciting the housewives of the quarter to loot the food shops.

This invitation enabled me to become aware of the unity of views between the Chief of Government and the judicial services of the capital which I directed as attorney-general for the Republic. As is the case with all whose duty it is to assure respect for the law and the protection of persons and property, the President had no illusions about the heavy task which lay on the police and the magistracy in an atmosphere saturated with partisan passions, and poisoned by a foreign occupation that had become oppressive now that the resistance movement was employing violent and terrorist methods against the police and the magistrates.

On the one hand, it was necessary to moderate the activities of the parties which had sprung up out of the occupation and which had the more or less hidden support of the occupation authorities. These parties sought to substitute themselves for the state's protective organizations, and at the same time to prevent the German services from taking over the task of repression on the ground of the weakness or dilatoriness of the French public authority. This latter possibility was particularly to be feared; just as the President said to me, it would have been equivalent to a disavowal of the motives which had inspired his return to the government when, after an interview with Marshal Goering, he had sacrificed his own peace because he believed that he would be better qualified than anyone else for the task of saving France from a regime similar to that applied in Belgium, and perhaps even from a regime like that of Poland. It was therefore necessary to maintain control of repressive activities however unpopular this attitude might be for those who regarded it as their duty.

It was in this task that I was to collaborate in complete agreement with Pierre Laval. The decisions which we took were to save the lives of many men who would not have been spared by the German courts-martial if we, as prudent people had so often advised us to do, had abandoned to the occupying power, or to organisms which it controlled, the responsibility for repressing attacks against French people, attacks made either because of the victims' opinions or to satisfy personal vengeance, or as acts of banditry.

This situation was one of the aspects of the tragedy of the occupation. It was impossible, if control was to be maintained, to state publicly the motives behind the laws which were issued. I must point out, for the sake of complete truth, that these measures always had the high approval of Maréchal Pétain and that he was always in agreement in judicial matters with the Chief of Government and the Minister of Justice.

The Maréchal was always friendly toward the Minister [Gabolde], who had served under his orders in the 33rd Corps at Arras in 1915, and whom he had decorated with the Military Medal and twice cited to the Order of the Army. In addition I was linked in his mind with the years of his youth at the college of St. Bertin at St. Omer, where I had begun my judicial career and where I had known the sons of his fellow students. I mention these personal memories merely to emphasize the unity of views between the Minister, the Chief of Government, and the Chief of State, all of whom had the same thought, to keep the fatherland alive and to defend it against the audacious plans of the conqueror, against demagogic bids for popularity, and against terrorism.[1]

I

How had political criminal activity developed since the beginning of the war? Its development had been closely linked with the activity and the varying attitudes of the communist party.

The fact was that it had not been the Maréchal's government which had begun the use of repressive measures against communist intrigues. The Maréchal's government had merely applied, without intensification, the laws voted by Parliament on the initiative of President Daladier. The only modification was in giving the courts of common law in the occupied zone jurisdiction over offenses which had previously been dealt with by courts-martial. These latter no longer functioned in the occupied zone and it was necessary that they should be replaced.

The fact was that at the beginning of hostilities the communist party

1. Complaint has been made about the word "terrorism" which appears in many legislative texts. In a meeting of the National Assembly on 19 November 1948 M. Queuille described as "terrorist activity" far less serious deeds of which the communist party was then accused; the term is at present currently employed in the press in describing the situation in French Morocco or in Tunisia.

had been entirely against the war. Its propaganda developed the following themes based on those presented by Mr. Molotov in the séance of 31 October 1939 of the extraordinary session of the Supreme Council of the USSR: "Since the complete destruction of Poland the war has been meaningless. Its prolongation by England and France will bring economic ruin and will destroy the civilization of the nations of Europe. It is insane and criminal to continue the war in order to destroy Hitlerism even if that purpose is camouflaged under the banner of a struggle for the democracies. The true explanation of the hate of England and France against the German Reich is their fear of losing their colonial and commercial supremacy throughout the world. This is a war of imperialism and capitalism against proletarian nations."

The French communist party therefore vigorously supported the policy of peace with Germany and, something equally serious, the sabotage of war production [in France] which then began in factories of the Paris region (e.g. in the Farman factory at Billancourt and in fortifications in the Boulay region). Reports of some of their most typical operations had been put at the disposal of the Riom Supreme Court in 1940, and were consulted by members of the court.

President Daladier's government took action. On the parliamentary level those who in October 1939 had signed the letter demanding that President Herriot should summon the Chamber to meet were interned by order of the administration until their parliamentary immunity could be lifted. On the legislative level the government ordered the dissolution of the communist party, and made its reconstitution, and with it any activity linked with the Third International, an offense punishable by a maximum of five years in prison. On 22 February 1940 the Chamber decided, by the unanimous vote of 492 deputies present, to deprive the communist deputies of their membership in the Chamber.

The communist party's secretary-general, M. Maurice Thorez, was to be stripped of his French nationality. He had been mobilized in the auxiliary services of the army at Amiens and had clandestinely crossed the Swiss frontier near Thonon. The Germans facilitated his passage to Russia. A French court-martial condemned him to death, by default.

On 9 April 1940 those deputies who had signed the letter to President Herriot were given prison sentences by a court-martial and taken either to Algeria or to Puy.

All the actions undertaken in application of the decree-law of 23 September 1939, together with those dealing with sabotage in factories, came under the jurisdiction of courts-martial in accordance with the laws ruling during a state of siege. The ordinary criminal courts very rarely dealt with these affairs and only in cases where the military authorities took no action because of the insignificance of the matter.

Finally, the prefects interned many communists, or communist sympathizers, on administrative order. One of these internment camps was established in the jurisdiction where I then held the position of attorney-general, at Fort Barrau. I even received complaints regarding internments which were thought to be abusive and I made investigations in co-operation with the prefect.

Such was the situation when the armistice was signed. The occupation of the northern zone, which cut France in two, *ipso facto* brought the disappearance of the courts-martial.

After the Germans had occupied Paris the attorney-general asked for instructions from the government which had just been established at Vichy. The net effect of his inquiry was to raise not merely the question of judiciary competence, but also that of the very basis of the legislation on communist activities.

The new situation which confronted us was in fact particularly delicate. The communist party had placed itself in the forefront of collaboration in Paris. The newspaper *L'Humanité*, then being published clandestinely with the tacit consent of the occupying authorities, extolled fraternization between French workers and German soldiers (4 July 1940) and demanded that work begin again in the factories in order to aid the German war effort, inviting the workers to open the factories themselves (27 July 1940) if the owners showed ill-will and hindered the economic revival.

The police had arrested, on 20 June 1940, a member of the central committee of the communist party, M. Maurice Tréand. He was found to be carrying documents from the *Propagandastaffel* which showed that negotiations were in course between the two organizations [communist party and *Propagandastaffel*] with a view to the open re-publication of the newspaper *L'Humanité*. M. Tréand was imprisoned at the Petite Roquette with two women who had accompanied him, and the Parquet of the Seine began an investigation. On 25 [June] the [German] Counselor Fritz, who from his office in the Chamber of Deputies [occupied by the Germans] maintained liaison with the judiciary of Paris, demanded that these prisoners should be released. The first [German] intervention in the French judicial system was made in favor of a communist leader.

But the higher German chiefs [in the legal services] were reticent. They were themselves mobilized lawyers, notaries, and magistrates and were, quite naturally, not favorable to communism; but they were obliged to consider the directives from Berlin and the relationships which then united their country with Russia. Thus they saw nothing out of the way in an inquiry being made to the [French] government as to whether the Daladier legislation was still in effect.

The reply of Minister of Justice Alibert was in the affirmative. The ordinary criminal courts were competent to deal with these matters and were responsible for such actions as had already been in progress [at the time of the armistice].

The repression was a mild one and punishment varied between two and eight months imprisonment. The German authority, in the person of Colonel Fritz, *Militärbefehlshaber*, sometimes intervened to secure a milder sentence but in general showed little interest in the cases and I had no difficulty, from this point of view, until the break between the Reich and Russia.

The communist party, however, continued to receive the favors of the occupying authorities. Its newspapers and leaflets showed a visible desire for collaboration. The archives of the Parquet of the Seine, unless they have since been expurgated, should be very interesting. I cite the following at random from memory, from *Les Cahiers du Bolchevisme* [Studies in Bolshevism], published during the first quarter of 1941: "In the United States it is a dictatorship consisting of a few oligarchic families that now descends into the arena of war." *L'Humanité* said on 1 May 1941 under the heading *Les Assassins de la Liberté* [The Assassins of Liberty]: "De Gaulle, the General with a *de*, does not desire the liberty of his country but the triumph of capitalist interests; it is not the 'V' which should be marked on the walls, but rather the hammer and sickle." A leaflet, *Pour le Salut du Peuple Français*, published during the first quarter of 1941, demanded the creation of a People's Court of Justice to judge those who were responsible for the war, in addition to those who had been brought before the court of Riom; those named were M. Jeanneney, M. Herriot, M. Paul Boncour, M. Sarraut, M. Chautemps, M. Flandin, M. Pierre Cot, M. Guy La Chambre, M. Marcel Déat, M. Campinchi, M. Yvon Delbos, General Maurin, and General Denain.

During this same period the communist deputies who were held at Puy in the unoccupied zone, among them M. Billoux, wrote to the President of the Supreme Court of Riom a letter which must still be in its archives, asking to serve as prosecution witnesses against M. Daladier and M. Paul Reynaud.

In September 1940 a leaflet distributed by the communist section in Stains, with the title *A Date and an Anniversary*, denounced as among those who had "betrayed the people and sold France," M. Blum, M. Paul Faure, M. Ziromsky, M. Grumbach, M. Louis Marin, M. Jouhaux, and others.

In February 1941 another leaflet denounced M. Blum, M. Daladier, M. Auriol, M. Bedouce and M. Bastid as having facilitated the exportation of our aluminum and stated: "The general staff knew about it and kept silent because their palms had been greased; you will understand why the Court of Riom is in no hurry, and why Vincent Auriol has been released (*sic*)."

Some months earlier M. Forsin had given to the *Propagandastaffel* a letter signed by M. Maurice Tréand and M. Cathelas, both refugees in hiding, offering their aid in persuading the colonies to reject the propositions of England and of General de Gaulle, and not to break away from the homeland.

All of this explains the goodwill shown to the communists by the judicial services of the occupation in 1940 and during the first half of 1941. This propaganda did in fact bring the German army tranquillity and security in the Paris region. There was no sabotage in the factories, and the military could walk about at any hour of the day or night without fearing an aggression.

Thus the *Militärbefehlshaber* had authorized, contrary to the ban issued by the prefecture of police, a meeting on the Ile de la Grande Jatte [a Paris suburb] where the speakers, one of whom was M. Péri, praised—if my memory is correct, for I do not have the report at hand—a policy of closer collaboration than that into which the French government had timidly entered.

The only opposition which the Germans had to watch during this period was that of the Parisian bourgeoisie of Gaullist tendencies, but it was not dangerous. I remember that on 11 November 1940 some young people marched up the Champs Élysées with fishing rods [a visual pun on "deux gaules" for de Gaulle]. I had little difficulty in persuading Colonel Fritz to agree that they should not be punished. The same tolerance was shown to those who listened to the foreign radio, an act which was prohibited by one of the many ordinances which the military authority generously poured upon us. The only important questions during this period had nothing to do with the repression of opposition but concerned the removal of German property from [French] sequestration and the prosecution of German and Italian citizens for offenses under common law. The German military tribunal transferred to us at my request, without raising much difficulty, the jurisdiction for any offenses committed by Italians, and was satisfied with a monthly report of condemnations; complete indifference toward their allies was shown. I remember that the colonel who presided even recommended greater severity in dealing with the Italians who, in Paris, were black market experts.

II

In June 1941 there occurred an event which explains the change in the communist party, the altered attitude of the occupation authorities, and the creation of the punitive organizations made necessary by the circumstances. This event was the break between Germany and Russia. There was a delay before new instructions began to come into France from Moscow. Stocks of ammunition had to be built up, too, and working teams organized, for the new attitude of the communist party had nothing in common with the Gaullist opposition. It was no longer a question of writing V's on the walls, of listening to the London radio, or of street manifestations along the lines of the "deux gaules." The army of occupation was to be attacked in its work, its soldiers, its organizations, its communications, and its transport, and that army was to retaliate brutally and without distinction, like a lion driven mad by the stings of a gnat. It was then that there began a complete rupture between the population and the occupants which was to make existence impossible for both.

The new plan entered into application in August 1941, one of the periods which has left the most painful memories to those whose mission it was at that time to maintain order and to protect the legal institutions of the country. The first attacks, which as could be foreseen were to lead to terrible reprisals, occurred in Paris and were made by foreigners. It was among the refugees and immigrants from the east of Europe, and particularly among the Jews who had fled from Hitlerian persecution, that the first terrorists were recruited—the Zalkinow group, the Poles, the Czechs, and the Hungarians. The archives of the Parquet of the Seine may be consulted on this point.

The first of a long series of attacks took place on 12 or 13 August [1941], as far as I remember, in full daylight at a time of peak traffic at the metro station of Barbès-Rochechouart. At the moment when a dense crowd was entering one of the cars two shots fired at close range killed a naval cadet, Moser. The person who made the attack was lost in the crowd. On the following day a German army doctor who was walking along the boulevard Magenta in the dark on his way to the Lariboisière hospital was killed under similar conditions. The next was an attack against a [German] railway official as he was leaving his hotel near the *gare de l'Est*.

The first reaction of the chiefs of the *Militärbefehlshaber* was one of stupefaction because of the long period of calm which had followed their installation in the capital. The German police went into action and the French police on their side began investigations; such attacks ran the risk of bringing about reprisals against the population. But nothing was known of the new organization and the search was long and difficult.

The German high command, represented by the German army, being responsible for the security of its troops, planned a spectacular reply. They emanded that the authors of these attacks should be discovered without delay, arrested, judged, and immediately executed. Then, faced by the impossibility of acting so rapidly, they decided to shoot, in replacement of those who had been guilty, 150 persons condemned for communistic activity or interned on administrative order. This was the old German theory of tribal responsibility. It was a theory which bore no relation to the conception of hostages which had been put into practice during the first world war where the hostage was chosen in advance from among selected persons of importance who had great influence with the population, men such as prefects, bishops, attorneys-general, and so on.

The new theory was that replacements should be chosen from among persons who were presumed to share the ideology of those who had committed the attacks. We could not possibly agree to such a subtle argument and we protested against a theory which was condemned both by penal law and by natural law. The prefecture of police, directed by Admiral Bard, promised to do everything possible to find those who were actually guilty.

The German command also complained that the public was passive in their attitude when attacks were made, or that they even aided in the escape of the guilty. The German command were planning measures directed against the population as a whole, such as a ban on the movement of vehicles during the night, an earlier curfew to begin at 5 or 6 o'clock in the afternoon, and the closing of cafés and cinemas; if such measures were applied they would paralyze the life of the city and would, incidentally, cause as much trouble for German officers, who were clients of the restaurants and night clubs, as for Parisians, who would be kept at home by restrictions of all kinds. The French government's liaison agents in Paris, M. Ingrand for the Ministry of the Interior and M. Rousseau for the Ministry of Justice, informed their Ministers of this new situation.

In order to understand what followed, one must bear in mind the attitude which the government had taken toward the [French] administrative and judiciary authorities of the occupied zone since President Pierre Laval's removal from power, with the resultant postponement of his plan for easing the demarcation line. The division, not merely material but also spiritual, between the two zones was increased. The German authorities did not give us passes except after repeated demands; telephone conversations were listened to; postal correspondence was slow; and replies arrived with considerable delay. It seemed as though in Vichy they distrusted the chiefs of administration in the northern zone, and left them to get along the best they could, and yet this autonomy was devoid of the authority which could have been given only by governmental support in the eyes of foreigners, especially when those foreigners were as respectful toward authority as were the German officials and magistrates.

The [French] Ministers appeared very rarely in Paris, doubtless fearing another coup like that of 13 December 1940. Business was dealt with by correspondence. As far as the Ministry of Justice was concerned, liaison was maintained by the secretary-general, M. Dayras, an experienced and understanding official, but during this period he made only short and rare visits to Paris. I had gone to Vichy to pay my respects to the new Minister of Justice, M. Barthélemy. But, even speaking with all the respect which I owe to that eminent jurist, I must confess that he seemed to me to be more concerned with what was going on in the courts of Carpentras or Auch than with the difficulties created in Paris by the German occupation. He seemed to have resigned himself to the idea of being merely a Minister of Justice in the unoccupied zone and limited himself to telling me that he trusted in my diplomatic skill and my patriotism for the best possible settlement of incidents inevitable in a country occupied by a conqueror.

The disturbances caused by the telephone calls of Prefect Ingrand and Counselor Rousseau may be imagined. M. Barthélemy sent Secretary-General Dayras to Paris. In the meantime the German command had made a new proposition which they saw as an unhoped for concession. If the French government could obtain through its own courts ten death sentences, followed by execution, of notorious communists, there would be no execution of substitutes. It was a tragic dilemma. From the point of view of the interests of the French authorities, it would have been better to let the occupying authorities carry out their reprisals; but how many families would have been in mourning, and what a drama of conscience.

Dayras, quite rightly shaken by this alternative, decided that the decision must be made by the government and left again to inform his Minister. I do not know what happened in Vichy and I was not informed until the Government's decision had been taken. One afternoon Attorney-General Dupuich, who was serving *ad interim* at the *Parquet General* during the absence of Attorney-General Cavarroc, and I were summoned by Prefect Ingrand to a hotel near the Parc Monceau. We were given the text of a law, typed on onionskin paper, and we were told that this was a final text and about to be published in the *Journal Officiel*. It was being shown to us so that we could make sure that it did not contain juridical errors, in order that any details might be modified if necessary. I pointed out the dispositions which were unsuitable from the point of view of procedure in the trial of persons not present in court and made a pencil note of my comments.

The structure of this proposed law was as follows: in each court of appeal there was to be a new "special section" composed of the magistrates of that court who would judge all terrorist crimes as a court of last resort without possibility of appeal. These judges could pronounce any judgment provided by the law, including that of death. Extenuating circumstances were not to be considered. The law was retroactive. It was clearly a text inspired by the tradition of the period of the great [French] revolution.

The law came into effect immediately and its retroactivity made it possible to judge condemned persons for deeds committed previous to its publication, which was the only way of avoiding numerous executions of persons condemned in replacement. This retroactivity, which had so rightly disturbed the jurists, was not exceptional. The ordinances of 28 August 1944 and 9 November 1944 issued by the new French government were retroactive; the decree-law of the Polish government in London was also retroactive; so too was the law of 2 August 1947 issued by the Luxembourg government, to say nothing of the Russian Penal Code, in its law of application dated 22 November 1926, and the texts applied by the International Tribunal of Nuremberg.

The German authorities authorized the publication of the law in the occupied zone with unaccustomed rapidity.

A meeting was held at the Ministry of Justice under the presidency of M. Barthélemy who had come specially to Paris for that purpose. Those present were M. Villette, First President of the Court of Appeals, M. Dupuich, acting Attorney-General, M. Dayras, Secretary-General, M. Werquin, acting President of the Tribunal of the Seine, and I. The purpose of the meeting was to appoint the judges for the new "special section" and to deal with any matters submitted. President Cournet had been approached but had excused himself; it was President Benon, a glorious veteran of the first world war, who sacrificed himself in this patriotic duty. As far as current matters for consideration were concerned I stated that nothing was under investigation at the Parquet of the Seine which could come up for immediate judgment, and it was M. Dupuich who presented the files concerning those who had been condemned at their first trial and had appealed, and therefore were now to be dealt with before the Court of Appeals. This doubtless explains his embarrassment when [after the war] during the trial of the judges of the "special section" he appeared as a witness, and sought, as was only human, to place the responsibility on persons who were absent. It was also M. Dupuich who pointed out the attorney-general who had asked for the death penalty, M. Guyenot, but who in fact was merely following the same rules of authority and of fundamental obedience as are applied in the Parquets.

At the same time we had continued our efforts to have the number of condemnations to death reduced. Out of the ten which were demanded we saved first three and finally five.

The "special section" condemned only three. The drama of conscience among the judges must have been terrible. Demands for pardon were rejected by telegram from Vichy and the executions took place at dawn in a courtyard of the Santé prison.

This was the only time that the "special section" of Paris had to function under such conditions.

The same law was later applied in the unoccupied zone; death sentences, only rarely pronounced, were reserved for assassins who in ordinary times would have incurred the same punishment before a jury at an Assize Court.

No condemnation to death followed by an execution was pronounced by the "special sections" during the time that I was Minister of Justice. I carefully refrained from intervening at any time with the judges, for being a judge myself I knew how disagreeable such interventions were for those to whom they were directed. I defended the judges not merely against the German authorities but against the attacks of the extremist parties of the Militia and I allowed the disqualifications which some of them pronounced with the purpose of avoiding the strict application of the law. I must add that I was supported in all these steps by President Pierre Laval, whose natural inclinations were toward indulgence. I no longer was involved in the operations of the "special section" in Paris in my position as a prosecuting attorney for the Republic, because this section was the direct responsibility of my superior, the attorney-general. When I became Minister of Justice I arranged modifications of detail in the law which altered the procedure and provided the defense with guarantees which it had previously lacked.

III

But the problem of the repression of terrorist activity became more complicated during 1942, a time when I was in discussion with President Laval, again Chief of Government, at the Hotel Matignon. In addition to attacks against German military personnel there were now attacks against the French, either against important persons who had left the communist party, such as Clamamus and Gitton, or against those who supported the policy of collaboration. But there were also government officials among the victims, members of the police, gendarmes and other civil servants, victims of their professional duty. The attacks had now gone beyond the Paris region and were general in the occupied zone, and even in the unoccupied zone before the German army entered it.

In the occupied zone the German army retained jurisdiction over any attacks against military personnel, in accordance with ordinances in effect at that time, and used a heavy hand. Condemnations were continuous, as I was able to ascertain from the reports sent to me by the *Militärbefehlshaber* concerning matters dealt with at Mont Valérien.

After the bloody repression which followed the attack against the *Feld-Kommandant* at Nantes the communist party seemed to change its tactics. There were fewer assassinations of German military personnel and more assassinations of French people, doubtless because punishment of the latter was more discriminatory and less brutal. As these latter attacks did not come within the field covered by the German ordinances, the occupation authorities left them to the French police and courts. In the unoccupied zone the French authorities acted without any hindrance.

The government could not allow these crimes to go unpunished; regardless of the motive, sometimes obvious, which inspired them, they were crimes against common law, such as assassination, pillage, armed robbery, and destruction of buildings and crops, all of them punishable under the penal codes of civilized nations.

The repression of crimes of this kind, which from the point of view of public peace were far more serious than communist propaganda—it should be noted that the "special sections" punished such propaganda only by moderate terms of imprisonment, which incidentally enabled the convicted persons to receive a medal at the time of the liberation—was entrusted to the judges of the Court of Appeals whose training had prepared them in no way for the new task now imposed on them, but who were preferable, according to my profound opinion as shared by the Maréchal and the President, to partisan judges taken from among political adversaries as was being suggested even outside of the circles of the militant collaborationists.

Two of the "special sections," those of Lyon and Toulouse, had condemned assassins to death. The president of the "special section" of Lyon was himself assassinated at his home by terrorists dressed as German soldiers. In Toulouse the attorney-general who had led the prosecution was shot down on his way to mass with his wife and sister-in-law one Sunday morning. He was a gentle and charitable judge who had acquired an honorable reputation in the work of re-educating delinquent youth. The president of the "special section" had to have police protection at his home and I gave him an appointment on the other side of France in order to get him away from the threats of death which had been made against him. At Nantes the examining magistrate whose task it was to deal with terrorist attacks was killed in his office in the Palace of Justice. The examining magistrate at Béthune was the victim of an attack of the same kind. The president of the court at Aix was assassinated as he was leaving the Palace of Justice. Terrorists invaded the court room at Die to shoot down an attorney who was to plead a case that day. The attorney-general at Douai was warned in time that he was to be killed in the tramway which he took on Sunday to visit friends.

In spite of the indulgence which they showed in general, the judges of the "special sections" lived in an atmosphere of terror maintained by the spectacle of aggressions against their collaborators, the police, the prison guards, the commissioners and inspectors of the Sûreté Nationale and all the other members of that small world which revolves around the administration of justice. Truly the task was beyond the human possibilities of these judges, and I explained to President Laval that the system of "special sections" would have to be changed to avoid on the one hand an extension by the German authorities of their own competence to crimes committed against French people, and on the other hand the substitution of the Militia, then being organized, for the ordinary courts.

There was an incident at Riom. The "special section" of that court, in which President Laval took a personal interest, had to judge a particularly serious attack. The barracks of the gendarmerie at Arlanc had been invaded by an armed band and some gendarmes had been killed or wounded; one of them, dangerously wounded, had begged for pity from the aggressors, but they had merely completed his murder. The "special section" was presided over by a judge who made a show, at that time, of his loyalty and who had held positions in organizations created by the government at Vichy. The "special section," under threats and fearing for the life of its own judges, passed sentences of mere imprisonment. This decision aroused a wave of discouragement in the police services, which M. Bousquet reported to President Laval.

A conference was held at the Hotel Matignon. Present were the chiefs of the gendarmerie legions, the heads of the police, and the leaders of the Court of Paris. The Arlanc affair was discussed and I was harshly attacked, for, in the meantime, the condemned persons had escaped while they were being transferred to prison. At that time the prison administration still came under my Ministry. The chiefs of the gendarmerie and police demanded that courts should no longer be made up of judges, but rather of fearless and pitiless men, who would thus, consciously or not, have been playing the Militia's game. As I had decided to have nothing to do with a development which risked aggravating the civil war, I proposed, with the support of the Chief of Government, to hold a meeting either in Vichy or in Paris of the attorneys-general and first presidents of all the courts of appeal to consider with them what modifications could be made in the law and what means could be employed to harmonize the necessities of repression with the principles of law and impartiality indispensable to the proper functioning of any system of repressive justice. The Maréchal approved my proposal and decided that he himself would speak the words which the circumstances required.

IV

Two meetings were held in 1943, in Paris and in Vichy. All the chiefs of the courts of appeals were present. But the result was negative. Some—I do not wish to cite any names—proposed to hand over the work of repression to jurisdictions consisting of partisans, and even to the occupying authorities; their reason, needless to say, was not that they had confidence in them but that they wished to save their colleagues from the reprisals which threatened them.

Others proposed a combination of judges, policemen, and gendarmes which was a more reasonable suggestion and recalled the mixed commissions of the beginning of the Second Empire.

Personally I was opposed to the creation of new jurisdictions. My predecessors had multiplied these hybrid organizations with their badly defined authority and their proof that the legislative authority was powerless. Special tribunals had been established for nighttime aggressions, for the theft of cattle in the fields, for burning haystacks, and for offenses against the food laws; there had been a state tribunal, a court-martial at Gannat, which had lasted but a short time. There was no point in adding another to this list. A tribunal composed entirely of police and gendarmerie would receive the same threats which had paralyzed the magistracy. If the tribunals were entrusted to partisans, they would become instruments of reprisal and nothing more.

President Laval and I decided on a middle course. Of the five members composing the "special sections" there were to be but two judges; the other three would be appointed by the Chief of Government from secret lists of nominations made by the chiefs of the gendarmerie and of the police; there was however a requirement that all the judges must be officers of the judiciary police, which constituted a guarantee of juridical competence.

In order to test the new plan, it was to be tried only where the victim was a member of the gendarmerie or the police. Later it was extended to all assassinations of a terrorist character.

Thus the majority vote, that is to say, the responsibility for the decision reached, lay with men who would be jurors of a guaranteed character, whom the professional judges could counsel and direct.

This reform, which in fact was nothing more than a makeshift, combined with the effect produced on the higher magistracy by the very moving appeal of President Laval and by the energetic words of the Maréchal who had recalled the mutinies of 1917 and their repression, at first appeared to give good results because of the secrecy observed in the appointment of the military and police judges. But accidental or intentional indiscretions occurred and these men too were overcome by fear of reprisals against themselves and their families. As Pierre Laval said to me, with some humor, "Your judges are unquestionably good, honest men, but they're not at all daring."

An incident caused by the occupation authorities in the region of Dijon was to raise once more the problem of the participation of the Militia in legal repressions [of terrorism].

The incident in itself was an ordinary one; the reports of the attorneys-general included, every day, many similar ones throughout France. A French woman of Semur, a seamstress or dressmaker, had a liaison with a German officer. She was condemned to death by the local maquis and a young man appointed for the task shot her with a revolver. Believing that he had killed her he left and wandered about the city. To his surprise he saw an hour later that his victim, seriously wounded, was being cared for in a pharmacy. He went into the shop and completed her murder. Arrested by the local police he explained that he was merely carrying out orders given to him. The affair was referred to the "special section" of the Court of Dijon, composed in accordance with the new law.

At that time there was a particularly energetic counselor of military justice on the staff of the German general commanding the region; he had already caused a number of incidents which the diplomacy of the attorney-general had succeeded in smoothing out. He knew our laws thoroughly and knew that a death sentence was the only one applicable to this case. Therefore when the "special section," using as its excuse a disqualification which was juridically incorrect, merely sentenced the young man to hard labor, the German counselor, as soon as he heard of the decision, urged his own chiefs to order the arrest of the judges of the "special section" and deport them to Germany.

I was immediately informed of this by the local attorney-general and strove to save the magistrates by a personal intervention with General Ermerf, head of the judicial section of the German military authority at the Hotel Majestic in Paris, who would have to make the final decision. I was supported by two of his own collaborators, one a judge and the other an official of the Ministry of Justice in Berlin, Mr. Thierfelder and Mr. Bargatzki, who always showed understanding and humanity. The counselor for military justice at Dijon was ordered to drop the matter, but the danger had been intense and I now understood that magistrates were henceforth exposed to a new peril from the German side. They thus found themselves between two lines of fire, and not merely in the figurative sense.

Something else happened which caused me sharp anxiety. Until 1943 the military authority had administered occupied France and had established a correct liaison with those French services with which they were in relationship. The German officials were judges, lawyers, notaries, and university professors trained in juridical studies, courteous and conciliatory. As attorney-general of the Republic and as Minister of Justice, I had therefore been able to settle delicate matters and to avoid painful obligations most of which had to do with our attitude toward the German seizure of Alsace-Lorraine. (I refer to such matters as our refusal to accept decisions of German tribunals; to change the Christian names of Alsatians born in the occupied zone; to record on the [French] central registers any divorce judgments rendered in Alsace and Lorraine in application of German laws; and similar matters). It had been possible in all these affairs to put the question on juridical grounds, to gain time, and, as my own chief of cabinet, M. Cannas, put it, "to spin the papers," which made it possible not to give in and not to do anything which would limit us in the future.

But in 1943 the control gradually passed from the German army itself to the SS. The Hotel Majestic [army headquarters in Paris] without being stripped of its powers, particularly in its relations with the Ministry of Justice, nevertheless had to undergo control by the [SS] services in the avenue Foch, directed by General Oberg and Colonel Knochen. These new figures were partisan and authoritarian in spirit, determined to break by force any resistance to their decisions. They did not conceal their distrust and even hostility toward the regular agencies of the state and gave their confidence only to the extremist bodies and to the Militia whose pressure against the government increased day by day.

The SS, after a vain attempt by M. Bousquet to arrange an agreement acceptable both to the French police and the SS, obtained the removal of M. Bousquet from the position in which he had won the esteem and confidence of the Chief of Government and his subordinates. So far as my department was concerned the services of the avenue Foch lost no time in creating difficulties in the penitentiary administration which came under my authority. I had some interviews with Colonel Knochen during which I opposed any concentration of political prisoners in the fortresses of eastern France under the control of German police. Colonel Knochen did not hide his preference for the Militia and for the semi-military organizations of M. Doriot and M. Déat.

In the end the penitentiary administration was removed from the

Ministry of Justice and attached to the secretariat for the maintenance of order—which means that it was attached to the Militia. President Laval took this decision regretfully, in order to avoid the abandonment of the prisoners to the caprices of the SS police services. When this decision was reached the German army authorities ceased intervening in matters having to do with prison administration and I remember the remark of one of their higher chiefs on that occasion: "It's better for us and for you." This remark filled me with an anxiety confirmed by later events. Escapes doubled in number and there were revolts and harsh repressions, particularly at the Santé prison in Paris.

I understood that we were going to be presented with new demands and that we were threatened with losing control of the repression of terrorist activities, which would now pass, if not to the German authorities themselves, then at least to such organizations as the Militia. This fear was shared by the Chief of Government, who was only the nominal chief of a Militia which in fact was out of his hands.

V

One further consideration affected the legislative arrangements made at the end of 1943 and the beginning of 1944.

Though the term was not used, the country was in fact the victim of civil war. Both the maquis and the Militia were organized militarily. It was no longer a matter of isolated attacks but of military operations which included battles, the occupation of villages, raids, and the rest of it. This situation was strikingly similar to that of Spain during the French occupation of 1808-1812 when the Militia of King Joseph, supported by the French imperial army, waged a war of ambush with the famous guerrillas, who were being supplied arms and ammunition from England. As in the earlier example, the maquis—then the "partidas"—and the Militia included in their ranks men who were separated by contrary ideologies, searching the safety of their fatherland by different ways.

But both sides also included in their ranks trouble-making elements who took advantage of the confusion of opinion and the spread of anarchy to pursue their private ends, and to engage in operations of pure banditry. This struggle took place contrary to the elementary laws of war, particularly in regard to prisoners and the wounded. Leaders were powerless to prevent crimes committed by their own troops. Maquis leaders, at least those who had formerly been officers in the army, were the first to establish a certain discipline and to set up a form of court-martial to repress abuses and to pass summary judgment on their opponents. The Militia, for their part, demanded the right to establish similar agencies not merely against the maquis but also against the undesirable members introduced into their own ranks by hasty and undiscriminating recruiting. The Maréchal, above all else a military man, was not opposed in principle to the creation of courts-martial by the Militia. President Laval and I, on the other hand, were much more hesitant. It was remembered that at the meeting of the attorneys-general in Vichy the Maréchal had recalled the mutinies of 1917, and that his words had been favorably interpreted by the higher magistracy who would have preferred to see the special sections replaced by military tribunals.

The draft of a law which would have given the Militia—meaning the service for the maintenance of order—authority to pass judgment on any acts committed during its contacts with the maquis was prepared by a colonial magistrate, M. Mino, a member of M. Darnand's cabinet. He was a man who studied matters carefully, and I did not conceal from him the fact that President Laval and I had decided to limit the application of the text to persons caught in the act of assassination or of murder and then only if the guilty person had been captured in actual possession of firearms. On the one hand discipline would be strengthened in the Militia organizations and on the other hand summary executions would be avoided and the courts would be competent only where there was no possible doubt as to guilt. Such was the thinking of the Chief of Government in the creation of the courts-martial. The way in which the law was being applied was not known to us and it was only in July 1944 that the Maréchal's cabinet was informed that these new jurisdictions had given an unjustifiable extension to the application of the law. In this period, in fact, the secretary-general for the maintenance of order, supported by the German SS services, demanded the extension of his jurisdiction to all persons guilty of assassination and murder even though they were arrested later and therefore not caught in the actual act; he also demanded the application of the law to their accomplices.

President Laval and I refused this change in the law. The matter dragged on until 17 August 1944, at which time the government ceased to exercise its functions.

I was informed indirectly that a court-martial had functioned at the time of the mutiny in the Santé prison [Paris] and that its members had drawn a distinction between mutineers with criminal records under common law, and political prisoners who had joined in the mutiny and toward whom the judges showed indulgence.

VI

Other exceptional tribunals operated during the occupation. They had been formed previous to my participation in the government. These were jurisdictions similar to the "special sections" in their composition and in the range of penalties which they were allowed to inflict. Some judged thefts committed in buildings which had been bombed and evacuated by their tenants; the same tribunals judged aggressions committed at night in the obscurity made obligatory by defense against air attack. Other tribunals judged persons charged with theft of animals from the fields and with setting fire to crops. These tribunals received a certain amount of public approval because questions of personal safety and of food were of interest to the entire population; therefore propaganda hostile to the government abstained from criticizing their activities. I remember a death sentence which was pronounced at Agen against a bandit who had robbed farmers returning by night from a fair. In Paris, when Auteuil was bombed by British planes a man found stealing a bottle of liqueur from a shop was condemned to death. This punishment seemed to me to be excessive and I proposed to the Maréchal that he should reduce the penalty to hard labor as the man had been taking part in the work of clearing away the ruins of the buildings.

There were also special tribunals for black market operations and for illegal speculation.

The state tribunal was a creation of Minister Barthélemy. It was in two sections, one of which sat at Lyon and the other in Paris. Its president was a magistrate who was assisted by military or civilian judges appointed by the Chief of State. The Council of Ministers decided which cases should be submitted, in accordance with their seriousness. In fact it dealt chiefly with important prosecutions for illegal increase of prices and for speculation in, or possession of, rationed foodstuffs. M. Darnand was a member of the section at Lyon before he became secretary-general for the maintenance of order. So far as I know there was but one case in which he pronounced a death sentence actually followed by execution; this was against an abortionist of Cherbourg whom the Maréchal, a defender of the family and protector of births, refused to pardon.

In the definitely terrorist affair of the rue de Bucy the tribunal gave no death sentences though agents of the public forces on duty had been killed. A young student, Legros, son of an official of the Ministry of Finance, and the woman who inspired his actions, Mme Marzin, a suburban schoolteacher, thus escaped the death sentence. Mme Marzin later escaped at the gare Montparnasse [Paris] during a transfer. Young Legros was condemned to death by a German military tribunal for his part in an action against the occupation services. I intervened in his favor at the request of my friend Cathala, emphasizing his youth and the influences under which he had been placed, but in vain.

The operation attempted in the rue de Bucy by communist elements was repeated in the avenue d'Orléans but such activity did not please housewives who already had difficulty in finding food and who disapproved of rioting in shopping centers. The communist party therefore gave up this kind of activity as it might have compromised their influence on the working classes.

The problem of the prisons during the occupation
(1940-1944)

In 1940 the prison administration had already been under the control of the Ministry of Justice for a long time. Formerly it had been under the Ministry of the Interior; it had even been assigned to an under-secretariat of state created as a post for one of the most brilliant minds of the Third Republic, Anatole de Monzie. In fact it was quite reasonable to assign it to either one or the other of these ministerial departments because the application of penalties was a matter for the prefectoral authority, while the system for the prevention of crime was under judicial control.

The director whom I found in office when I took up my post in the Place Vendôme [Ministry of Justice] was not unknown to me. M. Contencin, a man of generous and sensitive nature, regarded his functions as an apostleship and dreamed of attaching to his name the credit for a great reform in the penal system, to consist of humanitarian changes and the application of methods for the education and rehabilitation of delinquents.

But in 1943 he was discouraged. His staff, affected by communist propaganda and disoriented by unaccustomed contact with political prisoners, had adopted a bad attitude. The number of people in prison had greatly increased not merely as a result of the application of the laws against subversive activity but particularly because of legislation on the food supply and the black market. The big black market operators had important resources and means of corruption which acted strongly on small officials who were poorly paid and had been recruited under sub-normal conditions because of the scarcity of candidates. In addition, the political prisoners impressed their guards by the relentlessness of their opinions, and often by their courage and dignity; these prisoners had nothing in common with the usual inhabitants of the prisons, common law transgressors who yielded readily to the rules of discipline in these establishments.

Parallel with the crowding of the prisons there came, unfortunately, a decrease in the accommodations available. In the northern zone the German authorities had requisitioned the best arranged prisons, the prison at Fresnes [Paris suburb] for example, where they reserved many sections for their own use. They acted in the same way in many large cities. Bombardments had damaged other prisons, as at Amiens; and those along the coast, for example the central prison at Caen, had been forcibly evacuated [by the Germans] because they were within the fortified area of the Atlantic wall.

The demarcation line prevented a fair numerical division of prisoners throughout the whole of the territory. One more difficulty was that the transfer of prisoners to French Guiana had been abandoned. Prisons were therefore extremely crowded; regulations intended to maintain hygienic conditions could no longer be observed; supervision was almost impossible. The food was notoriously insufficient. The prisoners, rationed like other people, were the only ones in France who could not make use of the black market, and the food parcels sent to them by their families were indispensable. When signs of indiscipline and rebellion began to be seen, especially in the southern zone—the fear of German reprisals in the northern zone led to greater prudence—my predecessor had used the vital necessity of the food parcels as a means of bringing a certain pressure to bear on prisoners in order to maintain good discipline. In this way the parcels for the political prisoners were limited and sometimes suppressed. I remember the visits of the weeping mother and sister of a communist general councilor of the Seine, a man who had been under my own orders during the war of 1914, when I was still attorney-general of the Republic. I succeeded in pleading the case of these poor women with M. Contencin by appealing to ordinary principles of humanity.

When I became Minister of Justice I explained the situation in the prisons to the President and in agreement with him I put a stop to the practice of attempting to maintain discipline by cutting off the family food parcels, and re-established the parcels privilege as it had always been before. This brought a new obligation for the prison staffs, that of verifying carefully the contents of the parcels. They were being used not merely as a means of clandestine correspondence but also often to carry small instruments hidden in the bread or other food to aid in escapes. I was shown nuts and eggs transformed into little masterpieces of human ingenuity.

Escapes increased in number under the often friendly eye of the guards, even when they did not act as accomplices. These escapes were prepared from the outside by resolute elements, often dressed in uniforms of the gendarmerie or the police. These pretended agents of the public authority, needless to say, limited their liberations to political prisoners; but common law prisoners took advantage of the disorder to escape as well. Some prisons were thus entirely emptied. It even happened that common law prisoners thus ejected from prison in spite of themselves, came back to surrender; but most of them left to join the different maquis where they accomplished all sorts of misdeeds. One police report informed me of the discovery of a corpse on which was pinned a note from a resistance court-martial indicating that the victim had been a malefactor executed by the maquis of which he had become a member after having escaped from prison.

The chief of penal administration discharged some guards, but their replacements acted in the same way at the first opportunity.

It was in this atmosphere of anarchy that the sensational escape of General de Lattre de Tassigny took place at Riom. I had met him in 1940 when I was at the supreme court of Riom and he commanded the region of Clermont-Ferrand. He was then a very warm supporter of the Maréchal but he had later modified his attitude and after the quixotic adventure of Montpellier he had been sentenced by a council of war and imprisoned at Riom. He was closely watched as much in his own interests as in those of the government. Ever since the incident of General Giraud the Germans had kept a close watch on military chiefs and we suspected that in case of an escape he would be taken to Germany, as had happened with General Weygand. President Laval was very liberal in all matters concerning food, and concerning his activities inside the prison—General de Lattre de Tassigny devoted himself to gardening in his hours of enforced leisure—but on the other hand he refused to allow the prisoner any visitors other than those of his religious confessor. I obtained from President Laval, relying on the fact that any appeal based on family sentiment was always successful, permission for Mme de Lattre to spend a few hours each week in his company.

The prison guards were themselves supervised by gendarmes who surrounded the prison walls, and it was with the help of these very gendarmes that he escaped. The director of the penal administration, who had taken every measure humanly possible, was in no way responsible. This escape was exploited by radio London and, in the contrary sense, by Radio Paris, which was inspired by extreme collaborationists. The German SS were greatly agitated and created new difficulties for the Chief of Government. He in turn appointed a commissioner-plenipotentiary, Colonel Bernon, to investigate, and in the end he demanded the removal of the director of the penal administration. I protested against this unjust decision and arranged for the President to see M. Contencin; the latter was then appointed a councilor at the court of appeals.

M. Contencin was replaced as chief of the penal administration by the prefect of the Ardèche, who had the same difficulties because the situation was irremediable. This official was soon discouraged and asked for another appointment. A particularly difficult problem had come to the fore when it was proposed that all political prisoners should be brought together in one or a number of prisons in the east of France under the more or less close supervision of the German army. This was a crucial demand made by the SS who were now convinced that the government was powerless to maintain security in its prisons. It was to be feared that once they were taken near the frontier they might be deported into some concentration camp across the Rhine without any warning or negotiations. The SS services in the avenue Foch [Paris], now responsible for all police and the security of the occupation forces, had chosen one of the Toul forts for this centralization of political prisoners.

I was summoned to see Colonel Knochen, General Oberg's deputy, and he told me what had been decided. I made some objections on the ground that the plan was physically impracticable and cited a report of an engineer who had visited the fort and listed its dilapidations. The fort had been pillaged, it had no doors, there were no bars at the windows, and we did not have the necessary metals and other materials to put it into condition. In this way I gained time, the only means of defense open to us. Colonel Knochen was not satisfied and complained of my ill-will.

This incident was not unconnected with the assignment of the penal administration to the Presidency of the Council. The administration was now entrusted to the Secretariat for the Maintenance of Order. I am sure that the President took this decision regretfully. But he was under pressure similar to that which had stripped the [German army command at the] Hotel Majestic of that same part of its powers. Prefect Esquirol was then replaced by M. Baillet, whom I had known at the Parquet of the Seine when he was assigned to the general intelligence service. He was a competent official and his father, the commissioner of police at Auber-villiers, had been a friend of M. Laval. But the functions now entrusted to him were beyond his capacity and he was soon dominated by disturbing elements from the Militia. Revolts were repressed with bloodshed, notably at Eysses. The staff of the central administration, which consisted of magistrates, was appalled and asked permission to leave that service. I then issued a decree permitting all who held the grade of magistrate to return to the chancellery.

If the penal administration had remained under the control of the Ministry of Justice we might have avoided an assassination such as that of M. Mandel, which so strongly shook President Laval. All who read the notes in his secret diary, found on his body, had sound reasons for regretting his death, since he was a supporter of national reconciliation.

I no longer intervened with M. Baillet except unofficially, and it was on the last day before our departure from Paris that I advised him to release the political prisoners from the Tourelles in order to avoid a massacre in case there was street fighting in the capital. My advice was followed and the attorney-general of the Republic at Laon, M. Amor, on whose behalf I had intervened, was freed. By the irony of fate he became chief of penal administration at the liberation.

The final telephone call I received, at nine o'clock in the evening, came from the mother of a prisoner at the Petite Roquette who thanked me for the return of her daughter to her home.

The Services in Alsace-Lorraine

The services in Alsace-Lorraine were attached to the Ministry of Justice and operated from Vichy. There had been no question of transferring them to Paris when I regrouped the whole of the central administration in the Place Vendôme.

These services were directed by a master of appeals in the council of state, M. Benoit, who had been an administrator in Alsace; being at the same time firm yet diplomatic he was perfectly fitted for this appointment.

Whereas most of the problems raised by the occupation were complicated, ambiguous, and changing, the question of Alsace-Lorraine had the advantage of being clear and precise. The French government considered as illegal, contrary to international law, and contrary to the armistice convention, all measures taken by the German government in an integral part of our national territory. Such measures included the removal of officials

who had been regularly appointed by their government before the occupation, the replacement of these officials by others appointed by the German
government, the expulsion of persons residing in Alsace and Lorraine, the
obligatory introduction of German practices in ordinary life and in public
and official acts, the attribution of the classification *Volksdeutsch* to the
people of Alsace and Lorraine, the introduction of German legislation, the
re-establishment of the frontier line of 1914, the obligation to serve in the
German labor force [youth labor service], military service as applied in 1944
to fourteen age groups, and many more.

On all these points the French government either directly or through
the services for Alsace-Lorraine had protested to the commission at Wiesbaden.

In April 1942 President Laval after an interview with Ambassador Abetz
had had a note drawn up which served as a model for all our protests.
This note affirmed the position of the government in principle. No provision of the armistice convention authorized the German government to
apply to the three departements of the Haut-Rhin, Bas-Rhin and Moselle
any different treatment from that of the departements of the occupied
zone; all measures taken by Germany in this region were illegal, being
contrary to the principles of international law. More than seventy protests
were made to the armistice commission. No response was given to any of
them, and when the French delegate expressed his astonishment at this
failure to reply, General Vogel told him that he had always sent them on
to the [German] Ministry of Foreign Affairs who had never sent him any
communication concerning them.

The only advantage which came to us from this activity of President
Laval was that we obtained a promise that refugees from Alsace and
Lorraine who had settled in the occupied zone would not be disturbed;
and after the German army crossed the demarcation line in November 1942
it was agreed that no measures would be taken against those who lived in
the unoccupied zone. This undertaking was generally adhered to and the
only regrettable incidents were those connected with the University of
Strasbourg in its evacuation to Clermont-Ferrand.

Once the question of principle had been dealt with there was nothing
for the services of Alsace-Lorraine and for the Minister of Justice to do
except to manage as best they could on purely practical grounds in each
difficulty, aiding and protecting those of our compatriots who had come
from the three departements and taken refuge in the two zones.

The German official at Vichy who dealt with matters concerning Alsace
and Lorraine was a young man, relentless in his conversations and difficult
to get along with: Dr. Diehl. The instructions were that he was always
to be opposed with the answer that "it cannot be done," and that the
maneuver of "spinning the papers" was to be used against him, a
trick of which I proved the effectiveness many times in dealings with the
German services.

In Paris, on the other hand, as attorney-general of the Republic,
and then as Minister of Justice, I was dealing under the best conditions
in all matters concerning the status of individuals, legislation, and procedure,
with Consul-General Quiring, an old diplomat who was willing to make
some sort of arrangement on any question of detail so long as it was not
taken as a decision in principle. Many Alsatians owed their tranquillity
during the occupation to him, through my intermediacy.

The Alsace-Lorraine services disposed of rather large special funds which M. Benoit managed scrupulously. I made the decision, one which in fact was the same as that of my predecessors, that these funds should be used entirely for the relief of the distress of refugees. Whenever the prefect of one of these departements, evacuated to the southern zone, reported some case of misfortune I left it to M. Benoit to determine the amount of the aid to be given to the person in question through his prefect. A subsidy was granted automatically to a certain category of refugees whenever some family event involved extraordinary expenses, as for example a birth, marriage, first communion, and so on.

In addition, regular help was given to important people from those areas. This was for example the case of the aged Canon Muller, a former senator, of most of his colleagues in parliament, and of the artist Hansi who had settled in Switzerland.

Further, I entered a protest every time I heard of the unjustified arrest of an Alsatian because of his attachment to the mother country. I remember particularly the case of the arrest of Mlle Sigolène de Wendel.

Although the services of my department were competent to deal with matters concerning any official from Alsace and Lorraine, in fact those questions referring to members of the educational services were dealt with by the secretary-general of the Ministry of National Education. M. Terrachet was a high official, jealous of his authority, and he felt that all matters concerning Alsace-Lorraine should be dealt with by his services. It was for this reason that I was not aware of the tragic incidents connected with the University of Strasbourg, evacuated to Clermont-Ferrand, until the situation had become irreparable. Professors and students of this university had been brought together at Clermont-Ferrand in the unoccupied zone, an arrangement which had no inconveniences before the total occupation of France. But in 1943 it could be feared that these students and professors would be a target for the numerous SS organizations in the Auvergne, and prudence suggested the advisability of scattering them throughout the various universities of the south of France, all the more because they were violently hostile to the German occupation, a very natural reaction on their part. Some professors shared this point of view. I remember a letter from the widow of a professor who was killed by the Germans. She wrote to thank me for the help which I sent to families of victims after the bloody events which had occurred in the local universities when the Germans had claimed they had to conduct searches to find students belonging to resistance organizations. If the students had been scattered at the right time many precious human lives would doubtless have been spared. The university was finally dispersed, but unfortunately too late.

The clergy of Alsace and Lorraine, both Catholic and Protestant, were also dealt with by my services, since both priests and pastors were government officials because the Concordat was still in effect in the provinces of the east of France. M. Benoit dealt with these questions through the aged Canon Muller who had formerly been one of the chiefs of the autonomist movement but had returned to better sentiments and was now living in poverty in a monastery at Vichy. I had the pleasure of dealing personally with Lorraine affairs with Monseigneur Moncelle, brother of the former mayor of Metz, who had the confidence of the bishop of that city, evacuated to Lyon with Cardinal Gerlier.

During the first world war I had known Monseigneur Ruch, Bishop of Strasbourg, at the staff headquarters of General Balfourier of the 20th Corps, and I could not forget the spiritual and material aid which he had so generously bestowed upon so many of my comrades. He had taken refuge in the Dordogne, and though his health was poor his determination was unaffected. At the time of the exodus from Alsace he had taken with him as he had the right to do the precious objects of the mass and pontifical possessions, now carefully preserved at the Château de Hautefort. The Germans demanded the return of these objects and were keeping the cathedral closed to all church services until they had been returned. Monseigneur Ruch refused to comply with their demand, and I shared his point of view entirely. When the free zone was occupied the Germans seized part of the treasure by force but it was possible to preserve the rest. All that I was able to do was to deposit a complaint with the commission at Wiesbaden as a basis for future action.

Among the difficult questions raised by the German government were those concerning the status of individuals, the civilian records, and the validity of actions taken by the new tribunals now installed in our provinces by the Reich. Alsace had been combined with the Grand Duchy of Baden, which complicated the problem still further from the juridical point of view.

The administrative services of the Rhine provinces had the idea—a ridiculous one to say the least—of germanizing all Christian names and making the same changes in all the civilian records. The question had already been brought up while I was directing the Parquet of the Seine and I had refused to make similar changes in the civilian records of the occupied zone, basing my argument on juridical grounds. In this way I gained time, which was the great objective, in such a way that this demand was never met.

As Minister I adopted the same attitude toward divorce proceedings, disavowals of paternity, legitimatization of birth, recognition of a child born out of wedlock, and so on, regardless of the difficulties which might result for the families, and the law suits which might arise later because of the differences on the two sides of the Vosges mountains in matters concerning family status. To have accepted the changes made by the Germans would have been to recognize implicitly that the three departements were no longer a part of France; and on the other hand, to order the transcription of these German decisions into French registers of civilian status would have been a heresy, as the decisions had not been made in the name of the French people. Some of the resulting situations must have been inextricable, particularly in cases where one of two divorced persons remarried.

At the same time, in a spirit of conciliation, I did agree that judicial commissions of inquiry should be allowed to operate in the usual way and that judicial papers should be accepted when there was similarity between the two legislations. In application of this principle no commission of inquiry was accepted in the matter of a divorce based on insanity in one of the parties, as this is a ground not admitted in French law. M. Quiring accepted this restriction and did not insist.

To sum up, no decision was taken which constituted an explicit or implicit recognition of a situation created in Alsace by the occupying power through the use of force and contrary to international law. This point of view coincided with the firmly expressed determination of the Maréchal and President Laval. It cannot be forgotten that President Laval, in May 1941, when he was no longer a member of the government, had the courage in an interview given to the American press agency, United Press, to speak of the drama of Alsace-Lorraine at a moment when the result of the war was for the least uncertain, fully realizing the risk, entirely unknown by those who spoke at the London microphones, which any Frenchman who remained on his native soil ran in making any public statement.

The Secret Societies

The legislation against the Freemasons had been one of the first indications of political activity on the part of the government of Maréchal Pétain. A law had suppressed all secret societies, of which the most important was that of the Freemasons, though even such very small bodies were included as those of the Theosophists and the cult of Memphis-Misraîm. Membership in a secret society which had been dissolved now became an offense. Every government official had to make a declaration stating whether or not he had belonged to any secret society. As two declarations had to be made, there were confusions which created juridical difficulties for the courts. False declarations were to be punished by penalties of the same kind as applied in the case of crimes. Former dignitaries of secret societies were excluded from public office and their names were published in the *Journal Officiel*. The definition of "dignitary" was extended by the service for secret societies to all the upper grades, which gave extraordinary length to the lists published. All property which had belonged to secret societies was placed under sequestration, and its administration and liquidation was entrusted to the direction-general of domains [controllers of all state property] under supervision of the Parquets.

The service for secret societies had originally been attached to the Maréchal's cabinet. M. Bernard Fay was placed in charge. A staff of officials had been especially set up and the administration included headquarters at Vichy and in Paris, with representatives in all departements, a propaganda service, and a special police service. When President Laval returned to power he found that various abuses were being committed and that unrest had been created in state administrations by the partisan activities of those who were directing the service for secret societies.

The chief of these services at that time was Admiral Platon, secretary of state attached to the Chief of Government. The admiral was a valorous sailor of an upright but passionate character. He considered the fight against Masonry as a crusade against the infidels and he surrounded himself with demobilized officers, such as Colonel de Verchère, as ardent as he was. Admiral Platon proposed to President Laval a draft law which would extend the application of the law against secret societies even to employees of public services which operated autonomously, and to new dignitaries. President Laval refused to sign the proposed law, and a struggle ensued between the admiral and the Chief of Government. The special police for secret societies created incidents, and the prefects protested. M. Bousquet, secretary-general for the Ministry of the Interior, had difficulties with a member of this police force during a journey in the departement of the Marne. President Laval complained of the publication in the *Journal Officiel*, before the matter had been referred to him, of the names of high officials who were former dignitaries of secret societies.

President Laval had attached to the services operating under his direct authority a commission of which the task was to examine all claims relative to the application of the law; this commission had previously operated under the Maréchal's cabinet. President Laval appointed as president of this commission a president of section in the council of state, M. Reclus, whose impartiality he knew well. New members were added to the commission, among them a magistrate, M. Cannac, who became chief of my own cabinet. Admiral Platon was displeased with these appointments. M. Reclus offered to resign and maintained his position only on the insistence of President Laval.

In the meantime Admiral Platon had to terminate his membership in the government, and Laval asked me to accept the attachment of the service for secret societies to the Ministry of Justice.

I had had no personal connections with Freemasonry, and it had always shocked my religious beliefs. Nevertheless after years of judicial discipline I believed that a law must be applied honestly, without excessive harshness and without favors which would distort its application. This conception was the same as that held by President Laval and our agreement was always complete on this subject.

I then tried to find as director for the service some magistrate who had no connections with Freemasonry, who enjoyed the approval and respect of everyone, and who was without personal ambition. I had the good fortune to find someone who met all these requirements, M. Sens-Olive, an Honorary Counselor at the Court of Final Appeals. His diplomacy succeeded in overcoming the hostility shown at the beginning by Colonel de Verchère, who had been the confidential collaborator of Admiral Platon. He introduced into the service methods which were more in harmony with the traditions of French administration. This new orientation did not please everyone, and I learned that careful search had been made in the archives of all the Masonic lodges to find out whether I myself had been a Mason. It was insinuated that possibly I had been prudent enough to cause the disappearance of any traces of my membership, but this campaign of insinuations became so ridiculous that it died out.

I decided that publications of names would not be made in the *Journal Officiel* until after communication to the Ministers of the departments concerned in order to avoid any more incidents such as that of the prefect of the Cantal. I gave my full confidence to the Reclus commission because it was working with an impartiality which deserved praise.

I had, in fact, previously felt doubts regarding the professional honor of certain officials in the Service for Secret Societies when a M. M..., former minister, was listed as a Masonic dignitary. He was linked to me by an old family friendship; I had full trust in his word, and his own affirmation contradicted some notes in a quite different handwriting on the registers of a lodge to which he had belonged in his youth. I also discovered a tendency in the service to create difficulties for the Chief of Government when it was discovered that one of his immediate collaborators, a commissioner-plenipotentiary had, long before, been a Mason.

A troublesome search was made in the home of one of my former chiefs, a higher magistrate already in retirement, who came much shaken to tell me of his fears. I reacted vigorously and forbade such practices. I finally decided that all who were suspected of false declarations should be allowed to present their own defense and should give their explanations before the Reclus commission before any action was taken against them, a precaution which proved to be quite useful.

In my own department I noted that the list brought to me contained little more than the names of interim judges of the peace, who, as everybody knows, are volunteers, unpaid magistrates, serving in the cantons as substitutes for judges of the peace. To recompense them for the aid which they brought to the service of justice by imposing disagreeable publicity on them seemed to me somewhat inelegant, and I therefore asked them to resign before any names were published, unless they preferred to appeal to the Reclus commission.

In concluding this note on the activity of the service for secret societies I shall make a comment. Contrary to what might be thought, the dignitaries of Freemasonry who held high positions in politics and in state administration under the Third Republic were few in number. The lists of dignitaries contained the names of the illustrious unknown—minor officials, tradesmen, pharmacists, doctors, and lawyers of the small cities.

(Document No. 207)
Fr. ed. 619-642

[*Not dated*]

GABOLDE

[*M. Gabolde deposited, with the preceding, another declaration of eight pages, entitled "From Wilflingen to Fort de Montjuich." This may be consulted at the Hoover Library; as it does not deal with the period of the German occupation of France, it has not been translated here.*]

THE MINISTRY OF JUSTICE

HENRY CORVISY

Director for Criminal Affairs and Pardons in the Ministry of Justice

I the undersigned Henry Corvisy, born at Saint-Omer 9 November 1893, and now living in Paris; former Director of Criminal Affairs and Pardons in the Ministry of Justice; Counselor in the Court of Appeals, revoked by the provisional government; Chevalier of the Legion of Honor, military section; certify under oath the truth of the following recollections.

June 1940.—When I was summoned to Bordeaux during the negotiations for the armistice I called on M. Fremicourt, first president of the Court of Appeals, who had just been made Minister of Justice in Maréchal Pétain's first government. Our conversation was most cordial. The key idea emphasized by the new Minister of Justice was as follows: "The armistice is inevitable. It is the least of the possible evils. Nevertheless if the Germans demand that we hand over the fleet we cannot agree and rather than give in to such a demand we will undergo the worst misfortunes, for the honor of France is at stake." At Bordeaux I tried to find some way of joining General de Gaulle, a military writer about whom there had been some talk, who, it was said, wanted to continue the fight on his own account, together with such Frenchmen as could join him, by acting with England. It was impossible to leave.

July 1940: Vichy.—M. Fremicourt instructed me to go to Paris to reorganize the services of the Ministry of Justice in the capital; the government was uninformed as to what was happening there. My instructions were very broad: I was to do the best I could. After the vote of the National Assembly which transferred the power of preparing a constitution to Maréchal Pétain, the mission which had been entrusted to me by the previous Minister of Justice was confirmed by the new Minister, M. Alibert. I was in fact unable to reach Paris until 8 August because of the closing of the line of demarcation.

The English radio.—I listened for the first time to the voice of General de Gaulle and was astonished by the stupidity and the unworthiness of his proposals. I no longer regretted that I had been unable to join such a person and resigned myself to doing my duty to France, in the position in which circumstances had placed me.

The Creation of the High Court of Riom.—M. Cassagnau, Attorney-General for the Court of Appeals, accepted the position of prosecuting attorney with the High Court. On the day of his acceptance I had a talk with him.

"It is necessary to be very prudent," he said, "for we must judge no one except those responsible for the defeat. Under no circumstances should the question of responsibility for the declaration of war be touched on." M. Cassagnau maintained this point of view to the very end.

Law regarding government servants of foreign origin.—Government employment was now forbidden to all persons who were not French by birth and of French fathers. The principle of this law was easily justified; the particular case which had inspired M. Alibert in the matter and which had led definitely to the immediate adoption of the law was that of M. Palewski, whose origin was uncertain, and who on being naturalized French had been chosen by M. Paul Reynaud, then Minister of Justice, as his chief of cabinet.

This law, adopted too hastily without sufficiently calculating its consequences, has proved to be difficult in application, and often unjust. This was true, for example, in the case of the sons of Belgians, and above all for persons of Spanish descent in the department of Oran. Various special cases proved to be particularly grievous. For example, M. Germain, a magistrate under the Ministry of Justice, born in Metz of a Lorraine family before 1918 [when Lorraine became French again], was ruled out by the law because he had been a German. He was kept in office temporarily until the necessary suppleness could be given to the provisions of the law so that he and others, particularly those of Alsace and Lorraine, would have their full rights as French citizens.

In 1936, when the Popular Front government was formed, M. Siben, former attorney-general at the Court of Colmar, was deprived of the pension which had been conferred on him when he retired. M. Siben held patriotic and anti-autonomous views [this refers to the Alsace separatists] which were not approved by the Blum government. This unprecedented measure directed against a high magistrate who was universally respected had caused a scandal in Alsace. Justice in this case was rendered as soon as I brought it to the attention of the new Minister of Justice, M. Alibert.

8 August 1940.—On this day I took charge of the services of the Ministry of Justice in Paris. My first solicitude was to disguise and hide such files as might interest the Germans, particularly those dealing with spies, with the sequestration of enemy property, and with certain cases of naturalization [this refers to the naturalization of Jews]. The Germans came to the Ministry to make a search and found nothing, but as they had been unwilling to say what they were looking for, I was not much worried. Circumstances led me to exaggerate the importance of my functions at this time and to act as an uncontrolled dictator over all the judicial services in the occupied zone. It was scarcely possible to receive any instructions from the government [in Vichy] and in any case the government would have been unable to give me instructions based on a knowledge of the facts as they did not have the necessary information, and the transmission of my own reports was most uncertain.

In my office at the Ministry I received a large number of people of all origins and levels. There was never a case in which the legitimacy of the Maréchal's government seemed to arouse the slightest doubt in anyone's mind—even in the mind of M. Mornet, who had been retired in 1940 because of his age, and who came to me personally to offer his services to the government, and to ask for a favor.

I assumed the title of "Under-Director of the Ministry of Justice of France," instead of the previous official title of "Under-Director of the Ministry of Justice."

An example of the application of the first law concerning the Jews.—M. Brack, formerly Director of Civil Affairs and of Justice, who had been made a counselor at the Court of Appeals by the Maréchal's government, was born of Jewish parents. Nevertheless as he was of illegitimate birth and as his blood relationship to one of his parents could not be established, he was regarded as a non-Jew in the sense of the first anti-Jewish law. When the second anti-Jewish law came to be applied, his case was deliberately overlooked.

M. Lyon-Caen, Attorney-General at the Court of Appeals, asked that an exception be made in his favor. It was not made.

M. Durand, an Algerian Jew, had become ineligible for the magistracy because the Cremieux decree had deprived him of his French citizenship. He was retired and asked for a pension; this was given to him because of the very favorable opinion expressed by the author of these notes.

M. Alibert paid a brief visit to Paris. He and I were on terms of mutual confidence, and he told me of his aversion toward the Germans, and his apprehensions. He feared the physical extermination of the French people and based his hopes for the future entirely on supple and skillful policies which would make it possible to gain time.

I obtained authorization from the government to recommence action against the communists under the Daladier decrees of September 1939. The communist party was now starting its agitation all over again, strong because of the good will of the Germans, who as soon as they entered France had released the militant communists who were interned or imprisoned at that time.

In theory the occupation authorities gave their agreement to the government [that the Daladier decrees should again be enforced], but in practice they prevented any effective repression. The way things went was as follows: as soon as a militant communist was arrested, the German military courts took charge of the case, and would consider only some minor infraction, such as obstructions of the public way, sentencing the communist to some very small fine or punishment. French justice would then be helpless because of the legal principle of "not twice in jeopardy."

Regarding the law on secret societies, I note for the record that only a very few magistrates stated definitely that they were Freemasons. No magistrate was troubled because of such a declaration.

22 December 1940.—I learned with surprise, through a telephone call from M. Dayras in Vichy, that I was to be appointed, that very day, Director of Criminal Affairs and Pardons. As soon as I reached Vichy the Director for Personnel, M. Dallant, gave me the text of the proposal made to the Maréchal in my favor. I saw with some emotion that it was my war services which had been emphasized.

January 1941.—I took possession of my new post in Vichy. M. Alibert told me once more, in confidence, what his policy was: "Save everything that can be saved; maintain everything that can be maintained; re-establish everything that can be re-established." There was complete agreement between the Minister and his director [the author, Henry Corvisy].

As had been the case in Paris, so too in Vichy there was no question whatever as to the legitimacy of the Maréchal's government. I had a conversation with my predecessor, at that time my friend, M. Battestini, who on his own request had been made a counselor at the Court of Appeals. This high magistrate was politically a man of the left, inspired by the attitude which was later to be called "the spirit of the resistance." He was quite ready to criticize the acts of the government. Nevertheless he declared that the Maréchal was not merely the only desirable chief under the circumstances, but the only possible one.

M. Battestini, in August 1944, accepted the position of technical counselor in the cabinet of a certain Willard, a communist lawyer, who seized control of the Ministry of Justice and inaugurated the "purification."

Pardons.—The Maréchal expressed a desire to be precisely informed as to his rights in the matter of pardons and amnesty. I prepared a long note in which I expressed my own ideas on the way in which his right was to be exercised. In particular I emphasized that it was legal to grant individual amnesties. Further, I proposed the institution of letters of remission which without having the full effects of an amnesty would make it possible to save some meritorious person from the sequels of his punishment, often more grievous than the punishment itself. The Minister of Justice, M. Barthélemy, approved my note without raising any difficulties and the Maréchal accepted my point of view. This method was followed for three years and gave excellent results. It should be noted that the system which I proposed would scarcely be applicable except under a strong centralized power, completely honest and free from political influence. In this connection it should be mentioned that from 1940 to 1944 the cabinet of the Maréchal did not intervene with the criminal direction even once, under any circumstances, to suggest that a pardon should be given to anyone. All the pardons granted by the Maréchal were based on the absolutely uninfluenced proposals of the Director of Criminal Affairs.

At the same time the cabinet of the Chief of State had let it be known that the Maréchal would use his right to pardon in certain affairs such as offenses against the Chief of State, the laws against the Freemasons and the Jews, and so on. On the other hand he would refuse on principle to use any clemency in abortion cases.

The Direction of Criminal Affairs never at any time, in any case, either before the war, during the war, or after the war, proposed any measure of clemency for anyone who had given any aid of any kind to the Germans or the Italians.

Those who were prosecuted for having taken up arms against France, as in the Dakar Affair, were not condemned to death unless they had not in fact been captured. Those who were captured with arms in their hands—for example, Hettier, known as de Boislambert—were merely deprived of their liberty. Most of them escaped and little trouble was taken to prevent them from doing so.

M. Barthélemy, Member of the Institute, Professor of Law in the University of Paris, Minister of Justice, felt deeply disturbed, as his predecessor had been, regarding the fate of France in case Germany won a final victory. One day when I called on him in his office I found him in a state of despair. He had just had an interview with Abetz who had told him that we would never recover the departements of the Nord and the Pas-de-Calais.

It was from M. Barthélemy that I learned of the existence of Tito, whose achievements aroused his enthusiasm.

M. Barthélemy's sarcastic spirit led him to criticize the acts of his colleagues and he thus appeared on occasion to be in opposition, even though he was a Minister. His sympathies lay with the movement which was not yet known by the name of "resistance." One day I met him in the office of someone named Massigli. The conversation was particularly cordial and unrestrained and I admit that I was rather scandalized by the freedom of the remarks made by the Minister of Justice in the presence of a man who was known for his hostility to the government's policies.

M. Barthélemy was very human in his reactions. He had never wished to hand over to Spain the Spanish revolutionaries who were living in France and whose return was demanded by their government; his attitude was not due to any sympathy for their cause but simply because he feared that he would be sending them to their death.

Regarding the communists, it was only German threats which had forced him to ask me to prepare a law establishing the special sections.

For M. Barthélemy I had great esteem but little friendship. I believe that he felt the same toward me.

General Revers, assistant to Admiral Darlan, seemed to be extremely devoted to his chief.

3 June 1944.—On this day I saw the Maréchal for the last time. After a lunch to which I had been invited I had a private interview with our Chief. I had not seen him for a rather long time and I found him looking older and tired. Nevertheless his fine intelligence was not affected. Our interview dealt at first with the military institutions of France and with military discipline, and then turned to current events. The Maréchal said to me, "The Americans will make a landing very soon and the Germans will be beaten. I shall have an extremely difficult role to play in order to defend the interests of France. Fortunately I have friends in America."

(Document No. 227)
Fr. ed. 643-647

Paris, 4 August 1954

H. CORVISY
Henry Corvisy

CHAPTER XII

FREEMASONS, JEWS,
AND PERSONS INTERNED
BY THE FRENCH GOVERNMENT

FREEMASONS

MAURICE RECLUS

Member of the Institut de France

I the undersigned Maurice Reclus, Member of the Institute, President of Section in the Council of State, living in Paris, make the following declaration under oath.

I knew Pierre Laval in 1918 when I was foreign political editor of *L'Avenir*, a newspaper of which Henri Lillaz was the financial backer and chief inspiration, and Pierre Laval the legal advisor. We felt drawn toward each other at once and became real friends. I knew him as a simple and a direct man, free of dogma and metaphysical conceptions, supremely intelligent without posing as an intellectual, and above everything else profoundly humane. I deeply admired the fact that his patriotism came from his ancestors and from the land itself; that he was a patriot whose country lived in his very blood.

Though our relations were neither very frequent nor very intimate, our relationship continued to be most affectionate on both sides. As a journalist I had the opportunity to support his policies on many occasions. Sometimes when he was President of the Council he would advise me by telephone of one point or another which he regarded as most important. During that period I used to give important luncheons at Lapérouse, half literary and half political. I was happy to invite him and to see him there, equipped only with his intuitions and his good sense, for he held his own against writers, lawyers, and orators all of the highest class, yet outclassing them by his skill and finally making them ashamed of themselves. I remember in particular one contest at my table between Pierre Laval and a political rival, a prominent member of Parliament who had been a minister and was later to be a President of the Council of Ministers; it ended in Pierre Laval's triumph, which he accepted with modesty.

In September 1940, I think it was, when he was the Maréchal's chief

Minister, he offered me, through M. Marquet, the prefecture of the Seine. Marcel Peyrouton, who was then secretary-general of the Ministry of the Interior, came from Vichy to Royat, where the Council of State sat, to make sure that I would accept, and to tell that my successor in the Council of State had already been as good as appointed. I declined but Pierre Laval did not hold it against me and even asked me later, on two occasions, to become an ambassador; again I refused.

After his return to power in 1942 he again asked for my co-operation, this time under conditions which did not permit me to refuse.

The Vichy laws on secret societies forbade important officials of Freemasonry to hold public positions, but exceptions could be accorded by a commission for secret societies which had the power to maintain in their posts those threatened with removal by this law, or to reinstate those who had been removed. The commission was particularly severe in its method and had granted only an extremely small number of exceptions, a fact which Pierre Laval, personally deeply opposed to this type of legislation, could not accept. He decided to change the composition of the commission and urged me to accept its presidency.

I was deeply disturbed. I disapproved absolutely of the measures which had been taken against Freemasons and I was most reluctant to become associated with them even for the sake of softening their effects. I therefore kept out of the way as much as I could, broke my appointments, and kept my telephone off the hook. But I was a government servant and I belonged to a corps of officials whose members are normally asked to preside over commissions; I could not avoid the subject indefinitely.

When Pierre Laval summoned me personally to the Hotel Matignon I explained to him without any subterfuge both my scruples and my dislike of the whole matter.

"Good heavens, I know all that," he said to me, "and it's exactly why I thought of you. My ideas on the matter are the same as yours. It is against democratic liberty to punish people for their political and spiritual loyalties, and to create misdemeanours of opinion; and in this particular case it is bad policy because it arouses uselessly the anger of a part of the middle classes who tend to be more or less anti-clerical. I want to act against this injustice, against this error. Help me by instilling into a regenerated commission a spirit which will be systematically liberal, granting every possible exception and trying to bring the expelled Freemasons back into the administration, the magistracy, the Army, and the universities. In that direction, go strongly ahead, as strongly as you wish. I will protect you completely by official orders."

I struggled against the suggestion for a long time, defended my point of of view carefully, and explained to Pierre Laval my very good reasons for not wanting to get mixed up in the matter. He appealed to my Republican principles and to my liberalism. Without for a single instant abandoning the tone of affectionate cordiality in which he always dealt with me, he let me understand that in any case I was going to be appointed.

He added that to this task of classification and of at least partial reparation of wrongs done, to which he was inviting me, he would add another task equally useful. Admiral Platon, under whose jurisdiction all matters concerning secret societies fell, had prepared a draft law which would greatly increase the harshness of the anti-Masonic measures. It had been officially agreed that the text of this law would not be submitted to the government until it had been examined by the commission for secret societies. "You must gain time," Pierre Laval said to me. "Take weeks and months to examine it before expressing an opinion. Propose amendments, change it so that it means nothing, sabotage it, and finally reject it entirely if you can. I am back of you. And in any case I am protecting you and will continue to protect you. . . ."

I will not recount the details of the work which I was able to do as president for the commission for secret societies, and the struggles I had to wage against the services dealing with the matter, which showed themselves relentless in their attempts to destroy Freemasonry and against Admiral Platon who was a true madman of sectarian bigotry and repression. What I shall recount is intended only to indicate the points on which Pierre Laval attained his ends, and how he supported me without wavering, and in such a way that the credit for the results obtained really belongs directly to him.

First of all, the commission which in its former composition had given almost no exceptions at all—perhaps one out of twenty—now reversed the proportion, reinstating nineteen out of twenty, *at least*, of the Masonic officials who has been ejected.

This was not accomplished without difficulty. Admiral Platon had partisan supporters, even in the new commission, who made our liberal policy extremely difficult. In fact I did not have a majority on the commission, and my friends and I had to persuade, and when necessary, to bluff. I used Pierre Laval's orders, of which I made no mystery, as my authority. I let it be understood that in limiting and softening the application of the laws of exception regarding Freemasonry we would be furthering Pierre Laval's personal policies. In any case we did succeed in bringing back into public service hundreds of the sons of the Louve [stonemason], thus giving bread to hundreds of families who had been wrongly injured.

On another point we were able to render certain dispositions of the law much less harmful and particularly in a matter which interested Pierre Laval, namely that of the persons who had made false declarations as to their membership in Freemasonry. All government servants had been forced to declare on oath whether or not they belonged to any secret society. A number of Freemasons had not felt able to admit their membership, and by making false declarations they became liable to punishment, even including prison.

"I don't want any of that," Pierre Laval had said to me. "Get them out. You are a lawyer: invent anything—twist the texts, turn white into black, and black into white—anyway, get out of it somehow. Here again I'll give you my protection."

Against all likelihood we succeeded in setting up a legal system which enabled us to get all the authors of false declarations out of their difficulty. Not one of them, on any occasion, was punished. We were rather proud of this accomplishment; and as for Pierre Laval he was delighted.

But all of that was not accomplished without upsetting and really exasperating Admiral Platon and his anti-Masonic office. He openly declared war against me. The Gestapo heard of the matter; I need not recount how I lived under their continual surveillance for over three months and how during that time I was refused a pass allowing me to go from Paris to Vichy in order to exercise my functions as president of the commission.

I now come to the leading event of my presidency, the commission's examination of the draft which Platon had prepared to increase the severity of the anti-Masonic laws.

It would take too long to explain the nature and the methods of the changes by which the law was to be made more severe. I simply point out that thousands of French families hitherto spared would have been punished, and not only families of those in public administrations but also of those in the liberal professions, in intellectual careers, and in the entire economic life of the country.

Pierre Laval would not hear of such an interdiction, alloting to Freemasons a fate very similar to the odious treatment given to Jews. In agreement with him I decided to have the commission reject this draft law, as horrifying as it was stupid. But, I repeat, I did not have a majority on the commission. Admiral Platon and his representative kept close watch, declaring, and proving as well, that they were immovable, and even making veiled threats. They were really determined to get their law put into effect. I didn't want it. The credit was not really mine as I knew that I was supported wholeheartedly by Pierre Laval; but those of my colleagues on the commission who shared my ideas then showed an extreme independence and true courage to which I pay full homage in a spirit of affectionate gratitude.

I did not conceal from myself the fact that Pierre Laval could not intervene openly in this matter of the draft law. If he took too blunt a position against the laws of exception, he might have awakened certain susceptibilities in those around the Maréchal and thus aroused even more the partisans of Admiral Platon and his policies against the Chief of Government. Therefore he was obliged to act through intermediaries, putting me in the forefront. I realized this but had no doubt that if necessary he would be able to force the acceptance of my solutions and his decision.

In the end of the commission did reject the Platon draft, refusing it purely and simply, without bothering to suggest an amendment either in form or in purpose. It was a narrow victory—the vote was exactly equal, four against four—and a majority was obtained by the deciding vote of the President, myself.

I am very proud of having thus rendered so important a service to the liberal cause by resolutely barring the road to those who wished to ban Frenchmen from the activities of our national life and by saving Freemasonry in the most definite manner when it was threatened with the worst persecutions. I remain grateful to the memory of Pierre Laval for having allowed me, in this matter, to make the right side prevail, for having permitted me to play this part, and even, as will be seen, for having completely and absolutely protected me.

What happened was that immediately after the vote of the commission had been taken, Admiral Platon sent Pierre Laval a violent demand in which he accused me of pro-Masonic prejudices, of partisan opposition to the National Revolution, and of conducting a dishonest maneuver with the purpose of forcing the commission to reject his draft law. Admiral Platon concluded by demanding formally that I should be removed from my position as president of the commission.

It is certain that if I had not been supported I would have run serious risks. But Pierre Laval paid no attention to Admiral Platon's demands and kept me in my position. Even better, at my request, he added to the commission two new members whom he had chosen personally and whom he instructed to follow my directives. Thereafter I had a majority and was able, without any more opposition, to increase the number of exceptions made to the anti-Masonic laws, and to protect those who had made false declarations from being punished in any way.

From this brief account, and from the numerous documents which I have in my possession, it is clear that Pierre Laval did everything to limit, in a liberal Republican spirit, the effects of the interdictory measures, which he entirely disapproved.

I testified in this sense before the Interrogating Commission of the High Court of Justice and my deposition must be included in the testimony for the defense recorded during the Laval trial.

(Document No. 122)
Fr. ed. 651-654

Paris, 31 May 1950

MAURICE RECLUS

FREEMASONS — ADMINISTRATIVE
INTERNEES YOUTH CAMPS

ÉMILE BERNON

*President of the French Legion
of Combatants in the Aveyron;
Plenipotentiary Commissioner, 1942*

I the undersigned Émile Bernon, former plenipotentiary commissioner, former chief of the French Legion of Combatants for the departement of the Aveyron, a political prisoner at Fresnes (Seine), having been personally summoned in due form by Maître Charles Amable Desmé, bailiff of the High Court of Justice, to appear as a witness in the case brought against Pierre Laval before the said High Court, at the session of 4 October 1945, at the request of the indicted person; having not been taken from my cell by the prison administration as is required by the regulations; having in consequence been unable to appear before the High Court, there to reply at any session whatever to the call for witnesses cited by the defense; and having as an unheard witness the strict duty to contribute to the establishment of the truth; do make the following deposition of that which I would have said before the High Court under oath.

I did not know President Laval before 1942.

As departemental president of the French Legion of Combatants for the Aveyron, I was present at many meetings of the officers of the Legion, held at Vichy, where President Laval spoke as Chief of Government.

At the first of these meetings, in the spring of 1942, President Laval told us about certain German plans of which he had some knowledge, plans that would in his opinion make conditions under the armistice worse and would be decisive for the fate of the country. He told us that he believed it was his duty not to leave the Maréchal in ignorance of these German plans, and that it was also his duty to abandon, despite the difficulties and risks, and also despite the advice of the occupation authorities, his continued refusal to accept a position of power. He added that his passionate love for his country had led him, regardless of his personal interests, to accept a position heavy with responsibility, difficult, dangerous, and bringing only ingratitude. He asked the French Legion of Combatants to help him in his task.

After the luncheon which followed this meeting, presided over by the Chief of Government, Maréchal Pétain, Supreme Chief of the Legion of Combatants, gave his legionnaires the same details about the conditions under which he had asked President Laval to take power in this difficult hour which threatened to be so serious for the country. The Maréchal ended his address with these words: "I ask you to aid President Laval in his task. I am in complete agreement with him. There is no longer any difference or cloud between us; all has been wiped out. Henceforth, we proceed hand in hand."

Later, in 1943, at other meetings of the same officers of the Legion of Combatants, I had occasion to note that the general staff of the Legion, guided by some of the departemental and regional officers who were particularly militant and mistrustful, and who were undoubtedly influenced by the vice-presidents and by the Maréchal's own cabinet, was moving farther and farther away from the Chief of Government, reproaching him particularly for his lukewarm attitude to the National Revolution, and for his resistance to any application of the exceptional laws decreed against Jews and members of secret societies, even though the Legion itself had received from the Maréchal in person, during the summer of 1943, an order to aid the chief of the French Militia, and more precisely again in January 1944—the 25th, I believe, or in any case after Joseph Darnand had been imposed on President Laval as secretary-general of the police.

In December 1942, together with Colonel Marmod, I was presented to the Chief of Government by the director-general of the French Legion of Combatants, to be appointed, on the Legion's own nomination, a plenipotentiary commissioner. Thus it was that from this time I was in contact with President Laval and received his direct instructions and orders of mission.

Two of the permanent missions assigned to me stand out from the others. The first was to preside over the commission for the liberation of persons interned by administrative order; and the second was to serve as vice-president of the special commission on secret societies, to aid Councilor of State Reclus, its president.

The commission for the liberation of persons interned by administrative order had been created by President Laval in January 1943, in order that every such interned person might have a legal possibility of requesting that his case be studied within one month after the request was made, at the expiration of which period a decision, either of liberation or of continued internment, was to be presented to the Chief of Government.

This commission had to overcome the passivity, and often the resistance, of certain prefects who had themselves issued the orders of internment. The commission also had to overcome the timid inertia of the government's central administration. In overcoming these difficulties, the commission had President Laval's total support.

I ascertained and reported to the Chief of Government the following: (1) that the very great majority of persons interned by administrative order, apart from persons engaged in black market activities, had been arrested by the preceding governments of President Daladier and President Paul Reynaud; (2) that among them were thousands of internees whose dossiers were empty, so that it was impossible to discover the reasons for their internment; (3) that many internments had resulted only from vindictive denunciations, and that many political internees had been arrested only because of their opinions, often unexpressed, or for having belonged, at a period when it was not forbidden, to the political party which had been dissolved by President Daladier's government.

I then asked President Laval to authorize me to give more of a character of appeasement to the work of this commission than had been previously envisaged. Not only did President Laval authorize me to present for his signature the greatest possible number of authorizations of liberation that could be considered compatible with the maintenance of public order, but he simplified the procedure to be followed in order to speed up the examination of demands. He instructed me to arrange liberations by telegram; to make sure that decisions were carried out, and not held up by administrative routine; and to avoid sabotage of these decisions. Finally, when the chief of the Militia, on taking control of the police secretariat, insisted that his own office should have the right to veto any liberations decided on by the commission, I was supported against everyone by President Laval in my protests, and as a result the commission kept all its former powers.

Thus it was that out of a total of about 25,000 persons interned by the administration, including persons interned for their economic protection and persons who had been engaged in the black market, about 20,000 political internees—communists, labor union members, and Gaullists—were liberated by President Laval on my proposal. Of the liberated persons, about 14,000 were in the southern zone.

These liberations were hotly criticized by persons around the Maréchal but not by the Maréchal himself. They were criticized also by the collaborationist parties and movements, and in short by those who believed in large-scale repression through imprisonment and political cruelty, holding that such methods are the sign of strong governments, though in fact they are a sure sign of weak ones.

Concurrently with this first permanent mission, I was named by President Laval, in the decree of 7 March 1943, vice-president of the special commission on secret societies; and President Laval maintained this nomination in spite of the demand of Vice-Admiral Platon, secretary-general for Masonic questions, that it be annulled.

In this field, President Laval's policy was to block, weaken, or deaden the virulence of the special legislation against secret societies, as he did not have the power to suppress these laws. The work of this commission was criticized by the same elements that had regarded me as suspect in my work as president of the commission for the liberation of persons interned by administrative order. These groups did not perceive the incompatibility between the appeals made by the Maréchal and President Laval for the union of all Frenchmen, and the bans that they themselves hoped to maintain, and at times to intensify, against citizens whose only guilt was to have belonged to secret societies at a time when they were not forbidden by law, and which in any case were no longer secret now that the laws had been passed.

My appointment to this post enabled me to arrange many more meetings of the commission and to swing the balance in favor of reinstatement demanded by civil servants who had been removed from their posts because they had been Freemasons. The number and quality of these reinstated persons was such that opponents of this policy of justice and appeasement, working with the anti-Masonic police and Militia-recruiting authorities, did not hesitate to fabricate false evidence and to prepare declarations which were completely invented. In this they were supported by a Paris press campaign on the orders of the German *Propagandastaffel* in an attempt to have annulled the decisions which the commission had taken while I presided over it.

In connection with the various missions assigned to me by President Laval I was a witness of his thoroughly humane action toward the political internees; of his reactions against the German demands for laborers; and of his confidential instructions intended to make more liberal, or even to block, the measures adopted under pressure from the occupying power, and to make ineffective the steps taken against rebels of various kinds, against Jews, and so forth.

When in January 1944 the suggestion was made to me that I might take temporary charge of the new office for youth work camps, I learned from President Laval that as the result of unwise negotiations between the general commissioner of this organization and the German authorities in Paris some groups of work camps were operating under the orders of the German Air Force or of the German Army, and that all the work camps had received assignments from Wiesbaden to work with the Todt organization. I declined, saying to President Laval that he knew very well that I would never be the slave of the Boches. He replied, "I do know it, and that is the reason why I ask you to take charge of the work camps until a director-general is named. There have already been enough blunders; they have put their head right into the wolf's mouth. It will be your job to get them out of this dangerous situation. That is your mission as a plenipotentiary commissioner."

The work camps were threatened with dissolution by the Germans if their instructions were not carried out. They were endangered also by an internal crisis following the arrest of the general commissioner, because the officers of the work camps, appointed on the sole decision of the general commissioner, had succeeded in building up a sort of mysticism around him, and no longer concerned themselves with maintaining their organization, staffed and organized by the only laws to which the French were still obedient. The youth work camps were thus doubly threatened by German levies.

President Laval ordered me to keep this force in existence and to keep it in France at all costs. Therefore, on the pretext of reorganization in order to carry out instructions from Wiesbaden, those work groups under the orders of the German Air Force and the German Army were withdrawn. On the pretext that the recruiting law for the work camps did not apply to the northern zone, the groups that had been designated to work there were retained in the southern zone. On the pretext of arranging normal practices in the command, the living conditions, and the organization of the sections assigned to the Todt work camps, for which we had already made demands in principle that we knew full well were inapplicable, we first delayed, and then cancelled, the departure of all young men on Todt assignments. These maneuvers were rendered delicate by the attitude of those chief officers of the work camps who had been particularly devoted to the general commissioner. These persons had expressed a satisfaction, that no one had asked them to express, regarding the assignment of sections to the German

Air Force; and they gave their complete acceptance to the plan of working for the Todt organization, provided only that they be dressed in blue and not in green.

The fact that President Laval had consented to be a shield, in order, as he put it, to protect the country from even greater evils, brought him attacks from all sides. He made use of these attacks just as he used the unpopularity which he seemed to be cultivating. One evening in the autumn of 1943, when a member of his staff, speaking to him in his own office, remarked how much easier the task of the Chief of Government and his colleagues would be if only President Laval would make himself more popular, the President answered, "When you understand the use I make of my unpopularity in my own country you will understand many things."

In all the many circumstances in which I was in contact with President Laval I found in him always the most profoundly humane feelings and the most passionate love for France and peace. But in all things he was understood too late, for he was wrong in being right too soon.

(Document No. 8)
Fr. ed. 655-658

> [*The text translated above was deposited with the Hoover Library by M. Bernon. A request for a signed copy was sent M. Bernon, who died before the request reached him.*]

JEWISH AFFAIRS

XAVIER VALLAT

Member of the Chamber of Deputies
Commissioner General for Jewish Affairs

> [*M. Vallat deposited with the Hoover Library a text of about 20,000 words which he had written in 1947 while in prison at Fresnes. The following is a translation of part of that text, from the middle of page 23 to the middle of page 46*].

. . .The government of Maréchal Pétain decided to restrain this influence within proper limits by publishing on 30 October 1940 a law establishing the status of the Jews in France.

There are those who believed that this law was the result of pressure by the occupation authorities on the French government. Some accept this belief as a reason for excusing Vichy while others see it as one more element in the indictment against the government. Both are wrong.

The Alibert law—it is more convenient to indicate it by the name of the Minister of Justice who took the initiative in the matter—owes nothing at all to Nazism.

Proof of this is to be found first in the confidential statements made by M. Dumoulin de la Barthète, Director of the Civil Cabinet of the Maréchal, when he was interrogated on 26 October 1946 at the [police offices in the] rue des Saussaies by police commissioners Bugé and Collier.

In this declaration, during which he rather smugly allowed it to be understood that he was personally hostile to all laws of exception for Freemasons and Jews, he declared definitely that "Germany was not the cause of Vichy's anti-Jewish legislation. This legislation was, so to speak, spontaneous and indigenous."

The Alibert law was in fact issued several days before the first German ordinance concerning the Jews in the occupied zone, ordering the taking of a census.

Further, M. Raphael Alibert remained in Vichy during the entire second half of 1940 and so had no contact with the occupation authorities. On the other hand, no trace has been found in either the German or the French archives of any conversation on the Jewish question previous to the first quarter of 1941, when M. Alibert ceased to be a member of the government.

Finally, the French text shows essential differences from the Nuremberg laws, differences which we will point out during this study.

It is, however, thoroughly inaccurate to claim, as did M. Dumoulin de la Barthète, that the law of 30 October 1940 did not ban the Jews from political power and from government office. To suggest that M. Alibert thought it sufficient to ban Jews from public office in order to restrain sufficiently their excessive general influence would be to accuse him of most displeasing intellectual poverty.

In the Alibert law there were gaps which were to be filled later, but it contained in essence all the provisions by which it was to be complemented during 1941, in particular those which dealt with the participation of the Jews in liberal, commercial, industrial, and agricultural professions. It provided that later decrees would regulate the exercise of these professions.

The Alibert law may be summed up as follows. First, it defined the meaning of "Jew" as a person of whose four grandparents at least three were of the Jewish race. Next, it excluded Jews from all activity of direction in state administration. Jews could not hold any public office in the Ministries of Finance, of Foreign Affairs, of National Education, of the Interior, or of National Defense. Only the Council of State could suggest exceptions to these interdictions, which must be based on exceptional services of a scientific or literary character.

Public office in other ministerial departments was also closed, but in those ministries exception was to be made automatically in the case of Jews who were war veterans.

In the liberal and non-state professions the proportion of Jews to be accepted was to be established by special decrees, which implied the enforcement of the principle of 'numerus clausus' [limited number]. However, all professions connected with the press, radio, cinema, and theater were purely and simply forbidden to Jews.

It was in this way that the law, later to be amended but not to be modified in spirit, fulfilled, according to its author, the highly correct idea that Jewish saturation was not merely to be feared by the state when it affected the administration, but also was to be regarded as a danger when it reached certain liberal professions which exercised preponderant influence either through their purposes, as medicine and the law, or through their economic importance, as banking and exchange, or through their action on people's minds, as in the different forms of propaganda.

It is very clear that any racial group or political party which in any country controlled the majority of the newspapers, the cinemas, the radio stations, or which held the controlling power in the principal credit houses, would have no need, in order to hold true power, to include within its ranks under-prefects, counselors of embassy, professors, or inspectors of finance.

At this point it should be emphasized that in making these affirmations and in drawing the logical legislative conclusion M. Raphael Alibert was only adhering to a policy which found not only its source in a long national tradition, but also its justification in the position taken throughout the centuries by the Church with regard to the Jewish problem.

Let us understand this point clearly. It is not a matter of taking Rome as a shield, and of finding in ancient pontifical texts some absolution for a political fault. We are not pleading "guilty with attenuating circumstances." It is simply a matter of proving, in intellectual honesty, against those who accuse the Maréchal's government of having been a servile plagiarist of the Nazis, that this anti-Jewish legislation, as distinct from that across the Rhine, never went beyond the just limits established by the Church in accordance with the right of protecting the national community against the abuses and harmful influence of a foreign element.

In fact, the Church was led many times to take up a position on the Jewish problem, from the days of Saint Paul until our own.

It was the converted Jew Saint Paul who wrote, "The Jews are not pleasing to God and are enemies of other men." (Epistle to the Thessalonians, II, 15). This statement, if he had been living in our days, would have brought him two years in prison under the Marchandeau decree which doubles the punishment for libel if it is a Jew that is injured.

The doctrine of the Church on the Jewish question was recalled by Saint Thomas Aquinas in his Summa Theologia. It may be summed up as follows: Tolerance must be shown to the Jews so far as the practice of their religion is concerned. They should be protected against religious restrictions, and their children should not be baptized by force and without the consent of their parents. On the other hand, measures should be taken to limit their participation in society and to restrain their influence. It would be unreasonable to allow them, in a Christian state, to hold governing power and thus to reduce the authority of the Catholics. It follows, therefore, that it is legitimate to forbid their tenure of public office and that it is legitimate not to permit them, beyond a definite proportion, in universities and liberal professions.

The Church applied these policies as a temporal power in the Vatican state until 1789. Further, the Church generalized this policy for all Christendom through decisions of the councils and through papal bulls.

The Council of Vannes in 465, of Agde in 506, and of Epaone in the diocese of Vienna in 517, forbade Christians to eat together with Jews. The Second Council of Orléans forbade marriage between Christians and Jews. The Council of Clermont in 535 excluded Jews from the magistracy, and the Council of Mâcon in 581 excluded them from serving as collectors of taxes. The Council of Paris in 615 declared that they were ineligible for any public office.

At the beginning of the ninth century, Saint Agobard, primate of the Gauls, Bishop of Lyon, issued an extremely severe injunction entitled "Concerning the Insolence of the Jews."

Amolon, Bishop of Lyon, successor of Saint Agobard on the throne of Saint Irénée, in the time of Charles the Bald, published in 646, with the title "Against the Jews," another injunction in which he reiterates, in particular, that it is forbidden for a Jew to employ a Christian as a domestic servant.

The rowel, which was the yellow star of the Middle Ages, was introduced in 1221 by Pope Honorius III and extended to all of Christendom by the Council of Narbonne in 1227, and confirmed by seven later councils.

If the book written by Redocanacchi on the Popes and the Jews is consulted it will be noted that from 1217 to 1755 twenty-nine popes published fifty-seven bulls regarding the Jews, the purpose being to save the Christian civilization from Jewish encroachment.

If all these documents are classified according to their purpose, it will be found that they are divided as follows:

(a) Racial measures: those forbidding Jews to employ Christian nurses; and those forbidding mixed marriages.

(b) Political and economic measures against Jewish influence: those forbidding Jewish trade and certain activities; those forbidding entrance to the liberal professions, with partial tolerance for medicine; those forbidding the possession of real estate; and those forbidding usury.

(c) Social measures: those providing for segregation of Jews in ghettos; the general ban on cohabitation; those requiring the wearing of distinctive clothing; and the expulsion of Jews from certain territories.

Although nazi anti-Jewish policy added to all the above measures the horror of physical persecution and methodical organization of a scientific pogrom combined with social spoliation, French anti-Jewish legislation on the other hand remained approximately within the dispositions already taken by the Church throughout the ages. French anti-Jewish legislation was limited to measures restricting Jewish influence in political, economic, and cultural fields.

The Maréchal's government did not forbid mixed marriages for Jews. It did not forbid them to have non-Jewish servants. It did not forbid their access to public places. It did not shut them off in ghettos. It did not limit their circulation on public highways to certain hours. It did not force them to wear distinctive garments. It did not expel them from France.

Yet it could have done all these things while appealing to the historical precedents found in papal acts.

There is therefore nothing surprising in the fact that on 21 September 1941 M. Léon Bérard, Ambassador of France in the Vatican, wrote to Maréchal Pétain, who had asked him to send him information as to the Vatican's point of view on the measures taken by the French state regarding Jews: "An authorized person at the Vatican has told me that there will be no quarrel initiated against us because of our new status for the Jews. However, two wishes have been expressed to me by representatives of the Vatican with the obvious desire that they should be reported to the Chief of the French state: (1) That there should be no addition to the law regarding the Jews which would affect marriage. On that point we would meet difficulties of a religious kind. The Vatican has been deeply stirred by the fact that Rumania has adopted, on this important point, rules of law inspired by, or copied after, fascist legislation. (2) The second wish is that the law should be applied in accordance with the precepts of justice and charity. Those who spoke to me seemed to have in mind particularly the question of liquidating businesses in which the Jews owned an interest."

This discreet warning from the Vatican was accepted by the French government. When my successor at the General Commission for Jewish

Affairs, Darquier de Pellepoix, proposed to President Laval a text which would forbid mixed marriages between Jews and non-Jews, the Chief of Government refused to take it into consideration.

And though there were sometimes sordid manipulations involved in the liquidation of certain Jewish businesses, such action could take place only in violation of the rules laid down by the law of 22 July 1941, and by the later decrees for its application. On this point the clever dishonesty of certain individuals should be accused, and not the laws which, quite to the contrary, attempted to guarantee to the legitimate Jewish owner a fair sale of his business.

However we shall see later that eminent and highly respectable representatives of the French Church made severe and, in my opinion, proper protests at the end of the summer of 1942 against certain measures taken regarding foreign Jews who lived in the unoccupied zone.

In this connection I wish to point out to all impartial persons exactly why these protests strengthen my own affirmation that French anti-Jewish laws themselves were never criticized by the religious authorities.

This legislation was developed in detail during the second half of 1941. It consisted essentially of the law of 2 June 1941 which was merely a revision of the Alibert law; the law of 22 July 1941 which provided for the liquidation of Jewish property; the decrees dealing with liberal and independent professions; and the law of 29 November 1941 which established the General Union of Israelites in France.

The law of 2 June [1941].—The law published on 2 June 1941, dealing with the status of Jews in France, was not new; it was a revision and an adaptation of the law of 3 October 1940 which in practice had proved to be based on insufficient study and to contain important gaps. But neither the law of 2 June 1941 nor that which it replaced was a copy of foreign legislation, particularly of the Nuremberg laws.

Following are the changes which the law of 2 June 1941 made in the preceding law.

The law of 3 October 1940 had defined as a Jew any person of whom three grandparents were of the Jewish race, or of whom two grandparents were of the Jewish race if the person's husband or wife was a Jew. But in French law there is no juridical definition of "race." The administrative and judicial authorities responsible for applying the law therefore had no legal criterion for deciding whether a certain person was a Jew or not.

When the President of the Council asked M. Abraham Schramek, Senator for the Bouches-du-Rhône, to tell him if he belonged to the Jewish race, the Senator found it very easy to reply that he had no idea. He knew that his grandparents practiced the Jewish religion, that his parents did also, as he did himself; but he had no idea whether or not they belonged to the Jewish race. And no tribunal was able to reach a decision on that point.

Therefore it was necessary to furnish a legal criterion to the judges. This could consist only in the practice of the Jewish religion because, as we showed above, it is adherence to the law of Moses which preserves and marks off the Jewish people so that the Jews constitute a combined nation and religion.

Therefore Article 1 of the law was revised to provide that he is to be considered as a Jew who had at least three grandparents who practiced the Jewish religion, or who had two grandparents who practiced the Jewish religion if either he himself or his spouse is Jewish.

But how could it be known that the grandparents did or did not practice the Jewish religion, in view of the fact that the Jewish community in France had no archives similar to the French parish registers?

It could be done only by obliging the person in question to supply proof to the contrary, in the form of documents proving that the grandparents belonged to one of the religions recognized at that time in France, Catholic, Protestant, Orthodox, or Mohammedan.

And the atheists, it will be asked. The reply is simple. The grandparents under consideration would have been born in the first half of the nineteenth century and at that time atheism was almost nonexistent. All children were baptized and all marriages and funerals were religious. It was, therefore, simple for non-Jews to find documents proving that their ancestors had belonged to a religion other than the Jewish.

In practice this criterion proved to be perfectly satisfactory and made it possible to distinguish easily between Jews and non-Jews.

Article 2 of the law of 3 October 1940 had totally eliminated Jews from certain parts of the public administration and from parliament unless an exception were granted by the Council of State. The law of 2 June 1940 added merely a few additional points which unified these provisions, particularly in matters concerning National Defense.

The former Article 3 showed a serious omission. It provided that public offices other than those indicated in Article 2 were open to a Jew only if he could meet one of the following conditions: (1) to be the holder of a war veteran's card for the war of 1914-1918 (2) to have been cited in the Order of the Day during the campaign of 1939-1940; or (3) to have received the Legion of Honor, military section, or the Military Medal.

Through an oversight, the immediate family—parents, grandparents, wives and children—of soldiers who had died for France had been omitted from this automatic exception to the law. This regrettable oversight was put right in the new Article 3.

In its Article 5 the law of 3 October 1940 had provided an absolute interdiction for Jews to belong to any profession having to do with the press, the radio, the cinema, or in general with any public performance. The law of 2 June 1941 added to this list all professions having to do with speculation in its various forms.

The law of 3 October 1940 had not dealt with the special position of prisoners of war. Article 7 of the law of 2 June 1941 specified that the provisions of the law could not be applied to prisoners of war, or to members of their families, during their captivity.

Finally, the former Article 8 gave exclusive powers to the Council of State to free certain Jews from the bans provided by the law, and then only because of exceptional literary, scientific, or artistic services. The effect of this article was to require a long examination of the demands for exception, and to limit the right of exception to intellectuals and artists.

Article 8 of the law of 2 June 1940 remedied this double fault by giving the commissioner-general the right to annul all interdictions, excepting only those specified in Article 2, in the case of Jews who had rendered exceptional services to the French state, regardless of the nature of those services.

Complementary decrees.—The law of 2 June 1941 had not altered the provisions of the law of 3 October 1940 providing that later decrees would regulate the membership of Jews in the liberal and independent professions. These decrees were therefore prepared with reference to the liberal professions; industrial, commercial, and artisanal activities; and agriculture.

For the liberal professions the principle of limited number was adopted. If the proportion had been made exactly that of the Jews in France, the percentage would have been 0.8 per cent, and even 0.4 per cent in those professions for which French nationality is required. But in view of the fact that the Jews are much more inclined to enter the liberal professions than to do any manual labor, the proportion was set at 2 per cent. This figure was adopted for law, medicine, public and ministerial officers, architects, dentists, midwives, and pharmacists. In actual fact, the percentage restriction had to be applied only in the departement of the Seine and in North Africa.

Each of the decrees of application provided that war veterans and victims of the war would receive prior consideration wherever the principle of limited number was applied, even if the total number of such persons, as was the case in Paris, exceeded the proportion of 2 per cent.

The application of the quota principle to the liberal professions meant that it had to be applied as well to the universities. It would have been absurd to issue in profusion diplomas which theoretically gave access to professions to which the door was in fact scarcely open. The number of Jewish students admitted for each year in the courses of the various faculties, schools, and institutes of advanced learning was set not at 2 but at 3 per cent of the non-Jewish students enrolled for the same year's studies. Here again priority was given to war veterans and their children. In Algeria the application of the principle of limited number gave a proportion of 14 per cent because the number of Jews in comparison with the European population was very high. To have an idea of the extent to which the liberal professions had been invaded by the Jews in North Africa, it is important to know that the bar of Tunis includes 180 Jews out of a total of 220 attorneys.

The regulation of industrial, commercial, and artisanal activities set a more difficult and a more delicate problem. No legislative text was published on this subject, as the Germans refused to give their agreement for the occupied zone. But a circular issued by the commissariat-general for Jewish questions prescribed for the unoccupied zone regulations which express the spirit of the measures that had been planned. These were as follows.

Jews were not to take part in industrial or commercial activities through share corporations. But, on the other hand, any Jew who was a war veteran, or the ancestor, spouse, or offspring of a war veteran, or who had been established in his activities for a certain length of time and had a good business reputation, was allowed to carry on commercial or industrial activities freely so long as he did so under his own name.

In agriculture, not only was there no interdiction of activity by Jews, but the French government even attempted to direct Jewish activity into it by authorizing the purchase of farming land by Jews on condition that they cultivated it personally. In following this line the Maréchal's government was in harmony with the desires of the leader of zionism, Chaim Weizmann, re-elected president of the Zionist Federation of Britain on 6 November 1947, who had declared in an interview given in 1936 to a French journalist, M. Laporte:

"In all states where there is a certain proportion of Israelites, a fundamental misunderstanding exists between Jew and native. This is because the Jew . . . has abandoned the soil . . . and in the cities has

almost always avoided the manual arts, those activities which create true
riches, to establish himself in the parasitic professions and in the commerce
of goods and money.

"Thus the Jew has never succeeded in establishing that magnificent
bond between the man and his village, his province, and his nation, which
has meant that behind every real Frenchman, every real Englishman,
every real German, stand through the centuries those successive generations
who have watered the field and the workshop with their sweat." ["In Jewish
Palestine with President Chaim Weizmann;" *Revue de France*, 15 May 1936.]

It is therefore completely false to say or to allow it to be believed that
French anti-Jewish legislation allowed the Jews no liberty except that of
dying of hunger, by forbidding every paid activity.

The French state, desiring to defend itself against a harmful and dis-
proportionate Jewish influence in political and economic fields, removed
the Jews from directive posts in politics and administration and forbade
them to take part in the parasitical professions. But it left them free to
participate in the liberal professions in a proportion which was generous
if account is taken of their numerical relation to the total population. And
all activities for the "creation of true riches" remained open to them.

The law of 22 July 1941.—Did this same French state also strip the
Jews of their property, as too many people say and believe? The reply
to this question is also to be found in an objective study of the French
laws which regulate what has been called "economic aryanization."

In the occupied zone, this subject was regulated by three German ordinances. The first, dated 20 May 1940, was a general text which dealt
with business management and the administration of enterprises of all
kinds in the occupied territories of Holland, Belgium, Luxembourg, and
France.

The German ordinance of 18 October 1940 specified that any operation
which took place after 23 May 1940 in connection with a Jewish business
could be annulled; it further provided for the nomination of a trustee
manager for all Jewish enterprises.

The third German ordinance appeared in April 1941 and in effect placed
all the movable property of Jews in sequestration.

The ordinance of 15 October 1940 had led to the creation by the Ministry
of Industrial Production of a control service of trustee administrators
[*administrateurs provisoires:* French juridical term for temporary mana-
gers holding delegated powers.]

These trustee administrators were appointed by the French authorities,
but the German authorities retained the right to confirm their nominations,
and in a certain number of cases the Germans even imposed their own
subservient nominees.

The Ministry of Industrial Production found that it was necessary to
move very quickly in making its appointments: six thousand had to be
named in a single week. This, of course, meant that the French administration had not been able to make a very careful and individual examination of the moral qualities of these new manager-delegates. This in turn
made it urgently necessary for the French government to establish an
inspection service over this mass of little-known provisional administrators.
And it was even more important to inspect the operations of those administrators who had been named by the Germans. These necessities led to
the establishment at the end of the autumn of 1940 of the Inspection
Service for Provisional Administrators.

This important service was first directed by M. Fournier, former Governor of the Bank of France, and then, during the time when I was Commissioner-General, by two comptrollers-general of the Army serving successively, M. de Faramond and M. Bralley. These three high officials carried out their delicate task with a conscientiousness and a determination to act correctly which permitted no criticism and has given rise to no complaint on the part of those concerned.

When a commissariat-general for Jewish Questions was created by the law of 29 March 1941, this inspection service was logically attached to it, though without ceasing to be under the Ministry of Industrial Production, which itself continued to appoint all the provisional administrators in the occupied zone.

It was necessary to envisage the extension of this service to the whole of France as a result of Article 5 of the law of 2 June 1941. This article forbade participation by Jews in a certain number of professions and, therefore, it was necessary that regulations should specify under what conditions those activities should be managed and then transferred to non-Jews which could no longer remain in the hands of their first owners.

This was the purpose of the law of 22 July 1941, which applied to the whole of France and which dealt with economic Aryanization.

From the time of my first interviews with Dr. Blancke and Dr. Burandt, [German officials] who were responsible for economic organization at the Hotel Majestic, I had proposed the principle that the liquidation of Jewish property should be made so honestly that no one could raise a scandal. This did not fail to astonish the two officials to such a point that they distrusted me. (Interview Zeitscheld-Burandt-Blancke, on 23 April 1941.)

However the German authorities did not veto the publication of the law of 22 July 1941 in the *Journal Officiel*.

This was an empowering law, very general in its terms. Whereas the German ordinance obligatorily placed all Jewish property under provisional administrators, the French law said that it was possible to appoint a provisional administrator for all Jewish property. This was not a slight distinction between the two but an essential difference. For in practice, throughout the unoccupied zone, only those enterprises specified in Article 5 of the law of 2 June 1941 were placed under provisional administration, together with commercial and industrial undertakings in the form of corporations. Private property was only very exceptionally placed under provisional administrators, and then as a form of punishment.

In addition, some forms of property were exempted from sequestration: French state securities, and the securities issued by corporations controlled by the French state or controlled by French communities, or by countries under protectorate or mandate.

Regarding real estate, where the German ordinance applied to everything without exception, the French law excluded from possible provisional administration those buildings or premises which were used only for the personal habitation of Jews, together with their furnishings.

It was the duty of the provisional administrator to manage "as would a good father of a family" [this is a term with a specific meaning in French law] the enterprise for which he was responsible, and to receive offers of purchase made by non-Jews.

In order to avoid so far as possible any frauds and concealed arrangements between buyers it was made a rule that sealed bids must be made and that the highest should be accepted.

In both zones a consultative council with every guarantee of impartiality estimated the true commercial value of the enterprise or property which was offered.

In the sale of buildings in Paris it can be ascertained that no building was sold at a price lower than that approved by the consultative council. The following sentence is to be found in a report made after the liberation by M. Formery, Inspector of Finance, on the management of the Commissariat-General for Jewish Affairs: "The management of buildings was closely controlled, thanks to this well-constituted commission whose duty was to set a minimum price."

The Germans desired that the proceeds of the sale of Jewish property should be deposited in a private bank selected by them. This would have given ultimately an opportunity for them to get hold of these securities and funds on the first pretext that was available. The French law blocked these hidden purposes by specifying that the state Administration des Domaines should act as trustee of all Jewish securities specified by the German ordinance of April 1941, stipulating that the proceeds of the liquidation of Jewish property should be placed to the account of the Jewish owner in the government's deposit and consignment office, where interest was credited.

One tenth of all sums thus paid in on deposit and consignment was transferred to a separate fund in the same office to be used in aid of needy Jews.

Thus it can be seen that the liquidation of Jewish property was not confiscation, as had been the liquidation of the property of the religious congregations [in France] at the beginning of the century. It was a transference of real and movable property into cash, to which the title was guaranteed to the Jews by the French state.

Thus the truth is far from the legend which an attempt has been made to spread in France and elsewhere.

In order to avoid in the southern zone criticisms which had been aroused in the northern zone by haphazard appointments of provisional administrators, I arranged that my regional directors should prepare beforehand a register of persons whose professional and moral standing was such that any management of property which might be entrusted to them would not give rise to justifiable complaints of the correctness of their trusteeship.

The law provided that no provisional administrator could himself purchase the property which he managed.

As the occupation authorities had the right to approve the appointment of all commissioner-delegates and the liquidation of all enterprises in the occupied zone, it was difficult for the French administration to prevent the replacement of the Jewish interest in any undertaking by a German interest. However, the commissariat-general for Jewish Affairs and the Ministry of Industrial Production often opposed such a replacement successfully, particularly when the commissioner-delegate had been chosen directly by the Germans (see the Regelsperger note attached to the interrogation of 29 January 1947).

The principle followed by the commissariat-general, at least during my time, for enterprises which had branches in both zones was to appoint a separate provisional administrator for those interests which concerned the unoccupied zone and, except in the case of enterprises of purely secondary interest and importance, not to extend to the unoccupied zone the powers of a trustee in the occupied zone.

In adopting this attitude we were trying to establish as an absolute rule that the German authorities should have no concern, direct or indirect, with what was going on south of the demarcation line, where French sovereignty must remain intact.

The purpose was also to prevent indiscreet investigations in certain enterprises which were working for national defense, or which would be of interest to industrial competitors in Germany.

It can be proved easily that the action of the commissariat-general under my direction was directed toward the prevention of any control by the invader, of taking away from him everything which could be taken away, and of making certain that the French national economy did not suffer harm through Aryanization.

In the field of aeronautics, the patents held by Turbo-Méca and by Lévy-Messier, whose head offices were in Paris, aroused eager covetousness. It was in vain that the German Air Command attempted to impose on us a trustee manager appointed by the Germans. The commissariat-general appointed as provisional administrator the man who was recommended to us by [the French] General Bergeret. Things went the same way in the RBV Ballbearing undertaking, which was of intense interest to the German air force.

In connection with the sequestration of the Saprolip company, the German armistice commission intended to seize the machine tools of which it had records in the unoccupied zone. The president of the French delegation at Wiesbaden intervened personally on behalf of such a seizure. The commissariat-general formally opposed it.

In the matter of Berheim Brothers, the military authority wished to appoint a commissioner-manager of their own, Louis Thoman, editor of the *La Gerbe*. Not only was this prevented, but the Aryanization to which the German military command had agreed was not recognized in the unoccupied zone. In the Etam case, the German commissioner-manager was unable to get possession of the stocks in the southern zone. In the Électro-Piège sequestration, the inventor was able to transfer his stocks and patents to a new company working for national defense. In the Toutmain case, the commissioner-manager in the occupied zone was prevented from taking possession and from directing the shops in the unoccupied zone. In the Radio-Cité case, the Germans were unable to arrange a transfer of the title to themselves. The German controllers of the Galeries Lafayette were unable to take possession of the branches in the southern zone.

These examples explain why the German Director of Economic Affairs in France, General Michel, wrote to us one day: "Your action hampers my Aryanization program."

The U.G.I.F.

[Union-General of Israelites in France]

We know today from documents found in the archives of the German Embassy in Paris that already in January 1941 the Germans had made a plan for deporting all the Jews in Europe to Silesia. The first stage was to consist in separating the Jews from the rest of the population in all the occupied countries, and the Germans hoped that the French government would take over this task in France. Nothing about this plan was explained to Admiral Darlan, for he certainly would have informed me of it at the time when he entrusted to me the direction of the commissariat-general for Jewish Affairs which he had just created.

In the interviews which I had, as soon as I was appointed, with Ambassador Abetz and General von Stulpnagel, on the instructions of my government, in which I sketched for them the broad lines of my attitude to the Jewish problem, underlining its difference from the German attitude, the only indication of the plan was a question put by the general as to whether France intended to send back to their countries of origin all the Jewish foreigners who had taken refuge in France.

I pointed out to him that almost all of these Jews had come to France from the Reich or from countries occupied by the Reich, and I asked him, "Do you take your Jews back?"

I received no reply to this common sense question, but von Stulpnagel suggested to me that France might get rid of these foreign Jews by sending them to Spain, Portugal, or the United States. I pointed out that Spain was not going to create a Jewish problem on her own territory after having settled it four centuries ago, that Portugal was a tiny country already full of all kinds of immigrants, and that the United States had very strict immigration laws. The conversation ended there, but the two men with whom I was talking, as we know from the report of the exchange of impressions which took place between them the following day, were disappointed to note that they could not count on the French government for the accomplishment of their program. SS Oberstgrüppenführer Dannecker, Gestapo official responsible for Jewish affairs in spite of his youth—he was then only 26 years old—explained to me several days later the advantages of separating the Jews from the non-Jews. I replied that the ghetto seemed to me to be a ridiculous and stupid, old-fashioned idea of no interest in the modern world, and that anyway I did not see how the creation of a ghetto could be imagined in a city like Paris.

Undiscouraged, Dannecker, in a letter sent on 25 June [1941] to Otto Abetz, begged the Reich Ambassador to ask Admiral Darlan to express his point of view on the principle of separating Jews, including French Jews, from the non-Jewish French population, in view of the fact that "M. Vallat wandered round and round on the subject and showed no understanding."

The Admiral must have shown himself no more understanding than I had been, for he said nothing to me about it, and things remained as they were until the autumn.

On 29 August 1941 a letter from the military commander put to the commissariat-general the question of help given to needy Jewish families whose heads had been interned at Drancy, Beaune-la-Rolande, or Pithiviers after the raids organized on 12 August [1941] by Dannecker to gather in the foreign Jews.

The military commander expressed the desire that "such assistance should be given through a Jewish organization which would obligatorily include as its members all the Jews in the occupied zone and all Jewish religious organizations whose headquarters were in the occupied zone."

In concluding, the letter stated that "In case a law establishing such an organization could not become effective before 25 September [1941] the military commander would reserve the right to establish such an organization by decree."

The question was thus raised in precise form. Under the pretext of giving help to Jewish families which had been deprived of their normal support, the occupation authorities informed us that if the French government did not establish an organization which included all the Jews they would themselves issue an ordinance creating in the occupied zone an organization such as they had already established not only in Germany but in all the countries which they had invaded.

I informed my government and attempted to find out the full scope of the German plan. On 17 September [1941] I met at the Hotel Majestic the Ministerial Counselor Dr. Storz who showed me the text of an ordinance all prepared for publication. The dispositions were as follows. All the Jews in the occupied zone were to be grouped in a single organization, of which the Jewish religious associations would also be members. This organization was to have as its field all questions of philanthropic aid, of relief, and of instruction having to do with Jews. The funds necessary for the operation of this new association were to be supplied by individual variable subscriptions of which the rate would be fixed by the directors of the association. These directors, of course, would be named by the Germans.

Now I knew who the directors were to be. Dannecker had brought with him among his other baggage two Austrian Jews, Israëlovitch and Biberstein, whom he had already put in charge of a bulletin which claimed to be a sort of Official Journal for the Jewish community of Paris, in which Dannecker had his own orders presented by these two miserable creatures as wishes expressed by the Jews themselves.

If the French government did not act first it was certain that Israëlovitch and Biberstein would be made directors of the new organization where they would execute servilely the orders given by Dannecker. I therefore allowed Dr. Storz to understand that the French government had recognized the advantage of the suggestion of the military commander and that I thought that on my next journey I could bring back the draft of a law of which I indicated the chief points. It would therefore be unnecessary for the Hotel Majestic to issue an ordinance.

I immediately warned M. Baur of what was going on. M. Baur was a Jewish war veteran, about 50 years old, who had been reported to me as having courageously taken the initiative of coming to the aid of his unhappy fellow Jews since the beginning of the occupation. I had asked him to come and see me as soon as I took my position at the commissariat-general and I realized at once that this charitable and profoundly religious Jew had a noble soul and an upright heart.

I do not know what he thought of me, who held him in such high esteem. In any case, our relations went beyond those of mere correctitude and became trustful. He came to see me every week and told me what he knew, while I on my side hid nothing from him which concerned the fate of his racial brothers.

I showed him the draft of the German ordinance and he saw the serious danger which it threatened. I told him that, in my opinion, the only possibility was to put up a show by preparing a French decree in which care would be taken that behind a false front of words the fewest possible changes would be made in the status quo. I prepared a rough draft which I gave to him, asking him to think it over until the following day.

In this draft I specified first that all members of the administrative council of the UGIF must be of French nationality. Thus we got rid of Israëlovitch and Biberstein in advance.

The religious associations were not to be dissolved and were to continue to function under the French law providing for the separation of church and state. The UGIF was not to receive any directive except from the commissariat-general for Jewish Affairs, which would also have sole control of its expenditures. Thus we arranged for the directors of UGIF to avoid obedience to Dannecker's orders by replying that they [the directors] were not competent to make a decision and must refer the matter to the commissariat-general.

My proposed text was to apply, of course, not only to the Jews in the occupied zone, but to all Jews living in France, first for legal reasons and second because it would be more advantageous.

The Maréchal's government could not legislate separately for one or the other of the two parts of France, and never did so. To legislate for the occupied zone alone would have been sheer pretense since the rights of an occupying authority would give any German ordinance on the same subject precedence over the French law. To legislate for the unoccupied zone alone would have given the appearance of limiting French national sovereignty to the territories south of the demarcation line.

In both cases legislation for only one zone would have meant that different regulations applied simply because the persons concerned were at a certain geographical point, which would have been inadmissible.

The second reason for legislating for the whole of France, based on practical advantages, was that any law applying to the entire country could be more easily and more effectively used against the occupying authorities because of the serious repercussions which the violation of such a law by the mad sadist Dannecker would cause.

On the following evening Baur came to see me at my home, accompanied by Attorney Lucienne Scheid-Hass, a fellow member of the Paris Bar, who also had obstinately put her talent and her juridical skill at the service of her brothers.

They asked for several changes in the text of which the most important was that the word "instruction" should be omitted from the list of matters for which the UGIF was to be competent. I gladly accepted this suggestion.

In general they were too conscious of the serious danger of a German text not to be in agreement with mine. However, before submitting the draft of a law to the Hotel Majestic it was necessary that I should obtain written guarantees on two points which I regarded as essential.

Therefore in a letter dated 24 September 1941 I put three questions to Dr. Storz, whom I had seen at the Hotel Majestic on 17 September: (1) If the French government decides to create by law a Jewish organization which will combine all Jews living in France in order to obtain a general settlement of the social side of the Jewish question, is it thoroughly understood that the members of the organization's committee functioning in the occupied zone will be chosen by the French authorities? (2) Is it also thoroughly understood that the committee in the occupied zone, like the committee in the unoccupied zone, will receive its directives from the commissariat-general for Jewish Affairs, and will be supervised by it? (3) Is it thoroughly understood that the members of this committee responsible for representing all of the Jews in the occupied zone in their dealings with the public authorities will not be considered as priority hostages, and can be held responsible by the occupation authorities only for their own personal acts?

It was only after having received an affirmative reply to these questions that I presented my proposed law. The occupation authorities worked on it for two months.

This delay however was not enough to enable me to find nine important Jews who would agree to be members of the council of administration for UGIF in the unoccupied zone. In the occupied zone there was no difficulty in finding nine important Jews who were willing to sacrifice themselves by giving their names as heads of an organization which they knew would prevent the worst from happening to their fellow Jews.

I did not conceal from these noble-hearted men and women that I was asking them to take on a responsibility which made them, first of all, liable to be misunderstood by their fellows, and which also exposed them to the frenzied fantasies of Dannecker, in spite of the assurances which I had received from the military commander. Not one of them hesitated to accept so perilous a position.

But in the unoccupied zone the situation of the Jews was entirely different. Doubtless they poured abuse on the law of 2 June 1941 and even more on that of 22 July 1941, but they felt themselves to be in perfect security in that zone, as was proved by the daily flights of Jews from Paris, across the demarcation line, to take refuge in the unoccupied zone. Therefore the directors of the various associations existing in the unoccupied zone saw the creation of UGIF as meaning the dissolution of the associations over which they presided.

I had a difficult task to assure them, on numerous occasions, first orally and then in writing, that no Jewish charitable work would suffer and that all of them could come with their entire organizations intact into UGIF, there constituting each a special section. It took two months of discussions and endless conferences, with one sending a letter of refusal after having declared in my own office that he was satisfied with my statements, and another demanding that some adverb introduced into the text at the request of one his colleagues should be removed, as the other had first accepted and then retracted, though advising one of his friends to accept in his place . . . and so on and so on.

All this was further complicated by the petty intrigues of the grand consistory. I had first thought of offering the office of president of UGIF to President Hellbronner, precisely because he was already president of the grand consistory. When I told the Jews in the occupied zone of my plan there was a general outcry. Nevertheless, I gave M. Hellbronner, who visited me in Vichy from time to time, the text of my draft of the law, and afterwards changed it somewhat in accordance with his suggestions. I then asked M. Albert Lévy, president of the most important of the Jewish charities, the CAR (Committee of Assistance for Refugees) to be good enough to accept the presidency of UGIF.

M. Albert Lévy did accept, but only in order to assure the continuance of Jewish charities, and on an assurance from me that I would ask for no other activity whatever from UGIF in the unoccupied zone. And thereupon President Hellbronner led the permanent delegation of the consistory to adopt a resolution, on 18 January 1942 at Lyon, censuring this man whom he had previously described as the "Saint Vincent de Paul of Judaïsm."

After this useless hubbub everything calmed down. Because of the arrangements which had been made UGIF brought no alteration in the activities of the Jewish charities. If the reports made since the liberation by the two responsible officers, M. Edinger for the occupied zone and M. Gaston Kahn for the unoccupied zone, can be trusted, UGIF even made it possible for the Jews to camouflage a Jewish resistance movement in the two zones.

It must be emphasized that UGIF brought no aggravation of the situation of the Jewish people either in the occupied zone or in the unoccupied zone. However there are still Jews today who say that the creation of UGIF was an abomination and that it would have been better to leave to the Germans the responsibility of an ordinance forcing the Jews of the occupied zone to be grouped together in a Jewish association. That is an easy thing for those Jews to say who did not have to put the critical question to themselves, as did the leading Jews of the occupied zone, in agreement with me.

The following is the text of the official statement [on the strength of which M. Albert Lévy accepted the position of president of UGIF] submitted on 5 December 1941 to M. Raymond-Raoul Lambert, secretary of CAR, who served as intermediary between the Jewish charities and the commissariat-general for Jewish Affairs throughout these tedious negotiations:

"The commissioner-general for Jewish Affairs has no intention that the operation of the Union of the Israelites of France shall suspend, even temporarily, the activity of those charities which existed on 2 December [1941].

"These charities will transfer their resources and their goodwill to the Union of the Israelites of France. These charities must continue their philanthropic action while waiting for the union to take charge of the unfortunate persons whom they aid.

"The resources of the funds of Jewish mutual aid are not to be administered by the Union of the Israelites of France; they will be administered, in accordance with the law of 22 July 1941, by the deposit and consignment office of the government for the account of the commissioner-general. It is to him that the duty belongs of withdrawing from these funds such sums as seem to him to be necessary, and of transferring them to the council of administration of the Union of the Israelites of France, who will be responsible for the use of this money.

"Though gifts, legacies, and subsidies are not mentioned in the law of 2 December [1941] as being among the resources to be drawn on for maintaining the general funds of the Union of the Israelites of France, it is quite clear that the council of administration of the Union of the Israelites of France will always have the right to receive such payments, subject to the approval of the commissioner-general.

"It is certain that the establishment of the rates of subscription, as provided by the law, and the application of these rates, will require some time during which the Union of the Israelites of France cannot be left without regular resources. During this period, there would be no objection if the council of administration of the Union of the Israelites of France found equivalent funds through free-will subscriptions."

This official report summed up the concessions which the consistory had demanded from me through M. Hellbronner. On 14 December 1941 the central consistory, after a long session, advised the nine important Jews who had become interested, through steps taken by me, to accept. On 18 January [1942] the permanent delegation of the central consistory blamed M. Albert Lévy for his acceptance of the post [of president].

A tragic table of statistics gives us the answer. The other countries of Europe, invaded by the German army and deprived of any government of their own, found that similar groups were established in their midst by the occupation authorities. The table which was published as an annex to the official report of the Anglo-American Commission on the problem of Palestine makes it possible for us to know what happened to the Jewish population of the following countries:

	1939	1946	Decrease
Belgium	90,000	33,000	57,000
Czechoslovakia	315,000	60,000	255,000
Greece	75,000	10,000	65,000
Netherlands	150,000	30,000	120,000
Poland	3,351,000	80,000	3,271,000
Yugoslavia	75,000	11,000	64,000
Austria	60,000	15,000	45,000
	4,116,000	239,000	3,877,000

Only 5.8 per cent of the total Jewish population in these seven countries survived.

In France there had been 330,000 Jews in 1939, of whom at least half were foreigners. By 1946 there were only 180,000, of whom 160,000 were of French nationality.

In order to justify the responsibility which it assumed in the Jewish problem, the Maréchal's government has the right to say that 95 per cent of the French Jews are still alive, thanks to the policies which it followed.

Various measures taken against Jews.—As an examination of the anti-Jewish legislation of Vichy will show, none of its provisions went beyond the right which every government has to defend itself against a group which might establish a state within a state.

The impartial jurist who wishes to compare the sacrosanct non-sectarian laws [in effect, anti-church] which were established in France at the beginning of this century against religious bodies, on the ground that they too presented an internal danger for public authority, with the Vichy regulations concerning the Jews, will be obliged to agree that the earlier laws were infinitely more harsh on citizens who were all of old French stock, than were the new regulations concerning the Jews, of whom more than half were foreigners.

It may be replied that this is doubtless true, but that the Jews were forced to undergo not merely vexations and rough treatment but also torture, mass arrests, and deportation, of which the purpose was their extermination; and that such treatment was both detestable and criminal.

That is correct, but again, in speaking of these horrors, one must have the honesty to find out whether they were desired and committed by the Maréchal's government, or merely consented to. A slight examination of history will enable us to determine where the responsibility lay.

Vexations.—First, we must distinguish those measures which affected the dignity of the human being but did not affect liberty, health, or life.

The Germans asked me to forbid mixed marriages between Jews and non-Jews. I refused. They asked me to cancel cards of priority which had been given to Jews on the ground that they were ill, and to Jewish women who were pregnant. I refused. They asked me to establish a special private system of education for Jews. I refused.

The Germans asked that I should have all persons who were suspected of belonging to the Jewish race examined by a commission composed of German ethnologists. I refused. They asked me to force the Jews to wear a yellow star stamped with the seal of Solomon. I refused. They asked me to forbid Jews to enter theaters and places of amusement, restaurants, or, in general, any public place. I refused. They asked me to establish a special curfew for Jews. I refused.

Freedom of marriage continued to be guaranteed. Priority cards were still used by the Jews to whom they had been issued. Jewish students, as in the past, continued to attend the public schools. And as for the last three measures demanded by the Germans, when the French government refused to adopt them, they were issued as German regulations, but were applicable only in the northern zone, and then only just before the American landing.

Thus none of these bans or harsh regulations could be ascribed to Vichy.

Seizures of artistic objects, and infliction of fines.—Precious works of art and paintings by great masters having been seized by the occupation authorities from the homes of private Jews who came to me with their complaints, I protested immediately to the *Militärbefehlshaber*.

The French Administration of the Domain [in control of public property and of property held in trust], legal trustee for all property which had belonged to Jews who had emigrated and lost their French nationality, came to me to protest that the Germans had seized art collections which were the property of such Jews. I thereupon renewed my first protest. At the same time I submitted a very complete report on these various acts of pillage to the Delegate-General of the French government in order that it could take action as well with the German embassy and the Armistice Commission.

I received no reply from any of the occupation authorities and I thereupon took action personally in approaching Mr. von Metternich, who was the responsible chief in all questions of art. This Metternich was a member of the Rhineland branch of the family and was highly distinguished and an anti-Nazi. He did not conceal from me the fact that he held these actions to be wrong and that he regarded our claims as correct. Nor did he conceal from me the fact that I would never obtain an answer. . . .

But there, too, the French government did everything that it could to ensure respect for Jewish property.

The government's conduct was inspired by the same principles when on 17 December 1941 a German ordinance imposed a collective fine of 1,000 million francs on the Jews of the northern zone, following on attacks made against members of the German military forces.

This ordinance obliged the UGIF, which had been created only fifteen days before, and of which the administrative council had not yet been named, to pay that sum within a very short time, and ordered that after the payment had been made the sum should be recovered by the UGIF from all the Jews of the occupied zone.

It was an exorbitant demand, and one that could not possibly be satisfied. M. Baur came to ask for my advice and support. I went with him to the Ministry of Finance. I proposed that the Bank of France should advance the 1,000 million francs which had been demanded. This solution involved some difficulties, and I then suggested that an advance be made by the association of all the banks, which was done.

In these circumstances, again, the French government, far from being indifferent to a fine which was not the result of any action of its own, strove to lighten the burden on the Jewish community.

Arrests; raids for the seizure of Jews.—It was in August 1941 that the sinister Dannecker held the first raid for gathering in Jews from the central arrondissements of Paris. On that day 6,000 foreign Jews, whose original nationality had been that of countries which were neither neutral nor allied to the Reich, were arrested and interned in the camps at Drancy, Pithiviers, and Beaune-la-Rolande.

The Commissariat-General for Jewish Affairs learned of this raid only on the next day, through the official who acted as liaison between the police prefecture and the commissariat (M. Valentin).

On the following day forty Jewish lawyers were interned at Drancy. On 12 December 1941 another 700 Jews, all of them French citizens, were taken directly to Compiègne where they were placed with the 300 internees from Drancy.

All these police operations were carried out on orders given directly by Dannecker to the [French] police prefecture, without any previous notice being given to the Commissariat.

Not only can no responsibility be placed on the French government in this matter; in addition we made every effort to have a certain number of these unhappy people released and in all cases to have their conditions of internment improved. Thus there were released from Drancy 850 persons who were ill, 700 of them at the end of October, and 150 on 12 November [1941].

I asked the [French] Prefecture of the Seine to give them supplies for bedding and heating, as the camp at Drancy was entirely unfurnished on their arrival. I asked the occupation authorities, and succeeded in my request, that parcels of clothing and food should be allowed to be sent to those interned at Compiègne.

On three occasions I repeated my appeals to the *Militärbefehlshaber* on behalf of war veterans who had been interned.

However, I refused to visit the camps as I was unwilling that my presence there should be interpreted by the internees as an indication of agreement with measures which in fact were the responsibility of the invader alone.

On 20 February [1942] I had a violent argument with Dannecker which led to a notification by the German authorities through M. de Brinon that I was forbidden to live in the occupied zone. At the same time they asked Admiral Darlan to replace me.

Up to that date there had been no deportation of Jews.

The first convoy of deported Jews left Compiègne for Germany in mid-April [1942].

My final act as Commissioner-General, as powerless during the last eight weeks as would be a bishop in a land occupied by the infidel, was to transmit to the Maréchal a letter entrusted to me by the qualified representatives of the Jews of the northern zone, in which they asked that the French should not forsake them.

As regards what happened after I left the northern zone I obviously could know only what the public in general was able to learn.

It would be improper for me to pass judgment here on the attitude taken by my successor. It will be sufficient to say that President Laval, who was of a peaceful nature and detested violence, blocked most of his tendencies and insisted that French anti-Jewish policy should be guided by directives which differentiated it essentially from Nazi policy. In particular, he did not allow the fundamental legal texts to be changed.

However, in the spring of 1942, President Pierre Laval did accept a measure which aroused the vivid protests of the French clergy.

After a visit by Dannecker to the internment camps in the southern zone, where there were a number of foreign Jews who had been arrested at the beginning of the war by the governments presided over by Daladier and Paul Reynaud—whose Minister of the Interior was named Georges Mandel—groups of foreign Jews were sent to the northern zone and interned at Drancy and Compiègne whence they were deported to Germany.

Cardinal Gerlier, Bishop of Lyon, Monseigneur Théas, Bishop of Montauban, Cardinal Saliège, Bishop of Toulouse, and Monseigneur Delay, Bishop of Marseille, ordered that episcopal letters, in which they protested solemnly against these deportations, should be read from all the pulpits in their dioceses. In this action they were not obeying merely their own episcopal conscience, but certainly expressed the unanimous reprobation of the French people.

It should be particularly noted that in these individual protests, as well as in the appeal sent to the Maréchal on 22 July 1942 by the Assembly of the Cardinals and the Archbishops of France, neither the principle of the French anti-Jewish legislation, nor its application, was questioned.

There was an even more important point. Cardinal Gerlier made this declaration: "We do not forget that French authority has a problem to solve. . . ." Monseigneur Delay declared: "We are not unaware that the Jewish question does present difficult national and international problems. We recognize clearly that our country has the right to take such measures as are needed to defend itself against those who, particularly in the last few years, have done it so much harm, and that it has the duty of punishing severely all those who abused the hospitality which was so liberally granted them. . . ."

They all protested solely against the principle of deportation and against the "cruel dispersion of families."

In the eyes of the Catholic Church, as well as of the Protestant Church, which made a similar declaration at the same time, the state was not abusing its power except when it violated the basic rights of man and of the family.

And it is not necessary to be a religious believer in order to share this opinion.

It must therefore be recognized that the handing over of interned foreign Jews in the southern zone to the occupation authorities is an act, and the only one, for which the French government must offer a defense.

How could a man whose spirit was, by nature, so far removed from violence, and even farther from any form of cruelty, as was the case with President Pierre Laval, consent to such a measure?

His defense, if the High Court had not made defense impossible, would certainly have thrown light on the question.

My personal belief is that in this matter he was being blackmailed by the Germans.

Until the spring of 1942 only foreign Jews, and then only in the southern zone, had been interned, except for the raid made on 12 December 1941 [in Paris] which affected 700 French Jews, to whom must be added the 40 Jewish lawyers arrested in August. No Jewish woman had been seized, other than some delinquents, real or alleged.

At this time the occupation authorities announced to the French government that the security of the German army demanded the internment—which implied possible deportation—of all the Jews and Jewesses in the northern zone, including those of French nationality.

Of course it was possible to protest against this monstrous demand, and I have no doubt that the protest was made. But a protest alone could not possibly suffice to save the 75,000 French Jews who still remained in the northern zone.

President Pierre Laval, believing that it was his duty to give priority, in his defense, to French citizens, offered the removal to the northern zone of all foreign Jews who had been interned in the southern zone since 1939, as a payment to obtain relative peace for Jews of French citizenship.

The result was that the 4,000 Jews interned at Noé, the 2,000 at Brens, the 20,000 at Gurs, and the 15,000 at Rivesaltes, a total of 41,000, [1] were handed over to the Germans in exchange for [non-interference with] the 75,000 French Jews in the northern zone.

Thus anyone who is impartial must recognize that the one measure which, both in principle and in execution, went beyond the proper limits of the state anti-Judaism, which was the policy of the Maréchal's government, had been agreed to in order to avoid a worse atrocity. The tribunal of History cannot but find therein a justification.

To those who may believe that no one has a moral right to select some rather than others as victims, and that by making such a choice the French deliberately joined in the Nazi work of extermination, it is only too easy to reply that, for the French government as for the entire world, deportation in Germany was regarded merely as a harsh measure and not at all as equivalent to a sentence of death.

It was with horrified stupefaction that the atrocities of the concentration camps became known in the spring of 1945.

The French government in 1942, 1943, and 1944 was no more aware of these atrocities than were the Allies.

M. Grousset, in his horrifying book *Les Jours de notre Mort* [The Days of Our Death] publishes as an annex the report of the first journalist, a Frenchman, M. Lefèvre, who entered Auschwitz on the liberation of that camp by the American advance. Throughout an entire day he listened to the stories of the survivors, but when in the evening he returned to the officers' mess of the American division to which he was assigned and reported these terrible accounts, no one believed him. They had to visit the camp personally on the following day before they were convinced of the truth of what he said.

M. Léon Blum, who was held near one of the camps, declared that he himself had been ignorant of what was going on inside.

In the book which I cited above, *Drancy-la-Juive*, a Jew who survived deportation said, "We knew nothing as to the purpose of the voyage.

1. These figures are taken from the book, *Drancy-la-Juive*, whose authors, Jacques Darville and Simon Wichène, cannot be challenged by those who are pro-Jewish.

The radio had indeed spoken of gas chambers and crematory ovens, but we had been unable to believe it." [1]

This ignorance was so general that foreign Jewesses with children, when they were selected in the southern zone for internment at Compiègne and Drancy, desired to bring their children with them at all costs, and could not understand that the French authorities, in ruling that only adults could be included in the convoys, were merely attempting to save the children from the risk of deportation.

It would therefore be wrong to reproach the French authorities for not having known of abominations of which even those who became the victims did not suspect the existence, and to accuse them of having knowingly turned the Jews toward the gas chambers and the crematory ovens.

The fact is that if President Pierre Laval had washed his hands of the entire affair when a German edict was about to strike all the French Jews of the northern zone his legal responsibility would have been lighter, but his moral responsibility would have been all the greater.

(Document No. 184)
Fr. ed. 659-677

Paris, Fresnes Prison, 14 November 1947

XAVIER VALLAT

[*The final two pages of M. Vallat's declaration, which deal with the question of a Jewish state, may be consulted at the Hoover Library.*]

JEWISH AFFAIRS

JOSEPH ANTIGNAC

*Secretary-General in the
Commissariat-General for Jewish Questions*

[*This document is a note in M. Antignac's handwriting which was given by him to Maître Delz for transmission to Maître Jaffré in September 1945.*]

I believe that it would be of interest and of use to inform President Laval of my own declarations during my first interrogation by the judiciary police; I therefore present the following resume of points which I think would interest the President.

(1) I resigned from the Commissariat-General for Jewish Questions [CGQJ], where I had been director of cabinet for Darquier, and rejoined my family at Vichy on 4 May 1943. On 7 or 8 May the President, having learned from M. Darbou, his own director of cabinet, that I had resigned, asked to see me in order to hear what had happened at the Commissariat-General for Jewish Questions; he was all the more anxious to learn something

1. *Drancy-la-Juive*, p. 48.

as the Germans were complaining about Du Paty du Clam. He invited me to take office again but I refused on the ground that I could not work with Du Paty no matter what my functions were.

My motives for this refusal were (a) the incompetence of Du Paty; (b) his clumsiness in dealing with the German authorities who threatened to take over the direction of the CGQJ themselves, or to impose someone under whose orders I would not be willing to serve—Jacques de Lesdain or Louis Thomas, the latter being a friend of Déat and proposed by him; these two candidates, supported in various ways by the German authorities, had held meetings in Paris to prove that the CGQJ was doing nothing and that its president was hostile to any new measures; (c) the persons in the organization, who were only mediocre administrators; and (d) the hold which the Militia maintained over the CGQJ and which Du Paty accepted or tolerated. There had been numerous visits from Filiol and Bout de L'An, the latter being well acquainted with Du Paty and being the one, it was said, who had recommended him to the President.

Several days after this interview the President sent for me to see him in Paris. On 14 May 1943 he proposed that I should take over control of the CGQJ as secretary-general with full powers, replacing Du Paty who was being placed on the reserve list. I asked for forty-eight hours to think it over as I wanted to be sure that I would have certain people to work with me. When I had made the arrangements I had in mind I accepted the appointment and was put into office on 17 May 1943.

During my interviews with him the President gave me the following instructions; (a) do nothing except administrative work; (b) reorganize the CGQJ and take your time about it; (c) avoid complications with the AA [German authorities], for this would be the last attempt that they would allow us to make; be supple in negotiation and gain several months, which gave me to understand that we were near the end; and in a word prevent the AA from getting their hands on the CGQJ; (d) pass the propaganda over to Henriot; and (e) as for the [anti-Jewish] police, the President was in agreement that I should get rid of them and transfer them to Darnand, which was done at the end of July 1944.

To terminate our interview, the President said to me, "Manage things so that I shall hear as little as possible about you and the CGQJ and don't do like that crazy idiot Darquier did."

In spite of enormous difficulties I carried out this program, assuring the AA of the President's favorable attitude toward the new decrees which they desired to see appear, though in fact I was certain that the President would not sign anything.

Nevertheless I had the desired decrees prepared, and they were torpedoed by the Ministry of Justice, thanks to Dayras, the secretary-general with whom I entered into personal contacts.

(2) Denaturalization of the Jews who had been naturalized French after the end of 1927.

I was at that time director of cabinet for Darquier. These projects were imposed on us by the AA. The President gained as much time as possible, but in the end, forced by the AA, and also by Darquier who had attacked the President indirectly in a press conference in Paris when he declared "It is necessary to be determined," the President, unable to retreat further, signed the decree in June 1943, I think it was.

About ten days later we received an order, signed by Jacques Guérard [in Laval's cabinet], not to send the decree to the *Journal Officiel* for publication.

What could have happened? I was to learn on 15 or 16 August 1943, at a meeting in Vichy where I was present as representative of Darquier, who was then in a hospital, having broken his ankle.

This meeting was held in the President's office in Vichy; representatives of the German services in Paris were present, and also Guérard, Cadu, and I.

The President explained that he had been obliged to annul the decree as the Maréchal had pointed out that he alone had the right to deprive any French citizen of his nationality. After having shown his own good faith in the matter, the President promised to prepare the decree again and to persuade the Maréchal to sign it.

Time passed and a month later the Maréchal refused to take any collective measures. He agreed that such punishments could be inflicted but only individually and in so far as the person concerned had broken French laws.

My personal belief, and I am not alone in so thinking, was that the President had "put on an act" in order to gain time, to show that he was not personally hostile to the measure, as he was being heavily attacked by the press in Paris on this subject, finally relying on the Maréchal who gave his refusal.

Beginning at the end of September 1943 there were again widespread arrests all over France and particularly along the Riviera, as reprisals. I saw the President on the following day before going back to Paris and though he did not make any confidential statements to me he was prudent and my opinion was then clear on what had happened in regard to these arrests. The President was not anti-Jewish. On many occasions he had suggested that the operations conducted by the CGQJ for economic Aryanization should be transferred to the Ministry of State Property. A decree approved by Cathala was even presented to the Germans, I believe, who refused this clever though elegant burial of the Commissariat-General for Jewish Affairs. This economic operation was in fact the only reason for the existence of the CGQJ. It could not go beyond its powers, which did not at all permit confiscation; the results of the sale of any commercial property or business or of any building were paid in to the state's trust and deposit fund to the credit of the person concerned.

One day I told the President that certain publications accused him of being pro-Jewish. He answered, "Why should I be anti-Jewish? The Jews don't bother me. In my country, the Auvergne, there weren't any; we ruined them all."

The truth regarding the responsibilities of those who governed France cannot yet be presented. The wounds are too new and spirits are too overexcited by propaganda whose political purposes become clearer day by day. History will pass a better judgment on a Maréchal of France and on many others who in good faith sacrificed that which was dearest to them, their honor, in order to save the French from suffering the worst.

That which is certain is that henceforth and without hesitation the guilty men can be pointed out. They are those who for personal interests or from stupidity denounced to the Germans the actions of our leading men of state, complicating in this way all that our leaders were doing to resist. 'Resist' is the right word, for it is an act of resistance to hand over only 100,000 workers when they demanded 300,000.... etc.

(Document No. 135)
Fr. ed. 678-680

September 1945

[Not signed]

JEWISH AFFAIRS

ALEX DELPEYROU

Journalist

I the undersigned Alex Delpeyrou certify under oath the accuracy of the following statement.

It was on 16 August 1944 that I saw President Laval for the last time. We had talked together in the Hotel Matignon in the presence of M. Guérard. I had come to report to Pierre Laval on the mission which he had entrusted to me at the Delegation-General of the government, where I was in charge of the press services.

I had been appointed to that post on 1 October 1942. My work consisted on the one hand in being present at press conferences given by the *Propagandastaffel* as the French government's observer, to listen to instructions given to the Paris newspapers, and to send them to the President in Vichy either by teletype if urgent, or otherwise through the diplomatic pouch; and on the other hand to report in the same way those articles in the Paris newspapers which did not adhere to the general instructions given by the Ministry of Information, or which carried on a campaign against what might be described as the 'delaying' polices of Vichy.

On 16 August 1944 I reported to President Laval the refusal that I had just given to Ambassador de Brinon who had called to his office the chiefs of service from the Delegation-General and asked them to follow him to Germany.

"I have nothing on my conscience," I told President Laval. "To leave France at the very moment when the occupying forces are getting ready to evacuate the country would be to disavow the policy of remaining in France, a policy which I have approved and defended for four years. Therefore I remain no matter what happens."

"You are right," Pierre Laval said to me. "But I fear for your safety. All those like you who have served my government are running serious risks. So go and hide."

The President then asked me what was the attitude of the people of Paris at that moment. I did not hide from him the fact that now with deliverance coming near the great majority of French were getting ready to shout for General de Gaulle with the same frenzy as only a few weeks earlier they had cheered Maréchal Pétain.

"There's no doubt," I added, "that tomorrow you will be the most unpopular man in France."

"I know it," he answered, "but don't forget this: it is my unpopularity which has enabled me to serve my country to the utmost.

"And do you know what is going to happen now?" he continued. "The men of London have promised that abundance will now return. They have lied. The privations which we have suffered during four years of occupation have been nothing compared with those which now await us. Build prosperity on ruins and cemeteries! Years of misery, years, do you understand, that's what the future holds for us.

"Unlike M. Blum I am not fond of prophesying. But nevertheless I can predict among other calamities an inflation of living costs, the collapse of the franc, and if great care is not taken, a civil war.

"For two years I have denounced the communist peril. Some people have thought that I was waving a scarecrow for my own purposes. I know Stalin and I know his appetite. After crushing Germany he will devour Europe.

"Those who reproach me for some of my attitudes—I wonder if they know the advantages I obtained in return? Later, very much later, they will have to agree that I was right and that my policies never had any purpose except the interests of my country.

"I know that you have no doubt of it yourself, but what about the others? Those who attempted to get out of their own responsibility by asking me on every point for precise instructions—as though, face to face with the occupying powers, I could possibly define my true position. There were things I could say and there were others which had to be guessed."

Before leaving the President I assured him one last time of my deep affection. I was very shaken and could not repress my tears. He then took me by the two hands saying in low tones, "Adieu, and good luck."

On the following day, 17 August 1944, Pierre Laval was taken by force to Germany.

Six years have passed. Events have given the most striking confirmation to the predictions of a man who several months earlier had told me in his own office this other confidence.

"The fanatics of collaboration," he said—he was speaking of Déat and Doriot, whose campaigns in the *L'Œuvre* and the *Cri du Peuple* the President had asked me to watch very carefully—"do more harm to France than the maquis. By denouncing every day what they call the delaying tactics of Vichy they put me in an impossible position, both with the Germans and with the Maréchal. Do you understand?

"The PPF, the RNP, the single party . . . what will they accomplish? Nothing but the installation of a Gauleiter. And do you know what a Gauleiter means? It means the crushing of France under Allied bombs, it means mass deportations, it means famine, and it means the steady massacre of those who disobey German regulations. And if you get a chance to do so, tell them so from me."

At the beginning of 1943 Pierre Laval, on a visit to Paris, summoned me urgently to his office in the Hotel Matignon.

"If I asked you to help me in a matter which has nothing to do with your work in connection with the press," he asked me, "would you refuse your aid?"

"Certainly I wouldn't refuse it, Mr. President," I answered.

"Well, I need you, and this is what it is," he said. "You know Darquier de Pellepoix?"

"Yes, Mr. President. M. Léon Bailby made him assistant secretary-general of *Le Jour* in 1934 when I was chief of the political services on that newspaper."

"What do you think of him?" the President asked.

"Nothing in particular, except that he was president of the Association of the Victims of February Sixth," I answered, "having himself been

— 651 —

seriously wounded on the Place de la Concorde. And also that well before the war he was already violently anti-Jewish."

"Too much so. He exaggerates," the President said. "In the Commissariat for Jewish Affairs he takes on himself to do things which go beyond the government's directives. He is a fanatic and a madman when it comes to anti-Semitism. Because of him I have had constant trouble with the Germans. I need someone like you to tone down his fanaticism. I have just arranged with Dr. Knochen the liquidation of an agency which operated in the rue la Boétie in liaison with the French Commissariat for Jewish Affairs under the direction of a certain Captain Cézil. This agency was nothing less than an organization for secret denunciations, paid for by the German services. But Knochen demands that it be replaced by an autonomous association exclusively French, established like all associations, under the law of 1901, with an administrative council at its head. I want you to act as president. Do you agree?"

I objected that I had a great deal of work at the Delegation-General since the government had in the meantime appointed me as a member of the censorship committee for the cinema, which was headed by Paul Morand, who was later made French Ambassador in Berne. But President Laval insisted.

"I do not ask you to do a lot of work," he said. "Except for one meeting of the administrative council each week you will have nothing to do except to let me know what happens at the Commissariat for Jewish Affairs, as you are already doing for the newspapers of Paris. I saw Darquier this morning. He agrees that you should become president. I will undertake to get you accepted by the German authorities. The association will be called the French Union for the Defense of the Race. I am the one who found that title for it. Knochen wanted it to be called the Federation of the Anti-Jewish French. I finally made him accept my idea. It has the merit of being more vague. The purpose assigned by the Germans to this association is to support the anti-Jewish propaganda of the commissariat by leaflets, booklets, conferences, press notices, and so on.

"Now understand me correctly, Delpeyrou," he continued. "I don't want any of that sort of thing. Your directions are to delay, to postpone, and to appear to be doing something when you are doing nothing. The commissariat will allot you the credits for setting up the offices. Use up these credits for furniture and fittings, in securing personnel, in buying office supplies, but keep away from any sort of propaganda outside the office. Gain time—that's all I ask of you. And if things slip up, I shall be there to protect you. You understand?"

In accordance with my instructions I presided over the association for eight months, attending one meeting of the council of administration of the UFDR every week. I refrained from any form of propaganda. In addition I kept President Laval informed in detail of the plans of the commissariat and particularly of the famous draft law which Darquier de Pellepoix prepared under German pressure and submitted to Pierre Laval; its purpose was to withdraw French nationality from all Jews who had been naturalized after 1923.

In this connection here is the artful plan by which the President succeeded in preventing the proposed measures from being applied. On many occasions Knochen, von Gerlach, and General Oberg had harrassed M. Antignac, successor to Darquier de Pellepoix at the head of the Commissariat for

Jewish Affairs, in their attempt to get the proposal out of the files of the President of the Council. Before having been turned out by Vichy as having 'resigned' Darquier had assured the Germans that his proposed law had been signed for some months by Pierre Laval and would appear any day in the *Journal Officiel*. In fact the President, warned by my reports, kept the draft in his own hands.

Their patience exhausted, the German chiefs for Jewish questions ordered M. Antignac to demand an interview for them with President Laval, and to go with them to Vichy. When this delegation entered the office of the Chief of Government, President Laval after pretending to look for it for some time pulled out of a drawer the text of the draft law. It did in fact have his signature on it, and he made the following declaration to his visitors.

"The delay in publishing this law in the *Journal Officiel* is not my fault," he stated. "The proof is that I approved it and signed it, just as M. Darquier de Pellepoix told you. But in signing it I thoughtlessly went beyond my powers."

And to the astonished Germans Pierre Laval then added the following explanation.

"This matter, gentlemen, is an affair of the rights of the person," he said. "And because it has to do with such rights it is in no way an affair of the Chief of Government, but only of the Chief of State. You are certainly not unaware of the extent to which the Maréchal is jealous of the rights which are his under the constitutional laws. Of course in fact it is a simple formality. It will be taken care of at the next Council of Ministers."

On the following day, at Pierre Laval's request, the Maréchal, with the approval of the Council, informed the occupation authorities that although he was in agreement with the measures proposed by Darquier de Pellepoix he considered that the cancellation of acts of naturalization could not be effective collectively but would have to be done individually after a careful examination of each case.

And this was the burial, thanks to Pierre Laval, of a law which if it had been applied would have handed over tens of thousands of Jews to Nazi ferocity.

I add that after eight months during which I had, in accordance with my instructions, imposed complete inertia on the management of the French Union for the Defense of the Race, I was summoned to the German embassy where von Gerlach, with Knochen at his side, after reproaching me for having accomplished no act of anti-Jewish propaganda told me that I would soon hear from him.

Eight days later the UFDR was dissolved by the Germans and its staff expelled from the building which it occupied. I owe it to President Laval that I was not arrested at that time.

None of these considerations prevented French justice from condemning me on 13 July 1949 to national degradation for anti-racial propaganda.

Though my testimony is treated with deep suspicion at the bar of the special tribunals which have raged throughout France since the coming of the Fourth Republic, I imagine that it will retain all its value before the tribunal of History. My memories as reported above show, as do so many others, that Pierre Laval, assassinated by order of General de Gaulle, until his very death placed at the service of his country the incomparable power of exhausting effort, brilliant intelligence, and a patriotic ardor which, unknown to the immense majority of his contemporaries, was as praiseworthy in its concealment as it was in its stubborn persistence.

(Document No. 119)
Fr. ed. 681-684

Paris, 11 April 1950

A. DELPERYOU
Alex Delpeyrou

JEWISH AFFAIRS

GEORGES MONIER
French Minister in Lisbon

I the undersigned Georges Monier, Master of Appeals in the Council of State, retired, former Minister of France in Lisbon, living in Paris, make the following declaration under oath.

In 1930, when he was Minister of Labor in the Tardieu cabinet, I met M. Laval for the first time. I was then director for social security in the Lyon region.

In 1931 M. Laval became President of the Council of Ministers. He chose as his director of cabinet M. Léon Noël, then prefect of the Haut-Rhin. M. Léon Noël also acted as secretary-general in the Ministry of the Interior for President Laval, and as director of the Sûreté Générale. Two months after the formation of the cabinet M. Léon Noël added me to his staff. M. Léon Noël's offer is explained by the fact that I had been his close collaborator in the Rhineland. M. Léon Noël had been, from 1927 to 1930, the delegate-general of the High Commissioner of the French Republic in the Rhine Provinces of Coblenz. From 1920 to 1930 I had been chief deputy, and chief of juridical services, in the High Commissariat of the French Republic in the Rhine Provinces. Thus I came into contact again with President Laval just at the moment when his government was overthrown in 1932.

I was a member of the French mission presided over by President Laval at the Berlin conferences of 1931, in Chancellor Bruning's time, and at the London conferences of 1931 in connection with the Young Plan.

In 1935 I was attached to the secretariat-general of the Council's presidency as a technician. My work was to prepare and to write the texts of the economic decree-laws which concerned the Ministries of War, Interior, Public Health, and Labor. I had not seen President Laval again from 1935 to the end of 1940. In September 1940 I was repatriated from Syria where I had been captain on the general staff for the French forces in the Levant. At this time I resumed my duties as Master of Appeals in the legislative section of the Council of State, which had been evacuated to Royat.

In October 1940 M. Laval summoned me to Vichy and asked me to join his cabinet. I pointed out first that my health had been seriously affected by my service in Syria and would not permit me for some time to participate very actively, and second that having been a member of the French occupation of Germany for twelve years and having thus dealt with the Germans as a conqueror, it would be very painful for me to resume my relations with them as one of the conquered.

On those grounds I declined the offer which had been made to me. President Laval accepted my reasons kindly but remarked, "Like you, Monier, I have often dealt with the Germans when I represented the conqueror. I believe that it is now the duty of all of us to maintain our presence in order to save what can be saved. My attitude and my acts are dominated by the desire to preserve for France her independence and her integrity, and those means which will permit her at the end of the war to take again an honorable place in the concert of the nations. I do not insist on keeping you with me; take up your place again in the Council of State, but be sure to tell those around you that my policy is just as I have explained it."

From that moment until May 1942 I had no relationship with members of the Vichy government.

In May 1942 one of my colleagues in the Council of State, M. Blondel, a friend of M. de Menthon, asked me to go to Vichy in order to report to the President of the Council of Ministers what had been done to M. de Menthon at Annecy by the Legion, and to arrange that proper measures be taken for the liberation of M. de Menthon and for punishment of those responsible. I did make these demands. M. Laval received me in his office. I told him what had been done to M. de Menthon a few days earlier at Annecy. I told him that I was making this appeal in the name of some of my colleagues, that I was not personally acquainted with M. de Menthon, that M. de Menthon himself did not know that this appeal was being made, but that my colleagues and I were very disturbed to see that for some time past things had been happening which were of a nature to stir up something very close to the spirit of civil war.

M. Laval said to me at once and without the slightest hesitation, "I thank you for having let me know. In any case I would have heard of what happened to M. de Menthon and I would have acted, for, believe me, no appeal is necessary to convince me. Everything which I do and everything which I try to do, under painful conditions which no one other than myself is aware of, with the purpose of maintaining France, would be perfectly useless if I allowed the pogroms of a civil war, of which the certain result would be the destruction of France by the French themselves. This possibility has been a nightmare to me since the assassination of Max Dormoy, though as you know he was not always my friend."

On the same day President Laval sent Dr. Grasset, Minister of Public Health, a heavily wounded veteran of the 1914-1918 war, to Annecy in order to make an investigation and to inform the local council of the Legion that it was suspended from all activities until the end of that investigation. I learned afterward that M. de Menthon was freed and that punishments were inflicted.

After the conversation which I have just reported President Laval asked me what I was doing in the Council of State. I told him that as Master of Appeals in the legislative section I dealt with the legal work of the Council in the matter of the special laws for Jews and for the children of foreigners. I told him that the first decision taken by the Council at my request had had the effect of blocking more or less completely the laws of exception. M. Laval completely approved my attitude and said, in the presence of many high officials who were then in his office, "There you see the man I need in the Commissariat for Jewish Affairs to neutralize the activities of Darquier de Pellepoix and if possible to destroy that entire organization, which day by day becomes more inhuman."

I cried out against this idea but M. Laval became more definite and imperative, saying to me, "It's the question which disturbs me the most just now. I must clear it up."

After some discussion, and although it was an effort for me to accept, it was understood that for a month I would act as secretary-general with powers equal to those of the commissioner-general, and that I would use this time to gather information and make a detailed report on the kind of matters that were being dealt with by the commissariat and the way in which they were being handled. As a matter of fact I did not have to prepare the report because in a very few days I learned enough to tell the President of the Council of Ministers immediately what the situation was, and in consequence to give him my oral resignation. M. Darquier de Pellepoix on his side, after the one and very stormy interview which I had with him, demanded that I should be immediately removed from my position as my attitude was not at all, in his opinion, an appropriate one.

The President of the Council of Ministers thanked me but did not accept my written resignation until a month later. (See Annex I). On receiving the precise information which I brought him he asked me to draft a law which would suppress the Commissariat-General for Jewish Affairs and would divide its work between the Ministry of Justice, section dealing with personal rights, and the Administration of State Property, trustee section, an arrangement which in President Laval's opinion, and mine as well, would remove the poison, so far as possible, from these laws introduced under German pressure.

A first draft prepared under this plan was rejected by the occupation authorities. Slightly modified it was re-presented repeatedly by M. Laval, and finally accepted after two months of discussion. A copy of this version, signed by all the ministers interested in the matter, is certainly in the archives of the Ministry of Justice.

Unfortunately just as this text was about to be published and to become effective, the Chief of the SS, Captain Dannecker I think it was, who took a particular interest in Jewish matters, persuaded the higher German authorities to withdraw the agreement which they had previously given.

My attitude throughout this matter had brought upon me the attention of the German police. I was soon informed of that attention by the President of the Council of Ministers himself, and he sought means of protecting me from possible reprisals. Many months passed. The body to which I belonged, the Council of State, had left Royat and was again installed in Paris. My chief, M. Porché, advised me to remain hidden for some time with my family in the Auvergne. M. Laval gave me the same advice. In November 1942 the Germans entered the free zone. I was not particularly disturbed but I learned that my residence was known to them and that I was being watched by the German police. In December 1942

I decided that I would run no greater risks in Paris than in the Auvergne and I asked that I should be allowed to take up my position again.

M. Laval then summoned me to Vichy again and said in substance, "I believe that it would be unwise for you to go back to Paris. At the first opportunity they would arrest you and I am afraid that I could do very little to help you. Besides, I know your feelings and in particular I know the anguish which comes to you at the thought of a civil war among French people. That is why I want you to represent France in Lisbon. I have only one order to give you: do everything which can be done through your attitude, your actions, and your proposals, to take advantage of any opportunity to bind together again the two parts of France." I attach as an annex to this report a letter drawn up by President Laval in which he defines the mission which he entrusted to me; this letter was addressed to Mr. Caeiro da Mata, a confidential advisor of President Salazar, and at present Minister of Foreign Affairs in the Portuguese government (Annex II).

At the end of April 1943 I took up my post in Lisbon, a post which I was to leave with the full agreement of the Portuguese government on 24 August 1944. During this time by agreement with M. Laval I sent no political telegrams to Vichy lest they should be intercepted by the Germans. I went twice to Vichy during that period, once in September 1943 and again in April 1944. On my first visit in September 1943 my interviews with President Laval were limited to reporting the very courteous reception which I received from the Portuguese government, and to telling him that I had encountered no particular hostility on the part of the Allied missions. On the contrary, in April 1944, my final interview with President Laval, I spent difficult hours in Vichy. On this matter I limit myself to reproducing the report which I made to the Garde des Sceaux on my return to France (Annex III).

To conclude my present testimony I wish to say that in my eyes President Laval had no ambition other than that of serving, unyieldingly and tirelessly, the permanent interests of France and of the French people.

(Document No. 99)
Fr. ed. 685-691

Paris, 28 March 1949

GEORGES MONIER

ANNEX I

GENERAL COMMISSARIAT FOR JEWISH AFFAIRS

Vichy, 26 June 1942

Monsieur le Chef du Gouvernement,

By a decree dated 6 May 1942 you were good enough to assign to me the functions of secretary-general in the office for Jewish Affairs and to ask me to aid, in this capacity, the Commissioner-General for Jewish Affairs under the conditions described by Article 3 of Law No. 545 of 6 May 1942.

Believing that it is my duty, as it is that of every government official, to serve the State in the position which is assigned to him according to regulations, I began my work at once. I was all the more anxious to do my duty as this indication of confidence was so great a one, particularly as I had been named without any solicitation whatever on my own part.

The complete sacrifice of one's self may be demanded in the carrying out of a duty; the renunciation of all dignity and honor must not be demanded.

In acting any longer as assistant to the present commissioner-general in accordance with his conception of his work, as would be necessary under the law, I would be carried beyond the demands of duty.

For this reason I find myself obliged, after a month and a half of service, to submit my resignation.

I shall be deeply grateful to you if you will accept it.

Signed : Georges Monier

ANNEX II

Vichy, 5 April 1943

Mon cher Ministre et Ami,

I have read your message with great interest and I was pleased to learn that the delay of the departure of M. Monier for Lisbon was not due to anything in the relations between our two countries.

I understand your regret and I am touched by the feelings which you express as a friend of France when you consider the possibility that the French in Lisbon might by their attitude cause difficulties for the representative whom I have appointed.

As Minister of Foreign Affairs I deplore the fact that French people abroad, poorly informed, might show themselves unsympathetic and unjust toward the French government; nevertheless this consideration has but little importance in my opinion. What is important above all else is that confident relationships should be maintained between Portugal and France through normal channels. It is not normal that my country should continue to be represented in Lisbon merely by a chargé d'affaires.

I have no doubt, my dear Minister, and I wish to express my personal thanks in advance, that on the Portuguese side a warm welcome will be given to M. Monier. The new minister is a man of duty, extremely tactful, who will know how to avoid any action that might embarrass the accomplishment of his mission. I propose therefore to ask M. Monier to take up his position in a few days. I would have liked very much to have him wait until your return before leaving for Lisbon but I know from your chargé d'affaires that you will probably not be back until after Easter.

I need not tell you how deeply I was touched by your two messages, which show me once more the excellence of your feelings toward me and at the same time the friendship which you feel for my country.

Croyez, mon cher Ministre et Ami, à mes sentiments affectueusement dévoués,

Signed : Pierre Laval

ANNEX III

At the end of April 1944 I was summoned to Vichy by the President of the Council of Ministers and Minister of Foreign Affairs, as a result of German complaints regarding the use that was being made, more or less generally, of the diplomatic pouches. I had been in Vichy several days when I received from the Minister of Foreign Affairs a formal order to leave France on the same day and to take up immediately my post at Lisbon.

The exact date of my departure is shown on the diplomatic passport which, in accordance with usual procedure, I handed back to the direction of personnel in the Ministry of Foreign Affairs last May when I returned definitely to France.

On the same evening I left France by plane. At that time no reason was given for this sudden order for my departure. I was all the more surprised by it as I had just asked for and obtained, that very morning, authorization to spend a week in the Auvergne with my family.

Here are the reasons as they were given to me, and explained on my return to France by M. Hervé Bigot, chief of the personal secretariat of the President of the Council of Ministers and Minister of Foreign Affairs, at Vichy. On the day of my departure at eleven o'clock in the morning M. Bigot had been called to the telephone on the Paris line by M. Guénier, chief of the personal secretariat of the President of the Council of Ministers in Paris at the Hotel Matignon. Conversations on this wire were of course listened to by the German services of the Gestapo. M. Guénier read over the telephone some ten rumors which had been published in the Paris press. Among these ten, two concerned me, and attacked me under the heading "Of what use is the Lisbon Diplomatic Pouch?" I was accused of passing military documents on to the Allies. After reading these texts M. Guénier added only a single remark—"You've understood."

M. Bigot had in fact understood, and at once went to see the President of the Council of Ministers. He repeated the conversation that he had just had with M. Guénier. After listening to him M. Laval made a short and violent remark which I hesitate to reproduce here. He then asked M. Bigot to find me and to warn me that he wanted to see me immediately. It was only at one o'clock in the afternoon that I was able to reach him. He then ordered me without any comments to leave France immediately. He instructed M. Bigot to give me the car and gasoline necessary to go to Lyon-Bron in order to take the five o'clock plane after making sure that I had all the necessary visas.

Early the following morning the chief of the Gestapo in Vichy, Captain Gessler, with two of his acolytes, entered M. Bigot's office. He stayed there for two hours asking questions about me, my attitude, my activities, and the documents which I received or sent. M. Bigot replied that he received from me occasionally, for distribution to friends or prisoner comrades, such rare and minor items as cigarettes, soap, chocolate, and so on, and that while all this was not perhaps very strictly in accordance with regulations, it did not seem to justify M. Gessler's obvious state of excitement. M. Gessler then stated that the accusations against me, of which he had proof, were extremely serious and that he was going to have a talk with M. Laval, and that he would ask that the diplomatic pouches which I might send or receive should be examined. In fact he did call on the President of the Council of Ministers and immediately afterward on the secretary-general of Foreign Affairs, and he did examine the diplomatic pouch which had arrived that very morning from Lisbon. He found nothing in it. The services of the French military authorities had been warned in time by the Secretary-General, M. Rochat, and the necessary precautions had been taken. This inspection was repeated afterward in spite of the protests of the Ministry of Foreign Affairs. M. Taddei who was at that time chief of the diplomatic courriers and is today an official in the direction of personnel of the Quai d'Orsay was present at the dispute touched off by the German police and can testify on that point.

Without wishing to betray any secrets, I can say that military documents which passed through the diplomatic pouch, and concerning which the German police seemed to be precisely informed, were so important that my arrest and immediate execution was envisaged by Gessler. And in fact, if I had been arrested and executed, the Germans would have been following the laws of war and in this case would for once have been acting legitimately.

M. Bigot, M. Guénier, and M. Taddei are ready to testify, each one on points with which he was concerned, and if it is necessary to do so, regarding the absolute exactitude of what I have stated above.

I ran these risks voluntarily. The members of my family also voluntarily accepted for their part the danger of the reprisals which the Germans never failed to apply in such matters, and with those methods which everyone knows about. Each of us did no more than his duty. That is the only point which I wish to establish and the only point which I should like to see recognized.

CHAPTER XIII

FOREIGN AFFAIRS

THE FRENCH EMBASSY AT THE VATICAN

LÉON BÉRARD

French Ambassador at the Vatican

[*This declaration is in the form of a letter addressed to M. René de Chambrun.*]

Paris, *3 November 1955*

Mon cher Ami,

As I told you in my letter of 2 July, I planned to use my vacation time for assembling the memoirs from which I could derive material for the written testimony which you were good enough to ask me to give regarding the occupation years. Various obstacles, which you will no doubt excuse me from describing here, prevented me from doing what I had expected. Please therefore allow me to summarize very simply the essential points of what I think I should place on record.

I reached Rome on my mission as ambassador to the Vatican toward the end of November 1940. The seat of the Embassy had been moved in June, when Italy entered the war, to the Vatican City. It was there that I was to establish my residence. Technically, in spite of the June armistice, we were still at war with Italy. The Italian government would not allow a French diplomat accredited to the Vatican, and a subject of an enemy power, to reside in the capital of the kingdom or even to have free access to the capital. During four years we never left the Vatican, my family, my collaborators and I, except with special permission from the Italian authorities and under the guard of a police officer appointed by them, who however was always tactful in carrying out his duties as a guide and guard. We were well lodged, thanks to the administrative services of the Vatican, and under the same roof as the Minister for Great Britain and the Ambassador for Poland. The regime imposed on us by the Italian state was the same as that for those diplomats whose governments were still more effectively at war against the Axis powers. I mention these points to reply, if necessary, to the false rumors which were circulated at a certain time.

From 1940 to 1944 our Embassy maintained the representation of

France with the Head of the Church and at the center of the Catholic world. Aided successively by two embassy counselors, who have since deservedly been elevated to the rank of ambassador, I took care during those unhappy years that there should be no weakening of the rights, or even of the traditional prerogatives, of France in the various parts of the Christian world.

In this way we had the opportunity of rendering aid and support, with the benevolent backing of the Vatican, to our missionaries and especially to those in the Far East.

I believe that my actions were inspired both by broad views and by the feeling that France at such a time should maintain closer relations than ever with the high spiritual power from which so many nations sought approval or backing.

The Secretary of State for His Holiness several times asked me to call to the attention of my government the cases of persons of various conditions of life and religion who had been victims of injustice because of the occupation. I never failed to report to the Department of Foreign Affairs at Vichy the interest which the Vatican took in such cases. These requests or wishes were always taken into consideration. The government of the Maréchal strove to give satisfaction or, in so far as it was possible, to arrange that satisfaction should be given by others, as for example in the case in which we obtained the liberation of a General Superior of the Sisters of Charity who had been arrested by the Germans.

At the time when the Obligatory Labor Service was organized in France the cardinal Secretary of State expressed to me the views and feelings of the Vatican on this subject, on several occasions, intentionally limiting his remarks to questions which involved those religious or moral interests for which the papacy is responsible. The Vatican attached extreme importance to making the greatest efforts to exempt from work in Germany girls and women and students in the great seminaries, as well as to the maintenance of a service of priests for French expatriated workers. These were points which the cardinal had asked me to present urgently to our government. I had no doubt that the intentions and policies of our government were in conformity with the point of view of the Pope and his minister; nevertheless I sent very many letters and reports to Vichy on this subject. I dispatched them in a variety of ways to a number of different persons as our communications with France were sometimes not very certain, because of the occupation and the events of the war. I was most anxious that the thought of the Vatican should be made known to those who had to negotiate with the German authorities on problems of this character and of such importance.

In 1943, after the armistice concluded between the Italian government of Marshal Badoglio and the Allies, the Italian occupation troops in the southeast of France were replaced by German troops accompanied by the usual police forces. A number of Jews who had been in that region then took refuge in Italy where many of them lived a most difficult life. I asked the Department of Foreign Affairs at Vichy to establish a credit in my embassy so that I could give some aid and relief to these refugees. The Ministry hastened to accede to my request. As we could not leave the Vatican, this aid was distributed by the Swiss Legation at Rome, responsible for French interests in Italy; we transferred the funds to them.

Many of our compatriots in the departement of Corsica, who had been arrested by the Italian authorities for resistance, were now interned in Italy. Some of them were threatened with very serious punishments.

With the help of the Secretariat of State of the Pope I secured pardons for many of them.

In 1942 I spent two months leave in France. I had been able at that time to satisfy myself that the Chief of State, the Chief of Government, and the high officials of the foreign office approved the lines which I had followed in carrying out my mission. Toward the end of October [1942], and on the very day when I was about to return to Rome, the Maréchal was good enough to ask me to lunch with several highly representative members of the French religious body. Pierre Laval was among the guests. In a conversation which followed this lunch, Pierre Laval informed the Church authorities of the government's decisions regarding the subsidies which were to be given that year to the Catholic [educational] faculties of France.

On the same day I had felt it my duty to tell Pierre Laval of the situation of a young official, intellectually distinguished and of great merit, against whom he had been warned because of the young man's marked sympathy for the Free France organization. I had scarcely begun to explain the matter when he interrupted me to say that he had already been informed of the matter and had settled it in the way I desired before even knowing my opinion, as it would have been repugnant to him in such a case to break or interrupt so honorable a career.

That was my last conversation with Pierre Laval.

Veuillez croire, mon cher Ami, à mes sentiments affectueusement dévoués.

(Document No. 311)
Fr. ed. 695-697

LÉON BÉRARD

AMBASSADOR IN MADRID

FRANÇOIS PIÉTRI

French Ambassador in Madrid

I wish to point out first of all that I was among the members of the French Parliament who were hostile to France's entry into the war in September 1939.

Under the French constitution the two chambers should have been called on to make a declaration of war. If they had been asked to do so, I would have voted against such a declaration. But as everyone knows, we were not consulted except in being asked to vote credits for the government, "in view of certain international possibilities." The government when questioned by members of the Commission of Finance, and notably by me, as to whether this vote of credits implicitly indicated a declaration of war, answered explicitly that it did not. Nevertheless the government declared war two days later on its own initiative under very strong pressure from England. The government even refused to allow a debate on the subject and denied the demand for a secret session made by M. Bergery, and for which I voted.

Why was I opposed in this way to France's entry into war, at least at that particular moment?

(1) Because in spite of my hatred for Hitlerian tyranny and for Nazism, a hatred which I had shown in many speeches and particularly in the great meeting held at the Trocadero in 1933 in favor of the persecuted Jews—I thought that we ought not to shed French blood for matters of ideology or of domestic politics.

(2) Because the way Poland had acted in August 1938 toward Czecho-slovakia, supporting Germany in its *coup de force* and even going so far as to seize for herself a part of the Sudeten territory, had released us, in my opinion, from any obligation whatever toward Poland.

(3) Because I believed that the Danzig corridor, which had always been referred to as one of the points in the Versailles Treaty that might be revised, was not sufficiently important, even as a pretext, to be made the justification of a world war.

(4) Because the Russo-German alliance had just created complete disequilibrium between Franco-English forces on the one side and the adversary on the other side, especially in view of the fact that the United States had solemnly declared its neutrality.

(5) Because I knew perfectly well, as a member of the Sub-Commission for National Defense in the Commission of Finance, and as a former Minister of National Defense and as a Minister of the Navy during many years that even against Germany *alone* (a) we were in a condition of serious inferiority as regards planes and motorized equipment, and (b) our Maginot line, because it had not been extended to the sea, could be outflanked by way of Belgium whose defensive system was insufficient.

(6) Because I thought that Hitler's secret idea was to attack Russia before turning toward the west and that therefore Germany and Russia would very soon break their pact, and that in consequence it would be much wiser and more effective to await the outcome of that inevitable clash in order to impose our will on the conqueror, whichever country it might be, with means which could be improved in the meantime, used against a heavily exhausted adversary.

I communicated all these reasons to M. Daladier and other Ministers but only semi-officially since once the war had been declared and begun my patriotic duty obliged me not to discourage public opinion and morale by public intervention. Nevertheless after eight months of defensive sleep behind the Maginot line the Franco-British-Belgian army was out-flanked, attacked, and crushed in several weeks by an enemy which out-numbered it three to one and was ten times stronger in equipment. On 11 June 1940 the government fled precipitously to Tours and then to Bordeaux, inviting Parliament to follow it in its flight.

It was under these conditions that I found myself in Bordeaux at the time of the armistice. I declare that at that time the Parliament with almost complete unanimity, and the public in its immense majority, had three desires: (1) that a struggle which was impossible to continue, should cease; (2) that the government should remain in France; and (3) that full powers should be granted to Maréchal Pétain, the only one who was qualified by his past record to deal as best he could with the Germans and to limit the damages of occupation.

Of these points I can desire no better proof than that given by solemn appeals addressed to us by M. Herriot, President of the Chamber, and by M. Jeanneney, President of the Senate, asking that the reins of state should be handed to Maréchal Pétain and that the National Assembly should be summoned to meet at Vichy.

It is sheer trickery to have claimed afterwards that the armistice, the meeting of the National Assembly, and the transfer of full powers to the Maréchal had been the work of some clique and the result of intrigue. It is undeniable that M. Laval took the lead in such a movement, but it was a movement which corresponded precisely with the general desire of Parliament and of the mass of the people. There was no pressure from the occupying forces and the proof is that the eighty members of Parliament, out of 900, who voted against a change of regime remained freely in the unoccupied zone under the protection of French law. Those who were troubled later, rightly or wrongly, were not so troubled because of their action in this matter.

On 12 July 1940, after the decisions of the National Assembly, the Maréchal changed his cabinet and brought in three more Senators and Deputies. I was one of these three, being made Minister of Public Works and of Communications. This brought to five the number of members of Parliament who had been given ministerial posts: M. Laval and M. Marquet, from the Left, M. Ybarnegaray from the Right, and M. Mireaux, M. Lemery and myself from the Center.

Essentially my task was first to get the railways and the postal system working again; second to repair seven or eight hundred bridges which had been cut; third to get back to Paris and the north of France about ten million persons who had left their homes at the time of the invasion and were wandering about through the center and the south; and fourth to protect our rail and waterway equipment on which the Germans were making new levies every day.

In several weeks, not without great difficulty, these various objectives were attained, at least provisionally, and in such a way that there was immediate freedom of circulation. I reported officially on what had been done in a radio declaration on 11 August 1940.

Our conflicts with the Germans were rather harsh. They took place in the Armistice Commission and personally I did not have to deal with the Germans as I was in touch only with our own representatives on the commission. We had to give the Germans several hundred locomotives but on the other hand I succeeded in refusing to hand over 600 steel canal barges, thinking that they might possibly be used in an attempt to invade England.

I do not know what happened afterward, but I can testify that during the fifty days of my ministry the directives of the government, whether they came from the Maréchal or from M. Laval himself, were to resist German demands by every possible means. As a result there were constant conflicts to such an extent that on one of my visits in Paris I was ordered to leave the occupied zone within twenty-four hours. The ministers who had been members of Parliament were particularly subject to the defiance and hostility of the occupation authorities. At the beginning of

September 1940, probably for this very reason, the Maréchal dispensed with our services. M. Laval whose republican sentiments had remained very much in evidence had no part whatever in this change; in fact, the rumor was that he too might leave.

Several days later M. Baudouin, Minister of Foreign Affairs, asked me to accept the post of Ambassador in Madrid with precise instructions to try to establish permanent liaison with Sir Samuel Hoare, the British Ambassador, who had been Minister of the Navy at the time when I held the same position in France, and whom I therefore knew personally. I was appointed on 9 October 1940, I arrived in Madrid on 6 November and I presented my credentials on 7 December.

I cannot give the details of a mission which lasted throughout the life of the Vichy government, until 30 August 1944. I will limit myself to mentioning the principal points with which I dealt and the results of my activities during this long period, indicating in particular that at no moment was I disapproved by M. Laval even when I took initiatives which did not harmonize at all with what was called his collaboration policy—a policy which he told me himself, on one of my visits to Vichy, had no other purpose than to elude skillfully, or to soften as much as possible, the tyranny of German occupation.

So definite were these lines of conduct that in March and April 1943, as is shown by documents found in the Foreign Office in Berlin, the Germans demanded that I be recalled and replaced, and the Vichy government refused.

Activities of the French Embassy in Madrid from November 1940 to September 1944

(a) *Attitude toward the Spanish*

1.—Constant attention was given to the possibility that Spain might try to encroach on our possessions in North Africa. Aside from the sudden Spanish invasion of Tangiers a little before I reached Madrid, and against which I protested vigorously, as did also the ambassadors of the United States and of Britain, I gradually succeeded in convincing the Madrid government that it should drop its aims in regard to Morocco and Oran. This result was not achieved without a number of incidents. A Spanish plane was attacked by a French plane at Fedala in December 1940. There were anti-French moves by Consul Toca and by Abbot Manresa of Oran in April 1941; the publications *Arriba* and *Africa*, and others, carried on anti-French campaigns; and there was a demand for the expulsion of a Spanish press correspondent in Vichy in May 1942.

On a number of occasions, either directly or through an intermediary the Spanish government tried to engage me in conversations on Morocco, chiefly on the subject of revising the frontiers between the two zones as laid down by the Treaty of 1912. I always avoided such conversations. At the time of the Anglo-American landing in Algeria in November 1942 I appealed to Count de Jordana, the Spanish Minister of Foreign Affairs, as did also the ambassadors of Great Britain and of the United States, to maintain absolute neutrality and to refrain from any "protective" intervention.

2.—With the same care a continual effort was made to prevent Spain from entering into any agreement with the Germans and from giving them any sort of effective aid particularly through adherence to a tripartite pact. For this purpose, though the pretext was a simple matter of protocol and neighborliness, I had suggested and organized the meeting between Maréchal Pétain and General Franco at Montpellier in February 1941, a meeting which from this point of view was extremely useful.

The dispatch of the Blue Division to Russia was the only form of aid given by Spain to the Germans, but I was told in confidence that this move was made in order to prevent an attempt by the Germans to move troops through Spanish territory. In addition, all members of the Blue Division were volunteers.

3.—I signed many agreements with Spain in economic and cultural matters. They were all intended to establish good reciprocal relations and to maintain as long as possible a favorable attitude on the part of the Spaniards. These agreements included the treaty for the exchange of works of art in December 1940; a financial treaty in January 1942; and another treaty, both financial and commercial, in July 1943.

4.—With the same purpose I arranged for the participation of France in the exposition at Valencia in 1941, and at Barcelona in 1942, in order that the field should not be left entirely to the Germans. I also established many religious, intellectual, and other contacts, for example through the pilgrimages of Pamplona in 1941, and of Salamanca in 1942; the visit to Cardinal Gerlier in March 1941, a lecture by Abbé Breuil and others by Dr. Leriche, M. Hazard, and M. Bouvier, etc.; the presentation of plays by Claudel, Baty, and others; artistic and other expositions at the French Institute in Madrid; and French participation in the Holy Year exercises at Compostela in 1944. All these efforts were supported by the Vichy government and played a very great role in the improvement of Franco-Spanish relations, strongly influencing the Spanish attitude toward Germany.

5.—In spite of all this we always replied negatively to demands by the Spanish government for the extradition of important communists who had taken refuge in France, even when these demands were also justified by conviction for common-law crimes, such as robbery, murder, and so on. This was a particularly difficult struggle as Spain insisted intensely on these extraditions.

6.—Integrity of the territory of Andorra threatened for a time by Spain in 1942 was successfully defended.

(b) *Attitude toward the Allies*

1.—My first contact on arriving in Madrid in November 1940, even before I paid my official respects to the Spanish authorities, was with Sir Samuel Hoare. We agreed to remain in continual contact and to establish in Madrid a practical liaison, indispensable between our two countries. Thus we were in close relations at all times until March 1943 and then it was on the initiative of the British Foreign Office and not Vichy that these relations were interrupted.

During this period of two and a half years we agreed on many questions and we succeeded in solving many problems in satisfactory fashion. For example, we agreed on the commercial treaty with Morocco in February

1941, an exchange of prisoners in Syria in June 1941, a settlement of the San Diego affair at the end of 1941, on a plan referring to the blockade, and so on. On the other hand on different occasions we presented protests to each other from our respective governments. During our interviews we often discussed matters rather vividly but without affecting the cordiality of our relations. I have never understood why Sir Samuel Hoare, in writing his memoirs, said nothing whatever about all the matters of which I have just spoken.

2.—As regards the Americans it is necessary to divide the subject into two distinct periods, the first being that during which Mr. Weddell was there, from 1940 to 1942, and the second when Mr. Carlton Hayes was in Madrid, from 1942 to 1944. Mr. Hayes in fact arrived in Madrid just before the United States entered the war. My relations with Mr. Weddell were of a most friendly character, both affectionate and intimate. We often lunched or dined together. He told me many interesting things of a confidential nature which I passed on to Vichy. On the two occasions when Admiral Leahy passed through Madrid he was received by me at the French Embassy together with Mr. and Mrs. Weddell.

I would have been happy, in French interests and also in the interests of the Allies, if these excellent relations had continued with Mr. Carlton Hayes. At the beginning of his mission in Madrid, relations were excellent, and he was extremely friendly. But from the time of the landing in Algeria in November 1942, his attitude changed and unlike the English he believed that he ought to break off his relations with me. His memoirs on all matters concerning Vichy policies and the attitude of my Embassy are full of statements which are absolutely false and of which I can prove the falsity one by one. But all this is a purely personal matter, and details would be of little interest here.

(c) Attitude toward the Germans

Systematically and intentionally I had no relations whatever with the Germans during the four years of my mission in Madrid, not even at social functions. The closest approach to any relations was when the necessity arose of approaching the German Embassy on some visa or frontier matter, when my counselor, M. Lamarle, who spoke German remarkably well, took advantage of his necessary visit to ask a few questions and thus was able to bring us back interesting information. This attitude of withdrawal from contacts with the Germans was never disapproved by Vichy authorities who were in no way ignorant of it. Neither the Maréchal nor M. Laval at any time gave me any instructions to the contrary.

I must add that the two German ambassadors who were in Madrid during this time, Baron von Stohrer and Mr. Diekhoff—I do not include Count de Moltke, who died after being there only fifteen days—showed the greatest discretion toward me, making no attempt to establish contacts and remaining always on a basis of strictly correct protocol. This was not at all astonishing as they later showed themselves as being hostile to the Nazi regime, both being the object of attacks and having to take refuge in Switzerland. As for their counselor, Mr. Heberlein, the one who often saw M. Lamarle, he was recalled to Berlin, imprisoned, and persecuted. He was saved only by escaping to Spain, where he took refuge.

(d) *Attitude toward French Resistants*

It is not well enough known that it was thanks to the direct initiatives of the French Embassy in Madrid and to Vichy's tacit support that 15,000 young Frenchmen were able to pass clandestinely into Spain between November 1942 and July 1943 and to be sent to North Africa, where most of them joined the army.

The facts were these:—

(1) On 11 November 1942, when the emigration of young men out of France began as a result of the German army's entry into the southern zone of France, I approached the Spanish government with a written note asking that French immigrants should not be pushed back over the frontier but be permitted to remain in Spain. Vichy in no way disapproved of this request, when it was informed.

(2) I sent representatives with food and blankets to the concentration camp in Miranda where these Frenchmen were interned, and notes were made of their desires.

(3) To deal with this matter I asked for credits from Vichy and M. Laval himself soon informed me that he had sent me 500,000 francs. This credit was repeated three months later.

(4) I arranged the release from the camps or from the prisons of as many of these young men as I was able and I gave them passes which allowed them to go freely to Algeria.

(5) In February 1943, or thereabouts, with my agreement, convoys were organized by the Spanish Red Cross to move to Algeria the thousands of Frenchmen still remaining in these camps.

(6) A voluntary workroom presided over by my wife, and collections to which I was the first subscriber, were made in the French colony to aid these men. Many of them were sheltered in the French school and some in my own house.

(7) During this time the professors in the French Institute in Madrid and a part of the personnel of the Embassy declared that they were opposed to the [Vichy] government and that they placed themselves under the authority of the French committee in Algiers. I put no obstacles in their way and when I explained the matter in Vichy to M. Laval he approved my attitude, in spite of the vigorous protests from the Germans.

(8) The French colony though entirely on the side of the provisional government in Algiers from 1943 onward did not cease to be on very good terms with the Embassy and when I left my post in August 1944 they sent four delegates, from the French Club, the French Chamber of Commerce, the French Philanthropic Committee, and the French Hospital and Chapel of St. Louis, to express their regrets and their gratitude.

In June 1943 the Spanish government informed me that it was obliged to accept at Madrid a semi-official representative of the Committee of Algiers and to accredit a semi-official representative of their own government in Algiers. I made no opposition of any kind and only asked that such accreditation should not be regarded as diplomatic.

In September 1943 Count de Jordana asked for my approval of the nomination to these two posts of M. Truelle, a French plenipotentiary minister, and of Mr. de Sangroniz, formerly a Spanish ambassador. I gave my approval and had a long conversation with Mr. de Sangroniz before his departure for Algiers.

My sincere desire, of which I frankly informed Vichy, was to establish a secret liaison with M. Truelle and I think that the Allied cause would have benefited by it. But M. Truelle, badly advised by Mr. Carlton Hayes, who was determined to exaggerate his own role and to maintain division between us, would not take part.

Thus I was led to urge M. Laval, in about January 1944, to enter into direct contacts through Madrid or Lisbon with the White House, using as intermediary Mr. Fabry, a former minister who I knew was a personal friend of President Roosevelt. I also urged him to summon immediately the two Chambers and to get into contact with M. Herriot in order to prepare for a new regime in France. M. Laval seemed to agree, but events prevented him from carrying out quickly this double plan. When he was able to do so it was already too late.

At the end of August 1944 when I learned that a *de facto* government under General de Gaulle's direction had been installed in Paris, I informed the Spanish government that I would abandon my office and asked if my accreditation could be officially transferred to the representative of General de Gaulle. The Spanish government agreed and I handed over to M. Truelle the archives of the embassy, the seals, the code, and the buildings, without removing a single document, even of those which were purely personal in character and which might have been a danger to me.

Everything which I have stated above can be verified through documents which I left in the Embassy and which I handed over to my *de facto* successor.

The essence of all which has been stated above is that an error would be made and an injustice committed in thinking that the foreign policies of the government of the Maréchal and of M. Laval were dominated or guided by any desire to harm the Allied cause. I do not know the intimate desires or plans of either side. But it is certain that during my four years as Ambassador in Madrid, I never ceased to follow a policy of conciliation and agreement, and never ceased to avoid any kind of collaboration with the Germans. Vichy, and I repeat it, always allowed me to follow this policy and protected me against the hostile reactions of Berlin.

Proof can be found in the judgment passed against me in June 1948 when the High Court of Justice contented itself, in spite of my non-appearance, with condemning me to five years of national degradation, which amounted to an acquittal. During this trial my role as an ambassador was not in question, the only point under discussion being my ministry in 1940. But it is impossible to imagine with any reason that I could have acted for four years outside of or against the orders of Vichy.

In conclusion I add that M. Laval seemed to rely in all Spanish matters on his collaborators M. Rochat, M. Lagarde, and M. Bressy with whom I always corresponded and from whom I received constant approval, support, and encouragement.

(Document No. 120)
Fr. ed. 698-705

Paris, 12 April 1950

PIÉTRI
François Piétri

AN AMBASSADOR'S BOOK

FRANÇOIS PIÉTRI

Member of the Chamber of Deputies;
Minister; Ambassador of France

I the undersigned François Piétri, former Member of the Chamber of Deputies, former Minister, former Ambassador of France, living in Paris, author of Document No. 120, today deposit in the archives of the Hoover War Library a work entitled *Mes années d'Espagne, 1940-1948*, which has been published by Plon in Paris. The greater part of this book deals with the period of the occupation of France.

(Document No. 196)
Fr. ed. 705

Paris, 4 February 1954

PIÉTRI

THE UNITED STATES — TURKEY

GEORGES BONNET

Ambassador of France;
Foreign Minister, 1938-1939

In the spring of 1942 the ambassador of France at Ankara died suddenly. Jules Henry had been my cabinet chief when I was Minister of Foreign Affairs. He had also been with me as embassy counselor at Washington in 1937 when I was ambassador of France to the United States.

Several days after his death the government offered me the task of replacing M. Jules Henry and of leaving France as ambassador at Ankara. I refused. Immediately after the French defeat in 1940 I had declared that I believed it was my duty as a member of the Chamber of Deputies and as a member of the general council, and as a mayor, to remain in France in my own region in the service of my fellow countrymen who had shown their confidence in me by giving me their votes, and that therefore I would accept no other kind of position whatsoever.

However, several days later the radio announced that my nomination to the post of Ankara was imminent. I immediately denied this information and two weeks later I went to Vichy and called at the United States Embassy. I was received by the chargé d'affaires, Mr. Tuck. I spoke to him of the general situation, and I thought that I ought to refer to the plans for my nomination to the embassy at Ankara; I therefore said to him, "You have doubtless heard that there was some question of my being appointed to Ankara. I wish to say flatly that I made no request, having definitely decided to accept no appointment whatever; as soon as I learned of this plan I announced my refusal immediately."

"Well, speaking very frankly," the diplomat replied to me, "you are wrong not to accept. We regard you, in fact, as a very trustworthy friend of the United States, and you are in addition a skillful and experienced diplomat. Now it happens that at Ankara there is a German of whose maneuvers we are very suspicious, von Papen, a man who will do everything within his power to separate Turkey from the side of the Allies. We would have been happy if you had agreed to go to Ankara as ambassador of France to help us block Papen's maneuvers."

I was much astonished at what had been said to me, and said to Mr. Tuck, "Don't you listen to the London radio? You know very well that any Frenchman who accepts today any post whatever from the Vichy government is dragged in the mud and described as a traitor."

"You needn't listen to that crowd," the American chargé d'affaires answered. "They represent nothing. What matters is what we tell you." And picking up a paper from the table he added, "Besides, this is not merely my personal opinion, but it's the opinion of the State Department and in particular the opinion of President Roosevelt." And then he read me a sentence from a telegram which did in fact say that at Washington there was much regret over my refusal to go to the embassy at Ankara.

"I agree that you speak with very great authority," I replied, "but our conversation will be known only by a very few persons whereas the attacks of the London radio will be listened to and believed by millions of people."

"I assure you that none of that will have any importance," he replied. And he added that in his opinion it would not be the French rebels who would take over the power in France after the liberation. This opinion was also shared by all the Americans whom I saw at that time. They all thought that when the victory was won it would be M. Herriot and not General de Gaulle who would take power in France.

This conversation seemed to me to be so important that I repeated it immediately to M. Rochat, secretary-general of the Ministry of Foreign Affairs, adding that in my own opinion the American diplomats did not seem to realize the weight carried by radio propaganda, and that all the plans of American diplomacy would collapse under the movement of public opinion provoked by the radio.

(Document No. 201)
Fr. ed. 706-707

GEORGES BONNET
Ambassador of France;
Former Minister of Foreign Affairs, 1938-1939

THE UNITED STATES

GASTON BERGERY

Ambassador in Ankara

[*This declaration is in the form of a letter addressed by Ambassador Bergery to the Hoover Library, accompanied by extracts from a note prepared for the French press by Charles Marcepoil (attorney at the Court of Appeals of Paris; deportee at Buchenwald; officer of the Legion of Honor; officer of the Medal of the Resistance; Croix de Guerre with four citations) at the time of the prosecution of Ambassador Bergery at the Court of Justice of the Seine. The sections of the note are headed: (a) Before the War; (b) The Phony War; (c) the Armistice; (d) 1942: The Improvement in the General Situation; (e) From the Landing in Africa to the Liberation; and (f) After the Liberation. Ambassador Bergery also deposited a photocopy of a report of hearings before the Committee on Foreign Affairs of the House of Representatives of the 80th Congress, first and second sessions, on United States foreign policy for a postwar recovery program, pages 1215 to 1222; printed in 1948. Section (f) of the note, "After the Liberation," is translated here; the other material may be consulted at the Hoover Library.*]

Paris, 11 November 1954

Messieurs,

Count René de Chambrun has asked me to send you for your archives a statement of my thought and actions during the last war, particularly in my position as ambassador of France, first at Moscow from April to July 1941 and then at Ankara from July 1942 to 3 September 1944.

I have felt that a text written by me today when I know just what course events have taken since the end of the war would be less convincing than would a text which I wrote during the war, and another text written after the war by someone other then myself.

I therefore send you, attached to this letter:

1. A photocopy of pages 1215 to 1222, inclusive, of the official hearing before the Committee on Foreign Affairs of the House of Representatives of the United States, part 1, from December 17 1947 to February 12 1948.

In these pages will be found a part of the declarations made by Mr. Earle, who was successively governor of Pennsylvania, minister-plenipotentiary of the United States in Austria and later in Bulgaria, and on special missions to Turkey at the time when I myself was ambassador of France in that country.

Toward the end of my mission I had a talk with Mr. Earle regarding the USSR. This conversation so interested him that he asked me to dictate a note on what I had said. You will find in the document which I am now sending you the entire text of that note and also a copy of the letter written by Mr. Earle, transmitting it to Mr. Roosevelt, President of the United States, and Mr. Earle's own comments.

This text still represents my thought today, except for a single paragraph in which it now appears that I underestimated the determination of Serbia and Finland for independence.

Under these conditions if I wrote at the present time on the same subject I would have to add but one conclusion in order to take account of recent events, namely that we must simultaneously organize the defense of Europe and seek a basis for peaceful co-existence with Russia. These two purposes far from being contradictory are each one the essential condition of the other. That is a truth whose acceptance is difficult to secure from democratic peoples who do not agree to the sacrifices necessary for their own defense except when they are seized with panic; it is on an awareness of this psychological fact that soviet propaganda is based at this time.

2. An extract from a statement prepared for the press by my colleague Maître Charles Marcepoil at the opening of the political court action brought against me on my voluntary return to France, an action which was brought to an end on 12 February 1949 by an order of the Court of Justice of the Seine pronouncing my complete acquittal on every question raised.

This note covers the whole of my political activity before and during the war, and in particular summarizes the French interests for which I was responsible as ambassador in Turkey.

I thought that this text had some value because of the fact that Maître Marcepoil was a well-known "resistant." He was an officer in the Rafale and Andromède networks under the name 'Malo' and was a member of the general staff for the Ile de France [Paris region] of the Liberation Nord network; he was deported to Buchenwald; he was an officer of the Legion of Honor as a resistant and an officer of the Resistance Medal; he was awarded the Croix de Guerre with four citations of which three were for resistance.

Je vous prie, Messieurs, de recevoir ici l'assurance de ma haute considération.

The Hoover Library
Stanford University
California, U.S.A.

(Document No. 236)
Fr. ed. 708-709

GASTON BERGERY
Attorney at the Court of Appeals of Paris;
Ambassador of France;
former Deputy for Seine-et-Oise

ARCHIVES OF THE MINISTRY
OF FOREIGN AFFAIRS

LOUIS DE ROBIEN

Ambassador of France

The text deposited by Ambassador de Robien in the Hoover Library consists of about fifteen thousand words extracted from a manuscript which he prepared in Lisbon during March and April 1941 with a view to possible publication. From that text there have been selected the following sections referring to the archives of the Ministry of Foreign Affairs. References to the pages of the document deposited by Ambassador de Robien are given in brackets; e.g. [p. 9]. An annex entitled "Memories of Pierre Laval," which follows the sections referring to the archives, was written by Ambassador de Robien in Paris in January 1954.

[p. 7 *bis*] The Commission of Archivists, whose visit had been announced on 9 August 1940 by M. Epting, arrived unexpectedly at the Château of Rochecotte in the Touraine on the afternoon of 7 September. The commission consisted of high civilian officials, and included Dr. Winter, Dr. von Jagow, Dr. Matthessius, Dr. Sasse, and Dr. Ehrlich. Count Nostitz, from the Embassy in Paris, as well as a number of military officers, accompanied these specialists, who were difficult to distinguish at first sight from the officers, as many of the civilians also wore uniforms.

As soon as they had presented themselves the Ambassador[1] stated formally that he declined all responsibility in the matter of the breaking of the seals in various depots, particularly at St.-Étienne-de-Chigny and at Villandry. Their astonishment showed us that the acts in question were the initiative of other German administrations, acting outside the control of the General Staff and of the Service of Archives, once more proving the existence of dissension between the various German administrations.

After they had taken note of our protest the Commissioners asked us to conduct them to the various depots in the château and the other buildings, merely so that they could see where things were, as their actual work would not begin for several days.

Ambassador Dejean, I myself, Loyseau, and Vregille, who were alone at the château on that late afternoon, accompanied them and gave them all the information for which they asked. They made only a very rapid visit, without entering the rooms where the archives were deposited and without breaking the seals.

It was only on coming to Girollet that they broke the seals at the entrance,

1. [Dejean, who, with Robien, had been given full powers by the French Minister of Foreign Affairs to protect the Ministry's archives.]

and when we went inside the one who seemed to be their leader asked us to show them the Treaty of Versailles. We went up the stairway and took our visitors to the case, which we found just where we had left it when it was discovered. One of us lifted the lid. To our stupefaction, the case was empty. . . I must admit that I broke out in a cold sweat. Though not one of us had had anything to do with this inexplicable disappearance, and though we had repeatedly declined any responsibility since the time when a guard had been sent to Rochecotte, I had no doubt that they would regard us as responsible, and knowing the Germans I expected severe punishment. But contrary to what I feared, the Commissioners said nothing. I noticed, however, that they looked at each other in a way which showed that they were disappointed, but less astonished than we were ourselves.

I have never been able to know with certainty what was the truth about this strange matter. Had the treaty been taken during one of the 'pilgrimages' of which I spoke? That is not impossible. Nevertheless, I do not believe that was the case, and I am inclined to think that it was taken during the night of 4-5 September. It is probable that various German administrations were striving for the honor of discovering the treaty, and that the Gestapo, cleverer than the others, had little difficulty in getting in ahead of the German Embassy in Paris, the Army, and the Reich Service of Archives. It is even possible that the Gestapo had set the stage for the attack on the night of 8-9 August against Lieutenant Sauppe. From the inquiries which followed this attack they would have learned exactly where the treaty was kept, and as they had naturally been told that the Archives Commission was due on 7 September to carry away the trophy, the Gestapo had taken the initiative and seized the treaty three days earlier. That would explain, too, the cars that were standing in front of Girollet, reported to us by the neighbors, and the shots which were supposed to have been fired at a dog but of which the real purpose was to distract attention.

Whatever the fact may have been, the Commissioners, without showing their disappointment in any other way, had the seals replaced on the door of Girollet and we all went back to the château, making a point of talking about unimportant matters. Before getting in their cars they told us that they expected to go to see the other depots.

[Omission by Ambassador de Robien]

The German archivists began their work at Rochecotte [p. 9] on the morning of Monday, 9 September [1940].

Before they visited the depots Ambassador Dejean and I had a talk with their leaders and protested against a proceeding which, in spite of the formalities with which it was conducted, nevertheless constituted a violation of French diplomatic archives. To avoid giving the appearance of having consented to such an operation, we decided to abstain from being present.

[Omission by Ambassador de Robien]

I left again for Paris on 18 October [1940] in order to enter into personal contact with the delegation of the [French] Government in Paris and to clarify with the delegation the question of the archives, at the same time entering into contact with the German Embassy and the former Polish Embassy where the German Archives Service was now installed. I had the satisfaction of noting that my previous conversations had not been useless, as there was now no question of taking the whole of the political archives to Berlin, as had once been decided on the higher level.

A mongrel solution was adopted: on the one hand the files containing a part of the archives were to be brought back to Paris and placed at the Quai d'Orsay in the order in which they had been before their evacuation at the time of the mobilization; and on the other hand those archives which were not of a political character were to remain in the depots of Touraine, the seals were to be removed, and we were to have free use of the documents thus definitively released. A German commission was to go to Rochecotte on 5 November [1940] to make there the necessary arrangements for transporting the political archives to Paris, and for releasing the others. Therefore I returned that day by the morning train, with Leproux and my son Thibaud, in order to be at Rochecotte to receive the Commission which was to arrive during the afternoon. In order to do this, I abandoned participation in the funeral services to be held two days later for my father-in-law, a service at which, in the absence of his son Bertrand de Saussine, I was to have been the principal mourner.

> [*A note is omitted here. It reports the death at sea, on the same day, of Bertrand de Saussine, who had saved the crew of the submarine which he commanded, when it was sunk by the British. The final sentence of the note bitterly accuses the Vichy government's "double jeu" policy, of trying to please both sides at the same time, as responsible for the young officer's death.*]

[p. 10] At the end of the day, (14 november) [1940], I was called to the telephone to my great astonishment, as the line was, in theory, still cut. M. de Brinon was at the other end of the wire and told me that I had been appointed Ambassador in the Argentine. I thanked him for his message and at the same time told him that I was ready to renounce this appointment, which in fact fulfilled my greatest desires, if it were thought that my presence in France would be useful in completing the work I had undertaken. I had the impression that M. de Brinon was not particularly anxious that any important service of the Ministry of Foreign Affairs should be functioning in Paris; at any rate he told me that my presence would be more useful in Latin America. The Reich Commissioners, who happened to be present while this conversation took place, presented their congratulations on my nomination.

The Commission having informed us that it intended to suspend its work for several days, I took advantage of the opportunity to go to Fontevrault with Loyseau, his wife, Jankovitz, and my son in order to warn the director of the prison that the Germans would soon pay a visit. We examined the depot there, which we found to be in perfect condition, and we took advantage of the opportunity of seeing the church, with its Plantagenet tombs, and its ancient kitchen, which I think must be unique. (16 November) [1940].

On 17 November I received a telegram from the General Delegation asking me to come as quickly as possible to Paris. I delayed my departure by twenty-four hours in order to be present at Rochecotte the following day, when the Commission was to end its work.

During the afternoon of the same day a final convoy came to take away the files which were still there, in particular those on the control of foreigners and those of the Political Section, which we had brought from the Châtaigneraie and which had remained on the ground floor of the salon where the archives of the Protocol had been placed.

An Austrian Alpine chasseur detachment was on duty that day, commanded by a Feldwebel who introduced himself to me and said that he himself was an archivist, now mobilized from the reserve. He did not conceal his disgust at having to command the detachment for he believed that the archives were being taken completely away from us to be carried to Germany. Impressed by the labels on the Protocol files, some of which indicated that they contained documents relating to the religious coronation of Napoléon, his marriage with the Archduchess Marie-Louise, and similar matters, he asked if he could speak to me apart, and told me that he was ready to help us save the most precious of the files. I feared a trap and therefore only thanked him for his offer and explained that the files which had caught his eye did not have any political character and were therefore not included among those [p. 11] which his men were to load in the motor trucks. In order to thank him and to save him from having to watch an operation which he considered dishonorable, I proposed, with the agreement of Emilio Terry, that he should visit the library of the château where I had him taken by one of my colleagues while his men finished their ignoble task.

Just as their task was completed Dr. von Jagow arrived from Tours and told us that the order definitively freeing the archives which remained in our depots had been delayed because M. Abetz was absent, but that it had been signed and would arrive almost immediately. He himself was authorized to remove the seals without waiting longer, and he did so in our presence. I went in front of all the others to one of the doors on which the band had been torn accidentally several days earlier, an incident which had greatly disturbed Loyseau who had patched it up, at night, as well as he could; I tore the band off myself as though I were doing it to save the Germans the trouble, to the horror of Loyseau who simply couldn't get over it. . . . He kept the band as a souvenir. . . .

Dr. von Jagow also stated that the operation of removing documents was now terminated, a convoy having taken the archives from Fontevrault that very day. There remained only a few files from the Sub-Section for International Federations (international health agreements) and from the Section for the Supervision of Foreigners, which a single car could take away on one of the following days.

Thus when I left Rochecotte for Paris on the afternoon of 19 November with Raymonde Buretey and the usher, Guillot, the situation was quite clear. The political archives, contrary to the German decision that they must be sent to Berlin, were transported under the control of French archivists to Paris to the very place where they had been in the Ministry of Foreign Affairs at the time of the mobilization. The other archives were released and placed wholly at the disposal of the French administration. A note from the German Armistice Commission specified further that the political archives which the German archivists wanted the right to consult at the Quai d'Orsay, *in agreement with the French archivists*, would be returned to us intact at the proper time and place.

Thus ended the mission with which my colleagues and I had charged ourselves when we remained voluntarily in Touraine, with perhaps some presumption on our part. I am convinced that if we had not assumed this obligation, nothing would remain today [1941] of thousands of irreplaceable files which for the present are protected in their entirety as far as was possible.

As soon as I reached Paris I went to the Hotel Matignon to present myself to President Laval, who congratulated me on the results which I had obtained. I replied that these results had been secured only through the prestige of my chief, Ambassador Dejean, and the devotion of those who remained with us, and whom I recommended for his approval.

[p. 12] I wish to say that my interviews with this statesman dispelled the unpleasant memories I had retained from our first contacts when he was last at the Ministry of Foreign Affairs. I was struck by the lucidity of his intelligence and by the breadth of his political views, which went much beyond the situation of the moment. With him, patriotism meant love of his own country and not, as it did with most Frenchmen, hate for the countries of other people. He desired the well-being of the French, and he understood that it could not be obtained except in peace, through general European understanding. He was a true socialist in the good sense of the word, that is, an internationalist.

During one of these interviews, news was brought to him of the death of Chiappe, whose plane had been shot down off the Sicilian coast when he was on his way to Syria where he had just been appointed High Commissioner. I had the conviction that this accident was not fortuitous, but that it had been arranged by certain important men at Vichy who were jealous because this former Prefect of Police had been chosen for a post which many who were on the inactive list had desired for themselves. The English, too, feared the arrival in Syria, where they were so jealous of our position, of a man whose prestige would have served France, and they had an attack made on this plane of which the itinerary had been disclosed to them.

I also saw M. de Brinon, whom I had never met previously. He told me that I had been appointed Ambassador in Buenos Aires in spite of the candidacy of a number of politicians and ambassadors, among whom he mentioned Massigli, because I had known how to hold out against the Germans without irritating them and how to lead them by courteous means to accept my point of view. "That's the game you have to play with them," he added.

"I hope that while I'm flying across the ocean I won't meet the fate of poor Chiappe," I said to him jokingly.

"Buenos Aires too is a very good post," he answered, "and they will be against you for holding it . . . especially some of your colleagues and friends of the Quai d'Orsay."

"Well then," I answered, "I'm really not risking anything, for they don't usually distinguish themselves by their courage. I shall be able to measure the strength of their resentment by the warmth of their congratulations. *'Donec eris felix. . . .'*" [So long as you are lucky you'll have plenty of friends.—Ovid]

"I see that your experiences as chief of personnel taught you to know them well," he remarked.

Supported by the authority of President Laval and of his delegate in the occupied territory, I strove to obtain from the Germans a fulfilment of the promise made to me that at least a part of the administrative building of the Ministry of Foreign Affairs would be handed back to us. President

Laval was in complete agreement. "It is at the Quai d'Orsay and not elsewhere that the Ministry of Foreign Affairs should be located," he said to me. Therefore I thought that, thanks to his support, the task would be easier than the one we had accomplished at Rochecotte, where we were isolated and could rely only on ourselves. The principle itself was not contested by any of those to whom I spoke and I was astonished to find some of them reticent in a way which I was unable to explain. At the same time the French archivists, who under the agreement were to have had free access to the archives deposited at the Quai d'Orsay, met day by day more obstacles in carrying out their mission, so that gradually they had to give up trying to accomplish their task effectively.

There is no doubt that relations with the German authorities were becoming more difficult at this time. The same symptoms were appearing in public opinion.

[Omission by Ambassador de Robien]

One day when I was at the German Embassy for negotiations which I was conducting, I happened to meet Count Welczek in the courtyard. He told me that we must not deceive ourselves, and that the prolonged occupation of the country would lead to incidents which would become more frequent day by day.

"I know it from experience," he said. "When the French occupied my own country, Silesia, after the other war, they were received by the people with open arms. Several weeks later they were being cursed. It's bound to be the same no matter what is done."

The bitterness of his words doubtless revealed the feelings of an aristocrat, a career diplomat, toward the representative of the [Nazi] party who had supplanted him at the Embassy, and it was a good opportunity to criticize the policy of friendly relations which the latter was said to be following—at least in Germany.

But Mr. Abetz himself understood the true situation. He seemed to me in fact to be a very sensitive man, anxious to ease to the greatest possible extent all the inevitable friction, and fully aware that he would come up against many difficulties on both sides. During one talk I had with him, he happened to remark, "If we on our side don't succeed in establishing the climate of endurable occupation, then our military men will impose their own methods." And he added, "They're still worse than yours. . . . I know them."

It is certain that the policy of Montoire had some chance of succeeding only if the occupation did not continue for too long. . . . The fact that the Germans had not defeated England before the autumn equinox meant that there would be a long war and therefore a long occupation.

Lisbon, March-April 1941

LOUIS DE ROBIEN

The final fifteen pages of the Lisbon document, as shortened and deposited by Ambassador de Robien, are omitted here as they do not concern the Ministry's archives. They may be consulted at the Hoover Library.

ANNEX

MEMORIES OF PIERRE LAVAL

The prejudices which I felt in the past, and showed on occasion, against President Laval as a man, can only give greater weight to the testimony which I present today after having seen him at work in the most tragic period of the history of France.

The fact was that, like so many others, I had been influenced by the slanders spread against him in certain parliamentary or political circles which were jealous of his superiority. These people could not pardon him for defending the cause of peace to which their nationalist and Jacobin prejudices, usually at the service of some personal ambition, were opposed.

Besides, my first contacts with President Laval had left a bad memory. I had clashed with him when, as Chief of Personnel in the Ministry of Foreign Affairs, I had had to defend the ministry's credits against the general measures which he regarded as necessary and which called for a uniform reduction of ten per cent in all the expenditures of the State. I was perhaps not wrong in view of the fact that the credits were certainly already insufficient and that they referred to money spent abroad; but today I recognize that from a broader point of view it was he who was right in refusing to listen to my arguments. He knew better than I did the petty artifices of French bureaucracy and knew well that if he entered into a discussion of any point of detail he would become involved in a study of every objection that might be presented to him. The measure which he had conceived, certain regrettable results of which he doubtless foresaw, would thus have lost all the effectiveness which it derived in fact from his carefully considered determination to admit no exceptions. It was in full knowledge of the facts that he decided to sacrifice certain secondary interests to the general interest, acting not as a parliamentarian or a bureaucrat, but as a statesman.

He was to take the same attitude in the autumn of 1940. That which in France or abroad might have seemed brutal or extreme to those who did not know the true situation appeared, to the realist that he was, to be the only possible way of attempting to save what could be saved. Until that time, no statesman had ever been called to power under such tragic conditions, with the army annihilated and the country at the mercy of an invader who had divided it in two by the line of demarcation. No help could come from outside. President Roosevelt himself had replied in the most definite way that he could do nothing for France. The British fleet blockaded the French coasts as it would those of an enemy, waiting for Churchill to give the order to fire on the remains of our squadrons in refuge at Mers-el-Kébir. In our own country nothing could be done without recourse to the occupying authority; without such recourse the people who had fled before the invader could not return to their homes, the cities could not be supplied with food, the lines of communication could not be re-established, order could not be maintained, and a measure of economic activity could not be renewed. At Vichy itself, the Chief of State complicated everything by his senile changeableness, and above all by the intrigues of those about him, a group which included too many responsible for the defeat, too many newcomers without experience, and too many failures, most of whom dreamed only of gaining personal advantage from their unhoped for new functions.

It was impossible for him to explain his purposes to the French without coming into collision with the occupying authorities, and impossible to adapt these inevitable measures to any particular sentiment, however noble it might be. In the face of the isolation of France and the occupation of its territory in 1940, as in the financial collapse of 1935, only the most relentless decisions were possible. President Laval had the courage to take these decisions, unquestioningly envisaging from the beginning the means of adapting them progressively to events as they occurred, but obliged to say nothing of his plans, because talking about them would have lost everything.

The task which he undertook, though he did not know it then, was made more difficult by the fact that the Germans distrusted him in particular.

Among the contacts which I was obliged to make in the autumn of 1940 with the German Embassy, in order to protect the archives for which I had assumed responsibility, those with whom I spoke, doubtless in a confident mood because I used their own language, did not conceal their distrust of Laval, and confided to me that they would have preferred to deal with other politicians, some of whose names they gave me. "It was the French themselves who chose Laval," they often told me. "We didn't." But they added, "Now they should keep him, for we will never accept the usual methods of democracies, which consist in changing their responsible leader every time they feel like getting out of some commitment he has made in the name of the country. We will therefore support, against everyone, the man whom you yourselves have chosen."

I was therefore surprised when the Germans showed only a nominal reaction to the coup d'etat of 13 December [1940] and did not demand that M. Laval should remain in power. The fact was that in a few weeks they had been able to see what he was capable of doing and at heart they were not upset to be rid of an opponent whose skill, as they had discovered, was always sufficient to hold out against them, and who always protected what was essential while giving in on secondary points, the importance of which he excelled in emphasizing, however unimportant they really were.

I began to wonder whether certain German services, determined to prevent the liberation of prisoners for which the President had just obtained approval in principle, had not gone so far as to work, possibly even among those around Maréchal Pétain, for the departure of the man they knew to be the most dangerous opponent of the Reich because he was the most intelligent.

There is nothing surprising about this hypothesis for those who knew German administration under the Hitlerian regime, in which the different services continually blocked each other; the fact that the Embassy had shown its intention of supporting President Laval in order not to change the person with whom they had to deal was but one more reason for the Gestapo to get rid of him. It would be delightfully ironic if the Gestapo and the [British] Intelligence Service, without knowing it, in fact had "collaborated" on this memorable occasion.

What was already so difficult immediately after the armistice had become impossible at the time of President Laval's return in 1942. The French attitude of resignation towards the German armistice had changed to declared hostility. Because of the war against the Soviets, the communists who in 1940 had welcomed the Germans as allies of Moscow now became their violent enemies and took the lead in a resistance which until that time had been no more than a spiritual attitude unaccompanied by deeds.

In spite of everything, the President remained faithful to his line of action. He did not hesitate to override, in their own interests, the lack of understanding on the part of the French people, to whom less than ever he was able to unmask his true purposes. His policies seemed to them all the more shocking because he had made it a point of sacred honor not to appear to be playing the "double game" dear to so many other Vichy leaders, and because with both the enemy and Allies he insisted on acting honestly. His supreme skill, though it was in harmony with his character, was understood neither by one side nor by the other, and perhaps still less by the French to whom he could not possibly speak freely. But those with whom he was in close relations because of their work, or those to whom he had opportunity to speak from the depths of his heart, whether they were among the elite or the most simple and humble of men, understood very quickly. Few men could find the words, as he could, to convince such Frenchmen as were of good faith, because there were few so deeply French as he was himself. There again it would have been necessary for him to be able to speak openly to everyone!

From my first conversations with him in December 1940, he was able to win me over and to dissipate all the prejudices I might have had against him. He talked to me of the soil of France as only those can talk whose roots lie deep within it. He thought only of the French, without regard for distinctions, political, social, or ideological; his sole preoccupation was to defend their interests, and to put an end to their sufferings.

Before my departure for the Argentine, all that he said to me was this: "Do your duty as an Ambassador. See those whom you think it is wise to see. Preserve for France the friends whom she has over there. But, above all, think of the Frenchmen who are remaining here. Do all you possibly can to obtain for them all those things which they will lack more and more. Sacrifice everything in order that they shall suffer the least possible."

I remember something which seems to me to show his character clearly. When I returned to Vichy in September 1942 I happened to be lunching with the Ambassador for the Argentine; the President was there too. Rolls made from white flour were served, and Mr. de Oliveira made a point of mentioning that his cook had baked them with flour from the Argentine and that they were not from the black market. I can still see the President as he took one of these rolls, looked at it for some moments, and caressed it lovingly with his hands, so long and fine; I still hear him murmuring, "I would gladly give everything I have if all the French could once again eat rolls like these."

The fate of the prisoners of war and of the Frenchmen who were working in Germany was an obsession with him. He spoke of it almost every time that I saw him.

In matters having to do with my functions as chief of personnel he astonished me by the kindness he showed to all those who were unfortunate, no matter what their attitude may have been toward him. On many occasions he allowed me, in violation of the traditional rules of public accounting, to continue allocations to the families of officials whom he had been obliged to discharge. He even closed his eyes to the practice of paying salaries to those who had ceased work and were known to be in the maquis (notably true in the case of Mlle Borel, well known because she later married the president of the National Committee of Resistance, M. Bidault). In the case of the punishments which it was impossible not to declare in the case of our colleagues abroad, at least when they had taken the pains to give some publicity to their departure, with his approval, no practical application was made. All that happened was that notice of punishment was published, to avoid any reaction from the Germans.

He had the great merit of understanding that the interest of France, which he placed above everything else, was to reconcile those nations which by their history and geography were truly European. It was in this spirit that he spoke on the radio the famous phrase for which he has been so much reproached and from which, with obvious bad faith, the essential part is omitted. M. Laval never said, "I desire the victory of Germany" without adding the words "over bolshevism," which completely modifies the sense. I am all the more certain that in his mind these latter words expressed the true purpose of his thought because I met him on that very day when he was returning to the Hôtel du Parc with Paul Morand, on his way back from the radio station; he said to me, "You have heard what I just said. I think that you who have lived a long time in Russia will have understood." What he had wanted to say was that he desired the victory of Europe over a people who were not European either in their geography or in their mentality. Alas, throughout the world this point was understood too late and people pretended to believe that he desired the victory of Germany when in fact he was thinking only of the defeat of the communism which is natural in a country that had never been of the school of Rome, and could not conceive of freedom of persons and of property, bases of Roman civilization perpetuated throughout the west by the Christianity which was successor to the Cæsars.

Even in the final days of Vichy he had no resentment against the Allies or even against those Frenchmen who in their positions of safety far from France broadcast against him the most vile of calumnies. He never permitted the use of similar methods against them. One morning when I was in his office, M. Philippe Henriot came in to submit the text of what he intended to say that day on the radio. The President struck out a long paragraph, saying, "That's all true, but it could wound the feelings of certain men or even of certain countries . . . and I don't want that to happen."

I cannot conclude this testimony in a better way than by recalling the love for peace which together with his love for France inspired his entire life.

At the beginning of his political career he accompanied Briand to Berlin. He liked to recall stages of his apostleship for peace. To assure it for the world he would have done anything.

"I went to see Stalin and I went to see the Pope. I would go to see the devil if it were necessary," he said. He did even more; he gave his life.

This determination that there should be peace brought him the hate of the communists. They organized the resistance to get rid of Laval far more than to get rid of the Germans, because, for the latter, the Red Army would suffice. But the clairvoyance of Laval was a real obstacle to Moscow's plans.

The chiefs of the Kremlin wanted a long war and they achieved their desire at the price of two reversals of their policy, reversals which can be explained only if this deliberate intent is taken into account.

The war, and the misery which it caused, brought them the best possible opportunity to secure the victory of world revolution.

It was to prevent the crumbling of everything which constitutes western civilization that President Laval consecrated all his efforts to the re-establishment of peace and prosperity. There again he sacrificed the secondary to the essential.

They succeeded in assassinating the man, but his ideas are more alive than ever and are accepted again today by his enemies and even by his torturers.

(Document No. 198)
Fr. ed. 710-719

Paris, 21 January 1954

LOUIS DE ROBIEN

MISSION TO LONDON

LOUIS ROUGIER

Professor in the University of Besançon

I the undersigned Professor Louis Rougier, living in Paris, have deposited with the Hoover War Library as an annex to my declaration numbered 156 in the present series, and complementary to the documents attached to that declaration, the article which appeared in *Le Figaro* on 13 February 1953 entitled *Mission Secrète à Londres—Octobre 1940*, and also the article which appeared in *Le Figaro* on 23 February [1953]: *A Propos de Mission Secrète à Londres*.

(Document No. 180)
Fr. ed. 720

Paris, 30 March 1953

LOUIS ROUGIER
Professor Louis Rougier

CHAPTER XIV

FRANCE OVERSEAS

ANTILLES

GEORGES ROBERT

Governor of the Antilles;
Admiral Commanding the French Western Fleet

[*This document is in the form of a letter to René de Chambrun.*]

12 *December 1948*

Mon cher Maître,

During the interrogation which preceded his trial President Laval was asked for explanations of telegrams, signed by him, which I received in the Antilles during the second quarter of 1943.

These urgent telegrams instructed me to sink the warships and merchant ships under my control, to destroy the planes, and to sink the gold for which I was responsible. As he states in the written notes which have now been published through the filial piety of Mme de Chambrun, these orders were not executed and President Laval expresses his satisfaction that his inner thought was understood under such circumstances.

You have asked me to add my comments. I am happy to be able to bring this contribution to the work of documentation which you have undertaken in the interests of History.

Without wishing to go too deeply into matters I think it will nevertheless be useful to recall, in a few lines, the situation in the Antilles at the time when the telegrams in question arrived there.

For reasons more realistic than ideological our American possessions had been kept in obedience to the government of Vichy. It was necessary that they should remain in allegiance to a government even if it were only a government of fact in order that French national sovereignty should conserve its rights. To separate the Antilles from one government when no other had been recognized by the Allies could lead only to a third rebellion in the form of an autonomy of which the obvious feebleness would have given a full opening to any covetousness. Such is the result of all forms of feebleness.

In addition these possessions were physically incapable of living without financial support sufficient for their food supplies and, without running the risks just referred to, the Antilles could not find such support except from their legal protector. This support was always generously allowed by the governments of that period.

The result was that these colonies were able to live free and without need, spared the misery and social troubles which otherwise would have resulted, until May 1943.

The credits available for purchases on the American market were exclusively French and the federal authorities showed the greatest sympathy in permitting the conversion of these credits into dollars and in issuing the necessary export licenses. At the same time the facilities for entering American ports in order to ship the supplies were arranged. The net result was that the people of the Antilles were able to maintain an acceptable standard of life.

It was in May 1943 that the United States government demanded that we should renounce all obedience to a government of which the relations with the enemy seemed to be suspect; the penalty for refusing to do so was to be the destruction of the equilibrium hitherto maintained because all supplies and food would be cut off. I believed that it was my duty not to agree to this demand.

Quite apart from the fact that the basic argument of this demand did not seem to me to be established as I had no critical facts on which I could reach my own judgment, the practical purpose of such a detachment did not correspond in my opinion to any definite reality. I was receiving no political instructions from the Laval government. My relations with it were exclusively financial or administrative and were expressed entirely in telegrams of which complete copies in plain language were always given to the consul general of the United States. The obedience of the Antilles to the government of Vichy was already nothing more than formal.

To separate the Antilles from the Chief of Government while remaining true in spirit to the Chief of State, as was suggested to me as the best policy, seemed to me to be a formula of pure fancy. Finally, and apart from the fact that such a separation would have been a mark of sharp ingratitude toward a central power whose vigilant care had always been so valuable, our submission to the will of a foreign country seemed to us in principle unacceptable. Let us hope that History will throw some light on the secret motives of this injunction, as it is History's task to do. But it was an injunction which did not agree in spirit with the accords that had been previously drawn up and carried out, setting the modus vivendi for the Antilles.

But in the absence of such light I still do not understand today the reasons behind the blockade of May 1943, a blockade which brought famine to peaceful populations who could not possibly have the slightest contact with the enemy and who remained inevitably apart from any collaborationist tendency.

Further, as there was no question either, so far as the United States government was concerned, of putting me under necessity of giving up my post, since apparently I was to remain persona grata, the meaning of this action continues to escape me entirely.

I can be more definite in saying that despite the lack of liaison with France itself I realized the considerable difficulties which the increasing demands of the occupying powers created day by day for our government, and which had to be overcome by such means as were available to France, so long as the military action of the Allies had not succeeded.

It was this consideration which dictated my attitude toward the orders which were sent to me to sink the fleet. My attitude was at first one of delay and finally of refusal on the ground that it was materially impossible.

My attitude was to receive the full approbation of the French government when I returned to France many months later. On the other hand it prevented the occupation authorities from allowing me to cross the frontier freely. For many weeks I had to wait in Lisbon, on neutral ground, until the authorities had agreed not to oppose my entry and not to arrest me.

I owed the consent of the occupying authorities to President Laval and it was not easily obtained. This I realized later when I learned the terms in which Ribbentrop had expressed his opinion of my various agreements with the United States. This constituted proof better than words would have done that the orders to sink the fleet which had been sent to me were not an expression of the thought of the Chief of Government.

(Document No. 81)
Fr. ed. 723-725

ROBERT

ANTILLES

HENRI BLÉHAUT

Rear Admiral; Secretary of State for the Navy and for the Colonies

[*A letter addressed by Rear Admiral Bléhaut to M. René de Chambrun.*]

Lausanne, 10 April 1949

Mon cher Maître,

You have sent me a copy of the note which Admiral Robert prepared for you on the subject of the events which led to the secession of the French Antilles in July 1943, at the same time asking me if I can corroborate the Admiral's account, particularly in throwing light on the part played by President Laval in those events and the motives which were his in sending to Admiral Robert the telegraphic orders of which you are already cognizant.

It seems to me that in order to respond to your request I could do no better than to send you a part of the note I had written for my own defense, for the use of my lawyer, Bâtonnier[1] Poignard, in July 1945 when President Laval was still alive. I shall add only a few words intended to make some of the points clearer:

"From the beginning of the crisis in May 1943 the Germans demanded that Admiral Robert should be ordered to carry out immediately the

1. Head of the Bar of one specified court.

proposed measures for the destruction [or disposal] of war-ships, commercial ships, gold, planes, etc. I then proposed to M. Laval that in order to gain time he should send the Admiral a telegram which would remind him of his previous directives and at the same time assure him of the government's confidence that he would act for the best under the circumstances; the Admiral would understand and then later the most imperative orders could be sent without any fear that they would be carried out. M. Laval told me that the Germans would never permit the sending of a text which left the Admiral so much latitude. In answer to a question which I asked him, M. Laval told me with great intensity that he had no more desire than I had that the measures should be carried out but that he was obliged, at the risk of serious reprisals against the entire country, to give the Germans the impression that he demanded the execution of the orders for destruction.

"Under these conditions I told him of my decision not to have my name associated with any telegrams worded in that sense, fearing that the signature of the Secretary of State for the Navy on a technical order, such as that for the sinking of naval and merchant ships, would prevent the Admiral from suspecting the fact that the orders were being sent under constraint.

"Far from making the slightest objection to my reserve on this point, M. Laval found it wise and accordingly these telegrams were sent without my signature. Admiral Robert understood perfectly their political significance; his resistance to American demands [that the French in the Antilles should co-operate with the Allies] was sufficiently strong to save the French mainland from those measures of pressure with which it was threatened, without our having had to deplore any destruction. . . ."

I add that in my administrative relations with President Laval I was able to observe that he never had in view anything but the interests of France and that he placed those interests always before any other consideration. As he himself said, it is possible not to be in agreement with the means which he believed he ought to employ in order to attain his purposes, but when the truth is known no honest man can refuse to recognize his profound patriotism and his great foresight.

Je vous prie, mon cher Maître, de bien vouloir transmettre à Madame de Chambrun mes hommages respectueux et de croire à mes sentiments de très cordiale amitié.

(Document No. 105)
Fr. ed. 726-727

H. BLÉHAUT
Rear Admiral Bléhautnut

*Secretary of State for the
Navy and for the Colonies
from April 1943 to August 1944.*

THE ALLIED LANDING IN NORTH AFRICA

PAUL SAURIN

Member of the Chamber of Deputies for Oran;
President of the General Council of Oran

*Personal Memories of the Allied landing in North Africa and of the
entanglements of French politics from 1942 to 1944*

These few reminiscences are not intended to constitute a report of the
complex history of this dramatic period in the world war. They merely
present a few actual experiences of the author in Algeria. The conversations and incidents in which he took part and the intrigues with which
he was involved, generally unknown, will certainly contribute to the
clarification, one day, of the often unexplained sequence of certain historic
events.

I made the acquaintance of Robert Murphy at the beginning of July 1940
at the Hotel de Charlannes, above La Bourboule. I was still under the
shock of the tragic scenes of the French retreat in which I had participated,
in uniform, from Metz to Mendes. I had been able to join the government
and the members of Parliament who from Bordeaux had gone on to the
Auvergne in search of a capital. Clermont-Ferrand had been considered
before Vichy was thought of, and while a decision was being awaited I went
to rest for three days in this agreeable and comfortable mountain hotel,
undamaged, where Ambassador William Bullitt and Counselor Murphy
were staying. I found there too my colleague and friend Gaston Bergery,
who introduced us.
When we met again at Algiers our relations were soon marked by mutual
understanding and it was during repeated games of golf that we gradually
exchanged our views on the development of hostilities, the coming entry
of the United States into the war, the liberation of France, and the future
of the free countries.
The acute intelligence of "Bob," as he was called by his intimate friends,
facilitated confidences which gradually made us accomplices.
From the time of Pearl Harbor we talked with absolute frankness.
Murphy was aware of the hostility of the immense majority of the army
and the people of North Africa against General de Gaulle. In addition,
he personally did not like General de Gaulle. And further, he admitted
having received formal orders from the State Department to find another
military chief who could rally the French territories of North Africa to the
side of the Allies from the first day of a possible landing.
The State Department had no confidence in de Gaulle and wanted another
man or another formula.
I tried steadily to get him to accept my point of view, which might be
summed up in this way: In France governments directed by military men

have rarely been successful. It would be better to establish some provisional organization, presided over by an important civilian, which would include military chiefs, even of opposing tendencies, but which could be reorganized to meet the needs of a liberation which we foresaw as occurring by stages. Such a government should base itself on those who had already been elected by the nation, and I cited the Trevenenc Law, fundamental law of the French Republic, which stipulated that if the territory of the nation should be occupied, national representation should be reconstituted on a basis of the delegates of the general councils of those departements which remained free.

In the end, Robert Murphy told me that such a solution seemed acceptable to him and would have the approval of his government. But he made the objection that Algeria had no political figure of sufficient influence to be accepted by public opinion in the homeland.

I then suggested the name of my friend P. E. Flandin whom I could bring to Algeria at the right moment.

Bob wanted to have preliminary conversations with President Flandin and it was for this reason that the latter came, at my request, to Algeria in the spring of 1941, and that a first discussion took place on the Burkhardt road in the villa of the American Counselor. Agreement in principle was quickly reached and we undertook to work out the details of the political organization that was envisaged.

Flandin came back many times to Algeria to enter into contact with Murphy during the winter of 1941-1942, notably in the company of Pierre Forgeot, former Minister of Public Works.

On my side I made sure of the support of local representatives who had been elected by the people, and particularly of the presidents of the general councils of Algiers and Constantine, my friends Froger and Deyron. (I myself was president of the general council of Oran and took care of that part of the plan.) I secured the valuable support of Joseph Serda, member of the Chamber of Deputies for Constantine and chairman of the Algerian budget committee in the Chamber, and also of Senator Paul Cuttoli, whose powerful personality was a guarantee of success at Constantine.

As far as my part in the plan was concerned everything was ready when Robert Murphy, in July 1942, warned me that events would happen rapidly in the coming autumn. I left for the homeland and once more, in August, made certain of the agreement of P. E. Flandin, then residing at Saint-Jean-Cap-Ferrat, and of Paul Cuttoli who was resting in his villa at Cap d'Antibes.

In September at Algiers Robert Murphy told me of a final journey to Washington to receive definitive instructions. Without giving me the exact date of the landing he asked me to have our friend Flandin come during the first days of November.

I left for a final journey to the Côte d'Azur to arrange Flandin's journey. He landed at Philippeville on 5 November [1942] as agreed, while I was at Oran for my last contacts with my friends of the General Council.

On 7 [November 1942] we both reached Algiers, he at the Hotel Aletti and I at the Hotel de l'Oasis where I usually stayed. At nine o'clock in the morning I saw Murphy at the United States Consulate, 2 boulevard de France. He received me in the waiting room, rather hurriedly, as he was strangely busy and was in conference, in his own office, with Lemaigre-Dubreuil and several persons whom I was unable to recognize. We agreed that he would meet P. E. Flandin at five o'clock in the afternoon in my room at the Hotel de l'Oasis, a safe meeting place since my room was next to that of Mr. Cole, Consul-General of the United States, whom Mr. Murphy was supposed to visit.

Robert Murphy, in spite of his efforts to control himself, seemed to us to be nervous and preoccupied. The conversation was rather vague, for after Flandin had given him certain information (the Germans were preparing to occupy North Africa toward the end of November), Murphy merely said that everything was arranged, but he said nothing about the nearness of the landing. Before six o'clock he cut short the interview and made his excuses for leaving us ("We will meet again in the morning," he said), telling us that he was going to visit Admiral Fenard in order to meet Admiral Darlan who had come suddenly to see his son, then ill in Algiers.

At dinner that evening we exchanged our impressions of this bizarre interview, Flandin and I, without drawing any definite conclusion from Murphy's evasive and hurried attitude.

At two o'clock in the morning the first cannon fire (the glass of my windows was broken, and there were shell splinters on my balcony) revealed to us that the exact truth had been concealed.

From the first hours of the morning I tried to get in touch with Murphy at the consulate and at his home, but in vain. It was only the next day that I saw him hurriedly to compliment him (I remember having met General Weiss there as well), but I understood that, politically as well as militarily, everything was in order.

After several days had gone by, my discussions with Lemaigre-Dubreuil and then with Governor Chatel revealed Robert Murphy's admirable cleverness; he had been preparing several schemes at the same time and at the last moment had adopted the one which seemed to him the most profitable for his country and for the conduct of military operations.

With Flandin and me he had built up an operation on a "civilian and republican" basis, to which he was certainly not very strongly attached.

With Lemaigre-Dubreuil he made an agreement under which General Giraud was to be commander-in-chief, both civilian and military.

And at the last moment he had arranged with Admiral Fénard to bring Darlan to Algiers, had presented him with a *fait accompli*, and had forced him to sign a military arrangement infinitely more beneficial to the United States than that which had been laboriously negotiated by Lemaigre-Dubreuil on behalf of Giraud, mysteriously retarded in his submarine at Gibraltar.

He had accomplished what President Roosevelt wanted, a landing in North Africa and the support of the French, without recognizing de Gaulle in any way.

As the republican "Flandin solution" had been put aside, Murphy still had to reconcile the conspirators of the two military plans in which he had been engaged, Darlan and Giraud. It was not very easy. But in one way and another Robert Murphy, who wanted nothing changed in the administration of French Africa, did succeed, assigning the essential role to a high imperial council presided over by Admiral Darlan, civil and military commander-in-chief, delegate of Maréchal Pétain, and composed of three French pro-consuls: Governor-General Chatel at Algiers, the Resident-

General Nogues, at Rabat, and Governor-General Boisson at Dakar. (In Tunis, Admiral Esteva was in the hands of the Germans, to whom he had opened the way.)

General Giraud was most content with the role of generalissimo of the French army—he even dreamed of prancing on his white horse as far as Metz—all the more because General Juin, in actual command, remained at his post.

On the political side a committee was established, on a lower level than the high council, and the various commissariats or ministries were divided among the groups of different tendencies who longed for power.

Darlan presided over this committee. The vice-president was General Bergeret, former Minister of Air at Vichy, whose tendency was to favor Darlan. Relations with the Allies were assigned to M. Lemaigre-Dubreuil, whose tendency was to favor Giraud. The commissariat of the Interior was given to M. Rigault, collaborator of Lemaigre-Dubreuil and a member of the same team. Finance and Economic Affairs went to M. Alfred Pose, director-general of the National Bank of Commerce and Industry, whose personality was so powerful that he threw all caution to the winds and could endure no supervision. Foreign Affairs went to M. de Saint-Hardoin, a counselor of the embassy from the Weygand team, but above all a personal friend of Robert Murphy.

The oddest and the most disturbing person held only a secondary post: Henri d'Astier de la Vigerie, who was made under-commissioner of the Interior but through that post became chief of police.

I soon made the acquaintance of this throwback to the Florence of the sixteenth century; he told my friend Deputy Serda, whom he had met several days earlier, that he would like to meet me.

Henri d'Astier de la Vigerie was the real organizer of the French commandos which were to aid in the American landing. He had been an officer in the youth camps and had appeared to be only a subordinate of Colonel Van Heck. But, in truth, he had soon gone far beyond his associates because of his skill in the organization of plots, his audacity, and his adventurous spirit which hesitated at nothing. Beneath his bandit's mask he knew how to be charming.

It soon became clear that he was the key person in this complexity of plots, which developed from the earliest days out of a situation as paradoxical as that created by the "macedonian" government of Admiral Darlan. As chief of police, holding under strict control his two immediate collaborators, Commissioner Bringard and Commissioner Esquerre, he was all the more able to play his own game because no one succeeded in guessing what his political tendencies were.

He seemed to have joined Darlan's side; he made a point of royalist sentiments; he was very fond of de Gaulle; and he was the brother of Emmanuel d'Astier de la Vigerie, a communist and a notorious adventurer, one of the leaders of the resistance in the region of Lyon.

A few days after the Allied landing I prepared the text of a solemn letter to Darlan which was signed by the three presidents of the general councils of Algeria, and by Deputy Serda. This letter demanded the re-establishment of the Republic, the application of the Trevenenc law, and the formation of a government controlled by men who had been elected by the nation. This letter, published by *Combat* and broadcast by the London radio, brought me trouble. Darlan sent for me but "his" police were unable to find me. D'Astier then desired to make my acquaintance.

Our first interview took place in the restaurant Le Paris, with my friend Serda. I remember d'Astier as a disturbing but likeable man whose intelligence was fine and audacious but in whose character the love of conspiracy obscured all other characteristics. By nature he belonged to the race of fascists, a fact which made him scorn public opinion, laws, and customs, and directed his political activities entirely toward the search for ruthless agents through whom he could accomplish reforms which he believed could be realized only through a series of blows. As I talked to him I could not help but think of Morny.

He began by expressing his enthusiastic approval of my "letter to Darlan," and of the necessity of establishing a central power based on public opinion (he did not speak of the Republic).

He took me to his place several days later and there I saw a large portrait of General de Gaulle. But I also made the acquaintance of his immediate collaborator, a blond young man with the face of an angel and a manner that was both unctuous and gentle. His name was Cordier. I learned later that he was a monk.

During that same week Radio London announced that General de Gaulle had appointed General d'Astier de la Vigerie, brother of Henry and Emmanuel, as his second-in-command with authority if necessary to negotiate and make agreements on his behalf.

Henri d'Astier then introduced me, under the auspices of Alfred Pose, to a smiling young man with extremely agreeable manners and a great appearance of enthusiasm. His name was Marc Jacquet; he said that he had fled from the Gestapo at Lyon, and that he had been engaged by Pose at the African headquarters of the BNCI [National Bank of Commerce and Industry] at Algiers in order that he should appear to be employed. He knew nothing whatever about banking and didn't even bother about it. But he loved talking politics and dreamed of the great authoritarian upheavals in which he longed to take part thanks to his skill in plotting and in high-level intrigues. He soon told me that Henri, Count of Paris and heir to the kings of France, had been deeply impressed by my letter to Darlan and by the necessity of having a government based on public opinion.

Alfred Pose, to whom I talked about the matter several days later, confirmed that Jacquet, whom he knew in no other way, had been recommended to him by a mutual friend at Lyon and that he had found a place for him in the BNCI in Algiers, to enable him to live and to escape from the Gestapo.

Pose then spoke of the political confusion and confessed that he was very much attracted by the idea of a "lieutenant general" who might be the Count of Paris, and who might be aided by de Gaulle and Pétain. . . . which seemed to me to be slightly visionary, to say the least.

However I maintained my contacts with Henri d'Astier. I was then living on a property about 25 kilometers from Algiers at Rovigo, and my movements were becoming more difficult because of the scarcity of gasoline.

One day Henri asked me to come the next day to be received by his brother, the general, at the Hotel Aletti. Extremely interested, I made certain of keeping the appointment but insisted on going up by some back stairway for I noticed that the eternal police spies, who "doubled," in every sense of the word, the official police, were hanging about in the vicinity.

General d'Astier de la Vigerie had arrived suddenly on the previous day from London, coming in a plane which had landed at the Maison-Blanche

airfield without the knowledge of Darlan. The general received me with
great friendliness and undertook to prove that General de Gaulle was the
victim of unpardonable ostracism on the part of the American government,
and in reality a man who believed in order, a conservative, and a patriot
who had had many churches built in French Equatorial Africa, who had
the co-operation of many general officers known for their rightist sentiments. He told me too that the Count of Paris had been in contact with him
and had said that he was in agreement, that an arrangement could easily
be made between him and General Giraud, and in short that the African
Army and the people of Algeria, blinded by their devotion to Pétain,
were wrong in regarding de Gaulle as the representative of some sort of
general upheaval.

When I asked General d'Astier de la Vigerie what he thought was the
opinion of Admiral Darlan on this subject, he merely replied that, "If
we are thinking of de Gaulle coming here and making an agreement of
conciliation, it is only for a day in the near future when Darlan is no longer
there. . . . In any case his presence is not militarily necessary any more;
the Americans will soon realize that, and he will disappear. . . ."

This fascinating conversation was suddenly interrupted by the announcement of the visit from Robert Murphy, who was on his way up. Henri
d'Astier said that it was preferable that Murphy shouldn't know that I had
come to see his brother. I was to come back again on the following morning. . . .

But in the meantime Darlan had finally learned that General d'Astier
was in Algiers and had had him taken back to his plane at the Maison-
Blanche, with orders to expel him. The general returned to London; his
mission had been accomplished, I learned much later, because he had left
large sums of money with his brother Henri.

The following week, Henri d'Astier asked me to come to see him in the
rue Lafayette. . . . An atmosphere of conspiracy ruled the scene and I
was cautiously convoyed into an empty room where Cordier joined me to
say that Henri d'Astier was in conference with General Giraud but would
not be long. Then he said, quite suddenly, "It is here, in a room at the
back, that Henri, Count of Paris, receives his visitors. Wouldn't you
like to meet him while you are waiting?" Seeing my stupefaction he
thought it better not to insist, but to reassure me by saying, "There are a
lot of people in the next room that he has to see, particularly M. Alexandre
who represents the World Jewish Committee, and various friends of your
own whom you would be surprised to find here. . . ."

I heard whispers and surreptitious footsteps, but I saw no one. And
as d'Astier delayed a long time, I left.

Several days later I received a telephone call in the country; it was
from Marc Jacquet who asked me to come to see him on the following day
at the BNCI, at about six in the evening. When I arrived he got up and
asked me if I would like to meet a friendly person of importance who was
waiting for me in some discreet place. My curiosity was aroused and I
decided to play the game, promising not to try to find out where I was
taken on that pitch-black night. Marc Jacquet conducted me in a car;
I soon recognized the route and the building into which we went: l'*Algeria*,
easily recognized by anyone familiar with Algiers.

In Marc Jacquet's small apartment I was presented to a young man of
personable appearance: Henri, Count of Paris.

Slightly dazzled I listened to "Monseigneur" who spoke to me—he too!—

about my letter to Darlan, and about giving to those who had already been elected by the nation a share either in the government or in its control. He spoke to me of the intelligent action of Henri d'Astier de la Vigerie and of the acute political sense of Marc Jacquet, and he confided in me that de Gaulle and Giraud were ready to reach an agreement under his banner. . . .

The conversation lasted for about half an hour and I returned to Rovigo, perplexed and slightly amused by these comic opera conspiracies.

Three days went by. It was now 24 December [1942] and I was just getting ready, in my villa at Rovigo, to sit down at the table where we were to celebrate, quietly at home, both Christmas and our marriage anniversary. The telephone rang. It was Marc Jacquet asking me most urgently to come to see Henri d'Astier at his place. . . . "A most serious event has just occurred," he said. It was then seven o'clock in the evening. I left my wife, who was amazed and hurt to see me go at the very moment when we were going to celebrate our anniversary.

I reached the rue Lafayette. Henri d'Astier, with Marc Jacquet and Cordier at his side, told me that Darlan had been assassinated that afternoon by a young student from France, of the name of Morand, it was said.

"I have asked you to come, Saurin," he added, "so that you can give us your opinion on the new situation. Pose will be here in a moment and he would like to talk with you too."

Pose did, in fact, arrive and spoke of the great reconciliation among French people which we must now realize by formation of a government "including both de Gaulle and Giraud."

"De Gaulle," he told me, "will surely accept, for in this way he can get back into Algeria, which is his dearest desire. As for Giraud, he has been recalled urgently from the fighting front in Tunisia because of Darlan's murder, and he will be here tomorrow. His agreement is unquestionable. Henri d'Astier, having already sounded him out on this point, guarantees that he will agree. Now what will the general councils do?" Pose asked in conclusion.

I replied that I didn't have the slightest idea and that the whole subject seemed to me to be still extremely confused and most vague. I returned to Rovigo, promising d'Astier to come back on the following morning. He asked me to lunch at Le Paris for Christmas turkey. "By that time I will have seen General Giraud," he told me, "and we can talk more usefully."

On the following day when I reached Le Paris I found that I had been invited to a family gathering. M. and Mme d'Astier, their daughter, their son-in-law, Cordier—the secretary!—and I made up the party. When I went to the lavatory to wash my hands, I met there the former chief of press services for Governor Chatel who told me, "They've found the assassin. It's a young man named Bonnier de la Chapelle. I have just come from the *Dépêche algérienne* where I was with his father, the journalist, when the police came to tell him."

Without showing my feelings, I went back and sat down at the table beside Henri d'Astier to whom I announced the news while watching him from the corner of my eye. He neither frowned nor gave the slightest indication of surprise, but merely murmured, "Within an hour the entire city will know it."

I felt ill at ease but in my anxiety to learn the entire truth I agreed to spend the evening with d'Astier at his home.

There I was received, in the absence of the master of the house, by my old comrade Jacques Brunel, a lawyer, at whose home d'Astier had established his first center of operation when he had come to Algeria (because of an affinity which was both Gaullist and royalist.) Without my having to ask him any questions Jacques, still affected by the blow of the tragic events which he had just experienced, began to tell me of the fantastic preparations for the assassination of Darlan.

The meeting had been arranged by Henri d'Astier in a cellar in the rue Charras. Lots had been drawn and a young man from one of the youth camps had been made responsible for executing the orders of this little gathering. The young Bonnier de la Chapelle had turned white when he was ordered to go to Darlan and shoot him point-blank. Assurance was heaped on him that he ran no risk "since the police are in it." Bonnier was blessed by the monk, Cordier, who heard his confession and thus made him responsible for a "sacred mission." I was the first to hear this story which a number of writers have since recorded. . . .

"If only young Bonnier doesn't talk!" For Bonnier had been arrested, and General Bergeret, who had taken charge of the matter personally, had decided to bring everything into full light.

As everyone knows, Bonnier, in prison, made a complete confession and dragged everyone else into it with him. But it is also known that Commissioner Garidacci, who received his confession, prudently (?) kept it in his own possession, thinking to use it in bargaining for a substantial advancement, or, alternatively, in obedience to orders which he had received.

General Bergeret then made the error of having young Bonnier executed on the following night.

His suspicions were directed to all those who had been working with Henri d'Astier, but in his disapproval he confused all those who had been against Darlan from the earliest days, Gaullists of the *Combat* group, the conspirators of the commandos involved in the landing, and the men who had plotted the assassination. Without any proof whatever, he sent to a camp at Laghouat, all on the same basis, the security director, Muscatelli, the commissioner Bringard, the commissioner Achiary, Professor René Capitant, who was the leader of the *Combat* group, the two Alexandres, father and son, the three Alboulkers, Pierre Moatti and his father, Jacques Brunel, and so on.

Louis Perillier, who was then secretary-general of the prefecture of Algiers, was removed from office and sent to the front in Tunisia.

It was only several days later that Bergeret dared suddenly arrest and imprison Henri d'Astier and Cordier.

The judicial investigation dragged on and the only official punishment was the removal of the imprudent commissioner Garidacci.

When de Gaulle finally reached Algiers in June 1943, the judicial investigation was still dragging along.

Three months later, in September [1943], it was ruled that there was no case against d'Astier and Cordier and they were released with the approval of General Giraud. It may be well to recall here that General Giraud "shared" the power at that time with General de Gaulle and that General de Gaulle had appointed as commissioner of the Interior M. Emmanuel d'Astier de la Vigerie, a notorious progressive communist, but a brother of Henri, the royalist, and of General d'Astier de la Vigerie, the Gaullist. The d'Astier de la Vigerie family remained faithful to the Man of the Appeal of 18 June [1940].

In spite of the time that has since passed, complete light has not yet been thrown on the true plotters of Darlan's murder, of which d'Astier was the machiavellian organizer.

The truer Gaullists (including the *Combat* group with René Capitant, Alexandre, Pierre Moatti and the others), the pure Giraudists (including Lemaigre-Dubreuil and Rigault), and the pure royalists (including the Count of Paris himself, Pose, Marc Jacquet and Jacques Brunel), showed that, for the time being, they were all more or less happy about the disappearance of Darlan. Their obvious satisfaction gave credit, rightly or wrongly, to a number of contradictory legends.

The truth is that many of them were surprised by the assassination and that most of them were tricked, at least for the time being, by what happened.

The only unsolved question is this: for whom was Henri d'Astier acting?

It would be useless to expect to find the answer in any of the works of self-defense which the "great men" are publishing as Memoirs.

It will be of interest to record something of what happened politically to the more important of those who have been named above.

Royalist group.—The Count of Paris was politely taken to Larache in Spanish Morocco, where he usually lives. As is known, the Fourth Republic has abolished the law ostracizing the heirs of all dynasties which have ever reigned in France.

Alfred Pose was removed from politics in North Africa and then from the homeland. In the end the presidency of the BNCI was taken away from him.

Marc Jacquet, who had lived as a bachelor in Algeria, where he said that he was a bachelor, was married. He was elected a member of the Chamber of Deputies for the Seine-et-Marne and became a republican minister in the Laniel cabinet in 1953. It is true that he was suspected of having been responsible for security leaks in the military secrets of Indo-China and that a long-delayed inquiry was made by the Mendès-France cabinet, which also considered M. Emmanuel d'Astier de la Vigerie as possibly involved in the same leaks.

Jacques Brunel soon placed himself at the service, there in Algiers, of M. André Le Trocquer. He became a member of his cabinet in the various ministries through which M. Le Trocquer passed, particularly that of the Interior in 1946. He became prefect of the Yonne and then of Guadeloupe and is today cabinet director for M. André Le Trocquer, a socialist president of a National Assembly with a rightist majority.

Giraudist group.—Lemaigre-Dubreuil was gradually turned out of the direction of public affairs in Algiers. General de Gaulle, become all powerful, had him imprisoned at one time, but was obliged to release him. Lemaigre-Dubreuil abandoned public life.

As for Rigault, he followed his "boss," both in prison and to complete banishment.

Gaullist group.—René Capitant became one of de Gaulle's ministers.

Pierre Moatti became cabinet director for Soustelle, then an RPF [the Gaullist political party which was disbanded after a few years] in Paris, and then RPF president of the municipal council of Paris.

The Alexandres, father and son, and the three Aboulkers did not continue their political careers.

Muscatelli became prefect of Algiers when de Gaulle took power alone. He was afterward elected an RPF senator for Algiers.

Bringard has become director-general of general security in Algeria.

Achiary was made under-prefect at Guelma, but the executions which he was accused of having ordered in repressing the Mohammedan riots in the Constantine, in 1945, seem to have hampered his career.

Thus the disappearance of Admiral Darlan brought no benefit, for the moment at least, to any of those whose wishes it fulfilled.

A terse and categoric cable from President Roosevelt to Murphy refused the approval of the United States to any solution which had the Count of Paris at its head.

Murphy easily arranged a meeting of the high imperial council (consisting of Giraud, Noguès, Boisson, Chatel and Bergeret) to appoint General Giraud as commander-in-chief, civil and military.

This brave general, who in answer to every complex question was satisfied to quote the eternal and over-simplified formula, "I make war; I do not make politics," allowed to take place the most extraordinary kidnapping of a government that has ever been seen.

As soon as he came into action he reorganized his "cabinet" by eliminating Henri d'Astier de la Vigerie and Pose, and by bringing in several personal friends, among then Dr. Abadie. Harrassed by the more dynamic elements of the *Combat* group and by the systematic propaganda of the London radio, poor Giraud never was able to lay down a logical and considered line of conduct.

Very early in January 1943 Flandin and I visited him at the Lycée Fromentin, seat of the government, to explain our point of view, namely: "the re-establishment of the Third Republic; the application of the Trevenenc law; the meeting of the three general councils of Algeria to appoint delegates who, together with the Algerian members of the Chamber of Deputies and such members from the homeland as were then in Algiers, would constitute a qualified National Assembly on which Giraud could base his government."

The general objected that all this would mean the liberation of the communist deputies who had been locked up since September 1939, interned by Daladier, and who were then in the central prison of Maison-Carrée near Algiers.

Flandin, far from seeing any difficulty in this step, showed General Giraud that there was every interest in such a measure, at a time when the war effort necessitated the union of all French people who were determined to drive out the Germans (and the communists had been among their number since Hitler had been so imprudent as to attack Russia). General Giraud remained evasive and made no decision. Several days later he replaced Governor Chatel, against whom *Combat* [the newspaper] was pouring out its attacks, by Marcel Peyrouton, whose Algerian background and undeniable skill as an energetic administrator qualified him for such a post, but whose Vichy record made him a target for Gaullist attacks. London radio set the keynote and *Combat* took up the same line locally. For the first time, hostility to Vichy took the form of an insistent demand for a return to the Republic, but—and this is the most curious fact to be noted in the concert of recrimination orchestrated by General de Gaulle— without ever demanding the application of the Trevenenc law or even the establishment of any control by those who had already been elected by the people.

The Gaullists were already defining themselves as the sole representatives of the people, speaking in the name of all the French. They never abandoned this position, which they hoped would be accepted by world opinion without their being obliged to render their accounts until victory and propaganda had enabled them to transform their hopes into reality, a *fait accompli*.

General Giraud was the object of daily attacks and of defections from his ranks even among his own friends. Anxious to get along with de Gaulle, whose biting sarcasm disturbed him, he would have capitulated willingly if Robert Murphy had not been there to see that President Roosevelt's orders were respected: "De Gaulle is impossible and we want nothing to do with him."

A short conversation with Bob clearly illustrated this attitude. One day I was visiting Murphy in his new offices in the Health Center, where he received me in the midst of his collaborators and addressed me thus: "Saurin, you've come just at the right time; I was talking with my friends about the importance of de Gaulle's personality. Now tell me your opinion frankly: do you think that if de Gaulle had never existed the French people would have not resisted the German occupant?"

"There is no doubt about it at all," I replied. "They would have resisted just as much."

"You see," Murphy explained, "de Gaulle is of no use and there's no point in being encumbered by him."

"So that's how it is," I answered ironically, "you are thinking of causing him to disappear."

"Oh, I didn't say that," Murphy answered, laughing, "but I maintain that he's an impossible person, undisciplined, egocentric, and a man with whom it is impossible to arrange any concerted action. Never, absolutely never, will we tolerate his taking the power either here or in the French homeland."

But the pressure of de Gaulle's propaganda was not lacking in effectiveness and the British minister, Duff Cooper, gave him his strongest support.

General Giraud, on the advice of the Americans, had added to his group M. Jean Monnet, whose Gaullist role was to become evident only gradually. Little by little, General Giraud accepted an idea of a return to the Third Republic. He began by giving back to the Jews the full civic rights which the government of Maréchal Pétain had limited.

Several days later he announced officially that the Republic would be re-established with all its elected bodies. The old municipal councils in the townships and all the elected mayors, often replaced under the Vichy regime by appointed mayors, would take over once more their powers and their duties.

The general councils, suspended since the end of 1940, were to be legally summoned at the beginning of April 1943.

But Giraud still did not talk of "parliamentary control," and his "government" still lacked the juridical base which would have given it strength and which would have annihilated the effects of the violent criticisms from the London radio.

Lemaigre-Dubreuil was the first in Giraud's entourage who understood, and he visited me at Rovigo toward the end of March. He came to ask me to go back to my original idea that the general councils should be consulted in accordance with the Trevenenc law. But on this important point there was still no agreement with General Giraud and I showed him how difficult such an operation would be with a man who did not know just what he wanted or what he ought to do.

Freedom of the press was still non-existent but—a thing which seemed to go beyond all reason—a censorship had been organized favorable to de Gaulle; this censorship sabotaged the poor little propaganda efforts of the Giraudists. Under these conditions it seemed to me to be difficult to obtain from the three general councils a political attitude favorable solely to the concepts (?) of General Giraud.

In the meantime two odd personalities had reached Algiers from London, members of the group immediately around General de Gaulle: Admiral Muselier and M. André Labarthe.

I soon received from Governor-general Peyrouton an invitation to dine with these two distinguished guests, in company with my friend Froger, president of the general council of Algiers, and various distinguished persons of the country.

This was one of the most extraordinary and most dramatic dinners I have ever attended.

The obvious purpose of Peyrouton and his guests was to inform us about the personality of de Gaulle and about the activities of his committee in London, of which Muselier and Labarthe had been members.

My curiosity was completely aroused. Up to that time I had never heard any opinions about de Gaulle except those of Robert Murphy, General Giraud, and Lemaigre-Dubreuil, all hostile or reserved. I had never been able to follow the path taken by his political thought except through my own interpretations of his radio broadcasts. What I now heard was as I expected: the dinner was an experience not to be missed. Even if allowance was made for the bitterness which Muselier and Labarthe might feel toward their former chief, I expected nothing like the violence of their prosecution.

André Labarthe began by trying to show us what would have happened in North Africa if de Gaulle had landed there. His dictatorial character, his vanity, his arrogance, his unscrupulousness toward those who did not agree with all his opinions—we were spared nothing. André Labarthe told us that even in London torture chambers existed through which men who had escaped from France had to pass if they dared refuse to say exactly what de Gaulle wanted. He told us of the triangular bars on which they had to kneel—directly on the knee-cap—while blinding lights gradually extinguished their physical and intellectual resistance.

I thought I was dreaming . . . but Admiral Muselier (he was in full dress uniform) was to complete my nightmare. "I'm going to give you my opinion of de Gaulle," he began. "He's an assassin. . . ." And he overwhelmed the general with accusations of extortion and of causing men to disappear. Then he told of the expedition to Saint-Pierre-et-Miquelon, of which de Gaulle had been the leader. He said that President Roosevelt had formally opposed this expedition on the ground that it risked disturbing the general policy toward Pétain's France and Germany followed at that time by the USA, then preparing for war (an opposition formulated in agreement with the Churchill government); de Gaulle told the President that the order to land at Saint-Pierre-et-Miquelon would be given in spite of anyone and anything. I then began to understand Robert Murphy's attitude, and the hostile instructions of President Roosevelt. I understood less clearly the support which Churchill was still giving to the man of June 18th.

I was still perplexed when, the next day, we learned that Admiral Muselier had received from General Giraud the post of prefect of police for a large area around Algiers, while André Labarthe had been placed in charge of the reorganization of propaganda over Radio Algiers.

But without doubt de Gaulle had felt the storm approaching, for he had already negotiated with Giraud, through Jean Monnet, for the dispatch of a plenipotentiary to Algiers who would seek some basis of agreement.

It was thus that General Catroux, with great pomp, arrived in Algeria.

Catroux was scarcely installed in the Villa Ferrando when he asked me to come to see him. Originally from Oran and a brother of Alexandre Catroux, president of the Oran Chamber of Agriculture for that region, he had commanded the army division at Oran for a considerable time and had then become commander of the military region of Algeria. He had been a friend of my father, at that time a senator, and showed some sympathy for me.

"How's that old Pétainist, my brother, getting on?" was the first thing he said to me. And when I told him how highly I thought of his brother and how I approved of his attitude, General Catroux made this happy remark which throws much light on his own convictions: "Let me say that I understand you just as I understand my brother. I joined de Gaulle because I was then in Indo-China. I would certainly be a Pétainist if I had been in France in June 1940."

Catroux did not find it very difficult to get round General Giraud and his group. He had the art of handling negotiations with that off-hand manner which implies that men of good breeding always come to an understanding. He had no difficulties except with Lemaigre-Dubreuil, whose outright character was ill-suited to the mild and less sincere manner of Catroux.

In the meantime the general councils had met and given expression to public opinion, worn out by a division of clans and a guerrilla war among military men which it did not understand. Everyone demanded that agreement should be found between those who desired to liberate France.

Before signing a text which would begin to bind his own hands, General Giraud, urged by Peyrouton who had sent him a letter repeating the republican arguments which Flandin and I had championed, had a brief awakening.

He asked me to lunch, alone with Peyrouton and himself, and demanded abruptly if I would make my strongest effort to persuade the three general councils of Algeria to approve a Giraud government without de Gaulle.

I replied that the hour had gone by and that public opinion was no longer ripe for such an explosion.

And that was the end of Giraud's impulse toward independence.

The text of the agreement was signed between Giraud and de Gaulle, the influence of General Georges and, above all, that of General Juin playing an appreciable part.

On 30 May 1943 General de Gaulle arrived in Algiers, unheralded, and established himself in the *Villa des Glycines*.

On 1 June he received me in my capacity as President of the General

Council of Oran, several moments after having received my friends Froger and Deyron who were the presidents of the general councils of Algiers and of Constantine.

I will never forget this man's remarks. Their apparent self-assurance scarcely hid his uncertainty, not to say his disquiet, regarding the future. But his faith in his own star and his ambitious determination gave him unbelievable audacity. . . .

After congratulating me on what I had done in the Oran region and in the general council of Oran to maintain the spirit of resistance against the Germans, de Gaulle at once asked if I was ready to help him get rid of the last representatives of Vichy: Noguès, Peyrouton, and Boisson. I replied this was a matter for the government and that, as the modest president of a deliberative assembly, I could not involve myself in questions of personalities.

In return I asked him what were to be the broad lines of his policies . . . was the Third Republic to be re-established or not? What was his attitude toward the communists? and so forth.

I can still hear de Gaulle's reply. "It's going to be re-established, your Republic, Mr. President," he said. "You are an extraordinary man: here before you is the only person in the world to whom the communists give everything and ask for nothing in exchange; and yet you ask me whether I am going to associate them with my government or be suspicious of them. For the moment I have nothing to give them. . . . We'll see later."

On leaving, I had the feeling that he didn't like me.

Several days later the press announced that Peyrouton had sent his resignation to the governor-general of Algeria; his letter was published. That afternoon Peyrouton asked me to come to see him at the Villa Monfeld.

He told me of a nocturnal visit from Jacques Brunel and his brother-in-law, Colonel Jousse, who had come from General de Gaulle to suggest that he resign "in the higher interests of the country." Brunel added that apparently de Gaulle would be grateful for such a gesture and that no trouble would break out between him and Peyrouton. Peyrouton accepted this suggestion in good faith but had demanded that de Gaulle write a letter expressing his gratitude, and in fact such a letter was given to him a few hours later. It was published in the Algiers newspapers the following day.

In fact, Peyrouton was already beginning to realize how imprudent he had been in resigning, and he feared the days that were to come.

He had asked that he be allowed to enter military service again, and General de Gaulle had officially promoted him to a higher grade, that of major.

But several days later—just time enough for de Gaulle to make sure that he was on more solid ground—Peyrouton was arrested and thrown into prison. There was no longer any question of de Gaulle keeping his promises or respecting the word of honor which he had given. . . .

His personal policy was relentlessly pursued. In the two-headed "French Committee for National Liberation," Jean Monnet, chosen by Giraud, now played de Gaulle's game. In two successive changes of committee members the trick was turned, and General Giraud, feeling that he had been dropped—not to say hounded—decided to retire. After a tour of military inspections to save his face he was "asked" by de Gaulle to live permanently in a villa at Mazagran, near Mostaganem, 350 kilometers from Algiers. . . .

In October [1943] the second session of the General Councils began, and a Gaullist group was formed at Oran to demand elections for the renewal of the office of the joint congress. This was contrary to tradition, according to which no election is ever held in wartime. I agreed willingly, making the following statement: "I agree to the holding of elections because I know that you are aiming at me personally, unwilling to allow your president to be a man who voted for Maréchal Pétain. I accept, but I am still a candidate for the presidency."

I was re-elected, but already many of my friends had dropped me. I could feel that de Gaulle was trying to get at me and that he was methodically employing his tactics on every level.

The fact was that, anxious to give an appearance of approval by public opinion, de Gaulle had conceived the idea of a "consultative assembly" (consultative in this case meaning "without any real power") which would sit at Algiers. He personally chose all its members from resistance organizations, sometimes quite theoretical (delegates of "resistance" from South America were seated without laughter), but he was obliged to allow for elected delegates from the three general councils of Algeria.

Would that give opponents a chance to slip in? Don't believe it! General de Gaulle had more than one trick in his bag. By what he called an "ordinance" he decreed that in each general council of Algeria certain elected members, whom he named, would have no right to vote in the election of the members of the new Consultative Assembly. In the general council at Oran, eleven council members (of whom I was one) were notified of this incredible decision. I made an official protest. The governor-general, Catroux, wrote to say that I was right and he intervened with de Gaulle. But de Gaulle, who knew exactly where he was going, stuck to his ultimatum.

In this way only his "special pals" were appointed. In addition, de Gaulle was right about the passive attitude of public opinion.

Thereafter he became more bold, as all internal opposition was disarmed and public opinion, frightened, no longer reacted. He soon issued ordinances which enabled him to remove from office those who embarrassed him and make them ineligible for office for the rest of their lives.

The outline of the dictator became more and more clear: around him there gathered rapidly a "gang" who, thanks to Allied victories and the sacrifices of the French African Army, gradually seized power, without danger to themselves and without grandeur, and got their hands on the gravy bowl. The Consultative Assembly convened and elected its first president, choosing Félix Gouin, the indescribable deputy from Marseille. . . . The rest is known. . . .

Several weeks later there arrived from London Henri Queuille, former President of the Council of Ministers, and Louis Jacquinot, member of the Chamber of Deputies for the Meuse, who had recently been taken from France to London by an English plane. Both of them, anxious to secure information on the spot, got in touch with Joseph Serda and me; the four of us met at lunch at the Roman Baths near Algiers.

J. Serda who had succeeded in having himself appointed a member of the Consultative Assembly (it happened that he had been detained in Algeria on 10 July 1940 and therefore had not taken part in the vote which accorded full powers to Maréchal Pétain) joined with me in explaining what we knew of the personal aims and intrigues of General de Gaulle, whose dictatorial methods were no longer in doubt. We suggested to our friends that a republican league be formed, of which Queuille would be the president and for which we would furnish the leaders and the members. We thought that in this way, through public meetings, we could awaken the opinion of the people and have some influence on de Gaulle's policies.

Queuille soon confessed that he had already received offers from General de Gaulle to be a member of the "French Committee for National Liberation."

"I prefer to accept that invitation," he told us, "in order to be able to introduce the worm into the fruit."

Jacquinot, after confessing that he was no more Gaullist than we were, told us that he would follow Queuille in his tactics and would enter into the government. Queuille became vice-president of the council, and Jacquinot became Minister of the *Marine*. Thus the most skillful preferred to join rather than to struggle, and supported de Gaulle though they did not like him.

Queuille, who received me frequently in his ministerial offices, often confessed his disquiet and anguish at the errors which were being committed. "You do not see it from my manner," he told me, "but I am terrified." But he was too much of an opportunist to resign.

J. Serda had the courage to attempt some opposition in the Consultative Assembly itself, and to make criticisms. Punishment followed quickly. De Gaulle discovered that he had agreed to become a member of the financial committee of the departement of Constantine under the Vichy government and ordered his zealots in the Consultative Assembly to order Serda's exclusion.

Wishing to give a good lesson in advance to any who dared lift their heads, he did not hesitate to bring Serda before a "civic court" which ordered the confiscation of all his property.

Arrests were becoming much more numerous. Thousands of persons were deported to concentration camps at Laghouat, Bossuet, and Méchéria on the edge of the Sahara. In the departement of Oran alone a third of the voters lost all civic rights (by a simple decision of the "government"). Hitler and Stalin had found no better method of making certain that they secured the majority, and popular approval. Public opinion was decapitated. The most important persons were put in prison. General Noguès and Governor-general Chatel were able to escape to Portugal. But Governor-general Peyrouton, Governor-general Boisson, Secretary-general of Algeria Ettori, and still others, were imprisoned. Lemaigre-Dubreuil and Rigault who had arranged the Allied landing but were hostile to de Gaulle were arrested in Morocco . . . and were not released until their freedom was demanded by Robert Murphy.

Thus de Gaulle, suppressing all opposition, was going to rule as master. There were still some shadows, however, which disturbed him. P. E. Flandin, though he had taken refuge in the country 500 kilometers from Algiers, and General Giraud, though eliminated and in residence 300 kilometers from Algiers, could still be regarded as possible replacements if perchance the American government wished to get rid of de Gaulle. I myself was, more modestly, one of the last to represent the opposition as a member of Parliament and as President of the General Council of Oran.

Therefore we must disappear. . . .

My turn came, and the operation was quickly organized. The post of prefect at Oran was sought by one of de Gaulle's faithful followers, a certain Pompéi, who had achieved unpleasant notoriety in 1937 as chief of cabinet for the prefect of those days. His insolence, his pretentious excursions, and his notorious misconduct had turned the general council against him. I was already president at that time. Marx Dormoy, then Minister of the Interior, had removed Pompéi from his post at my request, remarking to me at the time, "I very much doubt that this young man will have a long prefectoral career."

Pompéi had been a member of the brain trust of General de Gaulle in London and was determined to return to Oran in triumph to have his revenge. General Catroux, governor-general of Algeria, and Henri Queuille, vice-president of the council, warned by me, opposed his nomination, and Catroux showed de Gaulle a photocopy of the checks without provision which Pompéi had drawn in 1937. De Gaulle paid no attention and appointed Pompéi prefect at Oran. Arrests multiplied, and terror began.

On 14 April 1944 I had sent General de Gaulle an open letter to denounce these excesses and the dictatorial methods of the government, and to express my indignation at the proposed ordinance, already published in the press, which was to ensure a monstrous campaign of political "purification." My letter said, in particular: "The bans explicitly pronounced against citizens, without any action on the part of the judicial authorities, will be too reminiscent of unbridled autocracy not to shock all true republicans. The French people, my General, have a liking for clarity, *fair play*, and justice. They have as good a memory as they have common sense, and that is why, though certain of their elected representatives seem to have failed in their duty, the people will know how to get rid of them in a proper way, without it being necessary to limit in advance their power of choice or to dictate the people's conduct. Great nations, and the French are among them, have always had a sense of equity and of generosity, the very qualities which belong also to strong governments."

Needless to say, this letter did not prevent de Gaulle from promulgating several days later his monstrous ordinance of 21 April 1944 which enabled him to declare ineligible [for any office] all men in public life who had not been willing to bow down before him. I was to begin the series.

On 25 April [1944] the newspapers published an official communique from the "Commissioner of the Interior" (at that time the crypto-communist Emmanuel d'Astier de la Vigerie, and his assistant was the virtuous Pierre Bloch), announcing that I had been suspended from all political office and removed from my position as president of the general council of Oran.

At once, my friends Paul Cuttoli, president of the general council of Constantine, and A. Froger, president of the general council of Algiers, made solemn protests. The result was the publication of a new communique from Emmanuel d'Astier de la Vigerie, declaring quite seriously: "No reasons of a political nature motivated these punishments. M. Saurin has been guilty of activities unworthy of the posts with which he had been entrusted." Thus libel was added to impudence. This "republican" government evidently did not shrink from any of the methods used by the lowest police. With no inquiry, with no complaint before competent judicial bodies, and without even hearing those who were accused, adversaries were vilified. An order was given to the press (the censorship was still in existence) to publish no denials from those who were defamed.

The prefect was ordered to threaten the internment of anyone who attempted to defend himself. Such was the regime installed in his own interests by the man who claimed to have a monopoly on patriotism.

I was forced to surrender in silence under this regime of terror. I had to wait ten years before my voters (my only judges in a Republic) could reply to de Gaulle and his gang, as soon as my ineligibility had been annulled, by re-electing me almost unanimously.

But the more important men were to meet similar and even crueler fates.

My friend Pierre-Etienne Flandin was suddenly arrested at his own home near Philippeville one morning at about five o'clock. Illegally thrown into a military prison under the most ignoble conditions, this former president of the Council of Ministers of France was treated like a common criminal. His cell was only six feet by five in size and was filled with an odor of pestilence from a gaping hole which served as his private water closet. I had to have a wooden cover made by a carpenter, and carried it to Flandin myself, to provide a little more comfort in that horrible cell.

And all this without any reason being given. It was the work of de Gaulle, dictating his orders to his War Commissioner, André Le Trocquer, whose joyous life provided the town with amusing gossip. The atmosphere at Algiers was such that when I asked permission to see my friend Flandin the honorable counselor at the court of appeals who had been appointed to serve as investigating judge with the military court of justice felt that he should warn me against the risks which I ran by daring to visit such a man.

P. E. Flandin, former president of the Council of Ministers, thus shared the detestable fate allotted to Marcel Peyrouton, former Ambassador of France, governor-general of Algeria, and to Boisson, governor-general of French West Africa, and so many others.

Robert Murphy, shocked, increased his attempts to bring this scandal to an end. De Gaulle, now feeling himself extremely strong, refused for a long time to improve the lot of these prisoners. But the pressure of the American government, in which Winston Churchill finally joined, was such that the general-dictator in the end transferred his political adversaries to a villa in the country, near Staoueli, surrounded with barbed wire and high fences like a chicken run. Troops from Senegal guarded the place under the orders of officers and noncommissioned officers, who were ashamed of the ignoble task assigned to them.

An increasing number of attempts were made, particularly by Mme Flandin who was admirable in her devotion and tenacity, to obtain the release of the prisoners on provisional liberty. They seemed to meet with no success until the moment when de Gaulle, in August 1944, desired to obtain recognition from the Allies of his "French Committee for National Liberation" as being the true government of France.

President Roosevelt and Mr. Winston Churchill, before accepting, demanded that all political prisoners should be treated in a less arbitrary fashion. De Gaulle promised to do what they asked.

He freed Flandin and assigned Peyrouton to demi-freedom on a property which the Shell Oil Company had placed at his disposal about 25 kilometers from Algiers.

On 23 August 1944 the "French Committee for National Liberation" was recognized as the government by the United States and Great Britain.

De Gaulle triumphed at the moment when France was being progressively liberated by the Allies, and by the French African Army which had landed in Provence on 15 August [1944].

On 25 August [1944] he had Flandin, Peyrouton, and the others arrested once again, just as they were getting up. They were taken to the airfield at Boufarik and transferred on the same day to the prison at Fresnes, near Paris, where they were incarcerated. . . . The elegance of the deed gives the measure of the man who ordered it.

One more shadow, however, still disturbed (God knows why) the surly spirit of that megalomaniac de Gaulle: the shadow of General Giraud, whom the Americans had already once placed in the first rank and whom they would be able to use once again, in case the insolence of de Gaulle, who knew that he was detested, became unbearable.

Confined in a remote residence, deprived of any possible means of political action, General Giraud had soon become resigned to the idea of not attempting to play a role that was too big for him. . . .

Yet he was the victim of three attacks on his life, of which the last was almost successful. Mystery still surrounds this strange determination to kill a man who could never have been accused of "collaboration with the Germans."

It happened that my family home at Rivoli, in the departement of Oran, unoccupied because I was living near Algiers, had been requisitioned by the army, and that the staff of a supply column was installed there. . . . Rivoli is only 4 kilometers from Mazagran where General Giraud lived.

It was "Colonel de Malglaive" who commanded the supply depot and who had installed himself on my property. The true and more modest name of this strange person was Luiz, and by profession he was a market gardener at Casablanca. De Gaulle, whom he venerated most ostentatiously and whom he tirelessly praised with sonorous and meaningless words, had made him a colonel.

There was one troublesome detail: when the Senegalese soldier who fired point-blank at General Giraud, piercing his jaw, in the garden of the villa at Mazagran, ran away while the orderly officer hastened to the victim's side, the Senegalese was picked up in a jeep which was waiting 200 yards away on the national road. . . .

Giraud's orderly officer was able to read the license number:. It was a car belonging to "Colonel de Malglaive" and it returned to the garage of my house at Rivoli that very evening. . .

Here I bring my scattered memoirs to an end.

They will have no other value than that of recounting undeniable facts, conversations, and incidents from my own experience. . . . They had brought me the regret of having known the other side of a "great man," and of having seen an unretouched picture of him, of some others, and of the events of which they made themselves the "heroes," which leaves me sceptical about the unselfishness of many men. . . .

Fortunately for me I knew and was close to young men of Algeria who when they were called to arms in November 1942 marched to fight against the Germans with courage and unlimited self-denial. Badly equipped, badly armed, they yet covered themselves with glory in Tunisia, in Italy, in France and on to the Danube.

Many of them were the sons or brothers of those whom de Gaulle imprisoned in his concentration camps.

Some of them were even pursued by de Gaulle's sectarian politics at the very moment when they fell on the battlefield, as was a certain captain who was killed at Cassino just when his colonel had received an order to send him back to Algeria to be interned at Méchéria. . . . The colonel wrote personally to "Minister" Le Trocquer to ask him if he must send the coffin. . . .

I knew too those admirable men who crossed the Pyrénées, worked their way through Spain in the face of a thousand difficulties, and came to swell the ranks of the French army of liberation. Among them, Rémy Flandin, son of the president, was able to reach Africa where he entered the army and covered himself with glory as a pursuit pilot while his father was still in a filthy cell. . . .

I knew too many resistants (like my former secretary, Lucien Gardellini, who often received information from me), men who were able, at peril to their lives, to organize clandestine struggle in France against the occupant. Enough can never be said regarding their high merit, and their glory, anonymous and without stain. . . .

The depth of my admiration for their heroism is equalled by the scorn I feel for certain brazen and shameless politicians I have known, whom History— so simple-minded is she—will consecrate as heroes.

(Document No. 238)
Fr. ed. 728-746

Paris, 8 February 1955

PAUL SAURIN

THE AMERICAN LANDING IN NORTH AFRICA

EUGÈNE BRIDOUX

General

[This document was written by hand in the prison of Fresnes by General Bridoux; on the original there is a note in Pierre Laval's handwriting.]

On 8 November 1942 at eleven o'clock in the morning, the Council of Ministers met at Vichy to examine the situation created by the American landing in North Africa.

Previous to this meeting: (1) The Maréchal had decided to offer armed resistance and had notified the civilian and military chiefs concerned, and also President Roosevelt, of his decision; (2) Admiral Darlan had asked that German planes be sent against the ships which were attacking Algiers.

When the meeting began, President Laval informed the Council of a communication he had just received from Paris through M. de Brinon. It stated that the German government proposed to give military aid to France.

The Council was to deliberate, with the Maréchal's approval, on Admiral Darlan's request and on the German proposal.

The Chief of Government immediately stated that he did not want any military aid. And he emphasized that to call on the German air force would be equivalent to "calling down the lightning."

But if he refused German aid, he would appear to be supporting the opposition; it is clear that his idea was to try to gain time. He was going to do it by trying to put the whole matter on the political level. As soon as the meeting was over he telephoned in this sense to M. de Brinon. The question was taken up again at a second meeting at a quarter past six that evening. The President said that he had received another telegram from Mr. Abetz, demanding for the German air force (a) authorization to fly across the southern zone, and (b) free use of the airfields there.

The Maréchal said that he was favorable to this idea. Under these conditions M. Laval stated: (1) that he would agree to flights by German planes across the southern zone (this was not new, as on the previous evening Wiesbaden had informed the French government that German planes were to fly across the southern zone beginning with the night 7 to 8 November 1942); and (2) that he wanted to wait, before taking a position in the question of the airfields, in order to obtain the opinion of the military leaders in North Africa and to confer on the subject with Wiesbaden [i.e., with the Armistice Commission].

In this way be continued to follow his idea of gaining time and not committing himself. He succeeded, because in the end no decision was made about the airfields. It was only on 11 November 1942 that the Germans occupied them, but they did it by force.

There was nothing new on the subject of flying across the southern zone, since no counter-order came from Wiesbaden.

Note: I have in my hands an unsigned summary of what happened at the meetings on 11 November, a summary which was found in the archives of the Maréchal. It is sheer fantasy: its author understood nothing either of President Laval's thought or of what certain ministers said during the discussion.

28 August 1945. — Note for President Laval

During November 1942, at a date which I do not remember precisely, Mr. Schleier, who for the moment was replacing Mr. Abetz at the German Embassy in Paris, came to Vichy and had conversations with M. Laval which lasted throughout an entire day.

In the evening M. Laval, who desired to ask Mr. Schleier to dinner invited Admiral Platon and myself, on that day the only Ministers present at Vichy, to join him at the Hotel du Parc.

Before dinner the President told me in confidence that Mr. Schleier had come to obtain fuller information on the subject of the attitude of France toward the United States, and that in accordance with instructions he had received from Berlin he was to urge the French government to declare war on the United States. M. Laval added that the talks throughout the day had been difficult, but that his position had not varied; he had rejected all the suggestions of his visitor. This was, too, in conformity with his attitude during the previous days. He had succeeded, on 8 November 1942, in pushing aside the intervention in North Africa by the German Air Force which had been both demanded by Admiral Darlan and proposed by the Reich; he had succeeded also, a few days later, in rejecting the alliance *durch Dick und Dünn* offered by Berlin.

During the dinner Mr. Schleier brought the conversation back, from time to time, to the talks which had been taking place, without trapping the President in a continuation of a discussion which he regarded as ended.

After dinner I went out with Mr. Schleier. During the few minutes that I spent with him he expressed his regret over the position taken up by M. Laval, and he concluded with these words: "That blasted President ———nothing can be done with him."

(Document No. 43)
Fr. ed. 747-748

[*This document is a holograph*].

THE LANDING IN NORTH AFRICA

EMMANUEL TEMPLE

*Member of the Chamber of Deputies
for the Aveyron; Minister*

Note for the Hoover Foundation

In 1942, at the beginning of the summer, if I am not mistaken, President Pierre Laval asked me to come to see him. During our interview, which was very short, he asked me to accept an important post in a prefecture in occupied France. This was the second proposal of the kind that I had received. I refused, as I had the first time, stating that as a veteran of the 1914-1918 war my relations with the Germans would be difficult if not impossible and that my replacement would become necessary in a very short time. Only an offer to go to North Africa, I added, would tempt me, as there the situation would be different; the task there, on the contrary, would be to protect the people from German and Italian propaganda. M. Pierre Laval replied that he was grateful for my frankness. And there the matter rested.

Shortly afterward he asked me to undertake a mission of investigation in economic matters of interest to North Africa. I accepted. Two American ships had taken food supplies to Algeria and M. Laval was extremely satisfied because of it, saying to me, "In addition, if you have an opportunity to see Mr. Murphy, please express my sympathy for him and his country."

Shortly afterward M. Laval nominated me to the prefecture at Algiers. I had thought only of an economic mission in North Africa, but time was running short and I accepted the offer in the form in which it had been made. Neither before nor after my departure did I receive any instructions from President Laval who, after what I had said, could not have been ignorant of my feelings. Maréchal Pétain, on the other hand, asked me to come to lunch with several important people and took me aside after the lunch to speak to me: "You will soon find yourself confronted with considerable difficulties in Algeria," he said to me. "What I have been told of you leads me to believe that you will know how to overcome them. You will have to receive people from many different nations. I ask you to give them all a proper welcome for, in one way or another, I am determined to save France."

During my first days in Algiers I brought together all the Alsatian refugees and told them that there was no possibility that France would renounce Alsace. I had no reaction from the government [in Vichy] on this point. The landing came soon afterwards. Taking advantage of the fact that our direct line seemed to be still free, I sent Maréchal Pétain a telegram telling him of the decisive character of the landing and begging him to take a decision which would bring unity to the French people. I hoped that he would leave [France] for Algeria. I had no reply. Between North Africa and France a curtain had fallen.

(Document No. 300)
Fr. ed. 749-750

Paris, 5 July 1955

E. TEMPLE
Emmanuel Temple

TUNISIA

PIERRE DE FONT-RÉAULX

Attorney at the Court of Appeals of Paris

[*This document is in the form of a letter addressed to M. René de Chambrun.*]

14 September 1955

Mon cher Confrère,

You have been good enough to ask for my testimony on events in Tunisia, during the war, of which I had personal knowledge. This testimony is to be a part of the study being made by the Hoover War Library. I bring you my testimony most willingly and I give it with absolute impartiality. You already know that I was director of cabinet for a minister who, in the events of 13 December 1940, played a certain part.

It was precisely as a result of the events of 13 December 1940 that, as a master of appeals in the council of state, I was led to accept the post, then vacant, of counselor on judicial and legislative matters to the Tunisian government.

Fearing that Maréchal Pétain might be led to go beyond those relations with the occupation authorities which were provided under the armistice convention, I desired, as did many Frenchmen, to go to North Africa, which seemed to me to be the jumping-off point for a possible re-entry of France into the war, when the United States was sufficiently prepared to come to our aid.

I reached Tunisia on 11 February 1941. I found a country completely calm, which had been protected by the armistice of 22 June 1940 from German or Italian occupation. I had not been a witness of the events which occurred there at the moment when the declaration of war by Italy, on 10 June 1940, had brought the outbreak of hostilities on the Libyan frontier. Nor had I been a witness of the events which occurred when the armistice was concluded. All that I know is that the resident-general of that time, M. Peyrouton, had refused to give way to the solicitations of the English consul, who had urged him to turn against the French government.

M. Peyrouton later became Minister of the Interior. He was replaced [in Tunisia] by Admiral Esteva who commanded the southern fleet and who had retreated to Bizerte after the armistice. Admiral Darlan's propensity for appointing the higher chiefs of the navy to posts of command is well-known. Admiral Esteva found that he was, if not actually under the orders of General Weygand, at least dependent on him to some extent. General Weygand had been made delegate-general of the government in North Africa in September 1940, at the same time that he had been appointed Commander-in-Chief.

The events which occurred in North Africa will not be understood if General Weygand's decisive influence is not immediately recalled to mind. It was General Weygand who had been able to bring perfect unity to North Africa. His ascendancy over the army was enormous and his moral influence over the French people of North Africa was no less great. General Weygand had a policy which he followed firmly. While remaining absolutely loyal to the Maréchal and acting vigorously against the troublemakers who would have ruined by their premature activities the plan which he had prepared, General Weygand was determined to make North Africa the base for the re-entry of France into the war. For that purpose it was necessary to take advantage of every possibility to strengthen the African Army and to establish a unified force. It was equally necessary that North Africa should remain absolutely secure. On the first point, the English aggression at Mers-el-Kébir had made it possible for the government to obtain some additional facilities, beyond what was provided in the armistice convention, to strengthen the North African armies. Further, France had the inestimable good fortune to be able, throughout the years to which I am referring, to rely on the absolute fidelity of the Mohammedans of North Africa. Neither in Algeria, nor in Tunisia, nor in Morocco was the authority of Maréchal Pétain ever contested by the great mass of the population. Particularly in Tunisia, Bey Ahmed, a man of a considerable age, reserved but clear minded, had the greatest veneration for Maréchal Pétain and no thought ever came to him of taking advantage of circumstances to present his own claims.

As counterpart of his plan, General Weygand was determined absolutely to oppose any encroachment whatever in North Africa by the enemy.

It was very soon after the armistice that the Germans understood what an error they had made, from their point of view, in leaving French sovereignty intact in North Africa and they tried by many different means to establish themselves there. General Weygand always resisted and it was precisely for that reason that finally, in August 1941, the Germans demanded his departure.

After he had left, his former post was divided. For civilian matters, a secretariat-general for co-ordination was entrusted to Admiral Fénard, a man who rapidly forgot, after the assassination of Admiral Darlan, how much he owed to him.

The supreme military command was entrusted to General Juin who continued the work undertaken by General Weygand and who with the aid of American equipment created the First French Army which covered itself with glory in Italy in 1943 and from which General de Gaulle, not without ingratitude, was to withdraw him after the Italian campaign.

To return to Tunisia and the events of which I was a more direct witness, I recall precisely that which I saw during the period of the armistice proper, up to 8 November 1942, and afterwards during the German occupation of Tunisia.

My functions as judicial counselor of the Tunisian government were not political. I did not belong to Admiral Esteva's cabinet and it must be added that the Admiral was by nature rather distrustful. However, I did receive some specific information on the general situation.

From the military point of view the French forces in Tunisia were not large. They included a small division of the armistice army commanded successively by General Audet, General de Lattre de Tassigny, and General Barré. A small naval force was at Bizerte under the orders of Admiral Derrien. There were also several air units under the command of General Péquin. These slight forces were sufficient to guarantee the security of the country, which in fact was not disturbed at any time.

The French Legion of War Veterans was, so far as Tunisia was concerned, nothing more than an association of former soldiers whose purpose was to maintain moral unity with a view to a later re-entry into the war and, at the same time, to maintain relations with Mohammedan soldiers. It must be pointed out at once, however, that Mohammedans in the large cities are exempt from military service as are also all Tunisian Jews. The French Legion of War Veterans, therefore, could not carry out this part of its task except with men of the countryside, who were rather primitive in nature.

Reduced in numbers though they were, French military forces in North Africa maintained all their prestige both in the eyes of the French and of the Tunisians, and they were uncontestably inspired by great enthusiasm after the service in Tunisia of General de Lattre de Tassigny, whose methods were often questionable and could even be made fun of, but nevertheless were extremely popular with the young men.

The French army in Tunisia had, in addition, been somewhat strengthened by contingents which had come from Syria. After the 1941 campaign, General de Lattre de Tassigny had welcomed them very warmly, praising their valor and their fidelity to Maréchal Pétain.

In the field of civil administration it must be said that we were still, to a great extent, in the stage of direct administration. The ministers of Tunisian origin were rather in the background and actual operations were in the hands of French officials. These men were under the orders of Admiral Esteva as resident-general, assisted by M. Lafond, the minister-plenipotentiary-delegate at the residence-general, and by M. Binoche, secretary-general, who had succeeded M. Georges Picot.

Admiral Esteva was an indomitable worker. He had a rather special command system which consisted in doing as much as possible by himself instead of supervising the work of his collaborators and directors. Behind his authoritarianism, however, he was a very kind man and in reality left considerable freedom of thought to his collaborators. For example, the delegate at the residence-general, M. Lafond, did not conceal his open sympathies for England. Though what was called the "resistance" existed in Tunisia in only a restrained way, M. Lafond was clearly its chief.

The work of the French administrations was extremely active. Tunisia had to be kept alive and prosperous during a critical period. It must be stated in all honesty that the French administrations succeeded in this task. North Africa was a country relatively fortunate from the economic point of view. Thanks to heaven, or rather to the rain, harvests were excellent from 1940 to 1943, and Tunisia was even able to contribute to the food supply of the homeland. The administration made intense efforts to take advantage of such resources as the country had in minerals and in soft coal. In short, from the material point of view, life was fairly easy in Tunisia during the armistice period.

The activities of the residence-general and of the administrations were not limited to material matters. Reforms of political structure, which would cover a long period to come, were undertaken in Tunisia. The ruling idea was that the French protectorate should continue and that one should work for the future on the principle that an end to the present regime was inconceivable. Among the long-term plans there were some in which I was concerned. This was particularly the case regarding the reform of the French court system.

Soon after the establishment of the protectorate in 1884, the other foreign powers had renounced the previous system of capitulations in favor of an acceptance of the French court system. Thus French tribunals were established in Tunisia as the sole courts for all cases in which a Frenchman or a foreigner was concerned. But there were only two French civil courts, one at Tunis and the other at Sousse. For both, the court of appeal was at Algiers. By a law of 9 June 1941 a French court of appeal was now created at Tunis and another law, of 13 May 1942, established two new civil courts at Sfax and Bizerte. These new courts, which answered an unquestionable need, had political importance. They showed that France intended to continue to fulfil in the most complete manner her role in Tunisia.

Reforms were also introduced in the organization of the mixed courts for land questions. Tunisia had a land system copied after the Australian Torrens law, and based on a land register. The fact was that Arab ownership was completely uncertain and registration of property was made only after a procedure which made it possible to find who was the true owner and to give him a guaranteed title. Needless to say, the work of this mixed tribunal, of which half the judges as well as the president were French, the other half of the judges being Tunisian, was of capital importance in carrying out this highly important program. Under the authority of Admiral Esteva I worked for the removal of certain abuses that had developed in the operation of the mixed tribunal. Its presidency was entrusted to a judge of the highest qualities, M. Rouillé, a former attorney at the Court of Appeals in Paris.

M. Rouillé and I have been the object of all sorts of persecution since the liberation. My purpose here is not to make any sort of defense of myself. I may be permitted to say merely that the intentions of those who have criticized us were certainly not entirely pure.

It would take too much time to follow the work of the French administration in all fields. I have given only a few examples. I must note also that a large number of the reforms and improvements of structure have endured even though there was a desire to bring about a spectacular annulment of the arrangements which had been made. When it was necessary to do something really serious there was no way to avoid repeating the same changes in another form.

Tunisia was obliged to apply the laws of exception which had been promulgated in the homeland for Jews and Freemasons, but they were applied with the very greatest moderation. When I reached Tunisia I found that the texts of the laws were already established. It was possible to get round them. For example, no Jewish doctor had to close his practice. The new regulations limiting the number of Jewish doctors were, in fact, applied but they had the right to take care of other Jews, and needless to say no one suggested that they should look into the question of the religion of people who came to consult them. At the Bar the regulations limiting the number of Jewish lawyers were applied, but far more liberally then in France. A proportion of about 25 per cent was allowed, and Admiral Esteva left the leaders of the judicial system free to make such exceptions as they thought necessary. These few examples show that behind apparent severity the regime was really complacent.

In cultural matters a very great effort was made by the Alliance Française whose presidency had been given by Admiral Esteva to M. Rouillé. M. Rouillé was able to secure the co-operation of eminent Tunisians, particularly that of M. Mustapha Kaak who, after the liberation, was to become prime minister of the country. Important lectures were given by eminent figures from the French homeland, and the maintenance of instruction courses in French literature, of concerts, and of theatrical performances maintained a most intimate cultural contact between the French and Mohammedan educated classes.

At the same time the relevant government service developed facilities for higher education by adding a center of juridical studies and advanced courses in the humanities and in science; the present Institute for Higher Learning in Tunis continues these courses. Even during the enemy occupation the services for higher education continued their work for French culture in complete independence.

Besides, Tunisia had served as a refuge during the war for many important people, which proves that life there was more agreeable than it was in the French homeland, even in the southern zone. Among the many refugees in Tunisia I must not fail to mention one Paris lawyer, M. Edgar Faure, who came many times to see me.

Relations between Admiral Esteva and the elderly Bey Ahmed were most agreeable. The situation changed somewhat after Ahmed's death and the installation of the new Monsef Bey in June 1942.

I was present at the installation ceremony for His Highness Monsef Bey. It was a traditional ceremony. Tunisia is in fact a kingdom, but the Bey is not the King of Tunis. He is simply the holder of the kingdom and that is his official title. Until the protectorate of 1884 Tunis was under the nominal suzerainty of the sultan at Constantinople. Since the beginning of the protectorate it has been the French government which installs the Bey in power. It must be made clear that the rules of succession are very special. Succession is not hereditary. As in Turkey, it is the oldest prince of the family who replaces the reigning bey, his cousin, when a bey dies. Monsef Bey, unlike his predecessors, wanted to take a more active part in the government of Tunis. Being far more interested in the development of a Tunisian upper class, Monsef Bey was, of course, connected with the two political movements, the old Destour and the neo-Destour. It must be explained that the word "destour" means "constitution." The essential purpose of both movements is that a constitutional monarchy should be established in Tunisia in place of the monarchy of the beys, which is in theory an absolute monarchy.

As soon as he had been installed, Monsef Bey made an address full of highly flowery compliments to Admiral Esteva. But relations between the two men soon began to turn sour. They became bad in September 1942 when Monsef Bey, in a letter to Maréchal Pétain, specifically demanded the recall of Admiral Esteva. On instructions from President Laval an arrangement was made and two events were scheduled to bind the reconciliation; one was to be a solemn session of the mixed tribunal for land affairs and the other a voyage to Kairouan about the middle of November 1942. The Allied landing in North Africa made both of these events impossible.

To complete what I have to say about the armistice period, I must add a word on the foreign representatives in Tunisia.

The diplomatic relations of Tunisia with foreign countries were maintained by the French government and, for that reason, there were no members of any official diplomatic corps in Tunis. There were only consuls.

The Swiss consul played a very important part as he was responsible for the protection of Italian interests. The consul of Spain was still there, together with those of many other countries and particularly the consul of the United States of America, Mr. Doolittle, whom I had occasion to see very often. Mr. Doolittle did not hide his feelings. When he called on me for the first time, according to protocol, he told me that if he had been a Frenchman he would have been a Gaullist and a refugee in London, and that if he had been condemned to death in his absence he would have regarded that condemnation as equivalent to admission to the Legion of Honor.

Somewhat surprised by his remarks, and speaking perhaps more diplomatically than he had done, I answered that I greatly admired the freedom of expression and the frankness of the diplomatic and consular corps of the United States. Mr. Doolittle, there could be no doubt, was an extremely active agent. He was, happily, able to escape from Tunis in time as the residence-general had given him all the means necessary for leaving and for saving his archives when the occupation of Tunis by the Germans became imminent.

I now come to the period of the German occupation of Tunisia.

The possibility of an Allied landing had frequently been discussed, but I think that no one in Tunisia guessed the exact date.

On 1 November 1942 I was at the races in Tunisia—they were the only amusement at that time—and had the pleasure of spending the afternoon with Admiral Darlan's son. That night, he was struck by the terrible illness from which he was never to recover. He was taken urgently to Algiers and that is where his father came to see him and so happened to be there, by chance, at the time of the landing on 8 November.

The announcement of the landing struck Tunisia like a thunderbolt. The famous remark of General Weygand was passed about by word of mouth: "If you are few, I will fire. If you are many, I will welcome you." But the question which concerned us most was that of knowing how far the American forces would advance and if they were going to make a second landing at Bizerte and occupy the whole of North Africa immediately. In fact, the American forces scarcely went beyond Algiers during the first part of the operation. Tunisia was in a tragic situation. From the day after the landing, 9 November [1942], a certain number of German military planes landed on the military field at El Aouina. What should be done? Since the armistice of 1940 the order had been not to allow anyone to come to North Africa. It was known that Maréchal Pétain's government had avoided application of the Darlan-Warlimont agreement of 27 May 1941, which had authorized the forces of the Axis to use the port of Bizerte and permitted the movement of Axis forces across Tunisia. The application of this agreement had been made conditional on political compensation which had never been granted. In November 1942 it was no longer possible to oppose a German landing. American troops were too far away and the French forces in Tunisia were too weak. The situation was a singular one. German planes were on the field at El Aouina but the French troops were in their barracks. Matters came to a head during the night of 12-13 November, when General Barré, commanding French troops in Tunisia, on orders from General Juin, removed all his forces 25 kilometers toward the interior of Tunisia. On the following day when the German troops landed at Tunis they found the barracks empty.

At Bizerte the situation was more dramatic. Admiral Derrien had first given orders to begin fighting again on 11 November [1942], but categorical instructions forced him to cancel this order. For some time the navy and the French land forces maintained a reserved sector at Bizerte in which neither German soldiers nor sailors entered. But on the day the fleet was sunk at Toulon Admiral Derrien was unable to carry out standing orders, in existence since 1940, for sinking the ships. Physically controlled by German forces which had invaded his command post, he was obliged to order the crews to evacuate their ships and the soldiers to evacuate their positions and to disarm, the enemy having threatened that if he resisted every member of the French armed forces, regardless of rank, would be killed and no prisoners taken.

The unfortunate Admiral Derrien refused to leave Bizerte at the time of the German collapse in Tunisia. When the Allies entered he was condemned to perpetual hard labor by the military tribunals of General de Gaulle. He died, blind, in the convicts camp of Lambèze in the midst of Arab prisoners. It is only with the most intense emotion that I can think of this naval officer with so brilliant a record.

The arrival of German troops in Tunis created a particularly difficult situation. Public order had to be maintained. The residence-general mobilized the Legion's forces of order, who were armed in order to prevent pillage by Arabs.

What was to be our fate in Tunisia? The French administration continued. From the material point of the view the situation was bad. There were no longer any communications with the interior of the country and the food supplies, already low, were still further reduced by the large quantities requisitioned for the German and Italian troops who landed. Added to that there were very frequent bombardments by allied aviation.

Morally the situation was still more painful as communication between Tunisia and the French government in Vichy was precarious. In addition, confusion was caused by the arrival in Tunisia of certain persons brought there by the Germans who, in fact, had no mandates whatever from the French government in Vichy and particularly not from President Laval.

One point remained obscure: what would be the reaction of the Tunisians themselves? The Germans hastened to bring back to Tunis the leader of the neo-Destour party, Habib Bourguiba, who had been interned in Marseille since the declaration of war in 1939. It is certain that the Bey and his ministers could have caused France the greatest possible difficulties, as the resident and his collaborators in Tunis now had no material means of action.

But nothing happened. In spite of disagreements which he might have had with Admiral Esteva, Monsef Bey did not take advantage of events to denounce the protectorate. On the other hand, the Germans formally opposed any seizure of power by the Italians.

Obviously it was by changing course back and forth between the Germans and the Italians that Admiral Esteva succeeded in maintaining the principle of a French protectorate.

I must point out too that relations between Germans and Italians were far from good. The Italian population of Tunisia had escaped mobilization since 1940. The Germans hastened to mobilize them all, and everyone at Tunis saw how brutally the German soldiers, responsible for training the new recruits, maltreated them.

At the beginning of the German occupation it was thought that it would not last long and an event occurred which was never understood by anyone. On 29 November [1942] American units appeared in the evening at a distance of 4 or 5 kilometers from Tunis. In the port the Germans were embarking. At the end of the day these American elements, which could have entered Tunis immediately, retreated about 20 or 30 kilometers. The hope of a rapid victory vanished and the occupation lasted until 23 May 1943.

It is useless, I believe, to recall the various incidents of the occupation. Admiral Esteva was obliged to submit to certain painful incidents such as the arrest of many of his collaborators, most of whom were taken to France. Prominent among them was M. Lafond, delegate at the residence-general, who several weeks after his arrival [in France] succeeded in escaping and returning to North Africa through Spain. But whatever may have been the extremely painful events of daily life, one fact remains: the Franco-Tunisian administrations remained at their tasks till the day when Tunis was liberated, and French courts continued to function. No one, at that time, said that the mission of France in Tunisia was at an end. It was, therefore, an unaltered relation with the Tunisians which the new French authorities found when they entered Tunis on 13 May 1943.

I cannot report on later events.

During the German occupation I had fought stubbornly, with such means as I possessed, step by step with Admiral Esteva, to prevent certain measures being taken. I had prepared many protests as a result of which the wearing of the yellow star was not imposed on Jews. I had also handed over to the president of the Jewish community the list of Jews so that its disappearance might be arranged. On 10 April 1943 I was summoned to the residence-general, where I found Minister Rahn and various German officers, who demanded the organization of an obligatory labor service to dig trenches around Tunis and to repair the damage done to the aviation camp by bombardments. There was a long discussion. I managed to prove, using racial arguments which were likely to please the Germans, that it was impossible to have Europeans take up pick and shovel where they could be seen by Arabs.

The result of my opposition was that in the night of Tuesday to Wednesday 14 April [1943] I was expelled and taken to Rome on a German military plane. There I had the good luck to be taken away from the Germans by the Italians, and to be transported by them to the French frontier from which I got to Paris. I heard through friends of what happened afterward in Tunis. On the second day before the Allies entered Tunis, the Germans had taken Admiral Esteva away by force.

After the Allies reached Tunis, General Giraud, badly informed as to what had been going on, brutally announced to Monsef Bey that he had been deposed.

I leave to the imagination what the repercussions of this event were throughout North Africa.

And this, my dear colleague, completes my summary of what I saw in North Africa. It is always difficult to write history and it is fortunate that institutions such as the Hoover War Library Foundation are engaged in collecting testimony. Unfortunately, that was not the case in the heat of the liberation when many officials, true Frenchmen—and I believe that I am one of them—were removed from their posts without any explanation. I am happy that the cordial welcome given to me by the Bar of Paris enabled me to renew my acquaintance with you and has now given me the opportunity to present this account.

I am convinced that the presence of France in North Africa is absolutely indispensable to the maintenance of stability in that part of the world. France has every ground for being proud of the work which she has accomplished there. Perhaps at certain times there has not been a sufficient awareness of the changes that have come among those upper classes which we ourselves have created. I believe that from this point of view the recent Franco-Tunisian agreements are based on an excellent principle. But I am convinced that many disturbances would have been avoided if the beginning had not been a systematic distortion of facts, of which the purpose was to debase, in the eyes of the world, those who by their loyal action had been able to maintain throughout these difficult years order, peace, and Franco-Mohammedan friendship in North Africa.

Can it be said, too, that the disquiet of the Jews, which the government of those days is accused of having molested, is today very serious? There is now a great exodus of Jews from Tunisia. Since 1948, 42,000 of them have left, and Jewish communities which had existed for a thousand years, like that of Djerba, have now disappeared. This fact proves much.

I am certain that the re-establishment of the truth, to which you are devoted, will bring conciliation and will put matters right again.

Je vous prie d'agréer, mon cher Confrère, l'expression de mes sentiments les plus dévoués.

(Document No. 305)
Fr. ed. 751-759

P. DE FONT-RÉAULX
Pierre de Font-Réaulx

INDO-CHINA

JEAN DECOUX
Admiral;

Governor-General of French Indo-China,
1940-1945

Having served for five years as a governor-general of French Indo-China during the most tragic period of the second World War, I was able to form an opinion, which I believe to be exact, on the origins of what has since happened in Indo-China and on the part played in this matter by the policies of the Maréchal from the time he took power until he left France prisoner. My belief is absolute on the following points.

(1) The government of the Maréchal never ceased from June 1940 to August 1944 to follow in all that concerned French Indo-China a national policy of resistance to Japanese undertakings. This policy, combined with the enormous prestige of the Maréchal himself among both the elite and the masses of Indo-China, enabled me to protect, until 1945, all that was essential to French sovereignty in that country.

(2) As long as it had the power to do so, and in fact until the outbreak of the conflict in the Pacific, the government of the Maréchal reported on many occasions to the Department of State in Washington the grave dangers that Southeast Asia incurred because of Japanese action against Indo-China. In the same way the government of the Maréchal insisted on all occasions that America should come urgently to the aid of French Indo-China as a part of the theater of war in the Far East.

(3) These appeals were not listened to. While there was still time Indo-China received no effective aid from the United States, though during the same period Siam, and above all Nationalist China, benefited by massive support from the United States. As far as I am concerned I deplore this failure. I persist in believing that if the government in Washington had better understood the situation when these events began, and if from 1940 and 1941 it had had the courage to accept its responsibility and to veto categorically the Japanese advance in the direction of the south, the government of the Mikado would not have insisted. The war in the Pacific would have been avoided and the war in Europe would have been shortened by many years.

(4) I remain convinced that the prejudices of President Roosevelt toward France and toward French Indo-China contributed largely to create chaos in Southeast Asia. Those prejudices are at the basis of the war in Indo-China.

(5) With regard to the French policy of resistance to Japan, to which I referred above, there is nothing whatever which would allow me to dissociate the personal actions of President Pierre Laval from those of the Maréchal, Chief of State.

(6) The policy followed from 1940 to 1944 in Indo-China in the name

of the government of the Maréchal constitutes in these respects one single piece without gaps or deviations. Until 9 March 1945 this policy proved its value. Its nature was such as to give back to France, at the end of the world conflict, an unbroken Indo-China whose function would be to serve as an essential element of order and pacification in the Far East.

(7) This policy was the only possible one. It was neither understood nor followed by General de Gaulle. Following the change of policy in France, and resulting from it, a wind of catastrophe blew over Indo-China. The catastrophe itself occurred seven months later when the goal was already in sight.

(8) This was a terrible misfortune not only for France and Indo-China but also for England, and even more for the United States.

In politics, as in the whole of life, our acts pursue us, and for each error a heavy penalty is paid.

(Document No. 150)

Fr. ed. 760-761

Paris, 29 February 1952

DECOUX

Admiral Decoux

FRENCH WEST AFRICA — MERS-EL-KÉBIR DAKAR — MADAGASCAR BRITAIN AND THE FRENCH COLONIES

LÉON CAYLA

*Governor-General, French West Africa;
Governor-General, Madagascar*

Even today, at the beginning of 1954, the moral atmosphere of France is still confused. The fact that ten years after the liberation of French soil followed by total victory of the Allies the country which during the first world war achieved a "sacred union" should now be divided on fundamental questions, is the subject of astonishment to the best of her friends.

Such a state of affairs can be explained only by recalling the circumstances which lie at its origin. The tragic situation of France in June 1940, the humiliation which it underwent because of the armistice and the occupation, and the reactions which followed, all gave birth to disagreements which only a broad policy of reconciliation could have dissipated.

It was certainly not a question of forgetting the criminal acts of those who placed themselves at the service of the enemy. Antagonisms which had to be removed as one of the essential conditions for the safeguarding of our common heritage were aggravated by confusing with a little handful of guilty men those thousands and thousands of French people who when faced by dramatic problems of conscience had no other thought than to preserve their country from the worst.

Between those who abandoned the territory where the controls of the armistice applied, and the countless others who accepted those controls under the pressure of circumstances, the chasm was often less deep than it seemed to be. In any case it was not by hurling degrading accusations at each other that the French could clear the way for the unity that was so necessary.

As time passes History will re-examine the records of those on whom it must pass its judgment, as past jurisdictions have so often had to do, revising some of the decisions reached in a revolutionary period. The judgment of History will then reinstate in public opinion all those good servants of the country who, victims of error, of party passions, or of personal vengeance were driven from public life at the very time when France had need of every asset in order to regain her position in the world.

It is right that the Frenchmen who in their various capacities exercised some part of the national sovereignty during those fateful days should now restate the considerations which in all good conscience they had then obeyed.

I had been appointed to the general government of French West Africa in the spring of 1939 and had scarcely taken over my post at Dakar when the war broke out.

In opening the annual session of the government council I emphasized the full meaning of a levy of black troops. Within a few hours of the issuance of the general mobilization order on 1 September 1939, its effects were being felt throughout the widespread area of French West Africa. War drums echoing the messages of the radio brought the call to the most distant places in the back country. Thousands of men began their march amidst the enthusiasm of the people. It was no longer a matter, as it had been in 1914, of signing up young recruits for instruction. Those who responded to the appeal were, as was also true in France, trained reservists, mature men long ago initiated, under the flag, in military life and obligations. The great Black Army came to life in a single bound. Those who were to take arms and those who watched them leave regarded as holy this war in which their fate and liberty were at stake. The great African federation proclaimed by its attitude that it was no mere geographic concept. Its fifteen million inhabitants of many religions and races, spread over five million square kilometers, affirmed with the moral unity which makes a people strong that they were completely integrated into the French community. No event could have consecrated in more striking fashion the profoundly human work accomplished there by France.

This noble sentiment of the troops and of the people did not waver. The Grand Marabout, Seydou Mourou Tall, as he toured the territories of French West Africa, branded with infamy Hitler's *Mein Kampf* in which colored men were considered as half monkeys.

In the atmosphere of ardent patriotism in which French West Africa was living, the cruel news that discussions were about to be entered into for the conclusion of an armistice aroused the most intense emotion. At first I refused to believe the reports sent through certain radio services. Remembering the order of the day in the defense of Verdun, "They shall not pass," I believed that a fierce resistance would meet the enemy everywhere that French land was still free, on the continent as throughout the empire. But many hours later confirmation came that the armistice had indeed been asked for. Though the night was already far advanced I sent my aide, Captain Renoncial, to General Barrau, the commander-in-chief of the land forces, with the message that I refused to associate French West Africa with the action that was about to be taken.

General Barrau's reply was approximately in these words: "Tell the governor-general that his feeling only increases the esteem in which I already hold him. However, I ask him, because of the gravity of the circumstances, to refrain from reaching any decision and to wait until I am able to express, after reflection, a reasoned opinion."

On the morning of the following day, General Barrau came to see me. At heart he agreed with me; but he pointed out that the insufficiency of our military equipment could place French West Africa in a perilous situation and that it was best to reflect further before launching ourselves in an adventure. In addition, he was assured that a considerable portion of the officers under his command would refuse to take any position against a decision made by Maréchal Pétain. I replied that there was no question of lightly engaging French West Africa in offensive operations, but only to protect its future. The lands of the empire must remain a powerful reserve of national force. They held large numbers of men who had previously been intended as reinforcements for the troops in France. They were far from having given all they could, their morale remained very high, and they were ready to fulfil to the very end their duty to the French community.

Nor did I allow the colonial department to be ignorant of the spirit that ruled in French West Africa; I informed them that the entire population was ready to continue the struggle.

Another conference was held at which the inspector-general for colonies, who happened then to be on a mission in French West Africa, was present. This conference was rather dramatic but did not enable me to secure the formal agreement of General Barrau. However, when I had declared that I could not agree to the objections which were presented to me, General Barrau asked me at least to wait until contact had been established with General Noguès before I made my determination public. I agreed, and a high officer of the general staff at Dakar was sent on a mission, by plane, to the commander-in-chief of land forces for North Africa.

At the same time, I had a long interview with the rear admiral commanding the Navy, who assured me of his co-operation. It was only the orders he received from the admiral of the fleet which led him, a few days later, to change his attitude.

The representative of Great Britain at Dakar, Mr. Cusden, told me that he was certain that French West Africa would receive the money necessary to meet its military expenses if it refused to agree to the armistice. In any case there was no question of an occupation by British forces of any part whatever of the territory of French West Africa.

Such was the situation when a first message reached General Barrau indicating that General Noguès would agree. All that was needed was a confirmation of this agreement. The confirmation did not come. The officer sent to see the commander-in-chief reported that General Noguès had not succeeded in obtaining the agreement of the Navy, which he regarded as indispensable, and regretted that it would be impossible for him to participate in what we had in mind.

To tell the truth I did not regard this reply, in itself, as setting an insur-
mountable obstacle to the line of conduct which I desired to follow. That
General Noguès did not wish to expose North Africa to a sudden attack
was understandable when it was considered that the troops still under
his command if deprived of support from the fleet might seem to him to
be too weak in numbers and in equipment to resist for long a German
operation on a large scale, then regarded as possible. But the situation
was different for French West Africa, where large contingents of reservists
were available and in front of which the desert zone of the Sahara was far
less easy to cross than was the Mediterranean. But what obliged me to
delay was General Barrau's formal opinion that a large number of the
European officers of the Black Troops would refuse to join in a movement
to which the naval forces were opposed. If I continued my plan, he
stated clearly, I must expect armed fighting.

Faced by the possibilities which General Barrau presented to me, I
replied bitterly, "By warning me that I risk forcing Frenchmen to fight
against other Frenchmen you bind my hands." And he replied, "That's
why I spoke to you as I did."

New objections were soon added to those of the military high command.
Those who expressed them, on the strength of information received from
France, based their arguments on the tragic situation in the homeland
where, in the spiritual and material confusion, the greater part of public
opinion desired that hostilities should be ended. Putting the empire in a
position of resistance ran a risk, they said, of worsening the fate of forty
million French people. It was on Maréchal Pétain, now responsible, that
fell the duty of limiting the disaster and preparing for the recovery of the
country.

This opinion was at first accepted only by a minority of the European
population but it gained considerable ground after the tragedy of Mers-
el-Kébir. That event completely upset most of the supporters of
resistance.

I had already made complaints to Mr. Cusden about the inadmissable
actions of certain British authorities in the colonies on our borders, who
without waiting longer had already undertaken in our frontier zones an
offensive propaganda regarding French administration and military command, whose officials and soldiers they were attempting to corrupt.

The consul-general [Cusden] had promised to report these facts to the
foreign office. However, after a visit to the English admiral who was
returning from Freetown to London, I found myself obliged to repeat
my protests to Mr. Cusden as we were returning to land in the launch. The
consul-general claimed that the governors of the British colonies had
certainly received the necessary orders from London. "I regret to note
that they have paid no attention to these instructions," I replied. "It
must not be believed that even after the reverse which they have undergone
the French would be disposed to allow anyone to trample on them."
Mr. Cusden again expressed his regret, which was certainly sincere.

The attack on *Richelieu* off Dakar by English torpedo-carrying planes
did nothing to re-establish calm. It increased the indignation aroused by
the aggression of Mers-el-Kébir.

After this aggression I had been obliged to place a guard on the British
Consulate, for I feared an incident might result from the excitement
then evident among the population of Dakar.

When it was decided that Mr. Cusden should be invited to go to Gambia

I placed the general government's micheline[1] at his disposal. He occupied it with his family and his staff. The governor of Gambia thanked me very warmly.

To sum up, as soon as negotiations for an armistice had been announced I had done all, within my power, to keep French West Africa entirely free. But the necessary support from the military forces had not been available, and further, my plans had been blocked by the inexplicable attitude of those whom I wished to continue to regard as allies.

In the meantime I had been appointed to take over the government of Madagascar. Some regarded this change of post as immediate punishment for my rebellion. Clarification of this point seems to me to be necessary. The fact was that President Albert Lebrun at the end of June had already ratified the order, countersigned by the Minister of Colonies. In doing this he had no thought, I am certain, other than to place Madagascar under the authority of a governor-general who for more than nine years had administered the Grande Ile, and whose personal authority was unquestioned. In addition, the Minister of Colonies, in notifying me of my new post, asked me to regard it only as proof of the government's confidence—a confidence which, so far as President Lebrun was concerned, was unquestionable in my opinion. It was only in December 1940 that the Secretary of State for Colonies, who could have no doubt on the attitude I had taken at Dakar at the time of the signing of the armistice, decided that to keep me in active service might appear as tacit approbation of my attitude, well known to the population of Dakar. A special regulation was therefore applied, reducing the age limit for governors-general, and I was told how much they regretted having to put me on the retired list. At the same time I was assured of the "gratitude of the government for the services which I had rendered to France and to the empire."

This point having been made clear, I now return to the situation in which I found myself at the beginning of July 1940 after the affair of Mers-el-Kébir. I had desired to maintain Franco-British co-operation on a basis of mutual confidence. I therefore found it impossible to understand the aggression committed against a French fleet that was bound under all circumstances, by instructions of which the English authorities, always well informed, certainly knew the general lines, to defend their flag to the point of scuttling the fleet in case of necessity. And in any case, what French sailor would have agreed to allow even the smallest ship of our Navy to fall into the hands of the Germans?

The tragedy of Mers-el-Kébir inevitably created a chasm between the British and their friends in French overseas territories. Thereafter my sole concern was to maintain to the highest degree French order and prestige, guarantee of the revival of my country.

The National Assembly, meeting at Vichy, soon invested Maréchal Pétain with full powers, on the pressing invitation of the presidents of the Chamber of Deputies and of the Senate. Maréchal Pétain, who had already been placed at the head of the government through a procedure which was not customary and which might lead therefore to a question being raised as to his authority, was proclaimed Chief of State by a massive majority of the elected representatives of the nation. Ambassadors and ministers-plenipotentiary of foreign powers were accredited to him.

It was under these conditions that I finally reached Tananarive at the

(1) Diesel railway car, originally fitted with Michelin tires.

end of July 1940. From the time I received notice of my new post I had limited myself to declaring that in Madagascar, as in French West Africa, I would defend French sovereignty. After what had happened in French West Africa and at Mers-el-Kébir I was more than ever determined to make it my first objective to have the rights of France respected, and its prestige maintained, on the Grande Ile. In the eyes of the native population France alone must be considered. Had the high authorities at Tananarive turned against the French government immediately after the armistice, I believe they would have been followed. Since that time British propaganda had intervened in a disquieting manner. A movement which in its origin may have been purely nationalist now scarcely hid the aspirations of these ancient rivals of French influence. The patriotism of the many French people in Madagascar had become linked with an intense friendship for the English. In certain circles the great dream was that English planes would arrive, and it was even hoped that English flags would fly over the Grande Ile beside our own. All this was happening under the eyes of a population among whom were many former leaders who had not forgotten past rivalry [between French and British]. It was true that much water had passed under the bridges of Ikopa since Gallieni had realized that the English were the only adversaries whom we would ever meet in Madagascar. The entente cordiale and the brotherhood of arms [war of 1914-1918] which followed had wiped out—at least in Europe—many points of friction. But other oppositions had become obvious. South Africa regarded the Grande Ile as its natural prolongation. Its chief, Marshal Smuts, was already preparing in his mind the humiliating words against France that he was to speak in London.

From the first I came up against the incomprehension of the enraged partisans of holy friendship for England, a state of mind ready to accept the worst British errors with regard to France. I was not however able to make open use of what had happened at Dakar in order to bring these people to a more exact evaluation of events. That would have envenomed a quarrel which already divided the French people on the island and would have provoked conflicts, possibly with bloodshed, which would have served as a pretext for foreign intervention. The Malgaches, closely attentive to everything that might affect their future, would have become more disquiet in the presence of quarrels which were incompatible with the conception previously given to them of the meaning of French peace.

To prevent all disorder, I was obliged to inflict punishment, though in very rare cases, and mostly of a light character, in order to reduce the divergence of those French colonists or officials who indulged in public manifestations harmful to French authority.

I did not, of course, make any protest against my being placed on the retired list.

Doubtless I would have been justified in being astonished that so much haste was shown in getting me out of a country to which five months earlier I had been so urged to return. But the action taken in my case, even though it disregarded the prestige which I had acquired in the Grande Ile, would seem justified to anyone who regarded it from the point of view of strict discipline. I had been a rebel before Mers-el-Kébir, and before the National Assembly of 10 July [1940]. I was being 'purified out,' and in the most proper fashion. The trick was turned with complete correctness, and I refused to adopt any reprisals against Vichy based on a purely personal matter.

I returned to France after spending several weeks in Algeria where I did not succeed in finding a place for myself. I had decided definitely on living as discreet a life as possible. And that is what I did for many months, until the British landing in Madagascar. I could not help being deeply troubled by an event which inevitably would strike a blow at French prestige. At the request of the secretary-general of the series of lectures which were then being given in the Théâtre des Ambassadeurs [Paris] I agreed to give a talk on what France had accomplished in Madagascar and on the right to outstanding respect which she had acquired there. A little later the British landing at Diégo-Suarez was followed by the occupation of the entire territory of Madagascar.

The danger to French influence increased sharply. A political party with which I had never had anything to do organized a meeting of protest and asked me to speak. I accepted this invitation only after having been assured that no partisan question would be discussed and that the meeting would be devoted entirely to the English intervention in Madagascar.

Some of my friends who had been resistants from the beginning told me later, without the least hesitation, that my opinion on the British attitude toward France in many circumstances was well founded but that I was wrong to express my opinion before the end of the occupation made it possible for the French people to say freely what they really thought. However, when I saw a certain British group striving actively to ruin the prestige of France in those territories in which it had survived the cruel afflictions of 1940 I could not restrain myself from uttering a cry of alarm. I had had relations so frankly cordial with the British that I did not believe that I was bound to any submission to them, submission which by very reason of my former offices in the Levant, in Africa, and in Madagascar, would have constituted a weakness close to cowardice. I thought that a voice which had been so much in harmony with their own could call some of them, at least, back to a respect for the traditional fair play which had been temporarily obscured.

When on the following 7 November [1942] landing operations began in the territories of North Africa I joined again with those who protested against these new and cruel losses inflicted on France. But once my first emotions had subsided I abstained from any further comment. The American authorities, in fact, were careful not to favor the anti-French intrigues which began to come to light in certain native circles. Further, as was known later, the landing had been preceded by an understanding with a group of French people, and had been followed quickly by an accord which put an end to a fratricidal struggle.

Henceforth I limited myself to the study of those economic and social questions which would inevitably arise after the liberation of French soil. I did this work in a spirit devoid of all party considerations, and in full liberty of thought.

When the liberation came I believed that it would allow France to realize its aspirations in an atmosphere of national reconciliation. My illusions endured but a short time. I personally was subjected to rather violent attacks and to monstrous denunciations which brought me before the courts of my country.

After a long preliminary examination, conducted, I must say, with great care for the truth, it was decided that there was no basis for the grave accusations that I had endangered the security of the state. But the examining commission of the high court maintained against me the fact that I had agreed to continue to serve under the orders of Maréchal Pétain. In addition, the commission found in the criticisms which I had expressed against certain actions of our Allies on French territory a form of conduct harmful to the morale of the population. Because of this attitude I was convicted of misdemeanor.

I will not repeat here what I said above concerning the considerations on which I had relied in the absolute conviction that I was serving the interests of France to my best ability.

In concluding this statement I express the hope that it will help clarify the reader's feelings regarding certain aspects of the drama in which so many French people, whose patriotism was unquestionable, took part in 1940 and during the following years. I have never inscribed my name on the long list of those who now claim to have foreseen something which has already occurred; but I think that an exact appreciation of events at the moment when they occurred would have saved France and its Allies from the disagreements and miscalculations of which the persistent effects still compromise the re-establishment of enduring peace.

There will be no concert of Europe worthy of the name so long as France, Great Britain, and Germany do not contribute in common, as is desired across the Atlantic, to the rule of harmony in a world which is today so troubled. The French themselves will not play the part which belongs to them unless they resolutely put an end to the internal quarrels with which their national life remains overburdened.

Must we wait for new generations to come before these quarrels which have so long retarded the return of the Sacred Union are forgotten?

France has never been and never will be a country of traitors. Today it has been weakened by the amputation of a part of its human assets. May it soon regain in the thought of the world all of that noble place to which it is entitled.

(Document No. 206)
Fr. ed. 768-769

Paris, 25 March 1954

LÉON CAYLA
Governor-General Cayla

MADAGASCAR

ARMAND ANNET

Governor-General of Madagascar

I the undersigned Governor-General Armand Annet, living in Paris, Governor-General of Madagascar from December 1940 to November 1942, deposit in the archives of the Hoover War Library the text of a book published in 1952, *Aux heures troublees de l'Afrique Française.* This book is an account of the events which occurred in Madagascar while I was governor-general of the island, events in which I was a participant and witness.

(Document No. 259)
Fr. ed. 770

Paris, 23 March 1955

A. ANNET
Governor-General A. Aunet

BRAZZAVILLE

JACQUES DOURDIN

Director of the French Statistical Service

I met President Laval once in my life; it was at the Hotel Matignon. I had come to bring him the results of a study which had been made of the attitude and morale of the people of Paris and their attitude toward the new government which Maréchal Pétain had asked President Laval to form.

I had taken the initiative of making such a study because, though I made it a rule never to do any work along political lines, it seemed to me to be particularly useful to make an exception in this instance because of the special circumstances of the occupation. Maréchal Pétain, who after 13 December 1940 had not hesitated to speak harshly about Pierre Laval, had now made it known, after two years of silence, that Pierre Laval had all his confidence, and that he had asked him to form a government.

I wanted to know how the people of Paris took this news, and I tested their reaction with very great care and very rapidly. The study was made within the three days after M. Laval's return to power.

This study gave results which were highly unexpected by everyone, including President Laval. To the question, "Do you believe that Pierre

Laval could work in the interests of France?" 40 per cent replied yes; 11 per cent said they hoped so, but were waiting to see what he did; 15 per cent replied no; 24 per cent said they had no opinion on the matter. The coefficient of error in such studies is about 2 1/2 per cent.

Careful examination showed that Pierre Laval had 51 per cent of the votes, a result which seemed to me all the more extraordinary when it was remembered that a year earlier, in an inquiry into the living conditions of persons who participated in the social security services of the Paris region, I had put a question regarding the popularity of the Maréchal and had received a vote of only 25 per cent in his favor, a result which was submitted to Maréchal Pétain himself.

When I took this study to President Laval he read it with mingled interest and scepticism and told me frankly, "I'm not worrying about popularity. If I wanted to be popular, I need only turn my back on my duty to France."

I even had the impression that he found a sort of comfort in unpopularity. And I asked myself if Pierre Laval fearlessly facing unpopularity was able to do his work, how great would have been his strength if he had believed himself supported, followed, and understood in his efforts by a large part of the population. Granted that there is nothing which changes quicker than feelings, especially those of the crowd, it nevertheless seems curious that in 1942 there were 51 per cent of the people of Paris who had confidence in the skill of Pierre Laval. And if such a result was hard to believe in 1942, it was still harder to believe in 1945 at the moment when misfortune struck Pierre Laval. This result will doubtless seem reasonable and probable after History has brought its judgment to bear on the life and work of this statesman.

One more detail. Though Pierre Laval judged that the information which I brought him about his popularity had only relative value, he was, on the other hand, greatly interested in the replies recorded in answer to the question "Do you know the names of the ministers in the new government?" To this question 88 per cent of the people replied "no." When he came to this point of the document he laughed heartily in a way that I can still hear.

Though I never saw President Laval again, I did have indirect dealings with him. It was at a time when I was trying to improve the material and general situation of my brother, one of the fifty-two officers who had given their word to General Testu at Brazzaville to remain faithful to the Maréchal, in accordance with the strict principles of military discipline. My brother and only two others had kept their word when Colonel de Larminat arrived at Brazzaville the next day. He paid for this apparently narrow conception of discipline by spending twenty-two months in the concentration camp at Lambaréné. In Vichy no one took any interest in the fate of these officers. I tried in vain to interest the Maréchal himself in their case, to get the support of Admiral Fernet, the Minister of Colonies, and many others. Everywhere I met the same attitude of polite indifference and the same slightly contemptuous sympathy. It was almost as though they said, "What are they doing on that side anyway?"

When I saw that I was not going to get any official help for these officers, in whom no one took any interest—the International Red Cross considered them "political;" the English and the Americans regarded them as enemies; the Free French called them traitors; and the people of France regarded them as those who were absent and therefore wrong—I decided to request authorization and facilities to go myself and discuss the matter in Lisbon with the representatives of General de Gaulle, or if necessary in London with General de Gaulle's general staff. I regarded it as a terrible thing that Frenchmen should put other Frenchmen in prison. I never imagined at that time that the same attitude would continue on a much vaster scale several years later.

I met with the greatest sympathy from Patrick Surcouf, cabinet chief for the Minister of Colonies at that time, and from Commissioner Henry Villar, who was with President Laval. They were ready to do everything possible to facilitate the task I had set for myself. By combining our efforts with those of Colonel Bro of the French Red Cross I obtained from President Laval an authorization for a mission of three persons to go to Lisbon. The three were to be Dr. Lejametel, the airman René Lefebvre, and myself. President Laval gave us the passports of official delegates and allotted us—I believe it was from the personal budget of the Chief of Government—the necessary funds for a mission which was inevitably costly, the value of the escudo being what it was.

We left on 13 October 1942, and two of us returned on 9 November of the same year, leaving the airman René Lefebvre at Lisbon; he later became a member of the Free French forces. Three months afterwards, all the officers who had been interned were set free, and they were finally reinstated in their commands. I have always felt the greatest gratitude to President Laval for having allowed me to accomplish what I considered to be a humane mission. It was a question not merely of the soldiers themselves, but also of their wives and children, who for the same reasons—that is, because they did not want to join the other side—were up in concentration camps at the mercy of Senegalese soldiers, a thing which for an officer in the colonial army is the greatest possible disgrace.

What I have said above would have been, in general, my testimony if I had been questioned at the time of Pierre Laval's trial.

(Document No. 39)
Fr. ed. 771-773

Paris, *1 December 1947*

JACQUES DOURDIN

NORTH AFRICANS IN FRANCE

GENERAL MAURICE GUILLAUME

Attaché in the Cabinet of Pierre Laval in Vichy
for Matters Concerning North
Africans in France.

I the undersigned General Maurice Guillaume, Commander of the Legion of Honor, Croix de Guerre, 75 per cent war disability, eleven citations, former director of the cabinet of Maréchal Lyautey, living in Paris, make the following declaration on my honor.

After the Allied landing in North Africa, the situation of the North

Africans living in France became particularly tragic. There were about 100,000 of them, cut off from their families and all their interests, and prey to the tendentious offers made to them by the occupation authorities.

In the face of this danger, President Laval decided at the beginning of 1943 to create a sort of ministry for North African affairs in France, though without the title of ministry. Its purpose was to co-ordinate activities concerning the Algerians, Tunisians, and Moroccans in France. As a former close associate of Maréchal Lyautey I was instructed by M. Pierre Laval to take charge and assume the responsibility of this very important service. It was agreed that I would act in complete independence, with no obligation other than that of keeping the Chief of Government himself informed of what I was doing. My task was to maintain order among these hundred thousand North Africans in strict conformity with French standards.

With neither exaggeration nor pride, it can be said that this task was fulfilled with the most striking success. The facts are as follows:

Obligatory Labor Service. Thanks to extremely delicate negotiations all the North Africans were exempted from compulsory labor in Germany. About fifty of them agreed to go to Germany to work of their own free will.

The Todt Organization. Here the result was the same. The large-scale recruiting planned by the Sauckel organization among the North Africans in France was prevented. Scarcely two hundred of them were requisitioned, an insignificant figure, and even among these two hundred almost half were able to avoid actually going to work, thanks to false medical certificates which I obtained from doctors who were my personal friends.

Escaped Prisoners and False Papers. Many thousands of North African prisoners succeeded in escaping from their camps and reported themselves to my agency for North African affairs. I supplied all of them with false identity papers to prevent their being picked up again by the Germans. They were then hired by French factories; or if they were too badly compromised in the eyes of the Germans, they were sent off to isolated farms, especially around Melun, as agricultural workers.

The North African Militia. In July 1943 Ministers Rahn and Auer [German] planned a North African Militia from the thousands of natives then residing in France. Very high pay was offered. An ordinary private was to receive 5,000 francs and officers up to 30,000 francs per month. Thanks to the measures which we took, and thanks to a propaganda as effective as it was dangerous, this plan failed completely. In November 1943 the German authorities abandoned their project.

The Arab Printing Plant. This is but a single detail, yet it is extremely significant. In Vichy there was but one printing plant with Arabic type. At the beginning of 1944 the Germans wanted to buy it or requisition it. Their idea was to use it in publishing tracts, which would be spread among the North Africans in France and dropped by plane in North Africa. Discussions were intentionally dragged on until finally the Germans were obliged to give up the idea of acquiring the plant, which would have been so useful for Goebbel's propaganda. And in any case, by a secret agreement with President Laval, I had made arrangements for the matrices and Arabic type to be hidden in a safe place in case the Gestapo should unexpectedly seize the plant. The Germans were never able to print any tracts in France in Arabic characters. They even became very spiteful toward the whole subject.

Arab and Berber Radio Broadcasting. Radio broadcasts were sent out every day from Vichy to North Africa in the Arabic and Berber languages. These broadcasts were made by persons in German pay and were particularly harmful for the French generals in North Africa. Advised of this by the directors of the radio station, M. Renaudin and M. Bouteille, I arranged to get rid of the radio officials who were favorable to German propaganda. I managed this without any publicity and replaced them by other Mohammedans of whose loyalty I was sure. The whole operation was completed in two weeks. Never again was there any Arabic or Berber broadcast hostile to the generals of the "opposition." The principle of French authority was formally maintained, in spite of the torrent of insults poured over Vichy by the Gaullist radio of London.

North African Resistants and Communists. I believe it was in May 1944 that I learned, through my intelligence service, that the Germans had found the names of a number of North African resistants and communists who had just begun to publish a clandestine newspaper called *El Hayat.* The names were in Darnand's possession, and a raid was to be carried out a few days later to round up all the active elements of the North African resistance in France. By a trick that need not be explained here I succeeded in getting hold of the list and in making it disappear at once. Darnand and the Germans demanded the list in vain. Informed of what I had done, President Laval "drowned the fish." I was already on the point of being arrested, quite apart from this new matter; but finally, thanks to President Laval, everything was arranged. Thousands of communists and resistants threatened by the Gestapo had been warned through our action. They had been able to flee from Paris and conceal themselves in safety in the provinces.

Intelligence Service. Though my mission did not include any form of intelligence service—quite the contrary, in the German's opinion—I strove, through the contacts I was obliged to have with German agencies, to obtain every bit of information that could possibly be useful to the Allies. President Laval knew about this, and on various occasions called to advise that I be extremely prudent in this dangerous activity because the Germans were keeping an eye on me particularly.

Thus I was able to send the Allies two months advance notice of the German attack against Russia, and of raids to be made in certain quarters of Paris against Jews and communists.

An extremely important fact was that with the support of President Laval we succeeded in saving General Juin from being arrested and deported to Germany, and prevented General de Lattre de Tassigny from being transferred from the prison of Riom, where he was guarded by Frenchmen, to a German fortress in Silesia under SS guard.

These facts are undeniable. They are proved by the declarations of important persons, attached to this present testimony.[1]

Through my contacts with the German services I was able to obtain passes for North Africans who were sent as liaison agents by the heads of intelligence networks. In the same way much other information was obtained from the same German sources and sent to the Allies, particularly through M. Noedts, director-general of general intelligence at the prefecture of police. He was a member of the Samson network and passed his information to M. Marcepoil, a lawyer and the Paris delegate of the intelligence service in London.

Information was also sent through M. Luce, of the general intelligence

1. [Not on deposit.]

service, now attached to the Tribunal of Paris, through M. Louit, a police commissioner, who was later condemned to death by the Germans and is today in the prefecture of police; through Colonel Touny, founder and president of the OCM, who was shot in 1944 by the Germans, and whose body rests at the Mont-Valérien; and through Mlle Cantan-Bacara, founder and president of the *La Flamme Française* network. All the testimony of these persons is attached to my report.[1]

Rescues of French Persons. Thanks to President Laval, who supported with all his efforts and all his heart my activities on behalf of Jews, Freemasons, and communists who had been arrested by the Gestapo and in many cases condemned to death, we were able to save hundreds of French people with no distinction as to their origin, their politics, or their religion. For example, we saved two young men condemned to death for their activity in the resistance, M. Bechu and M. Jacquard; their testimony to this effect is attached to this report.[1]

I must also call attention to the fact that in 1944 I went to President Laval to report two arrests: that of M. Jacob, *Syndic* [responsible spokesman] of the association of stock exchange agents and a brother-in-law of General Catroux; and that of M. Boissarie, a lawyer. M. Jacob is one of my friends, and M. Boissarie is the nephew of one of my intimate friends. Thanks to our combined efforts, the brother-in-law of General Catroux and the man who is now attorney-general of the Republic were not deported to Germany, and arrangements were made to allow them to escape without being troubled further.

I add to my declaration several statements which complete the details of the facts cited above.[1]

No comment is needed in any of these cases. The facts prove in a categorical and clear way that almost all of the hundred thousand North Africans living in France remained absolutely faithful to France alone. I have not wished to speak of all the purely administrative details through which the work for North Africans was done thanks to the sympathy President Laval felt for the Mohammedans. But it is certain that we were able to keep the North Africans wholeheartedly and exclusively on the side of France, not only through ardent propaganda, secret and continuous, which was carried on under our direction in all Mohammedan circles in France, but also by obtaining substantial and material advantages for them through our mission during the years 1943 and 1944. Let any North African or any Mohammedan be questioned; not one will be found who does not pay homage to all that was done for his people; not one can be found who will not testify that during the terrible trials of the occupation all these French North Africans stayed resolutely and completely faithful to France.

(Document No. 61)

Fr. ed. 774-777

Paris, *26 May 1948*

M. GUILLAUME
(Général Maurice Guillaume)

1. [Not on deposit.]

PART THREE

MILITARY

CHAPTER XV

ARMY AND NAVY

THE ARMISTICE OF 1940

MAXIME WEYGAND

General of the Army

The original cause of division among the French people, it is known, was the conclusion of the armistice of 1940 by Maréchal Pétain.

After the front had been broken at Sedan and the Allied armies had been split into two parts, after the battles of Flanders and Dunkirk, and after the seven days of fighting in the battle of France, the government and the Army Command agreed in their judgment that the French armies, cut to pieces and now alone, were incapable of preventing the enemy from conquering the entire territory of the country.

But their opinion differed as to the correct solution of this military situation. The High Command asked that an armistice should be concluded. The government refused and adopted the following program: it would go to North Africa, where the struggle would be continued, while the armies fighting in France would surrender and the territory of France would be abandoned to the enemy. So far as can be seen from the arguments and documents presented, this program of the government was impossible to realize. The Commander-in-Chief refused to capitulate and persisted in demanding an armistice. The government renounced its program and resigned. The armistice was then asked for, and concluded, by the government of Maréchal Pétain.

General de Gaulle, who had the use of the radio transmitters of the BBC, nonetheless continued to proclaim far and wide that the government's program would have assured the safety of the country and that the armistice, which he referred to as a capitulation, constituted an act of treason. His memoirs of the war present the events of June 1940, summarized above, in the same light.

It is necessary that so grave an inexactitude of history shall not be allowed to continue any longer. It is to dissipate every ambiguity and to re-establish the truth that I have appealed to the judgment of the men of today and of the historians of the future and have written a book from which I here present the two principal chapters.

Armistice and Capitulation [1]

When General de Gaulle speaks of the act which put an end to hostilities in 1940 he usually uses the word 'capitulation,' sometimes the word 'armistice.' In one place he even uses the two words, only two lines apart, to define the same act. Yet each of these words has in military and political language its own meaning, which makes it impossible either to use the words indifferently one for the other, or to confuse the two acts which they indicate. Either way it is a very serious error.

An armistice is a convention, both political and military in character, by virtue of which the belligerents undertake to suspend hostilities. The signature of an armistice leaves the state of war in existence. An armistice is a matter for governments, because governments alone have the power to bring hostilities to a stop, in the same way that they alone have the power to decide to commence hostilities. Military or civilian authorities when asked to sign an armistice convention can do so only if they have received special powers from their governments.

A short summary of historic facts with reference to the last hundred years makes any doubt on this point impossible. On 24 January 1871 Jules Favre, Minister of Foreign Affairs in the government of National Defense, went to Versailles to see the German chancellor in order ask for the conclusion of an armistice. He returned to Paris that evening to report to his colleagues the result of that interview; on that day the government took no decision. On the following day the government charged Jules Favre, this time with full powers, to see the chancellor again. On 26 January the two negotiators came to an agreement on principles, but Mr. von Bismarck demanded that anofficer should be present in order to agree with him on the clauses for the suspension of fighting. It was on the 27th that these clauses were discussed by Jules Favre, this time accompanied by General de Beaufort. On the 28th, signatures were exchanged. The *Journal Officiel* had already announced on the 27th the cessation of hostilities.

In 1918 the request for an armistice was addressed by the German chancellor to the President of the United States on 5 October. Negotiations between the Allies for establishing the conditions lasted until 4 November. During these debates, M. Clemenceau had occasion to inform Maréchal Foch specifically that his powers were limited in this matter to making proposals to the governments, the power of decision belonging to the governments alone. The Supreme Council charged Maréchal Foch and Admiral Sir Rosslyn Wemyss, First Sea Lord, with the mission of presenting the definitive text of the convention to the Germans, at the same time giving these two emissaries the power to sign the convention.

In May 1945, the Allied governments made the signature by Germany of a convention of unconditional capitulation the only condition for the cessation of hostilities, designed to show in that way that Germany must surrender without any right to further discussion. It was on the order of these governments that the Allied commanders-in-chief or their delegates signed this convention in Berlin on 9 May.

Finally I call attention to the declaration, already cited, made by

---

1. Chapter IV of my book *En lisant les Mémoires de Guerre du Général de Gaulle,* which I deposit with the Hoover War Library at the same time as this present note.

M. Reynaud at the Supreme Council held at Briare on 11 June 1940. The President of the Council emphasized, according to the minutes, "that the Commander-in-Chief has just given the most authoritative opinion on the military aspect of the question. But the problem of the continuation of the war is a political problem and is a matter for government decision."

Capitulation on the other hand is an act of an exclusively military character. It is a surrender after an agreement has been concluded with the enemy by the commander of a fortified place or by the commander of a force which lays down its arms in open country. Capitulation in open country is punished by death or by removal from military service. The following is the text of article 324 of the [French] Code of Military Justice: "Every commander of an armed force who capitulates in open country is punished (1) by death with military degradation if the result of the capitulation was the laying down of the arms of the force, or if before verbal and written negotiations he has not done everything compatible with duty and honor; (2) by removal from military service in other cases."

It is possible to think that General de Gaulle, who does know how to write, uses the word 'capitulation' not in its proper sense, but in order to qualify the armistice as a dishonorable action. That is to play on words and to create a confusion that causes error. For in the case with which we are dealing there are two opposing solutions of the cessation of hostilities: that of an 'armistice' demanded by the Commander-in-Chief, and that of a 'capitulation' of the armies asked for by the President of the Council, the two words being taken in their proper sense and defining different acts which have a precise definition from the military point of view. For the sake of the French army which I had the honor to command in these tragic circumstances, as well for my own sake, it is necessary not to be content with ambiguities but to know what we are talking about. Let us therefore recall the facts in detail.

At Bordeaux on 15 June [1940] at about quarter to four in the afternoon I had a private interview with M. Reynaud. He told me of his anguish in the matter of the decision which had to be taken. In his mind the problem was reduced to a dilemma; he could either act as Queen Wilhelmina of Holland had done in going to England and leaving to the Chief of Staff of her army the task of laying down their arms, or he could follow the action of the King of the Belgians who had stayed with his people after having negotiated with the Germans for cessation of hostilities. The President of the Council had chosen. He would not ask for an armistice and if necessary he would leave France.

It seemed to me unimaginable, and I said so at this point in our talk, that in a democracy, where the power rests on the will of the people, the people's representative could even dream of not sharing the fate of the masses, and of abandoning them, without support, to the hardships of an occupation by leaving the national soil in the hour of peril. M. Reynaud then suggested to me that I should do as the Chief of Staff for Holland had done, that is to capitulate with the land forces. I rejected this proposal both indignantly and resolutely, telling him that I would never agree to stain our flag with such shame. With this declaration on my part our interview came to an end.

It was then time for M. Reynaud to go to the Council of Ministers. Admiral Darlan and I were heard and I renewed my demand for an armistice.

We left the Council meeting room at twenty minutes to five. In case we could be of any possible use to the government we waited in the huge hall at the side, which was open to a winter garden and a gallery in which there also waited many officials and officers who had accompanied the ministers or commanders-in-chief. At five minutes to six the Council ended. On coming out the President of the Council came directly to me. "The ministers," he told me, "have decided that the land forces alone should capitulate and this capitulation must be asked for by the Commander-in-Chief." In order to render any ambiguity impossible I stepped back and told him again, speaking very loudly so that everyone could hear me, that I would never agree to soil our flag with such a stain. I reported this incident to the President of the Republic, in the presence of the President of the Council and Maréchal Pétain, and left for my head-quarters.

On the following day, 16 June [1940], I was unable to reach Bordeaux until after the Council of Ministers had been held. I presented myself to the President of the Republic and to the President of the Council and reported the increasing seriousness of the military situation. Another Council of Ministers was held at about five o'clock in the afternoon; I was not summoned. I was told that the ministers continued to insist on the capitulation of the land army and that they demanded my removal. But the council broke up without anything having been decided. In the evening M. Reynaud resigned and Maréchal Pétain was called on by the President of the Republic to form a new government which during that same night sent to the German government a request for an armistice. Such are the facts, and they leave absolutely no possibility of misunderstanding.

In order to reason fairly it must be recalled that General de Gaulle has said definitely in his memoirs, and repeated it several times, that the final battle was lost and that the recovery of the situation had to be sought outside of France. "On 30 May [1940] the battle of France was already lost, for all practical purposes. If the situation could not be put right in the homeland it would have to be put right outside it. The situation on the Marne could be corrected only on the Mediterranean.". . . "To get control once more it would have been necessary to disengage oneself from the tempest, go to Africa, and begin everything again from there. This implied extreme measures, a change in the High Command, the removal of the Maréchal and half of the ministers, a complete rupture with certain influences, and an acceptance of the idea that the homeland would be occupied by the enemy; in short, in an unprecedented situation it was necessary to abandon, whatever the risk, the ordinary pattern and procedures."

Such was the government program which was to be made possible by capitulation. As Commander-in-Chief I had the duty of estimating the value of the program and the possibilities of its realization. In my judgment it was a program that could not be realized; this is a subject of capital importance and I will deal with it thoroughly in the following chapter. But my judgment in this matter was one of the bases on which rested the unchanging resoluteness of my conduct from the moment on 12 June [1940] when I asked the government to conclude an armistice; that is why I present this judgment here. I therefore estimated the value of all the elements of judgment available to me: the state of our armies and the impossibility of receiving any serious and immediate support from our Allies; the necessity of saving a part of our national territory and our resources from enemy occupation, and of assuring in that way its political and economic existence; the possibility of maintaining a certain military force; the capital advantage of keeping the French fleet and French possessions overseas, because it was our determination, as is shown by the instructions given to our plenipotentiary, to refuse formally, no matter what the consequences might be, any demand of which the effect would be to place those naval forces or those overseas domains in the hands of the enemy. After carefully weighing all these considerations I decided to ask for an armistice and I refused to submit to an order to capitulate.[1]

One of the determining reasons on which the government solution was based was its anxiety not to break the word of honor given to England on 28 March 1940 and not to enter of its own accord into any negotiations with the enemy. Now it is important to know that the President of the Council said that he was ready to give me a written order to capitulate.[2] If therefore I had been able to agree to the capitulation of the armies, the government would have shared the shame. The capitulation of Dupont at Baylen and of Bazaine at Metz were those of isolated military chiefs hundreds of kilometers from their own government or deprived of all means of communication with their government. They acted on their own authority. But at Bordeaux, in a city still free of the enemy, where the Chief of the Government with his ministers, and with the confirmation of the authority of the President of the Republic available, was in constant contact with the Commander-in-Chief, the situation was entirely different. If, in spite of everything, I had been willing to commit such an act of infamy, the government with which I passed these tragic hours, and which implored me to commit it, would have been dragged into dishonor. In any case another situation was open to the government, that of allowing hostilities to continue and to embark for Africa under cover of the final resistance of the armies. The armies would have continued to fight as it was their duty to do. I would have obeyed, as was my duty, as long as it was a question of fighting. General Georges and I had already considered this extremity and we had agreed to share the fate of our armies to the very end, refusing to leave the national soil.

To sum up, I refused to capitulate because I was responsible for the honor of the army and convinced that an armistice was the solution to be sought. Thus I accepted my responsibilities and was entirely ready to bear the consequences. I would have understood it if they had said to

1. The complete support given to my decision by Maréchal Pétain certainly carried great weight, and doubtless was the determining factor in the decision of the Government. But I must make it clear that I took my responsibility as a military chief in demanding the armistice, without being influenced by any suggestion, and without any pressure being brought to bear on me.

2. Extract from the testimony of General de Villelume before the Commission of of Enquiry of the National Assembly: "But M. Paul Reynaud refused to (put a stop to hostilities) by means of an armistice. He envisaged only one solution, the capitulation of the army. When I reached Bordeaux, a few hours after him, he showed me a letter which he had just written to General Weygand asking him to capitulate, a letter which however was not sent so far as I know."

M. Reynaud said afterwards, "I asked him to cease fire." But this expression,"cease fire," came to his mind only much later, after he had returned from Germany. In fact it was always a matter of "capitulation." Further, here are my notes for Saturday 15 June [1940]: "If the general," M. Paul Reynaud said to me, "wishes to bring hostilities to an end he has only to capitulate with his entire army."

me: you do not want to capitulate; continue then to fight. I would have understood it if they had removed me from my command or if they had brought me before a Council of War for disobedience. I am a soldier and I did not claim the right to impose my will on the government of the Republic. But I did act in accordance with the right which can be denied to no man, and least of all to a chief, to act according to the commands of his conscience and of his honor. If I was wrong and if the government was firmly convinced that the safety of the country depended on the solution which it declared as correct, then the government's duty was to impose that solution and to take action against me. My will prevailed only through the government's resignation from power.

That is why I cannot pass over, without surprise and indignation, the fact that General de Gaulle wrote that the Commander-in-Chief "went in search of the solution available to him, namely capitulation"—here his usual little insult turns up again. "But since he had no intention of assuming the responsibility his method was to lead the government to assume it."

I have already said what I think of attributing to others the lowest and most cowardly motives. I regret to have to mention the subject again.

Let me be perfectly clear. There has been no attempt in these pages to show that I was right in asking for an armistice. I was convinced that I was right and otherwise I would not have asked for it; I am still convinced, and opinions in accord with mine are not lacking (Annex XVIII).[1] But I am obliged to point out, however modest I may sometimes be considered, that in these decisive circumstances I was the only one who took his responsibilities as military chief, and that the government, which General de Gaulle advised and of which he was a member, avoided its own responsibilities by resigning.

I am also obliged to declare that the creation of an ambiguity between capitulation and armistice has given birth to, and has perpetuated, an error in history against which I protest with absolute conviction and all my strength.

Transfer of the Struggle to North Africa[2]

Let us examine now in full objectivity the items of the government program for transferring armed resistance to North Africa.

To my note of 29 May [1940] informing the President of the Council of the conditions under which the battle for France was about to take place, M. Reynaud replied on the same day.[3] In the first part of his reply he expressed his agreement with my demand for reinforcements from the English. In the second part he asked me to organize a national fortified redoubt[4] in Brittany strong enough to resist for a considerable time; at the end of the message he informed me for the first time of his intention to

1. See page 231 of my book, *En lisant les Mémoires de Guerre du Général de Gaulle*, deposited with the Hoover War Library at the same time as this note.
2. Chapter V of my book, *En lisant les Mémoires de Guerre du Général de Gaulle*, deposited with the Hoover War Library at the same time as this note.
3. Annex V, p. 174, of the same book.
4. I made the obvious comments on the Brittany redoubt, a conception to which General de Gaulle says that he agreed only slowly.

strengthen the defense of North Africa. "I add that it is my intention to call up two military age-groups and to send them to North Africa in order that they may contribute to its defense with arms purchased abroad."[1]

The battle for France had been raging for five days when on 10 June [1940] I gave the President of the Council a new note explaining the gravity of the situation. His reply dated the 13th reached me on the 14th, two days after my demand that an armistice should be concluded had been sent to the Council of Ministers. Our armies, overwhelmed along the Seine and the Marne, were already in retreat. His reply first indicated the objectives which the armies should plan to protect during their retreat, and concluded, "If we fail we can still establish and organize the means of struggle in our Empire, making use of the freedom of the seas."

These were projects in early stages of conception, without order, and without any measures for preparing their realization.

Let us follow now in the text of the *Mémoires* how the same conception was developing in the thought of General de Gaulle. On 30 May [1940] he has no illusions; "If the situation cannot be corrected in the homeland it will have to be put right elsewhere. The Empire, the fleet, the people, and the whole world still exist." He then reproaches the High Command for having clung to the narrow field of the French homeland and for not having "played its ace, of enormous spaces, unlimited resources, and high speeds, thus bringing in the huge distant territories, all the alliance, and the seas."

In General de Gaulle's Corneillian [heroic: here used ironically] colloquy of 8 June [1940] the same idea is presented: "And the world, and the Empire?" On 10 June: "A recovery like that of the Marne [1914] was possible, this time on the Mediterranean." Finally, at the moment when M. Reynaud resigned: "To get control once more it would have been necessary to disengage oneself from the tempest, go to Africa, and begin everything again from there." Speaking of the day of 22 June he has told the reader of the Government's hesitations: "Two solutions were considered: Bordeaux or Quimper? . . . No formal decision was taken . . . of course I was in favor of Quimper, though I had no illusions as to the possibility of holding out in Brittany. But if the government had been evacuated to Quimper it would have had, sooner or later, no other way out than to take to the sea; there would have been no free area in Brittany because the Germans would necessarily occupy it in connection with their action against the English. Once on the ocean the ministers would most probably go to Africa, either directly or after having made a stop in England."

It can be seen that everything which had to do with this idea of going to Africa remained vague and hypothetical, and it will be noted how devious was the route envisaged by General de Gaulle, struggling with the indecision of the President of the Council, as the means of reaching a harbor of safety, that Africa whose name alone seemed to be a sheet-anchor but nothing more than a name, as no orders had been issued by the government responsible for the conduct of the war.

We must hasten to note that the Under-Secretary of State for War [General de Gaulle] from the time he took up his post on 7 June [1940] had

---

1. The time needed for execution when this intention takes the form of an order should be noted; to mobilize 500,000 men, transport them to Africa, train them, and obtain delivery of the arms to be bought abroad, would take at least four months.

teamed up with the general staff of the army in working out a plan for transporting as many units as possible to North Africa. Included were "the two classes of recruits who were being trained in the depots of the west and south of France. . . the navy estimated at 500,000 tons the additional cargo ships which would be necessary . . . this help would have to be asked from England. . . ."

During a first journey to England on 8 June General de Gaulle notes the determination of the Prime Minister and his refusal to lend the aid of of the British air force; apparently the general did not then raise the question of the shipping which we lacked, as he says nothing about it. General de Gaulle's second stay in London, on 16 June, was intended chiefly "to secure the aid of the English in our sea transport." In terms of considerable politeness toward our Allies the general gives us to understand that he did not obtain a single ton.

But let us turn to the facts, to a study of the elements of the actual problem posed by the government's conception. Let us examine successively what forces were available in North Africa in June 1940, with what reinforcements the homeland could increase their strength, what attacks North Africa would have to resist, and what effect the time factor would have on the entire problem.

In dealing with the first of these questions I wish to pay homage to the violent and patriotic reaction of General Noguès when he learned that Germany had been asked for an armistice. He judged that Africa was able to continue the struggle and he presented his attitude to the government in the most disapproving terms. As the days went by he was obliged to realize that France was unable to furnish him the help which he judged to be indispensable for the effectiveness of the aggressive defense which he had in mind and with a wounded heart he had to abandon his noble project.

What I knew of the insufficiency of the forces under General Noguès' orders and of the general military situation had never allowed me to share his opinion for even a single moment. The North Africa army had been stripped of all the units which it seemed possible to call to France without compromising its ability to resist an Italian attack from southern Tunisia. From September 1939 to 1 June 1940 North Africa had furnished the homeland 25 infantry regiments, 2 cavalry regiments, 4 groups of 75-mm artillery, 2 groups of 155-mm artillery, 1 tank battalion, 2 battalions of Senegalese, and some reinforcements which were not in the form of units. The total had been 2,975 officers, 9,370 noncommissioned officers, and 157,500 men.

At the beginning of June [1940] there remained in North Africa forces of a paper strength of 8 divisions. They were divided among 3 active divisions, 2 Moroccan divisions, and 3 territorial divisions responsible for internal security; in other words, between Sahara units [Algerian native units, regular army], fortress units recently created, and units under instruction in the depots. Aside from the goums and the divisions guarding the Tripolitan front these units were of very mediocre combat value. Some of them had just been hurriedly reorganized after the first German successes on the Somme. In the existing divisions [in North Africa] there was a considerable deficiency of anti-tank and anti-aircraft artillery, of mortars, and of communications equipment. There was no modern anti-aircraft equipment except for the batteries assigned to the defense of Bizerte and of Mers-el-Kébir. There was no rapid fire heavy artillery. The number of modern rifles was insufficient to arm all the men who had been mobilized.

The documents appearing in annexes VII, VIII, IX, X, and XI,[1] leave no doubt concerning these deficiencies. They are taken from depositions made under oath before the National Assembly's Commission of Enquiry on Events from 1933 to 1945, by officers belonging to the General Staff of General Noguès, to the cabinet of the President of the Council, and by an officer of the general staff whom I sent on a mission to Africa; there is also the testimony of a high officer of the Navy in the trial of Maréchal Pétain.[2]

I ask the reader to have the patience to study these extracts carefully. It is clearly shown that, as I have always stated, North Africa was unable to offer by means of its own forces any useful resistance to the armies of the enemy.

To what extent could it have been reinforced from the homeland?

"During the day of 12 [June 1940]," the *Mémoires* state, "I worked with General Colson on a plan of transport to North Africa. To tell the truth, the events which I had witnessed on the previous day and the isolation in which I was then placed made me fear that the spirit of abandonment had gained too much ground and that the plan would never be used. However, I was resolved to do everything in my power to make the government adopt the plan and impose it on the High Command." I have found no further details about this statement. I knew nothing at that time of any such work undertaken by the general staff of the army, whose task it certainly was. On my return from Germany [after the war] I read that the Under-Secretary of State for War [General de Gaulle] planned on 13 June to embark for Africa the 500,000 men available in the depots, together with the officers and technical units saved from our forces in Belgium, with 3 divisions to come from the Army of the Alps. I do not know whether this information is correct. But I can say clearly that it was fantastic. All the officers and French forces which it had been possible to embark at Dunkirk had been urgently taken from England to France, rearmed with equipment just coming from the factories, and sent into the battle again. As for the Army of the Alps, attacked since 10 June by Italian forces of considerable strength, it was truly unthinkable that 3 or 4 divisions could be taken from it just when they were being so remarkably used in a resistance which continued victoriously until the end of hostilities.

Regarding any forces which might have been sent from France to North Africa, the following is an extract from a note submitted on 7 June [1940] by General de Villelume to the President of the Council, to whose cabinet he was attached.

"There are at present in the interior and apart from territorial formations (which include 625,000 men) and the older classes which have been sent back to their homes for the present (1,000,000 men): (1) units immediately available for the armies, which are soon to be sent to the armies in their entirety, totalling 310,000 men; and (2) units under instruction which will be available about 1 August, totalling 180,000 men.

"All these units must remain in France.

"On the other hand it would be useful to send the following to North

---

1. See p. 197 ff of my book, *En lisant les Mémoires de Guerre du Général de Gaulle*, deposited with the Hoover War Library at the same time as this note.
2. The documents of both the enquiry and the trial were published and placed on sale.

Africa: (1) a first contingent of 120,000 recruits who are to be called up on 8 and 9 June; and (2) a second contingent, not called up, of 234,000 men.

"The problems involved here are as follows: (1) transport for 60,000 men per month if Italy is hostile or 90,000 men per month if Italy is not hostile so that if we use only our own resources we must ask the English for ships; (2) the problem of quarters, accommodation for only 20,000 now being available; (3) the problem of food supplies; and (4) the medical and sanitary problem."

In regard to these last three problems, General Noguès had telegraphed on 2 June [1940] that neither Algeria nor Morocco possessed quarters or sleeping and camping supplies necessary for such numbers; as far as clothing and arms were concerned all such supplies must be furnished by the home-land; for all training, the officers and equipment necessary must also come from France; and as for health and sanitary matters the incorporation of such forces in Africa under such precarious conditions and at the beginning of the hot season presented very serious difficulties. North Africa was not in a position to receive more than 20,000 men and could not even receive that many until the necessary arrangements had been made (Annex XII).[1]

General de Villelume states that his note was given to General de Gaulle by the President of the Council who told him to deal with the question, and that General de Gaulle on 9 July[2] [1940] issued the following order: (1) to evacuate urgently, to the destination already arranged, the heavier sections of the Ministry of War; and (2) to assign these destinations simultaneously to recruits in accordance to their importance: (a) Brittany, (b) North Africa, and (c) the Southwest.

Finally, to complete the statement on the reinforcement of North Africa by land forces, we must recall the negative result of the request made in London by General de Gaulle on 16 June [1940] "to arrange the aid of the English for our transport."

If all the forces for the transfer to Africa had been immediately available, which was not the case, and if all the ships necessary for their transport had been available, which also was not the case, and if the means of quartering and instructing them had existed in North Africa, which was not the case, nevertheless large-scale embarkation in the port of Bordeaux or in the ports of the Mediterranean, and the departure of the transport from these ports, would have been made practically impossible by the action of the German and Italian planes which ruled the skies of France (Annex XIII).[3]

The only reinforcement which could reach North Africa at this time was that of the aviation. Of course only those could go across which were able to fly over the Mediterranean, if necessary with a landing in Corsica. This passage was undertaken, with my agreement, from 15 June [1940] when, as the battle continued, our air squadrons were too directly threatened with destruction on their own airfields. The number of planes which crossed can be estimated at 700. Included were planes of the older types unfit for combat, and a considerable number of pursuit planes and of

---

1. See p. 211 of my book, *En lisant les Mémoires de Guerre du Général de Gaulle*, deposited with the Hoover War Library at the same time as this note.

2. [June].

3. See p. 213 of my book, *En lisant les Mémoires de Guerre du Général de Gaulle*, deposited with the Hoover War Library at the same time as this note.

first class pilots. But these squadrons arrived without their maintenance units and found in Africa only reduced stocks including a limited number of medium-sized bombs and no spare parts. Annex XIV[1] gives the opinion of the commanding air general for North Africa on the feeble combat power of these planes.

Such were the feeble forces available to oppose a large army with a powerful aviation, already actively exploiting its success. What attacks could they have resisted?

Masters of the entire area of France, the Germans would have been in direct contact with continental and insular Italy, as well as with Spain; thus without a break they could have attacked North Africa, all the more vigorously as the French government would have taken refuge there.[2] They had large forces available for such an undertaking as they had no adversary to fear on the continent of Europe since Russia was then their ally. North Africa could be attacked through Tunisia from Tripoli, already occupied by a strong Italian army which could be easily reinforced. North Africa could also be attacked through Spanish Morocco whose army had been increased to over 100,000 men, while Spain, passing from neutrality to a state of non-belligerence, had seized Tangier. Admitting that General Franco would not have wished to run the risk of entering the war, he could, nevertheless, merely open the way to the German forces whose landing in Africa would thus be effected through a friendly bridgehead. Maréchal Pétain knew all that, which was certainly the subject of his interview with General Franco.

The weakness of the Gibraltar defenses would not have allowed the English to oppose the Germans. The memoirs of Sir Samuel Hoare, of which an extract appeared in the *New York Times* in April 1946, established this point: "In the spring of 1940, the defenses of Gibraltar were still extremely weak, so weak that the governor of Gibraltar, Sir Oliver R. Hiddel, continually begged me to arrange three months of peace so that he could improve them. Heavy guns from Germany were already installed on the Spanish hills which dominate the straits. Tangier was already in Spanish hands and there was a large army in Spanish Morocco. With France out of the fight, our little army under reorganization, and the United States neutral, we would have been able to do nothing in the summer of 1940 to stop a German movement across Spain toward Africa. Hitler certainly had such a plan in mind."

On the other hand the Italian bases in Sicily and Sardinia were suitable for aero-naval action against Bizerte and Mers-el-Kébir. These undertakings would have broken up our means of defense along the thousands of kilometers of land and sea frontiers, and North Africa would have been powerless to oppose them. The Franco-British naval forces and our pursuit planes would have made the enemy pay a high price for his crossing on to African soil. But they would not have been able to prevent a crossing of the Sicilian channel and the straits of Gibraltar.[3]

1. See p. 215 of the same book.
2. It is useful to recall that the Germans soon realized the error they had committed in not occupying an area of such strategic value. They demanded from France on 16 July [1940], less than a month after the signing of the armistice, that the bases, ports, and railways of North Africa be placed at their disposition. Maréchal Pétain and his government, resting solidly on the terms of the armistice convention, formally refused.
3. British naval forces in the Mediterranean had been reduced in order to protect the threatened British homeland. A considerable number of their units had been made less available by work which was then in hand in fitting them with anti-aircraft artillery. The British planes at Gibraltar were reduced in number.

Thus the African Army, reduced to little more than its own forces, and struggling against infinitely superior armies both in numbers and equipment, which had a possibility of continuous reinforcement, would certainly have honored its traditions of valor and combative ardor but would have been unable to offer any effective resistance. This was the opinion which I expressed. It was shared by the chief of our naval forces.[1]

As for the time factor, it had to be considered from two points of view. The situation to be dealt with was so tense that each day and even each hour had its importance. None of the measures considered took this urgency into account. On the other hand it was not a question of winning some temporary success. It was necessary to hold out not for months but for years, this being the length of time recognized as necessary in order that the Anglo-Saxon armament should obtain a sufficient degree of power to enable it to intervene effectively. North Africa had none of the resources which would have enabled it to maintain a prolonged struggle. It did not have even the slightest war industry and it would have had to receive from France not only the means of completing its stocks of ammunition but also the French officers indispensable for the leadership of indigenous troops, already insufficient in number.

To transfer the struggle to North Africa in June 1940 would have been to lose it.

When decisions on which depend the fate of a country must be made, when the question to be decided is that of transferring the struggle to a new theater across the sea, then imagination, though indispensable in conception, is not sufficient. For execution, apart from moral factors there are imperative material factors: the forces, their quality, their proportions, the distances, the time available. It was a true evaluation of these factors which had to be obtained in order to prepare a practical plan. To take no account of them was to show unpardonable carelessness.

If the idea of the strategic role of North Africa as a part of the complete plan of national defense had been considered at the right time it would have led to the preparation of a special operating program with provisions for planning and execution, covering land forces, naval forces, and air forces, with reference to numbers, armaments, stocks, bases, and transport, some of these measures to be decided on after agreement with our Ally. For example, a line of defense would have been planned and prepared running from Cévennes to the Alps, broadly protecting Provence and its ports and the planned embarking operations. Thus if the grave decision of abandoning the whole of the national territory had been reached the Mediterranean could have been the basis of a recovery like that of the Marne.

But to envisage an enterprise of this scale for the first time on 29 May [1940], to decide on it in the total absence of preparation and without any measures of execution having been foreseen or studied—such an improvisation would have been nothing more than fantasy. "Freed of all contact with the facts they could think boldly," I might say, paraphrasing Balzac. These fantasies and dreams, even when expressed in a style that

1. The following is the conclusion of a note which Admiral Darlan sent me on 14 June [1940]: "To sum up, the continuation of the struggle in Africa would result in the more or less rapid loss of this territory because the British, particularly if they are threatened in their own island—and they will be—can send nothing substantial to Africa for many months and by the time they do finally send aid there will be no ports in Africa."

suggests endless resources, enormous spaces, and terrific speeds, all of them nothing but mirages at the moment when they were summoned up, are utterly useless in war, "an art that is all made of execution," and terribly realistic. The resolutions so tardily envisaged by the President of the Council and his government for the safety of France were, happily, utterly impractical; they would have led to the slavery of the homeland and the loss of North Africa.

(Document No. 262)
Fr. ed. 783-794

Paris, 28 March 1955

WEYGAND
Maxime Weygand

General of the Army, who commanded the French armies from 1931 to 1934, and was recalled to command them again in May 1940; Member of the French Academy

THE ARMISTICE ARMY
(1940-1942)

GEORGES REVERS
General

The armistice of 25 June 1940 officially recognized the defeat of France. Conquered, crushed, and occupied, at first in part and then totally, our country was to live through a material and moral crisis of which the sequels have not yet been entirely effaced today.

The army was beaten. It emerged from the trial weakened, wounded, and in part discredited. It is true that it had not found at its head such glorious chiefs as Joffre in 1914 or Foch in 1918. But whose fault was that? Who had chosen the chiefs who led the army into battle in 1939 and 1940?

The army did not have the equipment it desired, but who from 1919 to 1939 had refused to accept the costs of renewing its equipment?

Did the army find among its citizen-soldiers of 1940 the virtues of patriotism and sacrifice which were the glory of the men of Charleroi, the Marne, Verdun, and the Dardanelles?

On the country itself and its government must fall a large part of the responsibility for the defeat. The army did not deserve to bear alone the disgrace of misfortune.

That was the truth of 1940. That is still the truth in 1954. It is well to remember and to ponder.

Though the armistice was received by many French people with an unworthy feeling of relief, it must be affirmed to the honor of the army and of its leaders that they had an unhesitating sense of what they owed the fatherland.

Even before the obligations which the enemy intended to impose upon us were known, orders, some official and the others clandestine, were being issued to limit the disaster with a view to preparing the future rebirth [of the army]. It was necessary at the moment to surrender to the heavy demands of the adversary but it was also imperative to look to the future and therefore to save the army's corps of officers, its equipment, the Empire, and first of all Africa.

By 29 June [1940] measures for regrouping the army, for reorganizing it, for the taking of its inventories, and for making new preparations were already being taken. Several days later, at the beginning of July, the commanding officers of the armies and of the regions each received a handwritten letter from General Colson, Chief of the General Staff, asking them to camouflage equipment and supplies.

Provisional conditions of which we received notice reduced our forces to about one hundred thousand, of whom four thousand were officers. The air force was to be disarmed and placed under supervision. The navy was to leave the seas and enter ports, also under supervision. In Africa the total number of men was to be strictly limited. As a first approximation less than 50,000 men, or perhaps only 30,000, was spoken of as the permitted figure.

The great concern of the High Command at this time—and this remained true no matter what chiefs succeeded each other at Vichy: Weygand, Darlan, Colson, Picquendar, Verneau, and Revers—was to obtain from the occupation authorities the greatest possible means, chiefly for Africa, and to construct rapidly an army of the highest quality.

Our first proposals on 23 July [1940] were rejected by the conqueror. We were definitely ordered to reduce our force to eight military divisions arranged in two divisional groups. Each division was to include one staff group, three infantry regiments, one cavalry regiment, one artillery regiment, and engineering, communications and supply services. There was to be one legion of the Guard, as well.

In addition we were allowed two brigades of cavalry, horse-mounted. The motorization of this tiny army was strictly reduced and its armament was not very modern.

In North Africa, the original demand of our adversaries, particularly the Italians, was that the force be reduced to 30,000 men. Our intense efforts, strengthened by the effect of [British] actions such as those at Mers-el-Kébir and Dakar, enabled us to achieve a provisional allowance of 110,000 men.

Throughout two years of bitter discussions, in which we took advantage of every opportunity, we succeeded in maintaining this provisional arrangement, increasing our numbers, and securing as abundant an equipment as was possible.

The reduction in the size of the French army raised serious problems. In the first place, Germany forbade any form of conscription and made it a condition that all engagements should be for long terms. It was impossible to follow these instructions immediately. Permission had to be obtained to keep the youngest soldiers, those of the recruiting class of 1940, under the colors.

The demobilization of men who were not to be kept was difficult, equally because of the large numbers who were thus returned to civilian life and because of the disorganization of transport at that time. Finally, many of them found great practical and psychological difficulty in going back into the occupied zone. Officers and noncommissioned officers had to be cruelly reduced in number. Within a very short time, the total number of officers had to be reduced to 10,000, including Africa, although there had been over 30,000 in 1939. Very few of them could leave the army without a great deal of anxiety as to their means of living.

Above all, giving first place in their thoughts to the future and the rebirth of the army, the High Command desired to keep within its own control as much of its resources as possible.

A civilian corps was therefore created, based on the old army organization; administrative staffs were turned into civilians; and there were even some new corps created, such as the "chanceliers" [recorders or secretarial staff] of the General Staff, "administrative assistants" for combat units, a "building service" for the engineers. . .

Finally, many army services such as the geographic service and the armament manufacture service were transferred to such civilian ministries as those of Public Works and Industrial Production.

Some civilian government administrations received a certain number of military men. Some officers were taken into the prefectoral corps and some officers and noncommissioned officers into the government service for forest conservation.

The armistice forbade any form of conscription and we were obliged to disband the recruiting service. But there again the obligation was evaded. Thanks to the initiative of the Controller-General, Carmille, there was established a statistical and demographic service using the most modern mechanical equipment. The purpose of this service was to register and study the entire population as it was at the moment and in all its changes. (Controller-General Carmille was arrested and died in deportation.)

Demobilization documents were carefully drawn up in such a way that the military situation of each man would be known and kept up to date, together with his civilian status, to show his activity, domicile, family, etc.

With these facts available, and by making use of the new recording machines, mobilization was a possibility. This possibility was to be made use of.

The ban on all conscription prevented us from bringing together and training our young men. The establishment of youth camps was entrusted to General de la Porte du Theil; these camps, though military instruction was not allowed, did make it possible to assure moral and patriotic training, as well as the physical development of these future soldiers.

Provisionally this youth organization also made it possible to shelter men of the recruiting classes of 1939, and earlier ones, who were unable to go home to the occupied zone.

The youth organization was an improvisation and did not completely fulfil its purpose. However, the youth camps in North Africa did play an effective role at the time of the [Allied] landing.

As must be obvious the army of 1940 suffered a grave material and moral crisis. It was a material crisis because the officers were cut off from their home areas and, with meagre resources, were now mingled with refugees in overcrowded cities of the unoccupied zone. Now that a professional army was being created, servicemen could no longer be satisfied with the traditional advance money and with the obsolete barracks of conscription days. From the moral or psychological point of view it was necessary, not merely for the sake of army itself, but also for the country as a whole, to give some importance, and we may well say a certain glamor, to this new army. For these reasons a number of measures were taken which need not be listed in detail, in connection with pay, lodging, clothing, food, and quarters. In particular the question of uniform was the object of constant attention by the High Command.

Military ceremonies were emphasized and organized in the most precise detail. There were daily color ceremonies, reviews, participation in public functions, and so on.

The basic idea was correct but its application was sometimes defective in manner and extent. There were perhaps too many parades and military bands, to the point of rightly shocking some noble minds.

From 1940 to 1942 three phases can be distinguished in the evolution of the Armistice Army.

First phase, from 25 June to 25 November 1940. In this phase order was re-established. An enormous number of men had to be demobilized and both forces and territories rearranged. Everything was in chaos, aggravated by the successive categorical instructions from Germans and Italians, yet it was necessary to straighten things out.

We shall not go into detail but merely offer a resumé and outline. In the end we were allowed: —*In the French homeland,* 94,400 men of whom 4 per cent were to be officers and 16 per cent noncommissioned officers; to this number was added a little later the embryo of an air defense force of 15,000 men. *In Africa,* after having cut our forces to 30,000 men, we were allowed 110,000 on a provisional basis, to which 30,000 men in the French colonies were to be added. *In the navy and air force,* we were allowed 60,000 sailors, and 50,000 airmen.

Second phase, from November 1940 to November 1941. This was the phase of organization. General Huntziger was Minister of War, General Picquendar, chief of general staff of the army, and General Ollery and General Requin commanded the first and second divisional groups.

Third phase, from November 1941 to the dissolution of the Armistice Army in November 1942. This was the phase of consolidation and instruction. The new arm took form. It had re-established its material equilibrium and it had regained confidence. It worked for a future which it was determined to make a glorious one and which it hoped was near at hand.

In the French homeland the invasion of the unoccupied zone and the dissolution of the army brought these efforts to an end. But was all this work in vain? Certainly not. North Africa greatly profited by this intense activity. The formation of the army of Italy and its engagement in Italy under Juin, and the participation of the First Army under de Lattre in the victory, were due primarily to the effort accomplished in the formation of the Armistice Army.

It was too from the best of the officers and the men that the most valuable elements of the resistance were obtained.

General Huntziger was killed in an airplane accident on 12 November 1941. From the preceding 12 August Admiral Darlan had been Minister of National Defense. Working with Admiral Darlan, Admiral Auphan,

General Bergeret, General Verneau, and General Revers conducted and guided the evolution of the army towards its rebirth.

Military instruction was of course one of the most urgent concerns of the High Command. For the men the first task was both moral and physical, with technical problems next. The men had to be cleansed of the obsessions due to the defeat and had to be brought to such a state of mind that they could become combatants of the finest kind.

Within the framework of the general policies of the government, seeking at the same time not to indulge in any of the excesses which often characterized those policies, both national sentiment and military spirit were developed.

Above the ashes of yesterday's defeat the age-old glories of our country were visualized. All had to be brought to realize, and they were brought to realize, that one defeat does not kill a country which does not want to die.

The day might come when the army would stand again with the victors, and even in 1940 the army itself had decided who those victors were to be, though at times some of the men at the top seemed to have made a different choice.

From the physiological point of view the accent was placed on the athletic training which makes a combatant of high quality. It was a small army, and in the days to come when both former soldiers and youths would be called to the colors the men of the Armistice Army would have to act as leaders and instructors. They must be the most skilful and the most audacious; they must be models and examples.

The noncommissioned officers, and to a lesser extent the men who had signed up as professional soldiers, must be prepared for an ultimate return to civilian life. Therefore technical training for such life was developed.

The instruction of officers was based on the same attitude to the highest degree for the development of skill, physical resistance, and initiative.

Furthermore, the future had to be prepared for by knowing which ones could endure the trials that awaited us.

Under the pretext of seeking responsibilities a commission presided over by General Doumenc, with Major Schmuckel and Major Beauffre, analyzed unit records. In the second divisional group, on the initiative of the Chief of Staff, Colonel Revers, with the approval of General Requin, Major Jacquot visited the units and interrogated the officers in order to gauge their abilities.

There was also the important matter of creating a military doctrine adapted not to the past but to the present and suitable for the future. The lessons of the war were carefully analyzed, those of the first period being assigned to the Doumenc commission which has just been mentioned. In addition arrangements were made to keep informed as to conclusions to be drawn from the war in Russia.

It was difficult to establish this new doctrine; it was even more difficult to arrange its diffusion. At the beginning, in 1941, the maintenance of order was the only mission which the enemy allowed us to consider and it was in terms of this mission that the concept of rapid offensive action by small groups was presented and taught.

The new doctrine had to be a doctrine of offense, for a very small army can never defend itself and is reduced to making the attack its only activity. It must rely on rapid motorized detachments, for speed and surprise are its only two possible advantages. This doctrine was later to become that of the irregulars and the maquis when they were well led.

This brings us to the essential thought of the military chiefs. The basic idea, we insisted, must be that one day the French army will fight beside England and the United States, this time victoriously.

We would make certain, too, that the army and air force intelligence services never lost contact with London.

The army knew perfectly well that it could not attack the German army alone. All that it could do would be to help in an Allied landing.

For the second divisional group, with headquarters at Royat, which controls the divisions at Clermont, Châteauroux, Limoges, and Toulouse, the assigned objective was the liberation of the port of La Pallice. The plan was prepared personally by the Chief of Staff, Colonel Revers, in May 1941, and was approved by the two generals who commanded at Royat, General Requin and General Frère. The plan was tested at Caylus in October 1941, disguised as an exercise against an enemy attempting to land.

The first divisional group was concerned with similar matters. The epic drama of de Lattre in 1942 was somewhat related to this work, though with some illusions as to Allied reaction.

During the third quarter of 1941, and in 1942, the general staff of the Minister of National Defense, and then the Commander-in-Chief, acted along the same lines. The men concerned were about the same; for example; Colonel Revers, at first chief of staff at Royat, became a general, and Chief of general staff for Admiral Darlan at Vichy.

At the beginning of 1941 a modest organism was created at Lyon, in a villa unlikely to attract notice. There, under the direction of General Baures, short tactical explanations were prepared, dealing with everything that was known of modern warfare. Training courses for qualified officers were planned to take the place of our war school of which the reconstitution was forbidden.

Though the maintenance of order had been the chief objective in 1941, the principal theme of all the exercises of the military divisions in the camps at Courtine and Larzac in 1942 was offensive action by highly mobile detachments.

Such exercises did not at all fit within the limits imposed on us [by the Germans], and nearly always implied a duplication of our forces. And in fact precise preparations were made to split them into two forces. The army general staff, under Colonel Pfister and Colonel Zeller, discreetly made the arrangements for this reorganization.

The clandestine services under Major Mollard at the same time collected and camouflaged the necessary equipment. In particular the needed motor vehicles were disguised as the rolling stock of civilian transport undertakings.

Through the use of the statistical service at Lyon, already mentioned, preparations were made for a much larger mobilization of over twenty divisions. This, however, was somewhat theoretical in that it would be necessary to have equipment from the Allies.

All such work was dealt with in very short notes and sometimes only in verbal orders. Only reliable officers were concerned and these clandestine matters were not necessarily dealt with through the regular chain of command. For example, some captains knew more about everything, and played a greater part, than did their generals.

This was not because treason was particularly to be expected, but that quite apart from any unintentional indiscretion it was necessary to fear timidity due to age; too many years of strict discipline were not the right preparation for the role of an insurgent which, at the beginning at least, would doubtless be that of tomorrow's army.

In Africa control was less strict because contact was more frank and this type of work could be handled more easily. Further, General Picquendar, Generad Verneau, and General Revers believed it to be certain that the liberation would begin from Africa. Therefore a consistent policy regarding personnel and equipment was maintained, to further our preparation in Africa. For example, when promotions were made the youngest and best officers to be promoted were systematically sent there. Camouflage was practiced on a large scale by such ardent and convinced officers as Lieutenant-Colonel Allard. The manufacture of war material was also begun (Captain Oemichen).

In France the camouflage of equipment was directed by Major Mollard. This task was as thankless and risky as it was important. Much of our resources was saved from the German levies of 1941 and 1942. When the Germans entered the free zone [November 1942] a great part of these riches, however, did fall into their hands. Major Mollard, with the alias of Dubourg, was arrested and deported to Buchenwald.

One of the great desires of the High Command was to get a foothold in the occupied zone. The question of the repatriation of prisoners furnished a pretext. In 1942 regional commissariats for repatriation were established in the occupied zone. These offices served as solid points of contact which proved invaluable later. The commissariat in Paris, for example, under Colonel Coudraux, was a base for military resistance. It made it possible to take over on 25 August 1944, without delay, the command of the capital and the neighboring departements.

North Africa, as we have said, was a continuous source of anxiety for the High Command.

General Weygand during his proconsulate, that is, up to November 1941, had been able to inculcate in everyone a hatred for the occupant and respect for the order of the government. Because of this, all preparations for future action were easily made; but on the other hand the change to revolt against the government in November 1942 was from some points of view made more difficult.

In spite of some incidents the essential patriotism of the officers made it possible to avoid what might have been a difficult and grievous crisis.

Every incident outside of France, and even every threat, was used as a ground for demanding more equipment or force. In general the German commissions agreed readily enough because it was Africa which was in question. The Italian commissions generally opposed such requests.

The provisional agreement for 110,000 men was maintained and in March 1942 an attempt was even made to obtain an allowance of 120,000. At the same time units of Méhallas were created on grounds of internal security; they were described as a kind of reserve, but in fact were composed entirely of trained former soldiers. In October 1941 two air groups taken from France crossed the Mediterranean. Some navy ships were re-armed. All of this was of benefit to the Allies during the actions which followed the end of 1942.

The events at Dakar in 1940 and those of Madagascar in 1942 made it possible to secure some further forces for our colonies and in particular to arrange for the liberation of some prisoners.

In speaking of the colonies I must express here an opinion which I hold absolutely and which is shared by my closest companions in the clandestine struggle. The Allied attacks against our forces and against our possessions were serious errors.

There were certainly some so blind as to dream of using our distant bases in the reconquest of colonies which had become Gaullist, or even of conquering British colonies. But no responsible military leader became involved in such a maneuver. No German or Italian ever took action in our territories. The fleet was never on the point of going over to the enemy.

In any case, history has already swept away those contrived and selfish explanations which were built up in this connection.

The same is true for Syria where the case was even more complicated. We believe that the attack on Syria in 1941 was a bad operation. Frenchmen should never be made to fight against other Frenchmen.

In 1942 there began a serious crisis in the number of men available. Conscription was not permitted. Voluntary enlistments in the southern zone, where there was a smaller population, were not sufficient. The number who left on the termination of their engagements, on the other hand, was as usual.

In July [1942] our small army of nominally 100,000 men lacked about 20,000 (see note of 4 June 1942). The shortage had become 30,000 by the end of the year.

Studies were made and negotiations were entered into at Wiesbaden [Armistice Commission] to recruit 50,000 men beginning at the end of November [1942]. The reception given to this proposal was not absolutely unfavorable but the landings in Algeria and Morocco, the [German] invasion of the free zone, and the dissolution of the [Armistice] Army all took place before a decision had been reached.

While our forces were being first organized and then trained, and while they were being prepared for the tasks of tomorrow, some thought of the more distant future in the postwar period.

Admiral Darlan, Minister of National Defense, and then Commander-in-Chief, thought, with a touch of exaggeration, that all was not for the best in our army.

He was quite ready to compare our army with his unconquered navy, without realizing the difference between a small professional force with a strong officer corps and a people in arms. It was necessary to put up a fight against opinions which were exaggeratedly unfavorable.

But with this reserve it must be said that there were some absolutely correct things in his thought, and studies and preparation were begun.

We needed an army organized in another fashion, a better army, stronger in air units, and better trained. To show how realistic and modern our studies were it may be noted that we reached a conception of an army which included 30,000 parachutists supported by 20,000 planes. The desire to give dynamic character to our operations led us to decide on the dismemberment of the too heavy division, and to take a mixed half-brigade as our basic unit. The American tactical groups, 'combat team,' and 'combat command,' are nothing else than what we then had in mind, and the study of which we are speaking was made in December 1941, a year before the first US units were engaged in action.

It was necessary to recreate and reorganize the officer corps at the same time. In so condensed an army as ours had become it was not possible to maintain an excessive number of officers. Particularly, it was impossible to keep those who had shown themselves to be ineffective during operations, or those who might seem to have become prematurely old.

The country had been scandalized when it learned that between September 1940 and October 1941—when the army was reduced by three-quarters—more than a hundred new generals had been appointed.

In December 1941 a hundred high officers and generals were put on the retired list in advance of their normal time. This measure was based entirely on professional grounds; as one of those who took part in this action I can guarantee that such was the fact.

This measure of retirement must not be confused with eliminations based on racial or political grounds which were made elsewhere.

In April 1942 studies were being made and plans prepared for a single army, which involved the abandonment of water-tight compartments between corps. In the meantime the amount of inter-service training was greatly increased. Going still further, exchanges of officers were organized between the navy and the army from 28 July 1942. Through a closer acquaintance between the men it was expected that the cohesion of the army could be strengthened.

The intelligence services must be dealt with briefly. There were three —for the army, the navy, and the air force. The army and air intelligence services worked in close co-operation, directed by Colonel Rivet. The counterintelligence corps was particularly active under Major Pailhol, with representation in every region through the BMA (Bureau assigned to Antinational Conspiracies).

The army and air intelligence services were completely anti-German and remained actively pro-Ally. Contact was maintained with London, whom we informed through clandestine radio.

The naval intelligence service worked independently. Above everything else it was anti-English.

The Second Bureau was responsible for the use of the information. At the end of 1941 a new centralization agency was created in Admiral Darlan's own services, the Bureau of Documentation, or Bedoc. The civilian police services, first under Controller-General Rivalland, then under Prefect Bousquet, worked parallel with them in liaison with the army and without any special friction.

Yet anti-German action unavoidably led to incidents. In such cases the occupation authorities took action against the French government. The whole structure was threatened with ruin on several occasions. At the end of 1941 Admiral Darlan put the intelligence services under the orders of General Revers—though in fact the navy service still acted independently.

This work continued, but not without repeated difficulties. Admiral Darlan was aware of the pro-English activities of his subordinates and he reacted violently when the Germans attacked him because of it, but he did not interfere.

Life became more difficult after March 1942, when the government moved closer to the occupation authorities in its attitude. Certain leaders, for example General Bridoux and General Delmotte, wrongly gave in to German demands. Life became much more difficult when these same generals, in July 1942, agreed to the entry of the Gestapo into the free zone. Many clandestine radio posts were seized.

In spite of all such activities, liaison was maintained and London was kept informed. Confidence was such that from 5 November 1942 onward the British intelligence service warned its friends of the French intelligence services that the landing, to take place very soon, would concern us. This was a fine indication of esteem, and the highly important confidential information thus given was not for a moment disclosed.

At the moment when the Allies were about to land the structure of the French army was complete; the army's spirit was magnificent, it was hard at work, and it was full of hope. Re-entry into the war was being prepared through a plan of mobilization by stages, and by stocking arms, equipment, and supplies of all kinds.

The army was in liaison with a resistance movement which was being created in the northern zone. Contacts began with Captain Lejeune and Captain Passage, reaching General Revers through Captain de Beaufort.

The navy was in magnificent condition and its feelings against England did not affect the crews. The air force was led by General Bergeret, essentially pro-American and anti-German.

In Africa, all the officer elements of a very fine army were in existence. The excellent morale created by General Weygand still lived.

A solid clandestine organization maintained liaison with the Americans. Africa was ready to enter the war.

All of this had been accomplished by a few men whose names we have mentioned in the above report. They acted on their individual initiative, supported by the general spirit of the army. They worked together without any need for their efforts to be co-ordinated, for their patriotism was such that an orchestra leader, so to speak, was not necessary.

These same men were to be found soon afterward in the African army, working clandestinely, deported, or dead. They had done their duty and taken the risks which were offered them; they had accepted their fate, good or bad.

The government and the high chiefs of the country in general were intentionally or unintentionally ignorant of the work of the army, particularly of what it did clandestinely.

The Maréchal had become old and was content to be a symbol. He had not acted nor did he establish a line of action. Sometimes where individuals were concerned his old-fashioned conservatism led him to make bad choices.

Admiral Darlan contributed greatly to the successful development of the visible and official army. The impetus which he gave was good. He intentionally ignored the existence of clandestine action. He was entirely aware of the fact that his immediate collaborator, Revers, played an active role in this clandestine action. (It became known later, through a telegram from Krug von Nidda to Abetz, seized at the time of the liberation, that the Germans, informed by General Delmotte, had known of

General Revers' activities from July 1942 onwards.) Was this artfulness on the part of Admiral Darlan, or did his convictions suddenly change in 1942? We incline toward the acceptance of this latter hypothesis and give the credit to Admiral Battet who joined Admiral Darlan at the beginning of 1942.

President Laval never took an interest in the army. He never desired to intervene in military problems. This had been true before 1940. Already in 1935 and 1936 when we collaborated with his Minister of War, M. Fabry, we became aware of his attitude.

But it must also be said that he offered no practical hindrance to the underground action that was developing.

Circumstances did not allow the Armistice Army to enter the struggle. But it would be supremely unjust to consider its work as having been useless. It produced both the Army of Africa and organized military resistance. Their glory is also its own.

(Document No. 241)
Fr. ed. 795-804

Paris, 8 November 1954

REVERS
General Georges Revers

THE RECONSTRUCTION OF THE ARMY OF AFRICA 1940-1941

MAXIME WEYGAND
General of the Army

Maréchal Pétain appointed me in September 1940 as delegate-general of the government and commander-in-chief in French Africa. I took over all political and military powers in the three territories of North Africa and in the federation of West Africa.

My military action was of essential importance, its purpose being to reconstruct in North Africa an army which would be able, when the time came, to take up arms again against the enemy. Under the terms of my appointment I was commander-in-chief of air and land forces stationed in Africa and though I had no great resources at my disposal I did have a power of initiative of which I decided to make the broadest possible use.

In matters of organization my activities would be limited by agreements made with the secretaries of state for war and for air, General Huntziger and General Bergeret, a fact which offered no difficulties in view of our perfect understanding. But on the other hand my activities in this direction were limited, at least so far as visible forces were concerned, by the terms of the Armistice Convention, of which the application was under inspection by enemy commissions.

In the matter of moral and technical instruction of our military forces, everything would depend on the impetus which I might be able to give.

As to the use of our military forces the powers of the governors and residents-general, and of the commanding generals of these forces in each of the African countries, were not always sufficient to meet all the possibilities that might arise. I was obliged to modify these powers in order to be able to exercise my own authority as commander-in-chief to the full in case of hostilities.

The disorganization of the Army of Africa when I arrived was due to various causes, which included the magnitude of the levies made for the front in France, the continual rearrangement of those forces which remained in Africa, the delays and difficulties of the demobilization, and the great uncertainty as to the numbers and location of such forces as it might be possible to maintain.

At the time of the mobilization [in 1939] the forces of North Africa had included five divisions, one of which was a light motorized division, incomplete, which held the Tunis front; some new fortress regiments which held the fortifications facing Tripoli; some security forces, organized as divisions, to maintain order in the interior of the three countries, and some Sahara units consisting of mounted goums [Algerian Arab soldiers] or mixed foot and mounted units, with some motorized sections. Many of these units had been either removed or stripped of their best men, officers, and equipment, in order to improve new units intended chiefly for France but also for the Levant, for the Tunis front opposite the Italians, and for the Moroccan front against the Spanish. It will be remembered that, aside from the seven North African divisions organized in France, a first contingent of three divisions had been taken there during the autumn of 1939 and the following winter, and that a second contingent was sent for during the battle of May and June 1940; this latter included two divisions and important parts of a third division.

When the battle for France had turned against us, new units had been hastily formed in the base depots [in Africa], as a precaution, combining all services with units borrowed from the security forces, and sent even before they were completely organized into the areas regarded as most threatened. These groups were without cohesion, poorly commanded, badly equipped, and scantily trained; they were of very mediocre value.

After the armistice the process of demobilization increased the chaos, for it was necessary not merely to reduce the size of units which had greatly increased in size, but also to reorganize forces which had been put together in a disorderly way. The lack of transport had slowed down all movement; even by the end of November [1940] the 86th division had not returned from Syria.

Controller-General de Mesmay, on an intelligence mission in Morocco, had visited all the garrisons of that country between 2 and 25 September 1940. He had discovered that the pretended force of 75,000 men under arms was more illusion than reality, that many of the trained riflemen returning from France had not been organized into units, and that many of the existing units lacked officers, men, and training. Two months later, when I arrived there, improvement was still only slight. Some regiments existed only on paper, most of the others were in process of formation, and the shortage of officers was considerable. Demobilization had not been completed and there were in Morocco alone 15,000 Moroccans and 9,000 black soldiers above the permitted figure.

In Algeria, chiefly in the province of Oran, similar facts were noted. In the 19th Army Corps there were still 20,000 Senegalese and a large number of Tunisians still to be repatriated. Shortages of officers and French soldiers were so great that it was difficult to maintain the native units and impossible to form the colonial units and the African chasseurs. I ended a letter to the secretary of state for war with these words: "The impression given is shocking, the instruction and bearing of the troops is mediocre, and the commanding officers are inactive."

In Tunisia those forces which had been kept in condition to resist an Italian attack were the ones that had suffered the least of all. My first impression was more satisfactory than that which I had received anywhere else.

In French West Africa the inspections which I made on my first visits confirmed the reports of General Barrau. From the military point of view, things were worse than mediocre; the native soldiers were very young and only slightly trained, and there were not nearly enough officers, the colonial infantry alone being short by three hundred officers and four hundred noncommissioned officers. "These forces are in the midst of reorganization and incapable of doing what would rightly be expected of them," I wrote to Maréchal Pétain.

To sum up, except for a few special units such as the marksmen, the spahis, the [foreign] Legion, infantry or cavalry, and the goums, there was not really any army in Africa at all when I landed there.

Questions concerning the formation of the Armistice Army in Africa were debated between the Ministry of War, in the special section of the armistice services, and in the Italian armistice commission in Turin through the French delegation which was assigned to the Italian commission. This French delegation was under the orders of Admiral Duplat, assisted by General Parisot who had been in command of a division [during the fighting]. This general officer, of whose value I had been aware in the headquarters of Maréchal Foch, had acted successfully, just before the war, as military attaché in Rome. He knew Italy well and knew the Italian military chiefs, particularly Marshal Badoglio whose friendship for France was both faithful and helpful. General Parisot was skilful in our defense and often initiated measures which made it possible for the Army of Africa to exist; it is right that this fact should be recognized. In fact the Italians had originally insisted that the number of men should be reduced to 30,000, a figure which, on the strength of the most valid arguments, we refused to accept.

The regrettable events of Mers-el-Kébir and Dakar had the happy effect of warning our enemies of the risks run by an insufficiently defended Africa. During October [1940] we obtained agreement to plan for an army, to be known as "transitional," of 100,000, including officers, with 20,000 unarmed auxiliary workers. The loss of Libreville opened the debate once more. The Germans reminded us of our obligation to defend the colonial empire and we took advantage of their action by demanding that the figure be increased to 120,000 men. In February 1941 this figure was in fact obtained but only by including the goums. Another discussion followed because the goums were only a police force and should not be counted as part of the army. In the end we obtained an almost total acceptance of our case, and at the beginning of April I was able to bring the chiefs of the general staffs of the three countries together in Algiers to make definitive plans for a force of 127,000, which was to include 16,000 goums. This figure was really provisional, except for a few special points, as I indicated in a letter written in August [1941] to General Huntziger, in which I said that the Army of Africa was already in its fifth incarnation.

After the loss of Libreville we had obtained for French West Africa permission for the creation of a motorized group to be formed in Morocco, to include a regiment of Senegalese marksmen, a group of 75 mm field guns, a cavalry regiment, an engineering battalion, a transport company, and a medical section.

This did not mean that everything was settled; arguments continued on such important questions as the percentage of noncommissioned officers to be allowed, the proportion of French to native troops, the limitations on motorized units and, on anti-tank guns and the locations of the troops of which the Italians held that the center should be west of the meridian of Algiers. The government firmly resisted this last demand, the purpose of which was easily discernible. General Parisot, in agreement with me, secured permission in particular for a strong garrison at Bizerte.

Every event of any importance was used by us as an excuse for claiming reinforcements: Montoire [meeting of Chancellor Hitler and Maréchal Pétain]; the announcement by Admiral Darlan of a revival of the collaboration policy, and the [British-Gaullist] attack against Syria. In this way a new contingent of 900 marksmen, intended for the Levant, was created in Morocco, and Hitler promised in June 1941 that 1,100 officers, 800 noncommissioned officers, and 4,500 men would be liberated for our African forces and that 25 mm guns and anti-aircraft guns would be released to us.

But with the Germans, promising and keeping a promise are two quite different things. Their bad faith in fulfilling their engagements was made felt from the beginning, long before the German armistice commissions arrived in Africa.[1] The Germans did not hesitate to employ any means at all to retard the reorganization which we were trying to effect: repeated changes in the tables of permitted forces, the delivery of promised equipment in very small lots if at all, and particularly the indefinite postponement of the departure of volunteers from the French mainland. Many young men in France, attracted by the Army of Africa, volunteered to serve. The Germans systematically stopped them at Marseille where the chiefs of our forces in France, learning of their misfortune, tried to persuade them to enter their own units, with the result that I had to struggle at the same time against our own chiefs in France and the enemy. It was a day by day fight to obtain the officers, men, and equipment to which we were entitled.

The struggle to maintain the Foreign Legion ought to be recounted here. The attack against it began when the flow of recruits failed. The government of the Reich, knowing full well the value of the Legion, demanded the repatriation of all men of German blood in order to weaken it still further. Soon Italy, too, demanded the return of her citizens. It was

---

1. Until March 1941 there had been only the Italian commissions in Algeria.

an important matter; as is well known, the suppression of the Legion is a purpose dear to the German chiefs. If this Axis pressure did not succeed, a formal order could still remove from French command four solid foreign regiments (three of infantry, and one of cavalry). There again it was possible to limit the damage. Absolute shelter was first given to all those who had come in order to take advantage, under the Legion's flag, of its traditional hospitality which disregards the true name and past history of the individual. Then followed a bitter discussion. A compromise formula was finally found: those legionnaires would be repatriated who made a formal demand for repatriation. In fact, the only ones to ask for their liberty were those who were already compromised or of doubtful loyalty, and whose loss was not regrettable. The Germans received some apparent satisfaction and the Legion did not suffer too much from this "purification." In any case, the Legion survived; it has since proved that fact.

In spite of those obstacles the work advanced, each one doing his best, as did my own general staff. In the accomplishment of this heavy task I was greatly pleased by the efforts of the high commanding generals as soon as they had fully grasped the nature of the objective to be attained. I have already mentioned the high esteem I had for General Audet, an experienced and conscientious leader whose forces were the first to be ready. At the head of the 19th army corps I had found General Beynet, poorly supported by an incomplete general staff, whose turn of mind was rather too skeptical for my taste, but who was very intelligent and saw things as they really were. The commanding general in Morocco was General Vergez, a solid organizer and a calm and thoughtful leader.

Proof of the progressive strengthening of the " official " Army of Africa is given by two documents.

At the beginning of January 1941 I sent Maréchal Pétain a first report on the general situation. In North Africa, certain basic results had been accomplished; our forces were in their proper places, excess strength had been absorbed, equipment was almost entirely allocated and training was being conducted satisfactorily except in the motorized units. But there were still serious gaps; another 500 officers and 15,000 noncommissioned officers and French soldiers were still needed, equivalent to a third of the agreed total. Certain types of arms were still in short supply and vehicles in the armored sections were becoming worn out to a disturbing degree. In French West Africa a great deal had been accomplished in the organization and instruction of the 33,000 men who were under arms at that time. There, too, the shortage of French officers was strongly felt, the infantry alone having only half as many Europeans as were needed. The Germans had authorized the creation of a mobile group in the hope of hastening the armed defeat of the rebellion; its formation and operation required the liberation of prisoners who were noncommissioned officers or specialists, as well as the construction of barracks, the preparation of a base, and the increase of the stock of gasoline and oil. None of those tasks could be completed before the end of the dry season, a fortunate delay that postponed—without breaking off any of our arrangements and while still giving us the increasing benefit of supplementary forces—an enterprise into which we had decided never to become engaged.

To sum up, I considered at that time that a part of the African forces were ready to be employed and I concluded that if the demands which I had made were satisfied soon enough the entire force would be equal to any local tasks which they might have to accomplish by 1 April 1941.

The second document to which I referred above is the final general defense plan for Africa which I had to prepare at the end of September 1941. In this plan I had studied the attacks which might be made against North Africa under two hypotheses, that of an Atlantic battle and that of a Mediterranean battle. Under each hypothesis Algeria, less threatened, was considered as our final retreat and the reservoir of forces constituting my general reserve. In passing I note that this reserve amounted at that time to twelve battalions, seven artillery groups, ten groups of cavalry squadrons of which some were mechanized or motorized, and the entire air force.

In North Africa the forces, not including the goums, had reached the authorized figure of 111,555, of which 4,213 were officers.[1] The proportion of French to natives was still below the basic figure, and there were a certain number of reserve officers. The modern equipment included 69 guns of 25 mm, 117 mobile machine guns, and 150 tanks.[2]

In French West Africa numbers had increased considerably since the beginning of the year, having now reached a total of 56,500 instead of 33,000; included in the new total were 1,100 officers and 6,722 noncommissioned officers or French soldiers, of whom the proportion to the natives was still too low. General Barrau had received 70 guns of 25 mm, 50 mobile machine guns, and 22 modern tanks. In May 1941 General Barrau completed the organization of the French West Africa troops into three divisions, one for the Dahomey-Togo-Niger area, one for Central French West Africa, and one for Senegal.

It can be seen that we had patiently taken advantage of every opportunity and every excuse to increase our forces.

It is a pleasure to be able to add that Admiral Landriau, who came to French West Africa in August 1940, had soon brought the naval forces and the navy's land division into good condition.

I did not have the whole of the naval forces of Africa under my orders but I wish to say that I was always on terms of complete confidence and in full agreement as to purposes with the commanding admiral for the South, Vice-Admiral Ollive, superior navy officer in French Africa, whose headquarters were at Algiers. Similarly, the generals commanding land and air forces were pleased with the co-operation they received from Admiral Landriau, commanding naval forces at Dakar, Admiral d'Harcourt at Casablanca, Admiral Derrien at Bizerte, and Admiral Fenard at Algiers.

The Armistice Convention gave us no right to maintain any military air unit whatever. But it will be remembered that General Bergeret had obtained at Rethondes an undertaking that our planes should not be destroyed but merely held in reserve. In June 1940 about 700 French planes has crossed the Mediterranean and landed in French North

---

1. After hostilities in Syria had ended with the armistice of Saint-Jean d'Acre we asked for the repatriation to French North Africa of the forces which constituted the Army of the Levant. After a first refusal, and in exchange for my own recall, the Germans agreed in December 1941 to send 15,000 men, together with equipment which was to come from France.

2. We had obtained the release of this equipment from sequestration. But, faithful to their usual tactics, the Germans made us await a special authorization to use this equipment in the formation of units. How we managed things without their authorization will be seen later.

Africa.[1] I have said elsewhere that a considerable number of these planes were for the time being unsuitable for warfare because of their quality and the insufficient supply of ammunition and spare parts, in spite of the excellence of most of the pilots.

In accordance with the principle which had been adopted, all English or Gaullist undertakings and threats against French sovereignty were taken advantage of in order to obtain the re-establishment of our air units. Mers-el-Kébir brought us an authorization to reconstitute twenty-one air groups in North Africa and a few squadrons in French West Africa. But the units, arriving as available transport permitted, were disorganized; there were insufficient parts; and the equipment itself was a haphazard mixture. In addition, the control commissions watched to see that only strictly indispensable repairs were made and that actual flying-time was kept to a minimum.

By taking advantage of every incident we gradually obtained an increase in the number of planes in service, with corresponding facilities in schools, training, operation of fields where planes were kept, and workshops. It was under these conditions that, thanks to General Bergeret and General Odic, who commanded the air force in North Africa from October 1940 to July 1941, the fighting units were reorganized, the necessary services re-established, instruction begun once more, and mobilization prepared.

Infrastructure at the beginning included only a very small number of authorized fields. There again we succeeded in securing an increase.

Through the devotion, initiative, and discretion of air personnel of all grades remarkable results were obtained, without any disclosures, under the inspiration of General Odic and then of his successor in French North Africa, General Mendigal, and under the active command of General Gama in French West Africa.

In November 1941 there were in French Africa 8 pursuit groups, 5 reconnaissance groups, 13 bomber groups, and 2 transport groups, making a total of 28 groups, with about 400 planes.

The navy on its side had fitted out 2 pursuit squadrons, 7 bomber squadrons, and 8 exploration and torpedo squadrons, making a total of 17 groups with a little more than 100 planes. The supply of gasoline was satisfactory; ammunition was less abundant but was sufficient for two months' operations.

Thanks to arrangements made by General Bergeret, the dispatch of planes of recent manufacture was to make possible the progressive renewal of the Africa air force.

Everything which had been obtained in Africa remained available until the Allied landing, and constituted the principal elements of the French contribution to the campaigns in Tunisia, Italy, France, and Germany.

In spite of the progress which had been realized and the concessions which had been obtained the forces authorized by the enemy were not sufficient to enable the Army of Africa to re-enter the struggle at some

---

1. At the time when our airmen were once more allowed to fly, the Germans warned us that any clandestine departure of a plane would bring the suppression of the air group involved in the incident, the dismissal of the members of the group, and the destruction of all its planes. Anxious not to compromise the air force which we desired to conserve and bring to perfection, our airmen put duty before their natural fighting reflexes.

future date. It was impossible to be satisfied with such a situation. More arms and larger forces were necessary; mobilization must be prepared; fighting spirit must be given to the army. I shall now explain what was accomplished along these lines. Probably I ought to adopt the jargon of the day and call this part of my activity "resistance." It did not seem to me at the time when I did these things that they deserved any special name, because they differed in no way from the activity of my entire life, devoted to the struggle against the enemies of France, and because they were the natural continuation of the war to which the armistice had not put an end.

When I came to Africa three and a half months after the conclusion of the armistice an important supply of military equipment had already been concealed from the enemy in the most varied hiding places. Military chiefs of all ranks, particularly in Morocco, had understood from the very beginning the capital importance of keeping such equipment from any investigation by the control commissions. Each on his own initiative sought methods of concealment, often at great risk. The help of the civil administration and of private persons was not lacking. Clandestine transport of equipment was usually made at night under very difficult conditions. When I took over the command and found out what had been accomplished I ordered its continuation and gave my official approval to what had already been accomplished and what was still to be done.

Following is a statistical table of the most important hidden supplies of arms and ammunition, according to secret lists which I held:

	Arms	Ammunition
Rifles	55,000	26,000,000
Heavy machine-guns	1,500	
Machine-gun rifles	2,500	
81 mm mortars	210	40,000
Field guns: 25 mm and 37 mm	45	66,000
47 mm	43	4,300
75 mm	82	205,000
Light-field guns on caterpillar treads	24	
Self-propelled machine-guns	23	
Modern tanks	5	
Flame throwers	72	
Hand grenades		45,000
Land mines		8,000

It was impossible to try to conceal entire airplanes. Some light planes were concealed and spare parts were made secretly.

The air command made up for the reduction in the number of authorized fields by leasing appropriate grounds and maintaining them secretly.

The various military services competed in ingenuity and cleverness. The engineers established clandestine depots of equipment. The communication services, whose war-time role, as is well known, is of the greatest importance, deserves special mention because of the clandestine measures of camouflage and conservation which they were able to execute successfully. At the beginning, this latter service was directed by an engineer battalion commander, Guerin (who is today a colonel and director of communications in the Secretariat of State for War.) From August [1940] onward he was able to conceal from enemy investigations an important supply of "ER-2" radios by installing throughout Algeria a police radio-telegraph network which included sufficient apparatus of this model to equip two divisions. The same policy was followed in Morocco by increasing the size of the security network and by establishing a defensive network for linking the goums [Algeria] and tabors [Morocco.] In December 1940 there was established a monitoring service and a radiogoniometric network for locating any radio emitters installed by the enemies [Germany and Italy]. During this same period a station was established in Algiers to receive their clandestine communications and the messages of their military radios in Tripoli. All these arrangements were made in full agreement with the directors of the French PTT [Post, Telegraph, Telephone] and with their indispensable and patriotic aid.

The army medical services re-established a part of their supplies and the quartermaster corps built up stocks of clothing and equipment.

By establishing what pretended to be transport businesses it was possible to distribute among private persons about 6,000 army trucks and vans in satisfactory condition. About 200 special trucks, mobile workshops, tank carriers, tank trucks, and so on were hidden away.

Large stocks of valuable metals were also concealed from German investigation, including 17,000 tons of copper, most of which had been brought from France in June 1940, 2,400 tons of zinc, 1,650 tons of nickel, 1,000 tons of aluminium, 600 tons of molybdenum, 450 tons of lead, and 400 tons of tin.

Finally, in spite of the slight industrial capacity of North Africa, a certain amount of clandestine manufacture was carried out in the navy's workshops, or by individual firms. The more important manufactured articles included 37 mm cooling tubes used on board ship in gunnery practice, now transformed into self-propelled anti-tank guns; and armored trucks and vans for which the armor plate from the wreck of *Pluton* was used, these trucks being fitted with 75 mm guns or with machine-guns.

Communications equipment was constructed in large quantities, especially the "ER-40" model, some of which were made by Captain Oemichen, some under the authority of the PTT in civilian assembly shops especially created for that purpose, and some by private firms such as the Société Franco-Radioélectrique and the Société Africaine de Construction Radio-électrique.

Though the most varied means had to be used to manufacture and conceal these various kinds of equipment, and though the number of persons participating in such operations was large, the secret was well kept even by the most humble of the natives. During the thirteen months of my service in Africa only one clandestine equipment depot was discovered as the result of a denunciation. So far as Vichy was concerned I protected the officer responsible for the depot and I kept him out of the hands of the Germans.

It is comforting to think of the generosity and the scorn of risk shown by all these modest people who devoted themselves to the task, satisfied because they were doing their duty, proud to be preparing for the struggle still to come, and delighted in the extra satisfaction of making the enemy ridiculous.

These results seemed modest in comparison with the huge quantities of equipment that have since become so familiar. Nevertheless it was with only the equipment authorized for their use [by the Germans], augmented by what they were able to draw from these hiding places, that the Africa

Army fought so heroically and obtained the results which are so famous, from the time of the landing in November 1942 until they could be rearmed by the United States.

Forces in excess of the permitted number were maintained clandestinely, beyond those authorized. As was the case where equipment was concerned, all French authorities who were able to help did so most fully. I wish to pay homage to Colonel Gross, chief of the DDSA, who conceived certain ways of tricking the Germans which were really brilliant. We might note among his methods the clandestine passage of volunteers from France to Africa, the "provisional recruits," whose names were kept off the roster for a certain length of time, though there were 10,000 of them; the size of the guard detachments assigned to equipment depots, theoretically 55 men but in reality 200, all trained in the driving of armored cars;[1] the Moroccan auxiliary police which included 13,500 Mokrasnis instead of the permitted 600; supplementary forces of goums in Morocco and douairs in Algeria; and the military organization of 20,000 authorized "workers" who were supposed by the Germans to be unarmed.

The total number of trained men in these clandestine formations may be estimated at about 60,000.

But however successful these possibilities of reinforcement might be, it was of the greatest importance to prepare the Africa Army for active warfare. For this purpose its units had to be brought up to war strength and able to leave their bases in their entirety; to make this possible there had to be re-established the security forces which would replace them and supply services which would enable them to live and to fight. These objectives could be attained only through the procedure of mobilization.

At the beginning of 1941 the reconstitution of our forces was sufficiently advanced to enable us to go ahead along these lines without further delay. Colonel de Perier brought me the plan and I agreed immediately. We thereupon began preparation for our mobilization.

Captain Penette was a young officer who had come from Rabat to join our general staff. Colonel de Perier asked him if he would accept the task, with all the risks which it might bring, of being responsible for the clandestine measures intended to give the Africa Army the fighting power which it then lacked. He accepted enthusiastically. I received him shortly afterward, defined his mission, and ordered him to maintain absolute secrecy, even toward the Vichy authorities. An operations plan known as *Études* [studies], not dated, not signed, and without indication of source, was given to him to be taken personally to the various commanding generals, air commanders, and admirals, and to be communicated in strictest confidence to the civil governors and residents-general. These authorities were warned that no report of the matter was to be made. This memorandum specified the objective and the principles, but did not furnish details of the measures to be taken, as the means, needs, and possibilities differed considerably in the different areas.

1. General Dario recalled in a report which he had occasion to make in 1945 the unequivocal terms in which I asked him to evade German instructions when they released equipment to us without authorizing us to form units to use the equipment.

Captain Penette and the officers in each general staff who were especially responsible for these preparations were allowed great initiative, of which they made remarkable use. I was kept continuously informed of the progress of the work. Things had been moving along quietly when in April [1941] a liaison officer returning from Vichy warned me that the Minister of War had been informed that, contrary to the terms of the armistice, I had taken measures preparatory to mobilization; that the Minister regarded these measures as dangerous; and that the secret was not well kept. The fact was that one of the naval services had imprudently had printed in Algiers 10,000 cards to be used in calling up members of the reserve. I replied to the Minister that "being responsible for the defense of Africa, I would have been guilty if I had not taken indispensable measures." I presented to him the reasons for my decision without concealing from him the fact that I had ordered everything be kept secret even from him.

"In acting thus," I told him in ending my reply, "I accepted my full responsibility, leaving to the government to disavow me in all good faith if indiscretions made it necessary at some time."

I received no reply, which was the best reply that could have been given to me. Everything went on as though nothing had happened. In July [1941] I noted that because there was no official responsibility some chiefs were not performing this task with all of the zeal which they ought to have brought to it; I reproached them for this attitude and reminded them that they were completely responsible to me, the specialist officers being only the agents of their decisions in this matter. The preparations were completed by the special training of the officers and men necessary for the operation of the communications units in the field. These units were brought together and trained in groups under PTT control, listed as "temporary technical group for state transmission services, engineers and agents." General Merlin, who in 1942 was placed at the head of the communications services of French North Africa, succeeded in perfecting this organization, of which the work would be to provide an indispensable service to the forces in the field and to the general staffs.

It happened that the high commanding generals in North Africa were changed in July 1941. General Beynet was called to take the leadership of the French delegation at Wiesbaden, General Audet was given command of a region in the interior, and General Vergez was retired because of age. I succeeded in having them replaced by general officers of my own choice, General Koeltz at Algiers, General Juin at Rabat, and General de Lattre at Tunis. It is enough to give their names as they are inseparably linked with the victories won by the Africa Army. Nothing was spared that would make these victories possible.

Preparation for mobilization was well advanced when I was recalled from Africa. General Juin, who succeeded me in one of my functions, as commander-in-chief of the forces of North Africa, maintained and strengthened in every field the movement which I had initiated.

Captain Penette,[1] who was the key piece in this operation of mobilization, was able to note the results of the work when the Allies landed. Following are the conclusions of a report which he wrote in 1945:

1. Captain Penette was later promoted colonel, assigned to the headquarters of General Koenig at Baden-Baden, and then to service with the United Nations in the United States.

"It is no exaggeration to say that this clandestine preparation played a decisive role in the events of North Africa. It was this preparation alone which made it possible to compensate for the insufficiencies of the Armistice Army. Without this preparation the mission of protection assigned to a detachment of the French army in mid-November [1942], which proved to be indispensable for the concentration of the Allied forces, could have been carried out only much later and, without doubt, the rate of the Allied landings being what it was, only in positions considerably to the west of those along the Tunisian mountain range.

"The Africa Army was able to take the field from the middle of November only because measures prepared clandestinely had enabled it to be strengthened rapidly both in numbers and in equipment.

"The action taken by General Weygand, and continued after his departure by General Juin, was therefore one of the decisive elements of French success in the Tunisia campaign."

As I was responsible for the use of the African troops I insisted on laying down the principles in accordance with which they were to be instructed. The secretary of state for war had indeed given directives for the preparation of the Armistice Army in its mission of maintaining order in the interior. But the forces in French Africa had to be capable of entirely different action: they would have to fight. It was, therefore, necessary to give the Africa Army quite a different character, one which was suited to the conditions under which it would fight, and the one which would satisfy its military spirit. To give the Africa Army such an inspiration was the purpose of my directive of 10 February 1941 regarding the training of the troops.

This directive described first the nature of the ground and the kind of operations to be expected. Because of the great extent of the combat areas, the scarcity of good communications, and the aridity of the climate which emphasized the water problem everywhere, geographical and topographical conditions gave their full value to qualities natural in native troops, and offered great possibilities for maneuver. Maneuvers were all the more important because the Africa Army would have to meet surprise attacks coming from either land or sea but which in either case would allow us to defend from a position of strength against an adversary for whom it would be difficult to get a foothold in force on our soil.

The problem, therefore, was to convert an army which had been reduced in numbers and had only limited and often out-of-date equipment into a first-class force by making maximum use of its natural qualities, its mobility, its fighting spirit, its economy of operation and its endurance in order to maneuver, which was the only way of compensating for its inferiority in numbers and equipment. For such a force any fighting by units linked together to form a continuous front would be the exception. Any concept of linear or fixed defense had to be excluded. Night-fighting and difficult ground, so displeasing to any other kind of force, must be thoroughly mastered. Whether the task was to operate in the field in order to block the enemy's progress, or to support by outside operation the defense of a strong point which had to be maintained at any price, everything would have to be done by highly mobile tactical groups whose maneuvers would not be hampered by any worry about their communications to the rear. The command would have to be inspired by a strictly offensive spirit even when the over-all mission was a defensive one. The command would have to find ways of acting against the flanks and communications of the enemy and would strive to paralyze him by a multiplicity of attacks, each time striking a blow and disengaging at once. The vigor and the striking power of these tactical groups combined with air attack would inflict losses on the enemy, while offering only vague targets for his highly perfected military equipment. I summarized my instructions by saying that the objective was "to convert our reduced and poorly equipped forces, strong in their exceptional qualities of marching, endurance, and abstemiousness, into an extremely supple and maneuverable force, which could be integrated with units of any arm and inspired by a burning faith." After some detailed instructions on the way in which the program was to be realized my directive ended with these words: "Finally, officers and men must find the energy needed to complete this training in their love for the father-land, their spirit of sacrifice, and their desire for revenge." Everyone knew of this text.

My conversations with the leaders, the training exercises for officers, the alerts, and the maneuvers in the camps and in the field, at which I was present whenever my journeys and my economic and political work allowed me sufficient time, gave me the opportunity to keep this sacred spirit alive; waiting is always painful and few thought that the waiting would be so long.[1] Sometimes the flickering flame had to be revived, either because weaker spirits were discouraged by defeat or the stronger by the despair of not having yet fought. After one maneuver which had been conducted too languidly I even had to provide a stimulus to their insufficient energy and to remind the officers that the inertia of the men was the result of the listlessness of their leaders. But I came to feel more and more that the heart of all these Africans beat in unison with my own.

At the same time, faithful to the rule that I had set for myself, I never missed an opportunity to remind the government how I expected them to aid me in the moral side of my task. Here is a warning, one among many, which often appeared in my communications to the government: "As for the spirit of the officers," I wrote on 27 March 1941, "it is necessary not to lose sight of the fact that hate of the Germans is the dominating sentiment, and that any weakness [on the part of the government] which led the officers to doubt the government's attitude toward the temporary conqueror would run the risk of destroying their confidence."

Before leaving this subject I think I should speak of two occasions on which I intervened with General Audet, in order to show clearly the spirit in which I exercised my command, and toward what objectives I directed the activities of the forces.

The first of these two interventions occurred in January 1941. I had been advised by three reliable sources that the Axis was getting ready to attack Bizerte with German and Italian forces based on Sicily, and I telegraphed to General Audet that he was to "be ready to take all military measures suitable for defeating such an attempt." All military arrange-ments, land, air, and sea, were made for fighting against a violation of

---

1. One of my officers has reminded me that because I desired to avoid any ambiguity in the minds of his comrades who had met for the critical analysis at the end of a maneuver, I told them that of course they had the right to think as they wished but never the right to forget that the Germans had been, were, and always would be the enemy.

the armistice. The alert lasted several days. Nothing happened.[1]
The second of my two interventions came during the same period and dealt with an entirely different possibility. The British army in Egypt, commanded by General Sir Archibald Wavell, had launched a strong attack against the Italians in Libya on 9 December 1940. On 12 December the British had taken 20,000 prisoners. On 7 February, the British entered Benghasi, and on 9 February advanced British forces reached the frontier of Tripoli. The defeat of the Italians had led me to decide what action I should take if their retreat came so far as south Tunisia. I thought that it was our duty to disarm and intern the defeated troops who might try to find refuge there. During January [1941] I gave instructions to General Audet regarding the steps he should take in such an event for disarming the Italians and putting them in concentration camps. These precautions were taken in part. Although the territory of south Tunisia was, in theory, demilitarized the guards at the frontier posts were strengthened in spite of the presence of Italian control commissions in Tunisia. The Germans, however, did not permit matters to go so far. On 15 February there landed in Tripoli the advance forces of the Africa Corps which was to begin a counteroffensive and reconquer Cyrenaica. But eight months later, on 15 October 1941, the success of the new attack by the English made me put into force again the instructions which were still in the archives at Tunis. General de Lattre adapted them to the situation as it was then, which made it possible to prepare for the advance of the English at the end of 1941.

It was in this way that I strove to increase the power of the Africa Army by all means available to me, to give a definite direction to its activities, and to inspire it with an ideal. To maintain for France that part of its colonial empire which was still intact while at the same time preparing to aid in the deliverance of France was an objective well suited to satisfying the army's ardor, and to strengthening further its military spirit. When General Juin, at the end of the Tunisia campaign, addressed the army which he was about to lead into Italy with such brilliant success, he paid homage in the following words to the silent and resolute labor of its preparation, and to its military virtues: "It can never be said often enough that it is thanks to your courage and your tenacity that our Allies were able to fight in the heart of Tunisia and to get a stranglehold on the enemy. Enough cannot be said regarding the magnitude of your sacrifices. This noble mission, for which the interim army in North Africa prepared itself in secret, has been carried out by you with few arms, some that were allotted to us and some that were hidden."
The Africa Army in fact fought without respite from 20 November 1942 to 12 May 1943. It withstood the shock of the German tank attacks though almost unprovided with the necessary equipment, and in the end

1. We learned afterwards that the Germans had indeed planned a double operation in North Africa, against Tunisia and through Spain against Morocco; and that it was General Franco's refusal to allow the Germans to cross his territory which had led to the abandonment of the plan. Since the war this report of General Franco's attitude has been confirmed, particularly in the letters exchanged between Hitler and Mussolini, and in two books, *Mon Ambassade en Espagne* [My Embassy in Spain], by Sir Samuel Hoare, and *Entre Hendaye et Gibraltar* [Between Hendaye and Gibraltar], by Serrano Sunner.

dominated the enemy. The Africa Army played a leading part in the victory which gave the Allies complete possession of the African coast of the Mediterranean and marked a decisive turning point in the war in the western hemisphere. Through this army the bravery and the offensive spirit of the French soldier shone once again on the field of battle.

The Army of Africa had shown what it was capable of doing when it was face to face with its adversary and at last in possession of materiel which was equal to that of the enemy.

(Document No. 261)
Fr. ed. 805-818

Paris, 25 March 1955

WEYGAND

Maxime Weygand

General of the Army; commanded the French Armies for four years, 1931 to 1934; was recalled to command them again in May 1940; Member of the French Academy

THE CLANDESTINE ARMY AFTER DECEMBER 1942

GEORGES REVERS

General

[*This document was prepared with the help of Lieutenant-Colonel Madelin.*]

Before giving an outline of the action of the French army in the resistance we must recall briefly the situation in which that action took place.

Individual activity hostile to the occupants, it is known, took definite form from the end of 1940 in part as a "resistance movement," grouped around several important people in France itself, which carried on propaganda, secured information, and engaged in physical action, and in part as "networks" organized by agents of Free France or of Great Britain.

The principal resistance movements of the first group were united by their own agreement in the southern zone as the MUR (United Resistance Movements) which, by combining the auxiliary military elements of the various organizations, created the AS (Secret Army) under the direction of General Delestraint. The networks, on the other hand, remained rigorously separated, at least in theory, according to the standard practice of intelligence operations. In fact, they made use of the same men and covered the same ground. Contacts between "networks" and "movements" were continuous.

In another field, the communist party, entering the resistance after

June 1941 [when Germany attacked Russia], called on all the French people to unite with the communists in a "national front" which apparently had no immediate political aims, and created its own military-type organization, the FTPF.[1]

Up to that point, the other political parties had not played any role, as parties, in the resistance. The step taken by the communists led them to declare themselves as well, for otherwise the communists would have been able to claim that their party was the only one which did anything in the resistance, and even that they had themselves organized it.

Finally, General de Gaulle in London had to show our English and American Allies that he was not merely a "rebel," but the authentic representative of French opinion.

That was the chief reason why, when Jean Moulin, first delegate in France from General de Gaulle, created the CNR (National Committee of the Resistance) and combined under its banner all the resistance movements of both the northern and southern zones, he included not merely the representatives of those movements but also those of the former political parties of the Third Republic.

In 1942 Germany's needs for workers led to the creation of the STO (Obligatory Labor Service) which recruited and sent to enemy territory the French workers necessary for German war production. Up to that time the resistants maintained some official activity, real or pretended, as a sort of cover, apart from their clandestine activities, but at this time a new category of resistants appeared, those who had evaded the STO and who therefore, in order to escape deportation, had to take refuge in isolated farms, abandoned barns, and sometimes in especially constructed shelters, generally in mountainous zones difficult to reach; it was these who were known as the "maquis" [literally, underbrush and forest difficult to penetrate].

A fairly large number of officers and noncommissioned officers who had left the army for this purpose or for other reasons took part in this activity. To mention only a few: Captain Henry Frenay founded the movement "Combat;" Colonel Touny and General Lugand played an important part, the first in the OCM (Civilian and Military Organization) and the second in "Liberation Nord;" Major Loustaneau-Lacau created the "Alliance" network; and we have already mentioned General Delestraint who was the first chief of the AS. These were all purely individual activities. The French army itself, though in contact with many of these movements or networks, took no part in them.

The army had not felt the need of taking part, as far as it was concerned. The army existed only to re-enter the combat and was fully aware of that fact, especially in the homeland where it was in the presence of the occupants. In any case it could not have doubted that that was the reason for its existence, since certain of its leaders, particularly General Frère, did not hesitate to proclaim the fact insistently on all occasions; and many of its members were acquainted with the clandestine activity which was carried on within it, or at least suspected its existence.

Before December 1942 it would therefore have seemed absurd to most

---

1. *Francs-tireurs et Partisans Français.* It is to be noted that this organization never agreed to unite completely with the other movements.

of the officers and noncommissioned officers to abandon an army which was established with a purpose that was quite clear to them, and which was the normal framework of their activities, in order to join clandestine formations which had scarcely any real existence and of which the effectiveness seemed to them, at that time, much more doubtful.

The dissolution of the Armistice Army in November 1942 set a new problem.

An officer who had come from London to France wrote at the beginning of 1944 the following words, which express with some precision the situation and the attitude of the army in the homeland at that time: "The disbanded army is discredited in a way which has never been equaled. It is reproached with having lost the war, with having settled down comfortably in the defeat, with pompously claiming virtues which it was unable to practice, and with having been caught asleep in bed on the dawn of that November day when the fleet at Toulon, with some theatricality, it is true, scuttled itself. I happened to be temporarily in France and unable to move for the time being; among this humiliated army there were a number of my former comrades with whom I came into contact again. I was able to understand the thought of these comrades whom the affront which had befallen them left as strangers among the patriots of the resistance."

All of them longed only to prove, weapons in hand, that they had not merited the double insult which had been inflicted on them. Some of them went over immediately to the maquis. Others tried to cross the Pyrenees, because the first idea of any soldier who wants to fight is to join some regular unit; some succeeded, many failed. Soon they were turned away from such plans by their own chiefs, who showed them another way to take.[1]

In fact, a new organization had been immediately created around General Frère, who committed himself to it, under the leadership of those who having previously carried on clandestine activities in the army quite naturally continued in clandestine operations outside the army. At the head [of this new organization] was General Verneau, the army's chief of staff, assisted by Gen. Olléris, Gen. Gransart, Gen. Revers, Gen. Gilliot, and some officers from the army's general staff, together with Col. Ely, Col. Pfister, Col. Zeller, Col. Laurent, and Major Cogny. On the divisional level were the divisional officers who, working with them, had formally prepared the clandestine organization and the camouflage of equipment, such as Pommiès.

The new organization developed quite easily, in the southern zone, out of the ruins of the Armistice Army. At the beginning of 1943 General Verneau and Major Cogny went into the northern zone and there brought together the officers who had been scattered by the disbandment of the army, and founded new groups in that area.

Relations were established with London and Algiers through the Alliance network, and also directly. In London, Major Lejeune maintained liaison with Allied authorities through a British officer, Colonel Buckmaster.

These activities soon attracted the attention of the occupant who in

1. Passage across the Pyrenees was thereafter limited to specialists, drivers of tanks, air pilots, technical workers, and so on, who were needed by the Africa Army.

1943 struck heavily at the headquarters of the organization and at its field activities. In particular, General Frère, Gen. Verneau, Gen. Olléris, Gen. Gransart, Gen. Gilliot, Col. Boutat, and Major Cogny were arrested. The Gestapo was then able to boast, with apparent justification, that it had "destroyed" the new military organization.

But the broken threads were soon knotted together. General Revers took command, having under his orders Colonel Zeller in the southeast, Colonel Pfister in the southwest, Major Ailleret in the northern zone, and Major du Gareau in the Paris region.

Thus there were three military-type organizations in France at that time: the AS, the FTPF, and the organization developed from the army itself, which was soon to be known as ORA [Organization of Resistance of the Army]. The purposes of these three organizations were identical: to participate, under the leadership of the government of General de Gaulle, the CFLN (French Committee for National Liberation), in co-operation with French forces abroad and with our Allies, in the liberation of our national territory. The necessity of unifying their action was obvious to all. But whereas the first two organizations were based on "movements" or on parties which were more or less political in character, the third had formed itself, and intended to keep its specifically military character.

The army in France is traditionally non-political. It is unwilling to be either the tool or the support of a government, or even of a regime, regardless of whether the army approves or disapproves its purposes. On the other hand, the officers of the army were unable to imagine that two armies could exist, one abroad under the control of the CFLN and the other in France itself under the CNR and not under the control of the commander in chief. They belonged to the same army as did their comrades in North Africa, an army now cut in two by the landing and the events that had followed. This is why they naturally turned first in that direction. Further, military men desired to play their part in the common task, in their military role, just as the political parties and all the various social and professional groups had desired to do, for the same reasons. This feeling was sharply intensified among the officers, when they were reproached for the defeat and veritable capitulation which the dissolution of their army had in fact been, and in which they felt most deeply an unjustified humiliation.[1]

This special attitude, always firmly adhered to, and also, it must be said, certain rivalries between individuals, and especially the political ambitions of certain of the chiefs of the different "movements," made union difficult.

First contacts established at the end of 1942 between General Frère and General Delestraint came to an end with the arrest of the two leaders. Contacts re-established by General Verneau resulted, in October 1943, in an agreement with the AS. Negotiations which were entered into with

1. These feelings are to be clearly seen in the names under which the ORA was first known; an "organization sprung from the Armistice Army," the term used by General Verneau, showing clearly its origin and the fact that it was not a "movement;" the term "homeland organization of the army," used by General Revers to emphasize its unity with the army in North Africa; and the title which was finally adopted, "Organization of Resistance of the Army," was an expression of a fact even more than it was a name.

the FTPF at the beginning of 1943, in which Colonel Pfister served as intermediary, dragged on through the entire year and ended by a complete withdrawal of the representatives of the communist party, who claimed that as the result of an agreement made in October the AS had absorbed the ORA, and who also took refuge behind the authority of the CNR. But in February 1944, after long negotiations carried on by General Revers, the CNR finally achieved the union of the various formations which thereafter constituted the FFI.[1] General Revers, chief of ORA joined COMAC (Comité d'Action), an executive agency of the CNR. This was a logical solution; ORA maintained its non-political character and therefore its representative could have no place in the CNR itself, which was the highest political party of the resistance.

Then, in April 1944, General Koenig in London was assigned the task of co-ordinating the resistance in France in liaison with the Allied command. On 7 June 1944 he became Commander of the French Forces of the Interior, his control being effected through his representative in France, the DMN (National Military Delegate with the CNR) and the various DMR (Regional Military Delegates, one in each region). These representatives served as his liaison agents with the responsibility of transmitting his instructions, reporting to him on their execution, and allocating the available equipment and supplies.

This measure linked the activities of the French forces of the interior directly with those of the forces abroad and thus agreed completely, as we have seen, with the ideas of the officers of ORA. Thus in a singular reversal the same reasons which had caused the officers of ORA to be regarded as rebels in the resistance itself, because they offered their allegiance to the EM [General Headquarters] in Algiers, now brought them into close relations with, London, while the most ardent of the CFLN, jealous at the sight of an EM[2] abroad taking over the direction of their forces, began to draw away from London, and all the more because they feared that their political ambitions would be more or less disappointed at the time of the future liberation.

In spite of the profound unity of purpose, the differences which separated the various elements of the resistance had their effect not only on the kind of political activity which was carried on but also on the kind of military action to be undertaken.

The time had long passed for activities limited to sabotage, carried out by little groups, isolated from each other, who extended and increased the destruction of the bombings. The "movements" and military-type formations recognized the need for this policy, and its effectiveness, a policy which was still as a rule adhered to by the networks; but it was their intention that the resistance should participate more directly in the liberation of the national territory. Ideas differed as to the kind of action to be undertaken, and as to the right time for action.

Although such differences existed in the very heart of all the organizations, as a rule the military officers, whether belonging the ORA, AS, or the EM of London, being the heirs of the clandestine mobilization plans and of the

1. French Forces of the Interior. It must be noted carefully that the FTPF never united with the FFI and maintained a high degree of autonomy for political reasons.
2. [General Staff.]

tactical projects linked with them, thought that the activities, originally clandestine, directed by partisan groups, ought to lead to the reorganization of semi-military forces fighting openly, forces which finally would be absorbed by the French army when it landed. But, believing too, it must be remembered, that the struggle for the liberation of France would be longer than it was in fact, they feared that they would bring terrible reprisals on the country and would compromise future possibilities if they opened their campaign before the landing, while the occupying authority still had complete liberty of action against our interior forces. In any case these forces did not at that time have sufficient equipment and supplies[1] or the necessary officers.[2]

The opinion of those who came from the AS was fairly close to that of ORA. But as the AS were more closely bound to the local groups of a political character from which they sprang, they tended to consider the liberation of the region in which they themselves operated as an end in itself, and not as the commencement of further actions against the enemy army.

In view of these facts a complete plan for regrouping the maquis had been prepared by General Revers and sent to Algiers through Chevance-Bertin and Benouville. This plan envisaged the liberation of the southwest and center of France by French forces alone. These forces would in addition insure, by the same action, liaison between the two expected landings, the one from the Channel and the one from the Mediterranean.

The FTPF emphasized immediate action and therefore condemned what they called the "wait and see" attitude of the other organizations. They believed that enemy reprisals would merely strengthen the spirit of resistance among the people. They believed too that where arms were lacking the enemy should be attacked in order that his might be seized—an idea in contradiction of all experience, for on the whole the partisans in attempting to follow that policy lost more arms than they captured. In particular, they intended to make the resistance much more insurrectional than military. Relying on the People's Militia they concentrated far more on taking control of the country than on driving out the Germans.

In the end, at the time when the landing did take place, the highest levels of the resistance had agreed upon immediate action, limited to what was possible with the means available. They planned that destruction should be carried out over the entire country, that in the immediate rear of the enemy's combat forces there should be generalized guerilla fighting, and that in certain mountain regions, far from the landing beaches and

1. However, contrary to current opinion, it is probable that enough arms had been parachuted into France before the landing to supply all those who were able to use them. But it must be remembered that all forms of guerilla warfare are wasteful of equipment. Half of the parachuted arms were seized by the enemy before they could be used. The rest were badly distributed. And finally from 15 per cent to 25 per cent of the arms actually used were lost within two or three months. It must not be concluded, however, that equipment distributed among partisans is less effective than that which is given to the regular troops. The difference is that in a regular troop only two or three out of a hundred weapons used by individual soldiers are effective, whereas in a partisan group every gun which fires is effective.

2. In the French homeland in 1944 there remained about 9,000 officers who had belonged to the army of 1939. After allowances made for those who had become old, those who abstained, and those who belonged to the networks (there were about 1,400 of these), it was not possible to count on having more than 2,500 to 3,000 officers for a total FFI force of something between 100,000 and 250,000, according to the method of calculation adopted.

only weakly held by the enemy, a mobilization maquis should be created where available forces could be brought together and where they would receive parachuted equipment and the supplementary officers which they needed.

These activities were to be set in motion by twenty series of "phrases" broadcast from London, each being adapted to one region. The plan ruled out, at the beginning, the possibility of a general insurrection.

But though it had been possible to establish a certain unity on these high levels, and there is no reason for saying that there were any reservations, it was far from being the same on the lower levels.

To start an insurrection, to direct it, to prevent it, to delay it, or to stop it are all equally difficult. It must not be forgotten that partisans—resistants, maquisards, francs-tireurs, guerillas, or whatever name is given them—are volunteers. They are volunteers in every sense of the word which means that as far as they are concerned their obligations begin with their own free will and end in the same way. They are sometimes there when they are not desired, and sometimes when they are desired they are not there. They do not always do what is desired, but rather what they desire themselves. Their leaders are always rather like gang leaders, whether they wish to be or not, both the owners and the prisoners of their own troops.

Because of these things, union of all the groups, though achieved theoretically, existed only partially in actual practice and then through direct agreement between local leaders, agreement sometimes reached before the theoretical agreements on the higher levels, and in many cases limited to a sort of side-by-side operation of the units and the staffs, and sometimes only to a simple liaison between them.

The commanding officer of an FFI regional group, even though it was a region in which fusion appeared to have taken place, wrote on 20 April 1944: "In spite of our efforts, the attempt to make the FFI something more than a vague abstraction has not been successful. Since the end of January, as the result of the disagreement between the FTP and the AS, relations have not been re-established; today, though in some departements the work is being done jointly because of personal contacts that had been established, the region as a whole is isolated from the FTP." A CNR delegate in the southern zone, one scarcely to be suspected of prejudice against the communists, wrote, too, on 1 June 1944: "Regarding relations with the FTPF, I have been able to determine that throughout nearly all the regions contacts are nearly non-existent."

And on 6 June 1944, when the landing was announced, although from one end of France to another the program of destruction was carried out according to plan, at the same time wherever the occupants were not strong, insurrection broke out contrary to the clearly declared intentions of all the resistance leaders both within France and abroad.

In the Ain, the Alps, the Indre, and the western part of the Massif Central, large areas were practically freed, town halls and sometimes the headquarters of under-prefectures were occupied, and small German garrisons were isolated. "What happened in this area," wrote an officer on 15 July 1944, "was the beginning of a mass uprising in answer to appeals from the London Radio." The reference here is to propaganda and not to certain phrases used as signals, which as we know had been intended to set into operation a series of far more limited actions. Men rushed to join the various maquis in numbers exceeding all forecasts. In the Vercors, one of the best known maquis, there had been about 2,000 men just before the landing, but there were twice as many a few days later, and 8,000 by the beginning of July.

The unexpected magnitude of this movement set a serious problem for the chiefs of the resistance. They knew well that their partisans could not resist a strong action by regular soldiers. Further, they did not have the necessary equipment to arm and maintain even a quarter as many men as had joined them. Those leaders who were able to do so attempted to restrain this movement and to send back home the men who had not compromised themselves too much. The EM in London also urged them to take such steps, as their resources, though considerable, did not enable them to meet the demand so quickly.

But others had to accept the situation as it was and to try to make the best of it. One of the regional commanders wrote on 1 July 1944: "A number of localities have taken sides completely and we cannot reverse what has already been done. In most cases, it happens, these localities can be defended and are holding on well. Others, however, have had to be evacuated. . . ." They could not abandon these rebel villages to enemy reprisals without at least attempting to defend them. Further, by refusing to fight they ran the risk of being overrun by their own troops, and when everything was taken into consideration it was better to attempt to co-ordinate their activities. Finally, it must be said that after years of underground struggle the prospects of an open fight were sufficiently stimulating to turn the heads, somewhat, of young and ardent leaders. General Revers, reviewing the situation in the southwest of France, wrote to Colonel Pfister on 12 June 1944: "Because of the breadth of the activities, often anarchistic, of the resistance and the maquis, I believe that it may be necessary for you to undertake with your units operations of increasing importance almost at once, even if such activity is not specifically called for by London."

Within the restricted limits of the present report it is not possible to give more than a summary of the action taken for the liberation of the French homeland by the FFI, in the ranks of which the ORA was henceforth mingled.

In the southern zone, the Germans reacted. Beginning on 10 June 1944 they attacked the FFI in the Ain, Savoy, and the southern Alps with field divisions supported by artillery and air units. They drove the FFI back into the mountains. Their first attempts against the Vercors failed and they had to use two divisions, in July, to break up the maquis there, who then joined those of the Grande Chartreuse and the Oisans. In the Massif Central they were resisted in the east at Mont Mouchet, and in the west in Haute-Vienne. They massacred the population everywhere and burned villages.

In the northern zone, as the Anglo-American troops continued their advance the FFI guided them, supplied them with information, and cleaned up the enemy pockets left in the rear, finally reaching the Loire. Supported by a battalion of parachute troops they liberated Britanny while the American army reached Brest in a single rapid movement. Finally, on 18 August 1944, Paris revolted and isolated the German garrison in its various barracks; on 26 August General Leclerc, who had hastened to the city, received the capitulation of General von Choltitz.

But on 15 August 1944 the Franco-American army landed in Provence. With only fifteen divisions still in the south of France, the Germans were unable to deal both with this new enemy and with the maquis which was becoming stronger and more numerous on all sides; they had no other alternative than to evacuate the area.

The FFI immediately regrouped and undertook the pursuit of the enemy. By 20 August 1944, the Haute-Savoie, the Haute-Vienne except Limoges, the Corrèze, the Haute-Loire, and the Indre were completely liberated. German garrisons surrendered and all retreating German columns were harassed. The Pommiès independent group, the Schneider column, the FFI of the Cher and the Indre, the FFI of the Corrèze, and all the ORA units followed the Germans. On 12 September 1944, the German column commanded by General Elster, surrounded south of the Loire, was obliged to lay down its arms, giving us 18,000 prisoners in the hands of the ORA units commanded by Bertrand Chomel Fayard.

This was the end of partisan warfare. In actual contact with the enemy, divergencies were wiped out. The FFI became a part of the French army and while one section besieged the German garrisons on the Atlantic front, the other participated, in the ranks of the First French army, in the difficult campaign of the winter of 1944-1945, before continuing with the army into Germany.

Clandestinity and irregularity came to an end. Officers and soldiers were again a part of their normal organization: the French army.

(Document No. 242)
Fr. ed. 819-826

Paris, 8 November 1954

REVERS
General Georges Revers

THE ARMY
PÉTAIN AND DE GAULLE

ALFRED CONQUET
General; Intelligence Section, General Staff

Preliminary Note

When Maréchal Pétain was Minister of War in 1934 I was his private secretary for all matters and particularly for parliamentary affairs. After November 1934, when the Doumergue ministry fell, I was his chief of staff until the end of 1936, at which time I was sent to the Center for Advanced Military Studies on detached service. After that I took command of a regiment. When I did so, the Maréchal said to me, "I will recall you to my own service after you have completed your period of command." But the war of 1939-1940 took place.

The fact that I did not return to the cabinet of the Maréchal in July 1940 was due essentially to the opposition of Dr. Ménétrel, proof of whose attitude toward me will be given later. From 1940 to 1943 I first commanded the military departement of the Cantal and them served as assistant in territorial command to the general commanding the region of Clermont-Ferrand, which included six departements. Finally, I was arrested by the Gestapo and deported to Germany on 10 August 1943.

Thus though I could speak with every competence regarding the Maréchal's fruitful action between 1934 and 1936 (a study on that subject is in preparation) I have not the same competence for the period 1940-1944. From August 1940 to August 1943, however, I was able to be in touch with the Maréchal on many occasions; I was received by him, or summoned to his office, and was invited to eat with him. He made important confidential statements to me. On that subject, too, I shall write several pages. In the meantime I extract from my notebooks and take from my memories the following points from among those which seem to be the most significant of the Maréchal's thought. (I regret to bring myself into the picture, but how can I do otherwise when dealing with events in which I myself took part?)

September 1940

I was just back from a short convalescence following an appendicitis operation when my wife and I were invited to dine with the Maréchal before I went to Aurillac as commanding officer for the departement of the Cantal. (We had not been received by the Maréchal this way since 1937.)

That evening the Maréchal was in an exceptionally vivacious mood. After dinner he said to me, "You introduced me one day to a great book, *Intellectual and Moral Reform*, by Renan.[1] How topical that book is today! I am going to do everything in my power to revive in France the spiritual values which have been lacking among us.

"But tell me, you yourself have written a book on a great military disaster, to which I contributed a preface. The subject was Caporetto. I was certainly not particularly optimistic but I could not imagine that we too would come so quickly to a catastrophe of the same magnitude."

"M. le Maréchal," I replied, "you remember how confused the French people were in the years before the war. The study of that subject had been very close to my heart because war was coming nearer and I feared that we were moving toward the same disaster as that which the Italians had met and for similar reasons. I wanted somehow to sound the alarm, from my own position."

"I liked the conclusions you drew." the Maréchal told me. "What was it you said?"

"I had been struck by the thought which Voltaire expressed in the preface to his history of Charles XII," I replied, "His words were: 'It can be said of a man that he was brave on such and such a day. But in

1. It was in 1934 in connection with the talk which the Maréchal gave at the dinner arranged by the *Revue des Deux-Mondes*.

referring to the character of a nation it is necessary to state which government and which year is referred to.'   In this way I desired to emphasize the close relationship which always exists between the living force of a country at any particular moment and the quality of its government at that particular time."

"That's exactly right," the Maréchal answered.   "Yesterday the government of France was made up of politicians. Look where they led us. In the future they must be kept out of the government of France."

February 1941

When I was promoted to the rank of general in February 1941 I was told to report to the Maréchal, who asked me to stay for lunch.

"I take the liberty of bringing to your attention a book of topical interest," I said to the Maréchal as we were taking coffee in the salon, "although it is already thirty years old.   I refer to the book written by Captain Vidal de la Blache (killed in 1913) *The Rebirth of Prussia after Iéna*. I had studied it before 1914, pen in hand, at a time when we were the defeated nation of 1870."

"People have told me about this book; what do you think of it?"

"I think that there are a great many people who ought to read it, and that it should be made better known through the press.   After Iéna, the King of Prussia, when he was being urged by the Queen [Louise] to disregard everything else in order to resist with all his strength the Emperor Napoleon, held essentially to a single purpose, that of maintaining the framework of his country, reinvigorating its political and spiritual strength, and maintaining and protecting its unity while waiting for a favorable day. That policy was not unsuccessful for Prussia.   Our own rebels would find in this historic example, of which they are ignorant, a lesson in realism and patience."

"That's quite true," the Maréchal said.   "I will talk about it.   What it comes to is that de Gaulle is a Queen Louise who took the wrong turning.[1] The difference is that I will never go so far as to collaborate with the conqueror, as the King of Prussia did.[2] We shall re-establish ourselves without that.   I am quite sure of it."

June 1941

I had come to Vichy to obtain a passport for the occupied zone and saw the Maréchal for a few moments.

"Please allow me to present this little book to you," I said, *The War Record of the 27th Battalion of Alpine Infantry*.   I was made an honorary member of this battalion, which was one of the units in the division under my command in 1939-1940.   I myself wrote the introduction to this little

1. It is not surprising that the Maréchal was thoroughly informed as to the events of the 1806 period; he had studied that campaign in the greatest detail, and as professor of tactics in the War School he had analyzed the fighting which took place a few days before the battle of Jena.

2. "Never any military collaboration with the Reich!" We were to learn later that this had already been said in October 1940 to M. Rougier when he left for London on a mission.   It was repeated on other occasions and adhered to to the end.

book, and in it I point out the noble deeds of the battalion. I hope you will be good enough to read the conclusion: 'In remembrance and in hope: our faith that good will come surges up from these pages.'"

"In remembrance and in hope . . .," the Maréchal said. "That is the password for the journey from the tomb to the Resurrection. You could say nothing better. I truly hope to see this Resurrection."

December 1941

At this point I recall a strictly personal memory. I record it because it makes it possible to understand our interview of 30 December 1942. Admiral Darlan, already vice-president of the Council and Minister of the Interior as well as Minister of the Navy, had assigned to himself at the end of 1941, after the accidental death of General Huntziger, the Ministry of War.

The Admiral, who was regarded at that time as having a collaborationist tendency, took various measures concerning internal affairs: (a) he suppressed the departemental military commands, which had the effect of limiting the authority of the prefects, hoping by that step to secure a favorable reaction which would be helpful to him; (b) he struck off the list a large number of officers, including the most combative, with a view toward softening the attitude of the Germans. Army affairs were new to him and he obviously could not be familiar with the personality of the different officers. He therefore relied on others to inform him. He made his decisions very quickly, allowing himself to be made use of, sometimes by the prefects themselves and sometimes by certain zealous tools.[1] He placed me on the list of generals who were to be placed on the retired list, though General Frère, commanding the group of divisions in the very same month of December [1941], chose me as one of the four brigadier generals, out of a total of twenty, whom he recommended for promotion to the rank of general of division. I was told about these maneuvers. As a decision was about to be made I obtained an interview with the Maréchal who, greatly astonished, told me that he knew absolutely nothing about it—though every decree concerning general officers had to be signed by him.

"But what has the Admiral against you?" the Maréchal asked me.

"I have no official information at all," I answered. "I am all the more surprised because General Frère confided in me that he had included me as one of the four generals out of twenty whom he nominated for promotion, to the rank of general of division. But I've been told that the Admiral accuses me of having Gaullist tendencies."

"What do you mean by that?"

"M. le Maréchal," I replied, "you know me so well that I can speak freely, as I always do. If in fact I have Gaullist tendencies it is only in the sense in which you yourself might, in the depths of your heart. But for me there is nothing above the authority and the unity of the state. In telling you that I do not astonish you. It is the reason why I stand firmly in support of the Chief of State, in your support, in all fidelity."

"But that's very good indeed," the Maréchal said. "Obviously I can't

1. I myself learned sometime later the identity of the general officer who, in all his partisan passion, had worked against me in his relations with the Admiral.

get rid of the Admiral because of you, but I will send my representative to see him.[1] I talk to you this way because I trust you," and put a finger on his lips. "Shh . . . I'm looking after you."

And on the following day I was struck off the list which the Admiral had prepared.[2]

May 1942

The Maréchal one morning visited the camp at les Fontaines, near Clermont-Ferrand, and reviewed the troops of the division. The English had just landed on Madagascar. He spoke a few words extemporaneously, more or less in these terms: "The Army must work hard and efficiently in preparation for combat. No one knows what is going to happen."

For once he was prudent to the point of being enigmatic. It can be asked whether he was thinking of action against the British in Madagascar, or of war against England, or one against Germany.

I presented myself to him at the end of the review and saluted. He asked me what I thought of the effect of his words. I told him of the various interpretations which had been given, the result being that, contrary to what usually happened, approval was not unanimous.

I saw his expression darken somewhat, but he did not show any indignation. He never showed indignation. He merely replied, "Well, but you, who know what I mean?"

"M. le Maréchal," I answered, "I never have any doubt about your way of thought."

"Well then, tell them to follow me in complete confidence. I need their confidence more than ever."

June 1942

From the very first days of the month General Delmotte,[3] Under-Secretary of State for War, sent for me and spoke in approximately the following words:

"The government wants to form a combat division, made up of volunteers, and I am instructed to offer you the command.

"The present LVF [French Legion of Volunteers]," he said when I asked for explanation, "is not strictly under the control of the state. It includes only two or three battalions, which were raised with considerable difficulty. But we are going to facilitate recruiting of volunteers from the Armistice Army and the result will be a composite division rather like the Foreign Legion. The next step will be to take this division to a fighting front,

1. The representative was M. Romier.
2. I may add that a little later, this time better informed, the Admiral told M. Moysset, Minister of State, who had been his collaborator for many years at the Ministry of the Navy and was from the same part of the country as I myself, and one of my friends, "Yes, I regret that they almost made me split that man's ears for him (sic)." And in April 1942 when General Laure left he proposed that I should be asked to succeed him; later he offered me a command in North Africa, and following that a position as general of division (see below).
3. It was I myself who had brought Major Delmotte, in January 1935, to serve with me on the Maréchal's general staff, and who had arranged for his appointment at the Center for Advanced Military Studies at the end of 1936.

either in Russia or perhaps on the Turkish front. In this way we will obtain invaluable information as to the way the war is going.

"The Admiral is working very seriously on this plan. He promises you the rank of general of division within a year, and perhaps within only a few months. In addition you will receive large supplementary payments."

"I must decline a command of that kind," I answered.

"Good," he replied. "I have other candidates, one of whom is Colonel Perré." (On the following day I was able to warn Colonel Perré, then commanding a divisional infantry group at Clermont-Ferrand, and to tell him of my views on the subject. Colonel Perré was in fact approached on this subject.)

I withdrew and went to report the proposal to the Maréchal.

"You were perfectly right and I approve entirely," he said to me. "You could not take any other attitude; it is the attitude of a French general."

July 1942

During the summer of 1942 communist agitation increased and became intensely excited. The tribunals rarely pronounced death sentences. Nevertheless M. Marchadier, a fully committed extremist agitator and a very influential representative of the CGT [Communist-led federation of trade unions], was condemned to death; so was M. Calas, who did not belong to that particular region.

In my capacity of military commander at Clermont I was responsible for the execution of this decision made by the judicial system. Preparation had already been made on the hill where the execution was to take place, near the Clermont power plant. But in agreement with several important men, among whom were the Mayor and the President of the Red Cross, I went to Vichy. I asked for an urgent appointment with the Maréchal and when I saw him he said at once, "I will not have French blood on my hands. The point is settled; the sentence on these two condemned men is commuted."[1]

September 1942

My wife and I were invited to dinner on 30 September 1942. There were half a dozen guests, among them being M. Lémery, the Countess of S——, and some others.

In the course of the conversations in the salon someone was pleased to praise the Maréchal's qualities.

"Be careful," it amused the Maréchal to say, "General Conquet is here and he is the man who knows me better then anyone else does. He knows my qualities most precisely and he believes that everything said about me is exaggerated."[2]

"M. le Maréchal," the guest continued, "you are reproached for having established dictatorship. But the dictatorship which you have desired to introduce should be considered only as a dictatorship of noble sentiments."

1. No matter what happened the Maréchal himself never confirmed any condemnation of a French citizen to death. Have his adversaries the same scruples?

2. I mention this note of exceptional cordiality because it makes it easier to understand the interview which took place on 30 December 1942.

"A sentimental dictatorship is the right expression," the Maréchal answered. "At the beginning, what I did was readily approved by everyone or nearly everyone. But in view of the difficulties in which we are now involved, did I do the right thing? That is what I am asking myself now. Did you read my message? You certainly see that I am striving to preserve for France its moral and spiritual values; but does everyone understand it?

"Monseigneur Suhard, whose spirit is perceptive, has warned me; 'Above all, do not take sides with the church's organization.' And I have answered him, 'Don't be afraid. I am not on the side of the church organization. But nevertheless I shall always speak a word in their support.'"

The conversation turned to the University of Strasbourg, of which the Germans were demanding the disbandment.

"I must tell you," the Maréchal said to me, "that it is the Alsatian problems which bring me the greatest anxiety."

I mentioned that I was striving to maintain the University's prestige, in view of the fact that it was being continuously attacked, by asking its professors to give lectures to our garrison forces. The Maréchal congratulated me on the step I had taken and told me that I could do no better than to continue firmly along the same line.

12 November 1942

I saw the Maréchal for a few moments on the subject of the breaking of the Armistice terms.

"I shall not leave," he said to me. "A plane stands ready for me but in 1940 I promised the people of France that I would remain with them. When I took over the government I said to certain men, 'Go if you wish but I shall stay under any circumstances.' My determination before everything else was to protect the French people. Unhappily the situation remains the same. Honor commands me to remain. That which I have always sought is to save the country from greater tragedies, and to maintain the country's unity against division in order that my purpose may be attained."

He came nearer to me and said, "I would like to be, one day, the mediator between the parties. . . ."

Then he broke off sharply. It was only on 30 December 1942 that I understood the meaning of his sudden silence. On 12 November, the Maréchal was not yet prepared to speak in greater confidence.

(On that same day Madame Pétain told me that the Maréchal had recently had an interview with von Rundstedt who had been strongly impressed by "such greatness and such simplicity." Madame Pétain told me what was said, according to her, by those immediately around von Rundstedt: "It will be Maréchal Pétain who will make peace.")

30 December 1942

Taking advantage of the absence of Dr. Ménétrel, who was in Paris on a short New Year's holiday, the Maréchal summoned me by telephone from Clermont-Ferrand. The following is a resumé of our conversation.

"I feel that I am being kept informed more and more badly," he told me.

"In other days I was extremely well informed by you. I need someone near me in whom I have full confidence. I want you to come back with me."

"M. le Maréchal," I said, "it is perhaps a little late, for many critical decisions have already been made. Besides, there is Ménétrel between us. Under these conditions could I do anything useful? Nevertheless I am at your disposition."

"Very good. I relied on you. As for the rest, don't worry about it. You will work there in the little office right beside me just as you used to do at the Ministry [of War] and at the Invalides."

"Just as you wish," I answered.

"I will send you word next week to come and begin your service here, but I have something else to tell you," the Maréchal went on. "You know de Gaulle very well. I know that you were his comrade and friend".

"Yes, M. le Maréchal," I replied, "Perhaps you are thinking of the warm plea which I made to you in favor of his being promoted to the rank of colonel.[1] I had known de Gaulle since our days at the War School. Afterwards we were at Chem at the same time and later each of us had commanded a regiment at Metz under General Giraud. We were all the more in relation with each other because we had both been in your own service. Finally, we had very often exchanged ideas as sympathetic comrades are likely to do."

"Very good," the Maréchal said. " That means that you can easily get in touch with him, just as I knew would be the case. When the moment has come for me to transfer the power, I intend to send you to him, as a link between us, to transmit my proposals."

"You would be showing strong proof of confidence in me, M. le Maréchal. I would undertake such a mission with joy. But what do you think will be the right moment?"

"When the Allies have clearly won. But don't speak a word about this, needless to say," he added. "I shall see you next week."

Several days later, the Maréchal did in fact summon me again discreetly to his office. "Your transfer does not seem to me to be possible at this moment," he hold me. "There is opposition. But you will take over the direction of the Historical Service. That is important. Study the reports of our military correspondents very carefully. You will come to me to tell me about them. We will see a little later about your assignment to work at my side."

A little later... I was arrested by the Gestapo on 10 August 1943 and deported until 7 May 1945 when I was freed by the Americans. I was obviously no longer in a position to carry out the mission planned by the Maréchal.

Would he have adhered in 1944 to the proposal he had made in 1942? And in that case would General de Gaulle have listened to me any more than he did to Admiral Auphan?

My deportation, seen from any point of view, was the most regrettable incident of my life. It deprived me of what was perhaps the most exceptional opportunity to serve my country usefully. What a destiny would

1. It had become evident at the beginning of December 1935, according to what Lieutenant Colonel de Gaulle told me confidentially, that he was not being kept on the list for promotion to the rank of colonel by the competent commission. I had immediately informed the Maréchal who then intervened with General Bourret, chief of cabinet for the Minister of War.

have been that of France if General de Gaulle had consented to take over the legitimate power from the hands of the Maréchal!

The fact remains that the conversation reported above proves that in December 1942 the Maréchal desired to transmit to de Gaulle his legitimate powers on the day, which he already foresaw, of the liberation of France, in order that the unity of the nation might be firmly maintained. I testify to that fact.

(Document No. 243)
Fr. ed. 827-834

Fontainebleau, 1 February 1955

CONQUET
General Alfred Conquet

ARMY — (PIERRE LAVAL)

EUGÈNE BRIDOUX
General, French Army;
Minister of War

In the shameful haste which characterized what some have dared to call a judicial investigation preceding the trial of Pierre Laval it was impossible for me to give on his behalf the testimony which I owed to him, and to throw light on those events with which I was personally connected during the two years when I had the honor to serve under his orders, first as Secretary of State for War, and then as Secretary of State for Defense. The most I was able to do was to prepare two short notes, both referring to the results of the Anglo-Saxon landing in North Africa on 8 November 1942; these two notes are in the dossier of the trial.

It would have been interesting, above all, to throw light particularly on what I knew of the military part of his governmental action, leaving to others more qualified than I the task of bringing out the characteristics of his general policies, and of his action toward the German authorities in all the questions which day by day affected the life and future of the nation in the midst of the consequences of the war and the demands of the occupation.

A law of 16 April 1942 had given to Admiral Darlan, with the title of Commander-in-Chief, command of the French land, sea, and air forces, placing him directly under the authority of the Maréchal. Three ministerial departments thus were withdrawn, in theory, from the control of the Chief of Government and therefore he might quite well have left all the responsibility in military affairs to the man who had demanded it and who had obtained the highest position in that field. But it was not in the President's character to avoid realities; inevitably such matters must end up in his own office, either because of financial decisions to be taken, or because of approaches and arrangements to be made with the German command, or in order to reduce German demands in such matters. For my part, I never failed to report all my important actions to the Chief of Government, to solicit his opinion and his instructions, and to ask for his support. President Laval did, therefore, have a military policy.

"I have two great passions," he often said. "The first is my country. The second is peace."

He did in truth have a passion for peace, but with a noble feeling for the dignity and the grandeur of the country, and with a profound patriotism composed of love for the land of his birth, of pride for its past, and of unshakable faith in its future.

He had to the highest degree a sense of the meaning of the state and of his role as its Chief, together with a most true view of the Army's independence, of its power, and of its mission as a prime element in the nation's sovereignty. Military ways sometimes gave his wit full play but we soldiers who were near him knew that such remarks were not incompatible with his deepest feelings which were of sympathy, of affection, and of the need to have confidence.

The armistice convention of June 1940 had established for the mainland troops of France a maximum of 100,000 men, to be recruited entirely by volunteer engagement. The convention specified that the reason for the existence of this army was the maintenance of order in France. The convention was more liberal toward the French Africa Army and the colonial troops, whose mission was to guarantee the integrity of the French empire.

The recruitment of the Africa Army and the colonial troops presented no special difficulties, but the case was different as regards volunteers for the units on the mainland. By April 1942 their total was scarcely more than half the necessary number. The reasons for this failure were the discredit which had come to the Army by the events of the war, the difficulties resulting from the division of France into two zones of which that with the largest population was for the greater part not subject to the French government, and above all the impossibility of appealing to the mysticism of the soldier, an appeal which would have brought many young Frenchmen to volunteer.

On 10 May 1942 I submitted to the President a plan for a return to conscription so far as the first contingent of 50,000 men were concerned. He adopted it at once and waited for an opportunity to support it in discussion with the German authorities. He had realized at once, in fact, that aside from the material fact of bringing the Armistice Army to its full size, a return to conscription would break down one of the causes which most restricted our national sovereignty, would begin a return to our traditional institutions, and would prepare for the future by taking a first step toward the formation of reserves.

Negotiations on this subject were begun in the unfavorable atmosphere created by Hitler's reaction to General Giraud's escape from Germany, negotiations dragged on at Wiesbaden and at Paris until the end of August, at which date the German High Command announced its refusal.

I immediately asked the Chief of Government for authorization to start a system of cancellable engagements in the army, which might attract more volunteers than had the system of long-term engagements imposed by the armistice convention. My proposed system was in absolute contradiction to the spirit and the letter of the armistice convention. Nevertheless the President took the responsibility for it and from that moment our numbers increased steadily. The rate of increase rose sharply when the units of the Armistice Army, always by agreement with Pierre Laval, formed the first refuge for young men disturbed by the early requisitions for the Obligatory Labor Service. On 27 November 1942 when the Germans began the disbandment of the Armistice Army it had almost reached its full complement. This result could not have been achieved if the measures proposed had not been supported by the President in the most sympathetic manner, though some of them were of a nature to add serious complications to his relations, already very difficult, with the German government.

Although the situation of the North African troops and the colonial troops was in April 1942 more favorable than that of the troops on the mainland, it was none the less the duty of the government to strengthen them and first of all to improve their corps of officers. For this purpose a request was sent to the Armistice Commission at Wiesbaden in June 1942 that career officers and noncommissioned officers who were prisoners of war in Germany should be returned. This request was vigorously supported by the President and after difficult negotiations was accepted by the German High Command. They informed us, at the end of September 1942, that we could create a certain number of new units for which they would be ready to liberate several hundred officers and a corresponding number of noncommissioned officers. The execution of this plan was stopped by the Allied landing of 8 November 1942.

To increase the strength of the units which we were allowed to have it was not sufficient to consider merely the number of men. We also had to have modern means of combat, which the armistice convention had forbidden us either to manufacture or to use. The Chief of Government while attempting to obtain permission for the creation of new units in our forces overseas had also asked for authorization to begin the removal of military equipment from the supervised stocks in which they were held, in order that the new units could be equipped. This authorization was given to us in the autumn of 1942. On the mainland we had been able to get back some anti-aircraft equipment which formed the basis for a future force of modern artillery, though for any possible military action we could rely only on what were known as the clandestine depots.

As early as the summer of 1940 the Ministry of War had already been concerned with the problem of preparing supplies of equipment sufficient to permit the mobilization of a greater number of men than was authorized under the armistice convention. Officially the Government was supposed to know nothing of all this organization as both its principles and its activities were in strict opposition to the clauses of the armistice. The entire operation was inspired and controlled by the Army's own general staff. This equivocal arrangement did not suit Pierre Laval's character and as soon as I had told him about what was being done he insisted on becoming personally responsible and on giving his protection to all those who were engaged in the operation. He even went farther and at the end of October 1942 asked me to name a general officer through whom all questions of clandestine military equipment could be channeled. Reports were to be made to the Chief of Government through me.

If my memory is correct this general officer, testifying in the trial of

Maréchal Pétain, thought it a good idea to say that in this operation he was held as a hostage. I fear that the truth was less dramatic. He was a man already due for retirement because he had passed the age limit, and the choice fell on him in large part because this new position would give him the benefit of active service pay.

The German occupation of the southern zone on 11 November 1942 and the dissolution of the Armistice Army on 27 November gave a character of serious reality to responsibilities which up to that time had not really been threatened. Things began with the discovery by the Italians in Corsica and near Gap of hidden arms. The Italians made a demand for payment of indemnities which the Chief of Government rejected. Then the Germans came into action on their side and made demands which became more and more urgent.

These new demands came first from the military, but were next taken up by the Gestapo, and the President had to go to the utmost limits to protect French military personnel who were found and arrested. His method was to have his prefects deal directly on all such matters with the local German authorities on the spot, keeping for himself the task of dealing with Marshal von Rundstedt and General Oberg in such a way as to minimize the importance of what was going on. He took action every time an arrest was reported to him and though he was not able to prevent Colonel Mollard, the remarkable officer who had been responsible for the entire service, from being seriously mistreated and deported, he did at least succeed in saving him from execution.

The occupation of the southern zone on 11 November 1942 did not fail to arouse sharp fears as to the fate of the Armistice Army. The Chief of Government was the first to deal with the matter and during a visit to Marshal von Rundstedt he tried to ease the distrust which the Marshal felt for military units that were necessarily inspired by a spirit of revenge and which were now stationed in the rear of the German forces in the Mediterranean zone.

On 27 November 1942 at four o'clock in the morning the German Army and the SS began the disarmament of our regiments. On the same day the President outlined a program which would assure the continuance of our traditions and of our military institutions, and which at the same time would guarantee the material situation and morale of our officer corps and the protection of our equipment. On 29 November the German commander accepted our proposal. Our men were to be considered as on leave in their own homes and the officers as being on renewable leave. The central administration of the Army and the regional organizations would remain as they were with the necessary chiefs and staffs. The military services would continue to function in order to take care of military property and supplies. The Minister of Finance would take all steps necessary for the payment of all who were "on leave" and would set up a special budget to maintain those activities which continued, as just mentioned.

In the letter from the Führer announcing his decision to dissolve the Armistice Army there had been a provision for the possible constitution of a new national force. Pierre Laval, taking advantage of this provision, asked me to indicate a general officer who could deal with the representatives of the German general staff in Paris on all questions of principle having to do with this "new army." Pierre Laval was almost the only one in the government to feel that the disappearance of the French Army struck an extremely serious blow at the theoretical sovereignty which had remained to us since 11 November 1942, and he was making preparations to reconstruct that which had been destroyed.

This mixed Franco-German commission began to function in the first days of December 1942. It was supported by the personal efforts of the President who, on 11 January 1943, had a long talk with Marshal von Rundstedt, devoted entirely to military questions. As a result of these negotiations the German general staff showed itself favorable, on broad lines, to our point of view. It was from Italy that the opposition came, and it was because of this opposition that what had been planned had to be reduced. The agreement of principle with the Germans had covered the maintenance of an anti-aircraft force, and the formation of "government forces" of which the heart would have been the "First Regiment of France," as the President himself had baptized it.

Among the military establishments which were kept must be mentioned the preparatory training school and the military academy at La Flèche, both of which were important elements in our traditions. The military school at Saint-Cyr ceased to operate, but under an agreement with Abel Bonnard, Minister of National Education, the annual competitive examination was maintained in a disguised form, and those who were accepted were divided among the faculties of the higher institutions of learning, while waiting until a special military academy could again receive them.

The protection of military equipment was assured in so far as possible by the central administration of the Army and its different offices, through discussions and bargaining of which the bitterness often necessitated the personal intervention of the President, particularly every time another clandestine stock of arms was discovered, and at every German threat to take over the whole of our supplies.

The result of all this work was that on 17 August 1944 when Pierre Laval was taken to Germany with the members of his government he left behind him a central military administration with all its services and with regional agencies all ready to take up their role in the normal functioning of our military institutions. The officer corps were ready and all that needed to be done was to recall its members to active service. As a whole the military domain had been protected and, in fact, often improved.

At the beginning of my statement, I referred to some witticisms of the President in his comments on military men and methods. They were very often justified for although in theory the armed forces were not supposed to be under his authority it was always to him that the complaints and demands of the German services were presented and it was always on his shoulders that all responsibilities fell.

The Army was anti-German and could not be anything else. It showed its feelings without any discretion and there reached Pierre Laval's office almost every day, reports, complaints, and sometimes threats, from the control commission of the German Army, from the agencies of the Gestapo, and from German representatives of every kind who were operating in the southern zone. The activity of our intelligence services was particularly spied on and criticized, all the more because Gaullist intelligence services had also been created, with little possibility for the Germans of distinguishing between them. In addition to these two there were various other Anglo-

Saxon intelligence services and even private reporting systems. Pierre Laval accepted all this confusion with complete serenity, and took all the responsibility, even that which Admiral Darlan, the great chief of the intelligence services, should have taken. Pierre Laval took action at the German Embassy when things went wrong. His good will and his generosity were never failing.

He understood the necessity for personal contacts and shortly after his return to the government he had arranged a meeting for all the generals commanding divisional groups and those commanding divisions, in order to explain his policies. I remember his words: "I want to save the territory of France, all of it, and all of the Empire. . . . Without the agreement of France it is impossible to create a Europe that can live. . . . If Germany is not victorious we will still be neighbors and we will still have to reach an agreement with her in order that the youth of the two nations shall not have to meet in battle every twenty or twenty-five years. . . ."

His door was always open to any military commander who wanted to talk with him. General Juin, who commanded the army in North Africa under the direct authority of Admiral Darlan, came to assure him of the loyalty of the Army of Africa. General de Lattre de Tassigny, whose father-in-law he had known in the Senate, found great sympathy in Pierre Laval, and this sympathy followed him until his escape from the prison at Riom, an escape which Pierre Laval had announced to me personally and to others some fifteen days before it happened. Several months earlier he had approved the appointment of General de Lattre as chief of the mobile units which in the case of a retreat of the German Army, for any reason, were to enter the northern zone with the mission of reaching Paris as quickly as possible. He knew that this general officer held a letter of service which entrusted to him, in such an eventuality, the functions of Governor of Paris.

Many others came to him or benefited by his protection and afterwards showed him little gratitude.

It is not without interest to recall in this connection that the Gestapo attributed to his services, and indirectly to Pierre Laval himself, the responsibility for the departure from France of General Giraud on 6 November 1942. The French police had in fact known of all of General Giraud's movements in the south of France, and of all the arrivals and departures at the house where he lived near Antibes. No one doubted that General Giraud was preparing for activities far removed from the ideas which he had developed during his captivity (I allude to the written declaration on Franco-German collaboration which he prepared in 1941 as a prisoner, which must still exist in the archives of the French Diplomatic Service for Prisoners of War), and from the written engagements into which he had entered with the Maréchal and his government when he returned to France. The President knew all about it but he shrank from taking measures affecting a general officer in whose word of honor he still had confidence in the depths of his heart.

The occupation of the southern zone and the intensified activity of the Gestapo which resulted, led to many arrests of members of the Army who were on leave or on active service. Many of them owe their lives to action taken by the Chief of Government and it will be interesting to find records of these interventions in those same German files and documents which have so far been used only against Pierre Laval and almost always with the most complete intentional injustice. Ambassador Abetz, General von Neubronn who represented Marshal von Rundstedt at Vichy, and the

German police chiefs could speak in the place of those Frenchmen who up to the present have shown themselves little inclined to appear.

In the archives of the Reich will also certainly be found the voluminous correspondence exchanged between the President and the political authorities in Germany regarding the allocations of military pay to families of career soldiers fighting in North Africa and in other theaters where the Allies were carrying on the war against Germany. It will be seen that it was thanks to Pierre Laval that these payments were continued.

There will also be found the record of his intervention on behalf of the Gaullist combatants of Bir-Hakeim. It was Pierre Laval who obtained from the German command the arrangement that those Frenchmen who had been captured there should not be treated as irregulars. This decision was of capital importance because that was the first time that Gaullist soldiers had fallen into German hands.

The statement which I have just made does not cover as much ground, nor include as much detail, as I would have wished. I do not have at hand the documents on which to base a full statement and I have not wished to write anything of which I was not certain. But in any case it should be taken as testimony and it can one day serve as a basis for more complete presentation supported by official documents.

My testimony should also be accepted as a simple but very earnest homage to him who was my chief. With each day that passes I admire him all the more for the patriotism, the humanity, the relentlessness, the courage, and the farsighted vision of his actions.

(Document No. 128)
Fr. ed. 835-840

Madrid, 18 February 1951

BRIDOUX
General Eugène Bridoux

THE FIRST REGIMENT OF FRANCE

LOUIS LANGLADE
Lieutenant Colonel

I the undersigned Louis Langlade, Lieutenant Colonel, living in Paris, make the following declaration.

I had no occasion to become acquainted with President Pierre Laval before April 1943 when I was appointed by the Ministry of Defense to be chief of the military bureau of the Chief of Government, with an assurance that I would be concerned only with strictly military questions.

My initial mission was to organize the First Regiment in co-operation with the Ministry of Defense (the General Staff and its services) and with the colonel commanding the regiment, who like myself was a direct subordinate of the Chief of Government.

On this occasion I was presented to M. Laval in a very short interview. His expression was grave, and he scarcely looked at me. Nevertheless just as I was leaving he said to me, "There is to be one regiment for each departement. Therefore this first one must provide the officer corps for the others. To accomplish your task you must remain absolutely independent of everyone—of absolutely everyone."

The order was given and the line to follow was laid down. I kept to it in spite of the atmosphere of those days, the bitterness of some people, the hopes of others, the fluctuations of domestic politics, and all that was happening outside of France.

As often as possible I reported directly to the Chief of Government on the results of my mission. It was from him and from him alone, in spite of the pressure and solicitations of all kinds which came upon him in this matter, that I obtained the necessary support for my mission and, in particular, found the most complete understanding of military tradition, of the duties and needs of the army and of the necessity for maintaining the greatest political neutrality in all military questions. This was his attitude in spite of his reputation for neglecting military matters and of not wanting to know anything about them.

My visits lasted only a few minutes. The papers I presented were run through rapidly. He didn't seem to be interested in them. Nevertheless on every occasion the essential question was precisely put to me and the heart of the problem immediately reached. It was then only that he would sign.

There was never any exchange of views between us on questions outside my field except one day in January 1944. I think I had brought for signature a paper regarding military chaplains. After he had signed I asked him what general policy should be followed toward the occupying authority when, with the representatives of the Armistice Commission, I was obliged to discuss the handing over of munitions and military equipment.

"Get every advantage you can," he said. "Never refuse anything in principle, but above all never give in on anything. They asked me for a Franco-German alliance, and what did I answer? I said that there are three essential points which separate us.

"First, there is the question of Alsace-Lorraine. Hitler must repeat his words of 1938 and put his promises into effect.

"Then there is the question of prisoners; it is impossible to hold discussions so long as France suffers from their absence.

"And there is the question of those who have been executed. For them it is too late, but Germany is sufficiently powerful to give such advantages to the French that perhaps in some measure they will forget what has been done.

"When these three questions have been dealt with, and only then, can we begin to think about an alliance. That's all I said. And what had I promised? Nothing. I had left the door open without giving a thing. Do as I do."

From that day on, I understood Pierre Laval's methods and I was able to value properly his civil courage in defending the French heritage foot by foot.

It was by telephone that I heard his voice for the last time, just after the landing in Normandy. He was in Paris. I informed him of the bitter criticism of the First Regiment of France, a result of the situation in the departements of the Indre and the Cher. The maquis had prematurely begun extensive operations. A raid carried out on St. Amand Mont-Rond had resulted in the kidnapping of Mme Bout de l'An, whose husband directed the Militia. The First Regiment was reproached for having remained inactive and for having taken no action against the maquis. The matter was a serious one. The Militia wanted to take civil and military powers and organize operations against the maquis. The Germans had alerted two of their divisions and a group of bombers.

The President approved my proposal of entrusting to the commander of arms of the First Regiment the reglementary powers of a state of siege in order to avoid all excesses and to save the population from reprisals.

That was the last time I heard him speak. "I agree; do your best."

Orders were given through his chief of cabinet, M. Darbou, and calm was re-established.

Such are the circumstances in which I knew President Pierre Laval. I remember him with respect as a great Frenchman with civic courage, a flexible but relentless will, and exceptional intelligence, qualities which enabled him to save lives, to keep his country alive to the end, to restrain the claims of the occupying power, to protect intact the heritage and the sovereignty of France. Such is my deepest conviction.

(Document No. 123)
Fr. ed. 841-842

15 June 1950

L. LANGLADE

THE SCUTTLING OF THE FLEET

JEAN DE LABORDE

Admiral Commanding the French Fleet
at the time of Scuttling at Toulon

[*When Admiral de Laborde read a typed copy of this testimony he struck out a number of phrases and sentences as being "without interest." The same omissions have been made in the translation. The copy deposited with the Hoover Library contains the original text together with Admiral de Laborde's indications of revisions to be made.*]

I. 11 November [1942]

After receiving news of the entry of German troops into the free zone, I issued to the High Seas Fleet Order of the Day 169.E.M.I. (annex No. 1) and posted Communiqué 170.E.M.I. (annex No. 2).

In the evening, at the time of clearing for action, some cries from the crew of *Colbert* led to the gathering of about twenty men on the foredeck of *Strasbourg*, a gathering which was easily dispersed by the officers. It appears that the cries were, in effect, "We do not want to be caught by the Germans. Let's get under way."

That evening at about eleven o'clock Admiral Marquis telephoned me to say that Lieutenant von Fuault Frappart of the Armistice Commission would call to see me in ten minutes with another German officer, both being in civilian clothes and conducted by Captain de la Rochefoucauld. Admiral Marquis said that the purpose of this visit was to bring me a document to which he had given his agreement and to which he asked me to agree. He asked me to make a copy of the document as he had neglected to do so. I got up, as I was already in bed. About a quarter of an hour later the three officers arrived by car. Lieutenant Frappart gave me the document, which was a telegram from Chancellor Hitler stating that if I gave my word, as Amiral Marquis had done, that I would take no action against the forces of the Axis and that the fleet would defend Toulon, then the zone of Toulon would not be occupied by the Germans.

I read the document and made a copy (annex No. 3). I then said to Lieutenant Frappart that I was ready to give my word of honor as asked; but that I could not give it conscientiously unless I was sure that I would be followed by the commanding officers, their staffs, and their crews, and that he must know how difficult it is to maintain discipline in an inactive naval force, such as the High Seas Fleet; and that in consequence I asked for a promise that no German would come on board the ships nor would appear nearby. The companion of Lieutenant Frappart then remarked that a liaison detachment was provided for in the telegram. Frappart cut him short and told him that the liaison maintained by this detachment was to be with Admiral Marquis; Frappart told me that what I asked for was agreed to. I then gave my word of honor, pointing out that it bound me only to execute the orders already given by the Maréchal.

The visitors left.

Beginning at seven o'clock the next morning I had the officers of the staff convey to all commanders of ships the information that the zone of Toulon would not be occupied and that no foreigner would come on board the ships of the High Seas Fleet, telling them to make use of this information in case there were any manifestations like those on *Colbert* and *Strasbourg* on the previous evening. In fact no such manifestations occurred. I then prepared an Order of the Day (annex No. 4), and at nine o'clock I summoned the admirals and the commanders of the ships to my quarters. I informed them of the situation and I read to them my Order of the Day. I ended with the words reproduced in annex No. 5, demanding their word of honor that they would obey me. I then called them one by one, in order of length of service, and each gave me his word, taking my hand as he did so, except Pothuau, who was very much disturbed and asked me that he be allowed not to give his word of honor and that he would later give his resignation if necessary. I answered that that was an impossible situation and that he must give up his command immediately. I then ended the meeting.

I first offered Pothuau's command to Molas, who was then preparing to take command of *Strasbourg*. He accepted; but after half an hour's discussion with Pothuau he asked me to free him from his acceptance. I then appointed Glotin, who accepted and immediately took command. Molas replaced him on the staff.

I authorized the admirals to relieve any officer if they thought it necessary to do so. There were only two such cases. I also renewed my order, already repeated twenty times, to release any undesirable sailors; this resulted during the following days in a larger number of separations than usual.

II. From 11 to 27 November [1942]

This period, during which we remained in a state of alert, brought no events of importance for the High Seas Fleet. Liberty from noon to six in the evening had been re-established from the beginning of this period for the married men, and was then extended to the others. Overnight liberty was re-established on 26 November for married men.

A number of communiqués (cited in annexes Nos. 6-8, 10-13) were posted to keep the crews informed and to counterbalance the strongest of the false rumors which were circulating. Six battalions had been furnished, as soon as they were equipped, to assure the defense of the coastal zone from Sanary to Gapeau. This very difficult service for the High Seas Fleet had been interrupted only during the short period when troops had been supplied to assure this defense.

Two meetings had been held at Lamalgue on 14 and 16 November [1942] for the presentation by Admiral Wewer of Captain Hoffmann, who was chief of the German liaison detachment.

Admiral de Feo was president of the Italian detachment. After the meeting on 14 [November 1942] I published Order of the Day 183.E.M.I. [annex No. 9].

During this period all fires had been lighted under orders given on 12 [November 1942] on receipt of information from German sources, apparently quite correct but in fact false, that an English squadron with a convoy had been seen off Barcelona moving northeast at ten knots. Later an alert service in three-hour watches was established between the two divisions of cruisers and two groups of light forces. After several days, on 21 [November 1942] this alert service was brought to an end because of the expenditure of oil and because it was difficult for the battalions on detached service as far as Carqueiranne to return in less than six hours.

Admiral Abrial came to see the High Seas Fleet on 23 [November 1942]. He called together the admirals and the commanders of ships and renewed his directives for the use of the High Seas Fleet against the Anglo-Saxons if they attacked Toulon, and he confirmed his orders for scuttling, which had been permanent orders since 1940, if there was a threat of capture by anyone at all. We discussed several details, his idea being that scuttling should be done in such a way that refloating, even if it took a long time, would be possible.

After this meeting the group commanders were ordered to make suggestions for modification of instructions then in force. The first suggestions, those of the third squadron light forces, were received on board *Strasbourg* on 26 [November 1942] in the evening. In preparation for the time when the battalion on detached service would be given back to us we prepared a plan for the placement of all the ships, including *Strasbourg*, inside or behind the main jetty so that training could be renewed in a smaller anchorage elsewhere than at the Vignettes, which I now considered as too threatened.

I also ordered the preparation of a sea training program by very rapid sorties without anchoring at Salins, using the 2,000 tons [of oil] allowed for the six months.

In the evening of 25 [November 1942] Admiral Marquis proposed that he should come to see me the next morning, but at an early hour as he would be very busy. I replied that I had better go to see him, and we set our meeting for a quarter past eight.

Accordingly on 26 [November 1942] I visited him. He gave me the latest information on the military situation: the Italians had evacuated Hyères. The battalions of sailors had been taken to the beaches where defense works were being constructed rapidly. Two battalions of colonial troops were still in reserve. It seemed as though things were being arranged for sending the reinforcements necessary to liberate the battalions belonging to the High Seas Fleet. A smaller number of troops than before would be brought back, and they would be more carefully chosen. Admiral Marquis knew nothing about the results of my proposal that these troops should be made up of volunteers from among those war veterans who were members of the Legion. He asked me to return that afternoon at four o'clock to meet Admiral de Feo; the latter had requested it, as he had seen me only once, when he visited *Strasbourg* at the end of 1940. He wished to be able to tell the Italian generals with whom he had to deal that he knew me well and that he was sure of my reliability. Therefore I returned to Lamalgue at four o'clock in the afternoon. Admiral de Feo came and we chatted for some time in a very friendly way. The admiral seemed to know absolutely nothing about what was going to happen.

From Lamalgue I returned directly to my home, having ordered my barge to be at Tamaris at nine in the evening. I dined at home and returned to my ship at a quarter past ten. No important telegram had arrived that day and I went to bed early.

III. 27 November [1942]

At quarter to five in the morning there was a knock at my door. It was Guérin who told me at once that Rear-Admiral Dornon had just telephoned him that German troops had invaded Fort Lamalgue. It was Rear-Admiral Robin, Chief of Staff for Admiral Marquis, who had telephoned him; he had added that it certainly meant the complete invasion of the zone of Toulon, and he advised us to scuttle the fleet. I could not yet believe it. I dressed rapidly and told Guérin to try to get me into communication with Admiral Marquis. His line did not answer. Robin was called but he answered that there was somebody in his office; he asked us not to stay on the line, and hung up. I told Guérin to try to remain in permanent communication with Rear Admiral Dornon, to have the signal to prepare action sounded on all ships, to light all fires in order to destroy the boilers without the use of explosives if it was necessary to scuttle, and at the same time to take all the final dispositions for scuttling. Orders given on the command telephone system passed without difficulty. I ordered *Strasbourg* to get away from the quay. Dornon asked me if the order to scuttle should be given to all the ships in the region. I told him to wait a bit. He asked me if he should shoot in order to defend the arsenal. I said no, as we had been ordered at the time of the occupation of the southern zone to avoid any shedding of blood and that this order still was in force. I told him that if German troops came to the gates of the arsenal, he was to discuss the situation with them, and advise me immediately. By this time it was quarter past five in the morning.

At about twenty minutes past five Dornon telephoned that the arsenal at Mourillon had been invaded. I still waited. Finally at about twenty-five minutes past five, Dornon telephoned that the tanks had forced the Castigneau gate. I answered that he was to scuttle his ships. I had the same order given to the High Seas Fleet. It was now half past five in the morning. Very quickly the noise of the tanks increased from all parts of the arsenal. Planes then flew into the west at medium height; our searchlights found and spotted them. The batteries did not seem to be firing. The planes threw out light flares, and above the water could be seem huge parachutes carrying either magnetic mines or parachutists. A number of explosions, more or less distant, were heard but it was not possible to determine the direction nor to identify them.

During this time, operations for scuttling *Strasbourg* continued normally. The ship was got away from the quay; all members of the crew were at their alert stations. Suddenly at about twenty minutes to six the sound of a cannon was heard from the direction of the iron door in the arsenal wall, fired toward *Strasbourg*. *Strasbourg's* rear machine gun replied with a short burst directed against the flash of the gunfire. At that moment I was on the rear deck, in front of my office, as I was throughout nearly the entire morning; I immediately gave the order to cease fire, though without yet having understood what was going on. It was only a little later that I learned that a shell from an 88 mm tank had struck the corner of my quarters above the ladder to the upper deck and had gone into gun turret No. 5, wounding some of the men. At first it had been thought that a demolition charge in the turret had exploded. One of the wounded, Lieutenant Fay, was in serious condition; he had an open fracture of the thigh and died from his wound in hospital that same day. Some others were lightly wounded. It was the explosion of one of our own detonators, struck by a fragment of the shell, that had done all the harm.

During this time the evacuation of the ship by companies had begun on port side. The boats were being used and evacuation was proceeding rapidly. The men were being sent first to the bomb shelters, then to the depot. The noise of the tanks could still be heard in the direction of the arsenal and silhouettes of German soldiers could be seen on the quay. The moon was in its last quarter and veiled by clouds, so it was rather dark. The weather was calm.

It may have been about twenty minutes to seven when a German voice, speaking in French, called from straight behind us on the quay. At that moment I was near the catapult. I replied that it was difficult to hear from that distance and that he should come to the west landing stage opposite the open deck on the starboard side. In the end he understood and I saw him coming along the landing stage with two others. I went to the platform of the open deck on the starboard side, before which they had stopped. The interpreter then called up and said that his commanding officer was there and wanted to speak to the commander of *Strasbourg*. I replied that I was the admiral and that he could speak. After a moment be said, "Admiral, my commanding officer says that you must surrender the ship unharmed." I replied immediately, "The ship is already sunk."

As a matter of fact, *Strasbourg*, with all valves open, was down by the nose, and the bow was under water and aground. The fuses of the demolition charges had been lit for the last quarter of an hour in the compartments, along the keel, and in the boiler room, as the boilers were not yet sufficiently hot to be burned out. The destruction of the tubing and the superheaters had been completed some time previously.

When I gave my reply the three Germans consulted with each other. One of them pointed out to the others the submerged bow, and the interpreter spoke again: "Admiral, my commanding officer wishes to say that he respects you."

The three men stood at the salute facing me for some moments. I returned the salute. Then they went off rapidly toward the quay. At this moment the first demolition charges began to explode in the turrets. Then came the heavy sound of the explosions of the bombs placed along the keel.

I ordered all ships to raise the small ensign.

The day began to break. German detachments could be seen along the quay but remained behind the line of floats of the landing nets. The tanks arrived later. There were three together at one moment, and then there was only one, standing near the incinerator. Many motorcycles passed going one way or the other. All day long there was a rather confused activity but no attempt to come on board, although a floating gangway had been fixed between the quay and the port side at the stern as soon as the scuttling operation was complete.

Explosions had begun too on the other ships which could be seen from *Strasbourg*, namely *Colbert*, *Algérie*, and *Marseillaise*. As they began to go under they dipped at a sharp angle, but *Colbert* and *Algérie* came to an even keel again as they filled. In the end they sank on an even keel as did *Strasbourg*, now only slightly heeled. *Marseillaise* did not come to an even keel and rested at an angle of over forty-five degrees to port.

On board *Strasbourg* there was no fire except one on the bridge deck which burned out, some cables which burned for a time in turret 5, and an oil fire on starboard forward which poured out black smoke, and then white, for an hour and a half and then went out by itself.

On board *Colbert* fire broke out in the gun structure forward on starboard side, probably caused by the explosion of 90 or 203 mm shells, as the light armor was broken open on nearly all the turrets, though on *Strasbourg* it was intact. The fire on *Colbert* spread little by little through all the forward parts of the ship with successive explosions of the magazines which lasted until evening. The plane on the port catapult forward, when it caught, increased the fire's violence. Little by little the fire spread aft until all the upper works were burning, but it seemed that the lower decks had not been reached before water had fully entered. The fire became less violent at the end of the afternoon and appeared to go out during the evening.

On board *Algérie*, on the other hand, there did not seem to be any fire in the upper works at the beginning, but the bombs which had been placed under the boilers must have started a violent oil fire as the stack threw out torrents of black smoke, soon mixed with bright flame. The stack burned and spread the fire to all the upper works and probably to a part of the ship below decks before the complete entry of the water. Fire broke out later on *Colbert* and was much more violent. The explosion of munitions which began later was also much stronger in some places, particularly in turret 3, shaking *Strasbourg* violently and throwing up a column of smoke more than a hundred meters in the air. In the evening the fire still burned, casting huge red gleams over the water.

It was more difficult to see *Marseillaise* but it was my impression that there were no important fires or explosions as there had been on *Strasbourg*. In fact, I learned much later that a fire had been smoldering and developed violently in the evening, causing explosions as strong as those on *Algérie*. In the morning a column of black smoke from the oil began to rise in the direction of Missiemy. This column became enormous and lasted until the evening. It was one of the cruisers which was burning and I was told during the day that it was *Dupleix*. This fire must have been as violent as the one on *Algérie*.

Throughout that day I learned nothing more of the scuttling of the other ships.

On board *Strasbourg*, after the crew had been evacuated, there remained only I myself, my staff, and Lieutenant Seyeux, a total of seventeen officers in all, with four men to man the barge. The ship was on an even keel and there was no important indication of fire. Water level was about a meter below the after deck. My baggage and the baggage of the officers had been cleared, and I had mine placed in the launch; the officers had sent theirs to the depot with the final evacuations of the crew. I waited for what was to happen, having decided not to leave the ship except on orders from the government, or by force.

We paced back and forth on the afterdeck, photographed by many soldiers from the detachments who kept coming and going, and standing without any logical reason along the landing stage. From time to time these soldiers were scattered by explosions from *Algérie* and *Colbert*, as fragments were falling fast. The only incidents of this long day were the repeated attempts by the Germans to get me to leave the ship.

These attempts had begun at about nine in the morning. One of our own light boats, armed by Germans, hailed me from port side. An ensign wished to come aboard; the officers there refused to allow him to do so. He went back to the landing stage near *Colbert* and talked with other Germans. He came again at about half past nine and asked to speak to me. I was informed, and I said that he was to be brought to my cabin. He told me in German that the general ordered me to leave the ship with all my officers. I answered in German that I had the word of honor of the Chancellor, brought to me by Lieutenant von Ruault Frappart who, seated in the chair which I pointed out to the ensign, had received my promise. I said that I would not leave until the Lieutenant or his chief, Captain Hoffmann, had come to explain to me why the word of honor of the Führer had not been kept. The ensign then asked that at least the officers should go. I replied that as they were my staff they would depart with me. He insisted no longer, and left.

A little later in the morning there appeared a *lieutenant de vaisseau* or a *capitaine de corvette*—I didn't notice very carefully—with a most unpleasant and insolent manner. With him as interpreter was an army officer who spoke less French than I did German, which isn't much; therefore I continued to speak in German. He made, rather insolently, the same demand as the first had made, that I should leave the ship. I answered much in the same way as I had just replied to the other, and I asked why the word of honor of the Führer had been broken. He replied that Darlan had turned traitor and that the French admirals were traitors. I answered violently that I was not Admiral Darlan and that it was false that I had not kept my word. Somewhat deflated, he left.

At the end of the morning I was sitting in my office and saw Montrelay, in cap and cloak, just climbing over the rail after crossing the bridge of boats which had been established port-side aft. He explained that he happened to be near the fortifications with his evacuated crew and that a German general had come up and asked to speak to an officer. As he was the senior he had presented himself. The general had dictated an order in French, quite correct in its form, that I was to leave the ship. Montrelay had written down this order in pencil on two visiting cards. He took two other cards to write my reply, which was exactly the same as I had already given the first officers: that I was there on the word of honor of the Führer that the High Seas Fleet would not be touched. I stated in my reply that I would not leave the ship until Lieutenant Frappart, who had brought me the promise, or his chief, Captain Hoffmann, had given me a satisfactory explanation of what had happened. Montrelay, deeply moved, said goodbye to me and took my reply to the general, who had remained near the fortifications. The general left without insisting.

At noon we lunched sketchily on anything we could find in the galleys.

About two o'clock in the afternoon the insolent naval officer came back. Still haughty but more correct, he told me that this time it was necessary to go and that my officers and I had a half an hour to leave the ship. Having spoken his piece, he turned his wrist and looked fixedly at his wrist watch. After a moment of silence I calmly asked him if he had been ordered to use force. Obviously taken aback by this simple question, he stopped looking at his watch and answered, "No." I then said to him, "It's not worthwhile then to wait half an hour, because I have already told you that I am not going of my own free will."—And this time I added, "except, of course, on the Maréchal's orders." This seemed to strike him as a revelation and he left.

About an hour went by and another naval officer arrived with two interpreters from the army, both of whom together amounted to the equivalent of about half an interpreter; I therefore continued to speak German. He was a young man and hid his obvious timidity behind a manner which he tried to make severe. He told me with quite a bit of ceremony that he was bringing me the Maréchal's order to leave the ship and gave me an envelope containing a typed message in German as follows: "I have just learned that your ship is sinking. I order you to leave it at once. Pétain." Underneath was written "Certified, General E. M." The signature was illegible (annex No. 14).

I asked the officer why this message should be in German if it had come from Maréchal Pétain. This question obviously disconcerted him and he didn't know what to say. I then added that under these conditions nothing forced me to believe that it was a genuine message, that I didn't believe it was, and that I would not go. As a matter of fact, I learned later that the message was in fact a correct one; only the unbelievable error of translating it into German to bring it to me led me to believe quite sincerely that it was a fake. During the discussion I asked him once again why Lieutenant Frappart did not come. He irritated me by answering all the time, "I don't know," and in the end I said to him, "Well, I know; it's because he's ashamed."[1]

1. After preparing the above report I learned that Lieutenant von Ruault Frappart came to my house at Tamaris about 10 December [1942]. My wife was there alone, arranging to move our things. He had been presented to my wife the preceding year, at a concert given at the Theatre de Marseilles, by Consul-General von Spiegel. He was often at Tamaris and always greeted us when we met. He first told my wife

This further failure brought me another visit, about an hour later, from a tall fat colonel, a rather likable German, who in quite good French explained that he was responsible for communications and that he had been sent to re-connect our telephone in order that I might speak directly to Maréchal Pétain. I showed him that our telephone cable, in spite of our being some distance from the quay, was still slack. I said that we had been cut off at about half past five in the morning somewhere in the arsenal, probably by their own troops. He left, and I saw him quite a long time afterwards coming back along the landing stage with another officer and a civilian worker from the maritime engineering office, who began to do something in the telephone junction box on the quay.

By this time it was dusk and the work of repairing the telephone continued laboriously by night. It was completed when I saw the headlights of an automobile which was stopping on the quay. It was Commandant de Maupeou. Commandant de Maupeou, in civilian clothes, soon entered my office with a German officer. He told me that Admiral Marquis, left by the Germans as civil governor of Toulon, begged me to quit the ship, and that the Maréchal, and with him President Laval, Admiral Abrial, and Admiral Platon, implored me not to hamper the negotiations which were then being conducted. I asked de Maupeou if he had personally received this message. He said that he had not, and that he didn't know whether or not it had been received by Admiral Marquis. I then told him that I had every reason to believe, under these conditions, that the Germans must have shown Admiral Marquis the same message which they had shown to me which I believed to be false, and that I still would not leave. De Maupeou then asked me to give him one of my staff officers whom he would take to the maritime prefecture so that he could bring back conclusive proof. I sent Guérin.

About an hour went by and just as I saw on the quay the lights of the automobile which was bringing Guérin back, my telephone rang. It was Admiral Marquis who told me that he had indeed received the communication personally. I answered that under those conditions I was ready to leave, but that now that night had fallen I could not return home either by barge or by automobile without being arrested unless there were a German officer with me. He replied that an officer would come to get me but that he did not believe he would take me home. I was astonished; I still had no idea that I was going to be given the treatment, as absurd as it was unexpected, which in fact was reserved for me.

Some time afterward de Maupeou telephoned me that I could not leave by barge, and that I would be taken by car, probably first of all to the German general. I told him to insist that I should keep my own barge at Tamaris, still believing that I was going there.

Guérin on his return had of course confirmed the conversation of Marquis and had told me that the Germans had telephoned to Vichy not only that I

that he had learned that I had asked for him many times during the day of 27 [November 1942] but that he had been sent away from Toulon four days before and had only just returned. My wife told him that I had wanted to know directly from him, who had brought me the Führer's promise, why that promise had not been kept. He replied that what had happened was not at the desire of the Führer but of the General Staff; he did not understand what could have occurred as he himself had been congratulated in the Führer's name on the results of his negotiations with Admiral Marquis and myself. We believe, he added, that it was Darlan who must have given false information. When my wife asked him if he had some message to send to me he only asked her to present his respects.

would not leave but that I threatened to go down on *Strasbourg*, a suggestion which for a ship that was in water only up to its second deck was really childish.

Time went by and the officer that had been promised did not come. The night was extremely black, lightened only by great red flames from the fire on *Algérie*, which continued to burn, sometimes with violent explosions. It was now seven o'clock in the evening. We ate lightly under the same conditions as at lunchtime.

A few moments after we finished eating, one of my staff officers announced that someone had come to fetch us. A naval officer, loaded with revolvers and hand grenades, and surrounded by soldiers armed in the same way right to the teeth and evidently ready to give him instant aid, came into my cabin. The light was very dim as there was of course no electricity and the current came from the accumulators. The silhouettes of other soldiers could be seen through the door on the afterdeck. He asked me, not too confidently, if I wished to follow him. I replied that I would because the Maréchal had so ordered. He helped me to put on my coat and told me that I could take with me anything which I wished to take. I replied that I certainly expected to do so but that my baggage was already in my barge. There remained only the Maréchal's portrait which I took down. He wanted to take it from me to hand it over to a soldier but I refused and gave it to one of my officers. I went out closely followed by him and surrounded by soldiers who, though they dared not touch me, did not seem very sure of my intentions. I first walked toward the boat deck on port-side aft, but on deciding that the gymnastics which would be necessary there were hardly dignified I came back, still surrounded, toward the port barricade where the barge was waiting. As my baggage made it too full I told Hourdin to make a first run with the baggage while I waited. The barge went to the quay behind *Strasbourg* and then returned. I shook hands with all the officers, who stood in line before the barricade, and then embarked with Guérin. Seyeux gave the order, "About."

Once ashore, my baggage was placed on the ground under the guard of Hourdin. I took out what I intended to keep with me no matter what happened and left the rest in Hourdin's care, telling the German officer to give him a car as quickly as possible so that he could take the other things to my place, which in fact was properly done.

The naval officer then turned me over to an army officer.

I told the army officer that Guérin was to accompany me and that Hourdin was to stay there, after which we went on foot to the iron gate where the automobiles were waiting for us.

We left by the Lagoubran gate and on reaching the tram lines turned to the left; by following the Seyne station road we reached Ollioules. Through the narrow streets we came to a restaurant of which a small room one flight up was being used by the general as his office. He received me standing at his table, with three officers at attention. One of them was an interpreter. I had obviously interrupted his dinner as plates and glasses half full could be seen standing on the window ledge, poorly concealed by the curtains.

As soon as I entered with Guérin, the general began to speak, saying that the German authorities recognized that I had done my duty in sinking the fleet and that they expressed their respect. The interpreter translated and I made no answer. The general then said that to his great regret, on instructions from his superior officers, he could not leave me free to return home and was obliged to take me immediately to Aix where the other admirals were already. I did not permit any more translating and the rest of the interview was in German. I began by asking the general if it was the custom in Germany that soldiers should be punished for having done their duty. He made no answer. I added that I was not a prisoner of war and that he had no rights over me because on the word of honor of the Führer the High Seas Fleet was to remain free, and that I had not broken my own word of honor. I repeated what I had already said to the others regarding Frappart but I did not insist, as the general obviously knew nothing of the matter. But I told him energetically that he himself and those who had given him his orders were breaking the word given by the Führer and that I did not think that German soldiers could break a promise given by their supreme chief. I added that until that moment I had held a high opinion of the honor of German soldiers but that I now found myself obliged to change. Finally I asked him who had issued these orders. He told me that they came from the general of division at Sanary. I asked if I could see him. He told me that I could but added quite logically that the general at Sanary received his orders from the general of the army at Avignon and that he could only obey. I repeated that nothing justified treating me as though I were a prisoner of war. The general then told me that after the scuttling of the German fleet at Scapa Flow, the German admiral and his crews had been treated as prisoners of war. I replied violently that they were not English and that anyway there was no comparison between the two cases because the duty imposed on the German admiral by the armistice of 1918 had been to preserve his ships intact, whereas mine was to scuttle them rather than to allow them to fall into the hands of anyone whatever.

This conversation was broken throughout by long silences, the general standing, with one hand resting on the table, slightly bent, and with his eyes lowered in an attitude of manifest embarrassment. I stood before him on the other side of the table and from time to time took two or three steps in the tiny space available.

This went on for about half an hour. A fourth officer then came in, the one who was to accompany me to Aix. The general told me that I must go with him. I had realized in the beginning that there was nothing which I could do and I had prolonged the interview only out of exasperation over the absurd order to send me to Aix. I told him that as force was on his side I would follow, but that it was not of my own free will. I then said that I had too much baggage to be brought with me in the same car and that they should put my things in a second car. I added that Guérin, who had no baggage, should be taken back to Toulon to get his things before going to Aix.

The general gave some orders and the officer who had just come in went out to execute them. While he was gone the silence seemed interminable. The three officers were still standing at attention and the general was still leaning forward slightly with his hand on the table. Finally the officer returned and said that everything was ready. I then said to the general, "There's nothing for me to do but to go, but it will be written in history by you and by your chiefs that your Führer makes two kinds of promises; and I cannot believe that."

I went out with Guérin, followed by the escorting officer. Below I said goodbye to Guérin—who in fact followed me closely all the way to Aix that same night, after having gone back to the depot to get his valise. The journey to Aix took more than two hours as the driver went wrong at every crossroad in spite of the signs and I had to put him right every time. I finally reached Aix after midnight, and after a mistaken stop at the Hotel Sextius, where my guide thought I was to go, I arrived at the Hotel Riviera where the other admirals were already installed.

IV. 28 November to 5 December [1942]

On the morning of the 28th I met the admirals who were interned with me at the Hotel Riviera, Vice-Admiral Lacroix, Rear Admirals Bléhaut, Negadelle, Jarry, Robin, and Dambe, and also Guérin who had arrived in the night less than an hour after me. The six admirals told me how happy they had been to learn that nothing bad had befallen me. I then found that there had been rumors, some to the effect that I had been killed, and others that I had committed suicide; the latter version had found little acceptance among those who knew me well.

The hotel and garden were full of sentinels who ostentatiously loaded their guns at each change of guard. The officer responsible for us was an ensign, rather young, who seemed somewhat embarrassed by his responsibilities, but was always correct. There was no attempt to isolate us and we could write, telephone and receive visits without any control at all. The owners of the hotel, M. and Mme Swellen, gave us every attention. They brought us the newspapers and I read with stupefaction the letter of the Führer in which he accused me of having broken my word by giving the order on 12 November [1942] not to fight against the Anglo-Saxons, and by preparing the High Seas Fleet for departure on the night of 26-27 [November 1942] to join the English fleet.

Indignant over such infamous statements, I called roughly for the officer of the guard who was just down the hall. I held the newspaper under his nose. I told him that all of it was completely false, that those were abominable lies, and that the Führer had no right to dishonor anyone so baselessly. He remained silent before my burst of rage. I realized that he had not yet seen the communiqué; he went off to read it. A little later I found him again and told him that I was going to telephone to President Laval about it and that I would speak slowly as I wanted him to understand what I was saying. He replied that though he could read French he understood it too poorly for such a purpose and that he was going to ask for an interpreter officer. This officer proved to be an aviator from the Armistice Commission who spoke French extremely well. It was in his presence, and that of the ensign, that I had my conversation that day, making clear my indignation over the scandalous imputations of Chancellor Hitler. In particular I said, "No one, not even the Chancellor of the Reich, has the right to dishonor me by lies."

I have learned since, through a French married couple, literary people who knew him well, that the interpreter officer was Lieutenant Flasch, a Rhinelander highly educated in Romance languages, and that since this incident he has spoken of me with sincere admiration.

That was the sole incident of the day. I drew up an Order of the Day for the Forces of the High Seas Fleet of which I made a number of copies by hand, as I had no other way of reproducing it, so that my group commanders and my staff could each have one. As soon as I knew that they were leaving I would ask them to have the order reproduced and distributed in as many copies as possible to the commanders, staffs, and even to the crews, in so far as they still were waiting to receive them (annex No. 15).

The under-prefect of Aix, M. Gondrand, came to see us and with the greatest kindness placed himself entirely at our disposal for anything which we might need. At the end of the afternoon the ensign came to tell me that he had received an order to select three admirals who should return to Toulon on the following day to help in demobilization. With the agreement of everyone, I gave the names of Jarry, Robin, and Guérin. I learned later that Guérin as soon as he reached Toulon was expelled from the port zone and had to go to Marseille to a relative. The three left at ten o'clock on Sunday morning in a German car. Several sailors constituted a guard of honor which saluted as they left.

Scarcely had they gone when an order came that the other admirals, except me, were also to be freed during the afternoon. They left at half past four in gazogène taxis. ["Gazogènes" produced a gas for internal combustion motors by charring wood chips.]

In the meantime I asked a new officer of the guard, Captain Damscher, who had replaced the ensign, if my wife could come and live with me at the hotel. He agreed immediately without any hesitation. I then asked Bléhaut, who was alone in one of the taxis on leaving, to go and get her so that she could take that opportunity of coming. She arrived late the same evening.

On Monday evening neighbors who lived near me at Tamaris telephoned to say that my house was occupied at five o'clock in the afternoon in spite of the formal assurance given to me by Damscher that very morning, on the authority of the garrison Major von Gastell, to whom my demand had been addressed, that it would not be occupied. When I objected violently on learning this news Damscher, and then von Gastell, were sincerely indignant, and the latter reacted so effectively that later in the evening I learned that the occupants had been turned out at eight o'clock. I was assured that nothing had been touched and that it would not happen again.

I had also telephoned my complaint to Admiral Platon at Vichy and to Admiral Marquis at Toulon, but apparently the rectification was due to von Gastell who had acted first. Demands which I made to him for the recovery of my personal automobile, which was undergoing repairs, and for the security of my yacht, which was anchored in the care of the navigation police, were also quickly effective.

On the whole Damscher and von Gastell were very correct in their attitude, and even kind. The major came only once to the hotel, when the other admirals left. He was rather solemn but very well mannered.

From Monday onward all the sentinels and the guard detachment disappeared. My wife and I remained alone with Damscher and his aide in an entirely empty hotel, under requisition for the German airmen of Aix-les-Milles. They looked in every day, discreetly, to see if they could soon come to stay there, but Damscher calmly sent them away each time.

Except for the fact that we could not leave the garden our stay had none of the characteristics of detention. On 1 December [1942] news was brought to me at about two in the afternoon by von Gastell that I was free on condition that I did not live within about twenty kilometers of the coastline. That evening at seven o'clock, before I had left the hotel, which in fact I did not expect to leave until the following day, Admiral Platon told me by telephone from Vichy that the order had been countermanded by the High Command of the German Navy in Berlin.

On Thursday evening I learned from Admiral Platon that I was free on condition that I did not reside in the Toulon port zone itself; the written order reached Damscher only the following evening. I left the hotel Saturday, 5 December [1942], at ten in the morning, after having asked Damscher to give me a copy of the order for my liberation with an exact translation. He brought it to me Sunday morning at the Hotel Negre Coste.

During the final days his "supervision" had become more and more lax. Twice he even left, without telling me that he was off, to see the Major and I remained alone to guard myself during his absence.

(Document No. 191)
Fr. ed. 843-863

[*Not dated*]

J. DE LABORDE
Admiral

Annex No. 1

Strasbourg, *Toulon, 11 November 1942*
T. G.

HIGH SEAS FLEET
GENERAL STAFF
No. 169 E.M.I.

ORDER OF THE DAY

Officers and Men of the High Seas Fleet:

Events of exceptional gravity are bringing on our fatherland an even greater trial than that which it has already undergone. These events make more necessary than ever the union of all the French around the Maréchal, and your unwavering fidelity to the oath which you have sworn to him. Whatever happens remember that the dignity of your bearing, your calm, your discipline, and your absolute obedience to the orders of your chiefs, who like you have sworn to follow the Maréchal in everything which he orders, are the only means of saving the honor of France and of its flag.

Honor is our final possession; it is in no one's power to take it from a great nation; it enables us, if we protect it, to survive and to rise again after the greatest disasters.

ADMIRAL DE LABORDE
Commander-in-Chief, High Seas Fleet
(Signed) J. DE LABORDE

Annex No. 2

Strasbourg, *Toulon, 11 November 1942*

T.G.

HIGH SEAS FLEET
GENERAL STAFF
No. 170   E.M.I.

COMMUNIQUE

Following on the events in North Africa, the German government has notified the Maréchal that it believes it to be necessary for the security of Europe to take over itself the defense of the coasts of unoccupied France and of Corsica, which the terms of the armistice left as slightly defended as were the coasts of Algeria.

After this notice, against which the Maréchal protested on the ground that it was contrary to the conditions of the armistice, the German troops crossed the demarcation line and are now on their way to take up defense positions along our coasts.

The German government has given official notice that it is occupying these defense positions provisionally and only with strictly military purposes.

This does not imply any kind of encroachment on our fleet. In so far as our fleet is concerned, the order given many times by the Maréchal, with whom I am always in direct contact, that it must not fall intact into any foreign hands, will be strictly carried out if necessary.

ADMIRAL DE LABORDE
Commander-in-Chief, High Seas Fleet
(Signed) J. DE LABORDE

Annex No. 3

Telegram No. 771 from the Führer

Admiral Marquis gave a declaration of loyalty and asked that the defense of Toulon should be entrusted to the High Command of the French Fleet. The Führer agreed to this demand. The chief responsible for the command of Toulon should be asked to make a declaration on his word of honor that he will not undertake any action against the Axis Powers and that he will defend Toulon with all his forces against the Anglo-Saxons and against those French who are the enemies of the [French] government. If such a declaration is made the fortified area of Toulon should not be occupied, but a naval liaison detachment should be established with the commanding officer of the Navy at Toulon.

Military High Command West No. 00420h/42. *11 Nov. 42*

— 813 —

Annex No. 4

Strasbourg, *Toulon, 12 November 1942*

HIGH SEAS FLEET
GENERAL STAFF
No. 172 E.M.I.

ORDER OF THE DAY

The German government has agreed that the fortified area of Toulon shall not be occupied and that its defense shall be entrusted to the High Command of the French Navy.   On the word of honor of Admiral Marquis, the Maritime prefect, and myself, in agreement with the Maréchal, it has been arranged that the forces placed under our orders shall undertake no action against the Axis Powers, and will defend Toulon against the Anglo-Saxons and against those French who are enemies of the government of the Maréchal.   The fortified area of Toulon therefore remains entirely French and free.   Its defense will be entirely in French hands and entrusted to the Navy without any subordination to foreign command.

No foreigner may come on board a ship of the High Seas Fleet.

ADMIRAL DE LABORDE
Commander-in-Chief, High Seas Fleet
(Signed) J. DE LABORDE

Distribution: *Strasbourg - Al 1º E.C. - Algérie - Colbert - Dupleix - Al 3º D.C. - Marseillaise - Jean de Vienne - Al 3º E.L. - L'Indomptable - Tartu Vauquelin - Kersaint - Gerfaut - Cassard - Vautour - Guépard - Verdun - L'Adroit - Mameluk - Casque.*

Annex No. 5

I therefore ask you to give your word of honor that in these special circumstances I can rely always on your obedience without restriction, in order that I may keep the promise which I have made.

Annex No. 6

Strasbourg, *Toulon, 12 November 1942*

HIGH SEAS FLEET
GENERAL STAFF
No. 175 E.M.I.

COMMUNIQUE

In accordance with the agreement referred to in this morning's Order of the Day the German forces have stopped on the line Ollioules-Sanary and the Italian forces on the line of Gapeau.   The general alert given today was the result of a misunderstanding due to the fog, when *Impétueuse* was mistaken for a large enemy ship. No suspicious force has in fact entered Toulon waters.

ADMIRAL DE LABORDE

Commander-in-Chief, High Seas Fleet

(Signed) J. DE LABORDE

Distribution: *Strasbourg - Al.1° E.C. - Algérie - Colbert - Dupleix - Al.3° D.C. - Marseillaise - Jean de Vienne - Al.3° E.L. - Volta - L'Indomptable - Tartu Vauquelin - Kersaint - Gerfaut - Cassard - Vautour - Verdun - L'Adroit - Mameluk - Casque.*

Annex No. 7

Strasbourg, *Toulon, 13 November 1942*

HIGH SEAS FLEET
GENERAL STAFF

COMMUNIQUE

Fires were lit in the ships of the High Seas Fleet, and those of the region, because of information from an authorized source—which proved to be false—to the effect that a large English naval force with a convoy was approaching the coast of Provence. *Havraise* has dropped depth bombs at sea many times since yesterday because of sounds, caught by the listening system, which may have come from a submarine on reconnaissance duty.

ADMIRAL DE LABORDE

Commander-in-Chief, High Seas Fleet

(Signed) J. DE LABORDE

Distribution: *Strasbourg - Al 1st E.C. - Algérie - Colbert - Dupleix -Al.3° D.C. - Marseillaise - Jean de Vienne - Al 3rd E.L. - Volta - Indomptable - Tartu - Vauquelin - Kersaint - Gerfaut - Cassard - Vautour - Guépard - Verdun - L'Adroit - Mameluk - Casque.*

Annex No. 8

Strasbourg, *Toulon, 14 November 1942*

HIGH SEAS FLEET
GENERAL STAFF
No. 179 E.M.I.

COMMUNIQUE

The situation today is as follows:

The German forces on the west side occupy the agreed positions from Ollioules to Sanary. On the east, contrary to rumor, the Italian forces are entirely within the zone established to the east of the Gapeau. Neither

La Vallette nor Hyères is occupied. The reason for the rumors is as follows. When the [Italian] troops arrived the day before yesterday they did not know of the agreement that had been reached regarding the Toulon area until they had crossed Sollies-Pont. For that reason the point detachment of the vanguard reached La Vallette and the remainder of the troops passed by La Farlède and La Crau. Afterward all crossed Hyères in order to establish themselves at the east of the Gapeau. Only the command post of the general, about 150 men, who found no place to stay in the village selected east of the Gapeau remained temporarily in Hyères.

In addition to that we must naturally expect to see automobiles or motorcycles constantly maintaining liaison between the German line Ollioules-Sanary and the Italian line Sollies-Pont at the mouth of the Gapeau.

Yesterday *Impétueuse* twice dropped depth charges off Cap Capet against a submarine of which the periscope was seen twice. Rather a long time after the second attack a very large bubble of green gas rose to the surface indicating either the destruction of the submarine or at least very serious damage to the ballast.

ADMIRAL DE LABORDE

Commander-in-Chief, High Seas Fleet

(Signed) J. DE LABORDE

Distribution: *Strasbourg - Al.1º E.C. - Algérie - Colbert - Dupleix - Al.3º D.C. - Marseillaise - Jean de Vienne - Al.3º E.L. - Volta - L'Indomptable - Tartu - Vauquelin - Kersaint - Gerfaut - Cassard - Vautour - Guépard - Verdun - L'Adroit - Mameluk - Casque.*

Annex No. 9

Strasbourg, *Toulon, 15 November 1942*

HIGH SEAS FLEET
GENERAL STAFF
No. 183 E.M.I.

ORDER OF THE DAY

General staffs and crews of the High Seas Fleet:

In spite of the absurd rumors spread by foreign agents the fortified area of Toulon has not been occupied and remains entirely under the command of the French Navy, as does the High Seas Fleet.

This situation is due entirely to the admiration aroused in the high military authorities of the Axis by the heroic conduct of our comrades of the Second Light Squadron, and of the Navy in the Algeria and Morocco areas, who remained faithful to their oath to the point of sacrificing themselves.

These authorities yesterday evening asked Admiral Marquis and myself to accept their recognition of this conduct.

The maintenance of this situation depends on you. At a time when chiefs of the highest rank are losing their sense of duty you should show that honor is not measured by insignia nor by stars. Discipline without wavering, and perfect military bearing on land as aboard, are at this moment an absolute duty for everyone. The memory of our comrades who fell on the field of honor demands it. I have given my personal guarantee of your devotion to the Maréchal, whom I saw today and who asked me to tell you that he counts on you to save the unity and the honor of France.

I trust no one among you will be so without conscience as not to understand this duty.

ADMIRAL DE LABORDE
Commander-in-Chief, High Seas Fleet
(Signed) J. DE LABORDE

Annex No. 10

Strasbourg, *Toulon, 17 November 1942*

HIGH SEAS FLEET
GENERAL STAFF
No. 186 E.M.I.

ORDER

The Maréchal of France, the Chief of State, yesterday addressed to all the French people of mainland France and of the Empire the following message:

"Admiral Darlan dares state in a declaration that I am unable to express my intimate thought to the French people; he claims to be acting in my name. I am not the man to give way to constraint. To insinuate that I am is to insult me. At the moment when Africa was attacked I entrusted to Admiral Darlan the defense of French sovereignty, of which I am the trustee.

"From the time of the first engagement the Admiral did not hesitate to enter into contact with the attacker and, by giving a premature order to cease fire, disorganized the resistance and broke the morale of the troops. I confirmed repeatedly the order to defend Africa. He disregarded my order solely on the excuse that he was preventing a rebellious and traitorous chief, General Giraud, from usurping the command. Today he recognizes the nomination of that same chief.

"General Giraud was appointed by a foreign power who waged war on French territory. Admiral Darlan has thus placed himself outside of the national community. I declare him stripped of all public office and of all military command."

On receiving this order, commanding officers will remove and burn all portraits of Admiral Darlan which are on board their ships.

ADMIRAL DE LABORDE
Commander-in-Chief, High Seas Fleet
(Signed) J. DE LABORDE

Distribution: *Strasbourg - Al. 1st E.C. - Algérie - Colbert - Dupleix - Al.3º D.C. - Marseillaise - Jean de Vienne - Volta - Indomptable - Tartu - Vauquelin - Kersaint - Gerfaut - Cassard - Vautour - Guépard - Verdun - L'Adroit - Mameluk - Casque - Al. 3rd E.L.*

Annex No. 11

Strasbourg, *Toulon, 17 November 1942*

HIGH SEAS FLEET
GENERAL STAFF
No. 187 E.M.I.

COMMUNIQUE

Absurd rumors are being spread on the subject of our fleet at Alexandria. Telegrams exchanged between the Admiralty and Admiral Godfroy show that nothing has changed in its situation and that the crews remain unshakably faithful to the promise of the Maréchal not to deliver our warships to any foreign power. The English radio has denied the report that the ships were handed over to the English fleet.

At Toulon the French troops for the reinforcement of the defense of the fortified area continue to arrive.

No submarine has been heard on the listening apparatus by the patrols since the depth charges dropped by *Impétueuse* on 13 November [1942].

By arrangement with the maritime prefect all men stricken from the rolls for disciplinary reasons since 8 November [1942] will be expelled from the Toulon area on the day when their discharge becomes effective.

ADMIRAL DE LABORDE
Commander-in-Chief, High Seas Fleet
(*Signed*) J. DE LABORDE

Distribution: *Strasbourg - Al 1st E.C. - Algérie - Colbert - Dupleix - Al. 3rd D.C. - Marseillaise - Jean de Vienne - Al. 3rd E.L. - Volta - Indomptable - Tartu - Vauquelin - Kersaint - Gerfaut - Cassard - Vautour - Guépard - Verdun - L'Adroit - Mameluk - Casque.*

Annex No. 12

Strasbourg, *Toulon, 19 November 1942*

HIGH SEAS FLEET
GENERAL STAFF
No. 188 E.M.I.

COMMUNIQUE

We have just learned that Admiral Abrial has become Secretary of State for the Navy. You all remember his glorious role as chief of the heroic defense of Dunkirk.

Orders have been given to withdraw the supplementary troops which had been ordered to go to Toulon for the defense of the inner area. The Maré-chal desires that this defense shall be entirely in the hands of sailors. We all have at heart the desire to fulfil this task and to justify the confidence he places in us.

ADMIRAL DE LABORDE
Commander-in-Chief, High Seas Fleet
(Signed) J. DE LABORDE

Distribution: *Strasbourg - Al 1st E.C. - Algérie - Colbert - Dupleix - Al. 3rd D.C. Marseillaise - Jean de Vienne - Al 3rd E.L. - Volta - L'Indomptable - Tartu - Vauquelin - Kersaint - Gerfaut - Cassard - Vautour - Guépard - Verdun - L'Adroit - Casque - Mameluk.*

Copy: P.M. Toulon

Strasbourg, *Toulon, 21 November 1942*

HIGH SEAS FLEET
GENERAL STAFF
No. 193 E.M.I.

Annex No. 13

COMMUNIQUE

Leave for the occupied zone, which had been suspended, is now re-esta-blished for individual leave in cases of emergency.

Ordinary leave trains cannot be re-established, because of circumstances, until a later date.

To economize fuel oil the three-hour alert group has been altered to six-hours as on other ships.

ADMIRAL DE LABORDE
Commander-in-Chief, High Seas Fleet
(Signed) J. DE LABORDE

Distribution: *Strasbourg - Al. 1º E.C. - Algérie - Colbert - Dupleix - Al. 3º D.C. - Marseillaise - Jean de Vienne - Al. 3º E.L. - Volta - L'Indomptable - Tartu - Vauquelin - Kersaint - Gerfaut - Cassard - Vautour - Guépard - Verdun - L'Adroit - Casque - Mameluk.*

Copy to the Maritime Prefect, Toulon

Note: The preceding communiqués will be numbered as follows: Communiqué 170 E.M.I. of 11 November 1942 will be No. 1; Communiqué 175 E.M.I. of 12 November 1942 will be No. 2; Communiqué without number of 13/11/42 will be No. 3; Communiqué 179 E.M.I. of 14/11/32 will be No. 4; Communiqué 187 E.M.I. of 17/11/42 will be No. 5; and Communiqué 188 E.M.I. of 19/11/42 will be No. 6.

Annex No. 14

Kps. H.Qu., den 27.11.1942. 13.10 Uhr.
Folgender Fernspruch des Marschall Pétain
an Admiral de Laborde
wurde sœben von Generalfeldmarschall von Rundstedt übermittelt,
da Marschall Pétain nach Toulon keine Fernsprechverbindung erhält:
"Erfahre sœben, dass Ihr Schiff sinkt. Ich befehle Ihnen, unverzüglich
von Bord zu gehen." Pétain
Für die Richtigkeit:
Der Chef des Generalstabes

Annex No. 15

Strasbourg, *Toulon, 28 November 1942*

HIGH SEAS FLEET
ADMIRAL

ORDER OF THE DAY

General staffs and crews of the High Seas Fleet. Yesterday in order to
remain faithful to our oath of obedience to the Maréchal we had to do
that which for the heart of a sailor is the most grievous of all deeds, to
destroy his own ship in order that it shall not fall into the hands of a foreign
nation. You have executed this duty with a discipline and devotion more
meritorious than many acts of heroism.

In the name of France and of the Navy I thank you. You have heard
by radio and press the affirmation that the act of force against us which
brought us to this extremity was justified on the ground that I had violated,
from 12 November [1942] onward, the word of honor which I had given in
your name on the 11th; and on the further ground that the High Seas
Fleet were to depart during the night of the 26th to the 27th to join the
English forces.

You all know that both these affirmations are false; you know that I
never ordered you not to fight against the Anglo-Americans; that the only
general lighting of the boiler fires since the 11th was due to the false report
that an English squadron had been seen moving toward the coast of Provence; and finally that on the 27th all fires were extinguished on all ships
and that no arrangements for leaving were ever taken.

Throughout all these tragic events the honor of the High Seas
Fleet, and my personal honor, have therefore remained untouched. Of this
truth you will be under all circumstances the unimpeachable witnesses.

(Signed) DE LABORDE

Annex No. 15

ORDER OF THE DAY

28 *November 1942*

General staffs and crews of the High Seas Fleet.

[*In the papers deposited by Admiral de Laborde the
above Order of the Day is given twice, the second time
with a slight alteration in the heading of the paper on
which the order is written, and with an entirely unimportant change of one word, "Dans" becoming "De" at
the beginning of the final paragraph.*]

PART FOUR

SOCIAL AND CULTURAL

CHAPTER XVI

NATIONAL EDUCATION
AND YOUTH

NATIONAL EDUCATION

ABEL BONNARD

Minister of National Education

When Pierre Laval did me the honor of asking me to be Minister of National Education in the ministry which he was forming I had no other reason for accepting an office which would keep me from my literary work than a desire to try to accomplish a fine and important task, namely the reorganization of all national education, regarded as the most perfect expression of the rebirth of France. My decision was inspired by the idea that in the defeat which we had just suffered France must find the necessary stimulus for putting into effect those reforms of which she had already felt the need but which she had not had the energy to accomplish. The defeat must be forced to serve the very country which it had struck. There was nothing unreasonable about my ambition in this matter, nor even paradoxical. It is one of the most often proved truths of history that great nations have never shown their greatness more than when adversity has given them an opportunity to do so and has imposed on them the duty of retrenching within their own strongest virtues in order to be born again.

I shall summarize here, without adding any afterthoughts to the basic ideas which then inspired me, the spirit which was to animate this reconstruction of our various forms of education. The first and broadest principle was that all education, elementary or advanced, whatever the status of the pupils for whom it was intended, must meet simultaneously two requirements: on the one hand it must prepare the student to practice a trade or profession through which he could put his own abilities at the service of the society to which he belonged; on the other, it should prepare him to develop freely, outside his usual field of work, according to the nature of the soul within him, and of whatever unique gifts might be his.

Thus every form of education, even the simplest, should consist of a useful column, bearing a capital of culture. In elementary education, this culture would take the form of bringing to the pupils, beyond the practical training needed for their livelihood, a love of the countryside and of flowers, and a desire to protect animals, with the result that men thus educated would became kings of nature, if they were so fitted, even though they had only a modest place in society. In secondary education there would be variations. Parallel with the two forms of instruction already in existence, classical and modern, two other lines of education would be established, secondary technical and secondary agricultural. Each of them would achieve a culture of its own. The modern side would bring a broad and vivid understanding of the world as it is today, combined with a full knowledge of the most-used languages, and a knowledge of the world's geography, climate, races, and resources in minerals and oil. For those who were being educated in farm work, the cultural achievement, beyond a training in the best methods of agriculture, would be a sort of reconstructive knowledge of those masterpieces in which the great poets, from Hesiod and Theocritus to Virgil and Mistral, have sung of country life; for, however hard it may be, it is a life that blossoms naturally into poetry, blending the labor of man with the order and beauty of the world.

Technical education, entirely devoted to industry and the control of machines, would find its higher relaxation in visits to museums where art embodies the supreme technique, placed at the service of the human soul.

In the field of classical education the problem was more difficult. The quality of classical instruction in France has never ceased to deteriorate for many reasons, of which the first is that it had been designed for a social aristocracy of pupils who were not rigorously obliged to earn their own living; now that the same education is being given to pupils who are definitely under such obligation, its principles have become inapplicable. However, classical education has retained so great a social prestige that parents who do not provide it for their children believe that through this omission they have relegated them to inferior activities. The result is that classical education is overcrowded not so much in proportion to the fitness of its pupils as by the vanity of the families which force them into it. It is this dismal aura of prestige which must be abolished. My predecessor had believed he could stop the exaggerated rush of pupils to classical education by a preliminary examination. I, on the other hand, wished to prevent this invasion not by some feeble barrage but by giving to other forms of education the appeal which they ought normally to offer, so that the multitude of students would divide themselves into groups moving in different directions.

It must be added that the old ideal of *un honnête homme* [an honorable man] as it had been established in the France of the 1600s could not be maintained today; the sciences have developed much too far and the various professions have become too specialized to allow any one man, lazy in all probability, to be able to sum up within himself all the knowledge and all the culture of his time. So complete a union could now be obtained only by a harmonious association of different kinds and different individuals, and the precious essence of ancient culture could better be brought to such a community by a few who had studied profoundly than through many who had studied poorly.

I did everything possible to inspire the entire body of educators with the spirit which animated me. In Paris and at Rouen, Lille, Lyon, Marseille, Limoges, and Toulouse I spoke to the teachers and professors in all fields of instruction without bringing a single word of politics into my talks; my only purpose was to inspire my hearers with the love of their profession. I brought the rectors of the universities together many times, and saw each of them separately as well. I held many meetings of the academical inspectors and spoke to them with all the more pleasure because I thought I could feel among them the existence of most vigorous elements. I believed that no true reform can be achieved unless in changing things one also inspires men.

Some definite results were obtained. The salaries were increased so much that the tables prepared by the Ministry of Finance to show comparative pay between the various groups of civil servants showed that the teaching profession had been brought higher than before. When I joined the ministry I had changed the national bulletin for the teaching profession into a serious review, filled with important articles on a great variety of subjects. I bought slide projectors to be given to the most enthusiastic of the teachers, thus increasing their possibilities of interesting their students. I planned, too, to encourage those of the teaching profession, and they are very numerous, who of their own accord do special work in some particular field, such as geology, botany, local history, folk-lore, the observation of animals, or the culture of bees, not merely by supplying them with fundamental books needed in satisfaction of their curiosity but by putting them into close contact with experts among the professors of advanced education who might guide them in their studies and perhaps enable them, if they were sufficiently gifted, to become advanced instructors themselves.

When I joined the ministry I found there a plan for the reform of the system of medical education ready to be signed; it seemed to me too meager a plan for a matter of such importance and difficulty. There existed also on the same subject a study by Professor Leriche, a master of recognized standing, which had caught the attention and interest of the Maréchal. I reached an agreement with the Minister of Health, Doctor Grasset, who combined with his medical experience such qualities of honesty and fine spirit that it was a pleasure to agree with him. We formed a commission, made up of distinguished doctors, to study the plan prepared by Professor Leriche. The result was a reorganization of medical education which I believe was both good and fruitful. In addition I set up a commission to prepare a precise plan for a school of advanced administration where the finest civil servants and directors could be trained. I brought together the professors of advanced education in order to replace, with their advice, the school of history and geography by two separate schools, one for geography and one for history, which would be preferable. I increased the amount of time allowed for the study of history in secondary education and decided that among the four subjects in French composition from which candidates for a baccalaureate were allowed to choose, one must be historical. Educational activities were maintained in the prison camps and it was made possible to pass examinations there. I also made a collection of books, carefully chosen, and had them bound to send to the clubs of French workers in Germany, so that workers and prisoners would not feel that they were isolated and abandoned.

Particularly dear to me was my plan for limiting and decreasing the rush, greater year after year, of students who came to live, all jumbled together, in Paris. The provincial capitals of France are admirable, some of them more given to business, others to culture, but all of them more peaceful than Paris itself and all of them suited to serve as the most noble setting of activities of the mind while enabling students to live there closer to the countryside and to nature. It was my intention, and I said so most clearly, to make certain that the professors of the faculties should be regarded socially as among the most important persons of the city. I even planned to add to their salaries an allowance for entertainment in order that they could receive their pupils more often, could know them personally, and could find real followers among them. In spite of what might be believed, intellectual activities are far from being as highly honored in France as they ought to be. Nothing would have given me greater joy than to give back to them the standing which is rightly theirs.

The role of public education in any great nation is not merely to stimulate those natural tendencies which bear within themselves the genius and spirit of an entire people. Education must also complete and correct those tendencies to some extent. The French spirit, in the very agility and changeability by which it has often astounded or charmed the world, runs the risk of acting on a level which is above practical matters, forgetting to deal with things themselves, and confusing reason with logic. To this spiritual traveler, too quick in his movements, must be given the desire to carry his baggage with him, to burden himself with reality, for in that way his outstanding qualities will retain all their true value.

But as the cruelties of war struck France more harshly it became necessary to ward off continually recurring difficulties by the use of improvised measures, to protect the children in the schools to the greatest possible extent from the danger of bombing, to make their examinations easier while trying to maintain some value in them, and to add nothing to the sufferings of the families. The task of shoring up the existing structure replaced that of building. A great undertaking was no longer possible. Now that I look on these events after the passage of time I need make no effort to see myself as being well above whatever harm or evil they may have brought me. But when I think of that rebirth of an entire educational system which would have thrown its superb protection over a French youth widely differing yet united, and when I tell myself that it was not done, I must admit that I still suffer from an instinctive regret.

It is among these memories that I find again the image of Pierre Laval. He had a deep liking for self-instruction and as he was not born with the ready-made destiny of a young man of a well-to-do family it required determination to rise from the primary school all the way to advanced education. As Chief of Government it was his task to aid France at every point where she was threatened, and thus he had so much to do that I was not justified in tiring him with the details of my plans. But he knew their principles, and he liked them. His personality was both open and steady; as much in favor of reforms as he was against impossible dreams, he had a spirit which gave him absence of prejudice in his thought and absence of hostility and hate in his character. When I consider the contrast between his most humane nature and the harshness of his fate, a feeling of surprise would be blended with the suffering that I feel if we did not know, through the testimony of the centuries and the warnings of wise men, that there is no necessary relationship between the fate which a man merits and that which comes upon him.

(Document No. 270)
Fr. ed. 869-872

Madrid, 2 April 1955
ABEL BONNARD

FRENCH UNIVERSITIES

MAURICE GAIT

Secretary General for Youth

No educational establishment in France was closed during the hostilities, either in the southern or northern zone, except where there were German requisitions, of which the French authorities as a rule succeeded in securing the removal.

The seventeen French universities functioned normally; the 150,000 teachers of the primary schools, the 30,000 professors in the secondary schools, and the 6,000 professors of higher education remained at their posts, as did also those engaged in technical education and staffs of the apprentice centers created by the Vichy government to prevent unemployment among young people.

The fate of the University of Strasbourg was considered with special solicitude. The rector of this university, whom the government appointed, symbolically, as secretary-general of public instruction, divided his time between his office in Vichy—he did not have the necessary pass for crossing the demarcation line to go to Paris—and his office at Périgueux, to which city the administrative personnel of the University of Strasbourg had been evacuated.

The four faculties of Strasbourg University had been transferred to Clermont-Ferrand where they existed quite separately from the faculties of that city.

In spite of many attempts to force the government to follow another course the University of Strasbourg remained entirely French; it lost none of its rights and none of its property and it was able to re-establish itself in Strasbourg without any difficulty after the liberation of Alsace.

(Document No. 307)

Fr. ed. 873

31 October 1955

MAURICE GAIT

NATIONAL EDUCATION

JÉROME CARCOPINO
Minister of National Education

I the undersigned Jérôme Carcopino, Member of the Institute, former Secretary of State for National Education, living in Paris, deposit in the Hoover War Library that part of my book *Souvenirs de sept ans* which concerns the functions of the Minister of National Education which I exercised from March 1941 to April 1942.

(Document No. 267)
Fr. ed. 874

Paris, 20 May 1955

J. CARCOPINO
Jérôme Carcopino

[*This text may be consulted at the Hoover Library.*]

SPORTS

JEP PASCOT
Colonel of Artillery;
Under-Secretary of State for Sports

I the undersigned Jep Pascot, Colonel of Artillery in the Colonial Army, have the honor to make the following declaration under oath.

In September 1940 the Ministry of War placed me on detached service in the General Commissariat for Sports, at the request of M. Jean Borotra. During my military career similar orders had already been issued to me, but in this case my assignment was not based entirely on my competence in sports. General Blaizot, director of colonial troops, my immediate chief, and also General of the Army Huntziger, Minister of War, made clear to me the special interest they took in my new position. Doubtless they did intend to answer Jean Borotra's request by giving him the benefit of my special technical knowledge in physical education and sports, but they also had another purpose in mind.

The Minister of War was engaged in concealing the officer corps of the active army, which under the terms of the armistice he was obliged to dismiss. In the General Commissariat for Sports an officer so widely known for his sporting activities as I was could take steps to further this movement of national importance without arousing suspicions. Besides, no other government service was better fitted to take over military officer groups than the General Commissariat for Sports. It gave just the right conceal-ment and could get under way an effective military preparation which could one day make possible the reconstitution of the Army. It was in this same spirit and following the same instructions of General Huntziger that the Army's general staff assigned many other superior officers to detached service with M. Borotra, notably Colonel Maisonneuve, chief of the planning section and author of the "doctrine of general education" which was applied during the occupation in all branches of the educational system.

It was these directives of the Army's general staff which inspired my action, and it was with this feeling that I turned all my thoughts toward the young people of France.

I believe that I should recount the following facts here in order to show that President Laval was not ignorant of what was done, and that he intentionally protected all our undertakings.

I have never taken any part in politics. I had no acquaintance with any politician, nor had I even seen President Laval until 18 April 1942, the day I was promoted to commissioner-general. It seemed to me indispensable that the President of the Council should become better acquainted with me than would be possible in the few moments of an official presentation. I thought it was necessary too that he should be informed of the doctrine on which the General Commissariat for Sports was to be operated, and that he should know my own personal ideas for the pursuit and attainment of our objective.

He had been pictured to me as distrustful and secretive; people said that he was forced to give in a great deal to the occupying authorities. This seemed to be one more reason why I should be clear as to the intentions which had been ascribed to him in the matters which concerned me; and one more reason, too, why I should let him know clearly my own feelings.

I had some difficulty in arranging for the fifteen or twenty minutes with him that were necessary for such a conversation. Each time I met him it was almost furtively between two appointments more important than mine, as can be imagined. He threw me off, too, by his banter on these occasions—"I'm not much of a sportsman, and I'm not the worse for it, either . . . I trust you. You know what you're doing. Get on with it." However, an opportunity did come when I could really tell him what I wanted him to know and what I wanted to find out from him.

President Laval listened to me with close attention and great seriousness as I explained the points that I have presented briefly above: how I happened to come into the sports commissariat, what instructions I had received, the number of officers and noncommissioned officers who had been brought into the commissariat and hidden away, the doctrine of general education, and my own conception of the role allotted to the General Commissariat for Sports, namely that it was nonpolitical, and exclusively national, and that its mission was to safeguard the youth of France.

At the end of the interview, the President said to me very simply, "I have often joked with you, Colonel. But I was not ignorant of the seriousness of what you are doing. It is excellent. Save everything that can be saved: that is the essence of our task. Go ahead, prudently, but go ahead."

From that day on, my conviction was clear. This man who had been presented to me as crafty, secretive, rather Machiavellian, had shown himself to me, in his goodness and his simplicity, as direct, deep, and human. The impression I carried away was that he was dominated by the conception he had formed of his role as protector. Save all that can be saved!

On another occasion this attitude was even clearer to me.

From the beginning, the major preoccupation of the General Commissariat for Sports had been to acquire and build sports fields for the schools to make possible the application of the doctrine of physical education which had now been made obligatory and to endow France with sports equipment worthy of our country. From 1942 on, material and labor shortages made the construction of sports fields almost impossible. German building and construction regulations made things worse.

At the end of the financial year 1942, a great part of the credits allowed us were still unused, and a reduction in credits for sports equipment in 1943 was therefore threatened. In order to continue work which I regarded as indispensable from the national point of view, I explained to M. Gourdin, director of the budget, the new direction that I proposed to give to our sports equipment policy. The idea was to direct our principal effort to the acquisition of land for fields, and to work along as best we could in preparing them for use. I secured approval for this new program, and credits similar to those of 1942 were allotted.

Nevertheless, the acquisition of fields was not always possible without arousing discontent. The municipalities did rival one another in the diligence and energy with which they seized the advantages which the State granted them when they proved that they had purchased a piece of ground. They were granted 60 per cent of the purchase price; no government had ever done as much before. But, on the other hand, some of the owners of the fields we wanted were very reluctant to part with them. Though we chose ground with the greatest possible care, with every respect for cultivation, and in agreement with representatives of the Ministry of Agriculture, the office of the President of the Council received many complaints and criticisms of the General Commissariat for Sports.

President Laval summoned me one day, and I was led to explain to him what I had just stated above. His reply, engraved in my memory, was as follows: "You are making good use of the credits allotted to you. Keep it up. Spend the money. It's just that much more that the Germans can't get their hands on."

And when I talked to him of fitting out the fields with cross-beams for trapezes, ropes, and swings, with parallel bars, jumping equipment, and so on, all of which I was having built in spite of the ban placed on construction by the occupying authorities, he approved what I was doing in these words: "That's all right! Just that much more that can't be taken away and that will remain fixed to the soil of France. And just that many more men that Sauckel can't get away from me."

Thus supported, I was able to give myself entirely to the constructive and educational task of the General Commissariat for Sports. In spite of the occupation, its hardships, and its controls, the work accomplished was considerable. I will cite here only a few of the results.

(1) In 1940 there was not one school sports ground in France. By 1 January 1944, the state had bought for the use of the communes 10,335 sports fields. Of this number, a thousand were completed, another thousand were sufficiently advanced to be used, and the rest were being prepared.

(2) In 1940 we had only twenty-three approved swimming pools in France. On 1 January 1944 there were 460 approved pools, of which 250 were completed or in condition to be used.

But the physical side of what we did is less important than the spirit which inspired those who did it, a spirit I wish to emphasize here. The General Commissariat for Sports carried out during the occupation a mission in protection of the physical and moral heritage of France. All the organizations created by it, the national bureaus, the regional and departemental organizations, its schools and training centers, its medical examination system, and its sports equipment today continue to serve our country. It established a doctrine of physical and sports education which has been adopted by the Army. It preserved the young sportsmen and sportswomen of France from all contact with the Germans and with the Obligatory Labor Service.

There was nothing about this task that President Laval did not know, and nothing of its jealously national character of which he was unaware. He took steps to aid it, and he rejoiced in everything that could be done to the advantage of our youth in spite of the occupying authority.

I asked nothing from President Laval. I obtained no favor from him. In bringing my solemn testimony I am obeying only my sense of justice.

(Document No. 36)
Fr. ed. 875-877

Ribérac, 25 October 1947

J. PASCOT
Colonel Pascot

[Those doing research in the subject of the Pétain government's attempt to rebuild the youth of France through organized sport will find a detailed report on the subject, written by. Col. Pascot and deposited by him as Document Nr. 257, in the Hoover Library.]

YOUTH WORK CAMPS

PIERRE COSMI

*Director of the Cabinet of M. Jean Bichelonne,
Minister-Secretary of State for Industrial
Production and Communications*

I was Jean Bichelonne's collaborator during a period of twenty-one months, from December 1942 to 17 August 1944 when he was Minister-Secretary of State for Industrial Production and Communications; and also, during several months, when he was Minister of Labor.

At first I was a technical counselor and later chief of the technical services in the cabinet for Communications, and was charged by the minister with the task of directing the joint cabinet which dealt with the different ministerial departments that he controlled. This task was assigned to me at the beginning of August 1943 when Pierre de Calan, then Director of the Cabinet of the Ministry of Industrial Production, was arrested by the Gestapo.

A few pages would not be sufficient for me to tell, even in very condensed form, what I know of Jean Bichelonne's activities during this period. As I am obliged to limit my testimony I will deal particularly with a single point, namely his activities in connection with the Youth Work Camps, which, in fact, reveal clearly the determination and the technical skill so characteristic of Jean Bichelonne's various activities throughout four years in the defense of French interests.

I believe that it will be useful in the interests of clarity to explain first the general lines of the Youth Work Camps, leaving details to the two annexes to this statement which will make clear the development of the operation, or more precisely, of the operations.

The Youth Work Camps were reserved for the young men of the unoccupied zone. They were under the authority of the Ministry of National Education until the middle of 1943 when they came directly under the Chief of Government. It is well known that General de La Porte du Theil, Commissioner-General until the last months of 1943, had had the full confidence of Maréchal Pétain, whose interest in the camps was always strong.

These groups of young men in green uniform, organized with officers and under a military-type discipline, caused the German military authorities considerable disquiet which showed itself in demands for reports and in the close watch which they kept on the camps. During the period to which I refer, a decision of the Armistice Commission at Wiesbaden on 14 October 1943, limiting to 30,000 the number of young men who might be present in the camps at any one time, was a very clear indication of the state of mind of these [German] authorities. That decision was to be followed by many others; there was not a week, and sometimes not a day, when the close and constant watch kept by the German army over the young men of the camps did not show itself in intervention or imperative demands for information.

In answer to this continuous supervision and these repeated instructions, the French government replied by measures of which the general outline was as follows:

At the end of November 1943 the French government decided to assign those youths who were already in the camps, together with those who were being called up that month, to work which would be, in so far as possible, of value to the French economy within the framework of the Bichelonne-Speer agreements,[1] which were thereafter systematically cited in opposition to instructions received from the German army.

1. It is known that conversations carried on at Berlin in September 1943 between M. Bichelonne and the German Minister of Armaments Speer had made it possible to set apart various French establishments of economic importance of which the employees, thanks to this classification, would be guaranteed against being forced to go to Germany to work. It was not a question of establishments which were forced to work for German armament, nor even for Germany. An establishment could be classified as protected, with the identification "S," at the request of the French government whenever an important part of its activity was concerned either with

At this time (November 1943) the number of youths in the camps was limited to 30,000, made up of the November contingent and part of the July 1943 contingent. The excess beyond this figure, estimated to be 10,000, was to be placed at the disposition of the Minister of Industrial Production. It would be the balance of the July contingent that would be liberated in anticipation. These young men would be clothed in blue uniforms, which gave them their name, "the Blues," to distinguish them from the rest of the youths in the Camps who would be the "Greens." Blues and Greens would thus maintain the uniform which the Armistice Commission had wished to forbid. Like the Greens, the Blues would be organized with officers, though in proportionately smaller number, taken from the leaders of the camps; they would be obliged to lodge and live in common, in quarters prepared by the chiefs of the industrial establishments to which they were assigned. From the point of view of French labor regulations they would be considered as "requisitioned workers" in the sense of the law of 4 September 1942, and they would receive salaries.

The commissioner-general for Youth Work Camps was responsible for transfer of the youths to the industrial establishments to which they were assigned and for facilitating in every possible way, with such means as were available to him, the preparation of the living quarters. But once the transfer had been made, and the new organization put into working order, the officers and the young Blues would come only under the authority of a special service created for that purpose in the Ministry of Industrial Production.

The young Blues were allocated to different establishments coming under the supervision of the different divisions of the Ministry (Electricity, Mines, Chemical Products, Steel, Carburants, Machinery, or Aeronautics), but such firms as were classified "S," or about to be so classified.

The 30,000 young Greens, whose traditional assignments had been somewhat modified because of German orders, some being assigned to the preparation of pit props for mines in the Landes or to other French work places, thus remained alone under the direct authority of the commissioner-general.

Toward the end of December 1943 General de La Porte du Theil was removed from his post under conditions with which I was not precisely acquainted but which, as I remember it, were clearly connected with German pressure. The departure of the General and his temporary replacement by Colonel Bernon, Commissioner-Plenipotentiary named as Director-General, and the modifications in the assignments of the youths, created a very definite uneasiness among the officers and leaders, some of whom demanded that the organization be dissolved. But the government, by the law of 19 January 1944, placed the director-general under the

German orders for equipment, which could well be water taps, wire, or phonograph records, or for French orders to fulfill the program established by the competent ministries. More than ten thousand establishments were classed as "S." The statement of Sauckel, whose services were in the habit of calling the class "S" factories the "legal maquis," on this subject is well known: "I declare publicly that the abusive use of 'protected factories' combined with the general labor situation in France implies (he was speaking on 1 March 1944) a great danger for labor in Germany.... The term 'protected factory' in France means merely that the factory is protected against Sauckel." [1 March 1944.]

To one of his collaborators who expressed his disquiet on noting that German orders had been accepted and that nothing had been delivered, Jean Bichelonne replied—this was in December 1943—"All the better. I asked them to 'accept' the orders; but I didn't say anything about filling them." [December 1943.]

authority of the Minister of Labor—M. Bichelonne since the end of November 1943—and this decision was well received by the officers and leaders.

In his capacity as Minister of Labor, M. Bichelonne then placed under the authority of the Minister of Industrial Production all the Greens in the industrial establishments and in the pit prop workyards of the Landes. In this way they were assimilated to the young Blues whose special regime was outlined above, and in that way, behind the screen of the "S" classification, escaped control by the German military authorities.

The German Armistice Commission claimed jurisdiction, nonetheless, over the young workers in the protected sections. Visits to the factories, demands for assignment lists, etc., were frequent. But opposition to this action was much stronger in the Blue than in the Green Sector. Thus it was that numerous sections of the German administration were engaged in protecting the French economy.

Time was gained in this way, but pressure from the German authorities did not diminish. The French government, seeing that it had exhausted in its daily struggle all the means available to it for reducing a close and more and more threatening German control, began to think that the only solution would be to abandon the name "work camps." But M. Bichelonne desired to retain, for the benefit of the French economy, all these youths without losing the advantages in output which were assured by supervision under their own leaders. Therefore a move was made toward a formula which would provide considerable dispersion of groups with a reduction of the number of officers to an indispensable minimum.

Negotiations to this end were begun by the French government with the German Armistice Commission. But the commission ordered the immediate and complete dissolution of all Green and Blue formations. The young men thus became free workers and there was nothing left to do except to protect as well as possible all their equipment, their barracks, their trucks, their transport mules, their tools and so on, which the Germans immediately demanded.

The first annex to this present statement deals in some detail with the discussions relative to the assignment of the young men to the Todt organization. The second annex gives information of the same kind regarding the assignment of the young men to the German army. An account of simple facts evidently gives no more than a general idea of the vicissitudes of that continual struggle. It will be readily believed that incidents, minor or major, were numerous.

The difficulties which rigorous co-ordination, necessary there as elsewhere, brought on the French side should be understood. Negotiators on the ministerial level often found themselves in a difficult situation, for example, when the German adversary proved that certain statistics, in the presentation of which the French had exerted all their skill, had been falsified by being based on inexact data—intentionally but clumsily inexact—and again when it was necessary to claim, against all the evidence to the contrary, that thefts of equipment and food had not been prearranged with the maquis. But at least the young men and their officers, who never misunderstood the meaning of the measures taken by the French government during the Todt and Wehrmacht operations, were inspired by their own patriotism to find the means of supplementing such measures and making them fully effective.

I believe that I will not be going too far beyond the limits which I have set for myself if I recall the endless work days during which I saw Jean Bichelonne, in spite of the suffering brought upon him by the after-effects of his serious accident of April 1943, tirelessly bring all his strength to bear in all sectors of the ministerial departments, with their crushing responsibilities.

The results obtained by this constant struggle for the defense of French economic capacity will be established one day in books supported by statistics—correct, this time. They will point out, in the damage listed at the time of the liberation, the very large part due to bombardments and acts of war, in contrast to the part due to those German demands against which the activities of the French government could be brought to bear.

But there is at least one field in which the results of the steady action in that campaign of defense should have been immediately noticed, even if no one cared to acknowledge to whose efforts they were due. From the first months of 1944 the mines, the railways, the inland waterways, the vehicles, the generating stations, and electric transmission lines had been attacked by bombardments and by sabotage of which the intensity increased steadily, to reach a maximum between May and August 1944. All of Jean Bichelonne's collaborators, all the chiefs of the services having to do with these matters in the ministries, in the state railways, on the road transport services, and in the grain office, were witnesses of the fierce intensity which he brought to the defense of those essential elements in the French economy. Though some people were calling for disorder and disorganization on the ground that it was a form of combat against the enemy, Jean Bichelonne knew well that, in spite of everything, it was vital to assure a minimum food supply to the great city centers, to maintain a certain industrial activity in order to employ the workers of establishments which had been damaged or destroyed, and to avoid the unemployment which would have highly stimulated the demands of Sauckel.

Throughout this six months' struggle he was the impassioned leader.[1] Day after day, informed of breaks in the various lines of communication and in the power-lines, and of restrictions on the movements of trucks, he improvised solutions and means of protection. Right up to the liberation, Paris received each day, by rail, road, or water, supplies of coal and wheat, and its family parcels [authorized exceptions to the ration regulations, sent by relatives or friends in the country]. The electric supply was often cut, yet the factories continued working. Paris ate poorly, but Paris ate; and it was even possible to build up and maintain the little reserve supply of food which was to allow it to await the slow return of more normal supplies. I do not think it can be argued that Jean Bichelonne did not thus render eminent services to his country.

As others did—and perhaps with less reason—Jean Bichelonne could have avoided certain of the responsibilities which he accepted. But he always said, "If I don't do it, who will?" In the face of the mortal danger which France ran, convinced that the essential duty was to save what

1. And would it astonish anyone to learn that, obliged each day to take decisions of the greatest importance, exhausted by four years of crushing labor, and at the limit of his strength, he signed in July 1944, and to my personal knowledge signed without having read it, a manifesto of which the authors told him that it was merely some internal note intended for the government, asking that it be re-established in Paris?

could be saved, he fought, relying on his own strength, at every point where he believed he could fight better than another.   And he continued to fight until the last day,[1] pushing aside all advice that he should take care of his health, and all counsels of prudence.   He sacrificed everything—and I know that he did it in full consciousness of what he was doing—for his country, which, I hope will one day recognize that his sacrifice was not in vain.

(Document No. 177)
Fr. ed. 878-885

15 March 1953

P. COSMI

Annex I

Assignment of Youths to the Todt Organization

(1) At the beginning of October 1943 in a conference with Gauleiter Sauckel the French government obtained from the German government a general agreement on labor which was based on the Bichelonne-Speer agreements concluded in Berlin in September 1943, and which provided in particular for the German government's cancellation of its order that everyone in the Youth Work Camps should be sent to Germany and that the camps might be closed.

(2) The German Armistice Commission at Wiesbaden[2] by telegram dated 14 October 1943 fixed absolutely (on the order of the Führer) the maximum total figure for the camps at 30,000; and formally forbade, in consequence, the incorporation that had been arranged for 1 November 1943 of the remnant of the 1943 age group in the southern zone; this referred to 20,000 young farm workers whose calling-up had been postponed because of the needs of the food supply services.

(3) The French government replied, by a note from M. Bichelonne to Ambassador Schleier dated 27 October 1943, that the execution of the Bichelonne-Speer agreement demanded that account be taken of engagements previously entered into toward other German services, a total of 46,000 young men with their officers, whereas the total number of young men at that time was merely 28,000, and that therefore the incorporating of new recruits, which had already been begun, could not be suspended.   In actual fact, only 9,000 young men had been called up at that time.

(4) During a conference at the German Embassy in Paris on 3 November 1943, Lieutenant von Witzleben, representing the German Armistice Commission in Paris, announced that the German Commander-in-Chief West had drawn up a plan for assigning 50,000 [60,000] young men, as follows; 21,000 to industrial production; 7,000 to German air force construction: 11,000 to German army construction; and 21,000 to the Todt organization.

1. I myself witnessed his innumerable attempts, in full agreement with the Chief of Government, Pierre Laval, to make certain that the German armies and navy in retreat did not demolish the quays in the ports, the permanent structures—particularly the bridges—the electric generating stations, and the telephone exchanges in Paris.
2. CAA Wiesbaden = Franco-German Armistice Commission at Wiesbaden.

(5) On the evening of 3 November [1943], in the presence of the commissioner-general of labor, I received Lieutenant von Witzleben who announced that the German Armistice Commission at Wiesbaden, had withdrawn their opposition (noted in Paragraph 2 above) to the incorporation of young men arranged for 1 November [1943]. It was finally agreed, in addition, that the limiting figure of 30,000, about which there would be no further discussion, was not to include the necessary officers, that the French government would be free to conduct the operation of incorporating the new recruits, and that an extension of time up to 20 November [1943] would be allowed to make adjustments of the forces involved.

(6) On 4 November [1943] M. Bichelonne took note of these agreements, renewed his protests against the difficulties which the proposed measures would bring to the realization of the Bichelonne-Speer agreement, and emphasized the conflict between that plan and the one which had been announced by the German Commander-in-Chief West.

(7) On 5 November [1943] the Commander-in-Chief West confirmed his determination that the plan announced by Lieutenant von Witzleben —see item 4 above—should be put into operation.

(8) On 6 November [1943] the German Armistice Commission in Wiesbaden confirmed its former refusal to allow the new recruits to be incorporated, in spite of the assurances given by their representative in Paris on 3 November 1943—see item 5 above.

(9) On 10 November [1943] M. Bichelonne sent to the German Embassy in Paris a new protest insisting that these two opposing plans should be brought into harmony, and stating that in the meanwhile the French government would make no modification of the measures which it had taken.

(10) On 12 November [1943] the representatives of the German Armistice Commission in Paris contested the agreements given on 3 November —see item 5 above—by Lieutenant von Witzleben and again confirmed that they intended that their plan of assignment of the young men should be carried through. They asked that a table of available forces should be sent to them each week.

(11) An intense discussion continued until 17 December [1943], M. Bichelonne still defending the application of the Bichelonne-Speer plan against the plan of the German Armistice Commission. The atmosphere became more tense with each weekly presentation of the table of young men available.

(12) On 17 [December 1943] a telegram from the German Armistice Commission in Wiesbaden, dated 14 December 1943, was received, pointing out the difference between the figures in the tables given to the Armistice Commission's representatives in Paris, and the number of workers counted on the spot by the German control commissions. It was this telegram which assigned youths hitherto left in their work camp units, for such traditional labor as forestry, etc., to immediate work with the Todt organization. This order applied to 4,500 young men.

(13) On 22 December [1943] the Paris delegation of the German Armistice Commission set a delay of eight days after which the measures indicated above under item 12 were to be put into effect.

(14) The French government protested to the Armistice Commission in Wiesbaden on 4 January 1944. By two notes, dated 31 December 1943 and 4 January 1944, the Armistice Commission at Wiesbaden had insisted

on the "extreme urgency of the tasks for which the young men are intended."

(15) The French protest was rejected by a telegram from the German Armistice Commission in Wiesbaden dated 9 January 1944.

(16) On 10 January 1944 a conference was held at the office of the delegation of the German Armistice Commission in Paris. M. Guérard, Secretary-General of the Government, M. Bichelonne, Colonel Bernon, and M. Mouret were present. The new protest then presented was rejected by Major Meier-Faust. All that it was possible to obtain was that young men would be assigned to Todt construction south of the Loire, and therefore outside of the probable zones of combat. It was during this conference that M. Bichelonne stated his intention of placing engineers from the French Bridges and Roads service, who were already in contact with the Todt organization in connection with other engineering works of a non-military character, where they could serve as shock absorbers between the Todt organization and the young Frenchmen. To this the Paris delegation of the German Armistice Commission agreed by a note dated 12 January 1944.

(17) Meanwhile the German Armistice Commission at Wiesbaden had ordered by telegram dated 4 January 1944: (a) that some 17,000 young men of the Youth Work Camps, hitherto assigned to various kinds of work inside the organization, should be liberated from that organization on 20 January 1944 and reclassified as free workers, in the same places; and (b) that these young men should be replaced in the camps by those who would normally have formed the March 1944 contingent, but who would be called up earlier, on 20 January. This contingent was estimated at 20,000 from which the Todt organization would receive 17,000. If account is taken of the 4,500 assigned as noted above in item 12 the figure 21,000 [21,500] allocated to the Todt organization noted above in item 4 will be obtained.

(18) During the conference of 10 January [1944] at the Paris delegation of the German Armistice Commission (see item 15) M. Bichelonne had emphasized that it would be impossible to complete the incorporation of 17,000 young men within ten days.

(19) In a telegram dated 19 January [1944] the German Armistice Commission at Wiesbaden advanced the date for the completion of incorporation of the new group to 15 February [1944]; and rejected all suggestions presented for a modification of the assignments which it had outlined (see item 4 above).

(20) Operations for incorporating the new groups were begun, as were the transfers to the Todt organization (see item 12 above). On 9 March 1944, the Paris delegation of the German Armistice Commission sent an imperious note demanding that reasons for the delays noted in the transfers should be reported to the delegation by telephone. Up to that moment only 600 young men had appeared at the work places assigned to them.

(21) After 15 March [1944], the matter was dealt with by the new Minister of Labor, M. Déat.

15 March 1953

P. COSMI

Annex II

Assignment of Young Men to Work on Behalf of the German Army

(1) The plan of High Command West of the German Army provided for the assignment of 11,000 young men to the construction activities of the army. On 9 December 1943 the Paris delegation of the German Armistice Commission demanded for work in connection with these army construction undertakings 9,000 young men from the remnants of classes already called (see Annex I, item 2) and 2,000 young men coming from the normal contingent called up in November [1943]. The Paris delegation gave a list of the construction undertakings to which the young men were to be sent. They were to be at work by 17 December [1943].

(2) In a note dated 21 December [1943] M. Bichelonne informed the Paris delegation of the German Armistice Commission that it was not possible to meet this demand as all the young men were already assigned. He again pointed out the conflict between the various German plans.

(3) On 21 December [1943] in a conference with the Paris delegation of the German Armistice Commission I commented on M. Bichelonne's note of 21 December 1943. Major Meier-Faust and Lieutenant von Witzleben spoke with extreme violence and claimed absolute priority for their demands.

(4) In a note dated 22 December [1943] the Paris delegation of the German Armistice Commission at Wiesbaden set 3 January [1944] as the absolutely final date for the transfers which were to take place.

(5) On 28 and 31 December [1943] new conferences were held with the Paris delegation of the German Armistice Commission. I explained the arrangements planned for summoning the young men and for their transport. Three successive stages had been arranged at intervals.

(6) In a note dated 2 January 1944 the Paris delegation of the German Armistice Commission gave its agreement to the plan noted in point 5, on condition that all was completed by the end of the same month.

(7) Another conference was held on 19 January [1944]. It was recorded that results had "not been brilliant." Only 218 men had appeared for the first phase. No results were yet known for the second, but it was to be expected that they would be "no less disappointing." Lieutenant von Witzleben was "extremely displeased" and announced that "brutal measures" would be taken.

(8) On 26 January [1944] Major Meier-Faust summoned the chief of the liaison unit attached to the Paris delegation of the German Armistice Commission. He told him that this conversation was to be the "last" and that "if there were any more delay, the German Command would find itself obliged to take very grave measures to assure the execution of its decisions no matter what happened."

(9) M. Bichelonne created a new cause for delay by providing in the calling-up orders that any young men who were summoned but who were already working in a protected factory ("S") need not obey the summons.

(10) On 1 February [1944] a note from the Paris delegation of the Wiesbaden Armistice Commission "placed on record with astonishment that in more than one locality not a single worker had appeared."

(11) On 24 February [1944] the Paris delegation of the Wiesbaden Armistice Commission was informed that 8,600 summons had been sent out and that 340 young men had presented themselves at the collection centers.

(12) On 2 March [1944] the Wiesbaden Armistice Commission announced that the German army would carry out requisitions among the civilian population; but on 3 March [1944] the commission declared that it would abandon the calling up of the young men.

15 March 1953

P. COSMI

CHAPTER XVII

RED CROSS AND NATIONAL AID SERVICES

PUBLIC HEALTH

RAYMOND GRASSET

Doctor of Medecine ;
Secretary of State for Health

[This document consists of extracts from Dr. Grasset's testimony before the High Court, preceded by a letter to President Herbert Hoover.]

Dr. RAYMOND GRASSET   *Clermont-Ferrand, 31 August 1949*
   Clermont-Ferrand

Monsieur le Président Herbert Hoover
Président du Hoover War Library

Monsieur le Président,

I am asking René de Chambrun to transmit to you the enclosed documentation concerning my service in the Ministry of Public Health (1942, 1943, and 1944.)

These documents are extracts from the dossier of my trial by the High Court; they were the basis, after a long and meticulous verification, of the final decision that there was no case against me.

President Laval, Chief of the Government to which I belonged, was fully cognizant of all these matters for I scrupulously insisted on informing him regularly of my decisions.

This file represents, of course, only a minor element in the total operations of the Laval government in 1942. But it is to the credit of that government and should appear as an asset in drawing up the balance sheet of the work of Pierre Laval, who consistently gave his authority to the undertakings to which this file attests.

Je vous prie de croire, Monsieur le Président, à l'expression de mes sentiments de haute considération.

(Document No. 110)
Fr. ed. 889-899

RAYMOND GRASSET
Dr. Raymond Grasset

The Camouflage of Stocks Held by the Medical Service of the French Army

The medical services of the French army held enormous stocks in the southern zone, of which the approximate value, in the franc of that period, was 10,000 million francs. Part was held in ordinary military depots and the rest in innumerable hiding places established after June 1940.

Until November 1942 the medical services had refused to hand over these supplies to the French Ministry of Health. But on 11 November 1942 when the German army crossed the demarcation line I began discussions with Medical General Liégeois, director of the army's medical services, as to the best way of protecting these supplies.

When the French army was brutally dissolved on 27 November 1942 on German order I asked the President of the Council, both orally and in writing, to place the entire medical services of the army under my own authority in order to keep it away from German control.

The Chief of Government instructed Admiral Platon, Secretary of State without portfolio, to deal with the matter: letter from the Admiral, dated 4 December 1942.[1]

On 16 December 1942 I received alarming information and urged the Secretary of State for War to accelerate matters toward a final solution. The Ministry of War had retained control of the medical services and the quartermaster division.

On 2 December 1942 without waiting for my colleague of the Ministry of War to deliberate on the matter I informed all my regional directors in the southern zone of an agreement that I had succeeded in making with Medical General Liégeois, in accordance with which, thanks to antedated letters, transfers of supplies were made official and those who had camouflaged various hiding places were at least partly protected.

Finally, the regional directors in the services of Health and Social Assistance in the southern zone were summoned to Vichy, and then to Paris, and were given oral instructions to hide the military medical supplies by all possible means.

An important part of the official stocks deposited in the depots of the medical services of the army had been labeled "property of the civilian health service." Another part had been taken to hospital installations which also took over supplies from such hidden depots as would have been too easily discovered by the Germans.

This difficult work lasted for some months and achieved considerable results. I arranged with the Red Cross that all transportation be carried out under its flag. There were expenses. I dared not call on secret funds for fear of being immediately denounced. I therefore used a part of the funds belonging to the national lottery of which I shared the management with the French Red Cross, represented by M. Rousselier, a Councilor of State. Checks drawn on these funds reached the regional directors as being intended for "health education centers." But oral instructions had specified how the money was to be used.

1. Each date mentioned in this statement refers to an item of the dossier of the High Court; the most important of these pieces are reproduced below.

These operations succeeded in protecting a very large tonnage of precious supplies, bandages, and medicines. The German army used all its ingenuity in trying to discover our hidden depots and in trying to identify which of the transfers had been made recently. By all possible means they contested the correctness of civilian labels on the stocks of medical supplies when they discovered this system of marking. Such efforts on the part of the Germans continued relentlessly right up to the liberation.

We had made scarcely any use of the supplies which we had hidden and placed under civilian labels. So far as the open depots were concerned the Germans had recognized this fact. A message from Wiesbaden dated 4 September 1943, in the file referring to supplies hidden in the Indre, includes these words: "The stocks referred to always greatly exceed needs. During a period of over two years the civilian services have taken almost nothing from these stocks." This was true as our purpose was merely to keep these precious supplies from getting into German hands.

Finally, the value of such supplies saved through my efforts may be estimated at 900 million francs of 1939. Thus a good part of these supplies have been able to get back to the French army.

The civilian hospitals benefited greatly by another part [of these supplies]. At the time of the liberation my successor M. Billoux was able to announce that he was placing many truckloads of medical supplies at the disposition of the people of Paris. These supplies came from those which I had hidden in Vichy itself.

The following German note sent to the regional prefect of Limoges speaks openly of the concealments effected "with the knowledge of French official services and even with their assistance."

KONTROLKOMMISSION LIMOGES   *Limoges, 18 January 1944*
     Br. B No. 77/43 Ia/S

A Monsieur le Préfet Régional de Limoges

In answer to your request I confirm the summary of our verbal discussions of today's date. During the last few years the organization known as CDM [Camouflage of Supplies] has in conformity with its purposes hidden important war supplies. After the German troops entered the southern zone, and after the French army of the armistice had been dissolved, only a fraction of these supplies had been reported, as was required by the law of 5 December 1942, and had been taken over by the German authorities. Another fraction was handed over at the end of 1942 and the beginning of 1943 to groups belonging to the resistance movement. Again in the summer of 1943 the former officers of the French armistice army, working with resistance units, organized new clandestine depots for war materials, particularly for arms and ammunition. In certain cases this was done with the knowledge of French official services and even with their help.

An inventory of all war materials of every kind which have been hidden up to the present is not only a German military necessity of an urgent character, but is also in accordance with instructions of the French 'government itself, as our interview today clearly established once more. In consequence I ask you to give me all possible aid, as has been done in other regions, for making an inventory of war material which is still hidden. In particular I ask you: (a) to issue an appeal to the press asking the public to report to the services competent in the matter all war material which is still hidden, calling particular attention to the fact that not only must arms, ammunition and explosives be reported, but also war material of every kind whatever; (b) to get into contact, for the same purpose, with all services which may have information on the activity of the CDM in your region, and may know of war material of any kind which is still hidden; and (c) to send me not later than 3 February 1944 the result of these new investigations.

During our interview I called your attention to the question of vehicles which had been reconditioned by the CDM, the auto-machine-gun carriages at Sarlat and nearby, and the medical supplies from the French armistice army.

I promised you that I would guarantee that any late declaration by those who had received deposits of war material would not result in any action being taken against them personally. I also asked you to give me an opportunity in a later meeting, to which the director of the medical services would be invited, to make an arrangement for assuring that the needs of the French civilian population in medical supplies would be met.

Signed: Weyel

Protection of Medical Students Subject to the Obligatory Labor Service

Four annual contingents of young men were subject to the Obligatory Labor Service (STO).

In agreement with the dean of the Faculty of Medicine of Paris and the representatives of the hospital authorities of Paris, I took the initiative of having all medical students in these four annual classes assigned to my services, under pretext that they were needed for air raid defense and also to staff small-town hospitals which had no resident doctors.

It must be explained that these young men who were "studying" came under no authority other than that of National Education. To have them assigned to me it was necessary that the Chief of Government give his approval. After I had succeeded in my plan so far as medical students were concerned I had the same privilege extended to students in pharmacy. . . . And without even asking permission I added on the circular of notification the words "and dental students." It will be agreed that these dental students, being limited in their specialized knowledge to matters of the mouth, were not strictly of any use in air raid defense since they had received no instruction on first aid for victims of bombardments.

In this way 4,000 young men escaped from all labor service in Germany. In order to absorb them I had to set up permanent services in the little hospitals of the provinces—at Aurillac, Le Puy, Thiers, Moulins, Riom, and so on—and to force the administrative commissions to lodge and feed them—something that was not accomplished without protest.

Of the four classes of the Obligatory Labor Service thus dealt with, one, namely the class of 1942, was supposed to leave for Germany without any exceptions. There again I was able to obtain from the commission for laborers in Germany that students in the categories mentioned above should be assigned in Germany only to medical work and not to any form of production.

Opposition to German Requisition of Hospital Establishments and Psychiatric Hospitals

A very full dossier which I deposited in connection with my trial shows the intensity with which the government had to defend the hospitals and asylums against Wehrmacht activities.

The incident at Auxerre, 22 December 1943, resulted in a failure for us. That of the Vinatier at Lyon, 29 February 1944, was a success for us after I had conducted personal negotiations with the German Medical General.

In the meantime I had written to the Chief of Government, in my letter of 3 March 1944, threatening to open the doors of the insane asylums and liberate all the inmates if the Germans continued their requisitions.

Finally, the major insane asylums of Clermont, in the Oise, of Vinatier at Bron-Lyon, and of Albi were not taken over by the Germans.

In conclusion it should be noted that our strenuous efforts to defend our psychiatric hospitals were inspired entirely by patriotism and were intended to block the enemy's undertakings, since at this time the insane asylums had plenty of vacant places because the fight against alcoholism had reduced admissions for mental trouble due to alcoholism by 70 per cent.

Total Failure of German Demands to Make Levies on ¦French Production of Opium Alkaloids

In 1940-1941 France had perfected a method of producing morphine from the opium poppy [pavot à œillette] which was now being grown in France, to replace the morphine obtained from opium, which it was no longer possible to import from the Orient. These techniques belonged to Comar and Co. and the Franco-Pavot Co.

The Germans studied this process of production and checked it; and when the quantity produced became important they demanded a part of the morphine thus prepared.

Discussions of a commercial order were begun in 1942 and concluded in December 1943 with an agreement signed by the Minister of Industrial Production, in his capacity as representing the Organization Committee for Chemical Industries.

The first German claims were for 1,000 kilograms of morphine.

The figures established in June 1944 showed only 160 kilograms available for Germany; the accounts had been falsified and stock had been hidden with the acknowledged approval of the French authorities.

Dr. Rosenberg who conducted the negotiations on behalf of the Germans at the Hotel Majestic, with M. Yves Comar for the French side, demanded in June 1944 that these 160 kilograms should be delivered, and after a violent discussion witnessed by my representative M. Grégoire, chief of the central pharmaceutical service at the Ministry of Health, and M. Leprince, president of the Organization Committee for Pharmaceutical

Products, it was agreed to deliver 100 kilograms immediately and to postpone the delivery of the additional 60 kilograms.

Everyone strove to find means of delaying the delivery of the official papers which were necessary for this export of French products, though the German buyer was making daily demands from the Franco-Pavot Company that the goods should be dispatched immediately.

Thus matters dragged on until 18 August 1944 when a M. Strum of the Hotel Majestic desired, before fleeing toward the east, to take with him these supplies of morphine which had not yet been delivered. M. Yves Comar consulted with M. Harmist who warned the resistance and so arranged that the morphine should be stolen before the Germans were able to put their hands on it.

These hundred kilograms of morphine which thus escaped falling into German hands were but a very small part of the total which had been delivered for French medical purposes during the period June 1940 to August 1944. The total thus delivered to the French in pure morphine and in morphine derivatives was 4,000 kilograms.

Finally, in addition to the advantages thus obtained for the French health services, it must be emphasized that the production contract which had been arranged for the Franco-Pavot Company through the Ministry of Industrial Production and the Hotel Majestic had enabled them to obtain raw materials, coal, and electricity necessary for the production of a range of pharmaceutical products important for French health. It had also made possible the escape from deportation to Germany of almost all the workers of the companies involved in this industry.

And all this was accomplished without any counterpart as in the end nothing whatever was delivered to the Germans.

The continual control over this production exercised by the Ministry of Health, and the complete support given to M. Yves Comar in his maneuvers for tricking the Germans, were both made possible through a specific instruction of my own. I was kept informed by M. Grégoire, chief of the central pharmaceutical service in the Ministry of Health. M. Grégoire is now chief pharmacist for the French navy.

The Clandestine Importation of Scarce Medical Supplies into France

In 1942 the Germans having carried off all our stocks of rare medical supplies, the Ministry of Health received a petition from ophthalmologists in which they explained that they could not continue to treat diseases of the eye.

We succeeded in making an arrangement with the International Red Cross under which we were able to bring clandestinely into the southern zone four kilograms of cocaine and from four to five kilograms of pilocarpine which had been bought in Switzerland. The International Red Cross even aided in the payment.

The line of demarcation between the two zones of France was then very strictly controlled, and supplies of these drugs were brought across by one of my close collaborators who used the weekly Micheline [diesel rail car] which traveled between Paris and Vichy to carry ministers and high officials. These precious drugs were then delivered to the Darrasse laboratories to be used in preparing ophthalmological medications, and for distribution.

The Pasteur Institute

The following declaration, spontaneously sent, just after my arrest, to the instructing judge by the director of the Pasteur Institute, needs no comment. This declaration was not solicited by me.

12 May 1945

Monsieur le Juge d'Instruction,

I am able to report two precise facts which prove clearly that the only purpose of Dr. Grasset was always to keep French production in general, and in particular French therapeutic products, out of German hands by every available means.

(1) It was at the request of Dr. Grasset that the Council of Ministers in July 1942 decided to ask the Pasteur Institute to establish in the southern zone a production center for vaccine against exanthematic typhus. This center was, and still is, a large producer of anti-rickets vaccine on which the Germans were unable to make a single levy. This center enabled the Pasteur Institute not merely to supply the French prisoner camps in Germany, free of all cost, but also to establish stocks of vaccines in the different regions of France which would be used in case of epidemic.

(2) I can also report the invaluable aid given by Dr. Grasset and his Secretary-General Dr. Aublant during thirteen months of constant struggle between the Pasteur Institute and the Germans regarding the requisition of serum for the German army. In fact the Germans who had seemed, at the beginning of the occupation, to accept the scientific arguments which we presented them, had become more and more pressing and then threatening. Dr. Grasset then intervened personally and by his firm attitude obtained tangible results, of which I need give but one example. Out of 1,000 liters of anti-diphtheria serum, at 1,000 units per cubic centimeter, demanded by the Germans, he supplied them only ten liters. His intervention had great weight in making it possible for the Pasteur Institute to avoid deducting any serum whatever from its normal production intended for the French population, and to establish the condition that the Germans themselves should supply the horses which were to be immunized on their behalf.

The advantages were: (a) that nothing was taken from French stocks; (b) that considerable time could be used up in waiting till the horses supplied by the Germans could provide a serum with sufficient antitoxic strength; and (c) to delay considerably the production of this serum by allowing these horses to run all risks of immunization, through the use of horses unsuitable for the production of serum, through death, and so on. In fact, of 200 horses furnished to the Pasteur Institute only twenty still survived at the time of the liberation. They had furnished only a small quantity of serum.

Signed: Jacques Tréfouël

Member of the Academy of Medicine;
Member of the Committee of the
National Health Service of the Resistance;
Director of the Pasteur Institute

Return of French Doctors Who Were War
Prisoners in Germany

Doctors are "non-combatants," protected by the Geneva Convention. When they are taken prisoners they should be returned, except for the minimum number needed to care for combatants taken prisoner. This number is about one doctor for 1,000 prisoners.

In October 1940 the Germans therefore returned any medical staff in excess of the needed number. But captivity continued and those doctors who were prisoners became greatly disturbed, all the more because most of them were doctors belonging to the army reserve, and their practices at home were rapidly disintegrating.

The doctors who had been repatriated organized themselves and undertook negotiations, and in April 1942 Dr. Bour presented the first demand for a "relief shift on behalf of doctor prisoners in Germany." And it was in April 1942, that the Laval cabinet was formed.

A fact generally forgotten should be recalled here, namely that those members of the medical services who were taken prisoner with the army of 1939-1940 were conscripts and therefore military men, and that the military medical services of the army fiercely claimed the sole right to deal with them in any way. At the same time, Ambassador Scapini continually said in and wrote that the "Diplomatic Service for Prisoners of War, acting as protecting power for French prisoners is the responsible negotiator," and was therefore the only authority qualified to act in the matter. In short, the Secretary of State for Health, representing the civilian authorities, had no right to deal with anyone except doctors who were members of the army reserve, they being considered as civilians who were but temporarily in military status. But even then all that concerned him was to make sure that they had a place in the French medical community when they did return.

It was for these reasons that I arranged the prolongation of the law of 28 August 1942 on the reclassification of doctors who were prisoners in Germany.

Regarding the release of all doctors in German prison camps, subject to replacement by doctors coming from France, the Secretary of State could make only a suggestion and ask the medical services of the army, and Mr. Scapini, since he himself had no authority to negotiate with the Germans.

On 23 December 1942 Mr. Scapini reported by telephone from Berlin that his negotiations for the return of all doctors in the prison camps had not succeeded. He confirmed this when he came back to Paris.

Faced by this negative result I decided to attempt personal negotiations, since it seemed to me that up to that time matters had been badly handled, probably because Mr. Scapini was not himself a doctor.

On 2 January 1943 I arranged to be appointed by the Chief of Government as the sole French negotiator with the German authorities for the return of all doctors, pharmacists and dentists then in the prison camps in Germany.

I had an interview with Minister Schleier at the German Embassy in Paris, on 5 January 1943. On 14 January 1943 I discussed the same plan with Medical General Haubenreisser in Paris.

I used very simple arguments. I said that doctors were not combatants, that they had not been captured with arms in their hands, and that the Geneva Convention provided for their repatriation except for the minimum necessary to care for the other prisoners. After two and half years of captivity it seemed unfair not to authorize the exchange, head for head, of all French doctors imprisoned in Germany.

Schleier and Medical General Haubenreisser proved to be very understanding and promised to take action with the Wilhelmstrasse and the German High Command in order to facilitate a happy solution.

My negotiations were not at all difficult as I had but a single conversation with each of these high representatives of German authority.

On 5 February 1943 the German Embassy at Vichy asked for an interview with me in order to give me an important message. I received, at my ministry, Mr. Struw, chief of the embassy, who told me on instructions from his government that a general exchange had been agreed to but that the arrangement would become official only when means of carrying it out had been agreed on.

At the Council of Ministers on 6 February 1943 the Chief of Government reported an identical communication which he had received from the German government and he complimented the Secretary of State for Health on the success of his negotiations.

The result was as follows. The Germans refused authorization of exchange for about 150 doctors or students, in particular the Jews. Those who did return totaled 570. They were replaced in the German camps by doctors belonging to the active army, by 90 medical students in their second year, and by 27 doctors of the army reserve, surgeons or specialists.

For reasons presented in the documents of my dossier I kept the whole operation very closely in hand so that this medical exchange was first of all, and to a very large extent, made by sending career army doctors, who were without occupation at that moment since the French army had been dissolved in November 1942. The number necessary to complete the total needed for the exchange was made up chiefly of advanced students, that is of those who had all the qualifications of a medical diploma but had not yet entered regular practice. I called on fully qualified doctors only when it was necessary to replace, head for head and special capacity for special capacity, the surgeons and the various specialists.

This was a purely French operation and in reality it was rather embarrassing for the Germans. It was carried out with the greatest possible fairness. It was proof of a close solidarity within the French medical profession, and was an operation which it was only normal that the Minister, himself a doctor, should bring vigorously to a successful conclusion.

Medical Aid for Labor Deportees

My conscience demanded that I should bring medical aid to our workers. I proposed, therefore, a French medical service for French workers in Germany, organized under a system of control, and reserved for French only. The Germans rejected this proposal. They demanded that each employing company should have its own doctors, and that these should be entirely under German control. In general, the workers employed by each company were of many nationalities.

Discussions dragged on. The war developed more and more unfavorably for the Germans.

A demand for volunteer doctors failed. The appeals of Philippe Henriot and Déat, made after the Allied landing in Normandy, were unlikely to be favorably received if I opposed them even slightly.

In fact I violently opposed Déat and I resisted any departures of doctors for Germany. At the same time, always concerned for the health of our citizens, I arranged that Bruneton should propose to the Germans, on I July 1944, that they should make use of the many doctors who had been deported from France to Germany by the Gestapo in caring for French workers, and in the same way should employ any extra doctors in the prisoner of war camps. I had this proposition made again to the Germans on I August 1944 through the Armistice service.

Medical Secrecy

On 18 April 1944 the German government informed the Ministry of Health of its strong desire that the French government should promulgate a law obliging anyone who cared for wounds which had been caused by firearms or explosives to report the fact.

As soon as I received this information I went at once to the Chief of Government and told him that I would never agree to such a demand which was absolutely contrary to the traditions and honor of the medical profession.

"If they don't see your name signed to such a law," Pierre Laval said to me, "then mine will not be seen either. I am a lawyer and I know, as you do, the value of professional secrecy."

Realizing that it was a delicate matter he decided to conduct the negotiations personally and kept the papers which I had brought in order to have a talk, which he requested immediately, with General von Neubronn.

The German government abandoned its attempt to have the French government issue such a law, as is shown by a note from General von Neubronn to President Laval, dated 4 July 1944, following the conversation referred to above. Instead the German authorities issued a notice to the French people, through the press and by posters, placing the same obligations on them.

I protested again through the commission at Wiesbaden. My note of I August 1944 and that of General Debeney on 10 August 1944, which was its sequel, presented our arguments.

Aside from these official documents I had a series of semi-official conversations with representatives of the medical profession to prepare every possible defense against the menaces thus brought to bear on doctors who might be convicted of not declaring medical attention of that kind. In particular, I proposed that the reception office of the hospital should be held collectively responsible whenever the required declaration was not made rather than the doctor who handled the case. It would be difficult, if not impossible, to indict all the employees of the reception bureau of negligence when the required declaration was not made. As for the doctor actually treating the case I recommended that he should reply that as he dealt with wounded persons on certain days every week, it could not be his obligation to declare them as he himself had not selected them in any way, and as they on their side had not chosen him as their doctor. I personally took part in setting up such an arrangement at Clermont-Ferrand, and in that city it avoided all incidents.

The Feeding of Babies

The question of condensed-milk. The newspaper *Ce Soir* in October 1945 printed a story to the effect that I had allowed a number of babies to die because I did not supply enough condensed milk to the pharmacies.

Of course the story was untrue. Here is the proof that on the contrary, less than three months after I took my place in the Ministry of Health, I had been impressed by the danger which any restriction on condensed milk would bring to babies during the summer season.

Condensed milk was stocked and distributed by the Ministry of Agriculture and Food. The attached documents seem to me to prove clearly the nature of my action and the eagerness with which I sought to reach a solution, for which the most important element was lacking.

13 July 1942

The Secretary of State for Health
to
The Chief of Government

Following our recent conversation, I have the honor to send you herewith a note regarding the condensed-milk affair.

The Secretary of State
Dr. R. Grasset

13 July 1942

Note for the Chief of Government

The investigation which I have made carefully into the condensed-milk affair shows that there was certainly serious negligence or ill will. The stocks of condensed milk were sufficient to maintain throughout the third quarter of the year the same ration as during the second quarter.

In spite of that, and in spite of my efforts throughout the entire month of June, and also against the will of M. Bonnafous, who wrote to me that he had not succeeded in getting his instruction obeyed, there was a wholesale reduction in the ration cards for condensed milk in June, something like forty to seventy per cent in different departements. The departement of the Puy-de-Dôme was particularly badly treated.

Further, the departemental headquarters for food were unable to obtain, in spite of their pressing demands to their own ministry, instructions as to how the reduced rations were to be distributed.

Since no instructions had arrived by 1 July 1942 the situation was completely disordered. At Pau condensed-milk cards had been given only for babies who were ill, without any attention to the fact that cutting off the others from their milk supply would inevitably make them ill too.

Again, rations of condensed milk were refused for any baby over six months. In the Oise those pharmacies which had stocks of condensed milk had to refuse to supply it for babies two months old because the mothers did not have any ration tickets; and so on.

All of this has aroused intense feeling and violent protests, which are continuing.

I therefore thought it my duty to inform you on 3 July 1942 of this tragic situation and you then described as criminals those who had caused such disorder.

M. Bonnafous and I immediately took action to remedy the situation. But it is necessary to punish pitilessly the person who in June gave the order for this enormous reduction in the number of quarterly cards for condensed milk allotted to babies, and to punish the person who kept this order in force in spite of my almost daily protests to the Ministry for Food supply, and who deliberately did not specify what classifications of babies were to benefit by the small number of cards issued.

This intentional disorder during the warmest three months of the year ran the risk of causing a high rate of infantile mortality.

Today, 13 July 1942, orders for putting everything right have been issued everywhere, but their execution is meeting with the usual delays and I cannot guarantee yet at what date the supply of condensed milk for babies will be completely re-established.

The Secretary of State for Health

Dr. R. Grasset

THE RED CROSS

GABRIEL DE MUN

Marquis;
President of the French Red Cross

[*The Marquis de Mun's declaration is preceded by the following personal letter to René de Chambrun.*]

81, avenue Victor-Hugo   6 May 1947

Mon cher René,

You have asked me to prepare a statement on the relations which the French Government in general and your father-in-law in particular had with the French Red Cross during the time when I was its President.

Though I have prepared this statement from memory I hope it will give the technical details which are desired. As is emphasized in the preface to my note I took the greatest care to reduce relations between the government and the French Red Cross to a minimum as much to preserve the association's independence as to maintain the possibilities of buying food and medical supplies abroad for our prisoners and our civilian population.

Nevertheless I had to go to your father-in-law under exceptional circumstances, and each time with complete success:

I—To arrange that the central administration and the prefects should be asked to release to the French Red Cross the necessary food products for feeding civilian internees.

II—To obtain in 1944 a special subsidy of 100 million francs from the Ministry of Finance. The resources of the French Red Cross had been exhausted by the continual and unforeseeable increase of the charges imposed on us by events, such as the costs of evacuating the population of Normandy, to give one example.

III—To obtain the cancellation of instructions issued by Abel Bonnard, then Minister of National Education, which ordered the immediate dissolution of the emergency teams set up by the French Red Cross throughout France. The pretext given was that these teams which then included about 150,000 persons blocked the parallel recruiting of National Teams which Abel Bonnard was trying to create for political purposes.

IV—Finally when Marcel Déat was congratulating himself in the spring of 1944 of having brought the French Red Cross under the control of the Ministry of National Solidarity which had just been assigned to him, the Chief of Government vetoed the whole plan because of my absolute opposition.

The picture, however, would not be complete, my dear friend, if I did not refer to the services which your wife and you yourself so often rendered in alerting your father-in-law at all hours of the day or night when I came to ask you to intervene with him on the occasion of some new blow struck by the enemy against one of our fellow countrymen.

Croyez, mon cher René, à mes sentiments très amicaux.

MUN

*(Marquis de Mun, former
President of the French Red Cross)*

Relations between the French Red Cross and the French Government from 1942 to 1944

Under its statutes of January 1941 the French Red Cross was a private association recognized as being of public service. On this basis it was independent of the government. Its relations with the government were very limited as general questions of a broad character were dealt with by the International Red Cross at Geneva. It was chiefly to secure aid and food for war prisoners and for civilian internees that the French Red Cross entered into contact with the French government. The field was so vast that in fact the French Red Cross could not have fulfilled its task without government aid.

Prisoners of War.—Aid and food for prisoners of war were provided through collective action and through individual action.

(a) *Collective aid* was assured through funds placed at the disposition of the French Red Cross by the government. Using these funds the French Red Cross made foreign purchases which were possible only because its character of independence from the government enabled it to buy and to receive shipments.

(b) *Individual aid* was assured through the purchase of food products from the Minister of War by the French Red Cross for making up parcels.

The Direction for Prisoners of War under Général Codchèvre, transferred at the time of the liberation to the Ministry of Prisoners and Deportees, must have all the accounts relative to these two operations.

Gasoline needed for the Service of Prisoners of War was furnished to the French Red Cross by the Direction for Prisoners of War under General Codchèvre. The accounts were kept by that office. On the other hand, the gasoline necessary for the services of the French Red Cross was bought by the Red Cross itself, using permits issued by the government.

Civilian Internees.—The food and supplies for the aid of civilian internees were bought by the French Red Cross through permits issued by the government. The cost of these supplies reached so high a figure—25 million in 1943, and 60 million in 1944—that the French Red Cross was obliged to ask the Ministry of Finance in 1944 to reimburse them and to open a credit for further purchases. This request was granted.

The government also aided the French Red Cross on the two following occasions.

When the Germans entered the southern zone the Health Service in the Ministry of War sold to the French Red Cross, after camouflaging previous government ownership, important quantities of medical supplies.

At the same time the Health Service also gave the French Red Cross thirty ambulances.

The several million francs revenue from the property of the French Red Cross was of course insufficient to meet all these expenses. On the other hand, the French Red Cross in 1940 renounced its right to appeal to public generosity, that right being transferred to the National Aid. The National Aid undertook, in return, to supply the French Red Cross with necessary credits.

Beginning in 1943, after long discussions, the National Aid paid a flat sum of 20 million francs a month to the French Red Cross, which had complete liberty as to how the money was to be used. This sum proved to be totally insufficient, particularly after the heavy expenses of evacuating inhabitants from Normandy. By the spring of 1944 the treasury of the French Red Cross was completely empty. The Chief of Government and the Minister of Finance were personally informed of the situation and after a study of the activities of the French Red Cross they immediately granted a subsidy of 100 million francs.

(Document No. 79)
Fr. ed. 900-902

Paris, 6 May 1947

MUN
Marquis de Mun

RED CROSS — PRISONERS

AMÉDÉE ROUSSELLIER

Colonial Governor;
Vice-President, French Red Cross

One of the chief anxieties of the government after it had been installed in Vichy in 1940 concerned the fate of the prisoners of war. The Maréchal immediately thought of the services which the French Red Cross would be able to render in this matter.

Since the French Red Cross was affiliated to the central body at Geneva, which from the beginning of hostilities had organized a service of news and letters for prisoners of war, it was in a particularly good position to assist the government in the heavy task which now fell upon it, of easing the lot of our unhappy captives.

One difficulty, however, arose from the fact that there were three societies in France which, though having the same purpose and function, were working separately. It was now indispensuble that their efforts should be centralized and that a single policy controlled by a single authority should be followed.

These considerations led the Maréchal to consider the means of fusing the old societies; this fusion was accomplished at the beginning of August 1940.

For this new organization it was necessary to have a chief whose abilities had been proved and in whom the qualities of a diplomat were combined with those of an administrator; no one seemed more fitted for the post than Ambassador de Chambrun, who accepted the task. An unfortunate automobile accident prevented him from actually taking over the post, and the Maréchal's choice then fell on another prominent Frenchman, Ambassador François Poncet, whom the occupation authorities refused to approve. Thus it was that Professor Vallery-Radot was finally appointed.

After several months Professor Vallery-Radot asked to be allowed to resign and was replaced by Professor Bazy.

Under Professor Bazy's administration, the activities of the Red Cross developed more and more. Through its continual contact with the central committee at Geneva, the dispatch of packages and letters increased considerably and made possible a very quick exchange of news. For this purpose, a large goods depot had been established at Vichy, with an efficient workshop for making up packages, for which gifts poured in from all parts of the world, the Maréchal having made arrangements that they be allowed to enter France.

Apart from its official activities, the Red Cross maintained in addition a concealed activity which was as useful as it was dangerous. It gave help to escaped prisoners providing them with clothes, money, and false identity papers so that they could cross the demarcation line into the free zone. Further, the Red Cross gave invaluable help to Jews by preparing false identities which enabled a number of them to escape the persecution of the occupying authorities.

As was certain to be the case, the attention of the German authorities was finally turned to these practices, though luckily they were unable to discover any precise fact which would have permitted them to inflict punishment. They thought that the best way to put a stop to such activities was to strike at the head of the organization and they notified President Laval that he must replace Professor Bazy, the alternative being the appointment of a German gauleiter.

The nomination of the president must be made by the administrative council of the Red Cross; the council was at first unanimous in refusing to accede to German demands and decided to resign in a body.

President Laval, who was fully aware of the role played by the Red Cross both officially and clandestinely, and who was particularly conscious of the support which the Red Cross had been able to secure from the international committee at Geneva, did his very best to persuade the council to reverse its first decision, and to convince them of the necessity of appointing a new president and a new director-general while it was still possible to do so. The result was that the Marquis de Mun and the Count de Rohan-Chabot were installed in office to replace Dr. Bazy, who agreed to retire with a dignity and a spirit of self-sacrifice which makes due all the greater honor to his character and which, in fact, preserved the Red Cross for the final years of the occupation.

The Marquis de Mun allowed no encroachment on any of the privileges which the Red Cross could claim, always basing his position on international conventions, and using the necessary prudence and skill in preventing the discovery of his clandestine action, thanks to which policy it was possible to prevent the worst from happening. The explanation was certainly not that the occupants failed to do everything possible to trap him in some error. At one time they believed that they had succeeded and they arrested the Count de Rohan-Chabot, but finally they were obliged to release him for lack of proof.

It was especially in the final days of the occupation, during the campaign in France and the retreat of the Germans, that the Red Cross distinguished itself through the courage and devotion of its teams of workers and the spirit of self-sacrifice shown by its director-general. In addition, the director-general did not limit himself to a purely administrative role but entered into contact with the Norwegian consul-general, Dr. Nordling, through whom during the last days of the occupation of Paris he was able to obtain from the German government a relaxation of the harshness of the regime then in force, and even to halt at Compiègne a final train of deportees bound for Germany.

(Document No. 251)
Fr. ed. 903-904

Paris, [February 1955]

A. ROUSSELLIER
Governor Amédée Rousseller

THE RED CROSS

FRANÇOIS HAYAUX DU TILLY

Assistant Director-General of the French Red Cross

The circumstances under which I was received by President Laval

(1) I was secretary-general of the Anthroposociological Institute, directed by my friend Professor Jean Saint-Germès, an institution to which so many young Frenchmen of all origins, conditions, and religions owe the "certificates of prolongation of advanced studies" thanks to which they were able to delay their departure for compulsory labor in Germany. Because of my position I underwent two searches by the Gestapo, in April 1943 and again in June, both of which were without result. But as a result of a denunciation our activities were suspended and the Institute closed by Order No. II-Gal-E.V.-61/4 of Oberstürmbahnfuehrer Oehm, dated 1 October 1943.

President Laval must have been informed by his staff of what happened, for to my great astonishment I was summoned to his office in Vichy at the beginning of 1944.

Without any preliminaries, in the fashion of a man whose moments are all calculated, he said to me: "I know what you have done at the Institute, of your good work, and of what has happened. M. de Rohan-Chabot, director-general of the Red Cross, has been arrested and imprisoned in Fresnes. He is a great Frenchman; his imprisonment may continue for some time. M. de Bourbon-Busset replaces him, and he too may be arrested. The Marquis de Mun, president of the Red Cross, is seeking an assistant and we have thought of you. The position is not without risks, but in it you will continue to serve the country."

It was one o'clock in the afternoon and I was leaving when the President gave me a note, of which I attach a copy, saying, "Put that in your pocket. It's not only the French who love France. . . . Stay and have lunch with us."

At lunch, anxious and preoccupied, he nevertheless put everyone at ease by a few kindly words. He then asked a plenipotentiary commissioner and three or four prefects, who happened to be in Vichy and were his guests at lunch, about the bombing of factory centers and big cities, about the loss of lives, the material damage, the aid available, and the aid which should be arranged for, to give the greatest possible help to the people who suffered.

At the end of the lunch he sent us away with these words: "Off you go, gentlemen, and work hard; you can never do enough for the country."

(2) In May 1944, President Laval summoned me to the Hotel Matignon. He said to me bluntly. "The Marquis de Mun tells me that M. de Rohan-Chabot has been released from Fresnes, much the worse for his imprisonment. Take him as your pattern. You like to organize and travel about;

you will soon have the opportunity. The Red Cross relieves misery of all kinds and aids men of every sort. Give yourself to the work of the Red Cross without counting the cost."

I was taking my leave of the President when he added enigmatically, "Don't trust Déat."

I did not understand the meaning of this phrase until later, when I saw Déat's efforts to work himself into the activities of the Red Cross, efforts we were able to neutralize by standing solidly behind President de Mun.

(Document No. 35)
Fr. ed. 905-906

Paris, 3 October 1947

FRANÇOIS HAYAUX DU TILLY

Appendix

The following is a translation of the note referred to in M. Hayaux du Tilly's account of his visit to President Laval in Vichy early in 1944.

FRANCE!

Voice of sweet France, voice of immortal accents,
Sing ever in clear tones though cruel are thy days:
Gayety and mourning blend in a single glory.
O brave Anjou, O plains along the Loire,
O villages and castles, thoughts long sleeping
Are roused by you. And all thy voices, Paris,
All thy calls, still live: bridges, quais, the Louvre,
The Carrousel, the Seine, and that great door which opens
To our tears, great Notre Dame, where with trembling voice
And hands enfolded, we speak still to those who can no longer speak.
You who have died aloft in death that blends with beauty,
Like bird that folds its wings and falls;
You for whom the sea prepared a tomb,
And you who speak from deep within our prayers,
Blessed, sacred, shrouded in blood and light.
And thou, France, singest in noble song:
"That which was my beauty ne'er shall die."
'Tis thou who sayest, "The ordeal is beautiful and the suffering."
Now know us as we strive toward thee, O France,
Because thou stand'st erect amidst thy agony.
We keep our faith in thee. Thou livest in our hearts.

ALOYSIO DE CASTRO
of the Academy of Brazil,
July 1940

NATIONAL AID

G. PILON

Secretary-General for National Aid

I never met President Laval except in connection with my work as secretary-general of National Aid. I think, therefore, that I must first give a few brief explanations of this organization, as the most inexact statements possible have been made concerning it since the liberation.

The National Aid organization had been created during the war of 1914-1918 and a decree of 1915, signed by President Poincaré, had given it the status of an association of public service. In 1919 when National Aid under the presidency of M. Appel had ceased its activities, one could rightly have said that it had accomplished a miracle of unity and charity. It was logical that in 1939 when the new world war began the French government tried to recreate this miracle. A decree of 19 October 1939 reconstituted National Aid, therefore, under the high patronage of the President of the Republic. M. Georges Pichat, honorary president of the Council of State, became president of National Aid; M. Garric, well known as a leader in the formation of teams for social work, became the commissaire-general; and on the proposal of M. Dautry, Minister of Armament, whose assistant I then was, I myself was made secretary-general.

National Aid had already played an important role before the defeat of 1940. It had rendered assistance to the refugees from Alsace-Lorraine; it had aided the thousands of French and foreign people who had wandered over the roads of France during the exodus; it had supported the Red Cross; and it had aided all the relief teams who were working behind the front.

After the armistice, in the face of the country's frightful misery, it was logical that the National Aid should continue its work. A law of 4 October 1940 placed it directly under the high authority of the Maréchal of France, Chief of State.

In fact nothing in its previous organization was changed, the same officials and workers continuing as before, and the organization of National Aid remaining an entirely private operation.

At the end of 1940 National Aid had already organized a very important network of philanthropic agents throughout the whole country; because of that organization the importance of its work increased day by day. It was supporting 1,200 French people who could not get back to their homes, and foreign, particularly Belgian, refugees who dared not return because of their anti-German attitude.

It may be noted in passing that the motto of National Aid was that of Pasteur: "I do not ask you what your nationality is, nor your residence, nor your name; I want to know only of your suffering."

National Aid also organized soup kitchens particularly for old people. It established workrooms in order to help those who did not have sufficient funds to live. These workrooms later played an important part in the

— 859 —

nation's economy, producing layettes for babies, and making worn out garments into useful clothing.

National Aid also organized the exchange of two old garments for one remade garment, with the assistance of the workrooms, so that the war-clamazed people of France could be clothed. School canteens were established, and biscuits on a casein base, with added vitamins, were distributed. Holiday colonies were established for children, on a scale hitherto unknown in France. Regular meetings, with refreshments, were organized for mothers.

From 1941, beginning with the air bombardments of Dunkirk by the English, National Aid helped all those who suffered from war damage.

It may be a good idea to give some specific figures. For example, the number of layettes distributed was 35,000 in 1941, and again in 1942, rising to 75,000 in 1943, and 104,000 in 1944.

It is also important to recall that thanks to National Aid's casein biscuits, which were introduced for the first time by the organization, all French school children received substantial supplementary nourishment until 1944, and even afterward. During war operations in any locality it was the National Aid reserve of casein biscuits which, in most cases, made it possible to feed thousands of refugees.

These same casein biscuits were also the means of holding back thousands of tons of flour from the Germans, as this flour was always retained in addition to the agreed allocation for French rations. The casein thus removed from German control, at the request of the Minister of Food, would otherwise have been used in Germany for making moulded products of a military character, and explosives. These casein biscuits were also used for nourishing the English children on the islands of Guernsey and Jersey.

The Germans in the occupied zone, from 1940 onward, were fully aware of the operations of so large an organization as National Aid. From the first days of their occupation they tried to bring it under the control of a similar Nazi organization, German Winter Aid.

But thanks to the complete support of the French population, especially in the north, it was the German Winter Aid which disappeared, and French National Aid which continued its work.

Later in 1941 some French politicians of pro-German tendencies tried to set up, in opposition to National Aid, a French Winter Aid. This too met with no success.

National Aid was always able to take care of itself and to remain completely independent by emphasizing the fact that all of its departemental delegates, and those in smaller regions, were benevolent workers and that such a network couldn't possibly be replaced.

In addition, a very large part of National Aid's funds were secured through gifts from the public and this fact did much to protect the organization's independence. These gifts were a magnificent proof of public approval.

In 1942 President Laval could not ignore the fact that National Aid was assuming a more and more important role. In addition, the Germans and the young French politicians of a pro-German attitude were beginning to criticize violently the national attitude taken by the organization, regarding it as a form of resistance against Germany. Therefore they took every opportunity to attack it in their approaches to the President, usually when the Germans made some complaint about National Aid's activities.

The President sent for me and I must testify that I always found him understanding in the broadest sense and moved by a desire to maintain our work in its independent and French character. I will say something later of the more important of the interviews which I had with the President on this subject.

(1) *The Hidden Wool*

The first time I was summoned by the President, if my memory is exact, was the beginning of April 1942 in connection with the case of the hidden wool.

The Germans had just discovered a large stock of wool which had been hidden in the Nord, many hundreds of tons. The President asked me if National Aid could absorb this stock rapidly. I replied that in my opinion it could be done easily by dividing it among all our workrooms. Forty-eight hours later the entire stock had been distributed, and it was used to make layettes for French babies.

This policy of hiding raw materials through the operations of National Aid was thereafter followed systematically by the French government and in that way 1500 million francs worth of seized supplies [about thirty million dollars worth in the franc of that time] were handed over by the Services of Industrial Production to National Aid during the years 1941 to 1944.

(2) *Action in Support of the Salvation Army*

The Salvation Army was able to continue its activities in France until 1943. At that time the German authorities demanded that the Salvation Army should be dissolved on account of the propaganda it was conducting in favor of the Allies and because of the information that it was able to collect on their behalf.

By agreement with President Laval this organization was dissolved only outwardly, its entire activities being continued under the name of the Protestant Charities of the Deaconesses.

The testimony of those concerned with these two organizations can be obtained easily.

(3) *Action in Support of Quaker Activities*

In April 1943—I think it was in April—the Germans demanded that President Laval should order the dissolution of the Quaker charities in France.

The President summoned me. I explained very freely to him that there was the greatest interest in maintaining these charitable operations. I did not conceal from him that it was through their activities that we were helping all the English and American civilians who were still on French territory. The abandonment of these charities would condemn nearly all these people to death from hunger.

With the President's agreement the Quaker charities were maintained. On this point it will be easy to secure the testimony of Dr. Van Etten and Mr. Baxter, 5 avenue Victoria, Paris, who were the leaders in these charities and who continue their work.

(4) *Action in Support of Spanish Communists; and the de Hauteclocque Affair*

Throughout the occupation National Aid never ceased to give help to the Spanish communists who had taken refuge in France. This help was given through the charitable organizations known as Aid to Emigrants, led in its social work by Mlle de Blomay.

During the spring of 1944 the French newspapers of pro-German tendencies launched a very violent campaign against National Aid. They included in this campaign an attack on M. de Hauteclocque, a cousin of General Leclerc, who is now French Ambassador in Belgium. It must be recalled that M. de Hauteclocque who at that time was obliged by his political convictions to leave the French foreign office had been placed by me in the National Aid organization as secretary-general. He was in charge of the whole of our National Aid operations, a fact of which President Laval was fully aware.

As a result of this press campaign I was called to have a first discussion on the subject with President Laval. After that interview M. de Hauteclocque was able to continue his work for several months. Unfortunately a little later the Germans demanded his arrest and he was interned in the Caserne des Tourelles in Paris. We were easily able to remain in contact with him as National Aid was then helping all political internees, even in the internment camps, both French and German. I attempted to arrange his release through President Laval. The President assured me that he would do everything necessary to make sure that M. de Hauteclocque had nothing to fear.

At a second meeting with President Laval on this subject I explained plainly to him that we could very easily arrange for M. de Hauteclocque's escape. The President made it clear to me that he saw only advantages in such a course. The escape was organized several weeks later and succeeded completely. It was arranged by a National Aid agent, M. Colombo, now unfortunately missing, after bribing the Inspector of the Sûreté Nationale—with National Aid funds.

M. de Hauteclocque was hidden by the departemental delegation of National Aid in the Somme and it was through this delegation that I warned him at the time of the liberation that he should come to Paris as quickly as possible.

M. de Hauteclocque was then made secretary-general of Foreign Affairs in the provisional government.

It is quite clear that if President Laval had cared to make the slightest investigation, in view of what he already knew, M. de Hauteclocque would have been found without any difficulty after his escape. The President never had the slightest intention of taking such steps.

I can rely absolutely on twenty years of friendship with M. de Hauteclocque to guarantee that he is ready to testify in this matter.

(5) *The Garric Affair*

In April 1944 the Germans demanded that President Laval should discharge M. Garric, commissioner-general of National Aid, because of what they said was his anti-German attitude.

It is certain that M. Garric had never concealed his horror of Nazi methods. As a well-known Catholic speaker he could scarcely be favorable to German influence and his influence among young people was incontestable. President Laval summoned me to discuss the matter with him and I explained that it was exactly for the reasons given that M. Garric must unquestionably be retained in the services of National Aid. Otherwise our work would suddenly be paralyzed because of the influence that he had on young people and on the trained social workers.

After this discussion the President asked that M. Garric should be brought to see him. During a skillful interview which lasted more than an hour the President talked very freely with M. Garric and was surprised to learn that he belonged to the University and not to the Catholic University. I remember particularly that the President had asked at one moment what had been M. Garric's last position before he had come to France for military mobilization. On learning that this position had been that of assistant director of the University of London, the President answered in a vulgar exclamation of astonishment.

After the interview I was called back, on the same evening, and President Laval's exact words were, "He is an honest man. Let him stay where he is. I will protect him."

M. Garric was in fact able to keep his position in National Aid until the liberation and he even held it in the organization which replaced National Aid, known as French Mutual Aid.

In order not to make this testimony too long I will end by speaking of the most serious crisis through which National Aid had to go, a crisis which risked its very existence. I refer to the appointment of Déat as President of National Aid in April 1944.

At this time the pressure of the Germans on the French government had become very strong, and Law No. 169, 31 March 1944, gave the position of President of National Aid, on German demand, to the Minister of Labor. M. Déat had just been appointed to that position. The President of National Aid, M. Pichat, then left his post, but steps were immediately taken with the French government by the vice-presidents, and particularly by M. de Laboulaye and M. Cognacq, to secure the cancellation of this measure. Although such a decision was certainly extremely difficult because of the German attitude, President Laval decided to annul the law of 31 March 1944, and this annulment was accomplished by Law No. 197, 30 May 1944.

In taking this decision President Laval without question saved the existence of National Aid and enabled it to continue its work at a moment when it was most necessary. The Allied landing took place on 6 June 1944 and military operations increased day by day throughout the country. Public services were disorganized more as each day passed and it was National Aid which had to take action everywhere, particularly on the battlefields of Normandy and those of the Mediterranean landing. National Aid was doing so much that the Germans tried to set up in opposition to it a factitious organization, The Workers Committee for Immediate Help. This activity was carried on entirely by notorious collaborators and received unlimited credits from the Germans.

It would be easy to ask all the French people who suffered through war action to testify in these matters.

Could better testimony be given than that of General de Gaulle when he bestowed the Order of the Army on one of the social workers who was killed on the battlefield of Normandy, as were many other National Aid workers, while bringing help to the civilian population.

"Decision No. 136. On the proposal of the Minister of War, the President of the Provisional Government of the French Republic, Chief of the Armies, bestows the Order of the Army, posthumously, on Marguerite Lewandowska. Of distinguished personality and able to inspire those about her with her own force and ardent vigor, from the first day of the occupation she never ceased to work in the service of France. She gathered and transmitted important information, accepting all risks with the greatest simplicity and complete scorn for danger. As a volunteer she maintained relations between the most advanced elements of National Aid in Normandy. There she was killed by machine gun fire on the Falaise road, 31 July 1944. She leaves to posterity the highest example of generous and courageous intelligence. She is awarded the Croix de Guerre, with palm. "

Paris, 9 November 1944

Signed : de Gaulle

On 23 January 1949 M. Vincent Auriol, President of the Republic, bestowed the Grande Médaille d'Honneur on French Mutual Aid for exceptional actions of courage and devotion. The text of the citation was as follows:—

"From 1939 and throughout hostilities this organization was present and active everywhere that the population, afflicted or in peril, had need of it. It distinguished itself particularly during the Battle of France, during the exodus of 1940, and during the evacuation of danger zones, air bombardments, and the fighting for the liberation of the country. It continued its difficult task during the repatriations, and in Indo-China and Madagascar, and finally during the disasters caused by explosions, fires, cyclones, and floods, both in France and in the French Union. Its 35,000 voluntary workers and its staff have during ten years carried out a magnificent work of first aid and social welfare. Hundreds of thousands of French people were directly or indirectly associated in this magnificent accomplishment."

I think that so far as concerns everything mentioned in this citation regarding the activity of National Aid from 1941 to 1944 when President Laval was President of the Council of Ministers, nothing would have been possible if he had not, with full knowledge of the facts, permitted and often encouraged its activity.

(Document No. 94)
Fr. ed. 907-913

19 March 1949

G. PILON

RELIEF FOR WAR SUFFERERS

RENÉ MER

*Controller-General for Refugees;
Director of the Interministerial
Service for Protection against
war disasters*

General Introduction

The state's action in dealing with the problem of refugees began in 1939. At that time the first reception service to be organized was one for persons who had been evacuated from their homes by order of the French military authorities.

Vicissitudes of war in May and June 1940 imposed the grievous task of meeting the immediate needs of about four million persons driven out by the invasion, and then of repatriating all those who could go back to their homes.

At the beginning of the winter of 1940-1941 the task of the refugee service changed again. Refugees and those whose homes had been damaged by the war and who could not be repatriated had to be lodged and reoriented in their temporary domiciles. Later the same service had to be performed for those who could well be described as political refugees, the expellees from Alsace and Lorraine.

Large groups of war sufferers and refugees no longer arrived during the winter and in 1942; there were only small groups of expellees. And during this period, thanks to the continuous efforts of the government, certain categories of refugees were enabled to return to their homes.

It appeared to be the right time to alter the policies which had been established in favor of the refugees, by limiting their application and by considering more carefully the financial aspects. But at the beginning of 1943 new and difficult problems began to appear. Bombing started again, increased in frequency, and became more intense, with the result that after the refugee flow of 1939-1940 and the homeward movement of 1941-1942, a new refugee flood began to rise, more serious and sharper in its emotional impact, that of bomb victims whose property and, in many cases, families, had been directly affected.

The era of refugees had ended; that of people terribly damaged by war's destruction had begun. These people began to arrive at the very time when the service for refugees was engaged in the reform of its policies and a reduction of its budget. These new sufferers were caught in the alarming regulations intended for refugees and were being treated in just the same way.

There were reactions to the new policy. The events of the war became more intense in character. And a new government policy began to come into being. It was at this time that a qualified representative of the government declared: "What is now happening will sharply disturb both the fairness and the suitability of the measures adopted by the service for refugees."

A closer integration and co-ordination of all the services immediately concerned with the war seemed to be both useful and indispensable. For this reason the "interministerial service for protection against the events of war" was created.

When this new service was established the person responsible was led to a basic revision of the conception according to which the state should deal with war disasters. It was necessary to adapt the state's activities to the frequency and the wide geographical incidence of intensive bombing.

To accomplish the assigned mission it seemed necessary to reorganize the entire war service. The fact was that the different services concerned with the situation, both the service for refugees and civil defense, had formed such a conception of their task that it seemed they would hardly be able to make the necessary change in attitude quickly enough.

The service for refugees did not, in fact, have the necessary authority for making an effective co-ordination of the whole of the public and private organizations which were to participate in the protection of the population against war events. This was true both for such parties as the Ministry of Food, and for private agencies such as National Aid.

If the government, faced by urgent necessities, wished to take measures that would both utilize and go beyond the normal administrative framework in order to make its remedies effective, it would be absolutely essential that the responsible administration should be inspired by a definitely positive spirit.

In dealing directly with reality, a reality that is continually changing, it is impossible to cheat or pretend. The services dealing with war events were concerned with but one single purpose, that of seeking and obtaining practical results.

The work of this administration was realistic and rapid. It was inspired by a broad and sympathetic understanding of what was happening, without too great a care for the financial effects of its activities. The speed at which events then moved demanded boldness and imagination, combined with a relaxation of formalities which had sometimes become too rigid.

The task which the state had set for itself was to bring into working order a group of measures which would make it possible to realize its purposes to the greatest possible extent in accordance with the maxim "It is not the people who serve the government administration, but the administration which serves the people."

The interministerial service responsible for protecting the people against war events assigned itself the role of guardian in their new life for all who had been damaged by war or evacuated from their homes. It filled this role in dealing with both governmental and private administrations. The service also acted as guardian in matters affecting the interest of inhabitants of the areas to which refugees and evacuees were brought, such interests often being opposed or at least different. SIPEG [Service Interministeriel de Protection contre les Événements de Guerre] had been given the obligation, in its inaugural decree, of stimulating and guiding all services concerned with war events, and of enabling them to deal with such events.

There was no possibility of returning to the system of general evacuation such as had been used by the French military authorities in 1939. The action of the state had to be limited by an understanding of the technical difficulties and of the psychological disturbance which might result from any administrative decision.

Evacuation had to be kept at a minimum as regards areas affected and numbers of persons moved, and it was therefore proper to obtain the greatest possible amount of information, taking full advantage of the opinion of technical and area administrations, in order to determine which sectors were threatened and in order to select in these sectors those elements of the population with which the action of the state should be concerned.

When the susceptible areas had been determined and a survey of the persons concerned had been made, the next task was to find practical first steps which would produce a minimum of reaction and difficulties among those whom it was desired to protect.

After the state had succeeded in moving those who were threatened its anxiety would be to maintain them on some permanent basis far from danger and to treat them as refugees to be mingled with those who had been obliged previously to leave their homes at the time of the first bomb attacks, and those who had been obliged to abandon their homes for political reasons, namely the people of Alsace-Lorraine.

In this way all who had been driven from their homes by the war were brought together in one great group.

SIPEG, responsible for the existence and protection of this group, inspired all of its activities with understanding and feelings of humanity, a spirit which spread to the departemental administrations and inhabitants of the center and south of France, counteracting the lack of understanding and the poverty of imagination of those who themselves had never suffered directly from the war, finally reaching the refugees themselves and making them, in spite of their unpopularity, feel that all the measures taken were in fact in no sense directed against them but had been taken for their own protection as individuals and for the protection of their property.

The 1940 Exodus

Who will ever forget the heart-rending spectacle of the roads of France during the two months when they were crowded with hurrying men, women, and children driven from their homes by bombardment or by the fear of seeing their villages swept into the zone of combat against an enemy whose attacks were day by day more effective. They had left more through an instinctive urge than on any orders given to them, taking nothing, striving merely to flee from a nightmare which recalled only too vividly the events of 1914. It was during this flight that the armistice burst upon a people entrapped in an enormous migration, the largest movement of human beings that had occurred for many centuries. Within a few weeks more than 3,800,000 refugees, including hundred of thousands of Belgians, Hollanders, and Luxembourgers reached the center and south of France. The population of the central evacuation zone rose from 2,500,000 to about 4,000,000, and the population of the departement of the Creuse, for example, more than doubled. The government, in those tragic times of general retreat and defeat, took action to deal with the disaster. Through individual and group efforts, and thanks too to the good weather, it was possible to distribute the refugees among the cities and through the countryside, to lodge them in special huts or among the inhabitants, to feed them, to aid them, and to meet their immediate needs.

This work was first done through the office of the secretary-general for refugees, and then, under a decree dated 2 August 1940, by a special refugee service which was attached to the Ministry of the Interior.

When the first urgent tasks had been accomplished a triple duty fell upon the state: to enable refugees to start homeward; to re-install refugees in their former homes; and to re-adapt, gradually, those refugees who had been unable to return home or to take up once more their former employment.

The conditions under which repatriation had to be effected were far from favorable. The road system had suffered heavily, bridges and rail lines had been blown up, and equipment was scarce. Nevertheless repatriation was effected with the best of organization and discipline; precise plans for rail transport were established based on the possibilities of the system and the numbers of refugees in the various departements which had received them. The return by road of those refugees who used their own automobiles was made possible by the detailed organization of traffic and a closely supervised distribution of the necessary motor fuel.

In this way the government was able to organize the return, in a remarkably short time, of more than three million persons to their original homes. A few figures will show the rapidity achieved: in July [1940] there were 200,000 repatriations; in August, 1,700,000, of which a million were made by rail; and in September, 850,000.

By 1 November [1940] the first and most urgent task was nearing completion. Two million refugees had returned home by rail, which had involved the preparation of 2,000 special trains; and more than a million had returned by road, making it necessary to direct the movement of 200,000 cars, and to distribute 14,600 tons of gasoline.

Period of Relative Stabilization

At that time the refugee problem changed character. Whereas it had been chiefly a problem of immediate aid or transportation, it now became a problem of lodgings and of adaptation to new activities. In the case of refugees who had returned to their old residences, aid had to be given to make it easier for them to meet new living conditions. Those refugees who remained in the free zone had to be enabled to live a normal life there and had to be helped toward integration into what was for them a land of refuge.

The nature of this latter task was all the more interesting because it had to do with refugees whose stay would be a long one. They were people who had left their homes and land months earlier, and whose return could not yet be foreseen: persons evacuated from the forbidden zones, including the entirety of the departements of the Nord, Pas-de-Calais, Meuse, Meurthe-et-Moselle, Vosges, Haute-Saône, Doubs, and the Belfort area, and from a part of the departements of the Somme, the Aisne, the Ardennes, the Marne, the Haute-Marne, the Côte-d'Or, and the Jura.

In addition, there were the people from Alsace and Lorraine whom fate had struck relentlessly. In order to remain French they had left everything and lost everything. For them the idea of a return home was but a dream. A tragic light was thrown on their situation by the communiqué which the government issued on 14 November 1940:

"The German authorities in Lorraine have asked those people of Lorraine who speak French to choose between being transferred to Poland or leaving for the unoccupied zone of France. Our fellow countrymen have chosen France. Since 11 November 1940, the expellees have left from Lorraine in five to seven trains per day. They have been told, though certainly by persons who had no authority to speak, that this step was in accord with an agreement made by the French government and the government of the Reich. The French government denies absolutely this suggestion. A measure of such a character has never been considered in Franco-German discussion. The French government is informing the German armistice commission of what is being done."

Statistics: When the period of mass migration had come to an end the situation regarding refugees in the free zone was as follows: Of a total of 489,791 refugees, 257,644 had been aided. These were divided as follows from the point of view of their original homes:

From that part of the occupied zone in which movement was permitted,	16,781 who had been aided, 93,076 not aided
From that part of the occupied zone in which movement was controlled,	125,528 who had been aided, 86,159 not aided
From Alsace and Lorraine	97,743 who had been aided, 36,222 not aided
Foreigners residing in France	17,592 who had been aided 16,690 not aided.

In the occupied zone, up to the same date, 231,517 refugees had been aided and 94,749 had not received aid. These were divided as follows:

From that part of the occupied zone in which movement was permitted,	43,977 who had been aided 47,576 not aided
From that part of the occupied zone in which movement was controlled,	154,854 who had been aided 34,284 not aided
From Alsace and Lorraine	22,325 who had been aided 7,089 not aided
Foreigners residing in France	10,361 who had been aided 5,800 not aided
Of those whose property had been destroyed	48,385 who had been aided 48,616 not aided.

To establish all these exiles in a new country was a serious demographic problem which would have to be dealt with by a constructive immigration policy which would maintain the family unit under a new roof and reconstitute homogeneous human groups, each according to its affinities, in the center and south of France.

Inspired by these principles the state proceeded to deal with the various aspects of establishing the refugees, of course making use of all the administrative machinery of laws, decrees, official circulars, and ministerial decisions, but at the same time obtaining the co-operation of all the charitable agencies, National Aid, the various youth groups, and others, while also making an urgent appeal to the instincts of mutual aid and solidarity of those who lived in the reception areas. Laws, decrees, and steps taken by prefects were not enough; the personal participation and human understanding of those who had been preserved from war destruction was necessary.

To obtain these reactions of solidarity the government made a moving appeal: "The winter which is now beginning will be cruel for the many civilians who have been evacuated after being terribly struck by war and its consequences. Our hearts ache to think of the sufferings which threaten them. But the need is not for sympathy; it is for aid, and protection against the hardships of cold. Those still unable to regain their homes, those suffering close to a home which has been destroyed, and those whom the war has deprived of all resources, must be made to feel the warming spirit of solidarity and mutual aid which during the months to come must protect the health and life of hundreds of thousands of French men and French women."

Activities of the Service for Refugees

From 1 November 1940, therefore, the work of the service for refugees was of three kinds:

(1) To establish and support the refugees in such a way that they could endure without too much suffering a separation from their homes of indeterminate duration.

(2) To integrate them with the local population in order to bring to an end, so far as possible, that status of "refugee" which could not be considered normal.

(3) To attempt, at the same time, to arrange repatriations, chiefly for that part of the occupied zone in which movement was allowed, as returns to the forbidden zone could be dealt with only in partial negotiations because the occupation authorities always opposed any general study of the subject.

Living Conditions and Supplies for Refugees

Although under the pressure of events, and with some assistance from the good weather, the service for refugees had at first been able to lodge the refugees in huts and camps. Such accommodations, requiring as they did the organization of a collective life in dormitories and eating halls, were formally forbidden at the beginning of the winter 1940-1941.

The prefects were given the task of distributing the refugees through their townships and departements. They were to do this through friendly arrangements with residents or, where that was not possible, by the issue of lodging coupons, or by requisition. The purpose was to provide the refugees with lodgings that would not be merely momentary. The method of distributing them among homes made it possible to establish them under conditions of normal life, and it maintained the principle of family autonomy. In the same spirit of dealing with the problem, rental charges ere strictly controlled.

But although lodgings, heating, and beds were arranged everywhere with comparative ease, the problem of clothing the refugees remained a difficult one. They had arrived during the summer with little clothing, and their wardrobes had been very insufficiently completed by allocations and by the distribution of articles which had been obtained, on the one hand, through direct purchase from dealers or by requisitions, and on the other hand through the collection of 150,000 items which had been at first intended for demobilized soldiers and through the supply of a 130,000 pairs of shoes manufactured by the army's quartermaster service.

Through co-operation between the service for refugees and the Ministry of Industrial Production some alterations in favor of refugees were made in the rationing regulations, alterations which, without being veritable exceptions, did enable a refugee whose needs were the same as those of a non-refugee to receive allocation coupons for the purchase of clothes and other textile articles before the needs of the non-refugee inhabitants of that departement had been satisfied.

In order to enable refugees not only to buy vegetables and fruit cheaply and so to meet their immediate needs, but also to establish some reserves for the winter, the service for refugees, before any other organization, proposed and encouraged the creation and cultivation of gardens by refugee families. The service arranged the purchase of the ground and of seed and tools, providing the relevant departemental services with the necessary credits.

As a result of a strong publicity campaign more than 100,000 gardens were put into cultivation in villages and in large towns, and their produce made a definite contribution to the national food supply.

Refugees were not only able to take advantage of a system of lodgings organized by the state, but were also allowed to receive daily allocations if they would prove that they were unable to return to their homes and if they were in need. A condition of need was recognized whenever the total resources of the family was less than the total amount of the allocations in aid to which they might be entitled.

Those refugees who were receiving allocations in aid also received free medical assistance and such help as would be provided under existing social laws. A medical service was arranged wherever the conditions of the refugees required it.

The Re-integration of the Refugees

The state, while assuring satisfactory living conditions to those who had been obliged to abandon their homes, tried at the same time to act in such a way that a more lasting solution, and a more human one, would be achieved in a true integration of the refugees in the work of reconstructing France, there at the very place where fate had led them, far from their normal surroundings.

With this purpose, it was decided that every man over 16 years of age must be registered in the departemental employment bureau in order to qualify as an "aided" refugee. But it was made clear that the right to an allocation would not be automatically lost merely because a salary was being earned, so long as the total of allocation and salary did not exceed the permitted allocation by more than 50 %.

Those responsible for the refugees did not fail to note that the obligation to work would bring satisfactory results only if all possible dispositions were taken at the same time to secure social and professional re-integration of the individual.

A group of measures was taken in co-operation with the various ministries affected; there was a census of refugees showing their normal occupations, a planned distribution of expelled groups among the various areas, and the creation of centers for occupational re-training. These activities applied particularly to the young refugees for whom a number of centers were established in which they could be prepared for country life; in Corrèze, for example, such centers were established at Seilhac, Lissac, and Beaulieu-sur-Dordogne.

A census of land lying fallow or insufficiently cultivated was made with the greatest care. To such land were sent the farmers from Lorraine who, with their tenacity, knew how to give such ground a fertility that its owners had failed to seek. To encourage such farmers in this work advances of up to 200,000 francs were allowed to each farmer for putting abandoned land into condition again.

A considerable number of refugees were sent to North Africa to permit a permanent installation of those who, in answer to an appeal from the administration, had expressed a desire to establish themselves in the colonies. An Alsace-Lorraine mission was created in North Africa for this purpose, under the authority of the governor in Algeria and of the residents in Morocco and in Tunisia.

Repatriation: the Second Phase

Until 1 November 1940 refugees were permitted to return to their homes if they merely showed a repatriation certificate signed by the French authorities. But on that date the occupation authorities suspended such movements.

These returns began again on 1 May 1941, but only for places in that part of the occupied zone in which movement was permitted, and under the direct control of the occupation authorities who then had the sole right to deliver passes.

These returns were made by railway, in special trains, or in special cars attached to regular trains, arranged by the service for refugees and the SNCF [French state railways] under satisfactory conditions so far as speed and comfort were concerned. In view of the shortage of carburants return by automobile was permitted only if the refugee had enough gasoline to make the entire journey.

About 60,000 refugees crossed the demarcation line in this way between May and December [1941]. By 1 January 1942 the return of refugees to the permitted part of the occupied zone could be considered as practically at an end.

The return of refugees who had come from the forbidden zone was much more difficult and raised problems which did not fall within the sphere of the service for refugees.

However, through its special delegates to the occupation authorities, the service for refugees systematically continued conversations in an attempt to obtain a definite relaxation of regulations applying to the demarcation line on the boundaries of the forbidden zone.

The first returns to that zone were made under a commission for "family regrouping." Demobilized soldiers were also allowed to return to their homes in the forbidden zone and to try to bring back their families.

The occupation authorities had agreed to the repatriation of certain classes of refugees whose return would be of value to the economic activities of the forbidden zone. Heads and owners of agricultural, artisanal, or industrial undertakings, together with their families, were allowed to return under this rule. The effect was considerable and it is probable that over 100,000 refugees were able to reach their homes in the forbidden zone in this way.

The psychological and human aspects

In order to complete this rational organization for the protection of the interests of refugees, the necessity of establishing direct contact between government administrative services and the refugees themselves made itself felt. It was only in this way that the irreducible minimum of needs would be disclosed and improper demands suppressed. Such a contact was made possible by the co-operation of the social workers belonging to the health service in each departement, to whom was given the supplementary duty of visiting the refugees as they made their rounds.

In addition, a superintendent for refugees was chosen in each departement from among the refugees themselves. His task was to make visits through the townships to find out if instructions given had been properly carried out and to gather in each locality any demands and complaints. His activities were to be concentrated on the study and improvement of the material conditions of life of the refugees.

As a parallel activity the establishment of local associations of refugees was encouraged in order that they might serve as intermediaries and representatives of refugee interests.

The above report shows how complicated was the task of the service for refugees.

The execution of this task demanded continual attempts to co-ordinate the action of the various ministerial services interested in these matters; to stimulate the action of the departemental services whose inertia, it must be admitted, sometimes found its excuse, or even some justification, in the magnitude of the paper work which bore down upon them; to overcome in many cases the intentional resistance of the municipal services, too concerned for the selfish comfort of their townspeople; and finally to deal with the innumerable demands and claims of the refugees themselves whose lot was always a miserable one as is the case with any exile.

In accomplishing its task the service for refugees was the object of conflicting criticisms. On the side of the refugees some claimed that nothing had been done which could possibly be regarded as sufficient or even suitable to the occasion. Others claimed that the refugees were nothing more than lazy people, richly supported at the expense of the community, who refused to work.

But between these two extremes the service for refugees strove to maintain a fair balance, and though either point of view can be supported by a certain number of specific examples, it remains true that on the whole the conditions under which the refugees were lodged and lived were acceptable.

At the same time it is true that results were obtained because the service for refugees could deal effectively with the prefectoral administrations by using the special authority derived through being attached to the Ministry of the Interior.

(Document No. 291)
Fr. ed. 914-922

Paris, 26 March 1956

RENÉ MER

BOMB DAMAGE IN FRENCH CITIES

ALBERT CHATELLE

Member of the Marine Academy

I the undersigned Albert Chatelle, member of the Marine Academy, living in Boulogne-sur-Mer, Pas-de-Calais, deposit with the Hoover War Library a series of booklets concerning the following cities which were bombed during the occupation: Nantes, Montluçon, Rennes, Le Creusot, Le Portel, and Toulon.

(Document No. 253)
Fr. ed. 923

17 March 1955

ALBERT CHATELLE

[*These booklets may be consulted at the Hoover Library.*]

CHAPTER XVIII

INFORMATION AND THEATERS

INFORMATION AND PRESS

RENÉ BONNEFOY

Journalist
Director of French Broadcasting

The following notes regarding my activity in the Ministry of Information between 1940 and 1944 are necessarily incomplete because at present I possess no documents whatever. I happened to be in Paris at the time of the liberation when it was impossible to get back to Vichy where the archives and my personal papers remained. My family home in the Haute-Loire, where I also had some documents, was pillaged, and I am therefore obliged to rely on my memory. But everything I say in these notes will be exactly true and can be verified; I will omit nothing which could have been used against me personally.

I am a professional journalist and had been a collaborator of President Laval as editor-in-chief of his newspaper *Le Moniteur*.

In July 1940, when M. Laval became Vice-President of the Council, I was appointed director of the radio-news reports at Vichy, a post which I left after 13 December. On the President's return to power in 1942 I returned to Vichy. At first I was chief of cabinet for M. Paul Marion, Secretary of State at the Ministry of Information, and then, when he became Secretary of State attached to the Presidence of the Council, I was appointed (in October or November 1942) secretary-general at the Ministry of Information, a position I held until the liberation. My section included the press and the news agencies. I worked directly under President Laval in his capacity of Minister of Information.

Before beginning to speak of the Vichy period, it may be useful to say a few words about my journalistic activity and the tendencies of *Le Moniteur* in the years preceding the war and the collapse.

Those associated with the Vichy government have often been accused of being defeatists before the war, and already, even at that time, "traitors" who prepared the way for the defeat. If there ever was such a tendency it should obviously be found, more or less concealed, in the newspapers which those men edited or for which they were responsible. So far as *Le Moniteur* is concerned, to make certain of the contrary it is sufficient to study its files. It will be seen that far from ever having published anything that could possibly harm France, *Le Moniteur* never ceased, particularly during the years 1936 to 1940, to denounce everything that could have the effect of weakening our country and putting France in a bad position in the event of war. That theme will be found almost as an obsession at the time when disorders, strikes, sit-down strikes, party quarrels, and the decay of governing power made us day by day more unfitted to face the risks of a conflict. In the editorials which I wrote every day, I merely expressed the thought of President Laval and commented on his own public declarations. In one of his talks in Parliament did he not say in substance—I speak from memory, but the text can easily be found—"Take care that we do not fall asleep and abandon ourselves to disorder at the very time when across our frontiers another people forges new arms day and night."

Doubtless no one knows, or if they knew they have forgotten, that the first newspaper in France to tell the French people of the threat against them contained in Hitler's *Mein Kampf* was *Le Moniteur*. This book was brought to me by President Laval. At his request I personally translated the principal passages which concerned our country and they were published—with comments emphasizing the warning that we must not allow ourselves to sleep—in a series of articles which appeared on our front page under heavy headlines.

This shows that *Le Moniteur* never ceased to lavish upon its readers the warnings which the most elementary foresight and an undeniable patriotism demanded. It was evident that this newspaper could not be a warmonger at a time when it was only too clear that war meant enormous risks for us.

But when the war came, throughout the period which preceded the collapse, and up to the worst and very last moments, *Le Moniteur* had no concern except that of working for the re-establishment of French power. I defy anyone to find one single line, one single word, one single allusion of any kind that could weaken the morale of the army and of the people. France entered the war after a period of political, economic, and social feebleness and was beaten in 1940; the responsibility falls in no fashion whatever on those whose thoughts and acts found their expression in newspapers like *Le Moniteur*.

After the armistice I went to Vichy not only because of my ties with President Laval and the great admiration I had for his character and his qualities as a statesman, but also because I was personally convinced that in the unhappiness of France the most wise and the most realistic of the numerous policies then conceivable was to undertake nothing that might aggravate the sufferings of the country. The wise and practical policy would be, on the contrary, to do everything possible to lighten those sufferings, to help the country survive, and if possible, to re-establish its spirit during a grievous period of which no one could calculate either the length or the outcome. For all these purposes, contacts and discussions with the occupying power were necessary.

The field in which I was called upon to work, because of my professional training, was one of those in which the "emergency" justice of the liberation has been most unrestrained. In my opinion the department of information, in the situation in which we were at that time, was nothing more than a technical organization, just as was the department of agriculture or of public health; it had to play its part, as did all other organizations dependent on the French government, by carrying out in the service of the country the mission which I indicated above as the wisest at that time. Its alignment in the front rank along with the Ministry of the Interior, the Ministry of Foreign Affairs, and, after a certain turning point, the Ministry of Labor, and even more definitely the Chief of Government and the Chief of State, was only apparent.

They cannot, or do not wish to, understand the policies of Vichy, and particularly the policies of President Laval, who do not consider the entire program as a coherent whole and a single block, and who do not admit that these policies involved necessities of all kinds, some of which were necessarily disagreeable in aspects. That is why it is stupid to think—under the conditions which existed, and with a government devoted above all to protecting the French people—that the information and propaganda services could in general have acted otherwise than they did, for example by developing lines of thought that would have been aimed at the occupying power. On the contrary, it can be judged that on the way in which the Ministry of Information accomplished its tasks depended the results that could be obtained in other fields, results that would be concrete, tangible, and useful to the country. It is in this sense that I say that they carried out, all things considered, a task far more technical than political.

I do not believe that President Laval ever believed very much in the virtues of propaganda, and he looked after his own very badly. His official addresses were always rare, and he spoke only when he thought that he really had something to say. Even then he spoke only after long reflection and a careful study of the effect of his words. In this way he did not waste time in the field of information which he could give more usefully to more serious problems.

I never received strict and precise instructions from him. It was not his way, just as it was not his way to make confidential disclosures even to his most intimate collaborators. It was necessary to guess what he wanted rather than to ask him. Nevertheless I am sure that I express his thought exactly, as regards the general attitude that I was to take toward the press, in this brief formula: (1) get involved in as few incidents as possible with the Germans; (2) don't bother the newspapers or the journalists.

I never did anything except follow this double command, and I never received any criticism from President Laval.

Concerning my transfer to the radio and newspaper office in 1940, I will say only a few words. This was the era of Montoire. In this period I developed, in a way which was more definite and more sustained than at any other time later, the theme of collaboration. Aside from the fact that a German victory did not seem at that moment to be "unthinkable", in which case it would have been necessary by choice or by force to make arrangements with a victorious Germany, this policy was one which was being translated into substantial advantages for France when 13 December 1940 arrived to drive President Laval from power.

I shall deal at a little more length with my activity in the position of secretary-general for Information, from October 1942 to August 1944.

My sector included press services, censorship, and the OFI (Office Français d'Information, formerly Havas, and since known as AFP, l'Agence France Presse). We had no control over the newspapers and news agencies of the northern zone which were entirely under the *Propagandastaffel* and the German censorship.

The newspapers of the southern zone, on the other hand, at least until the Germans entered the zone, were under the sole authority of the Vichy government. It seems to me unnecessary to insist on the fact that the press of the southern zone, under the circumstances, could not possibly be a free press.

The censors who had been installed at the beginning of the war in cities where newspapers were published had remained at work. Foreign news was supplied almost exclusively from one source, the OFI. And the OFI naturally took care to give no news which might create incidents with the Germans. It was for this reason that the war communiqués of the Allies were not published—at German request. (I think I am right in saying, though I have no means of verifying it, that this obligation was imposed on us at the time of the armistice.) In these conditions, the work of censorship dealt almost exclusively with commentaries rather than with the news itself. Censorship was also responsible for seeing that certain reports marked "must" were published, since the newspapers naturally had a tendency not to use certain dispatches. Little by little, too, there was built up a set of censorship directives known as "general instructions," which had become really numerous at the time I took over. They were of all kinds, some of them rather stupid. Many of them had been imposed by the Germans. Others came from some of the ministries, who perhaps were taking advantage of the situation to prevent criticism of what they did.

Thus the press of the southern zone was not free. It could not write all it wanted to write, and it was even bound to publish as dispatches certain information supplied to it. But it was never once forced to say in its own locally written commentaries anything it did not want to say, and in particular it was never obliged to praise the Germans, or the Nazi regime (this it was never asked to do), or even to praise the policy of "collaboration," or the Vichy government. So far as the various concrete problems of domestic politics were concerned, the press of the southern zone had considerable liberty of judgment and criticism. It could make suggestions. And though it was subject to a regime of "guided information," and was obliged to be silent on certain questions which it did not care to deal with according to prescription—that is to say, all questions concerned with the war and with Germany—the press in the southern zone was never "tamed" to the degree to which, to take an example, the Soviet press or even the communist press is today in every country of the world. The owners of newspapers remained owners and kept control of their own businesses. Never once during all the time I was in office was any newspaper confiscated, or requisitioned, or banned, or even suspended for more than a week—and such suspensions were extremely rare. Paper was rationed, for material reasons much more obvious than those given for its rationing at the time I write these notes. But it was always divided among the newspapers as fairly as possible by an organization under M. Maillard's direction, an organization which had quite a high degree of autonomy, since the control of paper was not directly in the hands of the secretariat for information.

I can testify that the newspaper directors and journalists who have since often been condemned to prison—sometimes to the most extreme punishments—and whose enterprises have been confiscated, were not pro-German with very rare exceptions, even, I am sure, in the northern zone. I can testify that they had no anxiety, even when they joined spontaneously in the policy of "collaboration," other than to protect the interests of France. It has been proved that many newspaper owners who did not shut down their enterprises refrained from doing so out of consideration for their employees, and often at the specific demand of these employees, who otherwise would have been without work and in the end picked up by the Obligatory Labor Service. But by continuing to appear, these newspapers were obliged to obey the rules imposed on them by the necessities of the moment, just as the government itself had to do in the interests of the country.

Directors of newspapers in the southern zone met periodically in Vichy in their various groups to discuss their common interests, and on these occasions I always saw them. They expressed their grievances regarding the shortage of paper, they complained of the stupidities of censorship, the lack of variety in the news supplied them, and so on. All these complaints were evidently well founded, for the most part, but it was equally certain that I could not do much to remedy the matters about which they complained.

I was anxious, however, to give more suppleness to a system which had become very rigid because of the necessity of publishing almost the same news in all the papers, and always in the same stereotyped form. Therefore, shortly after my arrival at the secretariat-general of Information, I proposed a sort of compromise to the newspaper directors, an arrangement that would bring them, obviously not the chance to say whatever they wished, but at least greater scope in the presentation of their publications.

The press services published every day a "word of guidance" which presented in very condensed form two or three news themes that might be developed. I proposed to the directors of the newspapers to excuse them from publishing "musts" if they would agree to use themes from the "orientation note" in their editorials two or three times each week, it being understood that they could present the information as they wished, in the form they preferred, and in such places on the page or in the paper as they thought best. They were to bind themselves to follow in general the lines of the government's foreign policy, particularly in denouncing the communist peril and in sharing what would be Europe's fate if it were one day invaded by the Red armies.

The directors of the newspapers accepted my plan and each signed a contract to that effect, a contract which had been offered them without pressure or threats of any kind whatever. I had limited myself to stressing what a difficult and extremely delicate task the government was carrying out, and to pointing out that the press could do much to help lighten still further our country's burden. I am convinced that it was out of pure patriotic duty that the directors of the newspapers agreed to bind themselves in this way. Among the daily papers only three or four—particularly *La Montagne* of Clermont-Ferrand, *L'Action Française*, which was appearing at Lyon, and *Paris-Soir* of the southern zone, printed in Toulouse—preferred to keep to the former rules. Nearly all of the lesser newspapers accepted, each individually, the new contract.

Truthfully, they did not bind themselves to very much by signing it. The guidance notes were quite varied, and each contained at least one subject which was not too "burning" to be dealt with so that two or three times each week, on days chosen by themselves, the newspapers could present an inspired article. Many of them limited themselves to publishing the guidance note itself, and putting it in some less noticeable corner, sometimes preceding it with the words, "It is said at Vichy that. . . ." This was how *La Croix* dealt with the problem. In return, the new contract enabled them to make more use of variety and originality in their make-up and material, and sometimes to play down certain news.

I myself saw in the new arrangement an advantage related to the Ministry's technical *raison d'être*. The Germans with whom I had dealings in my work—who happened to be also the only Germans that I ever had anything to do with—believed in propaganda and studied our work closely, and examined the way in which the newspapers of the southern zone were conducted. They were always much impressed by the "statistics on the use of the guidance note" which we furnished them.

The task became more difficult after the invasion of the southern zone, when the Germans set up their own censorship almost everywhere, a censorship which paralleled and supervised our own. In theory the German censors should have concerned themselves only with news and commentary referring to military matters. But in fact they soon wanted to have a hand in everything. I was sometimes led to send certain German generals notes asking them to pay closer attention to the agreement.

At the meetings of the newspaper directors I frequently told them that I had a double mission; it was my duty both to bother them and to protect them, and sometimes to protect them against themselves.

I instructed the regional chief censors, whom I brought together periodically, always to act on the side of our newspapers in any trouble they might have with the German censorship, and always to remind the German censors that according to the agreements between France and Germany the French government was still sovereign power in the southen zone and that it, and it alone, could decide punishments that might be applied to the press. A time came when the German censorship office claimed the right to eject the French censors completely from the cities along the Mediterranean shore. I protested vigorously against their claim, always in the name of a national sovereignty which it was important to protect, no matter how slight it might seem to be. In the end I won. I do not pretend that the contents of the newspapers benefited much by this success, since they would clearly not have been noticeably modified, but I saw in it an advantage in the possibility of protecting those persons—in this case journalists and newspaper directors— who, if the principle of French sovereignty in the southern zone had not beeen maintained, would no longer have had the screen of French censorship between themselves and the occupying power, and that at a time when incidents would have inevitably occurred in greater numbers.

I will mention here that in general, though it was not my rule to resist the Germans stubbornly on the propaganda themes they offered me, I never gave in to any of their demands regarding individuals. To make this clear, I should state the conditions under which my work was done. At least once a day, and often twice, I received a visit from the press attaché of the German embassy delegation in Vichy. Even when the southern zone was not yet occupied, he brought me a bundle of texts, of press clippings, of themes to be developed, and of papers of all kinds which he himself had received from the Gœbbels laboratories or from the Embassy.

After the occupation of the southern zone, when it had become a "zone of military operations" and was officially thereafter known as such, I received in addition a more or less daily visit from the chief of the German censorship office, who also brought me an armful of copy. I put much of this material aside, giving as my pretext the small amount of newspaper space available. But I evidently had to take some of it. In any case I was personally certain, as I had been for a long time, of the total ineffectiveness of such propaganda on French opinion, all the more so because the Germans showed the greatest insistence in spreading news and ideas aimed at influencing French opinion. The net result was that we gave them nothing but a little hot air; yet even this was not useless effort on our part if it helped the government save the machines, the food, and the men of the country. I know that this was the opinion of President Laval.

The Germans with whom I had to deal in my work did not limit themselves, unfortunately, to bringing me texts. Sometimes they brought a list of people who were members of my services and whom they considered as suspect, demanding that I should get rid of them. I always refused, using every pretext in order not to do what they wanted. One day I even got up and, pointing to my chair, told my visitor either to stop asking such things of me or to take my place himself. He turned red and hesitated between rage and the withdrawal of his request. Finally he said no more. I think he was an honest man, and that he was affected by my reaction. But I might have had to deal with a brute. When I reported the scene that evening to President Laval, he said, "They want to humiliate us." I understood better then what self-sacrifice was necessary for him in order to accomplish his terrible task.

Shortly afterward I was asked to get rid of my own chief of cabinet, M. Feuyères. I refused with the same vehemence and he stayed with me to the end.

When the Germans intervened personally to "purify" the information services, I had a number of opportunities to warn those concerned each time that I knew which officials or journalists were running a risk. Along the same lines, I had to defend, this time against Admiral Platon, many of my collaborators who were accused of being Freemasons, and who perhaps were, but who conscientiously did their work. There again I received the most effective aid from President Laval.

One other minor point, just as it comes back to my memory. One day, I was asked by another representative of the German Embassy to get rid of the chief censor in Marseille on the ground that he was a colored man. The censor in question was M. Gerville-Réache, a journalist from Martinique, whose color was more or less that of café au lait, and who was always very cooperative. I temporized. The threat became very pressing. In order to avoid a serious incident, I was finally obliged to send M. Gerville-Réache off on a vacation. But he continued to receive his pay.

I know of no better way to explain my relations with the newspapers than to give a few examples.

One day I phoned M. Frossard, a politician, a talented journalist, and director of the *Mot d'Ordre* published in Marseille. I asked him to come to see me urgently, telling him that I was probably going to be obliged to take rather serious steps against his newspaper. He came immediately, very astonished, rather worried, obviously having no idea of why I had called him. I showed him a paragraph which had appeared the night before in his newspaper, in the literary section, in which in words scarcely veiled Hitler was referred to as being under the control of the devil. I saw him turn pale. He admitted immediately that punishment was necessary to protect my own service; the punishment was suspension for several days. We both expressed our great hope that the Germans would not notice the paragraph, which might have caused him and his staff the most serious difficulties. Happily they did not read everything, and they never knew anything of the affair.

Texts with double meanings, allusions, and apparently harmless morals drawn from fables were frequent in some publications. They never brought trouble to their authors so far as I was concerned. I limited myself to asking the directors of those publications, when I saw them, to use more prudence. Among others the director of *La Croix*, M.M. Michelin, could testify that I always gave him useful advice, as the attention of the Germans had been drawn to his publication on various occasions.

The *Action Française* was also very closely watched by the occupying authorities, who often asked me what measures I intended to take against that publication. I never took any, except to have some pieces by M. Maurras cut, since if they had appeared untouched they would unquestionably have led to the arrest of their author. I remember an interview which President Laval had with Schleier, who, at that moment, was acting as Ambassador. I was with the President because the interview was to deal with certain newspapers, and in particular with the *Action Française*. Schleier was aggressive and full of demands. I admired the President's skill and obstinacy in avoiding embarrassing questions, in "drowning the fish," and in getting off onto other subjects in such a way that nothing positive was decided with regard to the newspapers under discussion. And in the end nothing was decided at all.

Many letters could be found in my archives from newspaper directors in which they made it clear, often after expressing their inevitable grievances, that they appreciated the way in which I was dealing with them. I remember in particular a very intelligent and very subtle letter from M. Maurice Sarraut, director of the *Dépêche de Toulouse,* which showed that he had understood perfectly the difficulties of our task.

In the same way I may refer to my relations with M. Alexandre Varenne, director of *La Montagne* in Clermont-Ferrand, a newspaper which, as I indicated above, had not signed the new contract. All the difficulties which arose between this newspaper and the censorship, and they were numerous, were always smoothed out by my efforts. When M. Varenne wanted to "scuttle" his newspaper, several months before the liberation, he came to ask me how he should go about it, fearing that the consequences might be dangerous to him. He wanted to know what our reactions would be. I told him to send me a simple letter saying that *La Montagne* would cease to appear on a certain date and I would limit myself to acknowledging the letter. This was done.

M. Varenne often said to me, "You are wrong in not giving the newspapers more liberty . . . You will see . . . When we have the power in our hands, we will not trouble you as you are troubling us . . . You will be able to write just what you wish . . ." It is too bad that not all the resistants were modeled after M. Varenne.

I want also to make a note of the visit of M. Brisson, director of *Le Figaro*, when he too "scuttled" his newspaper. He came to ask that the government should bear the expenses of this operation, and should pay all the indemnities due to his personnel. It is true that *Le Figaro* did draw each month from the government an important subsidy and doubtless he thought it was only natural that the government should also subsidize its debt.

But if I continued, there would be no end of little incidents of this kind to record.

One word regarding the Obligatory Labor Service. It was the duty of the Ministry of Information to support in the press all measures taken by the government in this connection, measures thanks to which the departures of Frenchmen for Germany were infinitely less numerous than they would have been if the occupying power had made direct requisitions.

But at the same time that the texts prepared by the information services were being published, I was busy trying to arrange that as few as possible of those in my own services and those in the employ of the newspapers were taken for obligatory labor. Often, sometimes at the very last moment, I was able to arrange that departures were postponed, and in the end canceled.

In the same way we fought officially against the black market. Nevertheless the black market at that time was almost a vital necessity. I remember a remark President Laval made to me one day: "The black market? How could I be against it? The French have to eat and that's the only way they can."

The arrival of Philippe Henriot at the Ministry of Information, and particularly the introduction of Militia elements in the information services, brought about changes in our propaganda methods. I thought of retiring at that time, though it would have been agreed that I should keep the press section alone under the direct authority of President Laval. My task had become more difficult. Already I was the object of sharp criticisms from a part of the Paris press. One issue of *Le Pilori* devoted its entire front page to a denunciation of my methods. *Je Suis Partout* on a number of occasions accused me of corrupting the press in the southern zone. *L'Œuvre* devoted a very sharp article to the "shortcomings" of our censorship.

I realized that President Laval, though he cared less about the propaganda section, where only words were produced, did desire to keep control of the press section because of the concrete interests which went with it, the persons involved, the property, the enterprises, the paper, and so on, and because it was necessary to continue to protect the press.

I will not go into the details of this period. I will limit myself to reporting two or three typical matters which will throw light on it.

One day I received a note from a service near my own asking me in most urgent fashion to reduce the daily paper ration of the *Dépêche de Toulouse* by ten tons. I was told that this punishment was based on the fact that the *Dépêche* had removed one passage from a talk which President Laval had given to the Militia. I replied that since the President was involved in the matter I must consult him. I did, with a good idea of what his reaction would be.

He read the article referred to, looked at me, and said, "The cut made by the *Dépêche* was not done with any intention of harming me."

What he meant was, "In certain places I am obliged to speak in a certain way, which is not always the way I would choose if I could speak as I wanted to before France as a whole."

And he added, "Tell them that I will look into this myself."

Sometimes President Laval spoke—in half-sentences, as was his manner—before a little group of French people, for example, mayors from the villages of the Auvergne.

And in this connection I am going to report something else that happened.

There was in the Ministry of Information, created a short time before, a propaganda committee of which the duty was to work out themes in connection with the Obligatory Labor Service. A German from the Embassy, Diehl, took part in these meetings. I never attended them myself, but a member of my cabinet was always present, without taking any part in the debate. One day he came back saying that Diehl was stirring up a serious incident. One of the "propagandists" who was working out these labor themes had put in his paper that President Laval, in a recent talk to some mayors, had emphasized the great advantage to France in having a government which was able to arrange that departures for Germany were far less numerous than they would have been. Diehl talked of telegraphing to Berlin. I hurried to the President. He at once summoned the writer of the text, learned that he had indeed slipped into the mayors' meeting, looked at him carefully as though to ascertain whether he were evilly intentioned, or merely naive, made him say that there was a misunderstanding, and made him repeat his retraction before Diehl, whom he had also summoned. The President so managed the whole scene that when the German went out he didn't know what to think and almost offered his excuses as he left.

One more incident, a rather painful one. During the final months the German censorship became more and more overbearing and demanding. Incidents became more numerous. It was necessary to intervene and protest continually. One day the director of a newspaper in some city, of which I do not remember the name at the moment, telephoned me to say that the German censorship had suspended him indefinitely. I at once called the chief of the German censorship for the southern zone, whose office was in Lyon, and protested against the measure taken without consulting or even advising us. Astonished he replied, "But the suspension was ordered at the request of your own Ministry." It had come from a French service in a nearby building.

I have always thought that if the occupation had lasted another six months, we would have seen some elements—we might call them "extremists"—elements endowed with solid appetites that had no relation whatever with any convictions they might have had, begin to treat the press in much the same fashion as the liberation authorities have since done. By that I mean that whenever they had the opportunity to do so, they would have done as they wished with the property and personnel of the press. The assassination of Maurice Sarraut, publisher of the *Dépêche de Toulouse*, was like a prelude to a development that inevitably would have assumed greater proportions, under the pressure of a tiny minority of unscrupulous people who took advantage of the credulity and the often thoughtless ardor of Philippe Henriot, whose personal disinterestedness is in no way in question. It was against all that sort of thing, among other reasons, that President Laval—who, as I know, regarded certain methods as "abominable"—strove to the last to protect France and the French. I could do nothing better than to help him to the best of my ability.

One last word. Shortly before the liberation, the representatives of a press group with whom I had been consulting, asked me what they should do at the time of the liberation, and what instructions they should give their colleagues. I replied that I was not qualified to give them any instructions.

"You have seen the order that has been sent to all officials," I told them, "namely, that they are to stay at their posts and continue in their services. You are not officials. The government cannot give you instructions and has no instructions in particular to give you. But I can give you advice. If during the occupation you have done nothing except to conform to the government's orders and requests, if you have not sold out to the Germans, if you have never denounced anyone, then I believe you have nothing to fear and nothing to do except take care for a few days not to fall into the hands of the maniacs who will certainly be in evidence. But all that will soon settle down. For I certainly hope that those who will replace us will not be lunatics."

My one regret today is that I did not put these men on their guard against the risks they ran. But how could I know?

On 18 July 1946, the anniversary of the day in 1918, during the other war, on which I was given a fifth citation which later brought me the military medal, the High Court condemned me to death by default; such judgments of the High Court are final.

Search can be made throughout my private life and the exercise of my public functions. Not the slightest shadow of dishonesty, of compromise, or of impropriety will be found.

In writing these lines, I have tried merely to say what my relations were with President Laval during the hard years in which I saw him fight foot by foot to defend the "continuity" of France, and to enable his country to live through to the liberation.

(Document No. 65)
Fr. ed. 927-937

Paris, 3 July 1948

RENÉ BONNEFOY

THE FRENCH PRESS DURING THE OCCUPATION

ALEXANDRE CATHRINE

Director of Le Nouvelliste du Morbihan, *and of* L'Ouest Républicain; *Officer of the Legion of Honor; Croix de Guerre with five citations; Secretary-General of the* Groupement National de la Presse Spoliée Injustement Condamnée

It is the custom in times of peace to refer to the Press as "the fourth power," after the executive, legislative and judiciary powers. It is no less accurate in time of war to consider it as "the fourth force," after the forces of land, sea, and air. For information and propaganda in every modern conflict play a role and exercise an influence of which the importance is unquestionable.

It is for this reason that once war has been declared the press ceases to be free in the sense in which that word is understood in democratic countries. It is submitted to control and censorship. It will be shown in the first part of the present study how such control was applied in France from September 1939.

If the country, or a part of the country, is occupied by enemy armies, the occupying authority will clearly not give back to the press the liberty which the onset of the conflict had taken away from it; on the contrary, the occupying authority will place the press under a control in proportion to his distrust in it.

The armistice of June 1940 could not, therefore, have failed to bring to the French press as a whole the consequences which in fact did follow. On the one hand in the southern zone the regime of French censorship was maintained and adapted, while in the northern zone, on the other hand, German control was established in accordance with the particularly authoritarian and centralizing character of the occupying power.

How did the French newspapers conduct themselves and how did they exist under these two different regimes? What material and moral repercussions came upon them? And finally, what fate was reserved for them by the new national power which arose after the liberation? Such are the questions to which the present study is intended to reply.

The Control of the Press in Wartime

The control of the Press in wartime had already been provided for in peacetime.

To make certain that this is true it will be enough to consult the *Livre Vert* dated 1 June 1938 and published under the seal of the Minister of National Defense and War: "Instructions for the control of information in wartime or in time of tension in foreign relationships."

The principle which inspires these instructions is thus stated:

"In time of war or of tension in external relations the necessities of national defense will impose, without any possible doubt, the establishment of a legal status of the Press which will differ from that of normal peacetime, and which will include the prohibition of the publication in any form whatever of any information, military, diplomatic, economic, or other, which might be harmful to national defense.

"Consequently all periodicals, books, brochures, posters, printed matter of every kind, and films, will be submitted to the preventive control of a service placed under the authority of the government, which will have the right to seize or suspend publications containing information, articles, or pictures of any kind not authorized by this service."

This instruction, which determined the regime under which the Press existed during the war, had been prepared while M. Daladier was President of the Council; it included a number of rules which the governments of Vichy needed only to follow. Among them, for example:

"White space resulting from censorship must, in principle, be concealed by the printing of a text which has not been refused."

"Violent or systematic attacks against the government and parliament are forbidden."

"The publication of articles, declarations, or daily orders concerning the food situation in France is forbidden unless previously approved."

"Extremely close attention will be paid to all news concerning . . . the size and distribution of stocks of food . . . ."

Thus, when President Laval took charge of the Ministry of Information in 1940, he had to add nothing new. And if he is reproached for "notes of orientation" sent to the Press is it not known that during the war all journalists accredited to the Quai d'Orsay or to any other ministry also received instructions . . . It is sufficient to consult the newspapers of that day to be sure. And don't they also receive them in peacetime?

The Situation of the Press after the Armistice of 1940

The division of France into two zones as a consequence of the defeat of June 1940 raised new problems for the Press.

There were journalists whom the armistice or the demobilization caught in the unoccupied zone and who did not wish to go back to the northern zone, or could not do so.

There were Paris publications which had followed the government in the various stages of its exodus and did not wish to re-establish themselves in the northern zone; because of the division of France they were to lose an important part of their readers, the press of the southern zone being forbidden in the northern zone, and vice versa.

What did the government do?

Regarding the journalists. No journalist deprived of his employment was abandoned. All who found themselves in this situation were taken care of by the Ministry of Information, some in the central, regional, or local censorship services, some in various services created within the Ministry itself, and some as press attachés in other ministries.

Regarding publications evacuated from Paris. The Ministry of Information gave them subsidies not with the purpose of corrupting them but merely to enable them to live. The best proof of the purpose of these subsidies is that no regional journal received one, except in the case of one or two very small publications which the government wished to aid in order to prevent them from disappearing completely, and then because they wished to protect the staff.

The Organization of the Ministry of Information

All questions dealing with information, press, and the radio services were placed under the control of the Presidency of the Council of Ministers by the decree of 13 July 1940.

On 16 July 1940 the secretariat-general for information, press, and radio was created, with twenty other secretariats-general. M. Jean Montigny was the first chief, with M. Tixier-Vignancourt as his deputy for press and radio.

On 6 September 1940 when M. Laval, vice-president of the Council, became responsible for the information services, M. Cathala replaced M. Montigny. When M. Laval returned to power on 18 April 1942 he himself directed the Ministry of Information, with a secretary of state and a secretary-general. The Secretary of State for Information was M. Paul Marion who since February 1941 had been secretary-general for Information in the Darlan cabinet. The secretary-general was M. René Bonnefoy who was specially responsible for the press, being a professional journalist.

The choice of these directors for the press and censorship services, and other appointments to subordinate posts, indicate that M. Pierre Laval always desired that there should be only professional journalists in the key positions of the Ministry of Information. When M. Philippe Henriot became Secretary of State for Information and Propaganda in January 1944, M. Bonnefoy remained as secretary-general for Information with authority over the department of the press, which thus always escaped the supervision and control of M. Philippe Henriot. The administration of the Ministry of Information was taken over by Baron Mourre, inspector of finance, today mayor of Villerville in the Manche, whose collaborator as chief of personnel was M. Alphonse Juge, a member of the Consultative Assembly in 1945.

First Period: September-December 1940

This was the period of the installation of the Ministry of Information at Vichy. Unemployed journalists, as we said above, were put in various positions. Publications evacuated from Paris established themselves with their fellow publishers in the provinces. Journalists accredited to the government formed an organization. It consisted, for the greater part, of former parliamentary journalists who had followed the government and Parliament and who are now to be found, nearly all of them, in the publications which came into being with the liberation.

At the Ministry of Information the direction of the press section was given to M. Henry Prété who during the war had been the collaborator of Martinaud-Deplat, director of censorship at the Hotel Continental (Paris), M. Jean Giraudoux being High Commissioner for Information and Propaganda.

At Vichy M. Jean Duffour was made director of censorship with M. Gaston Guillaux as his immediate collaborator; both were "rebel" editors from Le Matin (Paris).

Second Period: under the Darlan Ministry

After 13 December (1940) and the temporary appearance of Prof. Portmann it was chiefly Admiral Darlan's 'sailors' who were to deal with the Press, bringing to bear on it the full weight of their incompetence.

How Did the Press of the Southern Zone Receive its Information?

Havas, the great press agency, which had followed the government throughout its exodus, established itself at Clermont-Ferrand and at Vichy. It was under the Darlan government that the French state became the owner of the news division of the Havas agency, renaming it OFI (Office Français d'Information) while the Paris section of Havas became AFIP (Agence Française d'Information de Presse) under double direction, French and German.

The Press of the southern zone had no relations with AFIP but only with OFI.

When President Laval returned to power in April 1942 he appointed M. Henry Prété as managing editor and M. Charles Morice as administrator. Both were old newspaper men. It should be noted that M. Charles Morice was chief of the political services of *Le Petit Parisien* before the armistice and had not been willing to go back after the armistice to a newspaper published in Paris.

There were negotiations between both OFI and AFIP. AFIP disappeared but OFI could send nothing but news of France to the occupied zone. On the other hand the German authorities could bring in only DNB (*Deutsche Nachrichten Büro*) which was thus the only international news agency. OFI had two branches, *Téléfrance* which distributed abroad articles written by important French people, and *Téléradio* which had two transmitters, at Bordeaux and at Lyon, and which broadcast news of France to foreign countries. These two branches continued to operate until the end of 1943, while OFI maintained a secret communication with Switzerland.

Another news agency survived the war. The Fournier agency, with offices at Lyon and Vichy, operated throughout the occupation without ever coming under the control of the occupying authority.

On the other hand the Interfrance agency opened a news bureau in Vichy with information which came chiefly from the German agency, Transocean. News issued by this agency was censored by the French censorship office before being sent to newspapers in the southern zone who subscribed to the service. This agency also had a service of articles for small local newspapers. But there was no time at which the Interfrance agency had any privileged position which might influence the newspapers in the southern zone in deciding what to do with its dispatches and articles.

An Unsuccessful Plan for Agreement

When M. Lucien Romier became Minister of State at the end of August 1942 he began, like the great journalist that he was and at the demand of his former colleagues, to try to ease the regime under which the Press operated. In January 1942 he submitted a draft of which the purpose was "to relax the censorship and improve the relations between the Press and the public administrations."

This draft plan brought no results although the Federation of the Press had sent an important representative, M. André François-Poncet, to deal with the government on its behalf and in its defense. A plan for an agreement between the censorship and the Federation of the Press was proposed by M. Marion, Secretary-General for Information; as it implied a total submission of the Press to the government it was refused by the newspaper federation. M. André François-Poncet abandoned his mission.

Third Period: April 1942-1944

The position when President Laval returned to power may, therefore, be summed up by saying that the bridges had been broken between the government and the Press in the southern zone, and that the Press was feeling the full weight of a censorship directed by seamen.

At this time there was a very great difference between the situation of the Press in the northern zone and that in the southern zone. The news-papers of the southern zone had no direct contact with the occupation authorities.

But several months after the return of President Laval to power, when the German troops entered the southern zone, the occupation authorities installed censors in all the publishing centers without giving previous warning to the government.

The Press of the southern zone then turned to the government for protection. The government secured an agreement that the German censors would be allowed to deal only with questions directly connected with military operations. In no case were they to have direct contact with the newspapers. Between the German censors and the newspapers there was always to be the screen of French censorship.

The government was concerned with protecting the press of the southern zone against German encroachments, and with loosening the pressure of French censorhip. With this in mind it conceived the plan of an agreement between the Federation of the Press and the Ministry of Information which, while giving the occupation authorities the impression that the government had the southern zone press well in hand, would at the same time give the press a little more liberty.

This was the purpose of the agreement proposed on 29 December 1942 to the four newspaper owners' associations which together constituted the Federation of the Press: The Association of Evacuated Publications of Paris, with de Nalèche as president; The Association of Regional Dailies, with Soustelle as president; The Association of Departemental Newspapers, with Gaubert as president; and The Association of Technical Publications. This proposal was the subject of an exchange of letters between the Ministry of Information and the Federation of the Press, represented by two secretaries-general, M. Maillard and M. Destin, on 6 January 1943.

The letter from the federation said in particular that "The Government's statement, in effect, informed the federation that in this way the federation would be helping to maintain the principle and some of the prerogatives of French sovereignty. . . ."

In his reply the Secretary-General for Information, M. Bonnefoy, said: "I do not doubt that important considerations of national interest have led to this decision. Your action will have the effect of aiding the govern-ment in maintaining the principle, and increasing the prerogatives, of French sovereignty. . . ."

Text of the Agreement between the publications named below, whose directors have given their agreement, and the Ministry of Information.

In order, on the one hand, to assure the government the complete and permanent support of these publications, and on the other hand to release these publications from a certain number of censorship obligations, to bring to an end the uniformity which at present characterizes their separate presentations as a result of censorship, and in general to give them greater liberty of expression, the following points have been decided on:

(1) The publications listed below are henceforth released from the obli-gation of publishing in a specified presentation those texts and headlines indicated by the censorship.

(2) In return for this release, these publications undertake to follow in the

most constant and loyal manner the general orientation given by the government and to support its policies in the most active way.

The publications participating in this agreement will have the right:

(I) To name a journalist, one for each publication, whose articles on general politics will no longer be submitted to censorship, whenever the publication desires this privilege, and who will write under his own responsibility.

(II) To present as they wish, by condensing, summarizing, expanding, commenting, if they so desire, or by editing in some special way, though without altering the spirit and tendency, all the texts, either commentaries or news, of which publication had previously been obligatory. (But publication of these same texts will continue to be obligatory for those periodicals which do not subscribe to the present agreement. Certain texts will be reserved exclusively for them.)

(III) To have the right of criticism, particularly in local affairs, aside from criticisms of a personal kind, it being understood that such criticisms will be fair and based on facts which can be proved. Criticism will be on food supplies, economic questions, the functioning of public administrations, and the life of society in general. The tendency of these criticisms should be in conformity with the spirit of the principles of the National Revolution. In order to facilitate the task of these publications in local matters, they are to have the right to appoint a journalist, who must be accredited by the prefect, who, for questions of local interest, and with the reserves just mentioned, shall be allowed to write on his own responsibility.

In return:

(1) The publications which participate in the present agreement undertake to follow permanently the political orientation given by the government. In particular they undertake to use a minimum of three times a week in their editorials and at their own choice the note of orientation which is issued each day by the services of the Ministry of Information, and on the other days of the week to develop general themes which are of a nature to aid the government's action. They will also have the right, in case they prefer not to make use of the orientation note absolutely regularly, with the intention of giving greater variety to their commentaries, to inform the Secretariat for Information of the themes which they desire to present. It is specified that the general orientation of the government, as it is brought out in the most recent texts and official declarations, is based in its broad lines on the following points: the fight against communism, collaboration between European nations; the action of the Anglo-Saxons in preparing the way for communism; France will find its salvation only in a regenerated Europe; the determination of France to base itself on Europe in reconstructing its empire; and urgency in applying the principles of the National Revolution.

(2) The publications undertake to give emphasis in headlines and in texts to all news which corresponds with this orientation and which is likely to have a desirable influence on public opinion.

In order to assure the proper execution of this agreement through permanent contacts, the publications which take part in it will maintain in Vichy a delegate who will remain in contact with the secretary-general and the information services. His task will be to transmit any demand made by the publications, to collect the orientation notes each day, and to settle with the secretariat-general all problems which may arise. The Secretariat for Information will have the right to ask the delegate to request one newspaper or another to be good enough to undertake some particular campaign which the government may believe to be useful. It is clearly understood that certain particularly important texts such as messages from the Maréchal of France, Chief of State, or from the Chief of Government, will remain on the obligatory list, as well as certain official communiqués particularly in matters of food supply. The Ministry of Information reserves the right to put a stop, if it considers it necessary to do so, to open conflicts which may arise between certain publications and which, in general, can only harm the work that is being undertaken as a joint effort. In particular, the publications taking part in the agreement will be specially protected against attacks which may be made against them by other publications. The Ministry also has the right to consider as ruptures of the present agreement any failure by any publication to carry out its undertakings.

Very strict instructions will be given to the censorship services by the Ministry of Information to ensure the correct execution of this agreement, and a watch will be kept to see that these instructions are strictly observed.

[End of text of agreement.]

The Federation of the Press chose M. Lucien Souchon, author of the book *Feu l'Armée Française* [The Late French Army] and secretary-general of the *Courrier du Centre*, whose anti-German sentiments were well-known, to represent it with the government and to look after the execution of the agreement. The government placed at M. Souchon's disposition in the Hotel de la Paix, where the Ministry of Information was located, a room which was between the offices of the Direction of the Press, and the chief censorship office. M. Souchon began his work on 15 January 1943.

Though it was definitely "directed," nevertheless the Press [of the unoccupied zone] did not undergo any actual constraint. While it had accepted certain obligations that resulted from the situation in which the country then was, many individual publications, it must be pointed out, did not sign the agreement offered them, a refusal which in no way prevented them from continuing to appear.

No Unification with the Press of the Northern Zone

In 1943 a new danger threatened the Press of the southern zone.

The press of the southern zone had always been violently attacked by the Paris press, all the more after the occupation of the southern zone by the Germans.

An organization committee had been formed, under the law of 16 August 1940, in all industries or groups of industries; these committees dealt with both social and general problems of their respective groups and in addition had some rights over the allocation of raw materials. Thus there was in the southern zone an organization committee for the Press, parallel to the Federation of the Press.

However, M. Jean Luchaire in the northern zone had created the Corporation of the French Press of which he was president. In 1943 M. Jean Luchaire decided to unify the Press of the two zones. If he had succeeded, the Press of the southern zone would have been placed on the same level as that of the northern zone, or in other words under German control.

Les Nouveaux Temps, M. Luchaire's newspaper, on 14 January 1944 published two official orders, one of them charging M. Jean Luchaire with the task of studying measures and presenting plans necessary for the unification of the corporative regime of the Press throughout the whole of France, and the other an order from the Ministry of Industrial Production and Labor which appointed M. Jean Luchaire as a special delegate with the High Labor Council to prepare and present a plan for organizing the printing trades, both economically and socially, and to prepare and present a draft of all measures necessary for co-ordinating that organization with existing Press organizations.

But these two orders never appeared in the *Journal Officiel* and therefore remained a dead letter; President Laval had acceded to the protests of the directors of the Press in the southern zone.

M. Jean Luchaire then strove to achieve a happier result by dealing with the journalists in the southern zone. But there already existed in the Ministry of Information a special service for the journalistic profession which had the duty of studying a status of the Press; in accordance with the desire of President Laval, the press [of the southern zone] was under no pretext to be a copy of the Corporative Press Group in the northern zone.

As the National Association of Journalists was now entirely dormant, a Defense Committee for Journalists was formed, uniting all journalists in the southern zone. This committee met in congress at Montpellier on 5 February 1944 and adopted a motion which had been proposed by the Lyon section, of which the purpose was to maintain the Press of the southern zone in its existing status until the end of hostilities. The text was as follows:

The National Congress of the Defense Committee for Journalists, meeting at Montpellier on 5 February 1944, desires to express its profound surprise on learning that a plan for the unification of the Press of the two zones in the form of a corporation which might shatter the present situation and the entire regime of the press in the southern zone has been in preparation without its National Headquarters having been consulted or even advised.

The congress, while affirming its desire that the labor charter should promptly be applied to the French press, desires not merely the maintenance throughout hostilities of the present regime of the Press in the southern zone, but also a return to a regime based on the law of 29 March 1935 and those later laws, decrees, and orders which extended its application....

Along the same lines, on 10 February 1944 when a professional statute was established for all who held posts of responsibility in the Press of the southern zone, the association for the defense of journalists prepared a plan for a reorganization of the Press which would have been adopted except for circumstances which occurred later.

In any case the resolution adopted by the journalists was an indication of the liberty with which they were able to express themselves; like their employers and the enterprises to which they belonged, they were able to escape German pressure to the very end, without taking into account all the arrangements made by the government which spared all press employees, journalists, office workers, and other workers, from requisition [under the Obligatory Labor Service].

Northern Zone

I. *The arrival of the Germans in May and June 1940*

At the approach of the first divisions of the German army the great dailies of Paris, following the example of the public authorities, emigrated toward the south. They were later to settle at Clermont-Ferrand or at Lyon. Their life during the occupation was, therefore, the same as that which was described above for the French press in the free zone.

Most provincial newspapers in the north of France, however, large, medium, or small, daily or weekly, remained where they were. For those who directed them a terrible problem was set: "If we continue to appear we risk harsh and continuous pressure from the occupying authorities, and a position like that of the famous *Gazette des Ardennes* of the 1914-1918 war. If we halt our publications entirely, the Germans will install in our place men from their own ranks or men who are on their side and the French public will never find in their newspapers anything but news, articles, and comments which are strictly German."

A very small number decided to abandon their publications with the result, exactly as had been foreseen, that German newspapers were installed in the place of the abandoned French papers—for example, *L'Écho de Nancy.*

Most of the publishers, having no means of living unless they worked, and conscious, above all, that they were choosing the lesser of two evils, continued to bring out their publications. Often it was the mayors, the prefects, and the members of Parliament who advised them to take this risk, arguing that the French administrations, in order to speak to the public, needed a tribune which was loyal to them. Thus in December 1953 several days before his election to the Élysée [as President of the Republic] M. René Coty, Senator from Le Havre, came to testify before the military tribunal of Metz which was judging M. Jean Lafond, director of *Le Journal de Rouen,* and declared that it was he himself who had incited M. Lafond to continue his newspaper under the occupation.

First contacts between the occupying authorities and the directors of newspapers generally went well. The "newcomers" would tell the director, or the managing editor, that they were fully aware of all that his newspaper had published to cast discredit on Hitler, on Germany, and so on, but that the past was the past and that they would not even remember it. Their instructions were limited to an order to publish (1) all German military communiqués, and (2) no attacks of any kind against the German army.

Aside from this double obligation, the Press was allowed the greatest liberty of presentation and subject matter.

This liberty was, in general, respected during the first weeks and even the first months of the occupation, though the attitude of the censors proved to be extremely variable from one city to another and from one departement to another.

For example, when the people of Lorraine were expelled in September 1940 and Maréchal Pétain's violent protest was broadcast, most censors in the northern zone forbade the Press to report the protest. Yet at Angers, after a telephone battle which lasted all night, *Le Petit Courrier* obtained permission to print the news on its first page, simply by making some slight modifications of headlines and size of type. The German service responsible for German relations with the French press was the *Propagandastaffel.*

Its geographic organization paralleled that of the occupation army. There was an *Oberpropaganda* service in Paris for the area which the Germans called "Gross Paris." There was another propaganda service at Saint-Germain-en-Laye, and later at the Vésinet for the northwest and the Paris region, another at Angers for Brittany, the west, the southwest; and one more at Dijon for the east and east-central area. The French press in the departements of the north was directly under the authorities at Brussels, being in the forbidden zone.

In each important city there was a *Propagandastaffel,* often installed on the premises of the principal newspaper. In Paris the *Propagandastaffel* services were very large and were installed at No. 52 avenue des Champs Élysées; here they dealt with press, radio, and cinema.

The *Propagandastaffel* organization for weekly publications varied from region to region as these were established chiefly in the under-prefectoral cities and less important towns in the departements. Sometimes it was enough for the responsible director of the publication to send his copy by post to the censor; in some places he had to take it personally to the censorship officer in the chief locality of the area; or sometimes the censor himself would come by car to censor each publication on its own premises.

The German army in general entrusted its propaganda services to specialists, men who were themselves journalists, writers or publishers. A curious detail was that authority was not always given to the officer who was highest in grade but rather lay with the one who was best fitted. For example, in the *Propagandastaffel* offices in the Champs Élysées it was a young lieutenant who acted as chief censor with captains and even majors under his orders.

The attitude and conduct of the *Propagandastaffel* officers varied a great deal according to the individual. Some of them were frankly full of hate and disagreeable; others showed themselves to be human and courteous; and with still others it was possible for journalists to work in an atmosphere of relative confidence. Some censors made a sharp difference between journalists who remained completely French under the occupation and those who were nothing more than courtesans of the occupying authorities. An officer of the *Oberpropagandastaffel* at the Vésinet said one day to one of our Norman colleagues, "After the war it will always be a pleasure to shake hands with men like you, who are true French patriots. But all that will be needed for M. X and M. Y (naming two fanatical collaborationists) will be a rope for hanging them." What a pity that this distinction, instinctively applied by German officers, could not have been maintained at the liberation by the French judges and 'purifiers.'

In principle it was the German language which ruled in relations between censors and publications. But in many places, notably in Paris, Normandy, and Anjou, the skill and determination of the journalists was such that in practice only French was used in these relationships, and respect for the customs and traditions of the French press was even imposed on the occupants—*Graecia capta ferum victorem cepit.*

II. *Publishing Enterprises under the Occupation 1940-1944*

Most of the publications of Paris which were evacuated to the southern zone when the Germans advanced were unable, or did not wish, to go back to Paris during the following months.

The only old titles used in the capital city between 1940 and 1944 were *Le Matin, Le Petit Parisien* (whose legitimate owners took no part in the management), *L'Œuvre* and *Paris-Soir* (of which the legitimate owners, like those of *Le Petit Parisien*, did not share in the management). New titles appeared among the big dailies of Paris: *Aujourd'hui, La France au Travail, Le Cri du Peuple, L'Écho de la France,* and *Les Nouveaux Temps.* They represented more or less the traditional shades of French political opinion with the exception of communism. The directors of *L'Humanité* had, however, asked for authorization to reappear; they did not obtain it. There was also a daily newspaper devoted to sports, *L'Auto.*

In the provinces the principal regional and departemental dailies continued to appear: *L'Ouest-Éclair,* at Rennes; *Le Journal de Rouen,* at Rouen; *Le Petit Courrier,* at Angers; *La Petite Gironde,* at Bordeaux; *L'Éclaireur de l'Est,* at Rheims, *La Dépêche du Centre,* at Tours; *Le Progrès de la Somme,* at Amiens, and so on.

Among the weeklies and bi-weeklies which had been so numerous before the war, many ceased to appear for various reasons or did not receive authorizations from the Germans, who never understood very clearly what their usefulness might be.

In all about 350 publications of various classes were published in the northern zone between 1940 and 1944.

Material problems were continuously and intensely difficult. Restrictions on supplies of paper, lead, coal, gas, and electricity involved each month the study of new problems whose solution required a wealth of ingenuity. On various occasions the newspapers had to reduce the number and size of their pages, and limit the space available for advertising. During the last months of the occupation most of them appeared in tabloid size and were set in 7, 6, or even 5-point type.

The greatest hardship which fell upon the press was the institution of the Obligatory Labor Service in 1943 and 1944, followed by requisitions of labor for Germany. The Press Corporation, of which we will speak later, engaged in epic struggles with the occupying authorities to avoid the threatened deportation of their employees. They were energetically supported by the Vichy government and so succeeded in obtaining a considerable reduction in the number which had been decided on by Dr. Sauckel's services. An average of about 80 per cent of their total employees was demanded from press enterprises but in the end this was reduced to about 10 per cent who were chosen by priority among young unmarried men or married men without children.

From the financial point of view, the situation of publications under the occupation was rather good. The circumstances themselves established what was in effect a control of the Press, standardizing sale prices and advertising tariffs, and securing a whole series of economies in newsprint and other supplies. The result was a quite prosperous financial situation for the publishers, and they took pains, in spite of official regulations to the contrary, to enable their employees to share largely in this prosperity, through the use of various devices such as indemnities and premiums.

From the moral point of view the situation was not at all the same. It was necessary to fight a subtle and continuous battle against the occupying authorities in order to maintain the national character of the organs of the press, in spite of the war communiqués and such commentaries as were more or less imposed on them. In general, the provincial newspapers succeeded better than those of Paris.

The news which they all received, apart from the orientation notes issued by Vichy and the German military communiqués, was distributed chiefly through two large news agencies, Havas, of which the Germans had taken 49 per cent of the shares, and Inter-France which in spite of certain legends was as a matter of fact until the summer of 1944 financed entirely with French money, from the subscribing periodicals and state subsidies.

III. *The Government and the Press*

Theoretically, the power of the Maréchal's government extended to the entire country, including the occupation zone. But in fact, in this zone the government's representatives, prefects, police chiefs, and officials of all kinds could take care of the population only with the consent, and under the control, of the military authorities.

It was even more true of the [occupied zone] Press, as it was not juridically attached to any public authority, that it escaped, for the greater part, all Vichy guidance. Those of the Paris newspapers which in their complete devotion to the occupying authorities had no intention whatever of following the orders of the legal government of France existed, in fact, throughout four years without any contact with that government.

Other publications, far more numerous, were able however to maintain connections with Vichy which, though not official, were nonetheless often very close. Their directors demanded an *Ausweis*, or pass, from the German authorities and once they had reached the provisional capital found the doors of the ministries willingly opened to them. The Ministers, the Chief of Government, Pierre Laval, and the Maréchal himself saw them privately or received them in delegations. In these talks the French authorities obtained information on the spirit of the public in the northern zone and on the conduct of the occupation troops and authorities, and could also discreetly give to their visitors useful instructions.

In addition the Ministers themselves or the delegates of the Ministry of Information frequently visited the occupied zone. They always brought the most active support to any publications which were having difficulties with the occupying authorities, support, unfortunately, which did not always prove to be effective.

At the Press Corporation a government commissioner was always present to maintain the liaison between the corporation and the French Ministry.

Finally, the information services at Vichy regularly distributed notes of orientation to the publications, and the German censors quite often allowed their use.

IV. *The Corporation of the Press*

In 1941 Maréchal Pétain, very deeply concerned with social problems, showed that he was favorable to carrying out several experiments in corporative organization at the time when he was preparing the labor charter. It was in this way that the farm corporation was established, and then a maritime fisheries corporation.

It was in this same spirit that the Press Corporation came into being in the northern zone under the initiative of Jean Luchaire.

This corporation was based essentially on the principle of equal representation for elements from the side of the owners and from the working side, including writers, office workers, and other workers, all being elected by their own groups.

There were five sections: Paris daily press; general periodical press, including publications specialized in arts, literature, technical subjects, fashions, theater, etc.; provincial press; news agencies; and press distribution services.

At the top there was a general assembly which included those elected by the employers and the employees from the different sections; and there was an executive committee of eight members, four from the employers' side and four from the workers' side, presided over by Jean Luchaire who was assisted by a government commissioner. Both the assembly and the executive committee sat each month and had to deal with all important problems, technical or social, which arose under current circumstances.

The organization of such sections as those of the Paris daily press or the news agencies, where only a small number of enterprises was involved, was relatively easy, but it was not the same for the provincial press which was numerous and scattered. In this case organization was slower and more delicate.

Vertically the provincial press was divided under three national commissions, one for the regional dailies, one for the departemental dailies, and one for the weeklies.

Horizontal division was by ten regions, the same as the new provincial administrative regions established by Vichy. Within each of these regions, Normandy, Brittany, Burgundy, Maine-Anjou, the Southwest, Lorraine, and so on, organization was according to the principle of equality for the owner and worker sides. Those who were elected by each of these regional organizations came each month for a meeting in Paris in the Passage Violet (rue Gabriel-Laumain) where an assembly of the provincial press was held twenty-four hours before the general assembly and council of the corporation.

In most cases it was the director of the most important regional newspaper who was elected president of the corporative group. There was one exception, however, in Lorraine. In order not to give the presidency to *L'Écho de Nancy*, a newspaper which was regarded as being entirely German, the director of an important weekly, Canon Polimann, hero of the first world war, member of the National Council, and a member of the Chamber of Deputies in the Third Republic, agreed to allow himself to be elected president of the corporative group. In the same way in Brittany, where the Germans had backed two or three publications, fairly powerful, which supported the autonomist program, steps were taken to see that the directors of these publications were not elected to any corporative office and that all offices went to truly French publications. The Corporation of the Press was slow in getting underway because of its rather complicated structure but it did operate completely for about two years, the last part of 1942, all of 1943, and the first half of 1944. There can be no question that, from the professional point of view, the corporation was a success and its oldest member still thinks of it today with a feeling of longing. Aside from the fact that it enabled the French press, in this most difficult period, to solve technical problems which without the corporation would have remained insoluble, it also created between directors, editors, office staff, and workers an atmosphere of co-operation and confidence which proved to be beneficial to all.

That does not mean that there were not conflicts sometimes between the different elements of some enterprise, or between competing publications. But the corporation had established "corporative tribunals," similar in their powers to consular jurisdictions or to French labor tribunals, which succeeded in settling such disputes in a fair and humane manner.

The corporation also established a certain number of philanthropic works and mutual organizations which, unfortunately, did not last when the corporation itself came to an end.

V. *The Germans and the Corporation*

The Germans did not receive the creation of the National Corporation of the French Press with enthusiasm. Under the old rule of "divide and conquer," many among them thought that it would have been easier for them to dominate a scattered and disunited press than a powerful and solid block in the form of a corporation.

Luchaire, not without some skill, convinced them that this grouping simplified matters for them and that certain difficulties could be settled more easily on a higher level than on lower levels. It was thus the principle of "the least effort" which in the end led them to accept this new institution.

But though the corporation was accepted in Paris it was often tolerated only with ill-will by the *Propagandastaffel* chiefs and censors in the provinces. As a result there were a rather large number of incidents which in the end were settled to the benefit of the publications and to the confusion of the local *Propagandastaffels*.

At the beginning of 1943 the corporation was an established fact throughout the northern zone and the provincial censors no longer contested its existence. Many provincial publications, especially among the smaller ones, owed to it their continued existence. In fact the dispersion and the great number of these little publications gave a great deal of work to the *Propagandastaffel* who pretended to be unable to admit that they had any use. Thus during the first period of the occupation they succeeded in purely and simply suppressing a certain number of them. The responsible corporative representatives of the weekly provincial press succeeded in convincing the German authorities at 52 Champs Élysées that they should stop this practice. Thereafter when a censor proposed a suppression of some publication he was unable to proceed until the president of the National Commission for Weeklies had been informed and had been allowed to plead the cause of his threatened colleague with the superior officer in Paris. The president of the commission succeeded in nearly every case. He even managed to demand and obtain the removal of some local censorship officers, notably in the Orne, whom he had found, by his own personal investigations, to be engaged in particularly reprehensible actions.

In the same way serious and delicate problems such as those having to do with the requisition of French labor for Germany were able to be solved in a relatively favorable manner from the press point of view, thanks to the corporative organization. Without the corporation questions would have been settled locally and without appeal. There is no doubt that the contingents of workers taken from the French printing plants would have been far larger and that the operation would have been repeated more frequently.

VI. *Relations between Publications in the Two Zones*

During the first two years of the occupation there were practically no relationships between Press enterprises in the northern zone and those of the southern zone.

After the creation of the National Corporation of the French Press, Jean Luchaire attempted to establish official contact but did not succeed.

At the beginning of 1943 the question was taken up again through the more modest and less disturbing channel of the smaller publications. Explaining his plan to the Chief of Government, Pierre Laval, and to the president of the corporation, both of whom approved, the president of the national commission for weeklies in the northern zone brought together in Vichy a certain number of his colleagues from all the departements of the southern zone. Thereafter they met every two months, sometimes in Paris, more often in Vichy. The Maréchal received them and poured encouragement upon them.

The purpose of this operation was twofold. On the professional level it was to promote in the southern zone an organization comparable to that of the corporation which had proved its usefulness on both technical and social grounds; and, from the national point of view, to bring the press in the northern zone more news and instructions of a purely French character.

In the spring of 1944 the foundations of a broader liaison between the two zones had been laid, for daily papers. Air bombing preparatory to the landing, and the landing itself, with the resultant complications and the stoppage of transport which they brought, did not permit further efforts along these lines.

VII. *The French Press and the Liberation*

After having to endure, more than other people, the servitudes of an occupation, the journalists had every reason to rejoice at the liberation of their country.   Further, as they had had to manifest, far more than many others did, those qualities of true "resistance" which in such a situation consist of diplomacy, courage, and tenacity, their consciences were at peace; they thought they might be recompensed, and they were certain that they would never be reproached.

The few directors or editors who had wrongfully practiced a servile "collaborationism" followed the Germans in their retreat. They were an infinitely small minority. All the rest waited tranquilly at home for those whom legend already called the "liberators," the patriots.

In so doing they were unquestionably very wrong. For all of them, or nearly all, were immediately arrested and after imprisonment of greater or lesser length were pitilessly dragged before courts of justice, indicted for "treason" under Article 75.

Convictions of those who had directed the press were characterized as much by incoherence as by injustice. For doing something which had been approximately the same with every publication, since the German demands and the Vichy orientation notes had been identical throughout the northern zone, the range of sentences pronounced proved to be strangely diverse; in some places they were condemned to execution; in others to hard labor; and in others to a few months in prison. In some departements, for example the

Loiret, journalists were simply brought before a civic chamber and punished by nothing more than "national indignity" [deprival of various civic rights including those of voting; holding office; taking part in such activities as press, radio, or cinema; or acting as guardian to a child].

It is true that the particular kind of punishment inflicted made very little difference to the "purifiers." The important thing, above all else, was that thanks to any condemnation whatever they should be able to get their hands on press enterprises which were known to be prosperous and which excited all the more for that reason the sharpened appetites of the newcomers. The proof of this pre-established determination lies in the fact that where no actual physical person was responsible a theory was specially produced for the circumstances which assigned responsibility to the legal entity of the publication itself, whether this entity consisted in a corporation or simply in the title of the publication.

Press enterprises were at once put under sequestration while new teams of workers installed themselves shamelessly in the offices and workshops of the periodicals and there brought out other publications for which they used the paper, the machines, the archives, the subscription lists, and even the funds of their predecessors. This procedure was to be "legalized" after the event by a law dated 11 May 1946 which confirmed the seizure of press enterprises and their transfer to a trust especially created for that purpose, the SNEP [Société Nationale des Éditions de Presse]. Thus was consumated the spoliation of the press which the former and future president of the National Assembly, Édouard Herriot, did not hesitate to describe as "theft."

An ordinance of General de Gaulle had ruled that every newspaper title which had appeared during the occupation must disappear. Thus the names which the public had liked the best, Le Matin, Le Petit Parisien, Paris-Soir, and so many others, disappeared from one day to the next. Periodicals over a century old (such long life was not rare in the provinces) which had been respected by six or seven different political regimes, two revolutions, and an enemy occupation, nevertheless received no mercy from the "liberators."

The liberators were not unaware of the fact that the ordinary reader becomes attached to a title. They therefore took pains in most cases to adopt names for the new publications which were linked as much as possible to the names which had been condemned to disappear. Le Matin existed no longer; Ce Matin was born. Instead of Le Petit Parisien there was Le Parisien Libéré. In the provinces L'Ouest-France replaced L'Ouest-Éclair, Le Courrier de l'Ouest replaced Le Petit Courrier, and so on. And as the format and typographical presentation of the assassinated newspaper was also maintained the good and naive public sincerely believed "that the bottle was the same and only the cork had been changed."

. . . Nevertheless, though robbed, ruined, and barred from professional activity, the former directors of the press, even those who escaped hard labor, today live most miserably while the men who robbed them triumph. In their extreme distress they can still congratulate themselves on having at least kept their heads on their shoulders. Not all had this good fortune, beginning with the founder and president of the Press Corporation, who, condemned to death after having been horribly tortured, died courageously under French bullets.

Such was the life and the struggle of the French Press in the northern zone during the occupation. Such, after the German retreat, was its cruel and undeserved end.

(*Document No. 209*)
Fr. ed. 938-954

[Not dated]

A. CATHRINE

[M. Cathrine states that the above declaration was prepared with the collaboration of M. Claude Hisard, Director of Press for the southern zone, and of M. L. M. Poullain, publisher of La Vigie de Dieppe, *who was president of the Corporation of Weekly Publications in the northern zone.]*

PRESS

GEORGES SERVOINGT

Director of "L'Espoir Français"

I emphasize the following points to show the basis for my declaration.

From 1928 to 1944 I was director of two reviews successively, both of them propaganda publications, *L'Animateur des Temps Nouveaux* and *L'Espoir Français*. These two publications were characterized by their violent campaigns against Nazi doctrine and policies, against the danger of war that was developing in Germany, and against Bolshevism.

During the war I published many articles, leaflets, and issues of periodicals, and I organized broadcasts. All had but one purpose, to incite the French to fight.

Before the war I was already on the Gestapo blacklist. I left Paris with my colleagues and employees, all threatened as I was, in June 1940. As soon as the Gestapo reached Paris, they ransacked my office and removed the contents. They did the same at my private residence.

I had therefore no reason—in view of my anti-Nazi convictions, my patriotic sentiments proved by a record which speaks for itself, and the harm both moral and material done me by the Germans after the armistice—to work in any way whatever for the policies known as "collaboration."

I published *L'Espoir Français* again in the southern zone in February 1941 after seven months of non-publication. I did so because I thought it was my duty to give my help, however modest it might be, to the Chief of State and to his government. It was in connection with an issue which I published in June or July, 1941, that I became acquainted with the Chief of Government, President Laval. It was he who asked me to come and see him. Faithful to a determination which I had maintained for twelve years in holding aloof from all political circles, I had abstained from asking for any interviews whatever.

In the course of our talk I explained to President Laval the spirit in which I was republishing *L'Espoir Français*. I renounced in no way the campaign that I previously had conducted against Germany; I simply wished to try to make the French people understand that the policies of the Maréchal and his government had no purpose other than that of gaining time while waiting for the liberation. This brought out the usefulness of making clear the necessity for such policies, a necessity which was not obvious to the people as a whole. The President said to me, "You are right. Continue. I will help you."

I knew that on several occasions he had taken steps to interest the Ministry of Information in the distribution of my review. Marion, who was then secretary-general in that ministry, tried to block distribution. A variety of difficulties were created by Marion's services to prevent or delay the publication of issues which were too "independent." Everytime I asked President Laval to intervene he supported my point of view, even though it was contrary to directives issued to the press.

After Marion's departure and his replacement by Creyssel in the propaganda office and by Bonnefoy in the information office, *L'Espoir Français* was more widely distributed. The interest in my efforts thus shown by President Laval was never subordinated to press directives or to any pro-German policy. Neither directly nor indirectly did he ever make any comments on the attitude we implied, nor did he ask me—as might have been done under the policy of playing both sides which was then being followed—to publish anything whatever along the lines of the German suggestions from which it was not always easy for him to escape.

I can affirm, therefore, that President Laval supported my efforts in full realization of what I was doing, that is, to make the French be patient in waiting for the liberation.

On many occasions I was present at conversations between members of his staff and visitors. When visitors came away from a conversation with the President they were always astonished that what he had said to them contradicted the official policies of some members of his government. So it was too with those who were present at the orientation meetings which the Chief of Government attended periodically. This made it very clear that his basic thought did not correspond to the official instructions issued by genuinely collaborationist elements of the government. These instructions, in any case, were often made ineffective by opinions which President Laval expressed during such meetings.

I could report many statements which I heard from those about him that bring out clearly the President's hostility toward any action against the maquis, and his clemency toward members of the resistance whose cases were brought to his attention. But I will not cite these statements, since I wish to speak only of what I knew at first hand. The following are facts of that kind.

One of my friends, Pastor Jean Lauge, today director of protestant chaplains for the French army of occupation in Germany, came to Vichy one day to ask me to try to prevent the execution of young Yves Toledano, who had been condemned to death as a spy by a German court. When President Laval was informed of this case, he said to me, "If I intervened with the Germans, that alone would be enough to make his execution certain." He then telephoned the prefect, instructing him to take the most effective steps possible in agreement with Jean Lauge, who would go and explain the matter to him. By an appeal to the Führer, which the prefect succeeded in getting the Germans to permit, time was gained. Then came the liberation and Yves Toledano's life was saved.

Two other friends of mine, André Borie, owner of the only big French construction firm which did not work for the Germans, and Marcel Hohberg, his son-in-law, were arrested by the Germans for some frivolous reason. But Borie was supplying food to all the various maquis of the Cantal with his motor trucks, and Hohberg was sought by the Gestapo because of certain contacts he maintained with the English. I had been hiding him and his wife for several weeks in my home. It was important that the Germans should not know exactly who Borie and Hohberg were. Once again, on my request, President Laval intervened with the prefect, who made use of his connections to get my friends released the day after they were arrested and before any inquiry could be made regarding their names.

One last important fact. I had been asked by two members of the "Goelette" network to find out the President's attitude toward an interview of which the purpose was to arrange a meeting between himself and General Kœnig with a view to a transfer of powers, and with the purpose of avoiding bloodshed between Frenchmen at the liberation. On my advice, the Chief of Government accepted the idea. But the two resistants demanded as a preliminary condition the liberation of three of their group, the Countess de La Chapelle, Mme Bonnet and Mme Dumazaud, who were held by the Militia and who were threatened with execution (according to a statement by Bout-de-l'An to Guérard) or at least with deportation. The President left the same day for Paris and told Guérard to take the necessary steps. Guérard soon joined the President, bringing with him one of the two members of the Goelette network. From Paris, the President insisted that the three women should be freed. Repeated approaches to the Militia by Darbou finally obtained their release.

Such are the facts with which I was personally acquainted. I report them today with complete objectivity, and with the sole regret that I was not asked to testify in the summary trial of the President.

(Document No. 27)
Fr. ed. 955-957

Paris, 10 June 1947

GEORGES SERVOINGT

THE PRESS

ANTOINE-MARIE PIÉTRI

Civil Servant in the Ministry of Information

I arrived in Paris on 20 January 1942. I came from Vichy where throughout the preceding year, I had served as chief of the press and censorship services in the Ministry of Information.

My new mission as press director in the capital—my exact title was "delegate for the press in the occupied territories"—had been precisely stated in instructions which I had received verbally, before my departure from Vichy, from M. Dumoulin de la Barthète, director of cabinet for the Chief of State, and from M. Paul Marion, at that time secretary-general of Information, as well as from Maréchal Pétain himself.

My instructions specified the attitude which I was to take toward the [French] press in the occupied zone, and toward the press and censorship services of the occupying authorities.

Available sources of information were in the hands of the Germans; censorship was entirely their own affair and I did not have even a theoretical right to concern myself with it. Thus my powers were reduced to the privilege of protesting, but only after the event, to the *Propagandastaffel* and the German embassy; and to the use of the power of persuasion—this I would have to acquire—over my former journalistic colleagues of the Paris press.

With regard to these latter, the situation was not good. In a resounding speech which the German censorship had banned, Maréchal Pétain had dealt in just the same way with the Gaullist rebels, who were pro-English, and the domestic rebels, who were pro-German, their essential elements being political parties such as the RNP and certain Paris newspapers. In such an atmosphere the press representative of the Vichy government had to move with padded footsteps. He was inevitably in complete accord with the opinions expressed by his chief, even if these opinions were to some extent unjust, and it was difficult for him, except in certain personal cases, to show a cordiality which would have been regarded as a disavowal of the policies being followed on the banks of the Allier [river on which Vichy is located].

The Germans themselves, strongly influenced by the journalists who were the most favorable to them, looked askance at a French civil servant who was trying to insinuate his own organization into a field of which they were extremely jealous. The greatest difficulties of my task, in fact, were due to the strength of Dr. Goebbels as third most important person in the Third Reich, to his belief that propaganda is an exact science, and to the way his agents in uniform worked havoc in Paris, under his protection.

Dr. Goebbels had not yet given up the plan of creating a separationist movement in France, pro-German and anti-Vichy. A typical maneuver for achieving this purpose was as follows.

Wartime controls barred any adjustment of salaries which was not approved by the occupying authorities. The Germans systematically refused all changes. The [French] press, controlled by the Germans, thereupon violently attacked Vichy, accusing the government of starving the working classes and of organizing a food blockade of Paris. There was no way of answering this propaganda and it was beginning to bear some fruit, though not really very effectively.

The press conferences of the *Propagandastaffel* were cleverly conducted and though on the understandable grounds of personal dignity I refused to be present at them I did have an agent there who was a French agent in the most noble meaning of that term. On many occasions the questions which he asked embarrassed the speakers, and from this fact it was possible to obtain important indications of what was happening, particularly when the recruiting of French workers for Germany was being first organized.

But the Germans also had their own agents in my organization, and it was for that reason, some of my remarks having been reported, that I had to put a stop to the press conferences which I had arranged.

30

However, in April 1942, when President Laval returned to power, there was the beginning of a friendly understanding between the French at Vichy and those in Paris. The new Chief of Government had realized, in fact, that in the news field he could not retain any political influence except by abandoning everything which concerned the technical and financial side of the press. It was in this way that Jean Luchaire, president of the Press Association [a "corporation" with official powers], himself became his own government commissioner, all-powerful in that field. Suddenly he showed no further hostility to Vichy and allowed me to work in a new atmosphere. As a result, in full agreement with the Chief of Government, I was able to begin to explain that, although the necessities of the occupation were real, there was no need to go farther than the occupant himself desired. If Germany lost the war the Paris press would have accomplished a mission of self-sacrifice, but it would be protected by the Maréchal only in so far as it had not forsaken him. This was precisely the meaning of a number of articles by Charles Maurras in L'Action Française, which had been evacuated to Lyon; it was being said, wrongly in my opinion, that these articles were inspired by someone on a very high level. Further, no one ever conceived the thought that the Maréchal would not continue to be the sole holder of the sovereignty of France, and the sole expression of the national will, or that the day would come when the legality and legitimacy of his power would be questioned.

Thus closer relations were established; they continued to the end, if exception is made of those men who went too far along the German road and were left with no alternative except to bet more and more heavily on disaster.

The conflict was limited to one in which the waiting policy of Vichy was confronted with varying collaboration policies, whose hues were multiple. There was no question of resistance, and even those who as a result of certain disappointments in dealing with the Germans, or because their thought truly moved along such lines, might have moved toward a policy of resistance, were stopped short in their tendencies by the assassination of Pucheu. This act of savagery, which foreshadowed so many others, confirmed in their fidelity to the Maréchal many hundreds of officials whose help to the resistance would have been effective.

The chief of the German censorship was Captain Junges, whose love of France was indisputable. I had succeeded in gaining his confidence, and in putting into effect a system which operated only as between the two of us. In accordance with a verbal arrangement he sent me the proofs of the weeklies, especially Le Pilori [anti-Jewish publication], and I made cuts, almost entirely in articles of denunciation and accusation. Captain Junges then took the responsibility for these cuts; in this way, for many months, the German censorship blocked maneuvers which in some cases were inspired by the Gestapo.

Unfortunately, the Gestapo made an investigation and Junges was saved only by highly placed persons who protected him. He was, however, sent in disgrace to Greece, with the prospect of being sent on to the Russian front if things did not go better with him. M. Gaston Guillaux, an old journalist who was my assistant at that time, was the only one who knew the secret of this extraordinary man-to-man arrangement.

My relations with the successor of Junges, Dr. Eich, inevitably were affected by that incident. Unwilling to undergo the fate of his unhappy predecessor, he treated me with a coldness which he thought would make him safe. But Junges had left me an extremely valuable contact in the *Propagandastaffel* in the person of Mlle Kuntzmann, his secretary. She always kept me informed as to the atmosphere of the moment, particularly regarding the waves of anti-Lavalism which at almost regular intervals would flow out of Berlin, in most cases stirred up by Gauleiter Sauckel, the great labor chief later hanged at Nüremberg.

In this way we were able to forestall many of the occupant's maneuvers, though we were sometimes caught. A standard lie was that if three workers signed up voluntarily to go to Germany, one prisoner could be designated by name for release. This led to the development of a black market in liberations, and the promises made were not kept. This piece of trickery obtained results in the provinces, and a number of days of negotiation were necessary before it could be contradicted. Along the same lines, we were able to put a stop to articles of German inspiration [in the French press] which invited women to go to Germany as workers, insinuating in only slightly veiled language that huge profits were possible, not at all derived from working in a factory.

President Laval had hoped that the German censorship would vanish, to be replaced by a purely French organization. At his request I had prepared a plan for such a change, to include the entire occupied zone. But though the German diplomatic service had accepted this point of view it met with a blunt veto from Gœbbels, who, natural protector of the German censors, all of whom were former newspaper men, was unwilling at any price to see them leave their comfortable posts for the fighting front. Further, as the Germans met with reverses in Africa and the East, distrust increased, and the entire occupation organization became more troublesome in their operations.

When Maréchal Pétain came to Paris in 1944 there was an absolute ban on any preliminary mention of his visit, in the press or on the radio. The Germans feared a nationalist explosion. The visit, however, did take place; as is proved by the newspapers of those days, hundreds of thousands of people, who in some mysterious way had known what was going to happen, crowded the route which he was to take, and the square in front of the Hotel de Ville.

The Maréchal's speech, given from the balcony of the Hotel de Ville, could not be broadcast but was nevertheless recorded by the radio services. This recording is certainly among those in the radio archives, and it is regrettable that there was no idea of having it heard in the High Court [special court created at the time of the liberation for the trial of persons accused of treason during the occupation.]

These journeys of the Chief of State in the occupied zone, which he had never entered until that time, set loose the same delirious enthusiasm in Paris as in Rouen, Nancy, or Dijon. Furthermore, we had been able to arrange that the censorship of the reports to be given in the newspapers was entirely in our hands, without any German interference, which enabled us to avoid any infringements of good taste.

This brings me to a rather tense incident that involved Mr. von Renthe-Fink, German Minister in Vichy. He was absolutely determined that the press should mention that when confronted with the damage done to the cathedral at Rouen by the British Air Force, the Chief of State had said that he "hated the English." I do not know whether, in fact, he made such a remark, but as the cabinet of the Maréchal had told me nothing about it, I saw no reason to accept such an item of news from Mr. von Renthe-Fink, who was thereupon extremely displeased. I had to put a stop to his only slightly veiled language by hanging up the telephone.

Several days later the landing was to harden the German attitude still more, and their nervousness increased. That is why the return from Germany of Philippe Henriot, Secretary of State for Information, relieved me of the effects of the occupant's bad mood.

I do not know whether or not the archives of the resistance contain a true account of that incident and the names of those who killed Philippe Henriot on 28 June 1944 at 5:30 in the morning. I know only that, as far as I am concerned, nothing in the facts of which I was aware at the time seemed to indicate that the resistance was responsible for the assassination. I shall mention two points in particular.

The first is that M. Rottee, Director of the General Intelligence Service, speaking in my presence to M. Bussière, Prefect of Police, several hours after the assassination, said to the prefect, "Once more it was those black Citroens [fast French automobile with front-wheel drive] on which the Germans forbid the French police to fire."

The second point is that Mme Philippe Henriot, who, according to all the newspapers of that time, had supposedly recognized her husband's assassin, a man who in turn was shot down by the Militia after being pursued across Paris, told me confidentially "How could I have recognized him? I scarcely saw him . . ."

I entrust these two observations to those who may investigate the matter in the future.

(Document No. 217)
Fr. ed. 958-961

Paris, 8 April 1954

A. M. PIÉTRI
Antoine Marie Piétri

CINEMATOGRAPHY DURING
THE OCCUPATION

ROGER RICHEBÉ

*Director of the Organization Committee
of the Cinematograph Industry*

I the undersigned Roger Richebé, President and Director-General of the Société des Films Roger Richebé, S. A., and film producer, make the following declaration.

The Memoirs of Goebbels, British edition, *The Goebbels Diaries*, published by Hamish Hamilton, London, contains the following words on page 159: *13 May 1942. . . . Great care must be taken to prevent the French from building a new reputation for artistic films under our sponsorship which could bring us serious competition in the European market. I shall arrange that the French cinema actors with the greatest talent are used more and more in German films.*

During the Nuremberg trial, the following documents were presented:

Translation of Document No. NG 5211
(Seal)
Strictly Confidential

(Seal)
Must be treated as strictly confidential

Telegram

(In secret code according to regulations)

Paris, 15 December 1943 at 1:35 a.m.
Received 15 December 1943 at 3:15 a.m.
No. 7814 of 14 December; very urgent; deliver immediately even at night.

Strictly Confidential

To be submitted immediately to the Reich Minister of Foreign Affairs at pol II (VS); continues telegrams of 9th instant No. 7716.

The commander of the Security Police and of the SD [*Sicherheitsdienst*] has a list of a total of 1,500 persons to be arrested in France during an operation planned for this purpose. Among the 1,500 persons there are 103 important persons in the highest positions in administrative, political, economic, and cultural spheres. In the preparation of this list there was complete agreement between the Embassy and the Military Commander on 67 of the persons named. The following, indicated as No. 2, is the list of these 67 persons, together with comments by the SD, on the subject of whose elimination there is complete agreement between the SD, the Military Commander, and the Embassy. (The remainder of the text is in clear, but the SD comments are in secret code). . . .

(63) Richebé, Roger, director of the COIC (Trade Committee controlling the French Cinematographic Profession) 15 avenue Victor-Emmanuel-III, Paris.

(64) Desbrosses, Jean, chief of the Film Production Service of the COIC, 4 rue Charles-Dickens, Paris. . . .

Following is a translation of comments in secret code;

Remarks concerning No. 1. . . .
No. 63: Responsible for continuous passive sabotage of German interests.
No. 64: Has a declared anti-German attitude; formerly with strong English connections.

The above having been presented[1]:

There is no doubt that the decision taken by the Germans with regard to M. Jean Desbrosses and myself on 15 December 1943 is the logical result of the blocking of the German cinema policy as it had been planned by Goebbels in 1942. I can certify that having been chosen by my fellow members of the profession as a member of the executive committee of the Organization Committee for the Motion Picture Industry, serving from April 1942 to 1 December 1943, and from that time until the liberation as executive-president in accordance with the unanimous vote of the members of the cinematograph industry, I was able in the exercise of my functions to observe and to have full knowledge of the action and directives of the government in this field.

The Germans had in France a producing organization known as "Continental Films," with great financial resources, which took care at all times to secure the best technicians and the best artists. They also had the Society SOGEC which owned an important circuit of motion picture theaters to which a number of others were added as a result of various juridical or extra-juridical devices. With these two organizations under their control, the Germans were able to bring considerable pressure to bear against any purely French cinema organization.

It should be noted too that the companies with German interests received unlimited support from both the civilian and the military German authorities. This support in many cases was not merely financial but also political and even of a police character.

Thus the resumption and maintenance of a purely French cinematograph industry encountered considerable difficulties, among which the following should be mentioned:

—Interference from the German administration, and demands by the censorship;

—the division of France into two zones and the extreme difficulty of communicating in any regular way;

—the shortage of raw materials and of electric current, which lengthened the time necessary for producing a film and developed a black market in certain indispensable products such as plaster, three-ply, etc.;

—the impossibility of exporting films, though before the war exportation had provided 40 per cent of receipts—only the German-controlled company, Continental Films, having the right to export French films.

In spite of these difficulties, it was possible to produce in 1942 and 1943 over 160 new films of which the quality constituted a victorious triumph on French screens not only over German films but also over films produced by the German-controlled French film company, Continental Films.

This work was obviously in the professional interests of the French cinematograph industry but it was also in a national interest, and I can say that the efforts of the members of the French industry were responsible for this success. These men were grouped together in the COIC [Organization Committee for the Cinematograph Industry] which served as a management board for all cinematograph activities; it was responsible to the Ministry of Information and was the executive agency for all government action in this field.

In spite of pressure from the German authorities and from certain French

---

1. M. Richebé uses a phrase traditional in French legal documents, *Ceci exposé.*

extremist elements, the General Executive Council for the cinema, directly responsible to President Laval, Chief of Government, concentrated on encouraging national production of films, on slowing down and limiting the action of companies under German control, and on hampering the execution of programs of political propaganda films, though it received requests for such programs and was even placed under a variety of pressures.

The COIC and the General Executive Council for the cinema were led to recommend and to take a certain number of measures for the organization of the French cinematograph industry. These measures were no more than an application of recommendations which had been made urgently before the war, particularly those in a general report prepared in 1936 by M. de Carmoy, Inspector of Finance, at the request of the French High Economic Council.

For the first time in the history of the cinema the government agreed to study special legislative measures in the interests of the cinema and to apply these measures. This legislation, it must be emphasized, was in general maintained after the liberation and is still in force.

The most important of these measures follow:

—the law of 26 October 1940 requiring permission to enter the cinematographic profession;

——the ban on double-feature programs;

—the requirement that the rental payment for a film must be a percentage of the door receipts;

—institution of independent auditing of door receipts;

—establishment of a public register of the cinematograph professions in which cession of, or mortages on, film receipts would be inscribed;

—authorization for the production of films, auditing of the financing of production and so on.

The purpose of these measures as a whole was to cleanse and strengthen a profession and industry which had seen an increasing number of failures at the outbreak of the war and of which the credit was seriously compromised.

In executing this program the government and the General Executive Council for the Cinema gave close attention to the desires of the industry itself. In my opinion the measures which they took, regarded as a whole, have greatly contributed to the fact that when the war ended the French cinema industry, though gravely hampered by the difficulties listed above, constituted a healthy and well-balanced instrument and was able to take its place again in the French market and in world markets.

Personally, I have never had any political activity. I have never belonged to any group or association of a political character. For the last thirty-five years I have devoted myself entirely to the French cinematograph industry, in the exhibition of films, in studio work, and in film production. It was because of the technical knowledge and general experience I acquired during my long career that my immediate associates, and later the entire industry, chose me to represent them and to defend them during the German occupation. Consequently my testimony can have no political implication and is simply a precise reflection of the truth.

(Document No. 104)
Fr. ed. 962-964

Paris, 14 March 1949

R. RICHEBÉ

THE THEATERS

RENÉ ROCHER

*Director of the Odéon
[State] Theater; President of
the Organization Committee
for Public Performances,
from 1942 to 1944*

Paradoxical though it may seem, and contrary to the legend in the creation of which such effort has since been spent, it is indisputable that the theater in France during the German occupation from 1940 to 1944 was at least as prosperous as it had been during the preceding years.

As soon as they entered Paris the Germans, for propaganda motives quite easily understood, strove to give the capital a normal life. With this purpose they encouraged and facilitated to the greatest possible extent the re-opening and the re-organization of all places devoted to public entertainment.

From September 1940, theater life gradually regained its normal rhythm. It is true that the first results of this activity were rather timid and not very interesting, but very soon the impetus given by the national theaters encouraged all the directors of other Paris theaters to follow their example. (The national theaters were at that time directed by Jacques Rouché, at the Opéra and Opéra-Comique, and Jacques Copeau at the Comédie Française and the Odéon.)

The four national theaters were under the exclusive control of the French government. Jérôme Carcopino was then Minister Secretary of State for National Education and Louis Hautecœur was Secretary-General for Fine Arts. But the theaters of Paris as a whole, during this first period, 1940 to 1941, were under the direct control of the *Propagandastaffel* and were dealt with only by this German organization.

However, when the occupation authorities realized the difficulties which they would have in achieving the proper operation of undertakings of which they were ignorant or with which they were only slightly familiar they put themselves in the hands of a certain Roger Capgras to whom they entrusted the task of aiding them in this difficult problem. They soon discovered that this Capgras had none of the necessary qualities and that, in any case, he was completely incompetent in theatrical matters.

The occupation authorities then relied for several months on Robert Trébor, president of the association of the directors of theaters, who was unquestionably the man best qualified to guide and assist them. Trébor, however, did not play his part of adviser for very long. Some rather unpleasant intrigues and more or less camouflaged denunciations led them to regard him as a suspicious person; he was soon discarded.

In January 1941 — when nearly all the theaters had re-opened their doors, and nearly all the cinemas as well — control of the theaters was entrusted to Gaston Baty, Charles Dullin, Louis Jouvet, and Pierre Renoir, in direct liaison with the *Propagandastaffel*. Since they had the full confidence of the occupation authorities, Baty, Dullin, Jouvet and Renoir had control over the whole of the theatrical undertakings. They were supported and aided by the members of the "Collaboration" group which had just been founded, the theater section of which was presided over by Jean Sarment.

Under this regime everything went along normally for several months. To a considerable extent because of the perfect working of the Metro [Paris underground railway which carried up to five million passengers a day during the occupation], the Paris public, hungry for distraction and quickly adapted to new timetables (performances began at about seven o'clock in the evening and ended before eleven o'clock), came to the theaters in masses.

And as the occupation lengthened and the occupants made themselves at home, certain technical and professional problems inevitably arose. The French government then perceived that the Germans, by encouraging the prosperity of the theaters, as they did, would soon be able to replace the influence of the French authorities by their own, and would be able even to turn out the French completely. The theater was thus running the risk of finding itself soon under the exclusive and absolute control of the *Propagandastaffel*; the four confidential directors, named above, were in fact no more than its instrument. If this situation continued it could become extremely serious.

It was to combat this danger that the Chief of State, acting on a report from the Minister Secretary of State for National Education, and in accordance with the law of 16 August 1940 which provided a temporary organization for industrial production, issued a decree dated 7 July 1941, at Vichy, establishing an Organization Committee for Public Performances (COES).

This decree met the situation perfectly. It made it possible to establish a specifically French agency for regulating and organizing the industry of public presentations — an industry which in fact had greatly needed such organization for many years. Above all, the new arrangement had the essential advantage of avoiding complete seizure and control of the theater in France by the German authorities. It is certain that without this beneficent decree the French theater would have fallen inescapably into the hands of a German organization under the absolute control of a German gauleiter.

It was true that the COES, modeled after all the other organization committees, could not act, and in principle ought not to act or develop its operations, except with the agreement of the German services; in principle it remained under the continual control of the *Propagandastaffel*. Nevertheless in actual fact it was soon to slip out of this foreign control and to come entirely under the French government.

Jean-Louis Vaudoyer, in his position as administrator-general of the Comédie Française, first French theater, was the first executive president of the COES. Vaudoyer, though an eminent man of letters, was not a "man of the theater." He was almost totally ignorant of the technique and procedure of the theatrical profession and of the customs and needs of those who belonged to it. He therefore retired after a few months without having taken any steps whatever for the organization of the committee which had been entrusted to him.

It was under these conditions that Jérôme Carcopino asked René Rocher, in his capacity as the director of the Odéon, second French theater, to be good enough to take the responsibility for organizing the COES. René

Rocher did belong to the profession, having directed many large theaters since 1923, and therefore seemed to be particularly well qualified. Nevertheless he declined the offer. Competely absorbed in the difficult task he had undertaken at the Odéon he feared that he would be unable to devote himself sufficiently to these new duties. It was only after being strongly urged by Jérôme Carcopino and Louis Hautecœur that he finally accepted. He received his official appointment as executive president of the COES in May 1942 and immediately organized the various services of the new agency in such a way that they functioned normally and to the satisfaction of all—except possibly the occupants—until August 1944.

As might be expected, the occupation authorities without opposing the COES in principle had not looked very favorably on the creation of a French agency which would substitute its influence for that of the Germans. However, by using ingenuity and diplomacy, the executive president succeeded in smoothing the angles and avoiding even the slightest incident. Everything went along normally until the beginning of 1944. At that time, as restrictions became more and more harsh, air raids more and more numerous, and difficulties greater and greater, everything became extremely complicated. Events were making the Germans more suspicious and more ready to take offense, and relations with them became more sensitive. On the initiative of certain advisers who were in fact French, the *Propaganda-staffel* thought it best to harden its attitude toward the COES and this led to further tension in the relationship. However, the worst was always avoided and the COES was able to accomplish to the very end the task which had been entrusted to it, without any serious incident.

It was the COES, in both the occupied and unoccupied zones, which was responsible, in addition to its control and regulation of all theatrical activity, for census and registration of all persons, both employers and employees, connected with such activities.

It was the COES which was responsible in both the occupied and unoccupied zones for the allocation of supplies indispensable for the normal operation of theatrical undertakings. It was thanks to the COES that all workers engaged in the theatrical profession were saved from being sent to Germany under the Obligatory Labor Service. It was thanks to the COES that the application of the racial laws to theatrical undertakings was avoided, not without difficulty. And it was thanks to the COES, it must be repeated, that the danger of direct and absolute control by the occupation authorities over the theatrical industry in France was disappointed.

Further, it was on the initiative of the COES that the "professional family of public performers" [1] was created by the decree of 17 April 1942.

Finally, and most important of all, it was on the initiative of COES that law No. 452, dealing with public performances, was promulgated on 27 December 1943. (This law was promulgated at Vichy under the signatures of Pierre Laval, Chief of Government, Maurice Gabolde and Abel Bonnard.) It must be believed that this law No. 452, finally regulating the exercise of a profession which had never previously been provided for in this way, brought undeniable advantages, as it was re-issued word for word by the "provisional government for the Republic" in October 1945 as ordinance No. 45-2339 of 13 October 1945 on the subject of public presentations, signed

---

1. ["La Famille Professionnelle des Spectacles" included those who appeared in theaters, music halls, circuses, night clubs, films and any similar activities.]

de Gaulle, Capitant and Parodi, and published in the *Journal Officiel* No. 242 dated 14 October 1945. It is still in effect in 1955.

It will not be possible to present here a list of all the steps taken by the COES from 1942 to 1944. To be convinced and to see clearly the extent to which this organization, established by the Vichy government, was able to aid theatrical enterprises while protecting them from absolute seizure by the German authorities, it will be sufficient to refer to:

(1) The complete file of *l'Officiel du Spectacle*, the professionnal publication of the COES, consisting of twenty issues numbered from 1 to 20 dated from September 1942 to June 1944. This *Officiel du Spectacle* was published as a supplement to *la Semaine à Paris* [weekly guide to events, sold to the public] by the staff of the latter publication but under the control of the COES, which was entirely responsible for the editorial side. It should be easy to obtain the entire file of these *Officiel du Spectacle* through *Semaine à Paris*, still published under the same director, Ribadeau-Dumas. *L'Officiel du Spectacle* presented each month the innumerable activities of the COES and the beneficial measures taken by it through the decisions of its executive president.

(2) The yearbook, *l'Annuaire Général du Spectacle en France*, in one volume covering the years 1942-1943 and a second volume for the year 1944; together with *l'Annuaire du Théâtre* for the year 1945 (one volume).

In these three yearbooks will be found a complete and detailed record of all the activities, both administrative and artistic, of theatrical life in France in the free zone as well as in the occupied zone during the German occupation from 1940 to 1944. This yearbook is at present still published by Éditions Ardo at 4 rue de Rome, Paris VIII, where it should be possible to obtain the three volumes referred to above which will confirm the information given here.

On the artistic side, too, it would not be possible to note here all the important theatrical productions which, by their value, would prove how astonishing was the vitality and true prosperity of the theater in France from 1940 to 1944. For such proof it would be necessary to obtain and use in support of what we are claiming the following publications which appeared under the official supervision of the COES and of the services of the secretariat-general of Fine Arts during this period:

(1) *Annuaire Général du Spectacle en France*, volumes for 1942-1943 and 1944; *Annuaire du Théâtre*, volume for 1945.

(2) The complete file of the *Revue des Beaux-Arts de France*, published by the Ministry of National Education and the secretariat-general of Fine Arts, nine issues, numbered 1 to 9, dated October 1942 to March 1944, through Éditions Vanoest, 3 et 5 rue du Petit-Pont, Paris V.

It is of special interest to point out that in *l'Officiel du Spectacle* will be found a series of articles on legal subjects signed by Robert Lecourt, doctor of laws, attorney at the Court of Appeals. It was at the urgent request of M. Lecourt that the executive president of the COES (Rocher) had finally agreed to entrust to him this series of articles in a "vichyite" publication, which of course *l'Officiel du Spectacle* certainly was. Robert Lecourt had acted as the lawyer for the COES in certain very small matters which concerned the organization.

Under the Fourth Republic, Robert Lecourt became a member of the National Assembly and a minister, and is today president of the parliamentary group of the MRP [Popular Republic Movement, new name for the former Catholic party].

We may note, however, merely for the sake of the record, a few of the most important artistic events from September 1941 to June 1944:

1941-1942

OPÉRA AND OPÉRA-COMIQUE :

150th anniversary of the death of Mozart: Don Juan, L'Enlèvement au Sérail.
Centenary of Massenet: Thaïs, Grisélidis.
Boléro, by Maurice Ravel.
Les Animaux Modèles, by Francis Poulenc.

COMÉDIE-FRANÇAISE :

Cyrano de Bergerac, by Edmond Rostand.
Iphigénie à Aulis, by Jean Moréas.
Hamlet, by Shakespeare (Guy de Pourtalès).
Iphigénie en Tauride, by Goethe (P. du Colombier).

ODÉON :

Le Comédien pris à son jeu, by Henri Ghéon.
César Birotteau, by Emile Fabre (after Balzac).
Le Bourgeois Gentilhomme, by Molière.
Napoléon Unique, by Paul Raynal.
Don Carlos, by Schiller (Jean Sarment).

ATELIER :

Vêtir ceux qui sont nus, by Pirandello.
Eurydice, by Jean Anouilh.
Sylvie et le Fantôme, by Alfred Adam.

AMBASSADEURS :

Échec à Don Juan, by Claude-André Puget.

ATHÉNÉE :

Comédie en trois actes, by H.-G. Clouzot.

MICHODIÈRE :

Hyménée, by Édouard Bourdet.

MADELEINE :

N'écoutez pas, Mesdames, by Sacha Guitry.

MONTPARNASSE :

Marie Stuart, by Marcelle Maurette.

COMÉDIE CHAMPS-ÉLYSÉES :

Candida, by Bernard Shaw.
Jeanne avec nous, by Claude Vermorel.

ŒUVRE :

L'Annonce faite à Marie, by Paul Claudel.

CHATELET :

Valses de Vienne, by Strauss.

1942-1943

OPÉRA AND OPÉRA-COMIQUE :

Marouf, by Henri Rabaud (L. Népoty).
Antigone, by Arthur Honegger (Jean Cocteau).
Pénélope, by Gabriel Fauré (René Fauchois).
Ariane à Naxos, by Richard Strauss (Paul Spaak).

COMÉDIE-FRANÇAISE :

La Reine Morte, by Henri de Montherlant.
Renaud et Armide, by Jean Cocteau.
Iphigénie à Delphes, by G. Hauptmann (P. du Colombier).

ODÉON :

La Duchesse en sabots, by J.-M. Renaitour.
Antigone, by Sophocle (André Bonnard).
Le Mariage de Figaro, by Beaumarchais.
Souvenez-vous, Madame, by Maurice Rostand.
La Vie et la Mort du roi Jean, by Shakespeare (Longworth-Chambrun).

ATELIER :

L'Honorable Monsieur Pépys, by Georges Couturier.

ATHÉNÉE :

La Part du Feu, by Louis Ducreux.

CHATELET :

Valses de France, by Henri Casadessus.

CITÉ *(Sarah-Bernhardt)* :

Richard III, by Shakespeare (André Obey).
Les Mouches, by Jean-Paul Sartre.

COMÉDIE CHAMPS-ÉLYSÉES :

Le Survivant, by Jean-François Noël.

GYMNASE :

Rêves d'Amour, by René Fauchois.

MATHURINS :

Deirdre des Douleurs, by J.-M. Synge.
Solness le Constructeur, by Ibsen.

MICHODIÈRE :

Père, by Édouard Bourdet.

MONTPARNASSE :

La Mégère apprivoisée, by Shakespeare (G. de la Fouchardière).
Macbeth, by Shakespeare (Gaston Baty).

NOCTAMBULES :

Le Bout de la route, by Jean Giono.

RENAISSANCE :

La Célestine, by F. de Rojas (Paul Achard).

1943-1944

OPÉRA AND OPÉRA-COMIQUE :

Othello, by Verdi.
Alceste, by Gluck.
La Tragédie de Salomé, by Florent Schmitt.
Guignol et Pandore, by André Jolivet.
Amphitryon 38, by Marcel Bertrand (J. Giraudoux).
Fantaisie Nocturne, by Alfred Bachelet.

COMÉDIE-FRANÇAISE :

Eleven new plays or revivals, including:
Le Soulier de Satin, by Paul Claudel.
Le Bourgeois Gentilhomme, by Molière (début of Raimu).

ODÉON :

Twenty-seven new plays or revivals, including:
Un fil à la patte, by Georges Feydeau.
Monsieur de Pourceaugnac, by Molière.
L'Étoile de Séville, by Lope de Vega (Guillot de Saix).

ATELIER :

Antigone, by Jean Anouilh.

ATHÉNÉE :

Am-Stram-Gram, by André Roussin.

BOUFFES-PARISIENS :

Les J-3, by Roger Ferdinand.

ÉDOUARD-VII :

Le Roi Christine, by Marcelle Maurette (with Cécile Sorel).

GYMNASE :

Le Maître de son cœur, by Paul Raynal.

HÉBERTOT :

Pygmalion, by Bernard Shaw.
Sodome et Gomorrhe, by Jean Giraudoux.

MICHODIÈRE :

Le Voyageur sans bagage, by Jean Anouilh (P. Fresnay).

MONTPARNASSE :

Hedda Gabler, by Ibsen.
Le Grand Poucet, by Claude-André Puget.

ŒUVRE :

La Danse de Mort, by Strindberg.

SAINT-GEORGES :

L'École des Ménages, by Balzac.
Fils de Personne, by Henri de Montherlant.

CITÉ *(Sarah-Bernhardt)* :

La Vie est un songe, de Calderon (Alexandre Arnoux).

VIEUX-COLOMBIER :

Huis-Clos, by Jean-Paul Sartre.

From 1941 to 1944 many subsidies were granted by the Vichy government to all French theatrical activities both in the free zone and in the occupied zone.   These subsidies were distributed by the Secretariat of Fine Arts and the COES to the most suitable undertakings.   It was thanks to this step that it was possible to create the various theatrical groups and most of the companies which are playing today.

(Document No. 254)
Fr. ed. 965-972

Paris, 29 March 1955

RENÉ ROCHER

PART FIVE

MARÉCHAL PÉTAIN

CHAPTER XIX

DECLARATIONS CONCERNING MARÉCHAL PÉTAIN

MINISTERS OF THE VICHY GOVERNMENT

PHILIPPE PÉTAIN

Maréchal of France

[*A statement made in September 1948 on the Ile d'Yeu by Maréchal Pétain to his attorney, Maitre Isorni.*]

« The French should recognize that during the four years in which I acted as Chief of State their vital interests were continuously and passionately defended by those who were charged with them.   Personal shortcomings are inevitable in all human undertakings.   The condemnations visited upon so many servants of the country, striking against their honor, their life or their liberty, and their property, are not deserved.   France was not betrayed by her chiefs, by her ministers, or by her civil servants.

« I owe this testimony to all those who, on my responsibility, having sacrificed themselves during the most difficult and most tragic hours of our history, have suffered unjustly because of it, and still suffer.

« I owe this testimony to all citizens, whoever they may be, who undergo these same hardships as a result of their fidelity to me and to the principles of civilization for which I stand.

« By rendering justice to them the French can find again the way to that union for which I never ceased to work when I was in power and which is essential to their safety. »

I the undersigned Jacques Isorni certify that the above text was prepared at the request of Maréchal Pétain, and in agreement with him, while I was on a visit to the Ile d'Yeu in September 1948.   It was his intention to copy it out in his own hand.

(Document No. 57)
Fr. ed. 977

Paris, 10 February 1958.

J. ISORNI

PETITION FOR REHEARING
PRESENTED ON BEHALF OF PÉTAIN
PÉTAIN'S DRAFT OF NEW CONSTITUTION

JACQUES ISORNI and JEAN LEMAIRE

Attorneys at the Court of Appeals of Paris;
Attorneys for Maréchal Pétain

A book entitled Requête en Revision pour Philippe Pétain *by Jacques Isorni and Jean Lemaire, published by Flammarion, Paris, in 1950, was deposited in the Hoover Library on 10 April 1951 by the authors, who had shared the defense of Maréchal Pétain, in the trial before the High Court in 1945, with the Bâtonnier Payen, leader of the defense. (Bâtonnier Payen had died in 1946.)*

The decision of the High Court of Justice on 15 August 1945 is quoted on pp. 7 and 8 of the book.

The petition for a rehearing was presented to M. René Mayer, Guardian of the Seals and Minister of Justice, on 16 May 1950. It is in three parts and is published on pp. 17 to 106 of the book. It cites evidence not available at the trial, and specific points on which the defense pleads that the Court was in error. This petition for a rehearing was presented in accordance with a note written on 7 September 1946 by Maréchal Pétain (pp. 17 and 18) in which he said:

"I have never recognized my condemnation. I have benefited by a pardon for which I did not ask. My only recourse is an appeal for a rehearing. Therefore I explicitly instruct my attorneys, Jacques Isorni and Jean Lemaire, when they have obtained the necessary documents, to secure a revision of the decision of the High Court on 14 August 1945, [night of 14-15.]"

Maréchal Pétain's draft of a New Constitution

The book ends with a bibliography of 53 sources, preceded by five annexes. The second annex is stated by the authors to be the complete text of Maréchal Pétain's draft of a new constitution, prepared by him in accordance with the decision of the French National Assembly at Vichy on 10 July 1940.

This draft is in six chapters, preceded by a statement of principles in which the fundamental rights and duties of both the citizen and the State are specified. The first chapter defines the executive power, the second the legislative power, the third the National Congress (of which the sole function is to choose the President of the Republic), the fourth the judicial system, and the fifth the local councils (municipal, departemental, and provincial). The sixth chapter defines briefly the French Empire and indicates the broad lines of its government.

The basic principle of the proposed constitution is the liberty and equality of individuals within limits established by the Constitution, under a representative government in which the legislative, executive, and judicial powers are separated. The President of the Republic is elected for ten years by a National Congress and has greater power than has in fact been given to the presidents of the first four French Republics.

(Document No. 232)

SUPPLEMENTARY MEMORANDUM IN FAVOR OF THE REHEARING OF THE CASE OF MARÉCHAL PÉTAIN

JACQUES ISORNI AND JEAN LEMAIRE

Attorneys at the Court of Appeals of Paris; Attorneys for Maréchal Pétain

We the undersigned, Jacques Isorni, attorney at the Court of Appeals of Paris, residing in Paris, and Jean Lemaire, attorney at the Court of Appeals of Paris, also residing in Paris, hereby deposit in the archives of the Hoover Library the text of a supplementary note in favor of the revision of the condemnation pronounced against the Maréchal Pétain. This note was handed personally to the Guardian of the Seals, Minister of Justice, on 15 September 1953.

(Document No. 232-A)

Fr. ed. 978

Paris, 23 September 1954

JACQUES ISORNI   JEAN LEMAIRE

[*This note, which may be consulted at the Hoover Library, presents details in support of the existence of an agreement between Maréchal Pétain and King George VI of Great Britain. Prince Xavier de Bourbon and M. Jacques Chevalier, former French minister, are stated to be available as witnesses of the truth of the statements made in the note.*]

DEPOSITIONS OF THE WITNESSES IN THE TRIAL OF PÉTAIN

JEAN LEMAIRE

Attorney at the Court of Appeals of Paris

I the undersigned Jean Lemaire, attorney at the Court of Appeals of Paris, residing in Paris, certify the exactitude of the essential passages in the depositions listed below:—

1. General Hering, general of the Army, formerly military governor of Strasbourg and military governor of Paris.
2. General Picquendar, general of Army Corps, reserve.
3. Vice-Admiral Fernet.
4. Jacques Chevalier.
5. General Campet, chief of the Military Cabinet of Maréchal Pétain.
6. General Debeney, chief of the Armistice Services at Vichy.
7. Charles Donati, regional prefect.
8. Jean Jardel, director of cabinet for Maréchal Pétain.
9. André Lavagne, master of appeals in the Council of State, assistant director of the civil cabinet of Maréchal Pétain.
10. Charles Bareiss, of Strasbourg.
11. General F. de Lannurien, formerly director of the War School.

These depositions were taken at the time of the trial of Maréchal Pétain in the High Court in August 1945 and the complete texts were published as a part of the report of the entire trial in the *Journal Officiel de la République Française.*

(Document No. 271)
Fr. ed. 979

Paris, 12 April 1955

JEAN LEMAIRE

DEPOSITION OF GENERAL
HERING IN THE PÉTAIN TRIAL:
THE ARMY — NORTH AFRICA

PIERRE HERING

General

*The High Court of Justice: The trial of Maréchal
Pétain.*
*Presiding Judge: Chief Justice Mongibeaux of the
Supreme Court of France.*
Ninth Session, Wednesday, 1 August 1945.

GENERAL HERING: Mr. President and gentlemen of the jury, I wish to present to you, in the light of my memories covering a period of forty years, the qualities of judgment and clearsightedness which the Maréchal has shown in exercising his high political functions as well as his military functions, and at the same time the profoundly humane character which brings all those who know him into close sympathy with him.

In the course of my statement I will deal more particularly with the part which the Maréchal played in the preparation for the war.

With his political activity you are all familiar. The Maréchal entered into political activities never at his own suggestion but only in answer to the entreaties addressed to him by men of every shade of political belief. His interventions in politics were limited to difficult times: in 1934 after the incidents of 6 February; in 1938 he agreed to serve as ambassador in Spain after the Spanish Revolution and because of our difficulties in dealing with the Spanish government; in May 1940 he became a member of M. Paul Reynaud's War Cabinet; and, finally, on 16 June 1940 he became head of the government.

In any case, aside from these most specific political roles—and I repeat once more that he did not solicit them—the Maréchal, in so far as I have seen him and wherever I have known the facts, has never concerned himself with political matters.

When he came to Vichy his first thought was to make personally certain that the governmental operations continued—I am speaking now of the administrative control of the government, as the higher control was in his hands at all times. He very quickly realized how impossible it was to combine the functions of Chief of State with those of Chief of Government, especially at his age. He therefore assigned to a chief of government the task of dealing with political matters and in particular with foreign powers, reserving for himself the two issues which he recognized as being of capital importance—this is something which he told me personally at the Villa Sévigné at the very beginning—namely the preparation of a new constitution, a duty which had been assigned to him by the National Assembly, and above all the material and spiritual rebirth of the nation through work.

Those were the two tasks which he most definitely reserved for himself.

In December 1941, I asked him how he was getting on with the work of drafting the constitution, and at what time he hoped to be able to promulgate it. The Maréchal answered, "The constitution is a long task. I cannot even think of promulgating a new constitution while the Germans are still in France. In any case, the task assigned to me was not to promulgate a new constitution but to prepare one." The Maréchal insisted definitively on acting in a legal manner. The words which I have just quoted are those which I wrote down myself on leaving the office.

And now as regards the rebirth of the nation through work. To be able to work it is first necessary to keep alive, and to be able to keep alive it was necessary to be protected against the demands of our oppressor and to ward off to the greatest extent his demands while in all cases saving the French people from the worst which might happen. Such was the theme of his entire policy.

It is in this dominant idea that the explanation of most of his actions is to be found. In the interests of brevity I shall cite only one example, the decision which he took in November 1942 to remain at his post.

I admit that I was somewhat astonished by his decision, all the more so because it was not in harmony with the conversations I had had with him three months earlier. The Maréchal answered me in these words: "The pilot of a ship must remain at the wheel throughout the tempest. He does not abandon the wheel. If I had left, France would have been placed under the same regime as Poland." And when I showed a sort of indifference—indifference is perhaps too strong a word: what I actually said was, "Well, then we would have had the same regime as Poland"—he answered, "You do not know what the Poland regime means. It would have killed France."

That was the purpose. And you find again, in this very answer, the profoundly humane character of which I spoke to you a few moments ago.

But in spite of the sacrifices which we had to make in order to avoid the worst fate, and in spite of the spiritual suffering of the Maréchal, he remained always supple in his adjustment to reality and in line with his objective, in complete clarity of spirit.

Why? We still had one sheet anchor, North Africa. If we lost it Germany would carry its domination across the entire Mediterranean area and liberation would be postponed indefinitely.

The Maréchal therefore strongly opposed all demands made upon him, in one form or another, that might enable Germany to establish its hold on North Africa.

In a word, what was it that he accomplished by acting in that way? He made the liberation possible. That was the chief point of his policy.

And now I approach the end of what I have to say.

The Maréchal, in spite of all the difficulties—and I am not speaking now of those caused by his own government for while it is true that he was not always well served it is also true that there were those who worked against him, and there was a point which made it even worse, that Hitler opposed his veto to the steps which the Maréchal had taken—what the Maréchal desired, in spite of everything, and in spite of any apparent weaknesses which he may have had, was to hold to that one idea that the enemy should be kept out of North Africa.

Note carefully that Hitler clearly perceived the error he had made in granting us the armistice without imposing any condition covering North

Africa. He tried many times afterward to do something about it. But on that point he found the Maréchal, whom he called the "old fox," immovable.

Whatever else anyone may say about the Maréchal's policy, this at least can be said, that it was probably the only policy which was both intelligent and humane.

What did this policy make possible? As I said a few moments ago it enabled France to endure, to live not too well and not too badly throughout four years; and it enabled our Anglo-Saxon allies to prepare their weapons. It made the liberation possible. That is the great point.

Far be it from me to desire to minimize in any way whatever the merits of our liberation and in particular those of my former colleague and friend on the general staff of Maréchal Pétain, General de Gaulle, with whom I worked until the war in complete harmony of thought. But the merits of General de Gaulle should not make us forget the eminent services rendered by the Maréchal in accepting at the age of eighty-five the crushing duties of the keeper of the goal. Because of these reasons, I have always refused to consider them as opposed to each other.

I am reminded of memories of my youth when I heard discussions of the problem of Alsace, between those Alsatians who remained in Alsace and those who came to France, having chosen France when the option was offered.

Was it better to stay? Was it better to leave? Well, gentlemen, there had to be two solutions: one part remained in Alsace to maintain the memory and the veneration of the lost fatherland and to restrain the German seizure of Alsace. The others came to France to prepare for retaliation. There you have two complementary roles.

In 1940 the same causes brought two men to the front whose roles again were complementary, Maréchal Pétain and General de Gaulle. Providence chose them well and placed each one where it suited him the best. For that we must be grateful.

Instead of devouring each other, instead of squandering our heritage or glory to the stupefaction of foreigners who watch us and no longer understand us, let us close our ranks, as the sergeants of another day used to say, to fill the gaps left by those dear to us who are gone forever. Let us think only of France, the unity of which must be, above all, established.

I have finished.

(Document No. 272)

Fr. ed. 980-982

[*See Document No. 271*]

DEPOSITION OF GENERAL PICQUENDAR
IN THE PÉTAIN TRIAL:
THE ARMY — HIDDEN STORES

ODILON PICQUENDAR

General of Army Corps

The High Court of Justice: The Trial of Maréchal Pétain.
Presiding Judge: Chief Justice Mongibeaux of the Supreme Court of France.
Thirteenth Session, Monday, 6 August 1945.

MAITRE ISORNI [one of the attorneys defending Maréchal Pétain]: We would like to ask General Picquendar what were the clandestine arms and military supplies of France after the armistice, whether the Maréchal knew of them, in what quantities they existed, and against whom their use was intended.

GENERAL PICQUENDAR: At the end of June and the beginning of July 1940 it was the idea of the entire military command to seek to hold back as much equipment as possible from the deliveries which were required by the Germans. In addition, just at the beginning of July, about the 5th or 6th, General Colson, Minister of War, personally sent a handwritten personal letter to all officers commanding military regions asking them to camouflage military equipment and supplies.

General Weygand, to my personal knowledge, insisted on the same kind of action in July [1940].

As the Germans seemed desirous of opposing the formation of a motorized army, the general staff of our own Army immediately gave its attention to the mass camouflage of automobile equipment. A general staff officer, Colonel Mollard, was especially assigned to this task.

I myself was made a member of the general staff of the Army on 20 October 1940, and it was at that time that I took charge of the service more or less auxiliary to the Army's normal activities, the purpose being to take care of camouflaged equipment.

The most important point of all was that neither the military command nor the government, in case of some discovery of clandestine items, could be accused of what was in fact a flagrant violation of the clauses of the armistice.

The amount of equipment thus camouflaged by individual initiative very soon proved to be considerable. It had to be inventoried, repaired, so cared for that it would not deteriorate, allocated according to the use we wished to make of it, and, above everything else, kept secret; and all this had to be done under the eyes of the German control commission.

It was done by a small staff chosen among former army officers who had been placed in retirement at the time of the armistice. They served under the orders of Colonel Mollard, together with a few noncommissioned officers, their number being similarly limited in order to preserve secrecy. This work was done with a devotion of which I need say nothing further here.

The extent of the transport of equipment which had to be undertaken may be imagined from the following figures: toward the end of 1941 in collaboration with Colonel Mollard, we estimated the value of the arms and ammunition which we had hidden as being 15,000 million to 18,000 million francs in value.

In addition, and of comparable value, there were supplies of every kind for the quartermaster services and for the medical services, and raw material, all of which we had concealed.

In this camouflage operation we had obtained support from the minor personnel in the administrational services of the police, gendarmerie, transport, and the Ministries of Finance and of the Interior. On the higher levels of those same services the support we received was more timorous and reluctant.

At the beginning we had had the moral support of the heads of the government administrations and of our own ministers, General Colson, General Weygand, and then General Huntziger. I myself, as a result of my own service in the Ministry [of War], knew quite a few heads of different services, who helped us. But this support gradually diminished.

However, in October [1940] the officers of the Maréchal's military cabinet assured me that we had his moral support. Very often this fact enabled me to obtain aid from other ministries.

The work which was done in 1941 had the following result. I can sum it up in the personal interview which I had with the Maréchal at the end of 1941 or the beginning of 1942. The Maréchal had sent for me to ask what was the situation regarding arms and supplies. I summarized it in the following way. We had recovered enough equipment, I said, to supply the eight divisions of the Armistice Army with their anti-tank and anti-aircraft armament, and with the necessary motor vehicles. We had supplies which enabled us to triple these eight divisions, more or less, as our total supplies of the equipment enabled us to fit out with light arms and provide with supplies the men of twenty-four divisions. Of course we had no heavy artillery and we had very few tanks. We had tried to send to the Allies a table of equipment which would be necessary.

In addition we had begun the manufacture of armored motorized machine guns in underground factories which were hidden in the Corrèze. These factories enabled us to complete 220 such vehicles by about October 1942.

We had also undertaken the manufacture of anti-tank grenades of an entirely new model, superior to everything then in use in the Allied armies. By about October 1942 we had already produced many thousands of these grenades.

The Maréchal—I can place this conversation with the Maréchal in about January 1942—the Maréchal congratulated me and said to continue because we could never have too powerful a French army.

As I said, at the beginning we had the advantage of the moral support of our own ministers, General Weygand, General Colson, and General Huntziger. This support was later reduced, unfortunately, toward 1942 to merely the moral support of the Maréchal because Admiral Darlan did not look very favorably on an increase in the land forces.

Later, beginning in April 1942, when there was a change of ministry, we had some apprehension regarding the collaborationist tendencies of the ministers.

However, in April 1942, when I put the question to General Bridoux, Secretary of State for War, he seemed to be well informed regarding our equipment and supplies. He told me that he could not deal with the matter personally because it was a violation of the armistice clauses, but that I was free to continue my clandestine work.

In May [1942], through the chief of cabinet of the Minister of War, I was able to be quite certain that M. Laval knew about what was going on, but that he did not seem to be interested in the matter.

Thus our support on the highest levels could be summed up as coming from the Maréchal himself.

In June I left the general staff of the army after some conflicts with Admiral Darlan, and I was placed on the retired list at the end of September 1942.

At that time I was maintained in the mission already assigned to me for several weeks longer, first of all because it did not trouble them at all to keep me as an inspector of camouflaged material, and also in order to have me on hand as a hostage if the day should come when there were difficulties with the Germans, the argument being, as I said at the beginning, that neither the government nor the military command could be involved, nor accused of violating the provisions of the armistice.

In October 1942, feeling sure that there would be serious events sooner or later that winter, I asked General Bridoux what the attitude of the army would be if the Germans entered the southern zone. He answered, "I can't consider such a hypothesis. It won't happen."

I put the same question a few days later to M. Laval, who gave me the same answer.

This convinced me that if the Germans did come into the southern zone the orders given by the government would not be favorable to military action against them. I therefore gave the following directives to all those working with me in the camouflage of equipment:

"In case the Germans enter the free zone, if the Armistice Army makes the slightest gesture of resistance, our mobilization plan, calling for the formation of a total of twenty-four divisions, will come into operation and you will place yourself at the service of the regional commanding officers. If the Armistice Army does not offer any resistance you will attempt to put the supplies at the disposition of Frenchmen who are willing to take the responsibility for them. You will try to camouflage the remainder in hidden depots in such a way that the owners or tenants of the places used cannot be accused. You will distribute arms and ammunition to all who ask you for it and who will accept the responsibility for what is given to them. You will attempt to destroy the remainder."

When the Germans did in fact enter the free zone in November 1942 there was no resistance. Needless to say, what we had foreseen did happen: the Germans in coming into the southern zone discovered by search and by other means at their disposal a large part of our supplies. Some of the depots were known to them through informers. But there still remained some which they did not find and I believe that I can say that these supplies were most useful—at least as far as arms and ammunition were concerned—to the resistance.

I am convinced that a great deal of heavy equipment still remains hidden and will be discovered in the course of the next twenty years.

(Document No. 273)
Fr. ed. 983-985

[*See Document No. 271*]

DEPOSITION OF ADMIRAL FERNET
IN THE PÉTAIN TRIAL:
THE ROUGIER MISSION

JEAN FERNET

Vice-Admiral

The High Court of Justice: The Trial of Maréchal Pétain.
Presiding Judge: Chief Justice Mongibeaux of the Supreme Court of France.
Fourteenth Session, Tuesday, 7 August 1945.

THE PRESIDING JUDGE: What is your name, Christian name, age, position, and domicile?

ADMIRAL FERNET: Fernet, Jean, 64 years, vice-admiral, retired, Paris. *(The witness takes the oath.)*

THE PRESIDING JUDGE: What questions do you wish to ask the witness?

MAÎTRE PAYEN, PRESIDENT OF THE PARIS BAR [leader of the three members of the Paris Bar defending the Maréchal]: Admiral Fernet knew, I believe, of the contacts which were established, beginning in the autumn of 1940, between Vichy and England. I believe that he can give us some details on that subject.

ADMIRAL FERNET: At the time of which I am going to speak I had been serving, since 22 July 1940, as secretary-general for the Presidency of the Council, for Maréchal Pétain.

On 20 September [1940] M. Louis Rougier, professor of economics in the university at Besançon, was received by the Maréchal at the Pavillon Sévigné. He had already been heard by M. Paul Baudouin, Minister of Foreign Affairs, and by General Weygand, who had just been appointed delegate-general of the government in French Africa. M. Rougier had come to the Maréchal to offer his services in attempting, in his own name, to negotiate with the British government in London, to which he insisted he had effective introductions, with the purpose of dissipating certain misunderstandings and of making certain proposals. The misunderstandings of which he spoke had to do with differences in the interpretation of the naval clauses of the armistice convention which concerned the preservation of the fleet. The proposals to which he referred were that ways and means should be sought to ease the blockade then established by the British government, which was seriously affecting the food supplies of the homeland and the economic activity of our North African territories, together with other proposals intended to put a stop to possible aggression against French economic bases, with a reciprocal agreement.

M. Rougier presented to the Maréchal exactly those points which I have just mentioned; the Maréchal completely approved the principle of the missions. Consequently, facilities were arranged for M. Rougier's exit from France through Geneva and for the continuation of his journey by way of Lisbon.

M. Rougier returned to Vichy on 8 November [1940]. The important persons who had heard him in September, when he had seen the Maréchal, were no longer able to receive him.

After the interview at Montoire [between the Maréchal and Hitler] M. Paul Baudouin had felt that his personal dignity made it necessary for him to resign as Minister of Foreign Affairs on the ground that he had been excluded from the negotiations. And General Weygand had left Vichy, on 3 October [1940] if my memory is correct, to take up his post in Algiers.

M. Louis Rougier was received by the Maréchal in my presence at the Hotel du Parc on 10 November [1940]. He reported the interviews which he had had the honor of being granted by the Secretary of the Foreign Office and by the Prime Minister in London. "These interviews," he said, "justified great hopes." And he gave the Maréchal personally a complete report of his mission.

The Maréchal thanked M. Rougier and also gave his entire approval to the conclusions presented to him.

The Rougier documents were then given to the Service of Control for Political Affairs, with a note which, according to Rougier, could serve as basis of an agreement of which the purpose would be to create the possibility of a mutual understanding on the questions involved.

The principal points of this agreement were essentially those to which I have just referred, namely:

Great Britain's guarantee not to attack those French bases and colonies which were still faithful to the Maréchal's government, in order to avoid at all costs an intervention by Axis forces in defense of such bases;

A reciprocal guarantee by France not to attempt to recapture those territories which were occupied by the Free French forces;

A relaxation of the blockade in order to permit the passage of certain foodstuffs essential for the French homeland, coming through the Straits of Gibraltar from West African ports and from Morocco;

The passage of the same kinds of foodstuffs from North African ports to the coasts of Provence as a result of classifying this traffic from the point of view of international law as "coastal shipping."

And a renewal of the solemn declaration already made regarding the absolute isolation and conservation of the fleet, in accordance with the promise already given.

Further steps were entrusted to the service for commercial matters [in the French Ministry of Foreign Affairs].

According to information which I received at the time I can state that arrangements were made immediately, by the Service for Political Affairs, through our diplomatic representatives in Madrid, to put the agreement into effect at the earliest possible moment.

In fact there had been, for two months, exchanges of views at Madrid between our embassy and the British embassy, dealing with approximately the same points as those which had been the objects of M. Rougier's benevolent mission.

That is what I have to say.

(Document No. 274)
Fr. ed. 986-987

[*See Document No. 271*]

DEPOSITION OF M. CHEVALIER IN THE PÉTAIN TRIAL: FRANCO-BRITISH AND FRANCO-AMERICAN NEGOTIATIONS

JACQUES CHEVALIER

Minister of National Education

The High Court of Justice: The Trial of Maréchal Pétain.
Presiding Judge: Chief Justice Mongibeaux of the Supreme Court of France.
Fourteenth Session, Tuesday, 7 August 1945.

THE PRESIDING JUDGE: Your name, Christian names, age, profession, and domicile?

M. CHEVALIER: Chevalier, Jacques, 63 years, professor and dean of the faculty of letters at the University of Grenoble, living at Serigny, Allier.

(The witness takes the oath.)

THE PRESIDING JUDGE: What question, Mr. President of the Bar and gentlemen of the jury?

MAITRE PAYEN, PRESIDENT OF THE PARIS BAR: M. Chevalier was Minister of National Education when he became involved in certain Franco-British and Franco-American negotiations. I would like him to explain what he knows of these negotiations.

M. CHEVALIER: Well, Mr. Chief Justice, I will limit myself to presenting the facts as objectively as possible. They are facts, I believe, which you will regard, as I do, as essential to the presentation of the truth.

On 4 December 1940 at quarter to eleven in the morning, just as I was terminating, in my position as secretary-general for public instruction, a meeting of the directors of my service, my private secretary announced the visit of Mr. Pierre Dupuis, Canadian Minister, who was bringing me a personal message from Lord Halifax.

Mr. Pierre Dupuis was shown into the room and gave me the greetings of Lord Halifax "to his most intimate friend." He then recalled certain memories and told me of the confidence which Lord Halifax placed in me.

At this point I take the liberty of introducing parenthetically an explanation. I had been on most intimate terms with Lord Halifax during the years when we were together at Oxford. In 1904 and 1905—when he was Edward Irwin—we had spent two years together at Oxford and during that time I had often been received as a guest in his home at Garrowby in Yorkshire, by him and by his father.

I met him again during the war of 1914-1918. I was with the British army during the entire campaign and was awarded the Military Medal.

Further, I was known and valued in England as one of the leading friends

— 935 —

of England and as one of the most violent enemies of Germany, as is shown by my books and lectures.

In short, then, Pierre Dupuis presented to me the compliments of Lord Halifax and said, "I have a message from him for you."

I ask your permission, Mr. Chief Justice, as this is a very important matter and I would not wish to misrepresent anything, to quote textually what I wrote down at that very moment at the dictation of Pierre Dupuis.

He first said to me, "Lord Halifax desires to re-establish contact through you as an intermediary. It is to you personally that he turns and it is on you that he relies. Now here is the message which he has asked me to give you."

This was the text of the message from Lord Halifax: "Please tell our French friends that we are in an extremely delicate situation. We cannot leap into each others arms. A state of artificial tension must be maintained between our French friends and ourselves. If Germany suspected our intimacy, Article 9 of the Armistice Convention would come into effect immediately. But behind this front of disagreement we must agree."

Mr. Dupuis added, and I made a note of his exact words, "The British are extremely well disposed toward you. All that they ask is that you shall not cede to the Germans either the air bases, the naval bases, or the fleet. You have two lungs: the colonies and the fleet. If the Germans got hold of them you would be weakened. Consequently we ask the French (1) to protect their fleet, (2) to protect their colonies, and (3) to do nothing to regain such of their colonies as have decided to continue the struggle at the side of England.

"If those conditions are met a working agreement will be arranged which will make possible, in spite of the blockade, your food supplies in essential products such as peanuts, wheat, sheep, items necessary for public health, and finally, and most particularly, gasoline, fuel oil, lubricants, and coal, it being understood of course that these products will not pass through Germany in transit."

In conclusion it was understood that the rule of silence and secrecy would be strictly observed, that we would keep to the solid basis of the Armistice—this was the English expression—, and that at all costs we would avoid bringing into operation Article 9 of the Armistice Convention, the article under which France undertook to do nothing harmful to Germany, and that between 'you the French and us the English' a state of artificial tension would be maintained in order not to alarm the Germans, which would have the possible risk of provoking their intervention. To such an intervention, Pierre Dupuis remarked to me, England is not for the moment prepared to reply.

On the following day, 5 December [1940] at 3 o'clock in the afternoon I went to see Maréchal Pétain who had just returned from Marseille. I explained the matter to him. He asked for more specific information regarding the colonies and told me that he accepted the plan of agreement with one reservation, namely that in the phrase "artificial tension between France and England" the word tension should be replaced by the word coldness. The Maréchal's precise words to me were, "No one is more ready than I am to agree to the English demands, with this single reservation."

That same evening in my office at the Hotel Plaza after my day's work I had a long talk with Pierre Dupuis. In accordance with my conversation with the Maréchal, the draft of the agreement was put into final form.

First, the phrase 'artificial tension' was replaced by 'artificial coldness.'

Second, as regards the colonies which continued the struggle on the side of England it was agreed that the situation of the moment would be maintained provisionally and that an attempt would be made, when the time came, to reach an understanding, it being agreed that these colonies would be given back to the French government through a simple substitution of police and military forces. Third, as regards the fleet and the colonies, the English promised to give us all the support which would be necessary and which they would be in a position to give us, in the proper way and at the proper time. Fourth, it was added that the English radio would henceforth refrain from interfering in French internal affairs. Fifth, as regards the vital question of oil, an agreement in principle was reached, it being left to technical experts to arrange the details in Madrid.

On the morning of 6 December [1940] I visited the Maréchal in company of Mr. Pierre Dupuis. The Minister, chargé d'affaires for Canada, read to the Maréchal the message of Lord Halifax and made some comments on it. He then presented to the Maréchal a long report in which the draft of the agreement had been formulated in detail. The Maréchal said that he was in complete agreement on all points.

On the following day, Saturday 7 December, Mr. Pierre Dupuis left again for England, and on Monday evening, 9 December 1940, I received this telegram from him: "All goes well," which meant, according to an understanding between us, that the British government agreed.

In accordance with the promise given to our English friends the agreement remained absolutely secret but came into effect immediately, as all the services having to do with the matter can testify.

M. Berthelot, for example, Secretary of State for Communications, General Bergeret, who was in the Ministry of Air, Admiral Bléhaut, who was with the naval general staff in Algeria, and many others knew about it and can testify to the following.

In the first place, maritime traffic, which had been greatly reduced up to that time, was re-established on a very large scale.

Further, the passage through the Straits of Gibraltar which had been forbidden to us up to that moment was now free for French ships, for example for those which brought men and equipment to Dakar, and for those which, with English 'navicerts' [permits] brought fuel and diesel oil to North Africa, as well as for ships carrying essential food supplies.

The gentlemen whom I have just named have since told me that they noted the facts and were intensely pleased, without understanding the reasons for what happened.

Thus the agreement was carried out for the greatest good—I am justified in using those words, and the English realize it perfectly—both of France and of England.

It was for the greatest good of France, in the first place, because the imports authorized by the English made it possible to avoid famine and above all to avoid the paralysis of our transport and of our industries, a paralysis which Admiral Auphan had told me would be inevitable from 15 January [1941], that is within six weeks, if we did not obtain permission to import oil products and lubricants.

Obviously the agreement was very useful for England too, first because of the solemn promise given by Maréchal Pétain not to hand over the fleet or the colonies, and second because by keeping absolute silence and secrecy we would not provoke an intervention by the Germans which would have brought into operation the famous Clause 9, enabling them to get their hands on North Africa, a step which, the English told me, would have been a catastrophe that might delay or even compromise their victory, and therefore our own.

As for the results, here they are.

To England, the Maréchal had promised that the colonies would not be handed over [to the Germans].

In the council meetings of 3 and 6 June 1941 Admiral Darlan reported a text in which the Germans demanded that certain bases in North Africa should be ceded to them, together with Dakar, in exchange for some political and economic counterpart.

Such an arrangement would have broken the engagements into which we had entered on 6 December [1940] and would have resulted automatically in war with Great Britain.

This German proposal was refused in the following manner. We greatly extended the political and economic counterpart, demanding from the Germans a formal recognition of French sovereignty and of the integrity of French territory.

The Germans of course refused this demand and thus we were no longer bound by the note.

As to the fleet, you know that in accordance with undertakings entered into by Maréchal Pétain with Mr. Churchill the order was given on 27 November 1942 to scuttle it.

Of what happened thereafter I shall say very little, as it is a matter which concerns the English.

All I can say is that relations continued in the most cordial manner, and that among all the ministries concerned, the government, the foreign office, and the admiralty, our attitude was somewhat reserved only in the case of the Ministry of Economic Warfare—the economic committee for war—which was having trouble in obtaining products of prime necessity.

As for Mr. Churchill, he was most favorable. He asked only that negotiations for arranging ways and means should be carried on in London rather than in France.

On 31 December 1940 through Mr. Matthews, first secretary of the United States embassy at Vichy, and on 25 January and 1 February 1941 through Admiral Leahy, Ambassador of the United States, who came to see me in my office, I received communications on parchment, in two copies, from "His Majesty's Government, desirous of encouraging the Chief of the French State in his resistance."

I also received other proof of the British attitude and other messages; each Thursday in February we were kept in contact by Mr. Dupuis.

Then on 6 April [1941] Admiral Leahy sent me from Marseille, where he was at that time, a personal message from President Roosevelt to Maréchal Pétain.

And finally on 11 April [1941] Colonel Benn sent me another important message from Lord Halifax.

Throughout this time, in addition, I was in intimate contact with the Americans, the Red Cross, the American Volunteers, and the Rockefeller Foundation, who with very great generosity had given us condensed milk and vitamin products for the children of our schools, and had arranged with the English for the passage of a large number of ships carrying those supplies.

As to the Maréchal's attitude in all these matters, he explained it to me at some length on 1 February 1941, at eleven o'clock in the morning, when

I was giving him an ultra-confidential message from his Majesty's Government, which I had received through Admiral Leahy.

The Maréchal said to me, "I am caught between two policies. One is that of collaboration with the English, a policy to which all my preferences go. The other is the rule of the conqueror to which I am forced to submit because the conqueror is here and because he imposes his rule on the people whom I must defend against him.

"I do not play a double game." And he repeated. "I do not play a double game. . . . I have but one promise to give, and I keep it. I am honorable in my dealings with one side as with the other.

"With those on one side I signed the armistice, and I respect the terms of the armistice. And I do so on the expressed and formal desire of the English, who say that a rupture of the armistice would result in a German intervention.

"On the other hand, I am true to the English and friendly toward them because within the limits of the field which remains open to me, and it is not a very large field, I do everything in my power to facilitate their task and to prepare their victory, which will be our victory as well. But at the same time," he concluded, "I resist to the greatest possible extent the demands of the Germans."

Of the Maréchal's resistance, as Mr. Churchill called it—he even used the English words "passive resistance"—I will give you two proofs of capital importance which made a great impression on our English friends.

The first fact which I cite is this: on 18 December 1940 I received a telephone call from Paris. At that time I had been Minister of Public Instruction for just four days, since 14 December. The Germans on that day had demanded that at midnight all personnel from Alsace-Lorraine [in the national educational services] who had been evacuated to the southern zone should be handed over to them, stating that if this were not done they would cross the demarcation line and invade the zone. I refused; I had to reply immediately; I took it on my own responsibility to refuse. I then went to see the Maréchal who completely approved of my attitude and signed my refusal.

The Germans did not come to repatriate those from Alsace and Lorraine [in the southern zone]. In this way we saved over eight hundred men and women teachers from Alsace and Lorraine, four hundred and fifty who had been studying to be teachers at Obernai and who had been evacuated to Solignac in the Haute-Vienne, and the professors of the University of Strasbourg who were at Clermont.

The second fact is this: Maréchal Pétain was extremely preoccupied with the problem of maintaining the rights of Alsace as a part of France. It happened that in April 1941, or even a little earlier, I was in touch with a German who said that he was an art historian and in Hitler's confidence. He seemed to me to be more reasonable, or if you prefer, less unreasonable, than many other Germans. His name was Herckmans.

Mr. Herckmans, who was in the confidence of Chancellor Hitler, said to us, "Unlike Goering and Goebbels we believe in a strong France and above all in a France which has no remaining causes of friction with us. In accordance with that policy we have decided to give you back your linguistic frontiers, which means that you will have Lorraine and even," he added, "the Wallon area, but not Alsace, because Alsace speaks a German dialect."

"Nothing of that kind can be done," I told him. "The Maréchal is absolutely immovable on the question of Alsace."

"Well, then," Herckmans said to us, "we could talk it over but there would have to be one agreed condition. The Maréchal would have to stop blocking all our demands by complete refusals and would have to support the policy of collaboration, whereas at present he always shows himself to be against it."

I can even tell you that he added at that moment, "The Germans call Maréchal Pétain, 'Maréchal Nein'—'Maréchal No'—because he always says no."

And it was a fact at that time, I fully believe, that among us the Maréchal was the only one who was able to make the Germans withdraw merely by his own prestige. The Germans feared him because he had conquered them.

Anyway, Mr. Herckmans did make his request through me, and I communicated it to the Maréchal on Easter Tuesday, 15 April 1941. This is the reply which the Maréchal dictated to me; I give the exact words:

"For Chancellor Hitler.

"We never know when we engage in discussions with the Germans what guarantees we have. Up to the present Chancellor Hitler has done nothing to ease the hardships of the occupation. We are pillaged of all our possessions. Our livestock and our agricultural products are requisitioned. We are forced to adopt a most rigorous diet. Nothing is done for our prisoners; no steps are taken to reduce the occupation costs, nor anything done to improve facilities for communication between the two zones. The Germans act toward us as does a bad school master; we are being hazed.

"The French people cannot accept German interference. The French people are hostile to their own government because of German demands. That is why the entire nation is violently anti-German, pro-English, and Gaullist.

"Under present conditions no discussions are possible," the Maréchal says. "My people do not desire them. And they know their true interests as well as I do and are even more skillful in discerning what they are."

I had this letter copied by my private secretary and I gave it to Mr. Herckmans at Mayet-de-Montagne that very day. He gave it to the Chancellor in the Balkans on Saturday 19 April [1941].

And now to say one final word on relations thereafter with the English. My relations with them continued on a personal basis when I ceased to be a minister on 13 August 1941 and returned to the faculty of letters at Grenoble.

At the time I continued to maintain extremely cordial relations with the English through Lord Halifax and Prince Xavier de Bourbon, who is my friend and my neighbor in the countryside of the Allier.

When I was arrested by the maquis on 25 June 1944 there was found in my possession a message from Lord Halifax transmitted to me by Prince Xavier, which is now in the hands of the judge and which begins with these words: "The thought of H (Halifax) and the thought of C (Chevalier) are identical; he can rely on me as I rely on him."

Several days after I had been arrested by the maquis Prince Xavier de Bourbon was arrested by the Gestapo and taken to Germany on the double charge of intelligence with the English and intelligence with the resistance, in particular with the communist party in the Allier. When he returned to France a few weeks ago these communists gave him a triumphant reception.

Since I was interned I have been able to correspond with Lord Halifax through the leaders of the resistance and I can tell you, that Lord Halifax, like the English, has not ceased up to the present to show his absolute confidence in me.

(Document No. 275)
Fr. ed. 988-993

[*See Document No. 271*]

DEPOSITION OF GENERAL CAMPET IN THE PÉTAIN TRIAL: AID TO VICTIMS OF THE OCCUPATION

JACQUES CAMPET
General

The High Court of Justice: The Trial of Maréchal Pétain.
Presiding Judge: Chief Justice Mongibeaux of the Supreme Court of France.
Fifteenth Session, Wednesday, 8 August 1945.

THE PRESIDING JUDGE: What is your name, Christian name, age, profession, and domicile?

GENERAL CAMPET: General Campet, Jacques, born 2 February 1888 at Dax, general on the available list, at present domiciled in Clermont-Ferrand.

(The witness takes the oath.)

MAÎTRE PAYEN, PRESIDENT OF THE PARIS BAR: General Campet was chief of Maréchal Pétain's military cabinet for three years, in 1941, 1942, and 1943. He is naturally fully aware of the Maréchal's feelings and of his activities, particularly with regard to the Germans. I ask him to be good enough to explain what he knows in this matter.

GENERAL CAMPET: Mr. President, members of the jury, on my return from captivity at the beginning of 1940 I was appointed chief of the Maréchal's military cabinet.

I remained at that post until January 1944 when I was ejected by the Germans.

Thus I occupied the post of chief of cabinet throughout three years and, if you will allow me to do so, Mr. Chief Justice, I will tell you what I was able to determine regarding the Maréchal during the three years when I held that position.

My essential duties were to keep the Maréchal advised as to the military situation. Every morning I entered the Maréchal's office with telegrams, communiqués, and maps, and I explained the situation to him.

Having performed this duty for three years I can affirm that the Maréchal could not possibly believe and in fact did not believe in a German victory. He could not believe in it because the information given to the Maréchal all pointed very precisely not to a German victory but to a German defeat.

It is not to serve the Maréchal's needs in this case that I make this statement. Since the Russian reaction at the time of Stalingrad, and since the Allies took control of the seas, the German defeat was written in the events and we had only to report the phases by which it arrived.

That is what we did. That is what the Maréchal's cabinet did, and it is what I myself was doing in presenting the facts to the Maréchal.

I regret that I am not able to show the papers which were prepared at that time, the detailed reports which I made each day, or at least every fortnight, to the Maréchal. But these reports were based on documents which may perhaps be found and which came from the office known as the "bur-doc," the bureau of documentation, which was an office attached to the secretariat of war, amazingly well directed, and concerned only with military operations. The results which this office obtained and the studies which it prepared were such that it did not please everybody, and had to fight for its own existence for a long time and on many occasions.

Therefore the Maréchal could not believe in a German victory and in fact he did not believe in it. His conduct proved it.

If the Maréchal had believed in a German victory he would not, as has been stated here [in this court], have agreed to the clandestine depots, the depots of arms which were prepared and of which the Maréchal had definite knowledge. I can personally testify to that fact because I often talked about them with the Maréchal.

If the Maréchal had believed in a German victory he would not have invited his regional commanders, or his officers commanding the military divisions, as the terminology was at that time, to prepare their arms and their forces for the day when they would be needed.

In the same way the Maréchal would not have had the interest which he did—I cite this minor fact as an example—in the statistical services, formerly known as the demographic service. The Maréchal took an interest in this service and went to visit it, or to visit its subsidiary services at Clermont, not to busy himself with demographic problems but because it was this office which was particularly responsible for preparing in the greatest secrecy under the direction of a remarkable man—who later died in captivity in Dachau, Controller-General Verminy—a military mobilization.

The Maréchal therefore knew that a German victory was impossible. He did not believe in a German victory and the question of saying that the Maréchal desired or did not desire a German victory does not arise because he did not believe in it.

For anyone who knew the Maréchal there is no question at all.

Questions of sentiment did not exist for the Maréchal; only questions based on reason were of importance.

It was not a matter of knowing whether the Maréchal desired the victory of the Allies or of the Germans, but of knowing who was going to win the war so that it would be possible to cling to the victor and to profit by his victory.

My second duty was to deal with the Maréchal's correspondence. It was very large, at certain times reaching 2,000 letters per day.

On this subject I can affirm that the larger part of his correspondence dealt with steps taken on behalf of those who were victims of the Germans.

There was no victim of Germany, no condemned person, no one deported or arrested, who did not, either personally or through his family, appeal to the Maréchal to ask for a pardon or a diminution of his penalty. The Maréchal insisted that a reply should be made to every letter and every request that was sent to him.

This was always done and I believe that there was not one victim of Germany who appealed to the Maréchal for whom he did not do something.

I saw in the newspapers that someone cited a figure, yesterday or day before yesterday, in speaking of an [internment] camp: 221 people owed their lives to steps taken, and an intervention made, by the Maréchal. But there were many other camps, and it can be said that the number of German victims who owe either the reduction of their sentence, or their lives, to actions taken by the Maréchal is considerable.

In connection with the Maréchal's correspondence you will permit me, Mr. Chief Justice, to speak also of his correspondence with prisoners. This was also very large. The Maréchal did a great deal for the prisoners. He established a commission to deal with their affairs—I forget the title of the commission—which sàt at Lyon, directed first by General Besson and then by General Codechevre. This commission did an enormous amount for the prisoners in both their material and their spiritual needs.

Food supplies had to be collected, the necessary meat had to be obtained from the Argentine, chickens had to be brought from Hungary, and fish from Dakar. All of that had to be sent off, money collected, help arranged, dispatches made, and railway cars found.

The Maréchal concerned himself in this work with deep feeling. His constant preoccupation was for the prisoners.

I must say that he was enormously helped in this charitable work by the Swiss Red Cross, to the benevolence of which organization I may be allowed to pay public homage here.

What I have just said to you, Mr. Chief Justice, is proved by the correspondence of prisoners who sent thousands and thousands of letters and messages of thanks and of devotion to the Maréchal, at least until 1942.

Afterwards this devotion was shown with a little less enthusiasm; but the generosity of the Maréchal himself never diminished and he continued to take care of the prisoners until the end.

My other functions concerned public appearances. I accompanied the Maréchal on his visits and his tours, and was with him when he received visitors. During these journeys and receptions I heard all the talks which the Maréchal gave, and all the words which he spoke. That which I heard enables me to affirm that the Maréchal most definitely had no pro-German sentiments. And what I am now saying, Mr. Chief Justice, can be confirmed by thousands of people who heard the Maréchal as I did.

In particular, at his public receptions which took place every week at the Hotel du Parc, at which the Maréchal received delegations of young people, of groups, of the mayors of France, of school teachers, and so on, he spoke words of such a nature that it was necessary to ask the press not to publish them, in order to avoid German reprisals.

Proof of what I am now saying, Mr. Chief Justice, can be found, and even heard, if the trouble is taken to find the radio records on which the Maréchal's talks were recorded. Needless to say these talks were not broadcast, but if a careful search is made they can be found and would furnish the proof of what I am saying on this particular point.

Some people have reproached the Maréchal on the grounds that he did not say enough, and others have reproached him for talking too much. In particular the Maréchal has been reproached for a certain number of statements or messages which certainly were not written by him personally even though they were signed by him. But no mention is ever made of the thousands and thousands of talks and addresses which he made in public, which everyone heard, or of his messages. Nevertheless in those words it can be seen that the Maréchal did not always, as he has been accused of doing, preach collaboration nor acceptance of defeat.

What he did preach in all his talks and in all his addresses, and on this point there can be a very large number of witnesses, was on the contrary the love of the fatherland. What he did seek was the conditions necessary for the restoration of the fatherland. The conditions for such a restoration, order and union—that is what can be found in all his messages, and in all the addresses, together with hope for better days, hope for a rebirth.

I will not cite here the Maréchal's messages or even parts of them; I do not know them by heart. But there are certain phrases which recur continually, for example, "Chance is not always misfortune," which the Maréchal repeated many times.

Once in a Christmas message he spoke of the stars which could guide our hopes. Some people with the best of intentions believed that the Maréchal was there referring to or calling upon the stars in the American flag. But in fact the reference was to those stars which have never ceased to shine in the sky of France herself.

That, I believe, is what can be said regarding the Maréchal's talks and addresses.

From another angle, it has been claimed that the Maréchal plotted against the Republic. This does not fall within my field, but I heard all the talks and all the addresses which the Maréchal made and I never heard the Maréchal urge anyone to revolt against the Republic nor even make any sort of appeal against the Republic. On the contrary I can give very definite proof that the Maréchal never sought to do anything against the Republic. In particular, in spite of all the solicitations which may have been made to him on the subject, he was always opposed to the removal from the town halls and public establishments of the busts [Marianne] of the Republic. He was always absolutely against it.

I can also give another proof of what I am saying. In spite of all the appeals made to the Maréchal, in spite of all the proposals which were prepared, the Maréchal always opposed a change in the State seals, and in the official stamps which carried the arms of the Republic, used by the various administrations. Nor was any such change referred to in his addresses.

There has been a great deal of excitement, too, over the fact that the Maréchal did not protest against the acts committed by the Germans in Alsace and Lorraine. I speak about this because in his receptions, where as chief of his cabinet I met his visitors, I often received people from Alsace and Lorraine who came to complain that they had been abandoned by the French government. On this matter I can assure you, but you probably know it better than I do, that not a single act was committed by the German authorities against the people of Alsace or Lorraine without a written protest being made by the armistice commission. And though, again, this does not come within my military sphere, I take the liberty of saying it because I had had a summary of these protests made to show to those from Alsace and Lorraine who, in their despair, came to present their complaints to the cabinet of the Maréchal.

I wish to say one more word regarding the interest which the Maréchal took in the young people and in the work done on their behalf.

The Maréchal took a passionate interest in an undertaking which he himself created or which was created at the beginning of his period in power and which, I believe, was a perfect success. I refer to the youth work camps.

Why did he concern himself with them? It was because he wished to make these work camps into schools of discipline, schools for the training of leaders, and I believe that the proof of his complete success is that all the young people from the youth work camps later proved themselves, without any doubt, either in the various maquis or in the army of de Lattre, and gave their blood willingly.

I have told you that the Maréchal devoted himself to the youth and the youth work camps. He also gave his attention to the scouts, who were not authorized in the occupied zone, but who were authorized in the free zone. General Lafont gave to their work a great development.

That, Mr. Chief Justice, is what I can say regarding the actions and feelings of the Maréchal. This objection has been made: but why did the Maréchal, his anti-German feelings being what they were, remain after 1942 when the Germans crossed the demarcation line?

This point again is not really in my field but I can tell you, because I often heard the Maréchal talk about it, why the Maréchal remained.

He could have left, and it was suggested that he should leave. He was even told in 1942 that a plane was ready to take him to North Africa. The Maréchal often said, "If I were seeking nothing more than my own popularity, there was but one thing to do, take the plane to North Africa."

But the Maréchal did not leave. It has been said, and it has been said repeatedly, that he was not willing to abandon his people in their misery. He had not been willing to abandon them in 1940. In 1942 he said, "Are the people of France less unhappy in 1942 than they were in 1940? I did not abandon them in 1940 and I will not abandon them now."

The Maréchal added too, "Sometimes a single grain of sand is enough to put a machine out of action, even the best constructed of machines, and the best arranged. I could perhaps put that grain of sand in the German machine."

The question was therefore settled so far as the Maréchal was concerned. He stayed because he judged that there was still something to defend, something to save, after 1943. The entire question is to establish whether or not the Maréchal succeeded.

This question is one to which I have neither the competence nor the audacity to reply. Nevertheless I may be permitted to say a word regarding the Obligatory Labor Service, the STO, and to point out that if the armistice had not been signed there would have been four or five million prisoners in 1940 instead of a million and a half, and if the Maréchal had left in 1942 and if he had not dealt with the problem of the STO, then instead of a million and a half men deported there would probably have been far more. The examples of Belgium and unhappy Poland are there to prove it.

(Document No. 276)
Fr. ed. 994-998

[See Document No. 271]

DEPOSITION OF GENERAL DEBENEY IN THE PÉTAIN TRIAL: THE MARÉCHAL'S ORDERS

VICTOR DEBENEY

General of Division

The High Court of Justice: The Trial of Maréchal Pétain.
Presiding Judge: Chief Justice Mongibeaux of the Supreme Court of France.
Fifteenth Session, Wednesday, 8 August 1945.

Christian name: Victor.   *Rank:* General of Division.
Age: 54.   At present in Fresnes prison.
(The witness takes the oath.)

MAITRE PAYEN, PRESIDENT OF THE PARIS BAR: Wasn't General Debeney chief of the armistice services at Vichy?

GENERAL DEBENEY: In April 1943 I became director of the armistice services at Vichy and in that capacity went regularly to see the Maréchal to report the chief happenings and activities of my service and to receive his instructions.

During these interviews I always noted that the instructions which he gave me were to resist German demands to the greatest possible extent, to maintain what could be maintained, and to avoid the worst.

In listening to the Maréchal's instructions and in noting the determination to defend step by step which they inspired in me I could not prevent my thoughts from returning twenty-six years in the past and seeing once more that tenacity of the defender of Verdun which so many Frenchmen of my generation came to know.

I gave up the directorship of the armistice services at the end of July 1944. At that time the Maréchal sent for me and told me that he was going to appoint me secretary-general to replace M. Tracoux who had been refused by the Germans.

I admit that this position frightened me somewhat. It was in fact political in character and I did not feel that I was particularly suited to it. I thought too that the fact that I was a soldier by profession would arouse some suspicion. I told the Maréchal of these doubts. The Maréchal replied that he insisted on having me with him and he repeated his order. I could only accede and I began my service as secretary-general with him on 1 August 1944, the day of the breakthrough at Avranches.

From that moment events moved very rapidly. I was at the Maréchal's side during all that tragic period from 15 to 20 August [1944], which ended in his being carried away by the Germans into captivity.

I was among those who were arrested at the same time. I followed him first to Morvillars and then to Sigmaringen, passing seven extremely hard and grievous months with him. Finally I accompanied him, when, on leaving Sigmaringen, he returned to France through Switzerland; I left him only at the Fort of Montrouge.

Such, very broadly, are the circumstances in which I had the honor to be near to Maréchal Pétain.

(Document No. 277)
Fr. ed. 999

[*See Document No. 271*]

DEPOSITION OF M. DONATI
IN THE PÉTAIN TRIAL:
PREFECTORAL ADMINISTATION

CHARLES DONATI
Prefect

The High Court of Justice: The Trial of Maréchal Pétain.
Presiding Judge: Chief Justice Mongibeaux of the Supreme Court of France.
Sixteenth Session, Thursday, 9 August 1945.

M. DONATI: Maître [title of member of French bar], I am pleased that you should give me this opportunity to make a statement on a point which concerns, I believe, not merely the region for which I was administratively responsible but also the whole of the regions in the northern zone [Region: an administrative group of departements].

You heard on another day the testimony of a prefect from the southern zone; throughout the four years of the occupation I was a prefect in the northern zone. I shall remind you that there was a certain difference between the two zones. The German regulations applied in the northern zone and not in the southern zone, in such a way that a certain number of problems existed in one of the two zones but not in the other.

In the northern zone we did not have to deal with the problem of the militia, unless it was in the very last months. We did not have the problem of the Legion [of War Veterans]. And we did not have the Jewish problem, as the Jews had all very rapidly crossed the demarcation line after the events of June [1940].

On the other hand we did have conflicts with those political parties of which the existence had been authorized, and we did not have sufficient forces under our control to maintain order. We were absolutely dependent on the Germans because we had no army. The southern zone did have an army until November 1942, but we for our part had nothing but the most ridiculous of arms, for each man merely one revolver of ancient model and four cartridges, with no cartridges for training. There were very many young police officers who had never even fired a gun.

It seems to me that after having heard the testimony of a prefect from the southern zone day before yesterday, and after hearing today the testimony of a prefect from the northern zone, the court will have a complete outline of the way in which France was administered during these four years. Thus you may regard my testimony not as the testimony of a single individual but as a sort of collective declaration.

I administered, directly or indirectly, fourteen departements which formed a solid strip of territory from Nantes to Belfort. My collaborators were twenty-five to thirty prefects. I was in contact with the people of the center, the west, and the east of France, and I am able to say what were the reactions in different areas.

We all felt a very great gratitude toward the Chief of the State from the beginning because of the fact that through the magic of his personal action he stopped the enemy in their course at a time when, because of what we had read in *Mein Kampf,* we had expected complete annihilation. At that time we did not know that the armistice, a day of French national mourning, was in fact sounding the knell of the German empire. In the distress which we then felt we were grateful to the Chief of State who gave us the opportunity to begin again to hope, and to regroup ourselves around a leader.

To this gratitude was rapidly added a feeling of admiration as we came to appreciate the grandeur of the sacrifice which the Maréchal had made, the nobility of his sentiments, and the value of the reforms he had imposed on the nation.

We all recognized the meaning of his sacrifice. We were personal witnesses whenever we went to Vichy; at whatever time of day he received us we were certain to note the attention with which the Maréchal listened to us, and his efforts to make himself available to each of us during his work-day, which began at eight o'clock in the morning and ended only at eleven o'clock in the evening, all without a moment of interruption because, morning and night, he received visitors at his table.

I have been received by the Maréchal in the morning and the afternoon; I have been a guest at his table at lunch and at dinner. We all deeply admired his physical, nervous, and intellectual strength as he gave us his concentrated attention, interested himself in all of our problems, and gave us the comfort of his tenacity and courage.

I must add too that this sacrifice of the Maréchal was of the greatest help to us in solving one of the first problems presented to the prefects at the beginning of the occupation, namely that of maintaining the municipal administrations in their activities.

The fact was that all the mayors of France after a very few months of the occupation were tempted to leave their posts. They had not been elected to do the work which they were now expected to do, to endure the pressure of the occupation authorities, to control the food rations of the people, and to supervise a niggardly allocation of coupons permitting the purchase of shoes or gasoline.

There was not a day on which we the prefects of the northern zone did not receive letters from mayors, and not a week in which we did not receive visits from mayors who desired that we should accept their resignations. All that would have been a veritable catastrophe if we had not been able to stop this flight of municipal officials, for the simple reason that the Germans would then have replaced them immediately by men under their own control and perhaps even by German military men.

Consequently it was absolutely essential to keep the municipal organizations in place. We succeeded, and we succeeded by using an argument which proved decisive in every case.

Every time we failed in our arguments with some mayor who insisted on maintaining his resignation we said to him, "Of course you are disgusted by the activities now forced upon you and you suffer because of the unpopularity which is now yours among your fellow citizens. But think a moment; there is one man who bears upon his head the sum of all the heartbreaks which you feel, of all the exhaustion from which you suffer. And that man remains at his post. That man is the Maréchal. He is eighty-five years old. Do as he does, you who are younger than he is and who have far less to endure."

This argument never failed. In my judgment it was the strength of this example of the sacrifice made by the Maréchal that enabled us to maintain at their posts the mayors who at the head of the 40,000 French townships were, from 1940 onward, the principal agents of our resistance and the effective executants of our activity in defense of French interests.

In addition to the value of the example of personal sacrifice, our contacts with the Maréchal enabled us to become acquainted with his feelings.

I wish to say a word regarding the Catholics. We were grateful to him because of his desire to restore spiritual values and because he believed with Poincaré that the country must be given back the soul it had lost and which only a return to traditional catholicism could give it. If Poincaré had still been with us—and I believe that no one could doubt either his republicanism or the strength of the resistance which he would have represented—I am sure that he would have been on our side in this matter.

We were even able to note the anti-German sentiments which the Maréchal made clear in his private conversations. I remember in particular one conversation with him during one of the first audiences which he granted me. I gave some examples of German exactions over which we were indignant, particularly the illegal requisitions; among other points I remember a figure of 20,000 pair of sheets, which had considerably annoyed me. The Maréchal said nothing.

I can tell you frankly that I asked myself whether he heard me or didn't hear me. Or did he feel nothing?

And then at that very instant I noticed that the Maréchal had clenched his fist so tightly that it had turned white. In that fact was revealed to me the spirit of a chief who was unwilling to lose control of himself, or to cause me to lose control, and who maintained his calm by an effort of will power, as though to say, "Of what importance are illegal requisitions in comparison with the vital interests for which I am responsible?"

Shortly afterward there was another incident which impressed me. It occurred when I presented the mayors of Franche-Comté to the Maréchal. You know that one after another all the mayors of France came to see the Maréchal, in small groups. Every week, thirty or forty mayors would be brought to see him. On that particular day I had brought a group of about forty from Franche-Comté and after the interview, after the Maréchal had said a personal word to each of them, one of them broke the circle surrounding the Maréchal and said, "May I have your permission to ask a question?"

"Ask it," the Maréchal said.

"Monsieur le Maréchal," the mayor said, "we sometimes ask ourselves where our true duty lies."

And the Maréchal replied without hesitation, in a single flow of words.

"I see what it is that disturbs you. There is a disturbing factor in France, isn't there? Well, assure yourself that I am the first to suffer from it."

A motion picture and recording camera was turning at the side of the room. It was quickly stopped to prevent what had just been said from creating an incident, as there were other than French ears which listened.

A third time I took the mayors of Anjou and Touraine to see him and one of them during the visit said to the Maréchal, "May I remind you that I had the honor of being presented to you on a certain day in 1940." It was the mayor of a township near Montoire. The Maréchal, with an involuntary gesture of disgust of which I was reminded a few days ago by an article written by the Tharaud brothers in *Figaro*, said, "Oh! I beg you, don't remind me of that memory." I mention this to show that the Maréchal did not go with satisfaction to Montoire, as it has been said he did.

Finally, the Maréchal's patriotic sentiments were for us unquestionable. In the first conversations which I had the honor of having with him he said to me, "What do people think of my policies?"

When I answered, "Your policy of collaboration is not understood, nor is it followed by French public opinion," the Maréchal replied: "Think a moment; I have but one purpose, to maintain intact the territorial frontiers of France, and that is well worth a few blows to self-esteem from time to time."

His words could be interpreted either way, and I consider that coming from a man who had reached the summit of honor and glory, they can be understood in all their greatness.

And if you would like me to give an example of one of those very blows to self-esteem I shall remind you of the message which he read, powerless to disclaim it, the message of which I spoke at the beginning of my deposition.

We also gave the Maréchal our admiration because of the greatness of the reforms which he imposed on the nation. This seems to contradict what has been said, and quite truthfully said, to the effect that the Maréchal was not personally responsible for the government administration.

It is true that the Maréchal had given his powers to the Chief of Government and that he did not deal with the detail of administrative matters. He studied them when they were reported to him but he was not personally an administrator. Nevertheless the Maréchal definitely left his personal mark on three kinds of activity, bringing three great changes which would not have been made without him. I refer to the creation of National Aid, the National Farm Organization, and the re-organization of state administration by regions.

I mention in passing that these three new institutions were criticized by the London radio which regarded them as the result of German interference in our affairs.

Yet now that the Germans are no longer here these three institutions are still maintained, with changed titles. There is no change except in the words. The three institutions remain.

National Aid is now called French Mutual Aid. The regional prefects are now called the commissioners of the Republic. The superintendents of police and the superintendents of economic affairs are now called secretaries-general of police and secretaries for economic affairs.

There is no longer a farm organization [corporation]; instead there is something whose name I have forgotten but which is based precisely on the same principles and renders the same services.

There is no necessity for presenting a long list of what National Aid accomplished. I wish merely to cite one fact which the public in general does not know about, namely that on the Maréchal's orders we made use of National Aid to bring help in every case and in every form of distress which could not be cared for through the normal budgets of the different ministries. Among other examples, it was National Aid which helped the families of all those who were arrested, and particularly of the communists for whom the Germans had forbidden us to grant any subsidies from official funds. National Aid enabled us to relieve suffering which we discovered and which we could not have dealt with in other ways.

I shall illustrate the effectiveness of the services rendered by the National Farm Organization in the matter of food supplies, the dominant concern of all prefects, by a single example.

Before the National Farm Organization was created in 1941 I was prefect of Eure-et-Loir. Like all the prefects I had to arrange for the quota supplies of potatoes. The potato is an essential food as everyone knows, and at that moment we did not have the means of establishing allocation figures for potatoes as we did not even know how many were produced. I asked the farmers to declare their production of potatoes; there is no need to tell you that these declarations were not truthful. To give an example, there were in Eure-et-Loir 30,000 acres planted in potatoes; only 5,000 acres were declared. I had to allocate a quantity of which I did not know the extent. My allocation figures were necessarily both arbitrary and incorrect. I asked one township for 200 tons though it was able to supply only 20 and I asked for 20 tons from another township which could have sent me 200. All this happened because I did not have the means at hand to work reasonably. The instrument for reasonable action was created, though in fact it was not created for this purpose but to defend the rights of the farmers. Nevertheless the farm organization had all the more merit for giving us its help when we asked it to aid us in our task of feeding the people.

In the following year, 1942, when I was asked to supply 50,000 to 100,000 tons of potatoes I was able, by an arrangement with the regional representatives of the farm organization, to apportion my requisitions in a precise and reasonable manner between the different townships, and then again in each township between the different producers of potatoes. And instead of making a failure of our potato distribution, we succeeded. Our success could be seen in the charts given to me one day by a doctor of an asylum or hospital, showing that in the winter of 1941-1942 the death rate had increased because of insufficient food whereas during the following winters, thanks to the farm organization, we were able to supply sufficient food to those communities whose nourishment was our responsibility.

(Document No. 278)
Fr. ed. 1000-1004

[*See Document No. 271*]

DEPOSITION OF M. JARDEL
IN THE PÉTAIN TRIAL:
11 NOVEMBER 1942
THE SCUTTLING OF THE FLEET
JEWISH AFFAIRS

JEAN JARDEL

The High Court of Justice: The Trial of Marécha
Pétain.
Presiding Judge: Chief Justice Mongibeaux of the
Supreme Court of France.
Seventeenth Session, Friday, 10 August 1945.

THE PRESIDING JUDGE: Please state your name, Christian name, age, profession, and domicile.

M. JARDEL: Jardel, Jean, 48 years, living in Paris.

THE PRESIDING JUDGE: You are not under indictment?

M. JARDEL : I am.

THE PRESIDING JUDGE: It is perhaps preferable, as I am hearing you because of my discretionary powers, not to ask you to take oath. That will not prevent you from telling the entire truth. What question do you wish to ask, Mr. President of the Bar?

MAITRE PAYEN, PRESIDENT OF THE PARIS BAR: I wish to ask M. Jardel, all of whose qualifications are familiar to me, what he can tell us of interest regarding the Maréchal's activities.

M. JARDEL: I joined the Maréchal in June 1942, strongly urged by M. Lucien Romier, Minister of State. I left him in December 1943, by German order.

When I first saw the Maréchal, one Tuesday morning in June [1942], he said to me at once, "Germany lost the war in 1918 because she was fighting on two fronts. She has lost the present war under the same conditions and for the same reasons. In all that you do, never forget what I have just told you."

I shall turn now to something quite different which happened on the morning of 11 November 1942. On that day the Germans violated the demarcation line and entered the free zone.

In the absence of the Chief of Government, the Maréchal summoned to his office General Weygand, who had come to Vichy to deal with certain African matters, M. Rochat, secretary-general of foreign affairs, and myself.

The Maréchal had decided to make immediately a solemn and public protest against this violation of the armistice clauses. The Maréchal was to read it to Marshal von Rundstedt as he was passing through Vichy. It would then be broadcast.

Marshal von Rundstedt arrived. He was brought to the Maréchal's office and the Maréchal read the protest to him. The interview was very brief and extremely cold. Marshal von Rundstedt seemed surprised and upset—he certainly did not expect the protest—and returned to his train.

In the meantime I had been informed that the ministers had met in one of the waiting rooms and were discussing the advisability of publishing the protest before the Chief of Government arrived in Vichy. He did return at about eleven or noon.

I went into the waiting room where the ministers were. I took the Minister of Information by the arm and led him to the Maréchal who gave him an order to broadcast the protest immediately.

It was broadcast, and as has been said, I believe, in earlier testimony given here, and as was commonly said at Vichy too, the protest facilitated, without any doubt, the operation in North Africa by tending to release the troops and officials in Africa from their oath of fidelity [to the Maréchal].

On the morning of the day the fleet was scuttled, I was in the Maréchal's office. The Maréchal was extremely sad; we were talking about the scuttling, and at a certain moment the question of the possible departure of the Maréchal came up.

"I have considered the question carefully," the Maréchal said to me. "But I gave my word that I would never leave the French people and that I would share their sufferings to the very end. Anyway, the path of duty is never the most convenient or the easiest, and for me it would be far easier to leave. My departure would save me from the mount of Calvary I am climbing.

"Well, my answer is no. I cannot abandon the French people. I serve as a sort of lightning rod for their protection. History will say later that I protected them from grievous developments. I can still protect them from some. I would stay even though I had to suffer far more."

Finally, I wish to cite one more fact, something that happened in June or July 1943—I don't remember the date precisely. In any case it has already been spoken of in preceding depositions.

The Germans had made a vigorous demand for the mass denaturalization of all Jews who had become French citizens by naturalization since 1936 or 1937. They had even prepared a draft of the necessary law. The question came up in a Council of Ministers. The council reached no decision. In order that a refusal should be certain and instantaneous the Maréchal then brought up the question himself. A note was prepared for the Germans, which he signed, refusing categorically any denaturalization. And this note was given to the Germans in Paris.

For some time, throughout many months, the Germans repeatedly demanded that the question be taken up again. They threatened the Maréchal with the arrest of his Jewish friends in Paris. I believe they did arrest one of them. The Maréchal never signed.

I have finished.

(Document No. 279)
Fr. ed. 1005-1006

[See Document No. 271]

DEPOSITION OF M. LAVAGNE
IN THE PÉTAIN TRIAL :
ATTITUDE TOWARD THE GERMANS
JEWS — OATH OF FIDELITY

ANDRÉ LAVAGNE

Deputy Director of the
Maréchal's Civil Cabinet

The High Court of Justice: The Trial of Maréchal
Pétain.
   Presiding Judge: Chief Justice Mongibeaux of the
Supreme Court of France.
   Seventeenth Session, Friday, 10 August 1945.

THE PRESIDING JUDGE: Your name, Christian name, age, profession, and domicile?

M. LAVAGNE: Lavagne, André, 37 years, a master of appeals in the Council of State, on the available list, living in Paris.

(The witness takes the oath.)

THE PRESIDING JUDGE: What questions, gentlemen?

MAITRE ISORNI [one of the three members of the Paris Bar defending the Maréchal]: M. Lavagne was assistant director of the civil cabinet of the Maréchal for two years. I would like him to tell the High Court what he saw during those two years at least so far as the chief facts are concerned.

M. LAVAGNE: The fact is—and I think this brief preface is necessary— that I held a rather special position, if I dare say so. I was to some extent involved in both the Vichy government and the resistance. I was a Master of Appeals in the Council of State and one fine day M. du Moulin summoned me and made me assistant director of the civil cabinet, retaining for himself the political direction of the cabinet.

I was rather upset. Like all French people, and there was nothing very original about this, I was against collaboration. Like most government officials with ten years' service I was rather hostile toward the new regime and toward the innovations which had begun to appear with the arrival of the newcomers of Vichy.

My reply was a refusal which was badly received; I was given a week to think it over. I returned and refused again. M. du Moulin arranged that others should urge me to accept. After three weeks of hesitation, reflection, regret, and refusal, he ordered me in the Maréchal's name to come to Vichy. Thus it was that I arrived there in July 1941. As an anti-German, if not a Gaullist, and as one who did not conform to the regime —this was my attitude to the end—I was, as I have just said, in touch with the resistance, with Chaveron, with Rollin, and others. I even made an offer to Chaveron that I would replace the man who gave information for the London radio and who had been captured. This happened in 1943. I did not carry out this promise because the Germans asked for my removal. I was nearly arrested but in the end the Germans only asked for my removal and I returned to the Council of State.

I had previously known neither the Maréchal, those about him, nor du Moulin himself. I had no feelings toward them, either for or against. In Vichy I never concealed my anti-German sentiments, and nothing I saw there disturbed me. Throughout the two years I never once received a German in my office. Only two pictures were to be seen in my office, one a portrait of the Maréchal, and the other a poster showing an Alsatian woman with high headdress praying at the grave of a French soldier; the words at the bottom of the picture were: "Remember that 1,500,000 French soldiers died in order that Alsace should become French once again."

I add further, in order to show that I did nevertheless render some service to the resistance, that in the Council of State, out of rather more than one hundred members, there were twenty-five who were removed [at the liberation], though their activities had been much less prominent than mine. I myself was merely placed on the available list for three years. This could be looked on as a sort of negative reward, but nevertheless a way of recognizing the services I had rendered.

There is another point on which nothing has been said but on which without wishing to quibble with the gentlemen of the resistance, I believe something should be said. The proportion of victims, deported and killed, among the resistance was I believe about ten per cent. I understand that the MLN has given an average figure of 800,000 for its members during four years; therefore if 100,000 is taken as the figure for deported and killed—which is to take it very much on the high side—the proportion of victims would be twelve per cent. Now, in the Maréchal's cabinet through the four years the Maréchal used, if I may employ that word, about twenty-five persons. Of these twenty-five, one was killed by the Gestapo, and four were deported, namely General Laure, my chief assistants Saivres and Estèbe, and Chaveron himself. In addition, two were arrested by the Militia, another, hunted by the Gestapo, only just escaped. M. Jardel and I, after having been in a rather dangerous situation, were finally able to get away. You see the proportion of twenty-five per cent in the Maréchal's cabinet is not so bad. We did what we could.

THE PRESIDING JUDGE: But the point under discussion is not what you did yourself. The question is what did the Maréchal do.

M. LAVAGNE: A rather strange fact is that every time the Maréchal had to let one of his collaborators go because of German demands he always replaced that person with another who was equally anti-German. This seems to indicate clearly that the Maréchal himself was not pro-German.

THE PRESIDING JUDGE: He chose his own collaborators?

M. LAVAGNE: Why, of course he chose them, at least those who were to be in direct contact with him. For those who did not have direct contact, for example those who were delegates on special missions, it was I who suggested the names. I would explain to him what their feelings were, and my reasons for proposing them. Sometimes he hesitated, sometimes he agreed.

I could repeat many of the sentences spoken by the Maréchal which reveal his own state of feelings, for example what he said at the lunch at which he received General Giraud for the first time. General Giraud talked at considerable length on the idea that Germany could not avoid being beaten in the end. The Maréchal said to him, "Everything you have just said to me you must explain to Laval. He has improved somewhat since 1940 but there is still a good deal to do. He has his own ideas, but you must make him understand that Germany will be beaten."

Another time he said to me, "America cannot be beaten." He had always had that idea. I still remember, also with reference to his conversation with General Giraud, that he said to him, "They have us by the throat. I am using my own body as a bulwark for the protection of France. I wait for the moment of liberation."

I saw, too, that the Maréchal was always extremely tolerant, an attitude which was in accordance with my own feelings. He had no kind of hate whatever for any French person, no matter who he might be. When some case was referred to him concerning a Freemason who deserved to be freed [from the restrictions against Freemasons], he was never opposed. In the same way in Jewish questions I always saw him show his feelings very definitely. On this subject it may be mentioned that Xavier Vallat got along badly with the Germans and that in February 1942 General Bridoux came to say that the Germans had asked for Vallat's replacement. When Darquier de Pellepoix came to see the Maréchal—I was not there personally but one of my friends, Saivres, reported the incident to me—he was extremely surprised by the way in which the Maréchal received him and by the fact that the Maréchal said, "I am very glad to see you. I hope you will succeed where Xavier Vallat failed. He did not protect the Jews enough." Obviously that had not been what Darquier de Pellepoix expected.

Another time I heard the Maréchal refer openly to Darquier de Pellepoix as a torturer.

I could also tell of the Maréchal's reaction when I told him of the deportations of the Jews, at a time when he no longer held the power and was faced by what had already been done by M. Laval and M. Bousquet, who in fact had an extremely thankless task and who did all that they could, but without advising the Maréchal beforehand.

In the matter of the deportation of the Jews we had at first resisted [the German demands] but had finally given in during July [1943]; but the deportations were completely stopped in September because President Laval, after a period of great tension, had refused to permit their continuance. When I spoke of these deportations to the Maréchal, his feelings of indignation and intense grief were clearly shown. "Reparation for all that must be made as soon as they [the Germans] leave," he told me.

Every time that we were able to protect a Jew, even if it meant sending him out through Spain, we did so. When there was risk of a French person being caught by the Germans the activity of the Maréchal's cabinet was always to protect him.

To take one particular case, I have heard it said that we refused to intervene on behalf of Maître Pierre Masse [a member of the bar]. I did not know Maître Pierre Masse but I guarantee that we tried to intervene and I do not know a single case in which we did not intervene with the greatest possible energy. Before the tension of 1941 the Maréchal had obtained reductions of sentences in fifty out of a hundred cases. I remember perfectly the Masse case, precisely because we intervened in that case many times; and I remember in particular having held in my own hands letters from his sister-in-law, who thanked me.

The Maréchal never refused to intervene in favor of any person whomsoever, and we did make thousands of interventions. Another point is that the Maréchal was not, as people so often seem to say, very strict on the question of the oath of fidelity [to the Maréchal]. It has been said that the Maréchal would have prepared his gas chambers and his deportations camps for those who refused to swear fidelity to him. I know quite well that there was the case of M. Didier, but we had not known about it. M. Didier was removed from his office without our being aware of it because the action was taken by a ministerial order and not by a decree [of the State].

The regulations concerning the oath of fidelity were applied in the Council of State. All members of the Council of State, including those who were active in the resistance and who have today reached the highest posts, swore fidelity to the Maréchal. There was one, however, who had the courage of his convictions and who believed that for the sake of honor some risk should be run: M. Blondeau refused to take the oath.

M. Barthélemy, who was indeed a good Frenchman, and M. Pucheu, demanded that M. Blondeau should leave, for an extremely simple reason. The reason was that they desired that one place should be vacant in the Council of State so that they could assign to it the director of the security police, whom they wished to replace. The conversation between M. Pucheu and myself on this subject was quite agitated. For my part I was unwilling that M. Blondeau should be removed. He had acted in accordance with his principles and I had said to myself, "There at least is a man of character." I had discussions on the matter with M. Pucheu, and with M. Barthélemy, who threatened to speak directly about the matter to the Maréchal, whereas I myself was not willing to tire him with details of that kind. Finally I did talk to the Maréchal about it, and the Maréchal said to me, "But let him come to see me."

M. Blondeau came, and after his visit the Maréchal said to me, "He told me of his scruples and we're going to arrange matters."

The result was that M. Blondeau took an oath which was scarcely an oath at all because it provided that he would not be obliged to act contrary to his conscience, nor in a way contrary to the Republic, the Declaration of Human Rights, and some other things. And the Maréchal was perfectly satisfied.

I apologize for talking so much about the rather delicate question of the oath, but there is, however, also the case of M. Watteau, a lawyer, an air force general on the reserve list, with a magnificent Croix de Guerre, who refused to take the oath and who said generally to the Maréchal, "I wish to be free of any obligations because of the Riom trial. Let us imagine that the result of the trial at Riom is to show that you yourself were guilty; I wish to be able to condemn you; I am unwilling to take the oath of fidelity."

And for that matter no member of the Court of Riom took the oath.

This same broad-mindedness was shown by the Maréchal in all fields. I always saw clearly that he desired that no French person should be troubled unless there were precise facts to be cited against him.

You know—and it is still the same today—that when anyone is put in a concentration camp before it is known whether he is guilty or not, all his financial accounts are blocked with the result that his family is forced to live under conditions which are difficult, to say the least. The families of those who opposed the government were somewhat in that situation, though less seriously.

This is the explanation. The military tribunals were obliged by the armistice convention to sentence, at least formally and by default, all members of the military forces who turned against the government. For the same reason, the tribunals were obliged to add, automatically, to these sentences the further penalty of confiscation of all property.

The Maréchal was informed of this situation. After a rather long exchange of letters on this delicate matter with the various ministries concerned, including war, navy, colonies, and the registrar's office responsible for the actual confiscations, all of these administrations being anxious to protect themselves, we finally succeeded in arranging in the Maréchal's name that such confiscations, which could be ordered only by military tribunals, would never in fact be made. The Maréchal insisted, even after judicial decisions in the matter, that the families of persons so condemned should continue to have the advantage of their property. I am in possession of letters which prove this point.

Along the same line, I also dealt with the question of pardons. My role was purely administrative, but it was I who transmitted the recommendations for pardon to the Maréchal.

The commission for pardons followed a policy which had been laid down on orders from the Maréchal. Needless to say, the Maréchal never opposed this policy of his own free will, and furthermore always acted to strengthen it.

The policy was as follows: Until 1942 there had been one zone which was completely free. The military tribunal, and the tribunals for misdemeanors in that zone often had to sentence French people for illicit dealings with the Germans, for having denounced other French people for crossing the demarcation line, for acts of espionage, for giving information to the enemy, or for having engaged in black market transactions with the Germans. I never noted a single reduction of sentence for French people condemned for such forms of collaboration.

On the other hand I never knew of a sentence against a Gaullist which was not reduced. Not only was no Gaullist ever condemned to death, but even in the case of other sentences the procedure usually followed was this: as a matter of principle a sentence of twenty years hard labor would be pronounced against a Gaullist. A short time later the sentence would be reduced to ten years in prison; then after he had served six months the remainder of the sentence would be remitted.

(Document No. 280)
Fr. ed. 1007-1011

[*See Document No. 271*]

DEPOSITION OF M. BAREISS
IN THE PÉTAIN TRIAL :
RESISTANCE IN ALSACE
THE ARMISTICE

CHARLES BAREISS

Strasbourg Veterinary Surgeon

The High Court of Justice: The Trial of Maréchal Pétain.
Presiding Judge: Chief Justice Mongibeaux of the Supreme Court of France.
Seventeenth Session, Friday, 10 August 1945.

THE PRESIDING JUDGE: Will you please state your name, christian name; age, profession, and domicile.

M. BAREISS: Bareiss, Charles Louis, age forty, a veterinary doctor, living in Strasbourg.

(The witness takes the oath.)

THE PRESIDING JUDGE: What questions, gentlemen of the jury?

MAITRE LEMAIRE [one of the three members of the Paris Bar defending the Maréchal]: Dr. Bareiss was until September 1942 the leader of the resistance in Alsace-Lorraine and as I desire that no ambiguity whatever on this point shall remain in the minds of the jurors I wish to read a certificate from the chief of the French Forces of the Interior in Alsace-Lorraine.

"Major Marceau certifies that Dr. Bareiss (Charles) was the leader of the first important resistance movement in Alsace in 1940; its work was the organization of combat groups, the preparation of lines of escapes for French prisoners coming from German camps, and the establishment of an information service for France and the Allies. Dr. Bareiss was arrested by the Gestapo in June 1942, brought before German court-martial, and condemned to death in March 1943. His execution was postponed. He was held in the camps in Bruchsall, Ludwigsburg, and Zwickau until he was freed by the Allied armies."

I would like, therefore, to put a first question to Dr. Bareiss. Can he tell us how it happened that he was not executed?

M. BAREISS: We were condemned, thirteen of us, on 10 March 1943. Our friends immediately appealed to Vichy and approached Maréchal Pétain who at once undertook negotiations. By making use of his personal prestige he obtained through Ribbentrop and through the chief of staff of the German army, Marshall Keitel, the postponement of our execution. I can state definitely that only the Maréchal's personal intervention saved our lives, because Gauleiter Wagner, governor of Alsace and Baden, was flatly opposed to any pardon for us and had demanded our execution, or at least my execution.

THE PRESIDING JUDGE: No questions, gentlemen of the jury?

MAITRE LEMAIRE: Another question: Could Dr. Bareiss tell us what was the general opinion in Alsace at the time of the armistice concerning the Maréchal himself?

M. BAREISS: I can say that at the time of the armistice all Alsace believed that the armistice was secured only by Maréchal Pétain and because of the prestige of his glorious record as a soldier. We believe that the armistice saved France from becoming a second Poland. It saved France from becoming an enormous concentration camp and from mass deportations.

Because of this fact it is certain that the resistance, regarded from this point of view, is an activity made possible only by the armistice which the Maréchal obtained, and I am certain that it was nothing but the pride of Hitler, drunk with military glory, unable to refuse the opportunity to receive the obeisance of the victor of Verdun, which obtained this advantage for France.

It is certain too that the armistice enabled France to maintain its North African positions intact, a fact which in my opinion was the first guarantee leading to final victory and to the crushing of Germany.

MAITRE LEMAIRE: Another question: what was the attitude of the German press in Alsace toward the Maréchal?

M. BAREISS: I paid very little attention to the German press until my arrest, but I read it regularly for as long as I was allowed to have a newspaper, while the case against me was being prepared. I can say that the German press never ceased to attack the Maréchal. It accused him of having constantly restrained Laval in his desire for collaboration. The German press held him responsible for forcing France to lose that position in the future and in the new Europe, which had been foreseen for it, the position which France would have been able to take if it had accepted its responsibilities and if Maréchal Pétain had not acted contrary to the good will of the collaborators and in particular of M. Laval.

In any case the Maréchal was continuously attacked by the German press and I remember clearly, on this point, an article in which Paul Shall, the specialist and second in authority in the German press in Germany, wrote—I am giving a precise translation—"His past proves that Pétain is not a friend of the Germans and that he cannot be."

I recall too that Gauleiter Wagner, governor of Alsace and Baden, said to M. Fuchs at the Hotel of Donnon, Schirmeck, during 1942, at some intimate gathering one evening—his remarks were brought to us by one of our absolutely reliable agents—"I have no confidence in Pétain. He is an old fox and he is playing tricks on us. In my opinion he is the very symbol of duplicity."

(Document No. 281)
Fr. ed. 1012-1013

[See Document No. 271]

GENERAL DE LANNURIEN'S DEPOSITION IN THE PÉTAIN TRIAL: A CONVERSATION WITH THE MARÉCHAL

DE LANNURIEN

General of the Army

The High Court of Justice: The Trial of Maréchal Pétain.
Presiding Judge: Chief Justice Mongibeaux of the Supreme Court of France.
Seventeenth Session, Friday, 10 August 1945.

At the beginning of 1942 I happened to be on a visit to Vichy. The Maréchal was talking about the general situation. I pointed out to him that he was being criticized. I can still hear the Maréchal's answer: "You may be certain that there is nothing, absolutely nothing, of what is being said in France against me, in France and outside of France, of which I am unaware. But I do not want to pay any attention to it. I shall keep on my own path no matter what happens, certain that I am working for the good of France. Do you imagine I wouldn't be far better off at home than here, faced by the difficulties which pile up day by day, amidst criticism from every side? But I shall not leave. I stayed in order that France may live. I will not fail in my duty."

In October 1943 I was back in Vichy again. The landing in North Africa had taken place. The question of the moment was still, "Ought he to have left? Ought he to have stayed?"

The Maréchal talked to me about it many times. In one of the first of these conversations he said, "I have been reproached with not having left when the Germans entered the free zone. Why should I have left? I did not stay here merely because it was a free zone. I stayed because of France, the whole of France, and perhaps still more for occupied France. The fact that today France is entirely occupied is one more reason for remaining. I have not left."

"I have been reproached for not having protested vigorously enough when the Germans crossed the demarcation line," he said another time. "I did protest, in agreement with General Weygand. But quite sincerely and in all reason, what more could I say? The Germans, from their point of view, were doing the right thing in crossing the line and rushing to the sea. They were threatened with a stab in the back by a landing on the Mediterranean coast of France. If they had not done as they did, they would have been acting like children. Well, they are not children. But my own duty did not change. I stayed because of France. I have not left."

In speaking of the general situation the Maréchal said to me, "I have to navigate continually through varied hazards. The Germans are still here in France and for the present they are the stronger. I cannot make a mess of what I have already done, for then we would lose the benefit of these three years during which we have maintained the safety of France. The English, the Americans, the Allies—at no price am I willing to break with them. I wish to wait till they are strong enough. At that moment I will take the necessary decisions. And those who are in rebellion against us—I do not wish to break with them but to open my arms to them when the time comes.

"My political staff and collaborators? They often hinder me. They believe they are doing the right thing, but they take me too far. You see how I have to change course all the time," he went on, "to get between the rocks and the sand banks. They call that 'playing a double game.' It is not a double game. I keep rigorously to the terms of the armistice, and for anything else I act freely. I am playing the armistice, which means merely a suspension of arms, in order to wait, to see what is coming, and to recuperate our strength. I am playing the card of France and I am determined to carry France to the very end in order that her voice shall be loud and firm on the day when peace is made.

"I am convinced that I am the only one," the Maréchal added, "who can still speak strongly enough, and can still dominate the Germans and the Allies, on the day when we sit at the conference table."

Another time, in speaking of rebellion against the government, the Maréchal talked of the problems of conscience which faced officials and many officers in France and in North Africa.

"Those who were on duty had only to obey," he said. "It was their duty to obey those immediately above them no matter who they were. If everyone began to discuss the order given him there would be no more army and no more state. The others, those who were in France, have acted according to their own consciences. There is nothing to be said about it. I wish to open my arms to everyone, even to the greatest, even to those who have fought against me the most, provided they create for me over there a strong army and a disciplined army, provided they allow me to maintain order in Africa and to take it back if it becomes necessary, and provided they allow me to take action in France when the right time comes and to speak in a strong firm voice on the day when peace is made."

One evening at table—it was the evening before my departure—a general conversation was being carried on. The Maréchal was absorbed in thought. One of the guests—I can still see him in my mind's eye—said, "Monsieur le Maréchal, the Germans will carry you away by force."

"And the Gaullists will bring you before a High Court," another remarked quickly.

I was somewhat shaken by this conversation. I said so to the Maréchal as we left the table, and the Maréchal, his hand on my shoulder, said to me in low tones, "You return to the occupied zone tomorrow. Now listen carefully. I have remained only in order that France may live. The Germans can take me away by force if they wish. The French can bring me to trial if they desire to. But so long as I am free I will not leave."

Today the predictions of that dinner table have come to pass. The Maréchal was taken to Germany by force. The Maréchal has been brought before a High Court. Another man than the Maréchal might perhaps have killed himself or sought asylum somewhere. The Maréchal returned. He is here today.

(Document No. 282)
Fr. ed. 1014-1015

[See Document No. 271]

JOURNAL OFFICIEL
THE TRIAL OF PÉTAIN

JEAN LEMAIRE

*Attorney at the Court of Appeals
of Paris*

I the undersigned Jean Lemaire, attorney at the Court of Appeals of Paris, living in Paris, deposit in the Hoover War Library, those issues of the *Journal Officiel de la République française* for the month of August 1945, which contain the proceedings of the trial of Maréchal Pétain in the High Court.

(Document No. 284)
Fr. ed. 1016

Paris, 13 April 1955

JEAN LEMAIRE

[*Further statements which particularly concern Maréchal Pétain are to be found in Chapter XV of the present translation, Document No. 243, Deposition of General Conquet; and in a large number of the articles and books deposited by their authors in the Hoover Library and noted here in the relevant chapters.*]

PART SIX

DECLARATIONS CONCERNING PIERRE LAVAL

CHAPTER XX

PIERRE LAVAL

ALSACE — LORRAINE

ERIC STOEBER

Doctor of Law;
Attorney at the Court of Appeals of Paris;
President of the Bar of Colmar

The undersigned Eric Stoeber, formerly president of the Bar of Colmar, makes under oath the following declaration:

In 1940 I left Alsace when the Germans arrived, in order not to be subjected to the regime of annexation which I foresaw. As a result an order of expulsion was issued against me by the German authorities. I took refuge in Paris, where I practiced law until the liberation of Colmar allowed me to return home.

In March 1943 I was advised that a certain number of important Alsatians, among whom was one of my personal friends, had been condemned to death by the Supreme Military Tribunal of the German Reich (Reichskriegsgericht) at Strasbourg on 10 March 1943 for acts of resistance. According to the German newspapers sent to me at that time, their names were as follows: Doctor Charles Bareiss, Mulhouse; Alfred Wenninger, Colmar; Manfred Brucker, Strasbourg; Frédéric Schaelderlé, Strasbourg; François Meyer, Strasbourg-Neudorf; Georges Henner, Mulhouse; Joseph Bossenmeyer, Haguenau; Robert Heitz, Strasbourg; Raymond Berchtold, Mulhouse; François Anklo, Mulhouse; Charles Vuillard, St.-Amarin; Émile Crémer, Belfort.

According to my informants, the Gauleiter for Alsace, Robert Wagner, was very bitter against these men and particularly against the intellectuals among them whose execution he desired to obtain at any cost in order to set an example.

I proposed, therefore, to ask the French government of the epoch to intercede in order to prevent this execution. Opinions regarding such a step were divided. Some had great hopes of a French intervention; others, on the contrary, feared that it would worsen the situation of the condemned in the eyes of the Germans. Since the dossier was in the hands not of the Nazi party or the Gestapo but of the very highest German military court, I was of the former opinion. Therefore I decided to ask for an audience with M. Pierre Laval, then Chief of Government of the French State. He received me at Vichy on 26 March 1943.

I explained to M. Laval that the accused had been condemned either for aiding in the escape of French prisoners of war, for having formed secret organizations which were to begin their work when the Germans left, or for having sent reports to France on the material and moral situation in which the Germans had placed the Alsatians. All these activities were classed by the Germans as "intelligence with the enemy," the enemy in this case, the beneficiary of the activities, being France. I stressed particularly the case of M. Robert Heitz, whose condemnation was based essentially on having sent to Vichy a report on the situation in Alsace and on the spirit of resistance among the people.

M. Laval readily agreed to take steps on behalf of my friends. He pointed out that he himself could not be reproached with being an enemy of Germany and that it was on this ground that he would base his attempt to get the sentences commuted. He promised that he would see the German minister Schleier, Counselor of the German Embassy and the right-hand man of Otto Abetz. On leaving me M. Laval twice told me, "I will do my utmost."

I know that the appeal he promised me was in fact made and that it was taken seriously, for a member of the German Embassy who had found my name on one of the notes submitted by M. Laval telephoned me a few days later to ask for some supplementary information. At that time he told me that the appeal of the French government would be transmitted with a favorable notation to Mr. Ribbentrop, the Reich Minister of Foreign Affairs.

After the liberation of Alsace, a counselor at the Court of Appeals of Colmar and a relative of M. Alfred Wenninger, one of the condemned persons, told me that he had had occasion to see during the war the German dossier, that a communication on the subject of M. Laval's intercession was in fact included, and that this intercession had had considerable influence on the decision of the Germans to commute the sentences.

On 9 July 1943 the situation of my friends seemed to have become worse, and I therefore made a new appeal to M. Laval. He agreed to appeal a second time to the German Embassy.

In the end all the sentences were changed to imprisonment. Today, according to information I have received, the condemned men have all been liberated and have returned to France. This result is due in large measure to the intercessions of M. Laval.

In support of my statements I attach (1) a copy of an undated note which I submitted to M. Pierre Laval on 26 March 1943; (2) a copy of my note of 8 July 1943 which I submitted to him on 9 July; and (3) a copy of a note of 12 July 1943, written after my second interview with M. Laval, to be sent to M. de Brinon.

(Document No 1)
Fr. ed. 1021-1025

Colmar, 13 October 1945

E. STOEBER

Annex 1

NOTE CONCERNING THE SENTENCES PRONOUNCED
AT STRASBOURG 10 MARCH 1943 AGAINST
M. ROBERT HEITZ AND OTHERS

The Supreme Military Tribunal of the German Reich passed judgment at Strasbourg on 10 March 1943 in a case in which several sentences of death were pronounced, including those on M. Wenninger, police magistrate at Colmar; M. Henner, police commissioner at Mulhouse; and M. Robert Heitz, under-director of social insurance at Strasbourg. M. Wenninger was accused of having aided the escape of French prisoners of war and of having attempted to create an organization which would enter into operation after the departure of the Germans. M. Henner was accused of having supplied false identity papers to escaped prisoners. M. Heitz was condemned solely for having tried to send to Vichy a report to the French government on the spirit of the people in Alsace.

These condemnations were based on Article 91B of the German penal code, which provides sentences of death or life imprisonment for any activity which tends to aid during wartime any power which is an enemy of Germany, and for any activity prejudicial to the armed forces of the Reich. These condemnations assume that France is an enemy power.

The sentence pronounced against M. Robert Heitz is especially harsh in view of the fact that, being legally of French nationality, he had done nothing more than try to inform his government on the state of opinion in Alsace. M. Heitz is an Alsatian of the first importance: a painter and literary critic well known and highly thought of; a French patriot, though without hostility toward Germany; and a determined adversary of the Popular Front, though not active in politics. He has many friends in Alsatian circles. The execution of the condemned persons would arouse in these circles a most intense grief, particularly in the case of M. Heitz, who must be regarded as one of the most eminent representatives of French Alsace.

The situation in Alsace has become tragic since the occupation authorities introduced obligatory military service. Many young men have taken refuge in Switzerland to escape this obligation. The authorities have responded by deporting the families of these young men. The execution of distinguished persons who in the eyes of the population have done nothing but act in accordance with their French feelings can only create an atmosphere incompatible with the efforts undertaken by the French government to bring about better understanding between the two neighboring nations.

Annex 2

NOTE

In March 1943 President Laval consented to intercede with the German government on behalf of the following persons: Doctor Charles Bareiss, Mulhouse; Alfred Wenninger, Colmar; Manfred Brucker, Strasbourg; Frédéric Schaelderlé, Strasbourg; François Meyer, Strasbourg-Neudorf; Georges Henner, Mulhouse; Joseph Bossenmeyer, Haguenau; Robert

Heitz, Strasbourg; Raymond Berchtold, Mulhouse; François Anklo, Mulhouse; Charles Vuillard, St.-Amarin; Émile Crémer, Belfort.

All of these men were condemned to death by the Supreme Military Tribunal of the German Reich, sitting at Strasbourg on 10 March 1943, for espionage and activity on behalf of an enemy power, namely France.

This intercession seemed to have been favorably received, and the lawyers acting for the condemned persons hoped that some clemency would be accorded to their clients. But it appears now that new difficulties have developed.

Under these conditions a further intercession by the Chief of Government, based on his desire to prevent executions of eminent Alsatians who have done nothing more than prove their attachment to France, would be extremely useful and might perhaps result in a decision favorable to the unfortunate condemned persons.

Such an intercession would appear to be most urgent, since a decision is to be reached very shortly.

Paris, 8 July 1943

Annex 3

NOTE

On 10 March 1943 the Supreme Military Tribunal of the German Reich (Reichskriegsgericht) sitting at Strasbourg, condemned to death for espionage and activity on behalf of an enemy power, namely France, the following persons: Doctor Charles Bareiss, Mulhouse; Alfred Wenninger, Colmar; Manfred Brucker, Strasbourg; Frédéric Schaelderlé, Strasbourg; François Meyer, Strasbourg-Neudorf; Georges Henner, Mulhouse; Joseph Bossenmeyer, Haguenau; Robert Heitz, Strasbourg; Raymond Berchtold, Mulhouse; Charles Vuillard, St.-Amarin; François Anklo, Mulhouse; Emile Crémer, Belfort.

At the beginning of April 1943 President Laval consented to intercede with the German government on behalf of these persons who had been condemned to death, basing his intercession particularly on the fact that even though legally France could be considered as being still at war with Germany, this technical description in no way corresponded to the actual relations between the two countries, and that therefore anything done by Alsatians on behalf of France ought not to be judged as severely as it would be if the power in question were effectively an enemy of Germany.

This intercession was favorably received, and it was hoped that some measure of clemency would soon be accorded all the condemned. However new difficulties seem to have arisen in this matter, and the reduction of sentence which was thought to have been obtained appears to be again under discussion. Under these conditions President Laval has agreed to undertake a new intercession in favor of the condemned men; this, however, cannot take place until after the return of Minister Schleier at the end of the week.

Since an intercession is at this moment believed to be extremely urgent, President Laval has decided while waiting for the Minister's return to ask Ambassador de Brinon to be good enough to present this matter personally to the German authorities without delay.

The affair is one which has aroused in Alsace intense emotion because of the character of the condemned persons, who come from the most varied circles and are all highly esteemed. They were above all motivated by their attachment to the French fatherland and had no intention of stirring up anti-German troubles. Some of them were charged with having aided in the escape of French prisoners; but there was never any intention of putting these liberated prisoners in the service of the enemies of Germany. Others, it seems, had thought to create organizations for maintaining order *after* the departure of the German forces. The espionage of which some were accused had nothing to do with military information but concerned merely the political situation in Alsace.

The moral suffering endured by the people of this province since the beginning of the war makes them extremely appreciative of any measure of benevolence. If the French government by its intercession should obtain a lighter sentence for these condemned men, it would be assured of the deep gratitude of the people concerned.

LAVAL'S PRIVATE SECRETARIAT

** ***

[*The following statement, numbered 2B, was prepared by two members of the private secretariat of* Pierre Laval *on 2 November 1945. Another statement,, more detailed, numbered 2A, was prepared at the same time and deposited with the Hoover Library, but on the condition that it should not be made public until 1970.*]

The voluminous mail addressed to M. Pierre Laval was dealt with each day by his private secretariat. Decision as to the action to be taken in connection with each letter was based on the principles and methods which had been followed by the two commissions for petitions, one for the Senate and one for the Chamber of Deputies, of the French Parliament.

There was no longer any activity in the two chambers, yet the right of petition is a traditional right recognized as belonging to all citizens. Ought they to be prevented from exercising that right? Or should they be permitted to use it, thus transferring to the executive branch—now the only one remaining—a task which until then had fallen to the legislative branch? Without attempting to find a technical solution of the juridical problem, a simple pratical solution was reached by applying in the secretariat of M. Laval the method formerly followed in the petition commissions.

Considered from this angle the problem appeared very simple. It was no longer necessary that the secretariat of M. Laval should be in intimate relation with him because it was not in fact the secretariat of a man but of a government service. It needed to deal only with routine cases; a secretariat of this type was by its very nature incompetent to deal with questions of principle or matters of a general character. Those who wrote were for the greater part poor people who presented their problems, their difficulties, and their misfortunes. In most cases the solution did not depend directly on services under M. Laval's direct control, and the secretariat transmitted such letters to the appropriate ministers and informed the writers of the action taken. The secretariat also asked the ministries to report the action which they took. In matters of special interest a report was made to M. Laval himself. The procedure was the same for personal visitors as for letters.

In addition to summarizing the basic rules of the private secretariat, in both conception and execution, in its co-operation with M. Pierre Laval, it will be useful to describe clearly the spirit which always inspired its activities. Those who constituted the private secretariat paid no attention whatever to the question of whether the petitioners did approve or did not approve the policies of the government. All that mattered was that they should be worthy of interest or sympathy.

What I have said above may be summarized thus: the members of the private secretariat belonged to no group and to no political party; M. Laval always left them free to act with the greatest independence of spirit and heart in spite of the increasingly heavy difficulties which the occupation and its consequences imposed upon our country. In the sector for which they were responsible they were humble workers in the great task of enabling the French to live despite the occupying power.

M. Pierre Laval knew of everything that was being done. Even though he intentionally paid no attention to the details, he knew the principles that were being followed, he approved the means, and he was ready to judge by the results.

From July to December 1940 and again from April 1942 to August 1944 tens of thousands of letters were sent out in the name of M. Pierre Laval. From the point of view of the most rigorous patriotism I do not believe that a single one of them could arouse the slightest reproach.

That is what the private secretariat of M. Pierre Laval was; that is how it functioned.

From July to December 1940, and from April 1942 to August 1944, the private secretariat did its work in the manner just described, except for some special tasks assigned personally to some members of the staff: (a) the first of these concerned the application of the law of 25 August 1942 regarding the internal administration of the Chamber and of the Senate; (b) the second concerned exceptions in favor of some high officers of Masonic orders who would otherwise be excluded, by reason of such office, from public service; and (c) the last matter concerned the painful problem of Alsace-Lorraine, which was present in the mind of every French citiz n, the German occupation there being more harsh than anywhere else.

(a) *Parliamentary Civil Servants*

Under the terms of the law promulgated on 25 August 1942 by M. Laval, the official staff of each of the two chambers had to cease operations after 31 August 1942. The presidents of the chambers (M. Jeanneney and M. Herriot) would no longer receive the various payments which they had in fact received up to that date even though Parliamentary activity had ceased in July 1940.

The functions of internal administration and financial management exercised up to 31 August 1942 by the two bureaus were to be entrusted to two secretaries-general, one for each of the two chambers. Each of these two was to be either the former secretary-general of the Questure [internal administration of a chamber] or a "secretary-general named by a decree on the proposal of the Chief of Governement."

The problem, generally speaking, was to maintain parliamentary institutions by assuring to the best ability of the secretariat the continuity of the internal administration of both assemblies. The employees and officers of Chamber and Senate asked their colleagues who were close to the Chief of Government to intercede to help clear up two matters which were among their chief anxieties, namely the choice of the two secretaries-general and the status of persons employed by the two assemblies.

The decisions of M. Laval conformed to the opinion submitted by this secretariat.

The secretary-general of the bureau of the Senate, M. de la Pommeraye, was at that time close to 68 years old. His colleague in the Chamber organization, M. Labrousse, was over 70. As the new secretary-general of the Senate M. Laval chose M. Miegeville, the Senate's senior official, oldest civil servant in the highest grade in the Senate's service. From the point of view of protocol the choice was irreproachable. It was as good politically; there is no indiscretion in saying that this appointment received the approval of M. Jeanneney. One can add, to confirm what has already been said, that M. Miegeville still occupies the same post. Moreover, by a regulation of 26 October 1945, signed by M. Jeanneney, he has just been named associate secretary-general for legislative services of the Constitutional Assembly.

For the Chamber of Deputies M. Pecheux was kept in his post of secretary-general by M. Laval; today he holds the same position. By the regulation of 26 October 1945, just referred to, he was named associate secretary-general for administrative services of the Constitutional Assembly.

Thus from 1942 the chambers had at their heads two civil servants of high grade, men particularly qualified both by their abilities and by their long experience.

The task was delicate. They fulfilled it exceedingly well. First of all they had to protect the buildings and parts of buildings, the annexes, the furniture, the archives, the works of art, the libraries, and so on, which were in constant danger through the presence of the Germans in both the Luxembourg and the Palais Bourbon.

Next they were responsible for internal administration and the management of finances; the use of the credits which were allocated, the expenses of administration, the payment of salaries to the civil servants and agents of the two chambers and the payment of pensions to members of the two houses (except those of Alsace and Lorraine, to whom during the entire occupation the full amount of their parliamentary salary was regularly paid).

Finally, the two secretaries-general had to maintain a staff of civil servants sufficiently large to be able to make a session possible without delay when the need eventually arose, and to make certain that such a session would be neither prevented nor retarded for lack of qualified personnel and equipment. The secretary-general of the Senate had the special task of keeping constantly up to date a list of all members of the National Assembly [i.e., of the two houses].

Each member of the administrative and legislative personnel of the two chambers had, since 1940, continued to be paid by the chamber which employed him, but only a small number were now actually needed to help the two secretaries-general. The majority had therefore been lent to various state administrations, ministries, prefectures, etc. But Article 4 of the law of 27 August 1942 stipulated that all civil servants and officers of the chambers should be definitively transferred to public administrations before 31 December of that year.

This provision alarmed the personnel of the two chambers; and the civil servants and officers of the Senate and Chamber so informed the private secretariat, which included two former Senate employees and which took up the defense of this personnel with President Laval. M. Laval informed them that he had no intention of applying this provision; and in fact it was never applied. Why? Because he thought that although it might be well to detach the personnel of the chambers for temporary assignments to other services of the State, they should nevertheless remain essentially at the call of the chambers themselves, where their services would be indispensable should it become necessary to convoke suddenly either the Senate or the Chamber, or both as the National Assembly.

(b) *Exceptions to the Law on Secret Societies*

The dissolution of all secret societies had been ordered by the law of 13 August 1940, signed by Adrien Marquet as Minister of the Interior, and Raphael Alibert, as Minister of Justice. The law provided two kinds of action: (1) the dissolution of groups or associations which were secret in character; and (2) an undertaking from all persons performing public duties, to the effect that they did not at the time of signing belong to a secret organization, and that they never would thereafter belong to such an organization.

The law of 11 August 1941 required (1) that the names of former high officials of secret societies should be published in the *Journal Officiel*, and (2) that such high officials should be forbidden to exercise certain public functions.

Under Art. 6 of the law of 10 November 1941 two groups were to be considered as 'high officials' of the dissolved societies: (1) those who as members of those societies had reached a higher degree than the third, or who had received honors in the third degree; and (2) those who, as members of those societies had been elected to any office or function in the lodges, obediences, congresses, or assemblies.

The public functions and offices which former high officials of secret societies were forbidden to accept or exercise were specified in Art. 2 of the law of 2 June 1941 referring to the status of the Jews, as completed by the law of 11 August 1941 (of which Art. 2 refers to Art. 2 of the law of 2 June 1941) and by the law of 17 December 1941.

The chief functions listed are those of the Chief of State and members of the government; all juridical functions including those of both the administrational and the judicial tribunals; the engineering posts in the services for mines, bridges, and roads; the service of Inspectors of Finance; all elective assemblies; all positions as arbitrator; in the ministries, all secretaries-general, directors-general, and directors; all posts in the prefectoral administration; all diplomatic career positions; all posts as professor or instructor; all commissioned and noncommissioned ranks in the land, sea, and air forces; and all positions of management in enterprises holding government concessions or receiving subsidies.

To this list must be added all posts in the colonies concerned with government, administration, justice, police, education, and so on, as stipulated in the law of 25 October 1941.

The effect was that former high officials and officers of the lodges were automatically placed in the position of having resigned from all the public offices just mentioned.

At the same time a procedure for exceptions to these regulations was established by the law of 10 November 1941. To a special commission was assigned the task of giving its opinion on all demands for such exceptions. On receiving the opinion of the commission the Chief of State might, in individual cases, cancel the exclusion from office which would otherwise be effective.

The commission was established as a part of the Ministry of Justice. It consisted of five members who were appointed by the decree of 2 December 1941 published in the *Journal Officiel* on 3 December.

Art. 3 of the law of 10 November 1941 provided that exceptions might be made in two cases: (1) when the person concerned had many years previously broken all connection with all Masonic bodies or their various subsidiaries and had ceased all participation in their activities, and (2) when the person concerned had rendered signal services to the French state and had shown clearly his total adhesion to the new order.

Demands for exception had to be examined by the ministry to which the person concerned belonged; such examination did not have the effect of suspending the exclusion (Art. 4, law of 10 November 1941).

The commission examined the dossiers thus prepared and was empowered by Art. 5 of the law of 10 November 1941 either (a) to re-establish the person in his previous post, (b) to reclassify him for employment in some other position, or (c) to maintain the decision previously taken.

Officials who were re-established in their positions were then dealt with according to the provisions of 3 April 1941 relative to admission to posts in public administrations (Art. 13, Sections 2 and 3):—"They will be re-established, on their request, in their administration and in the grade, class or section, and rank which they would have occupied if they had remained in office. In such cases, for the purpose of calculating their length of service, they will be regarded as never having ceased to exercise their functions and they will be paid an indemnity equal to half of the allowance, wage, or salary, with supplemental payments, which would have been paid to them during the period in which their service was interrupted, to which payments will be added, if applicable, the usual family allocations."

When Pierre Laval returned to power in April 1942 he wished to have all matters concerning the secret societies under his direct control. This was the purpose of the law of 21 June 1942: "All questions concerning secret societies referred to by the first article of the law of 15 August 1940 are now assigned to the Chief of Government who may delegate the powers thus conferred upon him to one of the secretaries of state who assist him."

A decision bearing the same date, 21 June 1942, assigned these powers to Admiral Platon, Secretary of State attached to the Chief of Government. The law of 21 June 1942 represented the first phase of a plan which Pierre Laval had thought out and carefully prepared. The second phase was represented by the law of 19 August 1942. Its first effect was to bring the special commission instituted by the law of 10 November 1941, previously assigned to the Minister of Justice, under the direct control of the Chief of Government. Its members were to be named by decree and "were to be chosen among important persons without attachments to the secret societies or their leaders." (Art. 1, law of 10 November 1941.)

It was also provided that "the commission may ask representatives of the administrations interested in the solutions of questions submitted for its examination to sit with it in a consultative capacity." (Art. 2 of the same law.)

Finally, the powers of the commission were extended. In addition to the three powers which it had already received from Art. 5 of the law of 10 November 1941, namely (a) to re-establish the person completely in the same office, (b) to reclassify him in another function, or (c) to refuse the request, the commission now had another power. This fourth power enabled it to propose the re-establishment of a large number of petitioners for a special period of two years. This was possible under Art. 3 of the law of 19 August 1942:—"Entirely as an exception, and apart from the cases covered by Art. 3 of the law of 10 November 1941 (see above), the Chief of Government after receiving the opinion of the commission may suspend, by special decision in an individual case, for a period of two years, the application of the bans and disqualifications which in accordance with laws and regulations in force had been applied to former members of secret societies. Such action may be taken on the double condition that the step is justified by the higher interests of the service affected, and by proof given by the persons in question that they adhere to the new order."

At the end of the two year period a new examination of the case would lead to a decision as to whether the person was to be excluded again, or freed from all bans.

The law of 21 April 1943 confirmed the powers regarding secret societies which it was the Chief of Government's intention to hold personally. This law revised the law of 21 June 1942 in the following terms:—"All questions concerning secret societies referred to by Art. 1 of the law of 13 August 1940 are assigned to the Chief of Government, who may delegate such powers to a Secretary of State."

The first to direct the work of this commission was a chief justice of the court of Riom, who has been made an honorary chief justice since the liberation. He directed the work of the special commission from its formation until he was replaced by M. Reclus, a President of Section in the Council of State. During this period exceptions were granted very sparingly. The members of the commission can testify to this fact and still better proof is given by the statistics of the commission's sessions.

A change came when Pierre Laval took power in 1942.

The law of 21 June 1942 and that of 19 August 1942 provided new grounds on which the commission could now act. The working instrument which Pierre Laval had sought was now available. The commission had the power to grant freely the exceptions for which it was asked. It was to do its work in a spirit of pacification and reconciliation between Frenchmen, in accordance with the desire of its president, M. Reclus.

M. Reclus thereafter presided over every meeting of the commission. Anti-Masonic bigotry, through which an opening had been battered within the commission itself, did however make a last effort to gain control when a draft of a law prepared under Admiral Platon's direction was submitted for an opinion.

This draft law provided a sharp increase in the harshness of existing legislation. It was submitted to the commission for opinion on 4 October 1942 but was not examined until 20 February 1943, when it was only barely refused, thanks to the deciding vote of the commission's chairman, M. Reclus, the vote of the members having been four to four.

Admiral Platon made a serious matter of this disapproval. On 2 March 1943 he sent a letter to the Chief of Government demanding that M. Reclus be removed from his position as chairman of the special commission.

But Pierre Laval did not share the views of Admiral Platon. Quite to the contrary; as this incident had shown that anti-Masonic bigotry still might dominate the commission he added two more members, M. Bernon and M. Cannac, by a decree dated 5 March 1943.

This decree was published on 7 March 1943 in the *Journal Officiel*. On 8 March Admiral Platon sent another letter to the Chief of Government expressing his astonishment, "on becoming aware of the thought of the Chief of Government only through reading the *Journal Officiel*," the decree of 5 March not having been submitted to him for his countersignature.

Admiral Platon in his letter was unable to prevent himself from "finding a close relation" between the incident which had occurred when his draft law was rejected and the nomination of the new members of the commission. "This is but one more effort," he said, "to try to convert into mere froth the anti-Masonic campaign which I have been conducting since June 1942." He ended his letter by asking the Chief of Government to cancel immediately the decree of 5 March 1943.

The decree was not cancelled. Thereafter the commission, of which the majority was no longer inspired by anti-Masonic feeling, gave itself to the task of granting in the most generous manner the exceptions asked for by previous high officials of secret societies.

In strict truth it must be pointed out that from the legal point of view this commission had merely consultative powers and that it was entitled only to state an opinion. But these opinions were followed by the Chief of Government in every single case, so far as can be recalled.

The percentage of exceptions allowed was high. It must have reached or perhaps exceeded 80 per cent of the number of demands presented. For precise details on this point the minutes of the special commission may be consulted, these archives having been taken in charge by the new government. It should be added that the legislation on this subject was never modified afterwards in an oppressive sense.

Thus through the work of a commission which faithfully followed, under the chairmanship of M. Reclus, the policies desired by the Chief of Government, the effects of the anti-Masonic laws were softened and even neutralized in application to most of the former high officials of secret societies who had been excluded on that ground from public office.

(c) *Questions Concerning Alsace and Lorraine*

First of all it must be recalled that the issue of the necessary credits made it possible to continue the operation of the services having to do with Alsace and Lorraine. Aside from the central offices of these services there were four divisions, religious, educational, social insurance, and local status. All these services had been moved from Alsace and Lorraine to the Dordogne.

The prefectures, including the prefects and their services, continued to function. The prefecture of the Bas-Rhin was at Perigueux, that of the Haut-Rhin at Agen, and that of the Moselle at Montauban. In addition to such administrative activities as were still possible these prefects had the duty of maintaining close contact with all who had been expelled from the three departements, and all those who had left as refugees. Mention should also be made of the municipal organization of Strasbourg which was evacuated to Perigueux where it continued to operate. The mayor, M. Charles Frey, received his salary throughout the entire occupation.

In the second place, the Chief of Government made certain that financial aid was sent every month to the more needy among our unhappy fellow citizens, particularly to those who had been evacuated or expelled by the Germans.

Quite apart from the money thus allocated each month to meet regular expenses, the Chief of Government granted large sums to organizations of public importance. For example, the civilian hospitals of Strasbourg, evacuated to Perigueux, one day received a million and a half francs, through M. Frey who is today still mayor of Strasbourg.

Unlike the members of the French parliament representing other departements in France, who received during the occupation a sum equal to what their retirement allowance would have been, instead of their normal pay, the senators and deputies from the Bas-Rhin, Haut-Rhin and the Moselle always received the totality of their normal parliamentary salaries.

In addition, as they did not have a pass permitting free travel on the state railways they were paid the expenses of such journeys as "expenses incurred on an assigned mission."

All officials from Alsace and Lorraine were maintained throughout the occupation in their normal posts and were always paid on that basis. Some of them were in fact lent to other administrations, but none were reclassified against their will in any service other than that to which they had belonged in June 1940.

"The compensatory indemnity" of 16 per cent of their salary continued to be paid to them though it was quite clear that the justification for that indemnity, the use of two languages in those three departements, no longer existed. But the government had wished to atone to this slight extent for the material losses of our unhappy fellow countrymen.

Such were the broad lines of the activities of the officials employed in the private secretariat, both in the daily tasks normally assigned to them and in the special functions allotted to many of them by M. Pierre Laval, which included the defense of the official staffs of the two houses of the French Parliament, of those high officials of Freemasonry who had been unjustly punished, and of our fellow citizens from Alsace and Lorraine. Members of the private secretariat were continually inspired in their tasks by the same principles and the same feelings, namely those of aiding the Chief of Government in the task which he had undertaken of preserving to the greatest possible extent the institutions and the men of our unhappy country.

(Document No. 2-B)
Fr. ed. 1026-1033

[*This document was deposited with the Hoover Library as a joint declaration of members of the private secretariat of M. Pierre Laval and is not signed.*]

PIERRE LAVAL'S NEWSPAPER,
" LE MONITEUR "

JEAN-FRANCISQUE BABUT

*Director-General of the Mont Louis Printing Plant at
Clermont-Ferrand*

In August 1927 President Laval bought a certain number of shares, enough to give him the majority holding, in the corporation which owned the daily newspaper *Le Moniteur* and the Mont Louis printing plant at Clermont-Ferrand, an establishment to which I had belonged since October 1912.

Thus it was in 1927 that I became acquainted with him. But from that time until 1939 I met him only occasionally, either in Paris or in Clermont-Ferrand.

From 1939 until 1944, as director-general of the company, I often saw President Laval, who was my chief. From September 1939 to July 1940 and from December 1940 until April 1942, not being in office at that time, he devoted himself energetically to the business. In any case the printing profession held a passionate interest for him, for in his opinion it was a profession which required intelligence and hard work.

Because I gained his complete confidence he allowed me to manage these important printing plants as I thought best. Due to the importance of his place in public life he enjoined me to be more obedient than anyone else to all regulations, and forbade me to do any work for any public administration, being anxious to avoid in this way the possibility that anyone should think that he used his personal influence in his own interests. As his remuneration, and only when funds permitted, he received the dividends on his shares and the repayment of certain of his expenses.

From 1940 to 1944, in accordance with his instructions, we rendered important services to a great number of persons who were menaced on different grounds; for example, a Polish Jew, an electrical worker evacuated from Alsace, whom we employed and even housed in our premises; and a British subject who arrived from England in February 1940 and whom we employed though he was not of the least use to us.

At the request of a militant member of the resistance, Georges Orliac, we took on as a helper on the rotary machines an Austrian who had deserted from the German army.

We had also in our various sections a certain number of Jews, escaped prisoners, and workers who were in trouble with the Obligatory Labor Service.

We gave work certificates to some fifty young men who did not work for us, with the object of protecting them from the Obligatory Labor Service.

Young people whose fathers had taken to the maquis were employed in order that their families should not be without resources.

We even lent out the company's vehicles to transport arms for the resistance, particularly to M. Emile Garant, known in the resistance as Master-Sergeant Mathurin.

We used our printing facilities to prepare journalists' identity cards for Jews (among them Serge Levy), special papers to aid in the return of prisoners by presenting them as returning free workers, baptism certificates for Jews, etc.

When the daily paper *La Montagne*, which belonged to Alexander Varenne, shut down in September 1943, we engaged one of its editors, Antoine Pourtier, and some of its office and plant workers, none of whom were needed in our operations. As we could not take on their entire personnel, and to avoid the requisition of the premises of *La Montagne*, we made a variety of efforts to find printing orders for our colleague.

There was not a day on which I did not take steps, either in conjunction with the services of the Chief of Government, or with him personally in particularly difficult cases, to aid persons who had been arrested or threatened with arrest.

I certify that during this difficult period I always received from President Laval the greatest understanding and the most complete support.

(Document No. 3)
Fr. ed. 1034-1035

Clermont-Ferrand, 1 November 1945

BABUT

GIRAUD — THE MAQUIS PRISONERS

FRANÇOIS HULOT

Bachelor of Laws; Captain of Artillery, Reserve; Journalist; Chief of Press Section, Commissariat for Prisoner Affairs

I the undersigned François Hulot, living in Paris; Bachelor of Laws; captain in the artillery (Reserve), holder of the Croix de Guerre (1939-1940), professional journalist since 1920, make the following declaration of my own free will and under oath.

My Relations with President Laval

I met President Laval for the first time when he was Minister of Foreign Affairs or President of the Council of Ministers, between 1932 and 1935, and I was a parliamentary journalist. At that time I was merely one journalist among many others so far as he was concerned, and I was acquainted only with such official and semiofficial aspects of his activities as his colleagues or he himself cared to present to us.

As editor of an important Paris weekly at the time of the Ethiopian affair, I began to have interviews of a more intimate character with President Laval while he was still at the Quai d'Orsay at the end of 1934 and after his voluntary departure from the government in the first months of 1936. At this time I saw him almost every week, and little by little I began to talk with him much more freely.

During that period, regardless of whether President Laval was in power or not, his point of view never changed. "There is but one policy for France to follow," he said, "and that is to remove the menace of war which lies heavy upon her. We must do everything to encircle Germany with the greatest possible number of nations, and we must also do everything to ensure that no one of these nations shall one day be tempted to unite with the power of Germany. My entire policy in the Ethiopian affair is to be found in these few words."

From 1936 to the declaration of war my conversations with President Laval were fewer.

I was called up at the end of August 1939, was taken prisoner with the Army of the Meuse on 23 June 1940, and was returned from captivity, on the ground that I was a veteran of the war of 1914-1918, on 17 August 1941. At that time President Laval had not belonged to the government in Vichy since 13 December 1940. He came irregularly to Paris; and it was only toward the end of October that I learned of his presence in the capital and visited him to talk of the problems raised by the captivity of thousands of prisoners, and to express to him in my own name and in that of many of my comrades our gratitude for what he had accomplished in our behalf. The armistice agreement had provided that we should remain prisoners until peace was declared. Yet only a year after the signing of the armistice about half the prisoners had already returned to France on various grounds. We were practically unanimous during this period, both those prisoners who had returned and those who remained in captivity, in thinking that this enormous mitigation of one of the hardest clauses of the armistice had been the fruit of the personal efforts of President Laval with the occupation authorities.

M. Laval was kind enough to express his appreciation of my statements, and I had occasion during the following months to see him many times.

When he returned to the government in April 1942 I was in charge of the press section in the general commissariat for prisoners, of which the chief was M. Maurice Pinot. I was also director of the newspaper for returned prisoners and the families of prisoners, published under the title *Toute la France.* Thus I was necessarily well informed on prisoner problems and had some influence in everything to do with prisoners.

These preliminary details are of some importance since they show: (1) that in April 1942 I was in no way bound to President Laval by any link of personal friendship, and saw him only from time to time; (2) that I was under no obligation whatever to him, from either a political or a professional point of view; (3) that as a former prisoner who had endured fourteen months of painful captivity, my feelings, like those of my comrades in misfortune, were more than reserved on what was commonly referred to as the "policy of collaboration." The thought of all our comrades still behind the barbed wire prevented us from deviating in any way on this subject.

First in matters which strictly concerned prisoner problems, then on much more general grounds, and finally in more intimate matters, I was an eyewitness of a number of precise incidents in the personal activities of President Laval which expressed his essential thought and at the same time the objectives he obstinately pursued. It is these precise incidents which I wish to record here.

I. *President Laval and the Prisoners*

In 1942 negotiations concerning the prisoners were dominated by the problem of General Giraud. This problem had canceled in great part the results of President Laval's efforts for our comrades, whose opinions were extremely divided on the subject of General Giraud's attitude.

Whatever may have been the innermost thought of the President and the judgment that he passed personally on the action of General Giraud, he repeatedly said to me: "A prisoner always has the right to escape. It is a matter of conscience for him if his escape has regrettable consequences. Even if the Germans demanded of me that I hand over General Giraud to them, I would refuse. I was merely asked to put General Giraud under close observation on the ground that he had been won over by the dissenters. I would not be worthy to hold the position of Chief of Government if I put the police on the heels of a General of the Army."

In November 1942 the free zone was invaded by the German army as a result of the Anglo-American landing in Africa.

There was intense emotion among the repatriated prisoners. We all thought of the fate of the seventy or eighty thousand escaped prisoners in the south zone. I broached the subject with President Laval and he told me: "Some French people reproach me for clinging to power in spite of the occupation of the free zone. Tell your comrades that if I have remained at my post it is because I have a duty to fulfill towards many Frenchmen in general, and towards the escaped persons and Jewish refugees in the south zone in particular. I hope to be able to get the Germans to agree that those who have escaped will remain free and not be sought. I am here to defend the French and I will defend them."

President Laval kept his word, and tens of thousands of escaped persons who had taken refuge in the south zone remained free.

During this same period occurred the requisition of labor. The probable first victims to leave for work in Germany were obviously the 700,000 prisoners whose repatriation was technically only "on leave from captivity," and who were obliged to report every fortnight to the German commander nearest their residence. These repatriates, so long as they were neither veterans of the first war, fathers of large families, nor invalids, could be sent back to Germany at any moment. In fact, they were in France simply "on leave."

Another interview with President Laval. He said to me: "The French say that I recruit workers for Germany. If I wanted to be popular all I would have to do is ignore the matter and let Sauckel go ahead. But look at the results: I said to Sauckel that it would be inhuman to send back to Germany men who had already suffered captivity for months or years. Sauckel wouldn't listen to me. I discussed it with him for weeks, and then one day I learned that he himself had been a prisoner in France during the war of 1914-1918. On that day I struck a sensitive chord in that stubborn man, and since then no prisoner repatriated on leave, or even any escaped prisoner, has been requisitioned for labor in Germany."

"I followed up this first gain," he said to me several days later. "Sauckel requisitions laborers in France as he does in Poland, Belgium, and all the other occupied countries. The other countries get nothing in return. I obtained the return of 50,000 prisoners. It wasn't easy. I'm not deceiving myself; no one is going to thank me. But I am doing my duty."

II. Some Comments of Pierre Laval, Chief of Government

I considered it my duty to discuss with any repatriated comrades, during the little meetings that we held regularly, what President Laval had been good enough to explain to me. He learned of this one day and said to me: "You understand what I am doing, but you see only a part of what I do. Come to a meeting of prefects in Paris or at Vichy. There are often, too, meetings of mayors, who come to see me in regional groups. We speak freely. It would interest you to listen."

It was thus that during many months I was privileged to be a silent spectator of his deliberations as President of the Council with his prefects, or as Chief of Government and Minister of the Interior with his mayors.

What was talked about at these meetings? Foreign policy? No. Collaboration with Germany? No. Gaullism? Never. The only topic was the increasing misery of the French and the desperate means that might be employed to diminish it. The essential anxiety was food, still food, and always food.

One day at the Matignon the black market was being discussed. Many prefects, particularly the prefect of the Mayenne, explained that it was impossible for them to stop the black market because it operated with the complicity of the Germans. I had never before seen President Laval really in a rage. I did that day. He issued a formal order to all his prefects to send him within a fortnight a complete and precise dossier on any actions of the German agencies which favored the black market, saying to them: "Give me names, figures, places, dates, and quantities. When my dossier is complete, I'll show it to Goering, and we'll see."

The dossier was made up. The President saw Goering, and on the strength of his dossier secured the suppression of the German buying offices and an order from the German High Command forbidding the German army in France to buy any food in France apart from the official levies.

Next to food came questions concerning the requisition of labor.

It did not take much intelligence to understand the inner thought of the President. He talked only of his disputes with Sauckel, of the violent resistance he put up against Sauckel, and of the delays he obtained. He explained that since he had obtained the exemption of all agricultural workers from requisition, it was necessary to classify the greatest possible number of French as farmers. The same rule applied to students. I listened to at least ten discussions on this subject. The inescapable conclusion that I drew from them was that if there was a fierce resistance to German demands, it was President Laval who was the heart of it.

Two or three times they talked of the maquis, and President Laval's comment was this: "There are maquis and maquis. We cannot permit terrorism to thrive among us; we cannot let farms be pillaged and crops be burned. But there are also conscientious objectors to the German labor requisition. I said to Sauckel that it was he who had organized the maquis. No French government over which I preside will ever bend to German demands regarding these objectors."

During 1943, President Laval asked me to bring together in the suburban town halls the municipal employees and important persons of the cities in the Paris region to explain to them what he was doing to meet the difficulties of the situation.

"You have heard me talk," he said. "You have heard me speak to the mayors and prefects. Take the essence of what I have said, and transpose to the municipal level the explanations that I have given on the national level."

It was thus that I had occasion to give private talks, in the evenings, in most of the town halls of the Seine area. I went to the districts which had been hardest hit by labor requisitions and by the arrest of hostages. I spoke with such frankness about what President Laval was doing that in the early days of 1944 the German Embassy, after demanding my arrest, insisted that these town hall meetings should stop.

III. Pierre Laval in Private Conversation

From January 1944 to 17 August 1944 I had the opportunity to become gradually more intimate with the President.

When I went to Vichy (for twenty-four hours, about twice a month), the President usually had me in for lunch with his immediate colleagues, about ten at the most. He spoke very freely, much more freely than with the prefects and mayors. The themes of his conversations were always the same: the misery of France, threats to France, the necessity of protecting the French in spite of themselves. As I listened to this man who said often and spontaneously, "If I wanted to be popular I would only have to turn my back on my duty," my feeling of admiration for him continued to grow. And each time he said it I remembered a phrase he had used in an unguarded moment when he received the mayors of the Cantal: "As Chief of Government in an occupied country, I am caught as though in a pair of pincers, one prong of which is German and the other French." And he added with a certain bitterness in his voice, "It's not always the German prong that hurts the most."

During the spring of 1944 President Laval did me the honor of inviting me five or six times to dine with him privately at the Hotel Matignon. Only Madame Laval, his daughter, and sometimes his son-in-law, were present.

Each time I listened to the President and his family talking at the end of a difficult day—a day beset with snares and difficulties, often cruel difficulties—I wished that everything they said could be heard by all of France. The conversation was on certain matters exclusively; they spoke only of the bad faith of the Germans, German demands, German cruelties— and in what terms! And on each occasion President Laval said, "I must stick to it; I must hang on. Yet how simple it would be to go back to Châteldon."

The last dinner to which I was invited was particularly dramatic, and I can bear specific witness to a fact of some historic importance.

On 9 August 1944 President Laval came to Paris. He had summoned to the Hotel Matignon the prefect of the Seine, the prefect of police, the president of the municipal council, and the president of the general council. He said to them: "The evacuation of Paris by the Germans is now only a matter of weeks, perhaps of days. My place is here. I have returned to Paris. Here I will stay no matter what happens. I shall summon the National Assembly."

His chief concerns, as he expressed them then to his colleagues, were these: first, to protect Paris; second, to maintain order until the Allied forces arrived; third, to arrange for a transfer of power in an orderly and dignified manner.

He strove for this triple objective to the very end, and it was in the hope of attaining it more effectively that he obtained permission from the Germans to ask President Herriot to return to Paris and resume his occupancy of the quarters of the President of the Chamber of Deputies. Armed with the agreement given by Abetz he left on 14 August 1944 for Maréville, where President Herriot was under house arrest. President Herriot freely agreed to return to Paris with President Laval, and to reside for several days at the Hotel de Ville in an apartment placed at his disposition by M. Bouffet, prefect of the Seine, while waiting for the mansion of the President of the Chamber to be made ready for his occupancy.

On the evening of 16 August 1944 President Laval asked me to stay for dinner.

It was almost ten in the evening before he was finally able to come up to the dining room, where his family was waiting for him. About eleven o'clock the telephone in the dining room rang. His daughter answered it: "Papa, the Hotel de Ville wants you." He took the receiver, listened for several minutes, and then said simply, "It's vile. I'm coming." He hung up. Turning to Madame Laval he said, "The Gestapo is at the Hotel de Ville. They have come to arrest Herriot. Abetz gave me his word that Herriot was free. I'm leaving. I want to be there." I can still see him removing his wallet, his personal papers, his keys, and other things from his pockets while he talked, and giving them to his wife, like a man who had a definite feeling that he would not leave the Hotel de Ville a free man.

The only car available at the Hotel Matignon at that moment was a little service car. President Laval got in alone, forbidding anyone to accompany him, and saying only to the chauffeur, "To the Hotel de Ville."

He came back at four in the morning, after persuading Abetz to postpone the arrest of Herriot. The arrest was to be made later that day at the same time that Abetz, in the name of the German government, summoned the French government to leave Paris for a city to the east.

Numerous witnesses have reported the complicated happenings of 17 August 1944, the verbal and written refusals of President Laval to leave Paris, the meeting of the Council of Ministers in the evening, and the transfer of the powers of President Laval to the two prefects of the Seine and to the presidents of the two municipal and departemental councils.

The Hotel Matignon's electricity was cut off that evening. With great difficulty half a dozen candles were found and it was in their light that we saw Abetz, flanked by agents of the Gestapo, arrive to effect the forced departure of President Laval and his ministers. The President said good-by to us.

"There is no longer a French government," he told us. "I am a prisoner like the others." He shook the hand of everyone and entered a car, accompanied by Madame Laval. I was never to see him again.

Today, 17 December 1945, two months after the execution of President Laval, I affirm that I never heard come freely from his lips any words except those inspired by the purest patriotism, and no matter what happens I regard it as an honor to have been called to work at his side.

(Document No. 4)
Fr. ed. 1036-1041

Paris, 17 December 1945

F. HULOT

STATISTICS OF GERMAN DEATH SENTENCES

CHARLES SAINT

First Secretary of Embassy;
Secretary-General of the General Delegation
in the Occupied Zone

The undersigned Charles Guillaume Arthur Antoine Saint declares under oath the following.

I was born in Paris, in the 16th arrondissement, on 22 March 1907. In 1930 I began my studies for the diploma of the School of Political Science, and I was ranked first in the diplomatic section in June 1932. I was ranked first also in the competitive examination of the Ministry of Foreign Affairs in June 1934. I was named attaché at the Embassy in Washington, and served as third secretary from 1934 to May 1937. I was then assigned to the cabinet of the Minister of Finance, and in April 1938 I was named associate chief of cabinet for the Minister of Foreign Affairs.

I was made a second secretary, and then a first secretary in 1939. During the war I was in the Air Force, at the Orly base. In December 1940 I was named representative of the Ministry of Foreign Affairs with the French government's General Delegation for the occupied territories. In April 1942 I became secretary-general of this agency.

At the beginning of April 1942 President Laval, who had been called to Vichy by Maréchal Pétain to form a government, asked me to come to Vichy. It was thus that I was present at the meetings held in the Pavillon Sévigné leading to the formation of a new government.

The evening before, President Laval had informed me by telephone of his intention of entrusting to me the direction of the Paris services of the President. He now asked me, when I saw him at Vichy, to describe to him the nature and extent of my work at that time with the General Delegation for the occupied territories.

I explained to him that after October 1940 I had created at the General Delegation a department known as the Special Delegation representing the

Administration. This was a part of that section of the Ministry of Foreign Affairs for which I was responsible, and devoted itself to the defense and protection of French persons who were arrested or sentenced.

It had a triple role.

— It centralized for the entire occupied zone all requests addressed by private persons to the government on behalf of persons arrested or sentenced by the German authorities, and also all demands of the same kind coming from different French ministries or administrations. By corresponding with all the prefects of the occupied zone it collected their information on any incidents involving the occupying forces in their departements.

— It intervened on behalf of our fellow citizens with the German military administration in Paris through German liaison officers assigned to the General Delegation. It supplied information to the Direction of Armistice Services at Vichy, and to the French delegation at Wiesbaden. It furnished the material for their dossiers and sent them such details as these commissions had need of for their negotiations and protests.

— Finally, in accordance with government instructions, the Special Delegation correlated all the dossiers of those events and matters which showed obvious abuse or extortion committed by the occupation forces, and prepared a general dossier of Franco-German differences for such purposes as were regarded as useful by the government.

The results obtained by the service to which my colleagues and I had thus devoted ourselves were already considerable. When I had completed my explanation, President Laval said to me, "You are doing a useful and noble work; keep it up. We will see later how things turn out and whether or not I should assign other work to you."

It was under these conditions, and in order to broaden my work, that I asked President Laval at this time for the post of secretary-general of the General Delegation; I obtained it.

From April 1942 to April 1944, at which time I handed in my resignation to the delegate-general, I saw President Laval many times. He interceded continually with the Germans to save condemned persons and interested himself particularly in what I was doing, which could not, for good reason, be too openly talked about.

In fact it was impossible for President Laval to make known to the public the work of an administrative department which was entirely devoted to the defense of the French, and which had bones to pick both with the French Ministry of Justice and with the arbitrary authority of the occupation forces. Nor was it possible to give publicity to the results obtained.

The Germans strictly forbade any publicity on this subject. They also forbade the proposed formation of a separate and important agency, a sort of general secretariat for civilian prisoners and deportees, which would have brought together the dossiers of imprisoned French persons and defended them before the competent German authorities. And furthermore, by notes dated 14 June and 13 December 1941, the commanding general of the German forces in France refused to allow intercession by a French administrative service on behalf of our arrested compatriots.

From this time on, at the risk of being ineffective, the long and patient activity of President Laval's government on behalf of such persons had to follow semiofficial and purely practical lines. Nothing could be demanded where the Germans refused any form of agreement and were willing to exercise only a form of tolerance. It was necessary to resort to argument and persuasion, to begin all over again each day, to make use of prestige, and to appeal to principles. That is what M. Laval told us to do.

In spite of these difficulties the following results were obtained by the special delegation for administrative matters during the first three years of the occupation:

ARRESTS

Period	Arrests reported	Interventions	Liberations obtained
Oct. 1940-Dec. 1941	4,500		500
Dec. 1941-Dec. 1942	37,609	7,443	2,871
Dec. 1942-Dec. 1943	about 50,000	over 12,000	over 4,000

DEATH SENTENCES

Period	Total sentenced to death	Military death sentences	Hostages sentenced to death	Reductions or suspensions
Oct. 1940-Dec. 1941	552	312	240	159
Dec. 1941-Dec. 1942	1,407 [sic]	858	540	290
Dec. 1942-Oct. 1943	473			146

Thus in three years of occupation the special delegation obtained over 8,000 liberations and saved 595 persons from death. Hundreds of letters of thanks testify to these results.

This is the truth which I would have stated during the trial of President Laval if his lawyers had been allowed to call witnesses concerning his work and his daily struggle to reduce the suffering of France during one of the most grievous periods of her history.

(Document No. 7)
Fr. ed. 1042-1044

Paris, 5 January 1946
CHARLES SAINT

YOUTH—JEWS
LAVAL'S ATTITUDE
TOWARDS GERMANS

FELIX OLIVIER-MARTIN

Assistant Secretary of State for Youth

Felix Olivier-Martin, living in Paris, declares the following under oath.

In February 1943, when it was suggested that I might succeed Georges Lamirand as secretary-general for youth, President Laval was nothing more than a name to me. I had never met him. Of course I had a general idea about him and his policies, but it was based on nothing more than newspaper reports and conversations in various political circles with which I was in contact. These conversations on the whole were resolutely hostile to President Laval as a person, not only in collaborationist circles in Paris, where he was held to be a traitor to the European cause, and in Gaullist circles, where he was simply called a traitor, but also in groups supporting Maréchal Pétain and General Giraud, where he was accused of having isolated the Maréchal. More than ever Laval, always a man alone, had no party. What had been true of his entire career was now still more cruelly true. He had scarcely any friends, and none outside the group most intimately in contact with him.

A certain technical curiosity, as it might be called, from which there might develop a sort of technical sympathy, nevertheless attracted me to this great political artist whose skill I had often admired. The presence of Abel Bonnard in the Ministry of National Education, and the half-friendly relations which I still had with him at that time, set up another barrier between the inner personality of President Laval and myself. Abel Bonnard, a sensitive man of letters, who had strayed into political activity through a singular ignorance of his own nature, had become, with a lack of seriousness that is difficult to excuse, though in entire good faith, a violent adversary and a particularly malicious and uncomprehending critic of the President's actions. The fact that I was Bonnard's subordinate, together with what remained of the admiration, now becoming weaker and weaker, that had formerly attached me to him, for some time kept me away from the President and gave my relations with him a sort of stiffness which prevented them from being really free on my side.

It was in March 1943 that I was presented to Pierre Laval. The suggestion was that I should succeed Georges Lamirand, who had announced his resignation, and the President wanted to become acquainted with me beforehand. This first interview was a brief one. The President clearly wanted to form an opinion about me. He had me talk about my previous career and about my work at the moment. He seemed to be pleased to learn that between the two wars I had taken an active part in politics, that

I had been elected a municipal councilor, and that I had had practical administrative experience on different levels.

After I had been appointed to the secretariat-general for youth I paid the President a longer visit. He said that he would not discuss technical questions with me. He had signed my appointment because he trusted me in this field and he would continue this confidence so long as I did not show that I was unworthy of it. As for detail, I must arrange that with his secretary general. He asked me if I were a writer, and seemed satisfied with my reply that although I was I had made it a rule to publish nothing whatever since the armistice.

"A man in political life," he said to me, "ought never to write anything except what is necessary for the solution of daily problems. He ought never to write on matters of doctrine or of theory. A moment always comes when such writing may turn against him and give his enemies a weapon. Above all, under circumstances such as those through which we now pass, he should speak as little as possible. Don't do like Masson; he talks a lot too much, and he embarrasses me."

He expressed the desire that I should have an understanding of public affairs, and he hoped that my experience in local politics would have given it to me. "It is in electoral skirmishes and in municipal life," he said, "that an apprenticeship for public affairs is served most usefully. Nothing can replace it."

He spoke very highly of Georges Lamirand, who, he said, had a real sense of public affairs. He regretted that the Germans had prevented him from making use of Lamirand in the diplomatic field. Then he spoke of Pelorson, who had tried to negotiate with the Germans over his head.

As to youth matters, what interested him particularly was that the Church was taking a hand. "Be careful," he said; "above all, don't get me into awkward situations with the priests." That was to be the chief point in my work. For the rest it was to be concerned with technical matters which he did not have sufficient time to deal with.

I did not see him again for several weeks. Then one day, toward the beginning of May, he sent for me. He showed me a long document in German which dealt with the question of Pelorson. He asked me to read it quickly to him. It was a long letter from Ribbentrop which expressed the confidence of the government of the Reich in Georges Pelorson and asked the French government to make him the head of the commissariat-general to be created for the purpose of looking after young French persons working in Germany. As an annex, in French, there was the draft of a decree creating this commissariat-general and naming M. Georges Pelorson as its chief. President Laval exploded. He emphasized the incorrectness of the procedure which the Reich Ministry of Foreign Affairs had followed in writing to him in German as though to a simple subordinate. This was a diplomatic matter, and the language of diplomacy was still French. As to the essence of the matter, the move was inadmissible; he still had the liberty of naming the high officials, subject to German agreement, but up to the present he had never been imposed on in so blunt a way. The draft of the decree aroused his particular indignation. "I would have done something for Pelorson," he said; "until now I had not regarded him as bad, but this move of his proves that he is an imbecile. If you see him, tell him to crawl back into his hole."

This, M. Laval said to me, was a striking example of the worst kind of the difficulties he had to fight against, namely those which came from the

French. "I can still make some arrangement with the Germans. I can wrest things from them, obtain concessions and delays. But in my work I find French people who themselves seek out the Germans and tell them what they ought to ask me to do. So when I can catch a Frenchman in the act, I don't miss."

It was agreed that he would not reply to Ribbentrop, and that he would ask the German Embassy verbally to settle the incident directly with me through normal diplomatic channels. Several days afterwards I did in fact receive the visit of Counselor Theilen, who presented to me in a very much reduced form the demand of the government of the Reich. His mission was now to express the demand in the form of a wish. I replied to the Counsellor that since M. Pelorson had directly provoked an intervention in his own favor it was impossible for the French government to respond to this wish. It was a question of internal governmental discipline based on a principle of which the Counselor would be sure to appreciate the value. The Counselor agreed after some discussion and the incident was closed.

Apart from the lesson in practical policy that this incident taught me, it had another altogether different importance. It revealed to me a Laval completely unknown, and made me reflect at length. Without expressing things to myself in so precise a way, I had nevertheless been accustomed for some time to regard the Maréchal as the head of the defense against German encroachments. To employ the obvious expression, Laval dressed up ["*maquignonnait*"] this defense much too carefully. All this led me to modify my conduct profoundly, and I decided to discuss directly with him certain difficulties that were piling up on my path.

Abel Bonnard continued to criticize not merely the President's policies, but also Laval himself. At the same time he gave me instructions contrary to what I was discovering to be the true thought of the President. Apart from every other consideration, it had been highly unpleasant for me to play the role, slight as it might be, of a weapon used in the war against him who under the constitution was my supreme chief. Regarding two questions which had a crucial interest for my section, that of the young Jews and that of subsidies for the youth movements, I determined to ask the President frankly if the instructions his Minister was giving me were really in conformity with the President's own policies.

It was at the Hotel Matignon one morning very early that I put the question to the President, begging him to treat my action as confidential. On the Jewish question he cleared the ground immediately of all theoretical considerations. "This is a political problem," he said. "On one side there is Germany, which desires to exterminate them; on the other side Italy and the Vatican, who are in agreement to protect them. This is an essential point of view. It is as important for me to get along with Italy and the Vatican as with Germany. In playing this game I can save many unfortunate people on the rebound. As for you, I ask you simply to let the matter lie dormant and to stifle any anti-Jewish initiative which may show itself among your subordinates. If it is the Germans who attack you, tell them that this is a problem of general policy and that you cannot do anything without referring the matter to me. And let me know at once."

In the matter of subsidies for the youth groups, he instructed me to refer the matter to him each time I thought that policy was involved. He would explain to Bonnard that this was of interest to him, President Laval, in his functions as Minister for the Interior, and that since he was responsible for general policy regarding parties he must harmonize with that policy any future matters which concerned the youth organizations.

As to Bonnard, the President told me that he admired his conversation and his intellect, and that really he liked him very much. "You know," he said, "I sometimes reproach myself for neglecting him and leaving him too much to himself. I ought to see him more often. But I haven't the time; and as soon as he starts talking politics he goes off the track. He writes wonderful articles, but he is more German than many Germans themselves. You seem to have more political sense than he does. Look after him, and gain some influence over him. Keep him from acting stupidly. This is the best thing you can do for me. Say to yourself that my task is arduous and warn me if you find that things are becoming serious." When I started to mention the ways in which I felt this new role might be a delicate one, he interrupted me: "Everything is delicate under present conditions. We haven't the right to let our conscience be too sensitive. After all I am your chief, and it is I that must carry on my own back the responsibility for the stupid blunders that M. Bonnard will commit or will make you commit. It is I who must always repair the damage. The least that can be done for me is to warn me. But don't come here [Hôtel Matignon]. I am badly placed here and am not on my own ground. And besides, I am encircled by inquisitive people. Come see me at Vichy regularly; I prefer to see you down there."

I left with a singular and quite new impression that I was to feel a good many times later. I had come rather timidly, both because of the very nature of the proposal that I was to make and because I was not sure how to solve these problems which had obsessed me for some time. And now I had discovered that practically nothing was changed. My procedure was still a questionable one, and my problems had not been solved. Yet something had happened within me. Peace of a kind had fallen upon me, driving out my worries and effacing my scruples. At the same time I had received an indefinable tonic and I felt suddenly able to take almost joyfully the decisions from which I had been shrinking for weeks. Very rarely, at least in my own experience, did the President dictate the solution that you were to adopt; but contacts with him altered things in such a way that you could find a solution yourself without effort. Contacts, I say, because it was something apart from his words themselves, something over and above what he said, and beyond the rather muffled voice in which he said it. It was something that cracked the shells of the most formidable problems so quickly and simply, almost childishly; that stripped them masterfully of all the intellectual and ideological trash with which our contemporaries knew so well how to entangle them; that went directly and without hesitation not so much to the essential as to the living point of the problem, a point, alas, which was very often bloody. And all with so much modesty.

From that day dated a great change in my relations with President Laval. The more I admired the skill of his policies, the more I discovered a man whose conduct, unexpected and disconcerting to my mental habits though it was, attracted me. I discovered a Frenchman who fought for his country in a manner which I still did not understand completely, but which I could not but feel to be genuine. I found too a chief, a man who commanded, and whom I felt myself impelled to obey. Because of this I went regularly from that time on, every Friday, to meet him at the Hotel du Parc, getting there before his car arrived in order to be one of the first to talk with him. More and more often, too, he got into the habit of having me lunch with him. It was thus that I had so many meetings with him, under the most diverse circumstances, talking about the most varied subjects. The inestimable value of these conversations can be imagined.

Thus it was that the second phase of my relations with Laval began; it continued to the middle of August 1943. At that time circumstances made it possible for me to penetrate far more deeply into political realities, and to share much more closely in the cares and the thoughts of the President.

What happened was that in the early days of August I was told by de Brinon himself of a maneuver of which the purpose was to throw out the President. Gauleiter Sauckel had come to Paris and had let it be understood that he would demand, in addition to workers already sent and being sent to Germany, a new contingent of 500,000 men. After telling me about this, de Brinon declared that he was certain that President Laval would refuse to agree to Sauckel's demands; that the German government would insist; and that one could thus foresee, within the near future, the fall of Laval and his replacement by himself, de Brinon. In a rather veiled way he let me understand that he was already thinking of how he would form his government, and that if I were interested, a portfolio could be reserved for me.

The whole thing immediately struck me as nothing but a lot of talk, and so I worked my way out of this thorny conversation with a few ordinary remarks. Nevertheless, I made inquiries and I found very precise confirmation of the intentions of F. de Brinon during a lunch at which were present Mouraille, who was then Abel Bonnard's chief of cabinet, Counselor Theilen, and myself. Going further into the matter, I sounded out General Medicus, chief of military administration in France, who had often furnished me interesting information. Medicus took out of his desk a list of those who were to constitute the future de Brinon ministry. I was on the list as a possible Minister of National Education, or of the Chancellery. The General also gave me to understand that the whole scheme had been got up by de Brinon with no support except that of the SS authorities in France, and that the Reich Ministry of Foreign Affairs had no part in it.

I went at once to Vichy and told the President about it. He was at first extremely surprised and made quick inquiries through Bousquet. These investigations soon verified what I said, and the President asked me to lunch with Krugg von Nidda, German minister at Vichy.

I repeated to the German minister, in sworn secrecy, the information that I had received, and the President made a long and violent protest—not at all in his ordinary manner—against the actions of his minister [de Brinon]. I had nothing to do, of course, with what went on after that, but I am certain that these revelations effectively aided the President in his defense of a position that was particularly dear to him and regarding which he felt deeply, namely his resistance to the transfer of French workers to Germany.

The definite position that I took up without hesitation brought me considerable personal difficulties both then and afterwards, but it also brought me the broader confidence of the President and allowed me to penetrate more deeply into his thoughts on a series of essential problems.

I am therefore in a position to bear witness, and I insist on doing so with some solemnity, to the fact that the essential concern of the President at this time was to stop the departures of French labor, and particularly of young Frenchmen, to Germany. I had striking proof of this very quickly.

In the last days of September [1943] information corroborated by different sources reached me to the effect that the German government intended to secure first a census of the military class of 1943 and then its mobilization. Armed with this news, I asked the President what the facts were, telling him that for me this was a matter of the very highest importance. My predecessor as secretary-general for youth had resigned in order to avoid being associated with the mobilization of the classes of 1941 and 1942. As for me, I was faced on that point by accomplished facts which I had to accept. But the mobilization of the class of 1943 would change everything; it would be impossible for me to continue to accept my responsibilities if this mobilization occurred. I therefore told the President that although I had no illusions on the importance or the efficacy of what I was doing, I would resign if even one French youth of the class of 1943 had to leave French territory. He pointed out to me with his habitual frankness the enormous risk in which such an attitude involved me. I answered that I had myself measured these risks and that I was ready to accept them. He then said that he agreed with me entirely on the fundamentals of this question, and that he authorized me, in the semiofficial negotiations which were to open on this subject, to announce my resignation. He said that he would firmly back the categoric point of view that I was going to adopt in these negotiations.

Negotiations began early in October. They did not go very far. In the first meetings I indicated my point of view as simply as possible, but very firmly, and underlined the fact that it was also the point of view of the President and of his government. Things went no further than that. The Germans gave in. The question was not taken up again until Déat became Minister of Labor in February 1944. But at that time it was fortunately too late for the measures which had been planned to bring about any serious results. I am therefore certain that the President's firmness in backing me up in this matter kept the class of 1943 from the tragic fate of the classes of 1941 and 1942.

The month of October 1943, so far as the President's foreign policy was concerned, was a time of pause during which he was justified in feeling that he might succeed in strengthening his personal position and in easing very considerably the situation of the French population under the weight which it carried because of the occupation. In fact, Marshal von Runstedt and Minister von Nidda had understood President Laval's point of view and they looked with some approval on the idea of allowing him to give his cabinet a more national character. All this is certainly already known, and so I will speak only of matters that I was able to know about personally. Along this line, the President longed to get rid of the collaborationist elements of his cabinet, and first of all of Abel Bonnard and F. de Brinon. As regards Bonnard he asked me for a technical note on the way in which the Ministry of National Education was being directed. He also asked me to give him some points about the kind of man who would be able to replace Bonnard.

This period of relaxation was not to continue. A stiffening of German policy took effect, first in Germany itself through the nomination of Himmler as Minister of the Interior, which was symbolic of the change, and then in France, through the departure of Marshal von Runstedt and the political annihilation of Krugg von Nidda.

It will be remembered that it was precisely at this moment of a stiffened German policy that the Maréchal's counselors suggested to him that he should send out a message convoking the National Assembly, which had been dormant since the events of 10 July 1940.

I learned of these intentions in a way that was very precise and also very embarrassing. Lucien Romier asked me, under the most rigorous oath of professional secrecy, to give my opinion as a lawyer on the wording of the message the Maréchal was to deliver. I thus had to limit myself to a purely technical opinion; moreover, the circumstances under which I heard of the message prevented me from informing the President of what had evidently been planned as a direct attack on him. But when the whole affair burst into the open with the disastrous results that everybody knows about I was able to tell the President what had occurred between Romier and myself.

This situation was a particularly painful one for the President, but though he eased an understandable fit of temper by a few violent expressions, he showed anxiety only over what he regarded as the general welfare. It was clear, he said, that his departure would bring his personal enemies only an empty satisfaction of their self-esteem. It would give the German authorities a unique opportunity to tighten their pressure on what might remain of the French State. Passing over the wounds to his own self esteem, he thought only of avoiding an open break between the Maréchal and himself. Such a break, he said, would have served as a justification of his personal policies, and would perhaps have given him an opportunity of getting out of a situation which risked ending in tragedy. But he looked higher and did not want to abandon, even for the soundest reasons, the extremely dangerous post that he had accepted in full consciousness of what was involved.

During the entire month of December 1943 he used me as a sort of semi-official intermediary between Romier, who had great influence on the Maréchal's thought and feelings, and himself, in an attempt to keep up appearances before the Germans and before France.

It was while I was carrying out a last mission of this kind, on which I had report to him, that the President told me that the German government had demanded my dismissal, together with that of some other ministers and high officials.

That was 31 December 1943. Under the shock produced by this news, I told him that the change would doubtless be my salvation and that I would thus escape becoming identified personally with the policies of a government which the addition of Darnand was going to make henceforth unacceptable so far as I was concerned. He then spoke in terms of his own situation and said that I was lucky to be able to leave under pressure, and therefore without deserting my post, whereas he personally was bound to his post and would not abandon it until either violence or peace tore it from him.

"It is necessary that I remain," he said, tapping the blotter on his desk with the tips of his fingers, "in order that France shall not be handed over to a Gauleiter, or to a band of adventurers."

I then spoke of the dangers that I saw in the arrival of Darnand, not because of his personality, for he was an honest man, but because of what he stood for in the minds of the Germans and of France. He replied that he shared my views entirely, but that he could do nothing against force. He said that he would try to neutralize Darnand, who was without political competence, by sandwiching him in between Lemoine and Parmentier, of whom he was sure. I asked him then to avoid at any price having Doriot forced on him. He told me that he would never accept him. I made clear my fear that the Germans would try to put Déat into the government. He told me that he was resolved to do anything to prevent such a move, and that in any case he would make the ministry to which Déat was assigned a meaningless one.

This was my last official meeting with the President.

(Document No. 9)
Fr. ed. 1045-1051

Paris, 23 March 1946

F. OLIVIER-MARTIN
Félix Olivier-Martin

EDOUARD HERRIOT

ANDRÉ JEAN-FAURE

Regional Prefect of Lorraine

In the first days of August 1944 I received a telephone call from President Pierre Laval, asking me if President Edouard Herriot had just died, as rumor said in Paris. I reassured him at once. The fact was that President Edouard Herriot was at that time under detention by the Germans in a pavilion of the psychiatric hospital at Maréville, near Nancy.

To give him complete assurance, I offered to President Pierre Laval to go in his name and obtain news of President Edouard Herriot. President Laval accepted at once. I therefore went to Maréville, saw President Herriot, and informed him of the object of my action. He asked me to thank the Chief of Government courteously.

In reality President Herriot was no longer ill, if in fact he ever had been, but his own doctor, Dr. Hamel, and those with him allowed it to be supposed that he was. They did this so that the Germans, thus deceived, should not decide to transfer him to some other detention point, or even to Germany, where his fate would become still more precarious.

On my return to Maréville, I tried to inform the Chief of Government, but he had already left for Vichy, where my message was to be brought to his attention.

However, since I had to go to Paris the next day on questions of food concerning my region, I went to the Matignon to give one of the President's staff some information about my visit to Maréville, points which I had not been able to mention on the telephone except by obscure and vague phrases because of German wire-tapping operations.

I felt it my duty to point out that President Herriot had told me about his friendly relations with President Roosevelt and about his relations with Moscow. This might make it possible, when the situation was right, to take some action favorable to our country; it was right, therefore, that the Chief of Government should be informed of them without delay. But I did not limit myself to this point. The role that President Herriot might be called on to play seemed to me to be of great importance. I wrote to President Laval to tell him of my feelings in the matter.

In my first letter, to which I did not receive a reply, I outlined what to me seemed to be the happy possibilities that could be expected from an intervention by President Herriot in the imminent negotiations with the Allies. I therefore asked President Laval to obtain from the Germans the liberation of President Herriot. Several days later, since I had received no reply and feared that my letter had been got hold of by the enemy censors, I entrusted to Colonel Germain, a plenipotentiary commissioner, who had come to Nancy, a handwritten letter in which I insisted strongly that attention should be given to my suggestion. My insistence was all the stronger because I knew that my letter would be handed directly to the Chief of Government.

On 12 August 1944 President Laval came to Nancy to fetch President Edouard Herriot. The two lunched together in private at the prefecture. They chatted familiarly about memories of their younger days, and about politicians whom they had known during the course of their careers. After dinner, when it was dark and the risks of bombardment along the roads were less, they went to Paris. President Herriot and Madame Herriot were received in an apartment which had been placed at their disposition by the Prefect of the Seine at the Hotel de Ville, until the mansion of the President of the Chamber should be evacuated by the Germans.

That evening a great hope was born, but, alas, scarcely a week had passed before President Edouard Herriot, this time under Gestapo escort, was brought back to Maréville for a brief stay before his transfer to Germany, while President Pierre Laval, stripped of all his powers, was forced to go to Belfort.

(Document No. 10.)
Fr. ed. 1052-1053

Paris, January 1946

ANDRÉ JEAN-FAURE

EDOUARD HERRIOT

ANDRÉ ENFIÈRE

*Member of the National
Constitutional Assembly*

RECORD OF NEGOTIATIONS WITH PIERRE LAVAL AND THE GERMANS IN THE DEFENSE OF PRESIDENT HERRIOT
(*1942-1945*)

Summary

I am writing this summary for those who have neither the desire nor the time to read my "Record of Negotiations with Pierre Laval and the Germans in the defense of President Herriot." To aid such persons to find the important passages quickly I indicate those which supplement the summary. A good idea of the entire matter and of my action in defending President Herriot will be obtained by reading, first, this summary; second, the principal parts of the record; and third, the letters in the appendix.

I was in constant contact with M. Herriot before his arrest, having known him for a long time though not intimately. My opinion is that my enlistment as a volunteer in the armies of the Republic of Spain had pleased him. When I began visiting him at Bretel, he was at first reticent. A visit from Albert Bayet removed his distrust. Herriot had imagined that I was sent by Daladier. Bayet put him right on that point, and his confidence in me began at that moment.

In protecting M. Herriot during his internment I took no step nor made the slightest move without previous agreement with Dr. Rebatel, his brother-in-law, who had great confidence in me, and whose acquaintance I had made one day at lunch at Herriot's home in Lyon.

The defense of M. Herriot made it necessary for me to have abhorrent contacts with important Germans. Mine were the natural feelings of a Frenchman during the war. This was particularly the case when the Germans concerned were members of that ignoble group of bandits, the Gestapo. My contacts with the Germans had but one purpose, the defense of M. Herriot. In other words, I never had any contact with any German for any motive other than this defense. I may be excused for insisting on this point: the Basile tribe is a numerous one.

The defense of Herriot made it my duty to see an important French politician whose policies I had bitterly fought before the war, Georges Bonnet. For the attention of those who are interesting themselves in handing out justice among human beings in accordance with their merits, I declare, in order to serve the truth, that M. Herriot owes a great deal to M. Bonnet. The defense of the interests of M. Herriot often obliged me to see Pierre Laval, in some respects very different from the stories about him.

At the same time that I was defending the interests, or rather the life, of President Herriot, I was in permanent contact with important represent tatives of the resistance, among them Georges Bidault, Teitgen, Lacoste, Coste-Floret, Blondel, and Albert Bayet, and with heroes of the secret service, such as our unhappy friends Cavaillès and "Maxime." I gave to anyone who had the right to receive it, information which often came directly from Pierre Laval himself.

I. M. Herriot a Prisoner at Evaux

On 30 September 1942, if I am not mistaken, the prefect, M. Angéli, came to President Herriot's home at Lyon and asked him to sign an under- taking that he would not leave France to join the French of the resistance. Herriot refused to give such a promise, not because he had any idea of leaving the soil of France, but because he thought it would be contrary to his dignity to sign any pledge whatsoever to the Vichy government. When the President of the Chamber refused to sign, Angéli, accompanied by armed men, took M. Herriot to Bretel, which was assigned to him as a place of enforced residence.

Several days before this happened I had seen the President at Grenoble. As usual, I had put him on his guard against the dangers which menaced his liberty and even his life; and as usual, the President had opposed his own optimism to my somber and sad opinions. He seemed always to be dominated by the odd idea that no one would ever dare touch the "Third Magistrate of the Republic," as he called himself with just pride.

I learned of the arrest of the President only on 5 October, in a train going from Marseille to Lyon. I can still see the railway worker sitting beside me, who was discussing it with his neighbor. I heard these words: "They've arrested him."

I listened more closely. I guessed at once that it must have been a person of importance, and unable to restrain myself longer I asked him who it was. "It's Herriot," he said.

My emotion was doubtless clearly shown, for the railwayman said in a friendly way, speaking in low tones, "I see we're among friends."

I reached Vichy on 6 October. I saw Terracher, Louis Marin, and Camille Bloch. What was to be done? I decided to leave for Lyon in order to come to some agreement first with Dr. Rebatel, Mme Herriot's brother, who had the confidence of the President, in whose home I had made his acquaintance. I left my hotel at four o'clock in the morning. It was still dark; I walked down a narrow stairway. I fell, I got up again, I felt a sharp pain: I discovered that it was impossible to walk. I had broken my leg.

Some terrible days followed, with the suffering that always accompanies the reduction of fractures, in this case combined with mental suffering because of my friend Herriot. Accursed stairway! At the precise moment when the President would have the greatest need of my help I had made it impossible for me to defend him and to devote my efforts to him. Those who have had a very strong feeling of friendship can understand the anguish that I suffered in those sad hours, immobilized in my bed. Three days after this accident I had myself taken to Grenoble on a stretcher. Getting into the trains, overloaded as they were, and getting out again could not be arranged without some danger, but there were no more accidents, thanks to a dear friend of the resistance, "Sister," as she was called.

What was to be done for Herriot? His family, and I too, like all people of common sense, felt that this enforced residence at Bretel was only a preliminary step, and that prison would inevitably follow his internment, only to end with his deportation to Germany. Max Dormoy had been assassinated, and this precedent obsessed our minds. We feared for Herriot's life after his noble letter—as noble as it was imprudent—returning the Legion of Honor to the "government" at Vichy had produced a veritable explosion of hate in those fanatical circles where assassination was an approved weapon.

Thanks to my excellent health I made an extremely rapid recovery. Eight days after a second reduction of my fractures, the first having been badly done, my leg was placed in a "walking cast," which allowed me to walk, though with two crutches. On the morning of 27 October 1942 I left for Lyon, and that same evening I went to Vichy where I had meetings with Louis Marin, who was in a state of rage, and with the Minister of Justice, Joseph Barthélemy. The latter was pained by what had happened. He desired that the resistance should believe that he disapproved of the measures taken against Herriot though at the same time he did not want to compromise himself in the eyes of the guilty government, of which he himself was a member with no thought of leaving. I asked him bluntly to take me to Laval. Barthélemy did nothing and I got nowhere with my plans. My heart heavy with care, and my spirit tormented by a thousand thoughts of which the only purpose was the defense of Herriot, I returned to Grenoble.

That which was bound to happen, happened. Prison at Evaux followed enforced residence at Bretel. M. Herriot stayed in this frightful prison (it was the Hotel Thermal transformed into a jail) from October 1942 to the middle of March 1943. As may well be believed, I did not remain idle. I did not accept inactivity on the pretext of having no means of action. I have always believed that when means do not exist they must be created. At Vichy I had just proved that my means, namely my connections with important people and the influence which might result, could produce no useful result. I decided that it was necessary to create other more effective means. I decided to visit M. Émile Roche, former director of the newspaper *La Republique*, for which I had written editorials before the war. My purpose was to consult Roche, and if the opportunity arose, to beg him to help me in trying to save President Herriot.

As usual Roche welcomed me most warmly on his estate at Vence, in keeping with his true feelings. Having suffered many disappointments in life he had become one of those who regard friendship not as a chain which hinders one's existence, but as a link which ennobles it.

Roche had been in close relations with Herriot before the war. I was therefore justified in believing it most probable that he would use all the means in his power, means which I imagined would be important, to help President Herriot. We talked and studied the situation. Roche said to me, "You must see Georges Bonnet." He picked up the telephone and after a long wait got Georges Bonnet on the line at Périgueux. Roche is a man of action; and when he recommends someone, he doesn't do it lightly. He introduced me to Bonnet in such a manner that the former Minister of Foreign Affairs, a man very suspicious by nature and even more so from experience, could without hesitation extend to me the confidence which was so necessary to the action which was to be undertaken. The following day I left for Lyon to tell Dr. Rebatel what was going on. M. Herriot's brother-in-law entirely approved of the idea of seeking the help of M. Bonnet. I therefore went to Périgueux, to the home of a man with whose prewar policies I had not been specially sympathetic.

I explained to Georges Bonnet the dangerous situation Herriot was in, the dubious state of his health, his anguish, and the fears of Mme Herriot and his family. I then came to the political problem. Herriot, I said, was necessary to France and it was our supreme duty to keep him out of danger and save the life on which so many political and republican interests depended. Such a duty would require supreme courage, but it was a necessary courage, one that brought with it the most perfect of all rewards, the honor of having defended against the enemy a Frenchman and a statesman who has himself brought honor to the Republic.

Never was there a more sincere plea than mine, nor a case more easy to win. Georges Bonnet said to me, "Herriot shall have the most complete aid that I can give him. I will spare myself no trouble, and if necessary I will go to see those whom I would most of all prefer not to see, if this dangerous and unpleasant step is necessary to the safety of Herriot. I am going to see Laval, and I shall tell him, with such arguments as are necessary, that this arrest is scandalous from the human point of view and stupid from the political point of view. I don't really want to go to Vichy for another week yet, but we shall leave tomorrow morning. We must not waste an instant in trying to improve Herriot's situation."

The conditions in which Herriot was detained at the Hotel Thermal, now transformed into a jail (with bars on the windows and barbed wire around the outside), were painful and uselessly cruel for any man, and particularly for a man of his age. M. Herriot could not receive a visit from his wife more than twice a week, and then only in the presence of a police officer.

"What is it that we want to obtain?" I asked Bonnet. "Evidently the supreme objective is his liberty, but in waiting to gain that, we can at least ease his situation, for example by obtaining for Mme Herriot the right to pay more and longer visits to her husband without the humiliating and embarrassing presence of a police officer."

The next day I left with Bonnet for Vichy. The former Minister of Foreign Affairs saw Laval and in the end obtained important results.

The decisive success, or rather, alas, the success that would have been decisive if Herriot had been willing to listen to my opinions, could not be obtained until about the middle of March [1943]. It consisted in obtaining for M. and Mme Herriot the right to leave the Hotel Thermal, and to rent a charming and roomy house for themselves alone in the city of Evaux, almost without any police supervision. Their guard was reduced to two officers whom it was easy to win over. Their right to take walks in the city and in the nearby country was tacitly admitted.

Many memories, some charming and others sad, come to my mind concerning those days which are so near to us and yet so far away when one thinks of all that has happened since.

I went to Evaux a score of times between November 1942 and March 1943. Those horrible trips! After leaving Lyon or Vichy, I reached Montluçon at three o'clock in the morning. Covered with a cape I squatted down in a waiting room of which the outstanding charms were a glacial cold, drafts which carried away one's hat, a sallow light which was too weak for reading and too strong for sleeping, and a repulsive dirtiness traversed by various species of vermin. In this waiting room one waited three hours. At six in the morning the train left for Evaux, to arrive at seven. When I got out of the train it was still dark, and I hurried to the little hotel where Mme Herriot was living. Breakfast awaited me and I ate it eagerly, as I was extremely hungry and stiff with cold. I brought Mme Herriot the latest news of Lyon, of her family, and of Bretel, and she told me how M. Herriot was getting on. His condition continued to get worse, and he became more and more nervous. This highly emotional man was rightly indignant about his imprisonment; the evils which bore down so heavily on France, and the powerlessness to which he himself had been reduced, made his life that of a martyr. When the time came I went with Mme Herriot to the hotel-prison, at the back of a sort of damp basin where the air was full of smells from a sulphur spring.

I was not allowed to go through the barbed wire fence. I saw the poor President behind the bars of his window, waiting impatiently for the arrival of his devoted and courageous wife. When he saw us he waved his cap with one hand, holding onto one of the bars with the other. He looked like a lion ignominiously shut up in a cage. I went back, sad and alone. When Mme Herriot returned I went down again to the barrier. Herriot was standing at the window and the same highly moving scene was repeated. More than once, Mme Herriot, a woman of great feeling, said to me as she noticed my suffering and my strained eyes, "Don't feel upset about it; it will all pass away. My husband knows what you are doing. He has confidence in you and loves you very much."

I should add that I had great need of some encouragement, but it would be surprising if I explained the true reason.

In the rough confusion of Pétain's Vichy a rumor soon got about that important people, whose names were not given, were busying themselves with the liberation of Herriot. Some groups, saying that they were friends of Herriot, now began to disapprove the various moves that might help the President. Some sublime souls, who were not all without ulterior motives, explained that any action on behalf of President Herriot ran the risk of "compromising" his immaculate virtue; it was better, they said, that he should suffer, and that his glory should be in proportion to his suffering. One individual who supported this point of view summarized his mighty thoughts in this formula: "Let Herriot have the crown of a martyr."

Neither M. Herriot's family nor I myself allowed ourselves to be turned aside by this singular opinion, an opinion, it must be said, which was scandalous coming from those whom Clemenceau called "those who watch while others act."

Dr. Rebatel has a clear mind, a doctor's mind. Mme Herriot is a woman whose courage has since been demonstrated. As for me, I am no evangelical sister of charity. Neither Dr. Rebatel nor Mme Herriot nor I myself ever acted lightly. Each of us thought things over carefully and weighed the points for and against. We calculated physical dangers which threatened Herriot's life and the political perils which exposed his prestige as a servant of the Republic to infamous calumny. Our reasoning was as follows, and I defy anyone to disprove it.

Our duty as friends, as relatives, and as republicans is to do everything possible to preserve for the Republic, when it is restored after victory, the strength, the national influence, and the international reputation of President Herriot. In order to preserve Herriot, two things, and not merely one, are necessary. Herriot's political prestige, both national and international, must be effectively protected against any attack, and our actions must thus be such that no one can ever say that Herriot compromised himself with Vichy. But there is also a second condition, namely that Herriot's health must be preserved. It must be admitted that he could render no further service to the Republic if he were not alive when victory came. This second point has that quality of self-evident truth which, according to Descartes, makes proof unnecessary.

Therefore we held firm. We thought that the crown of a martyr, however beautiful, is of no practical use when it rests on the head of a corpse. Until the last days of Herriot's imprisonment there were good apostles who still relied on the theory of a martyr's crown. They dreamed of this crown, those who ran no risk of having it on their own heads, even in the somber hours when Herriot was sick and isolated at Vittel. How can such mental aberrations be explained? I leave to others the task of finding out whether it was stupidity, lightmindedness, or an ignoble desire to see Herriot disappear forever from the scene—"Get out so that I can take your place."

Our little group, Dr. Rebatel, Mme Herriot, and Enfière, set for itself two objectives: to save Herriot's life and to protect Herriot's prestige. This double task involved endless difficulties. To save Herriot's life it was necessary to talk with those on whom it depended, Laval and the Germans. To protect Herriot's prestige it was necessary to find some dialectical system familiar to the Germans which would lead them to guarantee his life without demanding anything in exchange which could tarnish his prestige.

By squaring the circle? No. By astute diplomacy? Yes, certainly. Every policy must be judged by its results, and ours did in fact produce something, for we delayed the deportation of Herriot long enough to make it possible for him to regain his health completely. And we achieved this essential objective without hindering our second, namely his political prestige here and abroad. We were able to obtain these objectives because all of us continually acted with devotion, with tenacity, and with a courage that was perhaps at certain moments not without merit.

Let us return to Evaux. Time passed, and in spite of some improvements which were arranged, for example that Mme Herriot was able to see the President every day for three hours without any tactless supervision, the health of M. Herriot was still getting worse. He became more and more nervous, and black thoughts filled his days and nights with gloom. He scarcely slept at all; no food agreed with him; and he was losing his appetite. Sometimes Mme Herriot gave signs that she was beginning to get discouraged. I felt extremely sorry for her. When I was at Evaux and she was not at the prison, we walked through the beautiful countryside that surrounds the little town. I examined the countryside for means of escape, to find a temporary hiding place, and to see where an airplane could be landed. At Bretel, at Châtelguyon, M. Herriot had told me flatly that he would remain in France no matter what happened, but I never lost hope that in the end I would persuade him of the advantages of his being in London.

So long as the President was kept in prison, any escape seemed to be impossible, at least without the active cooperation of police agents; and of such complicity we were not at all sure at that time.

Toward the middle of March 1943 Georges Bonnet finally obtained, thanks to his skill and his rare qualities of perseverance, the right for Herriot and Mme Herriot to rent a private house in the town of Evaux. This change had immediate effects on Herriot. His appetite came back, he was able to sleep, and he began to read and even to write. Our joy was great but of short duration.

On 17 March 1943 I had a long conversation with the President in this house. I told him in detail what our efforts had been to obtain the excellent result of a change of domicile. The President, in a good mood, thanked me vigorously. For me this was a moment of joy and hope. But when I took up once again the question of his departure for England, the President held to his own point of view. Nevertheless, and this was an important indication, he did not put aside my proposal absolutely. He only wished to wait and see. Alas, this delay was fatal. He did wait and he did see. On 31 March he saw an entire company of German soldiers encircle his house. A German doctor examined him and said that he was in condition to be transported. The Germans took him away to an unknown destination. Thus ended the first phase of our activity.

I remember that Georges Bonnet had only just obtained—and with what difficulty—this famous change of domicile, when a whole crowd of people claimed to have gained this success themselves. At least ten of these thieves of victory could be named. I was indignant. Georges Bonnet smiled about it philosophically, and warned me paternally, in his wisdom, that I would see others like them. I did indeed!

II.—M. HERRIOT A PRISONER AT VITTEL, AT NANCY AND AT VILLE-ÉVRARD

April, May, June, July, August, and September of 1943 were frightful for M. Herriot, for his relatives, and for his friends.

For about fifteen days nobody knew where he was. Where had the Germans taken him? Where had they hidden him? Our anguish can be easily understood. We knew how delicate was his health, even though we knew it had improved after his change of domicile to Evaux. But his condition was such that a dangerous relapse could be expected at any moment. After days which seemed endless we learned that M. and Mme Herriot were detained at a house at Vittel, cut off from the world outside, in the most complete isolation. Soon we knew that M. Herriot's health was declining visibly. And a little later we learned that this seventy-year-old man was refusing all food and carrying on a hunger strike. The result was a frightening loss of weight. Through Mme Herriot's rare letters we could guess that her strength, even though she was endowed with prodigious energy, was wearing away. What would happen to Herriot if illness forced his wife to keep to her bed, or perhaps to leave her husband, for whom she was the only, the irreplaceable, support? Dr. Rebatel was desperate. We racked our brains for some way to save this relative, this friend, this statesman, the hope of a Republic restored after victory.

Aided by Dr. Rebatel, his calm and unshakable brother and brother-in-law and a sure friend, particularly in those difficult circumstances which open the way for human cowardice, I pursued the task that I had set myself, namely to defend Herriot's life by all means, to throw myself into this work without fear of what people might say, and if necessary to be willing so to compromise myself, without ever compromising the President, that the protection of his physical existence would never harm or embarrass his political personality. These tactics, so dangerous for me, were beneficial to our cause, and in any case were the only ones likely to produce results. I acted like a soldier charged with the protection of his unit, who bears the brunt of an attack in order to allow his unit to gain cover. At no moment of my action on behalf of Herriot did I misjudge the dangers I was running. I accepted them with full understanding. My confidence was based on the conviction that I was right, and on the knowledge of the importance of my mission, which was to save a glorious banner of the Republic, a banner which, in my eyes, was worth an army. Finally, my confidence was based on the idea, possibly naïve but surely beautiful, that the truth would be known on the day of liberation and that President Herriot himself would proclaim it. The hope that such a glorious day was sure to come sustained me, and renewed my strength when it seemed to weaken under repeated setbacks, disappointments, and dangers.

It was said in Paris not merely that General Medicus, chief of the German military administration, was not a fanatical Nazi, but that on the contrary he was a hidden enemy of Nazism, and a German army officer of the old school. General Medicus had the reputation of being distinguished, humane, and very intelligent; and it was said that consequently he was very disturbed by the way things were going.

I decided to establish contact with him. I succeeded, though not without difficulty, through the help of a member of the German army in one of the services of the Hotel Majestic, of which General Medicus was the supreme head. This German had been introduced to me as being very anti-Nazi, and he did in fact speak in a way which would have made the hair of a true Nazi stand on end. Naturally I felt a great deal of distrust for this man; I had the right and the duty to think that this member of the German army might be an agent provocateur. It must be said at once that he was nothing of the kind. He rendered great services to our cause, and he allowed himself to be executed by the Nazis in August 1944 without mentioning my name in the hope of saving his own head.

My German intermediary, when I had asked that a personal interview should be arranged for me with General Medicus, explained the whole matter to the anti-Nazi secretary of the general. On 19 June 1943 I was received by General Medicus. The interview was conducted in German as the General pretended that he didn't understand French well enough. (This was a lie, I learned afterward.) The conversation lasted more than an hour. I shall give a precise summary of this conversation because the ideas I set forth, and the arguments I used to support them, will never change, at least in their essentials. I had found the right plan of action for the defense of Herriot. Some may judge it severely. But I ask that the tree should be judged by its fruits. Let us see what these fruits were, without further delay: (1) the transfer of the President from Vittel to Nancy, and from Nancy to Ville-Evrard; (2) certain improvements in his treatment, as for example freedom to walk in the park at Ville-Evrard (in those days, happily now gone, the President's health, they always told me, depended on these walks); (3) the delay until the eve of the liberation of Paris (17 August 1944) of his deportation to Germany, a deportation which Mme Herriot and Dr. Rebatel considered certain to cause his death, since his health had not yet been completely restored.

With some variations due to the circumstances, the essential points which my talks brought out for the sake of their effect on the Germans were these:

"Germany has already lost the war. The cruel and inhuman methods which you are employing against the French of the resistance will inevitably create a terrible hate between the French people and the German people, one that will perhaps not be wiped out for many long years. You are laying France waste, pillaging it. How can you hope that the idea of collaboration should seem to the French anything but a sinister farce? You imagine that the French of the resistance are toughs and bandits. I tell you that they are brave men and heroes, and deep in your heart you know that what I say is true. You have only to recall your own history, the wars you call wars of liberation at the time of Napoleon, and more recently your own resistance during the years when the Ruhr was occupied. You have made Schlageter, Horst Wessel and other young Nazis into national heroes. From your point of view you were right; but what were these men if they were not members of a resistance?

"You think that the French are people who have fallen into decadence and you base your thought chiefly on three arguments, of which the first is our low birth rate. You forget that yours was even lower toward the end of the Weimar regime, and that we can well bring it up again just as you did with yours. Your second argument is that you were able in prewar days to build up friendships and to secure support in France, in the press, and among certain social classes; this leads you to believe that the French people are ripe for slavery. But the very action of the resistance shows you today that the French have not degenerated, because with all your strength you have not succeeded in putting a stop to it. You defeated us in 1940 with a rapidity which was indeed shattering. I tell you that your success was due less to the genius of your own generals than to the extreme inefficiency of our own. Put de Gaulle in the place of Weygand and everything would change. . . . The conclusion you should draw is this: you must not despise us; we will regain our strength, and you may well have need of us, more than you think at this moment. In any case, if you wish to save something of your own country you must stop this war as quickly as possible, a war which is already lost. And in the meantime stop martyrizing us and pillaging us.

"Once you have understood the true situation, if you have the courage to draw the conclusion to which it points, you must understand that President Herriot could play an important role and that it is in your interest to take care of him rather than to trouble him. Isn't Herriot an intimate friend of Roosevelt's? Suppose Herriot dies. What would be your situation in the eyes of the world? Even if he died a thousand times over from purely natural causes, the entire world would say that you have assassinated him. Your reputation is such that when anyone dies in one of your prisons, everyone believes firmly that you have killed him.

"Dr. Rebatel must be allowed to see Herriot freely. All measures which will hasten his return to health must be taken, and it is Dr. Rebatel who is the best judge of the situation, and not the German doctors, however eminent they may be. I must be allowed to talk freely with Herriot. If the necessity arises, I must be allowed to go abroad. If you want something done for you, you must do something for us." And I added with a mysterious air, "The President listens closely to what I say and has very strong feelings of friendship toward me. You will understand what I mean."

It will be recognized, perhaps, that such words would not leave the Germans indifferent just when they were looking for a good way to get out of their predicament. I may be permitted to flatter myself by thinking that such words were cleverly conceived from the point of view of their effect on a German; but on the other hand I do not wish to imply any hope that my words will be taken in that sense by people of ill will, who will not hesitate to accuse me of intelligence with the enemy.

Let us look more closely at my dialectic.

It was impossible to ask the Germans not to kill Herriot, unless at the same time it were proved that his death would have bad results for Germany and that the protection of his life would be good from their point of view. To anyone who dares to suggest the contrary, I ask this question: Do you believe that the Germans, our cruel enemies, were capable of acting from humane motives? Or, to use the familiar expression, would they be likely to go to any trouble "just for the sake of his beautiful eyes?" No, certainly not. Well, then! There remained only two possibilities, to do what I did or to hide behind a policy of doing nothing. I could not take refuge in withdrawal—always easy and often cowardly—for I was President Herriot's friend, supported in my efforts by his family, and holding political beliefs which led me to regard Herriot as a trump card of the first importance for the Republic and for France. I defy anyone, no matter who, to discover in my reasoning, approved as it was by M. Herriot's family, the slightest weak point. However one searched, however fine the arguments were spun, no weak point would be found; it is a garment without a seam. Either M. Herriot's life was important for France, or else it was immaterial to the interests of the nation. To those who hold to this second alternative I have nothing to say, but to those who believe the first, I declare that if this life was precious then it had to be preserved, and the proper means to preserve it had to be employed. It may seem superfluous to take so much trouble to break through doors which are already open. Alas! You, Dr. Rebatel, and all you relatives and friends of Herriot, have only to draw on your memories. Haven't we all known defenders and "faithful friends" of President Herriot who unanimously proclaimed the imperative necessity and the urgency of saving Herriot and yet whom nothing in the world could persuade to use the slightest practical means toward achieving a purpose already admitted and established?

"Those who watch while others act," as Clemenceau said, makers of fine phrases, all you who talked but said nothing, all you slanderers, where were you when Edouard and Blanche Herriot were imprisoned behind barbed wire, every instant in fear of deportation, perhaps of assassination; both of them ill, both seemingly at death's door? Yes, where were you?

You were making fine phrases behind doors and shutters that you had closed in your caution, for you were trembling before the Boche. And what were we doing? We were always on the road, to Lyon, to Vichy, to Paris, never hesitating to put our heads in the lion's mouth. Far from avoiding those odious contacts with the Germans whom we hated, we sought them out, because on these hated but temporarily powerful men depended the life of him who was the only object of our thoughts.

In my talk with Medicus, as in later conversations with other important Germans, I stressed the idea that Germany ought to make peace before it was completely beaten. This was not my true thought. In my heart I eagerly desired the total defeat of Germany, but I dare to say that even in those hours of intense feeling which the Nazi crimes justified, I never lost my head. My feelings never became absolute master of my reason. At the risk of shocking some people, I dare say this: that one could be both a very good Frenchman and a farsighted politician calculating that the complete destruction of Germany would give rise to other dangers. In any case, what I may have thought of the advantages or disadvantages of a compromise peace was without any practical importance, since I had no way of acting in either one direction or the other. When I argued with the Germans, it was not as a philosopher setting forth truths which he had discovered, but as an advocate pleading for the life of Herriot. It was necessary to give the Germans some reason for acting. My "concessions" cost little and did not bear heavily on the destinies of the world.

The pattern was "you give and I'll give"—but what I gave was nothing but words and vague promises; I had nothing else to give. They did have something to give, and they gave it. In exchange for a few phrases substantial results were gained, including better treatment for Herriot and above all the delay in his deportation, a deportation which would have killed him while he was still ill. This is the point that must never be forgotten if my actions, seconded by Dr. Rebatel, are to be judged fairly.

I invite thoughtful persons to ask themselves how my attitude could harm the cause of the liberation. I was but a tiny unit among millions of combatants, and my opinion had no practical effect. I bound only myself. I did not even engage the President, for I always took care to tell the Germans that I would try to obtain one thing or another from him and that success was possible—this was to give them hope— but that it would be difficult and slow—this was to gain time—and that the essential pre-condition of any effective action on my part was that he should be freed so that his health could be restored. For that was what I sought above everything else, to preserve his health and to gain time. In such tactics all the risks were on my side and all the benefits on the side of the President, and therefore of France and the Republic.

I have now explained my entire system of pleading with the Germans. Let us go back to the office of General Medicus.

General Medicus listened to my explanations with close attention. He did not interrupt me except to show his surprise at my more audacious words. And he did indeed have something to be astonished at, for here in the office of one of the highest German authorities in occupied France, one man alone, unarmed, dared to say to him: "You will be beaten, and you are already beaten." The General answered, "Your ideas are very interesting and I appreciate all their importance. I am a German patriot, and I am completely German. I am an officer and consequently my principles are those of chivalry—as befits a man of the old army." He added these last words in a low voice, turning his head so that he was not looking at me for several instants. In effect the General let me know bluntly that he distinguished himself from the Nazi brutes who represented the new army, and that he wanted the distinction to be perceived.

He went on, "Your ideas will certainly be favorably received in some German circles in Paris and in Berlin, but they will meet bitter hostility in other circles of which the influence and strength must not be underestimated. Personally, I can do nothing for President Herriot because I am not competent to act in such matters. You ask me to transmit your ideas to Dr. Knochen and General Oberg. I shall not do so. But I can put you in touch with them. Every decision relating to President Herriot must be made by them." And the General added, "I am a gentleman and I do not care to involve you in the presentation of your ideas to the officials of the avenue Foch. It is preferable to talk with the diplomats."

In taking me to the door, this high officer straightened himself and said firmly in a tone which was intended to convince me of its sincerity, "I believe in the victory of Germany; Heil Hitler!" I imagine that the careful reader will interpret the proposals of General Medicus the same way that I myself interpreted them: (1) General Medicus was certainly a German patriot and certainly not a Nazi. (2) Being intelligent and farsighted, he foresaw perhaps better than we ourselves, because of the information he had, that Germany's defeat was inevitable. (3) A "gentleman," as he described himself, he spoke with caution but nevertheless said everything that he could in his position to put me on guard against the brutes of the Gestapo. (4) He said, also with caution but nevertheless clearly, that my undertaking had some chance of success with the German diplomats.

I had striven to get in touch with General Medicus as quickly as possible after the removal of Herriot from Evaux and his imprisonment at Vittel. It had taken time to make the necessary arrangements, and it was only in June 1943 that I succeeded. My attempts to accomplish something with Adrien Marquet were made at the same time. I saw him a number of times in Paris and at Bordeaux. He had the reputation of seeing the Germans very often. What interested me most was the rumor according to which the celebrated Dr. Knochen, an important person in the Gestapo, and one who dispensed imprisonment, torture, and assassination, was Marquet's friend. This important German, one of the most terrible of the infamous Nazi police zoo, was the man I wished to "contact," to use a word introduced to our language by our English friends. The pleasure of my task can be imagined. My duty was to find, and to create, ways and means of defending the life of Herriot. For this purpose I hesitated before neither danger nor disgust. I set myself the repulsive task of seeing these butchers, these masters of assassination, these monsters of cruelty; but what dangers would I not have consented to encounter? What risks would I not have accepted to advance Edouard Herriot even another millimeter along the path of safety?

I have most unpleasant memories of my relations with Marquet. What a puppet he was, and how illiterate! How ignobly he enjoyed life in the midst of the miseries of a France invaded and pillaged! With his soul of muck he was a man without the slightest trace of dignity when faced by an enemy! Essentially, the life of Herriot meant nothing whatever to Marquet. He hadn't the least idea that Herriot could be of service to France when France was again free. For him there was but one man in the world that counted for anything, Adrien Marquet. Besides, at this time, Marquet was still completely convinced that Germany would win, and probably convinced too that a happy result of this victory would be the return to power of Adrien Marquet.

I shall recount one of my most horrible memories, one which can never be wiped from my mind. Marquet had allowed things to drag along. In visit after visit he gave me as my only consolation words and nothing more. He hadn't the least desire, I learned later, to lift his little finger on Herriot's behalf, but he wanted the contrary to be believed. Therefore he promised me that he would introduce me to his friend, that famous butcher Dr. Knochen. Finally the great day came. I went to one of those luxurious buildings in the avenue Foch where the Gestapo had set up its head-quarters. I refused to give my name, but when I said I was waiting for M. Marquet the guard stood at attention. I was taken to a special waiting room and asked to sit in an immense chair. Marquet arrived. "Wait a moment," he told me; "I must first see Dr. Knochen alone and then I will call you."

I waited, and I waited a long time, long enough to witness a spectacle which tore my heart and which today gives me a feeling of nausea if I think of it. A great door opened, and from where I sat I could see what was happening inside an office. Two German officers and three French boys in the "Youth and the Mountains" uniform were ending a discussion. As I listened I understood that these miserable French boys had just explained to the Boches a plan for propaganda in the "Youth and the Mountains" group to encourage recruiting for the Legion of French Volunteers [anti-communist military force]. When these unconscionable youths took leave of the enemy, they saluted in military fashion, clicking their heels in the German manner and jerking back the head. Had it been Maréchal Foch himself, no French soldier could have saluted with more enthusiasm and fervor. Shame! What shame! When these unfortunate youths had turned their backs, the two Boches, rightly satisfied, laughed heartily. I felt that I should faint from disgust, hate, and contempt. It seemed as though these feelings were going to make me burst. I made an effort to lock them within me as one would lock a prisoner in his cell. So that my feelings should not be visible in my eyes, I closed my eyes. Where could these three boys have come from? What were their families? Through what traitors' hands had they passed? They were as magnificent as young gods; their entire being radiated health and vitality. They were well-bred and magnificent animals. But had they any brains, and in those brains the slightest trace of intelligence, or conscience, or a single atom of dignity and honor?

These were my reflections when another door opened and Marquet came in, quick, alert and laughing, happy after the fashion of one who brings good news. "Off we go," he said. "There's no point in bothering more about Herriot. He's gone mad and will pop off very soon." And he burst out laughing.

"The news is certainly false," I said. "Give me some details, I beg you." His reply was that he didn't have the time just then, but that we could meet again. I never saw him again. If one day he should be punished, I would save my pity for others and give none to him.

That evening I left for Nancy in the hope of obtaining precise information about President Herriot. I was able to learn that M. Herriot was in fact suffering, and that an excess of urea was the chief cause of his doctors' anxiety. Somewhat reassured, I left Nancy to hurry to Lyon, where once again I met Dr. Rebatel and stiffened his courage with the recent and more reliable information I had obtained. I feared, and I was right, that the false news spread by Marquet would have got about rapidly in Paris and Lyon. We discussed the problem. I supported the point of view that in view of the present danger it was obligatory to adopt the most effective means available to us, namely, an appeal to some very highly placed official who could both understand and act. The person of whom I had already thought, and of whom I was now thinking even more definitely, was none other than the Minister of Foreign Affairs of the Reich, Mr. von Ribbentrop.

I wrote a letter along these lines to Georges Bonnet and Dr. Rebatel wrote another in support of mine. Georges Bonnet, who was devoted to Herriot on grounds of personal friendship, and completely convinced of the enormous advantage of safeguarding such a man for France, was ready to undertake anything whatever to save the President. Unfortunately, one weighty difficulty that had not occurred to me made any move through Ribbentrop impossible at least for the moment. An intercession of the kind we had in mind could succeed only on a basis of personal relations between the two parties; and contrary to what I believed, Georges Bonnet scarcely knew the German minister. He had seen him but once in his life, when the Franco-German declaration of December 1939 was signed; the presence of many political and diplomatic figures had made this ceremony anything but intimate.

Once again we were blocked. Those were horrible days. Mme Herriot's strength diminished slowly but steadily, and M. Herriot's vitality sank to a point where only a narrow margin separated life from death.

Once more I went to Vence, to the estate of Émile Roche. I explained my anguish; I painted for him in strongest colors the increasing risks that were linked with the President's death. I begged him to seek among his many connections some important person who could aid directly or indirectly in defending Herriot. Roche reflected for a long time and then said to me, "Yes, there is someone. He has already saved a resistance man from death, so he must have impressive methods and connections. I refer to Abbé Renaud."

"The 'pink baby' of the *Action Française* [French movement and title of its publication]?" I asked him with surprise.

"That's the one," said Roche.

The fact that Abbé Renaud had been a *bête noire* of that abject *Action* which was called *Française* in derision could only reassure me. Besides, I would have caressed the Devil himself if I had believed that from such an action our cause would gain some strength. Anyway, I did consult Georges Bonnet regarding this priest who had played a political role (particularly in the time of Benedict XV) and who, according to Roche, had been sufficiently lucky and powerful to win back from Germany the life of a French patriot. In talking with Bonnet I learned that the Abbé was an old friend of the former Minister of Foreign Affairs. Bonnet's description of him increased my desire to obtain his services, and strengthened my decision to approach him with constant caution. Bonnet confirmed that the Abbé had saved a Frenchman who had been condemned to death. But he warned me against the artful and incessantly intriguing character of this ecclesiastic.

Thus began the Renaud-Keller episode. The Abbé immediately put me in contact with Dr. Keller, who was a frightful individual with every appearance of being a good man. He was in reality an intriguer, crafty, ambitious, fanatical, not officially a Nazi—at least so he claimed—but a man who lived richly and who shamelessly used the most detestable means of satisfying his evil passions on women who desired to save a husband or son under German arrest. The vices and sadism of this man were not evident until flattery and alcohol stripped off his veneer. He claimed to be a practicing Catholic, and kept faithfully to the duties of his elastic religion. Such was the man with whom I now had to deal. During the course of my discussions with Dr. Keller, we did obtain one result, the transfer of Herriot from Nancy to Ville-Evrard, not far from Paris. It is impossible to say just what part was played in this happy move by the fear the Germans may have felt about allowing Herriot to die at Nancy, by Georges Bonnet's action, or by my own action through Dr. Keller.

Dr. Rebatel thought that the best way of restoring the President's health was to get him back to his own property at Bretel. Dr. Keller allowed me to hope that the return of Herriot to Bretel could be arranged in exchange for an important person who was then in the hands of the Allies, a person to whom the German police seemed to attach an extraordinary, and to me totally unforeseen, importance. The man in question was the engineer Bedaux, who several years before the war had played an important part in the affairs of King Edward VIII. Keller noticed my astonishment. "He is of capital importance for us," he said. "Obtain his liberation and we will give you Herriot."

It was then that we planned my journey to Madrid to negotiate with the British Ambassador, Sir Samuel Hoare, for the release and return to France of M. Bedaux, whose importance in world affairs, I had to admit, I had underestimated. To Gladstone is attributed this remark to a young member of Parliament: "The really powerful men of this world are not necessarily those whom the public knows." Was M. Bedaux one of that kind?

Perhaps it will never be known. His own testimony on the point in any case will be lacking, because he died in prison—if the newspapers are to be believed.

Suddenly Keller informed me that the Bedaux affair was blocked by other obstacles, on the nature of which he was at first silent. It took an incredible quantity of the best French cognac to loosen his tongue, but the result was that I then received some light on the internal struggles between the police, army, and diplomatic services of Germany. If I understood rightly, it was the diplomatic group and the moderate sections of the police and of the army (those sections which regarded the war as lost and sought a compromise peace) that wished at any price to get hold of Bedaux, while the supporters of war to a finish had no desire to allow their opponents to get their hands on an important person who perhaps might be able, through his connections, to get conversations started which would hasten the end of the war.

I never saw Dr. Keller again. A rather vague report has hinted that the doctor, who was implicated in the famous plot against Hitler in 1944, got across the Pyrénées in good time.

I now come to the episode involving Brinon, Grimm, and Hoffman. At my request M. de Monzie asked Brinon to see me. About this time, December 1943, the star of Laval seemed to be setting and a new sun appeared about to rise. It was said in Paris that Laval had given so little satisfaction to the Germans, that he had so repeatedly tacked about and created incidents of every kind to keep away from the Germans the greatest number of workers and the greatest possible quantities of equipment and raw materials of every kind, that German discontent had reached a point at which Laval's resignation and even his arrest were probable.

Common rumor, confirmed by my own sources, indicated Brinon, aided by Platon, as Laval's successor. I knew that Brinon was not without a certain intelligence, sharpened by the instinct of self-preservation. I felt sure that he would do something to aid us, even if it were only to create extenuating circumstances for use at a later date in case the Allies should be the conquerors—as Brinon was convinced they would be, according to the authorized opinion of Anatole de Monzie.

I saw Brinon at the Place Beauvau. I went to his office one morning. I had scarcely finished with the usual formalities of greeting when the telephone rang.

"My compliments, General (or Colonel)," said the slow and solemn voice of Brinon. It was Knochen at the other end of the line, the same Knochen with whom I had sought that ignoble contact. The Ambassador was admittedly polite, but I must add I was rather surprised by the obduracy which underlay everything he said, hidden though it was by an impeccable and icy courtesy. Some French people had been arrested and taken to Compiègne. The previous evening Brinon had asked that they be liberated. It was on this subject that the frightful Knochen was telephoning him. The butcher seemed to be raising difficulties.

"At least you can release the distinguished persons among those who have been arrested," said Brinon. I thought of Nathan speaking to Abner [in Racine's *Athalie*]:

> *A man obscure, to lowly fortunes bred,*
> *What matter if by chance his blood be shed?*

The result of my new efforts was that I had to see Professor Grimm and Counselor Hoffman of the German Embassy. Professor Grimm gave lectures on the future of Europe. His almost silly naïveté made him believe sincerely that he would succeed in convincing the French more and more of the necessity of building up a new Europe under the German banner. This same professor was charged by the Embassy with 'classified' missions of a political nature; that was why Abetz gave him the Herriot case to deal with. By way of introduction, the professor told me that he had always been grateful to M. Herriot for having been so "human" at the London Conference in 1924. At that time, it seems, German prisoners were still being held in France. Grimm, who was the German expert in London, had arranged with Herriot that they should be repatriated.

Grimm claimed that the matter on which I had come to see him was outside his field, and that he would have to refer it to Counselor of Embassy Hoffman. Oh, that German bureaucracy! Everyone feared everyone else and in self-protection tried to foist off on someone else every difficult problem.

I asked Hoffman for an authorization permitting M. Herriot's family to visit him. The doctor saw such visits as the best possible medicine because of their effect on the morale of our prisoner. My visits were necessary if we wished to make a clear plan for an escape; or for some political action. One day Counselor Hoffman telephoned me to say that all our requests were agreed to. I was delighted and immediately informed Dr. Rebatel, who took the train for Paris. There remained one more task for me, a horrible one, it's true, but necessary: to go to the avenue Foch to put in order the papers, passes, and details of days and hours of visits.

To go to the avenue Foch was not merely repugnant, but dangerous. It must not be forgotten that during all this time I was in permanent contact with members of the resistance, and particularly with Georges Bidault, then president of the CNR. Before entering the gestapian cavern I informed my friends Blondel, who has since been made a member of the Council of State, and Coste-Floret, since made a Master of Appeals in the Council of State. They were to give the alert if I had not come back by a certain time.

I entered the den of the butchers and the assassins. I wrote down my name. An agent called me and asked me to follow him. My anxiety, rapidly turning to anguish, may be imagined as I was taken into a room with two guards to keep me company. After a few moments I asked if there was not a misunderstanding. Without allowing me to finish my words, the brute thundered in German, "Just wait; you're not the only one who is going to be examined under a microscope."

"I don't understand what you mean," I said.

"Don't worry," he replied, "you'll have plenty of time to understand."

This time I'm caught, I thought. Deadly moments followed. I was taken into an enormous and very luxurious office, evidently that of an extremely important person. I found myself facing another brute, this one with officer's insignia. I do not remember his name, but I think it was something like Kessler (this fine gentleman could be traced).

"What do you want?" he said. "What are you doing for Herriot?"

To defend myself I said that I had come from Counselor Hoffman.

"Ah, ah," he remarked. *"Darüber werden wir nun einmal eine Untersuchung anstellen."* (We're going to look into that too.)

The brute rang and I was taken through long corridors to an office where two men of the Gestapo awaited their victim. Naturally I took shelter behind the Embassy. The remarks these superfanatics made about German diplomats, in front of a foreigner whose memory recorded each word carefully, were almost unbelievable. One of these gentlemen summed up his inmost thought in this expressive phrase: *"Das sind Diplomatenschweinereien"* (those are the swinish tricks of diplomats). The conversation of these gentlemen disturbed me, for I had no desire to be ground between the millstones of German diplomacy and the German police. But there was another point that reassured me: they had no desire to question me on my clandestine activities.

I finally left this place and hurried to Counselor Hoffman. He entered the room in a great rage. He telephoned another person of first importance, Mr. Beaumelburg, and I heard a strange telephone conversation, from beginning to end. I learned that there was an order from Abetz himself which specified that everything possible must be done to help restore the health of Herriot. I learned too that the Gestapo didn't take the orders of this Ambassador very seriously. Counselor Hoffman hung up the telephone receiver so violently that it fell to the ground. "Wait for me," he said, and went out.

Prudently I went out too, since I didn't want to remain alone in his office, and sat down in his secretary's office. Hoffman came back and said he had just been talking with Abetz, that the whole thing would be arranged, and that I was to go the next day to see Beaumelburg, a high official of the Gestapo. It seemed to me that I would not have the courage to go back again to the avenue Foch.

Let those throw the first stone at me who themselves have never been afraid because they have never been in such a situation. I admit that I hesitated for some hours trying to decide whether to return to the avenue Foch or to take refuge in one of my hiding places. My pride and my friendship for Herriot and his family struggled with my fear and were strong enough to overcome it. Friends of Herriot were rare in this period when to express friendship for him was dangerous and any reasonable calculation of his chances of survival was not encouraging. A voice within me said, "Will you be like so many others? At the supreme moment are you going to run away?"

It seemed to me that this was the voice of Herriot himself. Fear easily seeks for excuses and easily finds them. I was afraid, and others in my place would have been the same. But as I make humble confession of the fear I felt, I may also be allowed to add that I did not furnish myself with an excuse for it.

I decided to go back to the avenue Foch. On the following day I was once again in that despicable place, which I regarded as my battlefield.

Beaumelburg was a brute with the external appearance of decency. He agreed to authorize a visit to M. Herriot, but the authorization was to be for me alone and he insisted on accompanying me. This was doubtless the concession that the "order" issued by Ambassador Abetz had wrested from the Gestapo.

Painful negotiations resulted in a permit for Dr. Rebatel to see his brother-in-law.

The struggle between the Embassy and the Gestapo continued and became more ferocious as the general situation of the Reich got worse. If the Gestapo had not been obliged, nevertheless, to take the diplomats' wishes into account to some extent, it would have deported Herriot at once to Germany. This was our nightmare. It must be repeated that the doctors held that Herriot's deportation in his condition would mean death. Herriot had not yet gained the strength which would later permit him to stand so much.

III.—M. Herriot in Paris

The threat of deportation which weighed on President Herriot and his wife became more definite. In disguised phrases it had already been announced by Counselor Hoffman. One day we learned that our friend had left Ville-Evrard and had been taken to Nancy. The pretext was that he had been too near the capital to be safe. The fallacy of such an argument was obvious. In Nancy the possibility of an evasion was very slight. It is easy to hide a man in Paris, which is so enormous. It would be rash to wish to hide him in a city like Nancy. Any attempt to hide Herriot somewhere in the country would raise difficult questions of vehicles, of traces to be erased, and of a hiding place to prepare. We feared both his deportation to Germany and his assassination by the Militia. It will be agreed that the horrible death of Mandel justified our fears.

Once more we deliberated at Lyon. We asked ourselves if we ought to enter into contact with President Pierre Laval. We decided to do so, but only after long hesitation. Because of his position the help of President Laval was of capital importance. Yet it was also to be feared, or at least there was ground for thinking that it should be because of the false interpretations to which it might give rise, especially if ill will played its part, a possibility which it is always wise to expect.

Back in Paris, I had a talk with Georges Bidault. The president of the CNR thought that my contacts with Laval might be advantageous, particularly for getting information and, if the need arose, for obtaining aid for victims of the Gestapo. So far as Herriot was concerned, he thought that Laval would not want to do anything. On this point the insight of the future Minister of Foreign Affairs was at fault, as will be seen.

I had to have an intermediary. Émile Roche took me to Cathala, Minister of Finance and of Agriculture, whom Laval listened to readily. Several hours after my interview with Cathala, the President's office let me know that M. Laval expected to see me the next day. This meeting took place on 29 April 1944. The Chief of Government promised at once to see Abetz, but again matters dragged along. May was already at hand when I began to explain to Pierre Laval the plan which was to result in the event of 12 August 1944, the return of Herriot to Paris.

What was this plan? It is very important to me to explain it completely because I have been gravely reproached for it, and even though I omit mention of the dangers to my safety, for it almost brought me the unattractive honor of being assassinated.

To save Herriot at any cost: that remained the fixed point from which we never shifted our sights (when I say "we" I refer to Dr. Rebatel and myself). To wish to save Herriot was to take on the task of finding a means of restoring his liberty—and it could be restored only by escape or by the consent of his jailor.

At Ville-Evrard escape would have been relatively easy. I had examined the area with a team of members of the resistance whom my friend Blondel had specially recommended to me for their earnestness and their courage. But Herriot had been transferred again to Maréville, near Nancy, where such an operation, as I have already said, was extremely difficult and hazardous. Therefore it was necessary to use the only means remaining, namely the consent of his German jailors, obtained by artifice. It might seem mad to cling to the hope that the Germans could be persuaded to release Herriot when they had just taken him from Ville-Evrard to Nancy. Events proved that this hope was not absurd because it was in fact realized, at least in part.

In bringing Herriot back to Paris I had in mind two hypotheses. The first was that Laval would succeed in persuading the Germans or some German group to free Herriot and to leave him free; that would settle the matter. This hypothesis was not at all unlikely. It must not be forgotten that in the spring of 1944 the Germans were like people who were drowning and ready to cling to a blade of grass. And at this moment the blades of grass were the offers of Laval, which obviously, did not and could not engage President Herriot.

The second hypothesis was that the Germans would bring Herriot back to Paris in the fallacious hope of being able to make use of him. I thought it best to leave them this illusion, and then to benefit by Herriot's presence in Paris to arrange his escape, an easy matter.

Destiny chose the second hypothesis. Herriot did not agree to escape when he was at the Hotel de Ville, at a moment when escape was still possible; but that was not my fault; I did everything that could be done to persuade him. In my thoughts I even went so far as to use a narcotic, and though this thought never became a reality it was not from a lack of courage, but only because I knew of President Herriot's heart condition.

How could the Germans be interested in M. Herriot's case? It was most difficult. I did not know what Laval said to them (Mr. Abetz could give the vital information on this point) but here in any case are the points which I presented to the President of the Council.

(1) "Above all do not compromise Herriot. Besides, it is not to your interest to do so. Hold absolutely to the principle that President Herriot cannot enter into discussions with any German so long as the enemy is on French soil, and so long as he is not absolutely free himself. These are not mere words. I know the indomitable pride of the man and the memories of Rome and Corneille which saturate his thought and will force him to refuse disdainfully any move toward negotiations. I call to your attention the danger which could result if Herriot refused a compromise in stinging language. The Boches would become more vengeful toward him than before, and God knows what new sufferings they would inflict on him."

(2) "On the other hand, so far as I am concerned personally, you may

compromise me as much as you wish. Exaggerate, magnify my importance, tell them that the President listens to what I say on every subject, use the lowest and the most contemptible arguments, let them understand—or if necessary tell them bluntly—that I am acting for my own private benefit." (I may be permitted to recall that at these remarks and under these circumstances Laval made the same exclamations that Georges Bonnet had formerly made under similar circumstances: "President Herriot is lucky in having such friends.") "In short, give Abetz the hope that if he helps us, I will see that Herriot remembers when the day of reckoning comes."

I presented these ideas to Laval many times. In the end I persuaded him. He undertook to approach Abetz again.

Mr. Abetz felt that he could not make a decision on his own initiative which concerned the general policies of the Reich. The high opinion which he had of President Herriot further increased in his eyes the importance of anything concerning him. Ambassador Abetz informed his minister, Mr. von Ribbentrop, of Laval's demand. According to M. Laval, Ribbentrop too was unwilling to make a decision personally and took the matter to Hitler. However that may be, on Friday, 12 August 1944, M. Laval called me to the Hotel Matignon and told me that he had obtained German authorization for the liberation of M. Herriot. M. Laval added emphatically and with unconcealed pleasure, "Tomorrow Herriot will be free." My heart beat with joy, then with stupefaction when Laval added that he was going personally to bring back Herriot, though he asked me to accompany him.

The journey of Pierre Laval to Nancy was a serious error. It should have been foreseen that such an event could not be kept secret, and that once it received publicity it would inevitably give rise to comments from which both truth and political policy would suffer. But M. Laval did not cede to my arguments. He wanted to go personally to bring back Herriot. On another point, an essential one, M. Laval did follow my advice. He had at first wanted M. Herriot to stay with him at the Hotel Matignon. I was rather fortunate in proving to him that there would be grave disadvantages. After reflection he enthusiastically accepted my idea of lodging M. Herriot in the president's mansion at the Chamber of Deputies.

"It would be symbolic," I explained to him. "M. Herriot is still President of the Chamber of Deputies, and the acts of the government of Vichy are null and void in the eyes of the republicans. For us, the Republic never ceased to exist."

In my presence Laval telephoned to Abetz to ask that the President's mansion be evacuated by the German services which occupied them. Abetz consented and said that the evacuation would be completed in forty-eight hours.

We left the Hotel Matignon at three o'clock in the morning and arrived at Nancy without incident, continually passing German convoys moving back to the frontier.

At Nancy M. Herriot and M. Laval discussed the question of a lodging in Paris. Since the President's mansion was not habitable immediately, it seemed that the place offering the greatest security—for the Militia was to be feared—combined with some political neutrality, was the Prefecture of the Seine.

We arrived at the Hotel de Ville in Paris Sunday morning and settled down there. The Prefect of the Seine and Mme Bouffet with thoughtful friendliness placed the resources of their residence at the disposal of M. and Mme Herriot.

We had a most disagreeable surprise immediately. M. Laval had said to M. Herriot, "You will be free." M. Herriot was free only so far as a man could be who had a guard of Gestapo agents watching everything he did, stationing themselves behind and in front of doors, and never leaving him for an instant, day or night.

I complained to Laval about this; he himself was much embarrassed. He promised me to have it changed quickly. But it didn't change.

M. Taittinger sent a most friendly note asking that he might pay M. Herriot a courtesy visit. M. Herriot did not reply. M. Taittinger then sent Mme Herriot an enormous bouquet of flowers with a tricolor ribbon, accompanied by another letter. M. Herriot sent him a white visiting card, blank. Did M. Taittinger finally understand?

The day after we arrived in Paris M. Laval called me to the Hotel Matignon. "Was M. Herriot happy?" he asked me. "He is happy," I replied, "to be in Paris, but the German guard is always there. He would be much happier if he were sure that he was going to stay in Paris when Paris is liberated, but he is not sure."

"You should do for M. Jeanneney what you have done for M. Herriot," I told M. Laval. "It is necessary that M. Jeanneney come to Paris. M. Herriot is in full accord with M. Jeanneney, with whom he signed the famous letter concerning Pétain's violation of parliamentary rights."

I believe M. Laval had no time to follow up my proposal.

M. Herriot had adopted from the beginning the only attitude consistent with his dignity and with the interests of the Republic: so long as the enemy remained in Paris, he would participate in nothing, either directly or indirectly. I had told Laval that he was suffering from illusions if he imagined that members of Parliament would come to a national assembly summoned by him or by Pétain. M. Laval had strange advisers, Chichery for example. He had the idea of sending a car for Chichery to bring him immediately to Paris. Thanks to someone who tipped me off, I knew about this. I hurried to Laval and said to him, "I demand formally that you let Chichery stay where he is. He as a rival would inevitably give rise to comments which in my opinion would be harmful to the President." A telephone call put a stop to this adventure.

"It is impossible to get the Germans to recognize Paris as an open city," Laval said to me. "But I am negotiating to arrange the complete release of Versailles, where the National Assembly could meet, since the Germans are no longer in occupation there."

Laval had in fact conceived the idea of resigning his offices and placing them at the disposal of M. Jeanneney as President of the National Assembly [constituted by a joint session of Senate and Chamber.] In theory the Republic would have been re-established in this way, and one might well think that this solution would have brought important advantages.

Even before leaving for Nancy, I informed Georges Bidault of the imminent arrival in Paris of President Herriot. Georges Bidault knew, since I had already told him, that Herriot had not bound himself in any way, and though I had not yet had an opportunity to discuss the point with Herriot, I took it upon myself to say that he would never make any binding commitments. There were, of course, people who did not believe this, perhaps because they were hypocritical enemies of the President, hoping to damage him by letting him do as he liked while they were spreading a story which they well knew was false.

To give an idea of the unbelievable exaltation of our spirits in these hours, when the oppressor weighed upon us with all his weight but when the certainty of liberation renewed and multiplied our strength and our feelings a hundred times over, I will recall a memory of no importance to world history but of great and unquestionable importance for me because it was a matter of my life or death.

Professor Albert Bayet, to whom I was linked by a quarter of a century of friendship, once interrupted by a cloud which was later dispelled, was in the habit of eating in the same restaurant as I did. Albert Bayet, a first-class resistance worker, of course knew what I was doing to help Herriot and of my numerous visits to Laval. It was, in fact, thanks to one of his friends, who became one of mine, that I was able to travel clandestinely to Switzerland, as usual on behalf of Herriot. This celebrated professor, historian, sociologist, philosopher, writer, orator, astounding versifier, unequaled conversationalist, vice-president of the League for the Rights of Man, and most reliable friend, took me aside and said in a serious voice, like that of a priest in the confessional, "Some men in the resistance are convinced that you have brought Herriot back to Paris by agreement with Laval, the English, and the Americans in order that he may take over and block the way to General de Gaulle. They wanted to kill you. You would have been dead this evening if I had not interceded."

Thus the vice-president of the League for the Rights of Man, Saint Albert Bayet, prevented by this intercession a murder of which the reader of these pages is in a position to measure the iniquity. "O tempora! O mores!" cried Marcus Tullius Cicero. I too had an exclamation to make, one that will not be recorded in the world's literature, but which would have struck my assassins, had they come, as a bullet strikes the flesh. "Let them come," I said to my friend Bayet.

I feared for Herriot's life. At the Prefecture of the Seine we had no special guard to protect Herriot in case of necessity. As protection he had only four German policemen, and all our efforts were directed toward getting them out of the way. I asked Laval for a police group, to be armed with submachine guns and absolutely loyal.

The guard which was wrongly called "Laval's guard," as though it were some sort of Praetorian Guard, was in fact merely an elite unit of the regular police. It has since become clear that it was no exaggeration to call them elite police, for they defended the Paris Hotel de Ville gloriously during the insurrection. For a long time now, I had been forming true friendships with members of this guard. This was easily done because of my many visits to the Hotel Matignon. This entire unit, officers, noncommissioned officers, and men, was made up of patriots who asked only to be allowed to fight. I had had the chance to become acquainted with the officers and had been able to reach a reliable judgment on each of them. M. Laval granted my request and one section of them with their arms came to the Hotel de Ville and installed themselves there. Under the protection of this unit President Herriot was safe from assassins from whichever party they might come. (This small unit played a vital role in the defense of the Hotel de Ville: see the appendix to this report.)

When it became clear that the Gestapo would not release its prey despite the clear wishes of the German diplomatic staff, as expressed in the promise made by Abetz to Laval for Herriot's release, I proposed once again to

President Herriot that he take this last opportunity: escape was easy; the Hotel de Ville of Paris with its endless corridors, doors, basements, and service passageways, was splendidly suited to it. The Prefect of the Seine, M. Bouffet, and his courageous wife would have helped us. For whatever use might be found for it, I had already prepared a hiding place for the President, a hiding place where no one would ever have thought to look for him.

But President Herriot remained unshakable in his decision not to escape. I pointed out the perils to which he was going to be exposed once more. I remember well the vigor with which I fought the idea that the war would soon end. Georges Bidault said, "In a fortnight it will be over." We had to wait another ten months. It may be that President Herriot did not at this moment envisage a captivity as long as the one he was to undergo. However that may be, my arguments could not shake his decision not to escape.

The climax of this tragedy was now at hand.

I do not know what negotiations may have taken place between Laval and the German Ambassador, or between the Ambassador and Chancellor. I speak only of what I saw and heard, and of events in which I played a part.

In the night of 16 August 1944 Sturmbahnführer Nosek came to the Prefecture with an order, he said, to take away the President to a destination which he did not specify. He wanted to enter the room where the President slept. Our guard did its duty, which was to prevent Herriot from being taken away. Laval was informed. He hurried to the Prefecture in an unimaginable fury. He demanded that Abetz, who was in bed, should come immediately to the Prefecture. Abetz came and there burst upon him a storm which he has certainly not forgotten.

The rest of that night and the following day was spent in feverish negotiations in which I had no part. That evening the Gestapo took away M. and Mme Herriot. Several hours later they took away M. and Mme Laval and most of the ministers of the last government of Vichy.

I slept that night and the next at the Hotel Matignon, protected by the police group in which I had absolute confidence. Foreseeing that an insurrection was imminent, I took care to leave the entire section at the Hotel de Ville, where it had remained after Herriot's departure. "You are in the service of the resistance," I told them, "and you will share in the liberation of Paris."

All units of this force were filled with enthusiasm. They soon showed their patriotism, their courage, and their military worth by their acts. (See annex.)

IV. — HERRIOT IN GERMANY UNTIL THE LIBERATION

M. Theodore Steeg, a reliable friend of President Herriot's, then acting as president of the Radical and Radical-Socialist parties, gave me all possible help. Just as I did, he saw in Herriot a friend whose misfortunes should be eased, and a statesman who must be preserved for France. It was with M. Steeg that I undertook negotiations with Great Britain's Ambassador in Paris, His Excellency Duff Cooper. These negotiations produced no practical result despite the obvious good will of this diplomat, a friend of France.

Georges Bonnet, who had been in Switzerland for some time and was closely linked with the head of the Red Cross, Mr. Burkardt (later Swiss Ambassador to France), sought the aid of this eminent man, who because of his office knew many things and who was besides a faithful friend of France and of President Herriot. It was thanks to the Red Cross that M. Herriot's family was able to receive a brief note from the President and his wife saying simply "that they were well."

As the military situation of Germany got worse, our joy increased, but not our tranquillity. We feared that the Gestapo fanatics would execute their prisoners or would carry them away to the famous Tyrolean redoubt which was being talked about a good deal in the press.

In April 1945 Georges Bonnet asked me to come to Switzerland to receive important news about the President. Bonnet had learned through intermediaries that Krugg von Nidda, former Consul-General of the Reich at Vichy and a man to whom some importance had been attached and still was, had come to Geneva to make contact with important French people. Bonnet had refused absolutely to receive Krugg von Nidda.

In Geneva, Georges Bonnet and I paid a visit to Mr. Burkardt, president of the Red Cross. We learned that someone much more important than Krugg von Nidda was there and asked nothing better than to be able to speak. This man had the rank of minister and was called Berber. I saw him in the presence of a representative of the Red Cross. It was from him I learned where our President was. Herriot was near Berlin when all the intelligence bureaus in the world thought that he was in the Tyrol, in the famous redoubt. As a result of my action the embassies of France, Great Britain, and the United States learned of this fact that same day.

We understood that we could no longer act directly in defense of the President. Communication with the interior of the Reich was becoming more and more precarious. German diplomatic and consular agents themselves were no longer able to correspond regularly with their government.

One day in April 1945 great news reached us: the Russians had freed President and Mme Herriot. Our joy was immense; we believed that the hopes we had conceived when our friend was in enemy hands could at last be realized. Our satisfaction was increased by the feeling that we had fully accomplished the duties which were ours as patriots and friends.

ANNEX

The Hotel de Ville was defended by the FFI and the FTP under the command of my friend Lepercq, who became Minister of Finance and died in an automobile accident. But the Hotel de Ville was also defended by the section of the GMR which I had purposely left at the Hotel de Ville after the departure of Herriot, and by another section of the GMR, stationed at the Hotel Matignon [residense of the President of the Council], a section which I had taken by car across Paris while it was still occupied by the Germans.

In addition, I supplied to the command at the Hotel de Ville some machine guns and several million cartridges. I also supplied Georges Bidault with a sub-machine gun and ammunition for his own protection. The arms and ammunition had been stocked at the Hotel Matignon. At dawn on the day of the insurrection I "occupied" the Hotel Matignon alone with my friend Lieutenant "Dumas" (Pételot, from Nancy, a member of the "Lorraine" group, which was led by my comrade Fallaz, a member of the Provisional Assembly).

Deserved homage should be paid to the GMR, to the police officers of the Hotel Matignon, and particularly to M. Roure, their chief, to Lieutenant Chevalier, and to Inspector Courtès.

It must be left to historians to determine what would have happened at the Hotel de Ville when the Germans attacked it if our admirable GMR had not been there, or if they had been without machine guns and cartridges—in a word, without the men and arms whose presence at the Hotel de Ville was due to me.

(Document No. 15)
Fr. ed. 1054-1077

May 1946

ANDRÉ ENFIÈRE

A LUNCHEON ON 17 AUGUST 1944

JOSÉE DE CHAMBRUN

Daughter of Pierre Laval

I shall speak of a luncheon which it is my duty to place on record. It took place on 17 August 1944 at the Hotel Matignon; those present, in addition to my parents, my husband and myself, were President and Mme Édouard Herriot and the German Ambassador, Mr. Abetz. The luncheon took place, despite its unusual character, with the complete agreement of all those present. It marked the end of the attempt conceived by my father to convoke the old Chamber of Deputies and Senate in their capacity of National Assembly in order to assure a legal transmission of power without the disturbances which passion might produce. This was the last meal eaten by my father on French soil; he was arrested by the Germans that evening.

There are times when each minute, each word, each gesture, is engraved permanently in the memory of those who live through them. Such times are rare.

After a long period of anguish and of waiting, a sad page in the history of our country was coming to an end. Around this table we were living out the drama with special intensity because it had taken a particularly powerful hold on our own lives and on the lives of those we loved. I note that what I am about to recount took place on a wonderful summer's day, in the beautiful Hotel Matignon, with its windows wide open upon one of the finest parks in the world.

The Herriots and Abetz arrived together. Herriot looked out at the garden. "The first time I came here," he said, "I saw on the lawn a white blackbird."

"Is that possible, Mr. President?" I replied. "Wasn't it more like

Paul Fort's blue frog—the one that everybody talks about and nobody ever sees?''

He looked at me with both surprise and pleasure, and we went into the dining room. The lunch was excellent. Everyone strove to master his anguish and to rise to the occasion. Abetz began by asking if it wasn't at Lyon that there stands a statue of a German. "Oh, yes, you'd better ask my wife about that," Herriot answered. "She knows more than anyone else about the history of our beautiful city. You're probably talking about the 'good German.'"

"Oh, so there really is a 'good German,'" Abetz replied gently. Mme Herriot then told the story of the statue. I don't remember it very clearly; I think it was something about a rich German merchant of the sixteenth century who did many good things for the city. Herriot then told how he had been given a doctorate, *honoris causa*, at Oxford at the same time that the German scientist Max Planck, famous for his refutation of the theory of spontaneous generation, had been similarly honored. Everything that is said during these ceremonies is in Latin, and President Herriot wondered how Planck managed to prepare an address that would necessarily be full of scientific words. To Herriot's astonishment and wonder, Planck had begun by quoting passages from the "De Natura Rerum" of Lucretius. Herriot then asked if Abetz knew what had become of Planck. The Ambassador replied that though the present German regime didn't think very well of him, he had been able to get through these years peacefully.

This brought Herriot to the real heart of the matter. He insisted that no one had done more than he had to bring about good relations between France and Germany. He recalled that he had been a member of the government which, against violent opposition in France, had decided on the evacuation of the Rhineland; and that in spite of that he had been arrested by the Germans. He said that now, though he had asked nothing of anyone, he had been freed by President Laval because he was President of the Chamber of Deputies, in order that the convocation of the National Assembly, now made necessary by the turn of events, could take place. On returning to Paris, he said, he had refrained from any sort of manifestation at the Hotel de Ville and from official receptions or gestures of any kind, but in spite of his attitude the SS had come to arrest him during the preceding night. The Ambassador, he said, knew the rest. He added that he was ready to accept his fate, whatever it was, and asked only that he should be taken back to Maréville and not be forced to share the fate of the government. Abetz was very embarrassed, because the orders he had received were exactly the contrary, and he had already told Herriot before lunch what they were.

We were very shaken, for we felt that Herriot was absolutely right. Not only had he been arrested again, not only had the government itself been arrested, but now they wanted to force Herriot to leave at the same time the government left. My father and mother were leaving under German force, and we realized how equivocal the situation would look if this form of blackmail were practiced on Herriot.

My father judged that it was indispensable to summon the National Assembly in order that there should be a correct transfer of powers. His opinion was this: Exceptional circumstances had brought about the meeting of the National Assembly on 10 July 1940, at which the Assembly had voted to entrust all legal powers to Maréchal Pétain and to the government of the Republic. Now, new circumstances were about to put an end to these powers. It seemed indispensable that the National Assembly should take back to itself through correct procedure the powers it had delegated.

It was necessary at all cost, he felt, to make certain that there was continuity of government at the time of the arrival of the Allied troops, and to protect France from any possibility of action by adventurers. (And how right he was . . .)

But now, when Brinon and Déat, in haste to leave for Germany, had before their departure been busily stirring up the SS of Paris and Himmler himself, and the Germans in their fury at being beaten had listened to them, it disgusted us to find them once again interfering in our affairs and trying to compromise Herriot.

My mother spoke next. "Mr. Ambassador," she said to Abetz, "to leave under such conditions is impossible. Think of the grievous situation in which we would all be placed." And Herriot, lifting his arms, said, "Listen, Mr. Ambassador; it is France that speaks."

"It is true that these two men have not always been in agreement in the past," Mama went on. "There was always too much politics. . . . and France had too happy a life. But faced by a great danger these two are reunited, and you cannot justify an act which would make my husband seem the instigator of so unworthy a procedure, nor can you justify inflicting such a fate on President Herriot."

Herriot, lifting and throwing wide his arms, continued to repeat, "Listen! Listen! It's France that speaks." And in his turn he said that if he were thus forced to depart, everyone would be placed in a most difficult position. As for him, he would never be able to take the hand of Pétain. "For you, Laval," he said, "it's different; you can explain yourself. But to take the hand of Pétain, never. He is the enemy of the Republic. I have no more confidence in him than I have in de Gaulle. They are both dominated by ambition. And it is just for that reason that I come back here to Paris. And now I am being taken away again by force. There is nothing I can do except submit."

Abetz really seemed to be dying of shame. He knew too much, he loved France too sincerely, and he was too honest not to appreciate how hateful was the situation his superiors had created. He took it upon himself to say that he would arrange everything just as we asked it. This was very brave of him; it must not be forgotten that from this moment he lost the confidence of his superiors, and that he was stripped of his functions as soon as he returned to Germany.

Such a discussion could not be carried on for very long because our nerves were too tense, and so we returned deliberately to telling anecdotes. Papa and Herriot began talking about the days of Geneva. They recalled statesmen they had known together, Eden and Titulesco. Papa remembered something that Eden had said about the conversation that Papa had had with the Duke of Windsor, then the Prince of Wales, at the time of the Ethiopian affair. "You met our Prince of Wales in Paris," Eden had said to my father. "You seem to have got along very well with him." Then after a moment, he added, "Too well. We shall see that such conversations don't take place in the future."

My father brought out a watch in a fine platinum case which attracted the attention of Herriot. My father recalled that Titulesco, after a very childish scene, had given it to him as a kind of apology. Papa said that it was the most beautiful and the thinnest watch in the world; and he added that on receiving it he had said, "He gives me a watch; after all the trouble he has caused me, it should have been a clock."

All men must have their weaknesses, and Herriot's old vanity and his old rivalry with my father got the best of him. "Yes," he cried, "I knew about this business with the watch, and when I said to Titulesco, 'You gave a watch to Laval,' he sent me one just like it."

Papa, teasing him, said, "It certainly isn't as thin as mine. Mine is unique." He handed it to him, and Herriot admitted that he was beaten. This incident upset me, and if I had dared, I would have given Papa a good kick under the table.

We separated about half past four in considerable unity of thought, and very close together in our feelings. My husband promised to get some books and some cigars for Herriot and to bring them to him at the Hotel de Ville. He got there at five-thirty. The SS were on guard at the entrance. My husband, in agreement with the prefect, Bouffet, proposed to Herriot to get him out of the building through the drains, and hide him in the apartment of an American friend that had been lent to us. Herriot hesitated for a moment and then refused, saying that he would accept whatever fate brought him, and embraced my husband.

I tell the story of this lunch because it has remained engraved on my heart as one of those exceptional moments of which I spoke earlier, during which all those who were present made a great effort to act according to their finest natures. Why did Herriot in his public declarations momentarily repudiate the agreement he had made with my father? Why? Doubtless through cowardice.

I remember that during this lunch I felt the very greatest sympathy for him, for the false position in which he had been placed, for his scholarliness, and for the fineness of his conduct at the moment. And I said to myself, I who admire my father without any reservations whatever, why had my father not been in agreement with a man of so fine a spirit? The answer is a simple one, and I have just given it. It is that one of them often showed himself a coward, and that the other was the very incarnation of courage. I am convinced that if Herriot lives long enough he will realize that it was one of his greatest actions to forget so many old quarrels, to forget his imprisonment, and to unite with my father when the time came to preserve our ancient institutions. That was perhaps the finest moment of his life.

What of Herriot will endure for posterity? That he was President of the Chamber? It was almost childishly unimportant. That he was a statesman? He came to power only to precipitate the fall of the franc; he was the creator of the Popular Front. That he was a writer? He is already a little out of fashion.

His talent as an orator was great, but voices vanish and posterity does not hear them.

(Document No 25)
Fr. ed. 1078-1081

Paris, 2 May 1947

JOSÉE DE CHAMBRUN

AID FOR ARRESTED PERSONS

GEORGES RICHÉ

Bank Director

The undersigned Georges Riché, bank director and holder of the Croix de Guerre (1914-1918), living in Paris, declares the following under oath.

During the years 1942, 1943 and 1944, I had five or six interviews with M. Pierre Laval on the subject of the arrest by the Gestapo of 152 of my friends, members of an important information network which was in contact with the Allied High Command. It was my task to get them out of this situation and above all to try to find out as quickly as possible just what the German police had discovered about them and about that part of the network which was still in activity. The most practical way of doing this seemed to me to be to make use of the contacts which the Chief of Government had with the German authorities.

I knew the son-in-law of M. Pierre Laval, M. René de Chambrun; it was through him that I succeeded in being received for the first time by M. Pierre Laval shortly after the landing of 1942. I remember the exact words of his reply to me when I asked why he had not taken advantage of this landing to resign from office.

"I must stay here," he told me, "to defend the prisoners who are in France on leave from captivity, to protect those who have escaped, and to protect those of Alsace and Lorraine and all the rest of France, for the Germans are going to act with very great harshness."

My name was not unknown to the Chief of Government, for my brother had formerly been an under-secretary of state. But, in view of my own political affiliations and those of my friends, I had never thought that I would be received with so much spontaneity and frankness.

When I saw M. Pierre Laval again in March 1943, he knew all about the mass arrests of my comrades. He told me that he was prepared to protest. In fact he did telephone, in my presence, to the German Embassy to announce his visit to them and spoke in a tone of which the harshness surprised me. I am sure that he suspected the real nature of the matter, but he had the discretion to put no questions to me. I learned afterwards that he had personally guaranteed the innocence of my friends to the occupation authorities.

Shortly after this first interview I was asked to come to see him again, and thereafter from time to time as he took further steps in the matter. The information that he gave me was useful; but on the other hand he did not succeed in securing the release of my friends.

It was on this occasion that I realized how little weight he carried with the Germans. Relations between M. Laval and the Germans seemed to me rather like those of duelists making use of underhanded blows. Sometimes I saw him attack head on, sometimes he was evasive, and very often he was overcome and fatigued at the end of the day by the resistance which he seemed always to oppose to German demands. He said to me one day that the Germans reproached him with spending his time dissolving questions—which, he added, wasn't so bad when you didn't want to have to solve them. During my various conversations with him it seemed to me that this was his policy.

On the other hand, I ascertained that he was dominated, even obsessed, by the Chief of Government's responsibility for the protection of the French against the increasing encroachment of the German services. So far as I was able to judge he oriented his acts and words with a view to securing this protection with no thought for any other consequence, or even for his own personal security. I had a very sharp impression of this on the occasion of my last interview with him, a few days before the liberation of Paris. He had just managed to get back into the capital by overcoming the many obstacles along the way. When I expressed my astonishment at this decision to return as the Allies approached, he replied, visibly surprised by my question, that at a time when the Paris region was threatened by famine and by German reprisals, it was certainly necessary that the Chief of Government should be on the spot to organize aid and to arrange the convocation of the National Assembly, which he had already spoken of to me as the only way of uniting the French after the tempest. There was no lack of awareness of the situation on his part, but a considered plan, for he told me that he had had to overcome the resistance of those around him, who had urged him to abandon power and get away. Our conversation took place in the evening just before his arrest by the Germans.

I never asked the least favor from him nor did he show me any. I have here merely set forth, in all good faith, what I witnessed, as I would have done in court under oath.

(Document No. 11)
Fr. ed. 1082-1083

Paris, 14 May 1946

G. RICHÉ

MAURICE SARRAUT AND VICHY

ROGER PERDRIAT

Editor-in-Chief of La Dépêche de Toulouse

October 1940.

At the beginning of 1940 I was sent by M. Maurice Sarraut to Vichy with rather specific instructions. M. Sarraut had been asked very urgently to sell his newspaper, *La Dépêche*, and the person who had made this offer had told him that he was acting on behalf of the government. Was this true? My task was to secure information on this point from President Laval.

During that first interview M. Laval, in answer to my specific questions said: "I have never made an attempt to buy *La Dépêche*, or to have anyone else buy it. But a lot of things happen here at Vichy that I know nothing about, for which public opinion assigns the responsibility to me. Don't forget that the Maréchal has absolute power. He has more power than Louis XIV. And he or his cabinet give orders and make decisions without referring them to the ministers."

This remark, made under the circumstances I have just indicated, enables me to gauge the exact extent of President Laval's powers at that time.

The policy of the government was not clearly understood in the provinces; many legends about it were circulating. M. Sarraut asked me if I couldn't have an interview with M. Pierre Laval which would enable me to obtain precise information on this point.

I had this interview a short time before the Montoire meeting. Here is a résumé, as exact as I can make it, of what was said.

(a) *Domestic Policies.* I asked President Laval what should be thought of the attacks that were being made in many circles against the Republican regime.

"Unfortunately, I have no control over domestic politics," M. Laval replied. "That is the special field of the Maréchal and those around him. All I can do is limit the damage. I arranged that the text of the law which was adopted should include the words 'Government of the Republic.' Consequently I believe that the republican regime is not to be questioned. But is this everyone's opinion? I cannot say so."

(b) *Foreign Policies.* I asked President Laval what should be thought about certain rumors regarding the possibility of a separate peace with Germany, and about the uneasiness these rumors would arouse. M. Pierre Laval replied: "The essential fact, namely that we have about two million prisoners, is forgotten. Now when two million of a country's men are prisoners, that country cannot possibly have a free and independent policy. Besides, everyone in France thinks only of the return of the prisoners. For me too, this is at present, and it ought to be, my sole care. Think about that."

"And the policy of collaboration?"

"The policy of collaboration—that is an expression which Abetz and the Frenchmen on the France-Germany Committee invented. As for me, I have always been in favor of good understanding between France and Germany. But this understanding cannot be arranged until the Germans have left, the prisoners have come back, and on condition that at Berlin they do not try to take Alsace-Lorraine away from us."

December 1940.

At the beginning of December 1940, I noticed that the *Action Française*, without ever being censored, was emphasizing under ironic headings the fact that M. Pierre Laval's interviews, after five months, had resulted in the introduction of interzonal passes. It added that M. Pierre Laval was the only member of France's former Parliament who was still in the government. I mentioned these points to a member of M. Laval's cabinet, and expressed the fear that this press campaign would have serious consequences. A few days afterward M. Pierre Laval was arrested. At that moment

I was in Toulouse, where I had gone to report to M. Sarraut my interviews, and steps that I had taken. M. Sarraut then made this comment:

"The arrest of Laval is the same sort of thing as the 16th of May. Pétain really seems to me to have no other care than to re-establish some sort of monarchy, or some sort of dictatorship. He doesn't love the Germans, but he makes use of them and of the French defeat in order to follow his own domestic policy. As for Laval, he could have brought to a successful conclusion his negotiations for easing the terms of the armistice only if he had received some support from the government or from Parliament. But at this moment everyone seems to me to be trying above all to follow some personal policy for personal political interests by taking advantage of the defeat."

April 1942.

When M. Pierre Laval was summoned by Maréchal Pétain for an interview which seemed to be a prelude to his return to power I happened to be in Paris at M. Laval's office in the avenue des Champs Élysées, with a few friends. M. Pierre Laval said to us: "Don't think that you are going to see the prisoners come back from captivity in great columns. The hour for the return of the prisoners has passed. Germany is in the grip of too many difficulties, and the supporters of a policy of conciliation with France have been eliminated. I am taking up the task again only to avoid the worst."

"What do you mean by that?"

"I mean massive deportations of workers and Jews, and German control of all the industries of France."

June 1943: The People of Alsace-Lorraine.

In June 1943 M. Laval sent for me.

"The Germans are making preparations to mobilize the people of Alsace-Lorraine," he said to me. "I have protested to Berlin. I sent a note to Abetz and a letter to Ribbentrop. I have had no reply. I want my protests to be known, and I want people to understand that I have never accepted, and that I never will accept, the annexation of Alsace-Lorraine. The Germans have strictly forbidden the publication of my note of protest. Since there are many Alsatians in your part of France, *La Dépêche* must say this as clearly as possible. You will write an article in which you will indicate that this protest has been made, in spite of the instructions which forbid you to do so. The local censors will forget to read your editorial."

The article did appear. After its publication an Alsatian Deputy, M. Thomas Seltz, came to find me and said, "This isn't true. There has been no French protest. They would have said so if there had been one." I had great difficulty in explaining to him why the protest could not be published.

July 1943: The Militia.

In July 1943 M. Pierre Laval, faced by the increasing demands of the Germans, thought of reforming his cabinet in order to resist these demands more effectively. He asked me come to Vichy in order to request me to explain his intentions to M. Maurice Sarraut, whose opinion he desired to have. He explained his thought in something like the following terms:

"I am reproached for not standing out against the Germans. But I am almost the only one who tries to gain time, or even to say 'no.' I think that a government which brought about the union of all republicans and that really represented the country would have so much authority in the opinion of the Germans that they would hesitate. Ask Sarraut what he thinks of that."

"Maurice Sarraut," I answered, "thinks it would be better for you to withdraw."

"If I withdraw," M. Laval replied, "it will be Doriot who takes my place. The Germans are waiting only for my going, and Doriot; and you know what that means. That's why I stay and why I will hold on as long as I can."

During this talk the question of the formation of the Militia came up. I told M. Pierre Laval of the uneasiness this new formation would arouse. He answered, "The entire plan of the Germans is to surround me with people in whom they have confidence, in order to force me to leave. But I will not leave."

"But you are more and more alone."

"I wish for the victory of Germany for without it communism would establish itself throughout Europe."

When President Laval spoke these words which shocked the French I went to see him and found him rather depressed.

"What do people think of my talk?" he asked me.

"You can guess easily enough."

"My popularity hasn't increased much, evidently. In the position I occupy you have to talk in order not to act."

"They don't succeed in understanding you..."

Pierre Laval then made this remark to me: "Do the French believe that if the Germans were the victors I would remain in power? But with a German victory Doriot would take over the power, and I, and you, and Sarraut, would be hanged. How then can they suppose that I desire the victory of Germany? Nevertheless it isn't difficult to understand why I spoke as I did."

President Laval followed with close attention the events in the USSR. "The Germans will only get out of this by making peace with Stalin," he said. "If they don't, they're lost."

He asked me one day to send him a note about some dealings which the Germans had had with the Russians and regarding which some German newspapermen had spoken to me in confidence.

"An agreement of this kind," Laval said to me, "if it is in fact made effective, would ruin France, for it would enable Germany to hold out and to postpone her defeat. America and England will never give up. But the landing isn't going to take place tomorrow if the Germans can bring all their forces to the west. And it will be France that is crushed."

I told Pierre Laval that according to the information certain Germans had given me, Hitler's losses in the east had been frightful.

"Then Stalin will make no settlement," he answered me. "I know him. He is the most intelligent of them all. He knows what he wants, and if he makes things look as if he were negotiating, it's only because he's preparing to do something."

December 1943: The Assassination of Maurice Sarraut.

Just after the assassination of Maurice Sarraut a radio station in London or Algiers announced that it was an execution, and that this execution had been carried out by the resistance. I asked Pierre Laval what he thought about it.

"You can see what I think about it," he answered. "I have had the chief of the Militia arrested in spite of Gabolde and in spite of the Germans, who have ordered me to have him released. I refuse to have him released, and I will continue to refuse because the whole affair was staged by the Militia. And if the judge knows his business, he will not give way to them."

(Document No. 14)

Fr. ed. 1084-1088

[*This document, as déposited in the Hoover Library, is neither dated nor signed.*]

INSTRUCTIONS TO THE PREFECTORAL SERVICE

JOËL SERIEYX

Prefect of the Jura

I the undersigned Joël Serieyx, born 22 August 1909 at Lorient, and living at Nogent-sur-Marne (Seine), certify on my honor the absolute accuracy of the following testimony, which is merely a revision of notes I made several hours after the interviews to which they refer.

On 4 March 1944 I was called to Vichy by the Direction of Personnel in the Ministry of the Interior to fulfill various formalities preliminary to my installation at Belley (Ain), where I had just been named under-prefect. I was received at the Hotel du Parc by President Laval, Chief of Government.

After explaining that he made a point of making personal contact with new or transferred prefects and under-prefects, the President asked me if Belley suited me.

I did not conceal from him that I was very disappointed. My service record and my knowledge of affairs in Brittany had justified me in suggesting to my immediate superiors that I might reasonably be appointed to a first-class under-prefecture in Brittany, whereas I was now to be stranded in a little second-class under-prefecture, in an unknown arrondissement, apparently of no interest.

"You are wrong," the President replied. "The class of your appointment means nothing. Posts can now be graded only according to their sensitivity. You think the arrondissement of Belley is too calm? Go there. Within a few weeks, you'll have news for me. You are going to find yourself in considerable difficulty, with the Germans on one side and the maquis on the other. In the midst of all this you must govern, and you must protect the people for whom you are responsible, often against public opinion. It's neither easy, nor funny, day after day, believe me. I know what it's like."

"Mr. President," I said, "will you be so good as to tell me exactly what my attitude as a representative of the government should be toward the German authorities?"

"You must be the more intelligent," he answered. "You must get the better of them every time you can. You must give way when you are obliged to, but only as much as is necessary to avoid a rupture that would destroy the authority which you must necessarily maintain. Take the initiative, but let the general interest of France be your sole guiding principle. And understand clearly that you will be more and more alone.

"If you succeed in preventing deportations and German reprisals, no one will thank you," he continued. "They will merely regard that as natural. But if, in spite of all you can do, there are reprisals, you will perhaps be looked on as having sold out to the enemy, and as a traitor."

He continued: "I know what it's like. But when we have done our duty as Frenchmen every day, I for the State and you for your arrondissement, does the rest of it make any difference?"

"And about the various maquis, Mr. President," I added, "what should my attitude be toward them during the coming months?"

"You are right in saying 'various maquis,'" he agreed. "Yes, we must say 'various maquis!' Well, you will understand that the Chief of Government is in a legal position in which he cannot answer any official representative in any words except, 'the maquis are illegal.' But I can tell you this: our policy is to hold off.

"The direction in which the war is moving does not depend on my government. The result of the war does not depend on my government. But the maintenance of the French food supply and the maintenance of the French administration—that is, of public order—and of the daily life of the French people—these do depend on my government.

"The union of all French people does not depend, alas, only on my government. It depends on all French people—understand me, it depends on *all*, whatever their opinion of me may be and whatever opinion they may come to have of you."

When I rose to leave, the President said to me again: "Do not forget. Be the more intelligent; preserve to the utmost all French rights, defend to the utmost the French people, even those who insult you . . . . It is not their fault, as a rule . . . they don't see far enough ahead . . . and anyway, seeing ahead is not their business. Besides, they have no information on what the government is doing. Tell them about it. They have no information about the government's difficulties—nor do you.

"It won't be easy. Bon courage!"

Four months later, on 6 July 1944, I was summoned to Vichy by President Laval. In the meantime a certain number of adventures had befallen me, and I entered the door of his office without much confidence. I would have been far less confident if I had known that he was well-informed about most of my illegal initiatives.

The President offered me his hand. "Serieyx," he said, "wasn't it you who considered the post assigned to you at Belley too calm?"

"Yes, sir, but I've changed my mind."

"As a matter of fact, I have heard that you saved a certain number of your mayors by proposing to the Germans that they should execute you in their place. Well done. However, look out that they don't someday execute both you and the mayors together. That wouldn't be much help.

"I understand also," the President continued, "that to secure food for the sanatorium at Hauteville, you got in touch with the maquis. You were right, because you got the food.

"I have also learned that you arranged to be kidnapped and taken to Major Romans, the head of the Secret Army at Izernore near Nantua—just between us, it's not very secret and you can tell him so. There are about eight thousand men at Izernore; right?

"It seems that you stayed to talk with him up there for a day or two and that he sent you back by car. Apparently it didn't go off too badly," he added, smiling.

"I've also been informed that you refused to allow the Militia to set foot in your arrondissement," he continued, "and that you even advised your prefect to get rid of the arrondissement leader of the Militia immediately, or to accept your resignation. And I have heard a good many more little things of that kind."

"Mr. President," I said . . . .

The Chief of Government cut me off. "Mr. President," he said "doesn't want to know any more. I had you come to see me so that I can tell you this: I am making you a prefect. Does that suit you?"

"I don't quite understand, Mr. President," I answered.

"It's not complicated," M. Laval said. "You will understand. I am faced by three kinds of enemies. First there are boys who use the 'maquis' as their excuse to make absence of discipline their rule of life. They make trouble for everyone, perhaps even more for an intelligent secret army which knows how to wait for the time to act, than for the peaceful population.

"Second, there are dangerous imbeciles like Darnand, though he is a brave man, it must be noted, who with two or three others—clever men, but not worth the rope it would take to hang them—are forced on me by the Germans. Though you are not in politics you must know something of my troubles with them.

"Little by little, in order to avoid the worst, it has been necessary to give way somehow, to accept one, to place limits on another, and so on. That lot, while burdening me with their words, poison all my contacts and cut me off as much as they can from the people of France. As a result I am hated. I am hated—isn't that true?"

"In general, yes, Mr. President," I answered.

The Chief of Government smiled sadly. "You are not a courtier," he said to me. "But it's just as well. If you had said the contrary, I wouldn't have believed you. It's natural that I should be hated. But it's hard. Still, what can you expect? And yet if they only knew of our struggles. . . .

"My enemies of the third kind are the cowards, the ones who try to save themselves by crawling into a hole, the officials of every grade who say to themselves, 'The Americans are advancing; now is the time to turn my coat!'—as though there is any coat to turn when you are serving France.

"It is they who are chiefly responsible for the disorder, from which France will not rise again for a long time. I do not accuse the true resistants. We too are resistants. There are resistants who attack and resistants who defend. I accuse the turnabouts, those who run the risk of losing for France at the final moment all the benefits of my struggles, of our daily struggles during the last four years.

"All right," he said in conclusion. "So far as you are concerned, you are in favor of order and in sympathy with the Secret Army, a disciplined force, and against the germanized Militia. You have not turned your coat, and you have not yet become unacceptable to the German authorities. Therefore you shall be a prefect.

"I thought of the Jura for you, Lons-le-Saunier," he told me.

"The Jura? That's impossible, Mr. President."

"Why not?" he said. "It is the smallest of all the French departements at present. The arrondissement of Dôle is cut off from it by the demarcation line between the zones, and the arrondissement of Saint-Claude is in the hands of the Secret Army of the Ain-Jura."

"But, Mr. President, the administrative situation in the Jura makes it out of the question for me to take control there," I replied.

"On the contrary," he said. "You'll see. The prefect of the Jura was formerly under-prefect at Lorient. He says he is ill. He may even be cracking up. Either it's true or he is faking it very cleverly. But in any case for all practical purposes he can't do his job. His young secretary-general has taken his place. He is a Gaullist. All right. But if I know it here at Vichy, then everybody over there must know it too. So he's become of no use to anybody.

"The truth is that he's too young. The departemental delegate of the Militia has taken the reins of the prefecture away from him. It is the delegate who sits in the prefect's chair and who decides everything. Darnand finds all that very good. So do the Germans, doubtless. But not me.

"Well, there it is. I appoint you. You are going down there. You will leave to the ex-prefect—that is, to the man who formerly had the title of prefect—a few rooms in the prefecture; he is an old servant of the state. You will tell the young secretary-general to look after his general secretariat. You will cleverly get rid of the Militiaman and his Militia."

"But M. Darnand, Chief of the Militia," I objected, "is also Minister of the Interior.

"What if he is? I appoint you," M. Laval replied, "and I, I am the Chief of Government. So, you're going to turn out the Militia and you're going to push the German authorities away from the controls. If the Germans don't like it, they'll be forced to denounce me openly, because it is I who bring you forward and I who appoint you. Will they dare do so? I hope not. In this way, you will also prevent some elements of the maquis from creating confusion in your administration. It will not be difficult for you to arrange this with the chiefs of the Secret Army because you will find there, seen from the northern side, the same Secret Army group that you saw from its southern side in the Ain. There you have it. All right?"

"Aren't you forgetting one point, Mr. President?" I answered. "Today is 6 July. My appointment cannot be published in the *Journal Officiel*, even at your request, for about ten days. Before that time all the west and all the north of France may be in the hands of the Allies. The maquis of every kind will be in feverish activity because of these changes, and the Germans or the Militia will be carrying out maximum reprisals.

"Now it's impossible to succeed in less than a month or two in the complicated task you offer me. Before I succeeded I would certainly have been executed or assassinated, uselessly, by either the Germans or the Militia, because they will know that I was in touch with a maquis before throwing out the Germans and the Militia. They may find out from members of the maquis, men who feel that since I have been appointed by you and so in principle agreed to by Darnand, I must be a super-Militiaman and should be destroyed immediately. Perhaps even the Militia member that I evict will denounce me to the maquis. In short. . . ."

"All that is quite true," said the President. And he sharply added these words: "You said one word too many. First you said, 'I will be executed or assassinated.' Yes, that is quite possible, but you added 'uselessly.' No. I too will perhaps be executed. Not uselessly. Perhaps I will be heard. If I am heard, they will understand. . . . I hope."

"Is it yes?" M. Laval said.

"It's yes, Mr. President."

"Thank you, Mr. Prefect," said the President, shaking my hand. "And good luck."

But I never took office as a prefect. Eight days later I learned that the German authorities, taking Darnand's advice, had flatly rejected my appointment.

(Document No. 16)
Fr. ed. 1089-1093

Nogent-sur-Marne, 10 July 1946

signed: JOËL SÉRIEYX

AUBERVILLIERS

LOUIS PAGÈS

Mayor of Aubervilliers

I the undersigned Louis Pagès, born 14 February 1891 in Paris, former first assistant Mayor and acting Mayor of Aubervilliers, attest under oath, in full liberty of thought and action, to the following statement, which I was unable to make to the Court of Justice during the trial of President Pierre Laval.

I first knew Pierre Laval in 1923. He was then mayor of Aubervilliers, and I was engaged in commerce in that district.

As local delegate and later vice-president of my trade association, I dealt with him in connection with the defense of my fellow members, or of the association.

In 1925 I was put forward by the small traders in the municipal elections and I was elected on the Pierre Laval list. Since that time I have always been re-elected on the same list. In 1940, when the Germans arrived, the assistants to the mayor and the majority of the municipal councilors fled on the approach of the enemy; I was selected by the ten municipal councilors who stayed at their posts to act as assistant mayor and as mayor. This decision was ratified by the prefect of the Seine.

Later I was kept in office by the government, with President Laval remaining titulary mayor, but prevented by his high duties from actually serving. It was my duty to represent him and to take his place. Thus for twenty years, on the administrative and the municipal level, I was the close and also the intimate collaborator of Mayor Pierre Laval in the commune of Aubervilliers. It is on these grounds and in these circumstances that I had the honor to be able to judge him as a statesman and as a private citizen.

From 1925 to 1939 I always admired his love of peace, and the profound horror of war that he made felt on all occasions. He worked as hard for peace between individual citizens, calming them or arbitrating their feuds, as he did on the governmental levels where he did his best to avoid conflicts with foreign countries.

"I shall never put my signature to a call for mobilization," he often said. He said too, "When you want peace you must try to arrange it with your enemies or with those who may become your enemies, and not with your friends."

He loved the humble people, the workers, the old, and the little children. Every time I visited him to render an account of my acts of office, he showed his interest in what was happening to the working people of Aubervilliers and concern for their well-being. He often dealt with the smallest details, things having to do with the school canteens, or with food for the Old People's Home.

On every one of his journeys to Paris during the occupation, he had me come to see him and discussed Aubervilliers with me. He did not like the Germans. He had no confidence in them, but he knew that if they had occupied the entire territory in 1940 the French would have suffered more. That is why he saw but one way to save France and the French from total subjection; and that was to maintain for our country a national government which could diminish day by day the demands and risks of the occupation, while protecting our possibilities of defending our country when the peace treaties were at last signed.

I never heard M. Laval attack any country or any people. I remember hearing him say in the presence of the liberated prisoners in a meeting at the Salle Wagram, "They accuse me of being pro-German and anti-English. I am neither one nor the other. I am one hundred per cent French. I love only my own country."

I often found him heartbroken by dishonest or unfair German intrigues, the Germans' heavy-handedness, or by their incomprehensible tactlessness, and often too I found him grievously upset and dissatisfied because of the Maréchal or his reactionary group. M. Laval felt that there were too many French people who talked to and made arrangements with the Germans. He wanted to stand alone, to be the only one to carry on his shoulders the responsibility for this task, a responsibility which exhausted him physically. He was never discouraged. One day at the end of 1943 he said to me, "They will become harder and still more hard as their military disasters increase. I must stay at my post."

He knew about the activity of the resistance at Aubervilliers. I never heard him express any blame for the resistance. He always said, "But see that they don't act imprudently; the results could be serious." He never refused my requests that he should intervene on behalf of escaped prisoners, members of the resistance, or those who refused to serve in the labor levies. All my requests that he take steps to secure the liberation of political prisoners resulted in total or partial success.

Aubervilliers is proud of having been one of the most active and powerful points in the resistance network; all its activities were carried on under the benevolent and intentional ignorance of its mayor, Pierre Laval.

The President always strove to maintain the Republic. One day at the beginning of 1941, when Pierre Laval was again a simple citizen, the clerk of the Justice of the Peace at Aubervilliers sent me a letter, more than ironical and in fact aggressive, protesting against the fact that the bust of the Republic [Marianne] was still in the courtroom. I informed Pierre Laval of this letter and asked him what I ought to do about it. He answered in these words, "The Republic is not dead. You can reply —— if you like. But leave the bust in its place." He also ordered me to use, until they were all gone, those official forms and letterheads of the city hall which had the word 'Republic' at the top.

He always advised me to be very clever in dealing with the occupying authorities both in the interests of the people and in order to get as much as possible when an intervention was necessary, but never to have any personal relations or any cordial relations with them, and above all never to allow them to become involved in any municipal activity, never to make any advances, and never to invite them to any official city ceremonies, not even to a funeral ceremony for victims of an aerial bombardment.

One day in referring to the resistance, the communists, the 'let's-wait' group, and the collaborationists, he said: "Every day I must defend all those different kinds of people against the Germans, for they are all Frenchmen. My task is not easy." He fulfilled that task to the very end, without ever wavering.

(Document No. 17)
Fr. ed. 1094-1095

Aubervilliers, Seine, 26 February 1947

LOUIS PAGÈS

SITUATION AFTER THE ARMISTICE
LAVAL'S RETURN TO POWER
HITLER'S OFFER OF ALLIANCE
THE FLEET—BERNE

JEAN JARDIN

*[A letter addressed to M. Jacques Baraduc, defense attorney
for Pierre Laval at his trial; dated 9 October 1945].*

Mon cher Maître,

The turn taken by President Laval's trial leads me to abandon the silence
which I have observed during the last fourteen months in order that I may
bear witness, directly and indirectly, on his behalf as my conscience in-
structs me to do.

I am sending you with this letter a deposition made under oath.

In order to cover the subject completely I should have had to send you
a thorough report of all my activities as director of cabinet for the Chief of
Government from April 1942 until 1 November 1943, then as counselor in
the French Embassy, and later as chargé d'affaires at Berne until 1 September 1944.

Since there is too little time for me to prepare a document of that
character I must limit myself to indicating those facts which have seemed
to me, among so many others, to be significant, to prove some point, or to
have true symbolic value.

No better testimony can be given by a collaborator of President Laval
than to state why he was willing in April 1942 to serve under the President's
orders, why he continued to serve after November 1942, and why he accepted
further service in an embassy until the day of liberation. To set forth
those points is to say how I understood, throughout eighteen months of
daily collaboration, the purpose of his acts and the lessons of his patriotism.

From President Laval's actions, and from his extremely rare confidences
the following explanation of his presence in office and of his return to
power could be drawn.

I

In 1940 France was beaten, and England—as the testimony of that
country's own ministers proves—feared that it was about to be beaten.
Russia was allied with Germany. America was not in the war, and the
American experts, who were in a position not to be deceived, regarded
two years as the period necessary for war preparation. The armistice
did not wipe out France completely because it left her a free zone, a fleet,

and an empire. But Germany indicated no policy, and the future remained unknown. The President, who had formerly sought at Moscow and at Rome some remedy for France's isolation and for the German menace, and who in March 1939 (after Prague) had again denounced "the reaching out of the Hitlerian octopus" before the Senate's foreign affairs commission, in a speech that was both violent and prophetic, was obsessed by thoughts of the plan that had been stated in *Mein Kampf*, that of the London-Berlin axis.

In August 1940, in fact, it was not to France that Chancellor Hitler offered peace in an important speech, but to England. If someone had been in power who was less tenacious that Mr. Churchill proved to be, some government of the Chamberlain style, France could have found itself isolated and faced by a London-Berlin-Moscow axis. Now that the Allies have been victorious it is easy to talk about such matters; consider, for example, those who today criticize Munich, but who at the time called it a relief. In 1940, as anyone will readily see if he examines the question with the same objectivity that historians give to European diplomacy, to go to Montoire was a plain duty for the man who bore the responsibility for France. The doctrine laid down for us on this point was inspired by good sense and by history. In addition, it is always true that the conquered submits to the conqueror in order that he may live until the day when he can re-establish himself. The passions of the people can be so aroused that they forget these truths; but it is unthinkable that they should be unknown to statesmen worthy of the name.

In this light the armistice appeared to have two purposes: if everything was lost for the Allies, France could try to make an arrangement with her conquerors (a provisional arrangement, because during the thousand years in which there has been a France, France has known the meaning of alternation in victory and defeat); if the Allies were able to lead their armies to victory, then they would find, with us, in an intact Africa and a Mediterranean under their control, the conditions and the foundations for joint re-establishment.

After the event people want to deny this evidence; nevertheless, it is clear that without the French armistice Germany would have occupied North Africa, would have tried to control Gibraltar and Cairo, and, engaged in a different war, would no longer have attacked Russia. This is shown in an article in the *Times* dated 19 May 1945. Isn't it strange that some French people try to prove that in signing the armistice we were bad Allies, when the greatest London newspaper has seen in it an act of salvation?

II

In 1942, when President Laval returned to power, the situation was no longer the same. In particular, Germany had refused to authorize the development of the army provided for in the armistice and the rearming of North Africa, which would have been concrete signs of our return to the rank of a great power. Already eminent military men, whose pro-Vichy sentiments cannot be doubted, envisaged the rearming of France in conjunction with a United States landing in Africa. President Laval knew it. From the German side his last conversation with Marshal Gœring had left him no hope.

"You'll get nothing, no more than anyone else will," Gœring had told him. Under these conditions, why did President Laval return to power?

For two reasons: From the point of view of foreign policy, a compromise peace was always possible and it was not a French government in London that, in such a case, could defend our place at the conference table. From the point of view of domestic policy it was necessary to keep France alive as well as possible, or rather with as little damage as possible; to obtain the raw materials necessary for keeping our industries going, if we were to reach peace with our national equipment as nearly intact as possible, and if we were to prevent or limit the requisitions of manpower which were already being talked about. It was necessary to prevent divisions among the French people, so far as possible; to stop the promulgation of the laws of exception which the extremists demanded; and to prevent these extremists themselves from taking power. It may be noted in passing that M. Laval in two years dismissed the two Ministers who were most collaborationist in spirit, the only ones who had personal contacts with the Germans. The first had to leave in 1942, the second in 1943.

The men most opposed to M. Laval have often said that until the landing in North Africa his policies could be defended, but that they could not be after that time; that he should have left on 8 November 1942 or at least on 11 November.

To say that is to misunderstand the purposes of President Laval. If it had been necessary to keep France alive when she was half-occupied and still in close contact with her empire and the two Americas, how much more needed to be done to keep her living now that she was entirely occupied and cut off from the world? President Laval accepted this task, regardless of the steadily increasing danger to his popularity, his reputation, and his life.

During this period of 1942 I was present at a Franco-German talk of a semiofficial character, the only such talk I ever attended. It seems important to mention it here. It took place in my own home at Charmeil near Vichy one Sunday in July or August, 1942. There were present President Laval, the Minister of the Colonies, M. Brévié, Governor-General Boisson, M. Jacques Guérard and I myself on the French side, and for the Germans only Minister Rahn, who was then at the German Embassy in Paris. He had asked for a conversation with the President and Governor-General Boisson without his colleagues at Vichy being present, in order to tell them that the German general staff was just about to authorize our rearmament in Africa, and that all that was necessary was to make it easier for them. With this in mind Minister Rahn proposed to go to Dakar, whence he would return with a report showing the confidence that could be placed in our colony.

The President kept silent and Governor Boisson replied that he could not allow Mr. Rahn to go to Dakar. Mr. Rahn then suggested that the German counselor at Rabat should make the voyage. He would be discreet, he would have lunch with the governor, and on his return he would make a favorable report. M. Boisson replied that he knew quite well that if one German diplomat went to Dakar, there would soon be ten, then twenty, then fifty. Finally Minister Rahn offered that one of his assistants should go there with French identity papers, to which the governor-general objected that he could not deceive his own collaborators and that he would resign rather than do so.

President Laval remained silent for a time and deep embarrassment fell over the meeting. Finally, directly questioned by Mr. Rahn and begged by him to act as arbiter of the discussion, President Laval said, pointing to Governor-General Boisson, "It is such men as he who have made the empire, and who protect it. It is they who know what is possible. We must have confidence in them, and we must listen to them."

The conversation soon came to an end, and as I was seeing him to his car Minister Rahn said to me, "If I tell Berlin what I have just heard here, do you think the Laval government will last very long?" I made a vague gesture, and his chauffeur drove off in the direction of Paris.

III

From 8 November 1942, though I was personally much shaken by the demands of various eminent men who desired the government to resign and who claimed that they could prove the necessity of such a measure, I was able to measure the decisive importance of the presence of President Laval at the head of the government.

On 8 November 1942 at seven in the evening the German minister at Vichy gave President Laval a telegram from Ribbentrop according to which Chancellor Hitler offered France a total alliance. (The German text included the hunting expression *durch Dick und Dünn*, that is, through thick and thin, which could be translated for good or evil.) The reply had to be given that evening. In spite of pressure from those who saw in this an "unhoped-for opportunity," President Laval decided to gain time by asking to see the Chancellor himself, in order to be able to refuse without breaking up the situation as it was, that is, without causing a Paris government to be set up in his place which would have signed the alliance and declared war on the Allies.

He left on 9 November 1942 for Munich and underwent the attacks of the Chancellor during the evening of the 10th and the morning of the 11th. He built his refusal around the theme that "If I who have said publicly to all the world that 'I wish for the victory of Germany,' now say to you that this alliance is impossible, you ought to believe me." As the result of his refusal the free zone was invaded while he was still in Munich.

He had to return in December 1942 to defend France in another matter, that of the army provided for in the armistice. He had been asked to give an explanation of the arms and military supplies found—though in fact only a part was found—in the free zone by the Germans. According to the testimony of General Picquendar, the supplies, arms, ammunition, and food that were hidden (while some people were saying that Vichy was betraying France) had a value of about 100,000 million francs. President Laval handled the matter in such a way that General Picquendar was neither arrested nor disturbed by the occupation authorities.

On the morning of the sinking of the fleet the President, informed very early at Châteldon by the German minister at Vichy, who had gone there in person, arrived late at his office. The German diplomats had intensified their activity, and were extremely nervous. By the time President Laval arrived nearly everything had ended, except that Admiral de Laborde was still on his ship, which he refused to leave, being engaged in a violent discussion with the German authorities. It was then that the President proposed to the Maréchal in my presence that the following telegram should be sent to Admiral de Laborde: "I learn that your ship is about to sink. I order you to leave it."

From this time onward the President was even more silent, if that were possible, so far as any judgment on the general situation was concerned. If he said in his public declarations that Germany had kept all its strength, it was for reasons similar to those which had led him to speak the famous words, "I wish for the victory of Germany," at a time when he feared that a ministry would be formed under Doriot[1] within the week. But with us he kept silent, and even when we saw him return deeply wounded by the talks in Paris we were unable to find an indication of his suffering except in his expression.

The idea that everything was being reported during this time and that a whole gang of Germans were watching him, in order to restrict him or find a ground for getting rid of him and putting in their own men, clearly obsessed his thoughts.

The President lived these two years of French martyrdom in tragic isolation. He did not even have the consolations of the Maréchal, who filled the role of a legitimate final court of moral appeal and received visitors from different parts of France who came to tell him of the excesses committed by some administrations, or about certain policies that were getting more and more out of the control of the government. Already the President was carrying on his own shoulders the burden of accusations and reproaches. He listened every morning to complaints which the Maréchal passed on to him, for in his opinion that was the proper role, during the misfortunes of the fatherland, of the old chief to whom so many French people still turned in their anguish. A little after the landing of November 1942, when President Laval asked the Maréchal to give him full powers and the right to sign all official texts, he said to the Maréchal, "Monsieur le Maréchal, what is about to happen now will be terrible, and you are too great a man to be mixed up in it."

The President could allow his attitude to be perceived only by indirect indications, for example, in giving promotions, or in appointing to the most delicate positions those prefects who were the most skillful in handling the French while saving face before the occupation authorities. As is well known, he appointed Prefect Angéli to Lyon, and held out against the Germans when they wanted to send him away; it is also known that the resistance itself has given admirable testimony on behalf of Prefect Angéli. Among the seventeen prefects the Germans were to arrest and take away to Germany, many had come to my office to tell me, as they talked of the difficulties of their tasks, how deep was their affection for President Laval.

In September 1943 I received at the Hotel du Parc a mayor from the Puy-de-Dôme. He was a small industrialist who had hidden his workers when they were called up under the labor levy. He had been sentenced, and now, in order to get the Germans off his track, the French police were looking for him. He asked for my aid and said that his case was all the more annoying (a statement which was rather picturesque in view of the place in which he was talking) since he was to leave the next day for London by plane and stay there several days. He even asked me if I had anything I wanted done in London. I explained his case to President Laval, who solved it in the following way. The man was to go at once to the Regional Prefect at Clermont-Ferrand and give himself up as a prisoner; the Prefect would keep him in an office and notify President Laval, who would decide on his release, whereupon the prefect would release him the following morning. This was in fact done.

1. See the Paris newspapers of this period, concerning Doriot's activities in Paris; note also the communiqué of the Wilhelmstrasse following Laval's speech, and the recall of Doriot, forty-eight hours later, to the eastern front.

During the same year of 1943, but at the beginning (in January, I think), I heard President Laval praise General de Gaulle. During a lunch at which there were a number of guests, including two ministers, I offered a defense of General Giraud. President Laval reacted violently and expressed his opinion of General Giraud with considerable vivacity. He added, and these are his precise words, "There are only two men, I myself and de Gaulle. He's showing plenty of nerve; but for the moment all he can do amounts to no more than waving his arms in front of a tank."

Statements of that kind were rare, and thus should not be looked on merely as clever remarks. Under the circumstances this one should be taken as a watchword.

On 1 November 1943 I took up my position as Counselor of our embassy in Berne. On 1 April 1944, as a result of the death of Admiral Bard, I became French chargé d'affaires in Switzerland. Concerning the period from that date to the liberation I could give important testimony, if it did not affect our foreign policy and if it did not involve the highest permanent interests of our country. I will deal with only one point, after having given the necessary background.

In 1939, and throughout the war, the Chief of the French Intelligence Service in Switzerland was, in accordance with normal procedure, the Assistant Military Attaché, Major Pourchot. In July 1940, when the Germans obliged France to disband its intelligence services, Major Pourchot was placed on "armistice leave," and his name was stricken from the official list of military attachés in the Ministry of War. Actually, however, this officer, one of the finest Frenchmen it has ever been my privilege to know, continued his work in liaison with his superiors, who were then installed in the southern, non-occupied zone. Our representative at Berne had not had the elementary prudence to camouflage him in some advisory or diplomatic function, and his name therefore continued to appear with his former title in the Swiss diplomatic yearbook, a fact which obliged him to appear in uniform at official ceremonies. In November 1942, Major Pourchot's superior officers went over to North Africa, and he thus found himself in contact with Algiers.

In April 1944 the German authorities took steps intended to force President Laval to end the activities of Major Pourchot and his assistants on the staffs of our various consulates in Switzerland. I received a telegram from President Laval instructing me to dissolve the intelligence service, seal off its rooms and equipment, and send the army men concerned back to France.

I replied in a letter which ought to be available in the archives of the Ministry of Foreign Affairs, along with the telegram. I indicated that whereas perhaps at some past time there might have been an intelligence service operating in the embassy and in the consulates, this service had disappeared a long time ago, and the military men in question were now simply representing their country, the same as any other member of the diplomatic service. For greater security I moved the man in the Geneva consulate, the post nearest to our frontier, to an apartment in the city.

President Laval, who I was certain expected exactly the reply I gave, was able to use my letter against the German authorities. Some time later he thanked me for it, saying that I had prevented the arrest of General Caldeyroux, Secretary-General of the Ministry of War, and probably that of M. Rochat, Secretary-General of the Ministry of Foreign Affairs.

There was in fact an intelligence service which telegraphed every day to Algiers, sometimes directly and sometimes through Mr. Dulles of the United States Legation. This service was essential not only to the French general staff, but also to Allied Supreme Headquarters. From the texts of the telegrams it would be easy to prove that the services of Major Pourchot, covering as they did a part of France, Germany, the Tyrol, Austria, and the north of Italy, played a decisive part in the landing in France, in the operations at Avranches, and in the conduct of the war thereafter on the western front. Among a hundred points that could be cited, it must be mentioned that the firing bases of the V-2's at Peneemunde were pointed out by this service; these bases were then ready to function, but were destroyed forty-eight hours later by English air forces, thus delaying the bombardment of London by six months.

Major Pourchot, since promoted to Colonel, sent me on 30 August 1944 the letter of which a copy is attached; I did not ask for this letter. In fact, though I have had it for more than a year, I have made no use of it in spite of friendly requests that I should do so; nor did I ever seek protection from Algiers on the ground that the Vichy government's embassy at Berne saved "its" intelligence service by giving it diplomatic protection. The essential fact is that President Laval never taught his colleagues to play the "double game" to which so many government offiicials have resorted in order to save their places. President Laval taught them that there is only one game to be played, that of France and of the defense of the permanent interests of the country, which demands the abandonment of all personal interests and the complete self-sacrifice which we saw practiced by Laval himself.

In this particular matter it may well be asked who served France the better: President Laval's team at Berne, who protected and defended one of the essential mechanisms of the Allied army; or those diplomatic officials who had resigned five months earlier—and were sitting around Berne doing nothing on the pretext of resistance—after complicated negotiations with Algiers to learn what their new pay would be and what their position would be in the future?

I think that it is in such acts, accomplished by men whose respect, veneration, and faith toward President Laval never failed and never will fail, that the explanation, and above all the results, of his policies must be sought. There too must be sought the proof that in 1944 the two governments of France, that of Vichy, still represented in more than a dozen countries where it defended our interests, and that of Algiers, which was France not merely present but in action among the Allies, had become complementary. It is true that from the military point of view the successful operations were those of the secret service controlled by the army in Algiers; but it must be remembered that this service was tolerated and allowed only because it operated within, and under the cover of, the Embassy of a recognized government, that of Vichy.

You must remember, mon cher Maître, that only the necessity of defending my former Chief in a dramatic trial has led me to inform you, and thus to run the risk of also informing the general public, of matters about which I have kept absolutely silent up to the present, and which I would have preferred to keep completely to myself.

Veuillez agréer, mon cher Maître, l'expression de mes sentiments distingués.

(Document No. 18)
Fr. ed. 1096-1103

JEAN JARDIN

Annex to Declaration of Jean Jardin.

AMBASSADE
DE LA
RÉPUBLIQUE FRANCAISE
EN SUISSE
L'Attaché Militaire Adjoint
COPIE

Berne, 30 August 1944

Monsieur Jean Jardin
Chargé d'Affaires de France

BERNE

Now that you are bringing your activities to an end, I regard it as my duty to express my gratitude for the comprehensive and total aid that you gave to my service beginning 1 April 1944, when you took the position of chargé d'affaires.

Your first act at the beginning of April, an entirely spontaneous act, was to save the special services in Switzerland of the General Staff of the Army of Algiers. Vichy had ordered you in writing to bring these services to an end in the shortest possible time; you nevertheless continued to provide cover for them without thinking for an instant of evading your responsibilities.

Thanks to you, these services have been able up to now to operate without any hindrance, and to serve the cause of liberating our national territory in a way which on many occasions has been regarded at Algiers as very valuable.

Not only have you concealed their presence in Switzerland, but you have continuously shown your sympathy and your active and continuous interest in these services through me, on whom has fallen the honor of being their head.

On two occasions, 20 April and 28 July 1944, I reported by telegraph to my superiors in Algiers all that you were doing to help my service. Now that you are leaving your post I believe, in my conscience as a soldier, that I owe you this testimony of thanks; I am glad to give it.

Veuillez croire, monsieur le Conseiller, à l'assurance de mes sentiments les plus distingués.

MAJOR POURCHOT

Chief of Special Services of the
General Staff of the Army in Algiers

BERNE

The Capitaine de Corvette Captain Ferran, Chief of the Special Services fo the Navy at Algiers, joins completely in the sentiments expressed by Major Pourchot with regard to M. Jardin.

FERRAN

THE INFORMATION SERVICES

ALBERT DELOBEL

Official, Ministry of Information

I the undersigned Albert Delobel, born 9 October 1914 in Paris, now residing in Paris, give under oath the following testimony regarding the relations I had with President Laval from 1942 to 1944.

As a part-time journalist before the war I had had occasion to attack President Laval and his policies rather violently, at different times, after he came into power in 1935. In matters of doctrine I was opposed to him at that time. It was therefore with some hostility that I entered in 1942 a ministerial department of which he was the chief, the Ministry of Information.

My principal duty in this ministry was to direct the administrative sub-section dealing with provincial delegations and with the settlement of differences that might develop between the ministry's representatives and the prefects. In this activity I was able to understand at once how President Laval regarded and understood the role of propagandist for his government.

He had not the slightest idea that the representatives of the Ministry of Information should be propagandists for Franco-German collaboration as supported by certain Paris newspapers. On the contrary, he thought that the representatives should render just about the same services that a Deputy had been able to render before the war: to keep in direct contact with the people; to intervene as often as possible, in the difficult moments through which we were passing, with the prefectoral authorities and if necessary, when the official duties of a prefect prevented him from acting, directly with the German authorities; and to smooth out incidents which might develop from the occupation and its hardships. Most of the representatives of the Ministry of Information quickly understood this; it was only a few overly energetic persons, often appointed under pressure from the occupation authorities, who made his task difficult. He did not hesitate to say publicly how bad an opinion he had of what these persons were doing.

He brought together all of the provincial representatives of the Ministry of Information many times in Paris at the Hotel Matignon, each time in order to make clear his thoughts on what was happening.

Opposing those who desired a national revolution, he explained to the delegates how difficult, if not impossible, such an undertaking would be during occupation by a conquering force. He also showed how harmful a certain doctrinal propaganda, one too close to the ideas being presented by the German propagandists, could be. He asked the representatives to strive above all not to spread ideas but to keep the government informed of the state of the people's thoughts and feelings.

During these meetings he was many times obliged to take some action against some delegate who had not understood the meaning of his policy.

To one who had complained of the limited powers given him for opposing the activities of Gaullists or communists, the President replied in a scornful tone, "Doubtless you'd like to have the powers of a police commissioner!"

He went on to explain that it was the role of the government not to split the French nation into supporters of the government and "resistants," but on the contrary to defend all French people, whoever they might be, against the occupying power and its demands.

To Governor Bonamy, representative in the Morbihan, who complained because officials hostile to the government's policies were allowed to remain in office, together with some who had a Masonic background and others who were leftist, President Laval tried to show how clumsy a move it would be to deprive the townships of France of those administrators who had proved their ability and who understood perfectly the work of a mayor or a municipal councilor. He took advantage of this argument to protest forcefully against delegates who went outside their role of objective information and tried to play the part of official spies. On that same day he spoke in defense of several municipalities, among them Rouen and Vitry-le-François, whose chiefs were being attacked not only by the Paris press but also by hostile interventions of the occupation authorities.

The first effect of these remarks, which were made publicly, was the almost immediate resignation of the representatives whom he had thus put roughly in their place. In this way, little by little, he cleared out one of the administrative divisions of the French State into which there had slipped, after the events of June 1940, some men who—often without realizing it, it should be noted—had sometimes played the enemy's game.

In 1943 I came into direct contact with President Laval. The occupation authorities were astonished that the Ministry of Information did not maintain a delegation in Paris. It was not by chance that President Laval had always refused, or at least postponed, a decision on this matter. He felt that it would be dangerous to establish in Paris an information service which would necessarily be under the almost direct control of the *Propagandaabteilung*.

Nevertheless, it was a matter which he would be obliged to deal with urgently sooner or later.

Through the Ministry's secretary-general of that period he asked Maurice Mirabeau to organize, not a delegation, but merely a Paris information service. In order to keep this service from being subject to the supervision of the occupation authorities, as it would be if it were officially a part of the Ministry of Information, he attached it directly to the presidency of the Council of Ministers. But in order that the office should still retain the outward appearance of an information center, I was given the task of maintaining liaison between it and the Ministry of Information.

For some months we were able to work together in this way. Efforts were often made by the Germans to bring us into political activity of a more direct type, but Maurice Mirabeau and I were able to postpone the steps which they wanted us to take. In our most difficult moments we received the complete support of President Laval, both in our struggle against men who wanted to take our place in order to carry out the collaborationist ideas of certain Paris circles, and also in the moves we made through various French official services on behalf of Parisians with whom we were in daily contact. These interventions dealt with such matters as deportation to Germany, bomb damage, and resistants sought by the German police.

President Laval sometimes had us come to see him when he was in Paris and urged us to continue our activities of the sort indicated above, activities which in fact had nothing to do with what the occupation authorities would expect from an office of political propaganda. They fully realized what was going on, for in October 1943 they demanded that I be removed from the Ministry of Information and from any political service with the French government.

I was thereupon assigned to the Ministry of Food and given the task of liaison between the Presidency of the Council and the Ministry's cabinet. There was a weekly meeting of several such cabinet attachés, limited to those whom the President regarded as especially faithful to his policies.

During these meetings he sometimes encouraged us. We were concerned only with finding ways to help him perform the essential task of building up a series of protecting screens at all levels between the occupants and the French people. The more the political and military situation tended to become definite, the more President Laval was determined to remain faithful to the principles which he always defended, namely to resist the unjust demands continually being made, and with increasing violence, by the German government, through Gauleiter Sauckel, General Oberg, or other representatives of the Reich.

In this period we sometimes saw him on his return from difficult conversations with the Germans. He was often tired but never discouraged; he had "saved what could be saved," and he seemed relaxed and joyous because he had rendered service to his country.

The above statement indicates what would have been the general lines of my testimony if President Laval had been tried and if I had been called as a witness in the preparation for his trial.

(Document No. 21)
Fr. ed. 1104-1106

Paris, 2 May 1947

ALBERT DELOBEL

FOREIGN AFFAIRS—ADMIRAL LEAHY

CHARLES ROCHAT

Secretary-General
of the Ministry of Foreign Affairs

The Laval-Gœring meeting at Cracow in May 1935

On 2 May 1935 M. Laval signed at Moscow a treaty of mutual assistance between France and the USSR.

While he was in the Soviet capital he learned that Marshal Pilsudski had died in Warsaw and he decided immediately to attend the funeral ceremony. The official representative of the French government was to be Maréchal Pétain.

The body of Marshal Pilsudski was taken from Warsaw to Cracow, where burial was to take place at Wawell Castle. Thus all the foreign delegations met at Cracow. After the long ceremony the delegations were received by the Polish government, or more exactly by Mr. Beck, at the Hotel de France, where a luncheon had been arranged. Each delegation was at a separate table. Goering, when he entered the dining room, had himself introduced by Mr. Beck to Maréchal Pétain—who very pointedly avoided any conversation and limited himself to a few words of formal courtesy—and then to M. Laval, whom he asked for an interview. This interview took place immediately after lunch in one of the hotel rooms; I was present as interpreter.

After twelve years it is difficult to remember exactly what was said, but a detailed report was made at the time in a note which can doubtless be found easily in the archives of the Ministry of Foreign Affairs.

The interview began with a long monologue by Goering. He was clearly disturbed by the signature of the Rome agreement on 7 January 1935, and of the French-Soviet pact a few days before, and he bitterly reproached Laval with continuing the policy of encircling Germany, already begun by his predecessors. "The hand of France," he said, "appears in all the combinations that are being arranged against Germany."

Laval replied forcibly that only Germany could put an end to the isolation policy of which she believed herself the victim. He recalled that the Franco-Soviet pact had been conceived by Barthou; that it had definitely been intended to include on the same basis not only the USSR, but also Poland and Germany; and that it was only after the failure of this project, a failure due especially to Germany, that France had been brought to sign the Franco-Soviet pact. This pact itself excluded no one and was open to any state that wished to adhere to it.

The general tone of the interview was cold. Before any real discussion had got under way, a German officer came in to remind Goering that his special train was about to depart. The conversation came to an end without arriving at any conclusion.

Friday, 13 December 1940

At this time I was not Secretary-General of the Ministry of Foreign Affairs, since Charles Roux had not yet been replaced, but was its political director. One of my duties was to bring the department's letters to the Minister for signature each evening.

On 13 December M. Laval reached Vichy about noon, coming from Paris, where he had spent several days. I went to see him at his office about six-thirty in the evening to submit various papers for his signature. He said that he was very busy and asked me to come back around ten o'clock.

About nine o'clock he phoned and asked me to come to see him immediately. When I entered his office I found him in a state of agitation. He told me in a few words what had just happened at the Council of Ministers, expressing his indignation at the way in which he had been got rid of, and deploring the effect his eviction would have on conversations which were then in progress with the Germans. He gave me several diplomatic documents which he had been keeping either in a drawer of his desk or in his briefcase, and then went off with Brinon to have dinner at Chanteclerc.

About ten o'clock that evening he called me back again to give me several administrative documents that he had found in a drawer. While I was there, Heinzen, a correspondent for the United Press, came in to say that M. Laval's chauffeur had been arrested in front of the Hotel du Parc.

Then one of his secretaries entered, astonished to see the entrance hall of the Hotel du Parc full of police in civilian clothes. M. Laval tried in vain to get in touch by telephone with Peyrouton, and then with the Maréchal. He was even refused permission to speak to Mme Laval at Châteldon.

About eleven o'clock that evening Dumoulin de la Barthète and Ménétrel asked, through the doorman, to be received. About eleven-thirty M. Laval, a heavy briefcase stuffed with papers under his arm, and escorted by police, left the hotel and got into a police car which was waiting to take him to Châteldon.

"I wish for the victory of Germany because . . ."

Concerning the phrase "I wish for the victory of Germany because . . ." I have nothing to add to the deposition which I gave for the trial of the Maréchal, and which was published in the complete report of the hearings, *Journal Officiel*, p. 336.

From the time when Laval first spoke the phrase I had often talked with him about it. He repeated on each occasion that he had understood perfectly all the seriousness of his words at the time when he had put them into his speech. What he had wanted when he returned to power in 1942 was to create among the Germans, and more particularly in Hitler himself, "an atmosphere of confidence," thanks to which he would be able to resist more effectively Berlin's continually increasing demands, and perhaps to obtain some lightening of the rigors of an occupation that must be expected to continue, and to grow more strict.

It was better, he said, to compromise himself by words, words which in his opinion were without great importance and of which the purpose would be made clear to the French people by future events. He would secure immediate and practical advantages for France, whose existence must be maintained before all else, by putting himself in the position of being able on all occasions to cite this proof of an attitude of good will toward Germany, an attitude which this famous phrase would no longer permit his German interrogators to doubt.

For him it was a political operation, essential to his future actions.

In actual fact, during the many negotiations that he conducted thereafter with the Germans, whether they dealt with cooperation, the supplying of labor, or the delivery of any kind of goods, Laval always reminded the Germans of his declaration, claiming that if he, the man who had publicly "wised for a German victory," refused to agree to German demands, then it must be because those demands were truly beyond the possibilities of France.

The Laval-Leahy Talk of April 1942

On 18 April 1942 Laval formed his cabinet. He himself, in addition to being Chief of Government, became Minister of the Interior and Minister of Foreign Affairs.

As Minister of Foreign Affairs he was obliged by protocol on taking over his office to call upon each of the accredited ambassadors. Admiral Leahy, the United States Ambassador, was about to leave Vichy. Deeply affected by a cruel bereavement, he had already taken his official leave of the Maréchal, and had for all practical purposes ceased to act as Ambassador. Nevertheless, M. Laval went to see him at the United States Embassy, in the Villa Ica, on (I believe) 27 April. Admiral Leahy received him and Mr. Tuck acted as interpreter, since M. Laval did not understand English, and since the Ambassador from the beginning seemed anxious lest he should miss something of what M. Laval said to him.

I do not recall very clearly after four years the details of this conversation, but they were reported precisely in a note which is certainly in the archives of the Quai d'Orsay, and which was sent officially by telegram at the time to our Ambassador in Washington.

I remember, however, the very close attention with which Admiral Leahy followed Laval's explanations. After the usual formalities, and after expressing his sympathy over the death of Mrs. Leahy, Laval went immediately to the heart of the political situation. Admiral Leahy's attention increased when the Chief of Government expressed his personal feeling toward the United States, and referred to the family links which brought him close to that country. Laval concluded by affirming that he would never undertake anything against American interests.

Laval always considered this conversation as particularly important. He referred to it in all kinds of circumstances. He was quick to read to his visitors, whoever they were, the text of what was said, even after November 1942; and he made public the chief passages in it during one of his talks (I do not remember exactly when this was).

Admiral Leahy left Vichy for New York on 1 May 1942.

Jewish Affairs

As regards the Jews, I was not kept informed of German demands and of the means employed by Laval to limit or evade them. This question was generally dealt with in Paris, through the offices of the Ministry of the Interior. But whenever these demands were mentioned, I saw Laval react indignantly, describing as inhuman and hateful those measures which the Germans never ceased to demand, and which some of the Ministers (Platon and Darquier de Pellepoix) did not resist, in Laval's opinion, with sufficient energy.

When measures were proposed against foreign Jews in 1942, Laval summoned the Vichy representative of the German Embassy to his office, at my request, and protested in the very strongest terms. (I had prepared a note of protest for him; I seem to remember that he gave it to Krugg von Nidda after having toned down some of the wording, but my memory is not precise on this point.) Krugg von Nidda could only take refuge behind the instructions of his superiors.

For my part, I immediately reported the German demands to the Papal nuncio, in his capacity as dean of the diplomatic corps and as representative of the Vatican. I also called together all the chiefs of mission of the countries whose Jewish citizens were threatened, and advised them either to persuade their governments to act directly in Berlin, or else to repatriate their threatened citizens as quickly as possible.

I think I am right in saying that thanks to his personal relations in German circles the Spanish Ambassador obtained satisfaction in the matter of Spanish Jews, and also that delays were agreed to for the evacuation of the Jews of certain other countries: Rumania, Hungary, Bulgaria, Portugal, and Turkey.

The Sinking of the Fleet at Toulon

On 27 November 1942 at three-thirty in the morning Krugg von Nidda telephoned me at the Hotel du Parc to tell me that he had an extremely important communication to be delivered at once to the Chief of Government, a communication of which he could not tell me the subject.

I immediately informed the President by telephone at Châteldon, where Krugg and I arrived about four-fifteen. In spite of the icy cold, Krugg said that he would not see Laval until exactly four-thirty. Therefore we waited outside for about ten minutes, in the dark and the cold, until the specified time.

At four-thirty we entered Laval's little office. Krugg informed him of Hitler's letter announcing the German decision to occupy Toulon. Laval protested immediately in vehement terms. He protested against the action, and denied all the reasons put forward by the German government to justify it. Then he brought the interview to an abrupt end, asking me to go back to Vichy and summon to his office at the Hotel du Parc all the Ministers concerned.

By five-fifteen they were all in his office. Admiral Leluc, on Abrial's orders, called the Maritime Prefecture at Toulon, and learned that in fact the Germans had invaded the fortified sector of Toulon at four o'clock that morning and that the fleet had sunk itself. The scuttling operation was almost completed. The fleet had executed the order, given at the time of the armistice, to allow no French ship under any circumstances to fall into foreign hands.

Leluc hung up the receiver. It was a moving moment. "This," said Laval, "is one of the most tragic moments of a most grievous period."

(Document No. 22)
Fr. ed. 1107-1110

April 1947
CHARLES ROCHAT

END OF VOLUME II

---

*The table of contents is at the beginning of volume I;
the Index, at the end of volume III.*